Also by Darwin Payne

The Man of Only Yesterday
Owen Wister
Initiative in Energy
Dallas: An Illustrated History

Darwin Payne

BIG D

Triumphs and Troubles of an American Supercity in the 20th Century

THREE FORKS PRESS
Dallas

Three Forks Press
P.O. Box 823461
Dallas, Texas 75382

Library of Congress Catalog Card No. 93-60840

ISBN: 0-9637629-0-7

For Phyllis Schmitz Payne

Contents

Note

Although I have many memories and a lifetime of experiences in Dallas, this is by no means a book of personal reminiscences. Still, it is personal to the extent that rather than being a systematic study of the years covered, I isolated various topics and episodes which especially interested me and which seemed important to my own understanding of the city's past. It is my hope that these will seem to be important to a broader audience as well. Certainly my own views have been shaped to a large extent by the several years I spent as a reporter in this city for the *Dallas Times Herald*, for KERA-TV's *Newsroom* television show, and as publisher of *The Suburban Tribune*.

Concerning a matter of some sensitivity, I should note that I have sought to be consistent with the various time periods in my use of the word Negro. While that term largely has fallen out of favor today, it formerly was widely accepted in the black community, where it was a part of many official titles and designations, and among whites as well. As the 1960s arrived the word Negro was dropped in favor of black and then, in many cases, African-American. I have sought to reflect those changes in my manuscript.

PART ONE

A Yearning To Be Great

1

What Mattered Was Growth

The people of Dallas demand from her citizens some personal sacrifice for the general good.

–Citizens Association, 1907

Snapshot of a Growing City

In 1907 a local businessman rendered this thumbnail portrait of Dallas: "A city of skyscrapers, resounding with the roar of trade." In that year's city directory it was described as a place "where the wheels of enterprise and effort never cease their revolutions day or night." Boosterism, yes, but hardly an exaggeration. Much the same could be said, of course, about growing towns throughout the nation. This was, after all, an age when the basic culture of American life was being transformed from rural to urban, when urban population growth during the first decade of the century was three times that of rural areas. There was little time to stop and reflect about such matters, though. Growth and progress—that was what mattered. By most accounts, certainly in Dallas, the definitions of these two words were the same. Growth was progress and progress was growth.

A bird's-eye view from Dallas' formidable, fortress-like red courthouse showed three elongated primary streets—Elm, Main and Commerce—stretching eastward away from the Trinity River over land that gently rose and fell towards the state fairgrounds. Downtown bustled with commercial activity. It was crowded with electric streetcars, horse-drawn carts, and a few specimens of that noisy new contraption—the automobile. One could see lots and lots of people—well-dressed pedestrians, solitary riders on horseback, bicyclists, and a few loafers content just to stand and watch the hustle and bustle. Utility poles heavily laden with sagging electric wires, a visual nuisance which only a few minded, obscured the view to the sky. As for the "skyscrapers," a good number reached up five, six, even eight stories high. An even bigger one, the fourteen-story Praetorian Building, was under construction farther east on Main.

Of noise along these city streets there was plenty: factory whistles, church bells, fruit and vegetable sellers, clocks atop buildings ringing out the hour, newsboys, and, of course, racket from automobiles, streetcars, and wagon wheels. And the snorting of horses. Not to mention mules. Train whistles, too, for the Texas & Pacific Railway ran straight down the middle of Pacific Avenue, one block north of and parallel to Elm Street. They were good noises, an adventure for the ears. It was the chatter of commerce, a welcome sound.

While towns everywhere reveled in their emerging importance and growth, it is fair to say that Dallas' leaders harbored even higher hopes for the future than those in most other places. The city so impressed visiting railroad tycoon Jay Gould in 1887 that he predicted its population would reach 150,000 in his lifetime. It failed to do so. Gould did not allow it enough time, for he died five years after his prediction. Still, a group of businessmen who called themselves the 150,000 Club had been meeting regularly since 1905 to plan ways to reach Gould's prediction as quickly as possible. The larger Commercial Club, a forerunner of the Chamber of Commerce, had the same general goal of advancing growth and progress.

More than 93,000 residents now lived in the city that in 1890 had been the biggest in the state. Its size had doubled in the last five years, but to its leaders' dismay, Dallas now was only the third largest city in the state, trailing San Antonio and Houston. Nevertheless, Dallas certainly considered itself to be the commercial capital of Texas. Among the residents were a thousand drummers, traveling salesmen working an area extending far into bordering states. More than five thousand dwellers earned their livings as factory workers at some five hundred manufacturing firms. It was the kind of town where just the year before, at the conclusion of a popular three-week church revival, the downtown merchants all closed their doors between 11:30 a.m. and 1:30 p.m. so employees and customers could pray.

On all sides of town farmers worked a rich, productive soil. Here was the major source of prosperity. Dallas served as the farmers' staging area for marketing and distributing their crops, especially cotton. Within a 150-mile radius these farmers were growing one-sixth of the entire world's cotton crop. In servicing its surrounding agricultural enterprises, Dallas had become the world's leader in manufacturing cotton gin machinery, saddlery, and harness.

During earlier days when this land had been nothing but an unsettled wilderness in the infant but sprawling Republic of Texas, a wandering, ill-tempered Tennessean frontiersman named John Neely Bryan came upon a modest bluff at a meander of the Trinity River and concluded that the site was ideal for a new town. He claimed here in 1841 the 640 acres allotted to a single man, and he launched an immediate campaign to attract others to join him at this place he soon called Dallas. The location he chose was at a natural crossing of the river; the Republic of Texas planned a military road through the immediate area; it appeared likely that boats from downstream would come up to this point and no farther; the land was fertile and the climate mild. Of these reasons, none but those concerning the land and the climate proved to be of great significance in the years ahead.

It seemed inevitable that once the debris was cleared from the river the steamboats already plying the lower reaches of the Trinity and other Texas rivers would extend their voyages upstream to this turnaround point, exchange their cargo for North Texas' expected agricultural riches, then return to Galveston. A prosperous city surely would emerge at this transfer point. Indeed, just as Bryan hoped, Dallas had prospered, but to this day in 1907 the river had been a nuisance instead of a blessing.

Optimism, however, reigned almost exclusively in the city. A brother and sister (Herbert Marcus and Carrie Marcus Neiman) and her husband (Al Neiman) were making plans to open in the fall of

1907 a new ready-to-wear women's specialty shop. Officials of Sanger Bros., the dominant department store in the entire Southwest and a mainstay in the city since 1872, announced in March 1907 the purchase of a parcel of land for a new store on Lamar Street between Main and Elm for $100,000. (This was the same lot that pioneer settler and capitalist Sarah Horton Cockrell had bought for only $50 more than forty years earlier.) A. Harris & Co., another leading department store, was celebrating this year its twentieth anniversary in town. The canvases of Frank Reaugh, a local artist who painted romantic landscape scenes with cattle, were on exhibit at the Dallas Public Library, drawing good crowds. Vaudeville performers offered live entertainment at the New Lyric Theatre, the Majestic, the Dallas Opera House, Fair Park Auditorium, and Lake Cliff Casino. Curious folks who were intrigued with a new art form, moving pictures, attended the Nickelodeon or Theatorium. As many as 1,500 sports fans watched Dallas Giants baseball games east of town at Gaston Park, a rambling facility with semi-covered wooden stands extending far down the first- and third-base lines.

Under construction between Dallas and Sherman was something that in future years would prove to be popular and useful—an "interurban" rail line to carry passengers on electrically powered trains on the hour in both directions. More such lines linking Dallas to communities for miles around in every direction soon would follow.

Passenger trains bound for distant destinations posted cheap rates. A person paid just $25 to ride the Rock Island to California, or $10.30 for a round-trip ticket to San Antonio on the Katy line.

The automobile and explosive urban growth were arriving in Dallas simultaneously, a fact of great moment not appreciated or understood. Still, a faint glimmering of what was yet to come could be imagined. The growing number of drivers included a few show-offs. Police Captain E.S. Arnold ordered his horse-mounted officers to slow down those irresponsible speedsters by authority of City Code 295. This ordinance forbade hacks, omnibuses, buggies, carriages, wagons, drays, carts, cabs, sulkies, or vehicles of any kind from going faster than the walking speed of a horse or mule when crossing an intersection.

Just around the corner—about a year away—was the birth of a new kind of business related exclusively to automobiles. At the corner of Commerce and Prather there opened what some believed was the first drive-in gasoline station in the nation. "Hurry back," the attendant told his customers in a novel phrase that would be appropriated by an oil company and used as a national slogan.

All was not perfect in Dallas. Not even the most ardent booster would suggest otherwise. Growth brought problems, the sort being experienced by all towns in this era of rapid urban expansion. Dallas and growing cities everywhere had to cope with such matters as street and sidewalk improvements, sanitation and sewage, police and fire protection, regulation of public utilities, public education, municipal parks, and adequate water supplies. In this latter regard Dallas constantly flirted with disaster. A prolonged drought would be disastrous, and occasional droughts were the norm. No sooner would the prayed-for showers come, though, then gratitude turned to despair as streets and walkways became quagmires. "Lift Dallas out of the mud" became a popular cry to encourage more paving.

The river that Bryan believed seventy years earlier to be the key to the town's future looked no different now than when he had first seen it. Next to its banks the thriving downtown area reached a shocking line of demarcation. Here commerce yielded abruptly to an untamed barricade: a lazy, muddy river prone to occasional violent floods. In the spring of 1890 the water had reached a depth of fifty-two feet and a width of two miles. Chickens took to the tops of trees. Rabbits and snakes found refuge side-by-side on the elevated Oak Cliff railway.

Although John Neely Bryan had died without honor in a state insane asylum in Austin years earlier, his dream of navigation and the riches it would bring remained alive. Most people still thought the river could be controlled and used to the city's advantage. This very year workers from the federal government were constructing a series of locks and dams south of town to guarantee enough water for year-round navigation. Even now a few optimistic boats, anticipating the future, plied short stretches of the river, but not in productive fashion. In fact, the 1907 city directory described Dallas without qualification as being "situated at the head of navigation of the Trinity River." If that was not an out-and-out lie, it was such a stretching of the truth as to be farcical.

Just as the river marked an end to urban development to the west, the Texas & Pacific Railway tracks presented a different kind of barrier on the north. These iron rails, one block north of Elm, ran straight down Pacific Avenue for its entire east-west length. They stood as a formidable obstacle to cross-town movement. Rail traffic throughout the city was hampered by the existence of five separate terminals, causing difficulties for transferring passengers and interminable freight delays. Other problems unrelated to the rails included downtown streets that often zigzagged, abruptly halted, or were suffocatingly narrow.

There had been much recent talk about solving these problems and of beautifying the city, as well. In 1902 the Civic Improvement League was created for these purposes, but the tasks before it were too substantial for it to make much headway. In fact, the problems clearly exasperated the president of the organization. "There is scarcely a more slovenly community in the United States than this city," he lamented. Then, as an afterthought, he amended his comments—there was hardly a more slovenly community in the whole world.

BUSINESSMEN TAKE CHARGE

How could complex matters such as these best be handled? The past record of cities elsewhere was not encouraging. In these early years of the twentieth century notions concerning the proper management of municipalities were experiencing sweeping change. A careful student, Delos F. Wilcox, declared in 1913 that the ideas of city government that had prevailed just ten years earlier were on a par in their antiquity with the ethics of the pirate chiefs of the eighteenth century.

Influential people in Dallas, seeing the great reforms occurring in other cities, concluded that their own alderman or "ward" system of representation no longer could handle the city's increasingly tangled problems. The present system was a complicated one in which ten aldermen were elected from as many wards, and five additional aldermen were chosen to represent the entire city "at-large." Voters also elected the key municipal administrators, including the attorney, tax assessor, tax collector, health officer, three-member board of appeals, street superintendent, waterworks superintendent, and still others. Those elected were widely held not to be of the high-caliber needed to conduct the city's affairs. Those elected by specific districts tended to look first to the needs of their constituents, and only then to the needs of the whole city. More and more people thought this was the reverse of how things should be. The entire set-up was too cumbersome for an efficient, business-like operation at city hall.

In the 1906 city elections voters had approved a change to the innovative commission form of government in which only five elected officials—a mayor and four commissioners—would run the city, much like the president of a company and his vice presidents. Dallas County's delegates to the Texas Legislature and a committee of prominent local businessmen were devising in Austin a new charter to provide this form of government. None dared say it, but this commission plan with its at-large elections concentrated on five positions instead of more than twenty would diminish the power of the working classes and political minorities; it would enhance that of the upper classes. This was not clear to all, though, for included on that charter committee dominated by businessmen was an outspoken Socialist lawyer, George Clifton Edwards, who very much favored the charter change. Pleasing to Edwards and grassroots voters was a measure permitting the recall of elected officials who engendered widespread dissatisfaction.

The commission form of government had been introduced in Galveston to great acclaim after its disastrous 1900 flood. It was a plan greeted with enthusiasm in cities across the land; a hundred or so municipalities adopted its format in the decade following Galveston's breakthrough. In 1903 the *Dallas Morning News* printed a series of influential articles by its crackerjack reporter, Tom Finty Jr., describing its benefits. Finty had first-hand knowledge, for formerly he had written for the *Galveston News*, parent to its junior partner, the *Dallas Morning News*.

The genial man who presided over Dallas as mayor under the "ward" system, Curtis Pendleton Smith, amiably accepted the possible benefits people were saying would come from this new system. He favored efficiency; he would not stand in the way of progress. He had taken the popular cry, "lift Dallas out of the mud," to heart during his brief term in office, earning the nickname, "the man who does things." In less than twelve months his administration had paved 2.8 miles of streets, including nearly two miles on Ervay Street alone. Sidewalks had almost equal priority. Under the mayor's administration the city had built 10.5 miles of sidewalks in cement and 14.5 more miles in cinder. Seventeen miles of water mains had been laid. The mayor had arranged for "universal" streetcar transfers to permit passengers to travel the various city routes with far greater ease than before. He had brought about the installation of heaters on all those streetcars, too. Most folks were pleased that he had established a board of health. Indeed, he appeared to be concentrating carefully on providing the services that growth demanded. Mayor Smith, forty-three years of age, was dignified in demeanor and handsome in appearance. He carried out his duties with decorum, working from an office adjoining the council chambers at the fancy four-story city hall building at Commerce and Akard, built there in 1889.

The mayor had arrived in Dallas twenty years earlier holding no more than the stub of a railroad ticket, a law diploma, and a few dollars of change, a "a poor boy, a stranger in a strange land." Success had come to him because of hard work. That was how he viewed it. And while he surely was right about the hard work, his background had not really been one of poverty. His father, a prominent Indiana physician, sent him to DePauw University for both A.B. and A.M. degrees, then on to the Cincinnati Law School for a law degree. With these credentials in hand, to begin his career Smith moved to the city that was making so much noise down in Texas. Within a year he became assistant to the city attorney. Before another year passed he found himself frequently presiding as judge over City Court. Service on Dallas' public school board, two terms as city alderman from the Third Ward, and then four terms as city judge seemed to have prepared him well for his election to the mayor's office in 1906.

There were those, though, who did not think Mayor Smith had the skills necessary to continue serving the city in his lofty capacity. Under the new form of government the mayor and four commissioners would have broad powers and a great margin for error. A high degree of management skills would be needed for these positions.

Foremost of those ready for a change in leadership was the aggressive young business tycoon, Henry Dickinson Lindsley, president of the important new insurance firm, Southwestern Life, and son of a prominent Dallas lawyer. Despite his father and other family connections in Dallas, it would not be right to say that Lindsley had not accomplished great things in his own right, for not only had he organized Southwestern Life, he had proved to be an astute entrepreneur in finance, real estate, and insurance, outdoing his father and uncle. It seemed to Lindsley, who was thirty-five, that the new leaders of the commission form of government must possess strong business backgrounds. Mayor Smith seemed not to have this background. Recently, an overdraft in the city treasury of $122,000 had caused some alarm about his capabilities.

The kind of men whose leadership Lindsley believed city hall needed were people such as J.B. Wilson, head of the Dallas Consolidated Electric Street Railway Co. , who a few years earlier had built the eight-story Wilson Building; Royal A. Ferris, president of the American Exchange National Bank; Alex Sanger of Sanger Bros.; and C.C. Slaughter, the fabled cattleman and businessman. Of course, such men as these were too busy themselves to hold municipal office, but their expertise and leadership were there to be called upon, given the proper format.

To create that format Lindsley summoned the important men of Dallas together on Monday, March 4, 1907, to the Commercial Club to establish an association devoted exclusively to municipal politics. In this crowd of venerable, white-haired, mustachioed men, Lindsley's clean-shaven face, slicked-down modern hair-style, and protruding ears gave him the appearance of a callow high school boy. Yet, he confidently outlined for these businessmen an overall philosophy for the organization. The men listened and agreed to a concept that would be utilized for running the city for many decades to come. They would not themselves be candidates for office, but they would select men with appropriate backgrounds to be mayor and commissioners, establish a platform for them to run on, energize the city behind them, and then see to their election with the ample resources they commanded. Similar organizations had arisen in other cities after muckrakers such as Lincoln Steffens had exposed political bosses, spoils systems, corruption, and inefficiency. Examples of municipal reform existed in New York, Chicago, Philadelphia, Cleveland, Minneapolis, San Francisco, St. Louis, and Toledo. The fact that businessmen who were spearheading this Dallas reform movement was not surprising; business leaders were largely responsible for the wave of municipal reform in cities across the nation.

No political corruption had been discovered in Dallas. Mayor Smith was honest and upright. But the new form of government would give top office-holders much broader powers, and Lindsley envisioned accomplished leaders who would resist opportunities for private gain that might tempt ordinary men.

Lindsley, of course, was selected president of the organization, which took the name that first meeting of the Citizens Association, shortened in headlines to "C.A." and later to "Cits." Afterwards, Lindsley stressed especially that the Citizens Association would be non-partisan and open to everyone. Its whole purpose was for "the good of the city."

Soon after the Commercial Club meeting the Citizens Association held an open and public session at the club's auditorium. On the stage this night sat a committee of seventeen of the town's most prominent citizens, including J.B. Wilson, Alex Sanger, E.M. Kahn, George H. Schoellkopf, A.A. Everts, and Harry Seay. Also on stage were the group's new officers: president Lindsley, vice president Fred P. Wilson, secretary E.H. McClure, and treasurer Royal A. Ferris.

In opening comments Lindsley assured the crowd that the organization had no "political ambitions." Instead, its purpose was to see "that only good and efficient men are elected." The distinction was not a clear one. No candidates yet had been selected, but pledge cards to support these candidates, whomever they might be, were passed among the crowd for signatures. Some declined to sign, saying that they could not agree to vote for any man without knowing who he was.

Mayor Smith suddenly had found himself an outsider in his own city. Newspaper reporters asked for his impressions of the new organization. He had to plead a lack of information. Still, he couched an opinion carefully in theoretical terms. If such an organization had as its sole purpose securing the best candidates for city offices, then it should be encouraged. But, he observed more pointedly, if such an organization were created for selfish aims and self-aggrandizement, all good citizens would condemn it. "No clique or faction or set of men," he said, "should be permitted for one moment to abrogate to themselves the exclusive right of dictating a mayor and four commissioners to govern this city."

To make his own position clear, Smith confirmed that he would campaign for re-election as an independent. He would stress the same kinds of issues that had brought him to office: rehabilitating the water system, paving the streets and sidewalks, and finding better means for disposing of the city's sewage. "I do not propose to be dominated or controlled by any faction, sect or creed, but if given endorsement by the people again I will dare to do what in my judgment is right and proper, and let the criticism come afterwards, if there be any," he said in carefully measured phrases.

With no Citizens Association candidates yet named, Lindsley concentrated on building membership, especially from the "laboring classes." Less than a week after the association's initial meeting he reported membership to be 1,300, a healthy percentage of the city's estimated 7,800 eligible voters.

Lindsley announced a declaration of "principles" on which the unnamed Citizens Association candidates would campaign. Their goals were virtually identical to Smith's, except that they stressed changes in regulating utility companies serving the city. Lindsley and the Citizens Association took special aim at what had been identified in other cities as the manipulative, anti-democratic powers behind the scenes: the utilities. The C.A. would limit these franchises, including streetcar companies, to twenty-year licenses. It was alleged that Smith, in contrast, favored fifty-year franchises, an allegation he denied.

In April Governor Thomas M. Campbell signed the legislation authorizing the commission plan of municipal government for Dallas. This came two months after he had signed a similar bill authorizing Fort Worth to adopt the commission plan. (This Fort Worth had done on April 2 after a campaign extolling the same benefits envisioned for Dallas.) Dallas' plan provided for an annual salary of $4,000 for the mayor and $3,000 each for the four commissioners. The mayor would preside over meetings, wield important appointive powers, and possess veto authority that would require the votes of three commissioners to override. Each of the four commissioners would serve as the administrative head of certain city departments under the broad categories of waterworks, revenues and taxation, police and fire, and public works. Just after Governor Campbell's approving action, the Citizens Association announced on Saturday, April 14, its slate of candidates. All five men had strong business backgrounds.

For mayor the nomination went to Stephen J. Hay, secretary-treasurer of the Texas Paper Co. and a director of Lindsley's Southwestern Life Insurance Co. Hay, forty-three years of age, had moved to Dallas from Atlanta in 1887, taking a position at the paper company as a bookkeeper. He had been one of the founders of Trinity Methodist Church. He now was president of the Dallas school board. For the past six years he had chaired the board's finance committee. The fact that the school district had surplus funds in its budget was touted as one of Hay's special qualifications, one that stood in contrast to Mayor Smith's overdraft at city hall.

The four candidates for commissioner held similar business qualifications:

*William Doran, a native of Ireland, had been involved in the cattle business since coming to Dallas in 1875. Doran, his brother, and another man had founded the city's first packing company, Dallas Packing.

*Charles B. Gillespie, born in Arkansas, had come to Dallas as a boy of thirteen in 1867. For the past seventeen years he had been involved in real estate. Earlier he had served Dallas County as assistant treasurer and assistant tax collector, and from 1882 to 1890 he had been county tax collector.

*Harry L. Seay, a lawyer and the youngest candidate at the age of thirty-five, was a Tennessean by birth and the only Citizens Association candidate who held a college degree. He had moved to Dallas in 1893.

*Dan F. Sullivan, a native of Philadelphia, had been a resident of Dallas since 1878. Two years earlier he had retired from the plumbing and plumbing supplies business. He had served the city government previously as water superintendent and police commissioner.

Of the announced candidates, a political commentator in the *Daily Times Herald* observed in lukewarm fashion: "There is not a dishonest man in the bunch—not an extraordinary genius in the political corral. They are all average men—no more, no less—and there is not a man in the bunch who will be found unwilling, if elected, to draw his salary on pay day." Clearly, the afternoon newspaper had not jumped on the Citizens Association bandwagon, nor would it do so during this first campaign.

Citizens Association promotional material depicted the candidates as men who had risen from humble circumstances to high positions of confidence and respect. They could be entrusted with the public's affairs at this critical moment. They would hold public office "at a personal sacrifice, actuated only by the belief that the people of Dallas demand from her citizens some personal sacrifice for the general good." They were examples of unselfish citizens who were putting aside their private affairs for the good of the city. They represented the important principle of good citizenship in which the office seeks the man and not the man the office. Their election, it was claimed, would result in benefits "almost beyond calculation." Citizens Association campaign material said that there "will probably never be in Dallas an election of such deep concern to our citizens." The organization called upon "every patriotic citizen of Dallas for his hearty co-operation and support in the election of our entire ticket."

THE 1907 MUNICIPAL ELECTION

In its early days the campaign appeared to be conducted on a high plane, free of personal attack and based upon the qualifications of the various candidates. But behind the scenes the contest, which focused on the mayoral race, quickly became one of invectives which the *Times Herald* observed was degenerating into "one of the bitterest" campaigns the city had ever seen.

Smith complained that while the Citizens Association candidates themselves avoided personal attacks against him, their supporters, whose comments appeared regularly in the newspapers, did not. For instance, N.W. Goldbold, defending the association's decision to select just one candidate rather than several for each office, was quoted as saying that any other course would have divided the votes to bring a victory for the "lawbreakers and grafters." This could refer to no one other than Smith and the other independents. Constant references to the C.A. candidates as "honest businessmen" implied clearly that Smith and other aldermen were not. Smith, disturbed, asked voters to avoid distraction from the central issues of "more water, more paved streets, and more paved sidewalks." He vowed not to be dominated by "extremists" of any kind. "Conservatism will be the watchword," he pledged.

The most vigorous spokesman to emerge in Smith's behalf was Judge W.H. Clark, who declared that the Citizens Association had proposed a most startling proposition—that the "people of Dallas...are not capable of self-government." He sharply criticized the organization for having abrogated unto itself the right to select candidates without a primary. This, he said, was nothing short of a "dictatorship" such as had prompted the Boston Tea Party and stimulated the American Revolution. Judge Clark asserted that Lindsley and his committee of seventeen would be worse than Tammany Hall if their candidates won. Their characterization of Smith and other incumbent aldermen as political factions were "known by all Dallasites to be slander." As for the C.A. platform, it offered "nothing which our present city administration has not given us, namely, an honest, clean, progressive, and at the same time, conservative and economical administration." Judge Clark called Lindsley a "young prince of finance" who thought money ruled the world. Lindsley had no government experience, Clark observed, yet he wanted to be "dictator" of Dallas. Another person who spoke out for Smith was H.G. Jarrell, who after joining the Citizens Association at its inception now had resigned, declaring that the C.A. leaders selected the candidates without consultation from the general membership. "Secret political organizations are a menace to civic honesty and are antagonistic to the principles of free government," he declared.

Lindsley responded to such criticisms by charging that Smith himself had "begged" for the Citizens Association nomination by approaching at least half of the C.A.'s committee of seventeen. The C.A.'s basic strategy was to stress its candidates' integrity and business experience, with frequent derogatory references to Smith's $122,000 overdraft at city hall. Hay told voters that the overdraft reminded him of a story about a schoolboy who was told by his teacher to figure out this problem: "If a frog at the bottom of a well climbs up three feet each day and drops back five feet every night[,] how long will the frog be in reaching the top?" When the boy showed up at school with a slate overflowing with figures, Hay said, he told his teacher that he had not found the answer, but if he had more room on his slate and more time he would soon land that frog in hell. The city hall overdraft, it was contended, stood in stark contrast to the surplus that Hay had left with the school board before resigning to make the mayor's race.

As to the overdraft and accusations of financial ineptness, Smith responded in a detailed speech reviewing the city's financial position. Concerning Hay's surplus of funds at the school board, he said: "It has been easy for him to leave a surplus, but at what expense to the children of the taxpayers and citizens of Dallas! For, while he was saving up a surplus, and making what he presents as a record upon which to run for mayor, our schools were crippled for want of rooms and facilities for teaching limited. Why didn't he use this surplus to relieve the crowded condition of our schools?" (Overcrowding was an acknowledged problem; students were having to attend half-day sessions for lack of space.)

When the five C.A. candidates toured city hall offices, Smith confronted Hay directly. The mayor stepped out of his office and accused Hay of outright lying in claiming that he had lobbied for fifty-year franchises. He called on Hay to identify his source. Hay refused.

A rumor circulated a week before the May 21 election that in these race-conscious times had the potential for damage to Hay's candidacy. It was alleged that Hay's firm, Texas Paper Co., permitted a Negro foreman to supervise a number of white female employees. Hay produced a statement signed by twenty women refuting the charge.

Five days before the election the Citizens Association campaign manager appeared at Smith's city hall office with an unexpected demand. The man, W.T. Henry, clutched a list of twenty-eight election supervisors selected by Lindsley, and he demanded that Smith approve them for duty at each polling place. If he refused, Henry said, he would immediately start mandamus proceedings against him. Smith, surprised and unaware that the law provided for such a thing, agreed to respond by 11 a.m. the next day. "Nobody ever heard of election supervisors in Dallas County before this moment," the perplexed mayor said. Nevertheless, next morning Smith agreed to appoint all of Lindsley's choices. He could see nothing in the law that required it, but he observed that there was no harm in it, either. The independents could have supervisors, too, if they wanted, he said.

Voter turnout was unusually heavy on election day. Independents and Citizens Association candidates alike expressed full confidence in victory. By now, however, the results seemed foregone: 3,500 of the city's 7,800 eligible voters belonged to the Citizens Association. Before the evening grew long it was clear that the C.A. candidates had swept the race, carrying all five positions by similar margins of approximately 3-2. Hay had 3,196 votes; Smith, 2,396. C.A. supporters quickly organized a parade, complete with musicians who played "There'll Be a Hot Time in the Old Town Tonight" as they marched to the Commercial Club to summon the mayor-elect from its inner sanctum, hoisted him onto eager shoulders, and carried him to the foot of the Gaston Building, where Hay spoke. The parade stopped as well at the *News* to cheer that newspaper for its ardent support of the C.A., at the Federal Building, at City Hall (where the band played a mournful rendition of "Massa's in the Cold, Cold Ground"), at the Wilson Building for an appearance by J.B. Wilson, and finally at the Elks Club. Hay promised "no bitter or harsh feelings" toward his opponents.

Smith, watching election returns at city hall, left for home when his loss became apparent. He reported next morning that his wife was "immensely pleased" at the results.

The significance of the C.A. victory was summarized aptly by the "Old Politician" columnist in the *Times Herald*. It was "the power or organization, the potency of cash, the invincibility of numbers." It meant that "you cannot throw a mob against a well-organized and well-drilled army." The Citizens Association spent dollars; the independents, dimes. Smith's campaign expenditures of just more than $1,200 were dwarfed by the C.A.'s disbursement of $6,335 for its candidates.

Installation of the new officers came at 9 a.m., Saturday, June 1, before a packed crowd in the city council chambers. Congratulatory bouquets included a huge, horseshoe-shaped floral wreath prepared by Park Superintendent W.R. Tietze and emblazoned with the word "Success." At the beginning of the ceremony Judge J.J. Eckford called for Smith to step up front. He presented the outgoing mayor with a gold watch and chain on which was the engraved message, "From the City Hall Gang to Curtis P. Smith, the Mayor Who Did Things. June 1, 1907." Smith, visibly affected, briefly expressed his thanks in his last act as mayor.

The incoming officers vowed to uphold both the state and federal constitutions, and, as the times required, swore that they had never fought a duel with deadly weapons. Hay's acceptance speech fit not only his predecessor and himself, but almost all of the self-made businessmen of Dallas. "My mind goes back today to a morning twenty years ago when I arrived in Dallas, without money and without friends. Dallas has been good to me."

The *Times Herald* saluted Smith's term as mayor in a farewell editorial. "He made a first-class mayor, he was a doer of things, he paved streets and he built sidewalks and he did his level best to 'lift Dallas out of the mud.'" Despite his relative youth and his broad municipal experience, however, Curtis P. Smith declined to involve himself any further in Dallas' public affairs in the years to come. His short term of office soon was forgotten.

Three days after the election Lindsley announced that the Citizens Association would be a permanent organization that would concentrate on municipal affairs. While there would be no regularly scheduled meetings, he urged members to hold themselves "in readiness for a call to public duty whenever a crisis shall arise."

Two years after the election Henry D. Lindsley's father, Philip, wrote a massive two-volume book celebrating Dallas entitled *A History of Greater Dallas and Vicinity*. In it he extolled the accomplishments and characters of countless local citizens, but former Mayor Smith merited not a single word. In Philip Lindsley's mind, the Citizens Association founded by his son had won endorsement from "all classes of citizens, with wonderful unanimity." This was an exaggeration, but certainly his son had founded an organization which along with descendant organizations was to exert a powerful, compelling influence in the affairs of the city for years to come and give Dallas a lasting reputation as a place whose affairs were dictated by a coterie of powerful downtown businessmen.

A Devastating Flood

In the early hours of Monday, May 25, 1908, Erven Pemberton, a young stereotyper at the *Dallas Morning News*, finished his work and departed on foot in a steady downpour for his home on Eagle Ford Road (later Singleton Boulevard). It had been raining for three days in the upper watershed of the Trinity River. That morning's edition of the *News*, already running off the presses, carried headlines about awful flooding through Texas and Oklahoma. As Pemberton crossed the river over the long, wooden Texas & Pacific trestle, he could see below a frightening sight—the normally sluggish stream now swollen far out of its banks, churning and spitting as its waters powerfully surged downstream in the dark. Just a month earlier heavy downpours had brought the Trinity to flood stage at forty feet, its highest level in years. Fields remained saturated and creek and river beds still were swollen, and now there was even more rain. When Pemberton reached his house he found it already flooded. His wife and young child were safe on the opposite side of the water, but there was no way he could join them. He tried to wade through the current to rescue what belongings he could from his house, but the water was too high and rising. Thinking now of the newspaper and the need there for information, Pemberton ran toward the *News*.

As he crossed once again the T&P trestle he heard from below a man crying desperately as he clung to a piece of driftwood while the water carried him downstream. Pemberton tried to climb down to pull him to safety, but he could not, and the hapless victim faded from view still emitting "despairing cries."

At the newspaper Pemberton found staff members already gathering details about the flood and preparing for an "extra" edition to be published at 4:30 a.m. It contained as much information as could be gathered in these hectic pre-dawn hours, and the available facts clearly suggested that a major disaster was in progress. Pemberton's narrative formed a part of the frightening story which told of the Trinity's sudden rise between 10 p.m. and 3 a.m. from 28 feet to 41.5 feet with the water still climbing at press-time.

The special edition carried a number of ominous details. John M. Bassett, chief engineer of the city waterworks, said that by 4 a.m. the flood already was five feet higher than it had been in April. The water inundated the boiler room of the Turtle Creek pumping station, put out its fires, and stopped the steam-powered pumps, leaving the city without water pressure. The telephone company reported all lines to Oak Cliff down, and at 4:10 a.m. the Dallas Electric Light Co. told the newspaper that two feet of water already had flooded its power house (soon it would reach nine feet). The building was in darkness. Soon the entire city would be without electricity, water, and fire protection, a condition that would last for days.

Thus began what was to that point the most disastrous natural calamity ever to occur in Dallas. The Trinity peaked at a depth of 52.6 feet, spreading water over areas never known to have been touched by previous floods; four or five people--the exact figure was never determined--lost their lives; as many as 4,000 people were left homeless. Officials estimated early property damages at $2.5 million. The water swept away the "Long Wooden Bridge" erected in 1890 between Cadiz Street and Oak Cliff, and also the approach to the Commerce Street bridge, separating the city into two parts. Residents could reach the other side of town only by boat. Telegraph and telephone lines to the outside world collapsed. Rail service had to be cancelled because of high water and damage to railway tracks and trestles. The failure of the electric power plant—totally for three days and partially for nine—stopped all streetcar service. The flood water proved to be uncommonly slow in subsiding; twelve days after the first disastrous day the Trinity was still at flood stage, 31.1 feet.

The greatest single horror occurred at mid-morning on that first day before a huge crowd of mesmerized citizens, estimated at 15,000, who lined the water's edge on the high bank near the courthouse (as they were to continue to do for the next several days) to watch the yellowish water carry with it all sorts of debris—logs, outhouses, sheds, trees, and an occasional struggling, hapless animal. For a closer view a number of daring men stood directly above the water on the long, wooden Texas & Pacific trestle, the same one Pemberton had crossed. Some of them were railroad employees, evidently examining the structure's condition, for the constant force of the water had seriously weakened its foundation. Without warning the trestle pulled entirely loose from both ends, and tumbled downstream with the men desperately clinging to it. Some held fast to the framework; others tried to swim to shore. Horrified spectators shrieked as they watched the struggle for life.So awful was the scene that "women screamed and fainted, [and] hundreds of men ran from the place to avoid the sight of grim death." Some fifteen men who chose to hold onto the collapsed structure finally were rescued by motor launches. It was widely believed that as many as three of them drowned. Only days later was it realized that all had survived.

Volunteers on that same Monday and for several days to come set forth in boats of all descriptions to pluck hundreds of residents from roofs, tree limbs, and other precarious locations. The opportunistic captain of the small steamboat *Nellie Maurine* began charging residents 50 cents each to be carried between Dallas proper and Oak Cliff. Authorities asked him to concentrate instead on life-saving, but he refused. Sheriff Ledbetter and Judge Nelms, enraged, hurriedly conferred with County Judge Hiram F. Lively. The trio decided that the emergency situation warranted instant confiscation of the boat. This they accomplished before noon. The *Nellie Maurine* was placed in instant service for rescue work, and before dark it earned credit for saving some seventy-five individuals. For the next several days the *Nellie Maurine* continued to engage in rescue efforts, as did another steamboat, the *Anita Belle,* which was lashed to an electric launch, the *George A. Trumbull.* These and smaller boats made torturous journeys amidst treetops and rooftops, debris and wreckage, occasionally bumping into unknown objects beneath the brackish water's surface. One boat's crew no sooner rescued a family of sixteen from a rooftop than the house collapsed and disappeared. Police Chief Brandenburg estimated Monday afternoon that the many boats in service saved that day from 500 to 1,000 lives which otherwise would have been lost.

All of Dallas suffered from the flood in one way or another, by water damage or through the loss of services. Just three blocks from the heart of the downtown district at Young and Lamar, water was four feet deep. The McKinney Avenue and Cochran Street area, normally untouched by flooding, was under water. Particularly hard hit was West Dallas in the area where the West and Elm forks of the river joined. Scores of people there were homeless. In South Dallas water crept half way up the summit of Colonial Hill on Forest Avenue (now Martin Luther King Jr. Boulevard). On Parnell Street water measured eight feet deep in some places. Railroad properties suffered major damages, and the Katy, Santa Fe, and H&TC bridges south of town became so precarious that they could be used only at great peril.

Everywhere carcasses of drowned animals could be seen heaped up in piles and lodged against fences. Some pitiful creatures managed to save themselves. Fowls found refuge in treetops; dogs escaped by climbing on roofs and other high places; cats resorted to tree-climbing. Downtown crowds along the water watched and shouted encouragement to a desperate white stallion as it attempted time after time to find secure footing. They cheered loudly when at last it succeeded and trotted off into the brush with a triumphant whinny. A group of survivors in West Dallas watched another exhausted horse swim for six hours seeking safety. At one point the seemingly tireless horse struggled to climb onto the roof of a house, but the people who earlier had found refuge there fought it off because they feared the roof would collapse under the added weight of the beast. At a ranch in Eagle Ford seventy-five mules drowned. The *Anita*

Belle's captain rescued a pig and a Holstein cow swimming in midstream. The pig survived; the cow died shortly after being pulled aboard.

Homeless men, women, and children congregated in their woeful situations throughout the city at whatever high ground was nearest their flooded homes. Mayor Hay established a relief headquarters on Commerce Street. He quickly named committees to supervise—as best they could under the constrained conditions—distribution of food, shelter, clothing, drugs, bandages, disinfectants, and medical services. Some people had become so hungry that they were capturing pigs, chickens, ducks, and even dogs at the water's edge to cook and eat. State officials dispatched from Austin five hundred tents to be erected as temporary shelters, but they didn't arrive until June 1. Even so, an estimated 800 to 1,000 families used them. Located at several locations, the tent cities were given names such as Camp Hay, Camp Ferris, and Camp Bell.

If all these troubles were not enough, opportunistic vandals materialized. They manned skiffs and "every conceivable contrivance" to reach abandoned or half-submerged houses and to plunder whatever valuables they could find. This meanness extended as well to their rounding up of loose stock and then demanding payments from the rightful owners for their return.

As the water gradually subsided still other problems arose. The bodies of dead animals had to be disposed of. City and county officials made numerous stacks of an estimated six hundred and fifty heads of stock to burn. The value of these drowned stock—horses, cows, mules, sheep, goats, and hogs—was estimated at approximately $50,000. As the water cleared from houses and other structures it left deposits of mud. Before residents could reclaim their properties the city's board of health insisted that they had to be cleaned and disinfected.

PRIVATE RELIEF EFFORTS

With the Trinity still swollen and devastation rampant, Mayor Hay called the town's leading businessmen to a meeting at the Commercial Club. Royal A. Ferris of American Exchange Bank, appointed to head the finance relief committee, reported that his committee had raised about $20,000 during the week without requesting outside aid. But this was not enough. "At our last meeting we were not aware of the extent of the destitution, and I am afraid that most of us do not yet fully realize the extent of it, for the half has not been told." This brought him to the real focus for the meeting—raising money.

"I telephoned Colonel C.C. Slaughter to come," Ferris said. "He is here on my left. He knows what we wanted with him." So, by now, did the audience. They applauded loudly as the famed cattleman-businessman, now seventy years of age, stood up. Christopher Columbus Slaughter, who in the 1880s had been declared the state's largest single taxpayer, owned three West Texas ranches containing approximately a million acres. Along with his father, a friend of Sam Houston's, he had been one of the first Texans to drive herds of cattle north to Kansas along the Chisholm Trail. In 1870 he had moved to Dallas to enter banking and manufacturing. A prominent five-story limestone building bearing his name marked the center of town at 241 Main Street.

"When you need money, you raise it," the white-bearded septuagenarian declared. "That is the way Dallas has done heretofore." He proceeded to list the important projects energetic citizens had supported over the years, from the bringing of railroads in the 1870s to improving the Trinity River to raising money for the new YMCA building. Slaughter, a prominent member of the downtown First Baptist Church who had contributed $60,000 for its new building in 1890, spoke directly of Christian charity and urged that those businessmen in the audience be generous in their donations. As for himself, he was adding $900 to his original contribution so that it totaled $1,000.

Having had his say and with its meaning clear, he spotted in the audience C.A. Keating, the balding, white-haired farm implement manufacturer. "I am going to call on him," Slaughter said simply. Keating, born and reared in Nova Scotia, founder of the influential Texas Disc Plow Co., leading spirit of the Trinity River Navigation Co., and a noted civic leader since his arrival in Dallas in 1875, was ready. He noted that many of the flood victims who had lost all their clothing except for what they had been wearing were reluctant to come into town for help. He urged far wider distribution of clothing to these victims. And, yes, he would match Colonel Slaughter's pledge of $1,000.

Here was some momentum, and Ferris, assuming the floor once more, added to it. He announced that Sanger Bros. now wanted to increase its previous pledge to a total of $1,000. Then Ferris called on Ascher Silberstein, "a man who seldom has much to say." Silberstein, vice president and manager of Dallas Oil & Refining Co., got up from his chair to say, "You may put me down for $1,000."

George B. Dealey of the *Dallas Morning News* next spoke: "I am requested by C. Lombardi [the newspaper's publisher] to say that he will give $100 individually." Mayor Hay quickly responded, "Mr. Dealey, we are in the $1,000 list." "If that is the case," Dealey said, "you may put the *Dallas Morning News* down for an additional $500, making it $1,000." Ferris now singled out M.M. Phinney. "It's his time next," he said. Phinney, head of the Street Railway and Lighting Co. of Dallas, said: "We have already given $250. You may make our contribution $1,000." Thus, the movers and shakers of Dallas responded to the emergency facing the unfortunate flood victims.

Additional contributions of $1,000 arrived that afternoon from Dallas County Commissioners Court, American Exchange National Bank, R.S. Munger, City National Bank, and Captain W.H. Gaston. Then came smaller categories of $500, $250, $100, $50, and $25. What was raised that particular day is not known, but by June 5 the relief fund had reached $49,615.

A REALIZATION

The havoc wrecked upon the entire Trinity River basin was dramatized for readers of the *News* by reporter Tom Finty Jr., who rode horseback through the river bottoms all the way to Galveston Bay to chronicle the devastation. The damage and loss of life brought an immediate realization to Dallas' leaders: the Trinity must be tamed.

This realization coincided with a growing national awareness to address such matters. It was the age of city planning. The gathering of businessmen at the Commercial Club to raise money for immediate relief was the harbinger of future meetings and decisions with important results, particularly the creation and ultimate implementation of a city plan which changed the face of the city and provided a more orderly pattern for growth. But these and other improvements in the city were not to come without considerable effort and pain.

2

Eliminating the 'Social Evil'

Some hundreds of girls are kept in this district as White Slaves; Slaves to Lust, Licentiousness and Debauchery.

–J.T. Upchurch, 1912

An Emerging Metropolis

By 1913 the "City of Splendid Possibilities" had become, by self-proclamation, the "City of the Hour." A national news magazine, *World's Work*, commented with astonishment that only twenty years earlier Dallas had been a "border" town where visiting cowboys regularly shot out streetlights. Those untamed days seemed far away, part of a distant past when cowboys herded cattle to northern markets through town. Now Dallas had 131,276 residents, almost three times as many as in 1900, and almost 40,000 more than in 1907.

So far as the U.S. Census Bureau was concerned, Dallas was not yet a metropolis. It was an "emerging" metropolis, one of nineteen American cities with populations between 100,000 and 200,000. An actual metropolis was defined as a city with a population in excess of 200,000. Twenty-five of these bigger cities existed; almost all were older than Dallas and located east of the Mississippi.

Dallas could claim the tallest building in the entire state of Texas, the beautiful Adolphus Hotel, grandly presiding over a distinctive skyline visible for miles around the surrounding flat lands. In typical fashion, the city's leaders had determined to have such a hotel, and Mayor Hay, Henry Lindsley and Charles F. Bolanz traveled to St. Louis to persuade Augustus Busch, who in 1893 had rescued the new and grand Oriental Hotel with a cash infusion, to build it. Busch agreed, but only if leading Dallas citizens would take a 10 percent interest in the project. This was no problem. No matter, either, that the best location seemed to be the one occupied by the handsome, four-story Dallas city hall, constructed in 1889. It could be torn down and a new one built elsewhere. So the Adolphus, twenty-two stories high, was completed in 1912 at a cost of $1.87 million. Just around the corner Busch constructed a sixteen-floor office building, the Busch Building (later Kirby). Such tall buildings created a downtown canyon where gusts of wind made pedestrians' hats fly off. This, too, was a matter of pride. Such a wind tunnel, opined Alfred O. Andersson's lively *Dallas Dispatch,* was a sure sign that Dallas had passed from the village class into that of the great cities. "There are windy corners in both New York and Chicago, BUT SUCH A THING WAS NEVER HEARD OF IN FORT WORTH. Dallas is the only city in Texas that can boast of one."

DEALEY'S IDEA ABOUT THE TRINITY

The city now possessed a visionary design for its future development. It stemmed largely from the inspiration of George B. Dealey of the *Dallas Morning News,* who had been pushing the virtues of civic planning for several years.

In the winter of 1902 Dealey, then the newspaper's vice president and general manager, had walked onto the Commerce Street bridge overlooking the Trinity River to smoke a cigar. A native of England who had begun his career as an office boy at the *Galveston News,* Dealey had been sent to Dallas in 1885 to be business manager of that paper's new North Texas daily. He quickly developed an intense affection for his new home city; he was to be indelibly linked to its progress for the remainder of his long life. On this day in 1902, though, he had nothing in particular on his mind. As he nonchalantly puffed his cigar and gazed at the bottomland before him an inspiration suddenly came: this worthless land adjacent to the business district one day could become highly prized. Dealey determined immediately that he should buy some of that land, "notwithstanding the fact that I had no money to buy anything with."

He went to the nearby courthouse to see if he could learn the owners' identities. Unable to do so, he obtained the assistance of a friend knowledgeable in title-searching, asked him to obtain the information, and swore him to secrecy for fear someone would learn of his intentions and have the same idea. Dealey decided in his own mind that he would pay as much as $500 per acre for the property. Word soon came that a parcel of nearly 18 acres acres was available at $100 per acre. Dealey quickly borrowed the money and bought it. "When I went home I told my wife that some day real wealth would come out of it....My interest in the development of the valley and the reclamation of the big acreage down there started at this time, and continued," Dealey later would recall. Six months after his initial purchase, he bought a second adjoining parcel of land, and then three years later another. Dealey's life-long interest in taming the Trinity and eventually in city planning thus was born.

His formal thoughts on the matter came in 1909 when he delivered a paper on the virtues of city planning to an intimate circle of influential leaders known as the Critic Club, formed the preceding year by William Henry Greenburg, the rabbi at Temple Emanu-El, with Dealey and Cesar Lombardi, vice president of the *News*. To follow up on Dealey's talk, the *News* began a series of editorials and articles forcefully advocating a comprehensive city plan. After a stirring luncheon speech on the subject in 1910 by the visiting J. Horace McFarland of the American Civic Association, Dealey, the Chamber of Commerce, business leaders, and city officials organized the Dallas City Plan and Improvement League as an adjunct to the Chamber. To draw up a plan the organization hired George E. Kessler of Kansas City, a city planner with a national reputation who had strong Dallas ties. Kessler had grown up as a boy in Dallas with his widowed mother, an art and French teacher who determined that her son's education would include strong components of art and practicality. He had studied in Europe, travelling extensively, and developed a specialty in landscape architecture and civil engineering.

His credentials included work as a city planner for Kansas City and St. Louis, and he had some experience in Dallas, for in 1904 he had been summoned to Dallas to redesign the State Fair grounds.

Kessler harshly summarized the situation he found: "In exaggerated form Dallas today presents the difficulties attendant upon the expansion into a great city of a village at a temporary railroad terminus, no apparent thought having been given in the interim to the needs of a growing population." In 1910 he presented to Dallas a plan as grand and sweeping as it was detailed. It was too ambitious to swallow in a single gulp. But it was there, a City Beautiful blueprint for the years ahead about which the *News* reminded its readers by regularly printing excerpts. A year later, one of Kessler's key recommendations already was being acted upon: nearly $1 million in public funds had been spent to purchase land along Houston Street for a central railroad passenger terminal to replace five separate ones. (The new Union Station building, which opened in October 1916, cost about $1.5 million; other costs, including land, track and supplementary buildings, amounted to $6.5 million. It was owned and operated by the Union Terminal Co., itself jointly owned by the various railroads entering the city.) Among Kessler's other major ideas was the one Dealey particularly favored—confining the cantankerous Trinity River between levees to eliminate the perennial flooding and thereby opening up wide expanses of floodplain, including Dealey's, for industrial planning. Other aspects included eliminating the dangerous and obstructive Texas & Pacific railroad tracks from Pacific Avenue which had blocked downtown growth to the north, lifting the H&TC railroad tracks from Central Avenue to create a major north-south artery for automobiles, straightening and widening certain narrow downtown streets, and developing major new parks and graceful parkways.

Dealey summarized the import of Kessler's plan this way in a letter to him. "As I understand your ideas, the one great big project necessary for the proper development of Dallas is the reclamation of the Trinity bottoms with all that will follow." Dealey expressed to Kessler his "hearty agreement" with that, regarding it as the "fundamental proposition." As for the railroad tracks, that problem seemed insurmountable, for T&P had entered into a franchise agreement with the City of Dallas that guaranteed its right-of-way until 1941. Besides, a number of businessmen on Pacific Avenue relied on the

T&P tracks. Still, neither the T&P nor the H&TC tracks were absolutely essential; the city had an abundance of tracks, and alternate routes were available.

One important thing already had been achieved in the aftermath of the 1908 flood: the construction of an all-weather viaduct linking Dallas to Oak Cliff which could defy the greatest of floods. Voters had approved a bond election for $650,000 to build the viaduct, and when it opened in 1912 some 58,000 spectators came for the ceremony. The Oak Cliff viaduct, later known as the Houston Street viaduct, was billed as the longest concrete structure in the world.

LIFE IN A GROWING CITY

The people of Dallas these days represented just about every known occupation. Among them were 120 barbers, about 300 lawyers, some 250 physicians, sixty-one dentists (one of whom, Hiram Wesley Evans, was to become a few years later the imperial wizard of the nation's Ku Klux Klan), about 100 police officers, 145 firemen, fifty-seven blacksmiths, and two masseuses (Mrs. Julia Hughes at 1103 S. Ervay Street and Mrs. W.V. Looper at 1706 Canton Street). In greater number than any of these persons were prostitutes—as many as 400, many listed by name in the city directory. They lived and worked in an officially designated red-light district immediately north of downtown in an area known as Frogtown. The city also had more than 400 grocery stores, some 200 saloons, about 150 restaurants, five cigar manufacturers, twenty dairies, twenty retail coal outlets, twelve Post Office substations, 923 fire alarm boxes, some 120 boarding houses, four daily newspapers, twenty-five public "free" schools, and six "colored" public schools. There was even a bank owned by Negroes, the Penny Savings Bank of Dallas, located at 595 Elm Street.

Crime existed, certainly, but it was seldom of the sensational variety. Drunk and disorderly was the offense that involved by far the most arrests — 4,515 cases docketed between May 1, 1912, and May 1, 1913. The second most frequent crime was that of vagrancy, with 3,202 cases on the docket. At least twenty-eight persons were charged with murder during that one-year period, and five persons faced charges of reckless driving. Sixty-eight persons had been cited for associating with prostitutes. Police officers worked difficult hours: twelve hours on duty and twelve hours off, seven days a week. The department's new "dog wagon," instituted in June 1912, had proved useful. Nearly 2,000 dogs had been caught on the city streets since then. Of this number, 1,570 had been killed (euphemisms were not used in the year-end report from the Police Department), 353 were "redeemed," twenty had escaped the long arm of the law, and the police chief, for reasons unknown, had released to their freedom forty-seven lucky pooches.

"The City of the Hour" was booming in real estate. At the end of December local experts said that 1913 was the greatest year recorded for the sale of property in Dallas' history. Some $45 million had changed hands in property transfers. Two unusual transactions attracted special attention. In separate negotiations two 99-year leases had been signed, the city's first ever. An obscure young man from St. Louis, newly arrived and intent on establishing a network of movie and vaudeville houses, negotiated one of the leases for property on the north side of Elm Street at St. Paul. This individual, Karl Hoblitzelle, agreed to pay Mrs. S.A. Gibbs upwards of $4 million for use of the property. The other lease for 99 years had been made by Herbert Marcus as a site for a new Neiman-Marcus store at Main and Ervay streets to replace the original store, which had been demolished in a disastrous fire. As for residential property, new developments abounded. They included Munger Place, Winnetka Heights and Highland Park. A fine nine-room, two-story house on Forest Avenue in South Dallas was for sale at $6,500. On a wooded tract of land beyond Forest Avenue just south of the city limits, a new housing development known as Lincoln Manor had been developed for Negroes. Lots could be purchased for less than $50, and a number of Negroes were building frame homes there. In Highland Park a new seven-room brick house with servants' quarters was available for $5,000. The demand for housing was so strong in this growing city that citizens were being urged to build rent houses to accommodate the need.

Other real estate news was even more significant. Ford Motor Company paid $50,000 for a tract of land to construct an assembly plant in Dallas that would be the largest industrial facility in the city. (In 1914 the plant opened at Canton and Henry, where more than 5,000 cars a year soon were being produced.) Just north of town Southern Methodist University was constructing its main building,

Dallas Hall, in preparation for the first students in 1915. Across the street from the county courthouse a new, red-brick eight-story jail and court building going up was to be "the most modern and up-to-date building of its kind to be found anywhere." With the cells being located on the top floors, local officials believed it would be the world's first "skyscraper jail." The federal government had authorized funds to build a new post office, although many leading bankers and businessmen didn't like the proposed location. They sent a petition to Postmaster General A.S. Burleson to ask him to consider a site near the new union depot rather than the intended uptown location at Bryan and Masten streets.

That uptown area was flourishing. The old center of town around the courthouse had been extended as a finger all the way to Harwood Street, where three noteworthy and substantial buildings now stood. Two of them had been designed by the same architect, C.D. Hill. All were constructed in the neo-classic Greek revival style. One was Hill's stately new First Presbyterian Church, built at a cost of $135,000 and dedicated in March. Also designed by Hill was a new city hall going up between Main and Commerce streets. Just south of city hall was the magnificent Scottish Rite Cathedral. These three buildings joined on this far eastern side of the retail-commercial district the Carnegie Public Library, a handsome structure at Commerce and Harwood which had opened in 1901.

The city hall had become necessary when the former building, still a fine one, had been torn down to make space for the Adolphus Hotel. Taxpayers voted in 1912 to allocate the munificent sum of $475,000 for the new building. But by September of 1913 cost overruns were creating angry headlines. "$475,000 Is Sum Voted for New City Hall, Why Spend $600,000 Then?" asked the *Dallas Dispatch* in a banner headline. As costs mounted architect Hill was a principal target for criticism. By October some complained that this new structure would cost the taxpayers not $475,000 but $800,000! Hill also faced accusations of favoritism in awarding contracts. The project, when completed in 1914, cost $929,000—$585,000 for the structure and $344,000 for the land. But the building, made of Indiana limestone, would serve the city well into the 1990s and stand as a handsome, enduring landmark for the east side of downtown.

Residents continued to be concerned about the water supply, but great progress had been made here, too. A drought beginning late in

1910 and extending into 1912 placed the city in an especially difficult situation. At one point water lines stopped flowing. Residents had to fill tubs from forty horse-drawn water wagons. The water supply was down to six weeks when a big rain came. But now, just a year later, all agreed that the supply was plentiful. It was calculated that even if not a single shower fell for eighteen months no one would suffer for want of water. Responsible for this happy new situation was White Rock Lake, so new it was still filling up. The lake, planned by Hay during his time at city hall as mayor, already held 4.1 billion gallons of water, boosting the city's supply to 5.6 billion gallons. (Some had seen the creation of White Rock Lake as a waste of taxpayers' money, preferring the sinking of wells. "We do know that there is just as much water under the earth as there is on the earth, and the proper thing to do is to go after this water under the earth, as we have practical demonstration before us," wrote W.E. Hancock in the *Daily Times Herald*. (The "demonstration" to which he referred included the drilling of wells by such firms as Sanger Bros., Linz Bros., Butler Bros., and Southwestern Life Insurance Company to provide their water needs.) The city also had dammed up water for municipal use at Bachman, Carrollton, Record Crossing, California Crossing, and Turtle Creek. Now, at last, it could be said: "Never before in all her history has Dallas been in so favorable a position to defy drouth."

The city's growing reliance on the automobile was causing problems and serving as a manifestation of progress at the same time. The immediate problem was especially evident on the downtown north-south streets, many of them narrow and crooked and all of them designed for horse-and-buggy days. George E. Kessler called them a maze that needed remedying. Traversing this maze by the end of 1912 were 2,944 cars registered in the city. By mid-April 1913, that number had escalated to 4,544, roughly one automobile for every thirty men, women and children. Nearly fifty automobile dealers vied for this lucrative business. Commerce Street had become an "auto row" of more than thirty dealers soliciting buyers to upgrade their horse and buggy for a motorized vehicle such as a Franklin, Ford, Buick, Pierce-Arrow, Marathon, Overland, or Studebaker.

On workdays some 500 to 600 automobile owners drove their vehicles to their downtown jobs and left them there on the streets—

all day. This greatly constricted traffic. To remedy this nuisance the mayor and commissioners voted to prohibit parking on Main, Commerce, and Elm streets. This would be an inconvenience to many, reported the *News,* but not a severe one for those drivers employing chauffeurs. Several days after its adoption the parking ban—referred to as the "move-on" ordinance—was working "like a charm." It was pointed out that the ordinance actually offered a wonderful opportunity for enterprising capitalists to construct parking garages. Detroit already had one. Jackson Street seemed to be the best location to build one in Dallas.

Some 350 automobile fanciers formed an association, the Dallas Automobile Club. They were building their own facility in the Vickery area far north of town on a 36-acre tract donated by W.W. Caruth. Such a sprightly thing it was to be, with two or three bowling alleys, indoor golf, showers, smoking rooms, and dining areas. Members could fish, swim, and boat, for they planned to build a lake and create an outdoor recreational area. The fact that Dallas' automobile owners had chosen to develop their facility so far north hinted at the long-term impact of the automobile: the dramatic dispersion of city populations far from the center of town.

Another organization, more practical in intent, sought to improve conditions for motorists. This was the Dallas County Highway Improvement Association, formed in 1913 with the familiar slogan, "Lift Dallas County Out of the Mud." In an effort to do just that the organization sponsored in its first year a mammoth volunteer project to improve county roads. In newspaper advertisements the club urged citizens to bring their own spades and devote two days to hard labor. A suggested option was to mail a check for $5 so that a substitute could be hired.

The possibility of building a twelve-foot-wide bitulithic road between Dallas and Fort Worth was being explored by the two chambers of commerce. (The Dallas Chamber of Commerce was just a few years old; it had been formed in 1908 through the merger of the Commercial Club and the 150,000 Club.) The road was estimated to cost as much as $354,000. Such a project might seem startling in Texas, it was observed, but similar ones were common in the East.

While those who owned cars seemed to have caught on to a wave of the future, life was not all that intolerable for the vast majority without a powered vehicle. The city's transportation system, certainly compared to later decades, was remarkable. For travel within town there were four separate electric streetcar companies. For travel to surrounding towns the interurban railroad system, which had its first connection in 1908 with McKinney, now linked the city to a wide area. Two new lines established in 1913 gave Dallas four main routes radiating in all directions to places as far away as Waco to the south and Denison to the north. Passenger service for more remote destinations was available via eight railroad lines, all with regularly scheduled departures and arrivals.

Despite the proliferation and growing popularity of the automobile, "get a horse" was a cry that still could be uttered with some sincerity. Horses and mules continued to be useful as important if diminishing means of transportation. Fourteen liveries in town provided places to stable horses or mules while the owners worked or took care of other business. Farriers continued to make good livings. Two of them were shodding horses and mules on Elm Street, and others operated on Akard, Jackson, Camp, and Wood streets. Three dealers in horses and mules still found enough business to make a living.

Problems other than physical ones certainly existed in Dallas. Louis Blaylock, the sixty-four-year-old police commissioner now in his second term, worried about the evils of dancing. Down at the Queen Theatre ("Where Society Mingles"), men and women with nothing better to do learned the new and daring turkey trot. At other places young folks danced the scandalous "bunny hug" and the "Texas tommy." Alarmed parents were complaining. These dances, said Blaylock, were "all rot." In his opinion they were indecent and shouldn't be performed anywhere because they deteriorated the morals of young people. Blaylock asked City Attorney James J. Collins to formulate a city ordinance forbidding such "terpsichorean luxuries."

Yet another of Blaylock's concerns was the freedom residents continued to grant their fowl. These free-ranging chickens wouldn't stay out of the streets, and as a result Blaylock and the other commissioners adopted a so-called "chicken ordinance" requiring fowl to remain behind fences. It was way past time, many agreed, for the city to shed forever its old country ways.

SOCIALISTS MAKE A SHOWING

The chicken ordinance and others were the business of Blaylock, the other three commissioners, and the mayor. These offices had been filled without exception every two years since 1907 by Citizens Association candidates. The "Cits," as they now were called in newspaper headlines, continued to be supported by leading businessmen and voters as well. In 1909 voters had returned the entire slate to office by an astounding 8-1 margin. In 1911, a Citizens Association team headed by William Meredith Holland again won every city seat.

Now, in the 1913 elections, Holland was up for re-election. He had the distinction of being the city's first native-born mayor and also the youngest to date to hold that office. Just thirty-eight years of age, he was tall, clean-cut and youthful in appearance. Yet, he had experience already as county judge, a position he had resigned to run for mayor. Holland knew the city well, having grown up on North Harwood Street as the only child of an early Dallas attorney and his wife, W.C. Holland and Sarah Holland, both of whom had emigrated to Dallas from their native Tennessee. Holland's father had had his own period in municipal politics, serving as alderman in 1878, 1889, and 1890. He had been active in the effort to improve the Trinity River for navigation, and he was a trustee of the Trinity River Navigation Co. The Holland household on North Harwood had been a comfortable one; the young son had continued to live there at least until he was twenty-five years of age.

In this spring of 1913 Holland was campaigning on a platform of genuine accomplishments, including especially the vastly improved water supply at White Rock Lake. He also boasted of having brought a water purification plant to near-completion, of paving additional streets, of building the new city hall, of instituting the municipal collection of garbage, of working toward construction of the new union depot as recommended by Kessler, and of installing a sewage disposal plant. All this, he declared, had been achieved with no tax increase. Judge Holland was expected to encounter no difficulties in being re-elected, and the campaign was not worth a lot of attention in the newspapers.

One of his opponents, not expected to do very well, was running under the aegis of the Socialist Party, which had been founded in the city shortly after the turn of the century. Though small in number, Dallas' Socialists had functioned effectively and with considerable acceptance in behalf of the laboring classes. The "token" Socialist candidate for mayor this year was a native Dallasite who in 1906 had failed in his effort to be elected governor of Texas. He was George Clifton Edwards, son himself of a lawyer (W.M. Edwards) who had served as an alderman along with Holland's father. Edwards was a visionary. He had left Dallas to be educated at Harvard, studied for the ministry briefly at Sewanee, then returned to his hometown to be a school teacher. Having become a Socialist, he elected to live with the laboring classes in the cotton-mill district in South Dallas to see if he couldn't help alleviate their woeful conditions. Edwards and his wife found children as young as eleven working twelve-hour days, sun-up to sun-down, and sometimes longer. He described the situation as follows: "There is no home for the factory family; there is merely a place to eat and sleep; and some of these hovels here in Dallas, managed by the mill, are almost inconceivably crowded, wretched, and filthy. On the days when the mill does not run at night, the children hurry home at six-thirty, gobble down their food, and then take to the streets, seeking the electric light and the saloon corner as a relief after the monotony of the mill and the misery of their home." These words Edwards wrote in a letter in 1903 to the *New York Evening Post*. To assist adults and young alike to escape these conditions and to help them acquire power through knowledge, Edwards had begun on his own in 1901 to teach evening classes in South Dallas. He soon persuaded Superintendent J.L. Long to incorporate night classes into the Dallas public school system. Edwards' activism inevitably had led to problems. The board of education at first rejected demands to fire him for his political views, pointing out that they were irrelevant to the Latin and albegra courses he taught, but new board members who took office after the next election did not share that viewpoint and dismissed him. He then began to read law in his father's office, and upon being admitted to the bar he assumed the role of champion for the underdog by taking on unpopular causes and cases. His activism had not prevented him from serving alongside the progressive businessmen on the committee to write the new commission charter for the city in 1907.

Edwards' resolve over the years to battle for fair treatment of the Negro and to end lynching had been reinforced three years earlier through his personal involvement in one of the great tragedies ever to occur in Dallas. It happened in March 1910 when he was representing a black man in his late sixties named Allen Brooks accused of raping a three-year-old white child. An angry, lynch-minded mob gathered outside the jail after Brooks' arrest. Brooks was being held elsewhere, though, and the mob disbanded only after a delegation was permitted to search the jail. On the day of his trial a week later the mob returned to the courthouse, certain this time of his presence. They burst through the sheriff deputies' ineffective cordon, climbed the steps to Judge Robert Seay's second-floor courtroom where Edwards and court officials were present, grabbed Brooks from their midst, looped a rope around his neck, quickly tossed the other end of the rope to the mob below, and then watched the crowd pull the struggling Brooks through the open second-floor window to the ground, then kicked and stomped on him. Observers speculated that the head-first fall killed him. If so, it was merciful, for after pummeling him the mob next dragged Brooks' body at the end of the rope through the streets to the Elks Arch at Main and Akard streets. Here his body was strung up to twist slowly in the air. Mob leaders cut his clothing into pieces to distribute as souvenirs of the awful occasion. Afterward, law enforcement officers testified that they had not recognized a single person in the crowd. No one was ever charged with the vigilante action. Edwards had been powerless to defend his client, but for decades to come, his son later observed, in that "small, very southern city," he continued to be the labor lawyer, the ACLU lawyer, and the NAACP lawyer, as well as anti-Ku Klux Klan, pro-Prohibition, and politically a Socialist.

As expected, Edwards and his slate of Socialist candidates failed to unseat Holland and the Cits in the 1913 election, but their show of strength was surprising. Holland's margin was not nearly as one-sided as in 1911. Edwards won 1,809 votes as compared with Holland's 3,164. In so doing the Socialists increased their vote over 1911 by 358 percent; Holland's margin of victory declined by 44 percent. The *Dallas Dispatch* noted, "Another such victory and the Cits are undone—if, in fact, they are not undone already." Never before had the Socialists carried a single precinct in Dallas, but Edwards and the Socialist candidates gained a majority in three wards and nine precincts. Moreover, Dallas voters approved something Holland and the Citizens Association had opposed: the issuing of bonds to construct a municipal light plant.

Encouraged by their strong showing, Edwards and the city's Socialists continued to assail Holland's administration, even collecting signatures in an effort to seek his recall. Their persistent belligerence prompted a number of leading businessmen to meet at the Oriental Hotel and form a group which they called the Greater Dallas Association. Socialists and demagogues were ruining the city, they said, and someone must take steps to curb them. Actually, there was little need for the group. The Socialists never again were to reach the level of strength that they exhibited in 1913. Their rise and decline in Dallas paralleled the party's brief period of popularity in the nation.

OTHER VOICES OF CONSCIENCE

Certainly in Dallas there were many individuals other than the Socialists who displayed strong social consciences. One was R.C. Buckner, who in this year of 1913 celebrated his eightieth birthday. He had reason to be proud of the facility he had established for orphan children east of town. Already it was a revered institution, and such it would remain for decades to come. (Buckner, incidentally, had a strong sense of the past. On orphanage property east of town stood a window-less log cabin asserted to be the first home built in Dallas, that of John Neely Bryan. Another, larger two-story cabin on the grounds was the log cabin in which Buckner had been born in Tennessee. He had moved it to Texas as a reminder of his childhood.)

Dallas had a large number of prominent churches with God-fearing ministers. The churches included fourteen Baptist, fourteen Methodist, twelve Presbyterian, six Catholic, ten Disciples of Christ, five Congregational, one Christian Science, one Pentecostal and one Church of Christ. The 1913 city directory listed twenty-seven "colored" denominations as active, most of them Baptist. Four Jewish synagogues also existed.

Outstanding among the "colored" pastors was an individual whom white Dallas hardly was aware of but whose reputation in some circles was national. He was Alexander S. Jackson, pastor of the New Hope Baptist Church. He was a native of Georgia who came to Dallas from New Orleans in 1899 at the age of forty-two to be pastor of New Hope, the oldest Negro church in Dallas. New Hope had been founded in July 1873 in a log cabin in East Dallas at Juliette (now Munger) and Fairmount, and had thrived under a succession of outstanding pastors. In 1903 under Jackson's leadership the church built a fine new structure at San Jacinto and Bogel streets. Jackson, a former schoolteacher, principal, and college professor, eloquently stated in his sermons the need for racial justice. It was through his writings, though, that his intellect attracted attention. In 1920 he was to publish an analysis of Southern race relations entitled *The Rebirth of Negro Ideals*. The measure of esteem in which Jackson was held, as well as the secondary status then granted black citizens, is suggested by contemporary references to him as the "Negro Truett." He was to remain at New Hope until his retirement in 1933, at which time his son, Maynard Holbrook Jackson, succeeded him. (Some years later his Dallas-born grandson, Maynard H. Jackson Jr., was to be elected Atlanta's first black mayor.)

George W. Truett, with whom Jackson occasionally exchanged pulpits while enjoying a cordial relationship, was the famous pastor of Dallas' First Baptist Church. Truett's long and celebrated career at the church began in 1897, and now he was approaching his prime. Under his leadership First Baptist was well on its way toward becoming the outstanding church in the entire Southern Baptist Convention. A compelling and spontaneous preacher, the Baylor-educated clergyman also had strong organizational abilities and the kind of personality that gave him close ties with Dallas leaders such as Alex Sanger, a Jew. A tragic event had marred Truett's early days in the city. In February 1898, he had been on a hunting trip with the city's police chief of eighteen years, J.C. Arnold, when an accidental shot fatally wounded Arnold.

FALLEN WOMEN

Neither moral nor civic nor government leaders ever spoke publicly of one very visible aspect of Dallas: its flourishing trade in prostitution. The "social evil," as it was called, operated openly with official city blessings in a designated "reservation" a few blocks away from where John Neely Bryan had settled in 1841. This was immediately east of Lamar Street, from Cochran Avenue on the south to the MK&T railroad tracks on the north, and bounded on the east by a small stream known as Dallas Branch in the area sometimes called "Frogtown." (The area included especially the 2100 block of Wesley Avenue, the 1000 through 1300 blocks of Broom [recently changed from Ardrey], and the 2100-2300 blocks of Griffin Street.) City police and county officials permitted prostitutes to practice the world's oldest profession in this designated location without interference. The number of "fallen women" living and working in the reservation was estimated to range between 240 and 400, with the higher figure the most commonly accepted one. The rationale behind concentrating the prostitutes was to prevent them from contaminating the rest of the city. Unimpeded in their quest for customers, prostitutes had become increasingly bold in their behavior. One visitor to Dallas, a writer-researcher named Henry Bruere, said that day or night women could be seen "practically unclothed, always eagerly, sometimes clamorously soliciting trade." So immodest had the women become that Police Chief John W. Ryan ordered them to place screens over their doors and to stay behind them. But it was apparent to Bruere that once the patrol officers had passed out of sight the prostitutes opened their doors to flaunt their bodies again.

The first area set aside for prostitutes by the city had been in the "South End." The new charter of 1907 condoned its existence, but in a gesture toward propriety specified that no saloons could be located there. Judge W.W. Nelms, in making a charge that year to a new grand jury, observed that for many years "by either the tacit consent of our officers or the common consent and toleration of our people," prostitutes had been segregated in the South End. Because that property now was being taken up by the expansion of the railroads, prostitutes were dispersing to different parts of the city, inflicting a "condition" on reputable families which should not be tolerated. For the public good, then, the "social evil" again needed a precise, controlled location, and it had been found in Frogtown.

In 1910 Dallas' city commissioners adopted an ordinance specifically designating new boundaries for the prostitutes in Frogtown. They justified the creation of this "safe" area for bawdy houses along the lines advanced by Judge Nelms. A report prepared by three of the commissioners rationalized the decision this way: "We find that under the existing conditions bawdy houses and bawds are promiscuously scattered throughout the City, greatly menacing the decent neighborhoods and offending decent and respectable communities and parts of the City....We feel that the measure hereby suggested by us will entirely eliminate such objectionable characters from the decent neighborhoods of the City."

A preacher/reformer named J.T. Upchurch, who had been crusading since the turn of the century in Dallas against prostitution and had built a home for "fallen women" in Arlington called the Barachah Industrial Home for Girls, described it in a different way. What the city had done, he argued, was to create a place for the "despoiling of virtue, defaming of character, debauching of manhood, and the prostitution of girlhood." Upchurch said that from the street one could see women in the houses "without clothes enough on to flag a bread wagon." They wore, he wrote, no more than a single thin undergarment with "most of their person entirely bare." Every school child in town, boy and girl, knew the whereabouts of the reservation, according to Upchurch. And when electric streetcars passed along Cochran Street the passengers inevitably careened their heads to peer curiously down the reservation's streets. Writing in his publication, *The Purity Journal,* dedicated to the eradication of prostitution, Upchurch observed in scathing terms the contrast between Dallas' public proclamations of civic progress and this hideous, accepted evil in its midst. "Some hundreds of girls are kept in this district as White Slaves; Slaves to Lust, Licentiousness and Debauchery," he wrote. "Thousands of men and boys visit these White Slaves weekly and carry from that infamous Vice District moral pollution and physical disease to scatter it all over the land."

Most of these women worked out of "cribs," composed of two very small rooms, the front one opening onto the sidewalk and the other just behind. Crib "girls" would sit at their windows or doors to solicit the men or youths who passed by. Occasionally, a woman's "Mack" or "cadet" concealed himself in the back room, and robbed the unsuspecting patrons. Higher-class prostitutes worked out of so-called "parlor houses," where the "girls" were required to be properly dressed, in the parlor beginning at 8 each night, and on the job until midnight or until the last customer had departed.

One Saturday night Upchurch and two other missionaries toured the district to observe first-hand the sinful activities. They entered house after house. In one they found half a dozen nicely dressed white men "hugging and kissing as many negro women." On another occasion Upchurch went into the district to conduct an open-air service, accompanied by his wife and several supporters. Two skeptical police officers asked why he would bring his wife into such a disreputable area. Upchurch responded with his own question: What right did Dallas have to tolerate any street within its city limits where his wife could not go with perfect safety?

If Dallas' high-flown rationalizations for creating a haven for prostitutes were true, Upchurch wrote, then these women were not immoral tramps but martyrs, giving their lives to be burned out in a hell-on-earth to protect the city's pure women. "Why not erect a monument to their memory when they die, and why not give them rent at the expense of the Tax payer? Ah', bosh! Every intelligent man in the land knows that the women are not there to protect pure women, but they are there to gratify the unbridled passion of beastly men and to produce a few grimy, bloody dollars for the lords of the underworld."

If the vice district were truly a necessary adjunct for advancing the city's general welfare, he wrote, no one would raise objections if he reproduced in his publication photographs of some of the houses and the names of the absentee owners of these houses, not to mention photographs of some of the prostitutes—or martyrs—themselves. This is what Upchurch did in the October 1912 issue of *The Purity Journal.* The houses he chose to depict in his photographs clearly were not shabby structures; indeed, those pictured were handsome, two-story frame structures, many with substantial columns on the fronts. Photographs of the prostitutes showed them to be youthful, attractive, smiling, and dressed handsomely in ample white clothing. The owner of the two-story house at 2227 Griffin Street was identified as B.K. Boosterchill. At 2306 Griffin a two-story house with first and second-floor porches extending all across the front was said to be owned "and rented for immoral purposes" by R.M. Chastain (a clerk at Transfer Drug Co.). G.M. Ezell, a carpenter, was identified as the owner of the large rambling house at 1205 Broom Street. In the next block on Broom at 1301-1303 stood a house owned by George W. Louden, who himself lived at 3601 Live Oak. F.M. Donnelly was identified as the owner of a big house whose address was not given. And the "two immoral resorts" at 2116-2114 Griffin Street were said to be owned by the aforementioned Chastain and a local physician, W.W. Samuell, who practiced medicine from an office in the Wilson Building.

The identification of Dr. Samuell, to the reader of today, is a surprise. Here was a citizen already en route to achieving a lasting reputation for his good deeds. During the city's meningitis epidemic in the winter of 1911-1912, when schools closed, streetcars were fumigated, and public funeral services for meningitis victims were prohibited, Dr. Samuell had taken the initiative to contact the Rockefeller Institute in New York for assistance. That organization sent an authority on meningitis to the city to administer a newly discovered serum. Years later Samuell bequeathed to the city's park department an enormous collection of properties, many of which today bear his name, as do a high school and a boulevard. (This gift, the largest by far to be given the park department, was written on a prescription form.)

The profits to be earned through prostitution could not be denied. Henry Bruere learned that one landlord was earning $50,000 a year from several small structures that had cost less than $10,000, including the land.

Although Upchurch had shown photographs in his journal only of substantial houses in good repair, Bruere described the reservation as a place dominated by shacks. Prostitution existed elsewhere in the city as well, he said, despite the city's intentions to segregate it, and the houses outside the reservation tended to be of the "better grade or higher priced kind" frequented by persons who would not dare be seen entering one of the "cribs." Still, groups of bold young men had no such reluctance, and they made happy expeditions to the area. In summary, Bruere called the reservation "a most grotesque commentary upon the civilization of this 'best-governed city in the world.'"

In addition to Bruere's blunt criticisms in a prominent book on municipal government, the city faced condemnation as well at a meeting of the American Medical Association. In a speech to this influential organization Cincinnati's health officer said that the "Dallas plan" places prostitutes in the heart of the city and invites the world to come in and contract horrible diseases.

Finally, in 1913 the city's Council of Churches decided that it no longer would accept the rationalizations for the reservation's existence. Ministers representing the council declared that careful and prayerful investigations led them to conclude that the reservation's commercialized vice was the "greatest menace now confronting the people of this city." The organization announced a series of Sunday meetings in September in which prominent ministers would urge city and law enforcement officials to shut it down.

BREAKING UP THE RESERVATION

The Rev. George W. Truett was featured speaker at the first mass meeting at the First Methodist Church. His topic was "The Social Evil and Fallen Men." In harshest terms before a packed crowd Truett castigated men who were unwilling themselves to operate houses of prostitution but were perfectly content to reap profits by permitting others to use their properties for such immoral purposes. It was "one of the most severe excoriations on the violation of laws in this city ever heard in a Dallas pulpit," recorded the *Dallas Dispatch*. A prominent member of Dr. Truett's congregation was Dr. W.W. Samuell; if he was in attendance that Sunday he must have been squirming, for Dr. Truett mentioned in scathing terms the rumor that—yes—even church members were said to rent property for such purposes. If so, they were "moral cowards." In the several weeks that followed other ministers and speakers declared from various pulpits on Sunday afternoons that the Dallas system must end. They cited not just moral concerns but a terrible toll taken on women who in every house in the reservation presented "pictures of sin and disease and misery and hopelessness."

At the ministers' final meeting on October 5 they passed a resolution urging the dissolution of the reservation. Police Commissioner Louis Blaylock, who months earlier had cracked down on dancing in the city, was at the meeting. Reporters asked him afterwards what he thought. "It was a good meeting and good things were said," he acknowledged politely. "However, I am of the same opinion that I was before, that it would be unwise to break up the reservation to scatter these women over our own city or else drive them to other cities." Such an action, he said, would be like "tearing off the scab instead of curing the disease that caused it." Police Chief John W. Ryan, resplendent with his fine handlebar moustache, agreed with his boss. But County Attorney Currie McCutcheon had been won over. He announced that he would serve notice on the women in the reservation, advising them that they must move out by

6 p.m., November 3, 1913, or face arrest. Police Commissioner Blaylock and the police chief agreed reluctantly to cooperate.

The crusading ministers were not unmindful of the economic and social needs of the women themselves. They announced the opening of a "home for fallen women" called Hope Hall. Prostitutes were invited to enter Hope Hall for rehabilitation. There was a decided lack of enthusiasm. "Currie's a good fellow, but them church guys made him do it!" one of the painted women told a *Dispatch* reporter. One of the women said, "Remember Hawthorne's 'Scarlet Letter'? That's what they are trying to do with that offer of homes."

What happened on that long-awaited day, November 3, was described in the newspaper: "A veritable parade of moving vans, trucks, drays and carts loaded with furniture, trunks and boxes of personal effects moved from the reservation yesterday....Last night the section was dark and deserted. The houses were unlighted and apparently unoccupied. There was no sound of music or dancing."

But where had the women gone? That question worried Dallas in the coming weeks. Only five of the prostitutes accepted the offer to enter Hope Hall. Police matron Mrs. J.J. Farley was disappointed at the attitudes she encountered as she talked to the women. Many of them told her that their needs for money were too critical to give up this lucrative line of work, that they had mothers and children counting on them for support, and that they couldn't earn sufficient money any other way. Officers who had patrolled the area on its last day of operation reported that most of the women not only had left the reservation but also had left Dallas. But Chief Ryan observed that even while the reservation had been occupied, four times as many prostitutes lived outside it as inside it. He supposed that the reservation women had merely joined prostitutes throughout the city.

The Council of Churches was pleased, though. Its executive committee reassured those citizens who were concerned about the impact of the reservation's breakup. "If the people of Dallas could have been present last week when our representatives went through every house in the reservation, if they could have seen the pictures of sin and disease and hopelessness, if they could have heard the sad wail from many lips, 'We know this is no life for any woman, but we have sunk too low to turn back now'—if they could have seen and heard these things, we are persuaded they would agree with the description of one of the women, 'This is like a section out of hell' and none of them would ever defend a reservation again." Owners of the property, having lost their lucrative source of income, said they would convert the sites for business purposes, likely as a warehouse center. (This is what ultimately happened to the precise area, but not until later after an influx of Mexican-Americans who formed a part of what soon would become known as "Little Mexico.")

Scattered reports surfaced about the prostitutes' whereabouts. Fort Worth police were advised to keep these dislocated fallen women out of their city, and they notified keepers of known bawdy houses not to bring them in. A news item from San Angelo described twenty-two of the prostitutes arriving there. A week after the supposed exodus from Dallas, Commissioner Blaylock said that the prostitutes merely had spread throughout town, creating a condition that needed "stringent action." The Dallas County grand jury, acting at the behest of County Attorney McCutcheon, asked Judge Seay to assign two bailiffs to investigate the matter. Such a request, according to the *Dispatch*, in itself acknowledged that immorality now existed in almost every neighborhood of the city rather than safely within the confines of the reservation. A banker was quoted less than three weeks after the shutdown as saying he had been flagged down by a prostitute almost every night on his way home from work.

As the year ended the grand jury reported confidently that "the social evil" had not spread to other parts of town. Less than two months after the closing of the reservation, Dallas was praised for having achieved the biggest clean-up of vice ever made in the United States outside the Barbary Coast and Chicago. Atlanta, Georgia, said to have been made famous by its campaign against vice, had only a small amount of it compared to Dallas, wrote the *News* in a year-end summary about the good things that happened to the city in 1913.

While news about the reservation generally had been relegated to the back pages of the city's daily newspapers (the *Dispatch* excepted), front-page news these days centered on national issues of greater import such as the creation of a new Federal Reserve Bank system. Twelve regional bank headquarters would be established throughout the nation. Here was news that could mean something to the city's future. As 1913 ended, a group of bankers and chamber of commerce officials concluded that Dallas should be the headquarters for the Southwest, and they determined to win that prize.

3

The Boy Mayor Takes Over

If it is right for ten rich men of Dallas to meet in secret and pick the candidates for Mayor and Commissioners of this city, then it is right for ten rich Wall street men to meet in New York and pick the candidates for President and Vice President of the United States.

–James J. Collins, 1915

Winning the Bank

Nothing on his agenda was more important to President Woodrow Wilson than overhauling the nation's banking system. The vehicle for achieving this, the Federal Reserve Act, passed both houses of Congress on December 23, 1913. Wilson happily signed the measure on the same day. The de-centralized scheme recognized the growing importance of areas far from the Eastern seaboard. Cities selected as regional headquarters surely would become financial centers of large surrounding territories. Ambitious cities now entered a race of high stakes—to win designation as headquarters for one of the regional Federal Reserve Banks.

Dallas, "the city of the hour," became one of the first cities—if not *the* first—to proclaim its intentions to win a regional bank. Here was a project worthy of the urgency that won for Dallas its first railroads. Representatives of the local banks, the Chamber of Commerce, the Dallas Cotton Exchange, and the *Dallas Morning News* quickly moved to grab this plum. Telegrams were sent at once to President Wilson, Secretary of the Treasury William Gibbs McAdoo, and Texas Senator Charles A. Culberson. Three Dallas bankers, Robert H. Stewart, Royal A. Ferris, and John W. Wright, interrupted their Christmas holiday season to ride a train to Washington, D.C., to importune members of the site selection committee. This hurried trip failed to be productive. Secretary of the Treasury McAdoo said he was too ill to meet with the group. Secretary of Agriculture David F. Houston demurred as well, saying such a meeting could prove embarrassing to him as a fellow Texan and might compromise his objectivity.

Frustrated in this early setback, the Dallas men created a committee to coordinate efforts and to act more deliberately. In January they conducted a series of well-attended meetings at the chamber to devise a logical and forceful argument in favor of their city.

Bankers Nathan Adams and J. Howard Ardrey traveled to St. Louis to attend one of a series of briefings conducted by McAdoo and Houston. Houston commented that the twelve district banks probably would be placed in those areas which had registered the greatest economic progress in the preceding decade. This was encouraging because Dallas ranked high in this regard. Following up on this tip, committee members prepared an elaborate booklet marshaling economic facts to document the city's recent growth. Entitled "Texas and the Southwest Book of Facts," it claimed among many other things that Dallas now led every city in the Southwest in population (131,276), in wholesale business, in the number of wholesale houses, in factory output, in number of factories, in freight business, in postal receipts, and in new building permits.

At a federal hearing that spring in Austin the Dallas team was disheartened to hear Secretary Houston observe that agricultural Texas would benefit best by being placed in a district headed by a northern city with strong manufacturing interests. A link with St. Louis or Chicago, he believed, would create a more balanced economic unit. But Dallas spokesmen argued that Texas no longer should be thought of strictly as an agricultural domain. Nor was Dallas subordinate to St. Louis in commerce, for "the city of the hour" had captured a large trade territory formerly belonging to St. Louis. Dallas sold a greater volume of goods to Southwestern retailers than did St. Louis, the leaders argued, and 600 of Dallas' 2,200 traveling salesmen operated beyond Texas' borders. As for population, the number of residents within a hundred-mile radius of Dallas was just as great as that of the more widely known St. Louis and Kansas City. What's more, Dallas was *growing faster*.

Within the following weeks the committee orchestrated a steady barrage of similar messages to federal officials believed to have influence: President Woodrow Wilson's Texan aide, Colonel E.M. House; Secretaries McAdoo and Houston; Comptroller John S. Williams; and Texas senators Tom Sheppard and Culberson.

Then came an important break. Otto Praeger, a former correspondent of the *News* who just had been appointed postmaster of Washington, D.C., tipped off George B. Dealey that site selection committee member A.S. Burleson, postmaster general, was coming to Texas. Here was a man with powerful influence. Dealey arranged for his ace correspondent, Tom Finty Jr., to accompany banker Ardrey, who had taken a leadership role on the local committee, and intercept Burleson when he changed trains in St. Louis. They would accompany him to Texas and place before him Dallas' case in uninterrupted fashion. Finty, a veteran political reporter, could capitalize on his long-time friendship with Burleson. Ardrey was well-armed with economic data supporting Dallas.

Ardrey, thirty-six years of age and the cashier at City National Bank, was a solid citizen with impeccable credentials. Member of a prominent Dallas family, he had served as alderman and mayor pro tem from 1904 to 1906, and he was the first president of the city's highly visible 150,000 Club. Ardrey also had headed the City Plan League and played a role in persuading the city to hire George Kessler in 1910.

Finty, a native of Illinois, had been a store clerk, a railroad telegrapher, railroad station manager, court stenographer, and then lawyer before joining the *Galveston News* in 1894. As political editor for both the Galveston and Dallas newspapers, he had made wide acquaintances in influential circles. In this capacity he had known Postmaster Burleson for years.

Before the pair caught the train for St. Louis, Dealey devised a secret code that would permit confidential telegraphic communications between Dallas, St. Louis, and Washington. Arriving early in St. Louis, Ardrey and Finty checked into the Planters Hotel, where they read a coded message notifying them of Burleson's arrival hour. The two interpreted this as meaning the next day. They made plans to go to the theater that evening. For some reason, perhaps as a precaution, Finty first returned to the train station. To his great surprise he encountered Burleson already in the process of changing trains to continue to Texas. Finty raced to the nearest telephone, summoned Ardrey to come at once, and the two managed to board the train and reserve a drawing room. Burleson, travelling economically in a Pullman lower berth, accepted their invitation to relax in their drawing room. As the train rolled on to Texas through the night, Burleson sat in the drawing room with Ardrey and Finty until 2 a.m. "When the train conference broke up, I am convinced we had sold him on the idea," Ardrey later said.

On April 2, Dallas' efforts were rewarded. The city was announced as the site of one of twelve Federal Reserve Banks. Dallas' bank would serve all of Texas, two-thirds of Louisiana, half of New Mexico, one-third of Oklahoma, and a section of Arizona. Rejoicing was intense. A chest-thumping congratulatory newspaper advertisement by Dallas Trust and Savings summed up the local feeling that the selection meant the city was destined to become one of the most important cities of the United States. "It means a great increase in population. It also means a great expansion of our commercial and industrial interests. It means that many new and important enterprises will seek a home in Dallas. In short, Dallas is on the eve of an era of prosperity seldom if ever experienced by another city."

This, indeed, was a crowning achievement which acknowledged Dallas' emergence as probably the key city of the Southwest. It confirmed the city's self-image in that respect, and in more concrete terms it endowed Dallas with a full-blown banking institution of major proportions. The Federal Reserve Bank began with $6.5 million in capitalization as opposed to the combined capital of local banks of $5 million.

Dr. G.W. Benn of the Council of Churches reminded citizens to be thankful to God "for his goodness in giving Dallas the national reserve bank." And for Sunday, April 5, which was "Go to Church

Day," Benn urged worshippers to give special thanks in their prayers to God for remembering their city.

Ardrey surely would have continued to be one of Dallas' outstanding banking and civic leaders for decades to come, but two years later he moved to New York City, where he began a long and successful banking career. Finty, who ten years earlier had distinguished himself with his important series of articles espousing the commission form of municipal government, now earned promotion at the *News* by being selected as the first editor of its new afternoon newspaper, the *Dallas Journal.*

THE CITS HIT A SNAG

Since its beginning in 1907 the Citizens Association had won every mayoral and commissioner election by handy margins. When the founder of the organization, Henry Lindsley, announced his own candidacy for mayor in the spring of 1915, it was expected that the pattern of lop-sided victories would continue.

One who concluded, however, that the Cits' dominance must be challenged was former city attorney James J. Collins. "It is repugnant to me to see a city dominated by a few men, as this city is," he declared in announcing his own candidacy for mayor. Collins led a new political organization called the Peoples Independent Party (soon shortened in newspaper headlines to PIP or Pips; the election thus became the Cits vs. the Pips). Collins complained particularly about the closed-door methods by which the Cits named their candidates. "If it is right for ten rich men of Dallas to meet in secret and pick the candidates for Mayor and Commissioners of this city, then it is right for ten rich Wall street men to meet in New York and pick the candidates for President and Vice President of the United States."

Collins' running mates on the PIP ticket were J.O. Gill, an architect and builder, for street commissioner; H.L. Tenison, a businessman, for finance commissioner; J.P. Greenwood, an engineer, for water and sewer commissioner; and R.P. Keith for police and fire commissioner. With Lindsley on the Cits ticket were Otto H. Lang, an architect, for street commissioner; Manning B. Shannon, finance commissioner; A.C. Cason, water and sewer commissioner; and R.L. (Dick) Winfrey, police commissioner.

The race was easily the most hotly contested since 1907. The two major newspapers took opposite positions. The *News*, as usual, favored the Citizens Association slate. The *Times Herald* jumped ship to support the new organization, characterizing the *News* as "the bat boy of the corporations and the general flunky of big business."

Lindsley and his fellow Cits running mates stressed in their campaign a need to develop more local industry and to encourage outside investment in the city. They also displayed their progressiveness in their calls for free textbooks in the public schools and for more parks, playgrounds, and swimming pools. The PIPs pushed for lower rates from the gas, electric, and street railway utilities, and for free use by citizens of the city hall auditorium. Central to their campaign was a heavy barrage of criticism about elitist control by a chosen few.

The PIPs' difficulties in challenging a dominant political group were evident. In the closing days of the race the PIPs issued a "warning" to voters that Citizens Association businessmen were trying to "intimidate, cajole and browbeat" their employees to vote for their candidates. On the day before the election Cits campaign signs appeared in paint on the city's public sidewalks. On election day the PIPs' campaign manager protested against election officials wearing Citizens Association buttons on their lapels.

Voter turnout was the highest in the city's history. Better than 80 percent of the nearly 16,000 qualified voters cast ballots. Citizens Association candidates once again carried the day easily, though, winning twenty-eight of the city's thirty-three precincts. Lindsley's margin over Collins was 7,882 to 4,102. For the fifth consecutive municipal election Citizens Association candidates had won every single office.

At this point it seemed unlikely that the Cits ever would lose their tight grip on city hall. Heady with this record of success and confident in his abilities to guide the destinies of his city, Lindsley, looking not unlike a younger President Woodrow Wilson, set a commendable record of progress far into his single term of office. He spoke eloquently in front of the Liberty Bell when it stopped in Dallas on a national tour, and he pushed his pet, progressive projects at a dizzying speed: a public health board, a public welfare department, a free legal-aid clinic, a city employment office, reorganization of Parkland Hospital, and an overnight shelter for the homeless. Mindful of Kessler's recommendation to remove the T&P tracks from Pacific Avenue, Lindsley initiated a series of restrictive ordinances against the railroad—especially greatly curtailed speed limits—in an effort to force it to abandon the grade crossings. He set in motion a plan to streamline the city's franchise system for public utilities by creating a single street railway system and a single light and power company. These new franchise arrangements were to be submitted to voters for their approval in the 1917 municipal election. Under the new streetcar franchise the competing systems would be combined into one under the direction of C.W. Hobson, bringing anticipated lower fares and improved service. The new light and power franchise would be assigned to J.F. Strickland, and it too was touted to bring lower rates and better service. So successful was Lindsley as mayor that many speculated that his next political objective would be the governor's office in Austin.

On the last day of March 1917, two weeks after Russian Czar Nicholas II abdicated and with United States' participation in the First World War growing much closer, the Citizens Association held its biennial mass meeting at the city hall auditorium to approve a platform for the May 3 election. The crowd of about 1,200 men greeted Lindsley with enthusiasm. His speech, however, contained a bombshell that in coming days would split apart the Citizens Association and throw the mayor on the defensive throughout his campaign for re-election. He declared that he had changed his mind concerning the two new franchise agreements. He no longer endorsed the changes that he himself had prompted and arranged. He would vote against their approval. He now said he believed the property valuations were inflated (the basis for setting consumers' rates), the rate of returns they would be authorized were too high, and approval would place around the franchises a protective "Chinese wall" that never could be tumbled. They would become "perpetual," and this, Lindsley stressed, was wrong.

Dallas' business leaders, including the majority of the Citizen Association's own executive committee, were shocked. They had been convinced, in large part by Lindsley, that the franchise reorganizations were central to continued progress. Prominent businessmen immediately took issue with Lindsley, proclaiming their support of the franchises, the fairness of the arrangement, the investment of time and money already made, and their faith in the two men picked to administer them—C.W. Hobson of General Electric, who was to head the streetcar system, and J.F. Strickland, an interurban builder who would preside over the new power and light company. Alex Sanger, Leslie Stemmons, Royal A. Ferris, Nathan Adams, Edgar L. Flippen, Edmund J. Kiest, Horatio Adams, Jed C. Adams, H.C. Olmstead, Louis Blaylock, Eli Sanger, and Dr. E.H. Carey were among those who publicly avowed their support of the franchises and the benefits they would bring to Dallas. Three of the city's four commissioners, all Citizens Association men, also strongly supported them.

In the days that followed, Lindsley, out on a limb that perhaps he now preferred not to be on, suffered relentless pressure from newspaper reporters to explain his change of heart. But he would not back down. Strickland and Hobson contended that Lindsley had blatantly violated his pledges to them, and they placed a series of newspaper advertisements to prove their points. Lindsley spoke darkly of a "conspiracy" by the franchise leaders, further enraging them and their prominent supporters.

The Cits' lead candidate, founder of the organization, clearly was out of step with his own organization on a major issue. The Cits' dilemma was no more evident than in the campaign manager whose duty was to elect the entire slate of candidates *and* to win approval for the franchises. He was the retiring city attorney, Charles F. O'Donnell, who had drawn up the franchise proposals. He and top Citizens Association leaders could see no way out of their dilemma but to continue to press for voter approval of franchise arrangements and for the entire slate of Citizens Association candidates, including a mayor who urged defeat of the propositions.

This was more than many Citizens Association members could tolerate. Many began to search, even though the time was late, for a new mayoral candidate who would be acceptable to the business community and who also would favor the franchises. They found a candidate from within their own ranks, a grain dealer named Joe E. Lawther who announced for office as an independent on March 8, just three weeks before the election. Lawther yielded to what he said were endless solicitations from prominent persons and a petition signed by 2,400 voters. A clean-shaven man of forty-one with the profile of a matinee idol, Lawther had come to Dallas from Galveston in 1885 with his family as a boy of nine. On his steering committee were his four brothers, all Dallas residents. Central to his whirlwind campaign was his support of the franchises and his backing of all Citizens Association candidates save, of course, Lindsley.

Lindsley found himself under constant attack. Lawther portrayed him as a spoiled man of privilege accustomed to having his own way, a man who could tolerate no disagreement. "Lindsley talks about the Dallas spirit," Lawther said. "There is no man in this city who has less right to talk about it. There is no man in this city who has done more to kill the Dallas spirit by tearing Dallas asunder with sham battles and by arraying one class against another than Henry Lindsley....All he promises us on the franchise question is turmoil, strife and stagnation of business for years to come....He is activated solely by his own political aims and hope for advancement. He is using Dallas as a political football to help himself."

Lindsley's past feuds with two of his own commissioners, Lang and Winfrey, both of them up for re-election, were highlighted. Lindsley had said he would rather cut off his right arm than run on the same ticket with Winfrey, a comment he surely regretted. He had been publicly critical of Winfrey's police and fire operations, and it was said that he had attempted to withhold funds from police and fire operations in an effort to discredit him. Few were surprised when Winfrey showed up at one of Lawther's campaign rallies and drew wild applause. Yet, Winfrey maintained without enthusiasm that he supported Lindsley. Lindsley also was chastized severely for having slighted former Mayor William M. Holland's accomplishments by pointedly refusing to acknowledge them. Alex Sanger, who had sought to calm the furor over the franchise question, found himself described by Lindsley as a "meddler."

Nathan Adams, the banker, said: "No man ever tried to destroy his friends like Lindsley has. Wake up, Dallas people. Why should you sanction a mayor who allows no man to differ with him?" Attorney Jed C. Adams said, "The king is dead. Long live the people of Dallas." David D. Cahn emphasized the same point: "Russia has dethroned its czar, and Dallas no longer needs a dictator."

The *Times Herald* was particularly vehement in denouncing Lindsley. It carried page-one articles that made no pretense of objectivity. For days before the election the newspaper displayed on page one a prominent box under the headline, "How to Vote for Lawther."

Realizing the difficulty of his situation and his inability to focus the campaign on issues other than the franchises, Lindsley was reduced to pointing out that as the father of the franchise ordinances, he would be vastly more knowledgeable in supervising them than the inexperienced Lawther, whom he labeled a "bolter" and a "traitor" for defecting from the Cits to run as an independent.

On March 25 came word that Lindsley's wife had fallen ill in New Haven, Connecticut, where she was visiting the couple's son, a student at Yale. Lindsley halted campaigning to go to her bedside, not to return until after the election. Lawther, out of respect and fairness, suspended his own campaign activities. Both candidates' supporters continued to work in their behalf, but the fizz was gone in the final week.

On the morning of the election a full-page advertisement appeared in the *News* under the bold headline, "Prominent Citizens' Association Men Repudiate Lindsley's Conspiracy Charge." It was signed by Eli Sanger, W.A. Green, Edgar L. Flippen, Morgan Mayfield, Sam P. Cochran, L. Blaylock, Sam A. Leake, and Dr. E.H.Carey.

Balloting that day, April 3, was even heavier than in the record-breaking 1915 election. Lawther beat Lindsley by a count of 7,125 to 6,012. All other Citizens Association commissioners candidates won their races, although the one commissioner who had been identified as a Lindsley supporter, A.C. Cason, very nearly lost his seat. The new franchise arrangements won approval by a 2-1 margin, and in years to come proved to be entirely satisfactory to the city. In another matter, voters approved a plan to permit fishing in White Rock Lake despite protests about polluting the water supply.

Three days after the election, on April 6, President Wilson declared war against Germany. Lawther's administration during the next two years was destined to be overshadowed by the momentous events in Europe. Yet, much was accomplished during his term.

The new mayor maintained a low profile throughout his two-year term, content to do his work at city hall without summoning photographers every other day. He was said to have "kicked brass band methods out of the city hall." During his term he brought about significant improvements to White Rock Lake, making it truly accessible to citizens by constructing boulevards around its shores and beautifying the area with trees and shrubs (for which he would be remembered by the naming of Lawther Drive). The Commerce Street viaduct was completed; jitneys were removed from the city's streets in favor of total reliance on streetcars; streetcar service was improved; Ferris Plaza was purchased as a park in front of Union Terminal; and resolutions were passed to widen McKinney Street from Griffin to Lamar. Lawther also created Dallas' first city plan commission. He moved forthrightly on the T&P track removal issue, demanding meetings between T&P and city officials to achieve "justice" for the "long-suffering" public. It was Lawther who at last signed the contract on August 23, 1918, for the removal of the burdensome tracks from Pacific Avenue. The long-sought goal had not been easily achieved. T&P officials had proposed to solve the problem by elevating the tracks on a viaduct above the length of the street, and city officials at first approved the plan. But opposition, led by the *Dallas Morning News*, caused the city to change its mind in favor of total removal. On this issue the two newspapers took opposite stands, the *Times Herald* adamantly wanted the tracks to stay.

BOOZE AND BASEBALL

Elsewhere in town, other events gave grist for conversation. At the courthouse the sheriff, rough-and-ready Dan Harston, a former Grand Prairie letter carrier and assistant postmaster, instituted a series of reforms in the jail after his election in 1918. Harston, who sported a handlebar mustache and wore a large cowboy hat, abolished gambling among the prisoners, banned cigarettes for women prisoners, prohibited spitting on the floors and walls, and stopped inmates from striking matches on the walls. He was to be the last Dallas County sheriff who conducted executions in the old gallows in the county jail, for after 1922 prisoners sentenced to death would be transported to Austin for electrocution.

One of Harston's particular problems was in enforcing prohibition, adopted in Dallas in September 1917 three years before the 18th Amendment's nation-wide ban. There had been a thriving trade in Dallas in alcoholic beverages—both in consumption and production. Some 220 saloons and beer parlors were put out of business by prohibition, as were twelve wholesale liquor houses, a brewery, and two branch brewing plants. All of these represented an investment of approximately $3 million in property, equipment, and fixtures.

The sheriff, assisted by deputies Allen Seale and Hal Hood (both of whom later would become sheriffs themselves), arrested in one sixteen-month period more than 250 men and confiscated 150 stills. In one incident Seale and Hood raided a mammoth still at Turkey Knob west of Dallas (one of the hills on the north side of today's University of Dallas campus in Irving) around which breastworks had been thrown up and guards posted. The first guard surrendered after Seale and Hood shot the rifle out of his hands, and the second fled down a ravine with bullets raining around him.

The federal government established during these war years two important military facilities in the city that were related to aviation. A preflight camp at Fair Park known as Camp Dick trained aspiring aviators. North of town at Bachman Lake a 160-acre flying field was built to give final training to aviators before they shipped off to Europe. This facility soon would be known as Love Field.

This was the period when oil-field wildcatters discovered Dallas as a good headquarters for their operations in the Mid-Continent field and for raising venture capital. They filled the Sunday newspapers with huge advertisements that made extravagant claims. "This is not a gamble, but a business proposition," Mason Refining Co. said in its advertisement. "All the undesirable elements of speculation are gone and yet the dividends will be large enough for the speculator." Mason sold shares at $10 each. The Wichita Falls-Burkburnett Oil Co.'s advertisement showed a derrick spouting forth a bountiful stream of black gold. Investors who bought shares at $1.50 each were promised "quick action and large returns." Advertisements for other companies made equally bold promises.

While Dallas had for many years supported its professional baseball team, only in the spring did citizens have an opportunity to see major league players. This occurred when major league teams included Dallas on their pre-season tours through the South. In April 1919 the New York Giants and Detroit Tigers stopped in Dallas for an exhibition game at Gardner Field. One of the game's legendary players, Ty Cobb, the fiery and brilliant center-fielder for the Tigers, was a special attraction. An expectant crowd of 5,500 fans gathered at the stadium to see Cobb and other heroes. Only moments before the opening pitch did Cobb arrive, having just finished a round of golf. For his lateness he found himself a special target of derision from Giants' shortstop Art Fletcher and second baseman Buck Herzog. When Cobb singled his first time at bat, he shouted angrily that he was coming to second base on the next pitch. He did, his spikes flying high, ripping Herzog's trousers and slightly cutting his leg. The two instantly tangled with fists flying. Fletcher rushed to help Herzog. Police officers and teammates had to intervene to separate the threesome. The umpire ejected Cobb from the game, causing the spectators to protest strenuously because the star attraction was gone prematurely.

That evening at the Oriental Hotel dining room Cobb was finishing his dinner when Herzog approached and challenged him to finish the fight. The two agreed to meet in Cobb's room. Teammates cleared furniture for fighting space, and the two athletes engaged in a furious battle, with Cobb getting the best of Herzog. According to one report, the fight was stopped as Cobb was pummeling the prostrate Herzog. So severely beaten was Herzog that he was unable to play in the next day's game, also in Dallas. And Cobb refused to play against the Giants, choosing instead to sit in the stands. Another fiery chapter in Cobb's memorable career thus was recorded.

The Boy Mayor, 1919

As another municipal political campaign approached in 1919, Mayor Lawther announced early that he would be a candidate for re-election, "subject to the will of the people." He had performed capably and business-like in office. Royal A. Ferris backed him. So did former police commissioner Louis Blaylock, who said Lawther deserved re-election by an "overwhelming majority."

The situation placed the Citizens Association in a dilemma because Lawther had been elected as an independent. Should he now be anointed by the organization? Its leaders were of different minds. Some wanted to endorse him; others believed that Lindsley, now completing his war work in Washington, D.C., as a colonel in the Army, should be drafted for a second race. Among the latter was Leslie Stemmons, now chairman of the C.A.'s executive committee. "The only thing wanting now to start one of the hottest political campaigns in the history of Dallas is Mr. Lindsley's consent to make the race," commented the *Times Herald*.

The Citizens Association's executive committee was hopelessly divided. The split was so bad that a majority of the committee members bolted in early February and announced their support for Lawther. Those remaining, led by Stemmons and his friend John J. Simmons, sent word to Lindsley to return to Dallas to make the race. Lindsley declined the offer.

The dissenting pro-Lawther faction, led by Robert B. Allen and Dr. J.B. Cranfill, called a mass meeting at the Oriental Hotel in mid-February to re-group and to legitimize themselves rather than the Simmons-Stemmons faction as the actual Citizens Association. Those attending elected as their chairman Harry L. Seay, who had served as the city's first police commissioner. Stemmons and Simmons were ridiculed as attempting to establish an autocracy. "Brass collars are for dogs, not for men," Dr. Cranfill observed.

Stemmons was not about to concede that the bolters constituted the legitimate Citizens Association. He insisted that he continued to be chairman of the organization. As such, he offered the C.A.'s mayoral nomination to Louis Lipsitz, who promptly became the second candidate to spurn the offer. The *Times Herald* reported that Gross Scruggs was the next choice, with Judge Quentin P. Corley in line behind him.

Then, seemingly from nowhere, a dark-horse candidate named Francis P. Wozencraft emerged to take the nomination of both the Stemmons wing of the Citizens Association and the City Democratic Party. In a combined effort that came to be known as the "fusion ticket," the two parties chose not just Wozencraft but also an identical slate of commissioners. Stemmons was desperately seeking a viable candidate who could restore his Citizens Association faction, and the Democratic Party was eager to make inroads for the first time in municipal politics. Wozencraft, who by now had discarded his childhood name of Francis for the more masculine Frank, was a youthful lawyer just out of the Army. He had served as a captain under Lindsley, a colonel, in the war risk department in Paris. It seems likely that Lindsley, in declining the opportunity to run for mayor again, suggested that his bright young assistant would be a good candidate.

Although only twenty-six years of age, Wozencraft could make a claim to credibility despite his youth. He was the son of a well-known Dallas attorney, Alfred Prior Wozencraft, referred to as

"General" because of his service during the war with Spain when he organized Texas units to fight in Cuba and the Philippines. Recently deceased, he had been associated with the Southwestern Telephone and Telegraph Co. in Dallas. Young Francis, or Frank, born June 7, 1892, graduated in 1909 from Dallas High School, and then earned bachelor of arts and law degrees from the University of Texas in 1913 and 1914. He took a position with his father's firm, Southwestern Telephone, and with U.S. entry into the war he became commander of a Dallas infantry unit that departed for European service. The "Grays," as the unit was nicknamed, went on to see combat duty in the trenches, but Wozencraft was transferred to the safety of Lindsley's office staff in Paris.

Captain Wozencraft's nomination on a joint "fusion" ticket along with four other candidates, none of them incumbents, prompted a short-lived internal Democratic squabble. Some members of the executive committee declared "violent opposition" to the secrecy with which Wozencraft had gained Democratic Party approval. His connections with Southwestern Telephone were especially a matter of concern. By the same token, some members of the Citizens Association also took exception to sharing candidates for municipal office, especially with a political party. This seemed to contradict the very purpose for which the association first had been formed. Nevertheless, the nomination of a war veteran was a crowd-pleasing move, so much so that the "fusion" ticket also nominated for two of the commissioners' spots two other returning Army captains, Hal Moseley for streets and Lawrence E. McGee for police and fire commissioner. In fact, Moseley was still on duty in France, and he would remain there until after the election.

Even so, Wozencraft was the candidate of privilege. In a joint appearance with Lawther before the election he promised to serve in office without compensation. Lawther said he could not afford to make the same offer. "I am not so fortunate as my young friend here....I was not so fortunate as to have been born with a silver spoon in my mouth."

As the campaign developed Lawther's strategy was to avoid further confrontation. Wozencraft called for debate, but Lawther's campaign manager, Mike Murphy, responded that the people of Dallas needed to elect a mayor with "business ability" rather than a "silver-tongued orator." Because of Wozencraft's legal training,

Murphy acknowledged him to be better at oratory. "The greater part of Mr. Wozencraft's life has been spent in school, his honored father having been financially able to give him every possible advantage in the way of securing him an education," Murphy said. Lawther's own education had come from the school of hard knocks, from business experience, and he had "never posed as an orator or 'spell-binder.'" Wozencraft dramatized Lawther's refusal to debate by placing an empty chair beside him at his own campaign appearances.

Three soldiers from the Dallas Grays, newly returned from the war, declared their support for Lawther. One of them said: "If Frank will say to me that he didn't ask to be transferred from the command of the Dallas Grays in order to go into the war risk insurance bureau where he could have a limousine and an office in Paris while other Dallas boys were risking their lives daily in the mud-cluttered trenches and along the shot-swept battlefield, I will believe him and the boys who were on the firing line will feel differently toward him." Wozencraft did not respond.

On the eve of the election the *News* praised Lawther's courageous and efficient record, urging his re-election. Wozencraft, it was declared, was "utterly lacking" in public service experience and in the "ways of men and of the affairs of business." In his campaign he had "failed to advance a single idea that he has a larger and more enlightened sense of the city's needs than Mayor Lawther has." His candidacy, the editorial continued, offered nothing but a "personal ambition that is somewhat precocious."

That evening crowds gathered outside the *News'* office to watch election returns being posted. The result was close, but inside the building a reporter wrote the opening paragraph for the next morning's edition: "Captain Frank W. Wozencraft, lawyer, 26 years old, late of the United States Army in service in France, was elected Mayor of Dallas yesterday, defeating the Hon. Joe E. Lawther, present Mayor." Unofficial returns that night gave Wozencraft 5,025 votes to Lawther's 4,014. The entire "fusion" slate was elected, but the leading vote-getter on the ticket wasn't even in town to know it. He was Captain Hal Moseley, still in France. The inevitable election parade occurred when supporters converged at Citizens Association headquarters on Main Street, lifted Wozencraft to their shoulders, and advanced up Main to Akard, then down Elm Street.

The "boy mayor" of Dallas, the second native-born son to preside over the city's affairs as mayor, surely surprised even his most ardent supporters with his success in office over the next two years. It was true that he served during the post-war period, a time in which building permits soared and the new Magnolia Petroleum Building was started, but he did far more than merely watch this progress. When the telephone company announced a need for higher rates Wozencraft led the other commissioners in resisting, although the battle was lost in the courts. A similar effort to curb a rate hike by the power and light company was successful. Wozencraft also negotiated directly with the streetcar company when it sought higher fares, and the fact that he was able to hold the fare hike to six cents per ride instead of more was seen as a victory for the consumer. An extraordinary cold spell in December 1919 created an unprecedented demand for the limited supply of natural gas. To alleviate widespread suffering Wozencraft dispatched the city's wagons, trucks, and police and fire equipment to surrounding areas to haul in cords of firewood to sell at a good price at impromptu markets. He appointed a committee of women to investigate local milk prices. When General John J. Pershing came to Dallas on his triumphant tour in 1920 Wozencraft greeted him and rode alongside him in the downtown parade. He also entertained Mexico's president-elect, Alvaro Obregon, when he came to Dallas. During Wozencraft's tenure the last train passed on the T&P tracks on April 3, 1921. A new route carried T&P trains around the outskirts of town. In his last year in office Wozencraft instituted an annual award to be presented to the city's outstanding high school ROTC unit. In his first month of office Wozencraft appointed a new board of health which for the first time included two women. His enthusiasm for office even extended to crime-stopping, and he was with police officers when they solved the sensational 1921 robbery of the Jackson Street Post Office in which three men were wounded. Oftentimes the mayor could be seen at the scene of fires.

Wozencraft's performance did not go unnoticed elsewhere. When sixty-four of the state's mayors convened in Dallas toward the end of his term they urged that "on the basis of his record" he be named next governor of Texas. The mayor was obliged to point out that this was impossible—he was still two years below the constitutional age limit of thirty. In fact, Wozencraft had determined that his brief political career was over. He announced that he would not be a candidate for re-election. He had other important things to do, such as getting married. To his prospective wife, Mary McReynolds, daughter of a prominent Dallas physician, he said it now was time "to get to work and really make a living."

And this he did. He became an attorney for the new firm, Radio Corporation of America, handling its affairs in Texas. And when a vacancy occurred in New York City in 1931 he and his wife left the city of their birth and moved there, where Wozencraft soon had an office on the fifty-third floor of the RCA Building with a sweeping view of Central Park.

4

Embracing the Ku Klux Klan

There are sixteen known cases where citizens of Dallas have been taken from their homes and beaten or tarred and feathered and sixty-three cases boasted of.

—Arthur J. Reinhart, 1923

Growing Pains

The boom times of the roaring twenties did not overlook Dallas. Proud Chamber of Commerce officials predicted early in the decade that by 1930 the city's population would almost double to 275,000. Only twenty years earlier in 1900 Dallas had ranked a distant eighty-sixth among the nation's cities in population; now it was forty-second.

The new Magnolia Petroleum Building under construction at Akard and Commerce was a daily reminder of the city's progress and its claim to be the state's commercial capital. Workers maneuvered about the steel beams 300 feet above the ground with apparent nonchalance, dazzling spectators below. It was observed that by the time the top twenty-ninth floor was reached half of Dallas would be nursing stiff necks from peering upwards. Not only would the Magnolia Building be the tallest in town, it would be the tallest in the state and in the entire South. (Ten years later the oil company would place atop the building a huge, double-sided "flying red horse" which would become the city's most famous icon.)

The Magnolia Building gave powerful testimony to Dallas' growing ties to the oil industry. Despite the fact that there was no oil inside the county itself, the city was within easy overnight distance to all the oil fields of the Southwest and only seventy miles from the new field at Mexia. Oil tycoons and would-be tycoons wheeled and dealed from Dallas headquarters. In 1922 *Dallas* magazine declared that thousands of new organizations that had yet to bring in their first producers were prospecting for oil or gas.

Karl Hoblitzelle, who in 1913 had boldly taken out a 99-year lease on a piece of downtown property, made headlines in 1921 in a bigger way. His growing chain of vaudeville and movie houses, the Interstate Amusement Company, built a $2 million theater, making Hoblitzelle's dream of sixteen years come true. On opening night the new Majestic Theater on Elm Street attracted a handsomely gowned and groomed crowd, many couples arriving in big limousines amidst bright lights to see a vaudeville performance at what was said to be the finest playhouse in the entire South. The aging, white-haired Colonel J.T. Trezevant, who had come to Dallas in 1876 and established a leading insurance agency, spoke that evening and proclaimed the Majestic to be the finest theater in the entire world. Hoblitzelle declared it the greatest privilege of his life to have made Dallas his home.

Forty-one years of age with his greatest accomplishments in Dallas yet before him, Hoblitzelle had a Horatio Alger-like background. As one of thirteen children in a St. Louis family, he quit school to work in a soap factory to help support the family. He became interested in the entertainment field when he took a job as an office boy for the director of the St. Louis World's Fair, choosing this $5-a-week position over one in the auditing department that paid five times more. He preferred the fuller involvement with the overall operation he would get with the fair's director. When the fair ended, Hoblitzelle was placed in charge of demolition. Afterwards, using his savings of $2,500, he was joined by his brother George in opening what became a chain of vaudeville theatres in Texas. As the movie industry grew, Hoblitzelle gradually replaced the touring vaudeville acts with films, emphasizing those suitable for families. Before the 1920s would end, his chain of theatres, extending beyond Texas to Florida on the east and Chicago on the north, would bring him great wealth. He was destined before his death in 1967 to become one of Dallas' greatest philanthropists.

In this year of 1921 Dallas had three high schools—four if you counted the "colored" school, although few did. The old Central High School, renamed Bryan High, had been joined in 1915 by Forest Avenue High School in South Dallas and in 1916 by Oak Cliff High. Yet another new school, North Dallas High, was under construction. Dallas Colored High School, at Hall and Cochran streets, graduated twenty-five students in 1921. (When it moved next year to Flora Street it would be named Booker T. Washington.)

Thriving though Dallas unquestionably was, it still lacked certain essentials that first-class towns must have. Of one thing it was said there could never be enough—the famous "Dallas Spirit" (said to be a combination of "enthusiasm, cooperation, faith, courage, vision, perseverance, reverence, hospitality, and brotherly love"). Virtually all credited this special spirit with bringing the city to its present happy state. In times of crisis it was a reliable reservoir, always ready to be called upon. In addition to saying he could always use more of this invaluable asset, Charles Saville, the general manager of the Chamber of Commerce, presented his list of other needs: more highways, more interurban rail lines, more factories, more hotels, more houses, more development of Love Field and North Dallas, a new federal building, an athletic stadium, an opera house, a municipal golf course, and camp grounds for tourists. That still wasn't all. The city needed 20,000 more shade trees to "keep the glare of the noon-day sun off the residential streets." And it needed Pacific Avenue—soon to be free of railroad tracks as George Kessler had recommended—to be converted into a business street unobstructed by streetcar lines, wires, overhanging signs, sidewalk obstructions, and awnings. Utility lines, Saville believed, should be placed underground at this opportune moment. "Uniform architecture and broad sidewalks will turn the street into a real avenue, a show place and an object lesson," he said.

Sometimes reminders popped up that the veneer of civilization separating Dallas from the frontier was thin indeed. Just west of town in the Grand Prairie area an aggressive wolf was irritating farmers with persistent raids on chicken yards and sheep pastures. The farmers gathered sixteen hunting dogs, put them on the wolf's scent, and followed their dogs as they trailed it through the night. For twelve miles the desperate wolf sought to confuse the pack by crossing and re-crossing its trail, but the hounds finally caught the animal and brought it down in a "snarling whirlwind of fangs and fur." The party of hunters, following on horseback and foot, arrived in time to see the battle. Before the wolf died it left its mark on every single dog, crippling several, slashing throats, crushing leg bones, and tearing ears. The wolf, which turned out to be female, had been so far-ranging and industrious in her forays that it seemed certain she was feeding a litter of young ones. "Somewhere near Grand Prairie, probably in a hidden cave or under a fallen tree, a litter of whelps is waiting for their mother to bring them food," noted the *Times Herald* in its account of the episode.

THE PLIGHT OF BLACK DALLASITES

In the spring of 1921, with Wozencraft declining to run again, Dallas got a new Citizens Association mayor, Sawnie P. Aldredge, an attorney. Aldredge was joined in office, as usual, by a full slate of Citizens Association commissioners. The new chief of police, Elmo Straight, broke a longstanding tradition by leading a parade for the first time from the seat of an automobile rather than from horseback. "I don't know whether I'll buy a horse or not," he declared. "I like to ride in automobiles."

Mayor Aldredge announced that he would re-appoint Felix D. Robertson, a World War I veteran, as judge of the municipal corporation court. Judge Robertson's "courteous but thorough method" of handling those who violate city ordinances has earned him many friends, Aldredge said. (Perhaps Aldredge did not know that Robertson, a staunch Prohibitionist, was a member of a new and growing secret organization in Dallas, the Ku Klux Klan.)

One man who understandably may not have agreed with Mayor Aldredge's assessment of the municipal court judge was Roby Williams, a Negro who had moved into a house at 1128 Eighth Avenue in Oak Cliff at the corner at Cliff Avenue. He was the only black man on his block, although all residents on the adjoining block across Cliff Avenue were black. Williams' white neighbors asked him to move, but he declined. The neighbors' request had the force of law, for a municipal ordinance decreed the 1100 block of Eighth Avenue to be exclusively for white citizens; the adjacent one, the 1200 block, was designated for black citizens. Such ordinances were common in Southern cities. Municipal charges were filed against Williams for violating the ordinance. Judge Robertson found him guilty and fined him $150. Williams' attorney, William Hawley Atwell, who previously had served for fifteen years as the U.S. district attorney for the Northern District of Texas and who the next year would be the Republican gubernatorial candidate for the state, argued that Dallas' segregation ordinance was unconstitutional because of a 1917 U.S. Supreme Court decision, Buchanan v. Warely. Robertson disagreed, and County Judge T.A. Work upheld his decision. In January 1923 Williams and Atwell appealed once more, but a new trial was denied. (In the same month President Warren G. Harding appointed Atwell to the federal bench, where he began a long career to be ultimately confronted with decisions concerning the desegregation of Dallas' public schools, which he opposed.) Dallas' segregation ordinance and those of many other cities, however, had not long to exist because of that 1917 U.S. Supreme Court decision.

The Negro in Dallas, as in cities throughout the nation, was largely omitted as a factor in considerations of growth and progress. He was, as Ralph Ellison noted, "the invisible man." Negro hopes for advancement following World War I were shattered by a series of riots and mob violence in cities across the nation, north and south. Lynchings increased, tensions grew, and there was no relaxation of Jim Crow laws. Employment opportunities were severely limited. The poll tax in Texas and many states effectively restricted black citizens' power at the ballot box. Streets in Dallas' black neighborhoods lacked pavement. The two parks designated for Negroes had no playground equipment. Public swimming pools were strictly forbidden for any but whites. None of this, of course, was unique to Dallas; it was the way things were elsewhere, too.

Housing was a critical problem. A series of seven ordinances during the decade of the 1920s reinforced residential segregation despite the Supreme Court ruling. The growing number of Negroes in Dallas were hard-pressed to find places to live within their authorized confines.

A survey of available Negro housing in 1924-25 by the Civic Federation of Dallas' Inter-racial Committee, the first such survey in the city, showed that fully one-fourth of the city's Negroes, who made up about 15 percent of the population, were living in rented houses "unfit for human habitation." Those making the study examined 1,150 houses. Of these, 66 percent had neither bath, toilet, nor water. Half of the houses had no electricity or gas. The Mexican population, less than three percent of the city's residents, also lived in congested, unsanitary housing which often had no running water or sewage. Yet, even for this inadequate housing—most of it in the "Little Mexico" area along McKinney Avenue including the old "reservation"—rental rates were exorbitant. The report, awful though its details were, was welcomed by the black community, for it confirmed what Negroes already knew. It pleased them that some white residents were concerned about the harshness of their situation. As the *Dallas Express* wrote: "It is proof that there are men and women of the white race in Dallas...who are not afraid of facts, who will seek them and consider them, without passion and sentiment in an effort to make the wrong right."

Almost no black residents were willing themselves to agitate to improve their conditions. The risks involved were too substantial. This was exemplified through the experiences of an accomplished Dallas resident named William Sidney Pittman, a graduate of Tuskegee Institute and Drexel Institute of Technology. Pittman, who had met Booker T. Washington's daughter at Tuskegee and married her after graduation, was the nation's first African-American to win a federal contract to design a building, having gained that distinction in 1907 in being the architect for the Negro Building at the tercentennial exposition in Jamestown, Virginia. In Dallas, where he and his wife moved from Washington, D.C., he designed the multi-story Knights of the Pythias Temple on Elm Street. (In the 1990s it was the only remaining building in downtown Dallas that had been built, owned, and occupied by blacks.)

Pittman was not content with his personal success. In addition to his work as an architect, he published in Dallas a newspaper, *The Brotherhood Eyes*, in which he crusaded vigorously for social change. His aggressive stances shocked much of the black community and brought him only grief because of the reluctance to challenge the existing social system. Pittman's own wife, a music teacher in the Dallas schools, divorced him; he was convicted and imprisoned for two years for violating postal laws; and upon his release he continued to be ostracized by black leaders. Pittman remained in Dallas, though, and after such a promising start in life, he died a pauper in 1958.

In 1918 two black men, George F. Foster, a school teacher, and Ammon S. Wells, a lawyer, had emboldened themselves to organize a local chapter of the NAACP, but it had suffered from an unusual fate. The Dallas Police Department ordered that a police officer be permitted to attend all meetings. Under such a formidable presence, the chapter had been rendered all but ineffective.

A Klan Whipping

On April 1, 1921, a sensational event displayed a forceful, premeditated means of keeping the collar on black citizens, on other minorities, and on the moral behavior of all citizens, no matter their race or creed. On that day a reporter for the *Daily Times Herald* received an anonymous telephone call telling him to wait that evening at the corner of Main and Ervay for a car which would deliver him to a "good story." The reporter did as instructed. His hosts blindfolded him and took him in a caravan of six cars to a lonely spot about six miles south of town on the Hutchins Road. There, his blindfold removed, the reporter saw the men, now masked themselves with handkerchiefs, pull from a car a young Negro man they identified as Alex Johnson, an elevator operator at the Adolphus Hotel who had been snatched forcibly from his home at 3500 Roseland. Around Johnson's neck was a rope. Some of the men pretended to look for a proper tree for a hanging, and Johnson began to beg piteously for his life. One of the vigilantes pressed a six-shooter to his side. The men stripped off Johnson's shirt and tied him to a fence post. One of them addressed him: "Nigger, you have confessed to the crime, but we have decided not to hang you. Within five minutes from now you probably will be fainting." If he cried out, he was told, he would be shot; if the incident was reported in the newspapers he would be killed. Then the men, under the glare of headlights with the invited newspaper reporter watching, proceeded one at a time to flog their victim with a whip as hard as they could. The newspaper account which appeared the next day described the scene graphically: "The whip lash curled through the air and the negro's naked back writhed under its contact. At the third blow the negro gave a shriek of pain and the blood trickled down his shoulders. Again and again the whip fell, the negro groaning and trying to fall to the ground. The man was made to straighten up with each blow. 'Lord, have mercy on me. Don't kill me,' he prayed." After twenty-five lashes Johnson sagged against the post, but the men still were not finished. One drew near with a flashlight. Another produced a small brush and a bottle of acid. The men forced the victim to lift up his face while the man with the brush painted the letters "KKK" on his forehead in acid. Their work now done, the men drove back to town with their victim, and ordered him out of the car, shirtless and bleeding, to walk into the lobby of the Adolphus Hotel, where the alleged misdeed—a liaison with a white woman—had occurred.

The Dallas chapter of the Ku Klux Klan had spoken in a manner that won the tacit approval of local law enforcement agencies, many of whose members were Klansmen or Klan sympathizers. "As I understand the case," said Sheriff Dan Harston, a member of the local Klan's Steering Committee of One Hundred, "the Negro was guilty of doing something which he had no right to do. No, there will be no investigation by my department....He no doubt deserved it." An unnamed police department official said his office would take no action unless a formal complaint were filed. This was understandable, for not only was Police and Fire Commissioner Louis Turley a member of the Klan's Executive Committee of Ten, Police Chief Elmo Straight also belonged to the secret organization. Judge Robert B. Seay of Criminal District Court said: "Maybe it will be a lesson. It is time something was done in cases of this kind." Judge T.A. Work asserted that the moral lesson of the whipping and disfigurement would be beneficial. "If enough people hear of this it may do some good," he said. Judge Charles A. Pippen of Criminal District Court No. 2 had no comment, and next day he impaneled a new grand jury without mentioning the incident.

Three days after the whipping an anonymous letter appeared in the *Times Herald* signed by the "Black K.K.K." The writer advised that all Negro porters were being given information on what to do to prepare for another attack, including the shooting of any masked white man who might attempt harm. "After this week you had better be careful about using hoodwinks, as you may get them shot off," the letter stated. Another letter went to Harston: "We read your comments on this damnable outrage. . .and this is to tell you the matter is not settled and will not be for several days. Then your department will have something to do. Tell your white friends."

Inside the Klan

The Klan was new to Dallas, having been organized in the city only a few months before. Its appeals to morality, native Americanism, patriotism, and fundamentalist Christianity proved to be an appealing message, especially to those who were not well-educated and whose ties to small towns and rural areas remained close. Having been revived in Atlanta in 1915 by William J. Simmons, the Klan found fertile recruiting grounds in the Midwest and Southwest and especially in Dallas when in 1920 a nation-wide expansion program was initiated. The Dallas chapter, organized in late 1920 by Bertram G. Christie as Klan No. 66, swelled within four years to an estimated 13,000 members, the largest local Klan in the nation. Typically, a prospective recruit would be approached at work or at church, presented with copies of the Constitution and the Ten Commandments, and invited to a private dinner where important matters would be discussed. Only at dinner would the invited guests learn that the purpose was to recruit native-born, patriotic, Protestant members to Klan membership. Sometimes a Klan movie, "The Face at Your Window," would be shown. Especially receptive grounds for recruiting were Masonic lodges, other fraternal organizations, and law enforcement agencies.

Many charter members, though, were from the banks, the utility companies, and the professions. Certainly this was true in Dallas, for by the spring of 1922 the Klan's local Executive Committee of Ten included Police Commissioner Turley, three attorneys, a physician, and the assistant general manager of the Dallas Street Railway Co. Its Steering Committee of One Hundred included twelve lawyers, eight physicians, four Dallas Power & Light Co. officials, the superintendent of the local Ford Motor Co., a *Daily Times Herald* reporter, the Democratic Party county chairman, the county tax collector, a district judge-elect, a run-off candidate for district attorney (who would win), and a smattering of bankers, druggists, grocers, and others. The president of Dallas County State Bank, Robert L. Thornton, the man who later would win acclamation as "Mr. Dallas," was a member.

Despite such an impressive roster, which at the time was secret, a large number of men found fault with the Klan and its activities from the beginning. A young Rockwall boy of eight or nine years of age, Henry Wade, who later would become Dallas County's long-time and outstanding district attorney, one day heard from inside the house a leading Klansman approach his father outside to ask him to join the Klan. Wade's father, a Rockwall attorney whose first name also was Henry, not only rejected the offer, but he pointedly criticized the Klan as a threat to law and order. The Klansman responded, "Well, Uncle Henry, we may have to come around one night and put tar and feather on you." "You'd better be ready to kill me then, because I'll have my shotgun ready to meet you," Wade replied. The tense confrontation was one that young Wade never forgot.

A large proportion of Dallas police officers belonged to the Klan. While membership roles were secret, a typewritten list found years later listed as members not only Police Commissioner Turley, but also Police Chief Straight, the assistant chief, three captains, ten sergeants, and ninety-one other officers, or about two-thirds of the force. While this information was not available to the public, it was generally acknowledged that many law enforcement officers and officials were Klansmen. (Two of the young officers listed as Klansmen later would be intimately involved in the investigation of Lee Harvey Oswald. They were Jesse E. Curry, who was police chief, and homicide captain Will Fritz.)

Klan members were expected to support one another by showing preference to fellow Klansmen in their business dealings. "The Klan was quite a threatening organization--people were afraid to belong to it and afraid not to," Glenn Pricer of the *Dallas Dispatch* later recalled. "One of the main reasons for its growth was fear of boycott on the part of little businesses. And large firms encouraged their employees to join--they also feared the boycott."

The exalted cyclops for Klan No. 66 in Dallas was a dentist named Hiram Wesley Evans, destined soon to take command of the entire national organization. A 32nd-degree Mason, he was also president of the Union Publishing Company, publisher of the *Texas Freemason*.

A member of the Disciples of Christ denomination, Evans was a round-faced, smooth-talking glad-hander whose downtown dental office was on Main Street across from Neiman-Marcus and who lived at various times on Bryan, Worth, Fitzhugh, and Sycamore streets. It was later learned that it probably was Evans who had organized and led the whipping committee that lashed and branded Alex Johnson. Born in 1881 in Alabama, the son of a judge, Evans moved to Dallas shortly after the turn of the century from Jones County (where at the age of 18 he already was practicing dentistry!). By 1907 he was advertising "high grade dentistry at moderate prices." Six years later, as one of sixty-one dentists in the city, his two-column advertisement in the *Dallas Dispatch* read: "Gold crown, $3. Painless extraction, 50¢. We want your practice and guarantee to give you satisfaction!" So successful was Evans in Dallas that in late 1922 he moved to Atlanta and outmaneuvered Simmons to become the top Klansman in the nation, the Imperial Wizard, a position he would hold into the 1930s. When he ascended to the Klan's leadership and became a national figure, Evans described himself as "the most average man in America." *Outlook* magazine, though, called him a "natural orator" who spoke with the "softness and peculiarities of the South and with something of the tang and rotundity of the old-fashioned political oratory," and a man whose bland face gave the impression of "tremendous activity, backed by great force." In 1924 the news magazine *Time* showed its opinion of Evans' power by placing his portrait on its front cover.

One of Evans' personal friends in Dallas was the managing editor of the *Times Herald,* Philip E. Fox, who resigned that position in 1923 to join Evans in Atlanta to be the Klan's public relations director. As factions within the Klan struggled for control, Fox shot and killed an attorney for a rival group. At Fox's murder trial a bevy of Dallas journalists and politicians testified in his behalf as character witnesses. They included Mayor Louis Blaylock, Congressman Hatton W. Sumners, and the city editor of the *Times Herald,* E.K. (Sky) Mead.

KLAN DRAMATICS

Some six weeks after the Alex Johnson flogging, on a Saturday night when downtown streets were crowded, the Klan made its public debut in Dallas in a well-orchestrated and dramatic demonstration. At 9 p.m. there emerged from the old Majestic Theater (not Hoblitzelle's new one) a single file of shrouded, masked figures, marching silently ten feet apart behind an American flag and a flaming cross. It took an hour for the white-gowned marchers, 789 in number, to pass a single point. Every twentieth man carried a sign: "We Stand for White Supremacy," "Gamblers Go," "Parasites Go," "Pure Womanhood," "All Pure White," "Thieves Go," and "Grafters Go." Just as they had begun their silent walk the city's street lights conveniently went off, heightening the drama. (Asked later about it, workers at the power plant said vaguely that something was out of order.)

The newspapers gave broad coverage, including photographs of the parade, and published a statement the Klan had posted on trees and poles in various parts of the city. "This organization is composed of native-born Americans and none other....Our creed is opposed to violence, lynchings, etc., but...we are even more strongly opposed to the things that cause lynchings and mob violence." Next morning the pastor of Westminster Presbyterian Church, Dr. T.O. Perrin, told his members that the "hand of God may be working through the Ku Klux Klan" to make the country better socially, economically, and in other ways. Dr. C.C. Selecman, pastor of Dallas' First Methodist Church and soon to be the president of Southern Methodist University, said, "If the situation is such that a Ku Klux Klan is justified in Dallas, then it is a good thing." Dr. William M. Anderson Sr., pastor of the First Presbyterian Church, said the march showed that "someone is in earnest so things in Dallas can be straightened up." He said the secret order seemed to have the general approval of the Dallas ministry. District Attorney Maury Hughes called the Klan "a great help to law enforcement in Dallas County." Police Chief Straight and Police Commissioner Turley, themselves secret Klan members, said that if the organization stood for what it said, then it was a "splendid organization." The *News*, though, expressed its disgust in an editorial entitled "Dallas Slandered." "If freedom is endangered," the *News* wrote, "it is by the redivivus of the mob spirit in the disguising garb of the Ku Klux Klan." Those who marched through the streets were the "exemplars of lawlessness," their actions were "a fit subject for the consideration of the grand jury."

But on the same evening that the disparaging editorial appeared, the Klan struck again in a flagrantly lawless manner. A telephone dispatcher for the Union Terminal Co., a white man named John T. Moore, charged with aggravated assault on a twelve-year-old girl, posted bond and then was released by Sheriff (and Klansman) Harston into the hands of a masked and armed mob. The men, numbering fifteen to twenty, carried Moore to the Trinity River bottoms west of town. A *Times Herald* reporter, once again taken along to witness the event, wrote that mob members pulled Moore from the car with a rope around his neck. Moore wrung his hands and pleaded with his captors not to kill him. The mob had no such intention, though. They tied him to a small post oak tree, and a spokesman read to him the details of his alleged crime. His punishment: ten lashes with a blacksnake whip. The vigilantes took turns with the whip. The *Times Herald* reporter wrote next day: "The flitting of a myriad fireflies in the damp weeds of the humid bottom made the scene a weird one. The hoot of owls and croaking of frogs on the river bank drowned the victim's groans." Afterwards, the man was dumped out at Akard and Main streets as a lesson for all to see.

Neither did this incident disturb local officials. Louis Blaylock, former police commissioner now back in office as finance and revenue commissioner and soon to be the Klan-supported, two-term mayor of the city, said: "I have no say coming in regard to the Ku Klux Klan. I believe Moore got what he justly deserved." Police Chief Straight again declared the Klan to be right in its principles. "They must keep within the law, though." Sheriff Harston and District Attorney Maury Hughes, allegedly a Klansman himself, had no comment.

The whippings and tar-and-feather parties continued in Dallas throughout 1921, as they did in Texas, the South, and the Midwest. Klan members invariably denied all knowledge of the incidents, and on many occasions even offered rewards to help solve the crimes.

In late 1921 the *New York World* published a critical and sensational series of twenty-one articles revealing the lawlessness of the Klan. Many newspapers reprinted the entire series, including the *News*. The result was unexpected—the articles prompted even keener interest in the Klan, and membership rosters throughout the nation swelled. As one result for reprinting the series, the *News* became a target for extreme opprobium from the Klan and Klan supporters from throughout Texas.

From Dallas pulpits choruses of approval continued to ring out in support of the Klan's efforts to enforce morality. A sermon by the pastor of Forest Avenue Baptist Church, W.H. Wynne, "The Contribution of the Ku Klux Klan," was reprinted for mass distribution. The South Dallas preacher said he had investigated the Klan, observed what it had done and what it promised to do, and he approved of the organization. As for the Klan's refusal to identify members, this was "just one of the peculiarities of the organization." Indeed, he pointed out, much of its efficiency lay in its secrecy. The Rev. R.H. Tharp of Cole Avenue Baptist Church said the Klan's "whipping post" methods were the only appropriate tactics to use on those who were intent on "ruining our womanhood." Just how many local ministers belonged to the Klan is not known, but one of them, the Rev. Alex C. Parker of Rosemont Christian Church in Oak Cliff, was the cyclops of the Dallas Klan.

The Klan's efforts to affiliate itself closely with Protestantism were illustrated one Sunday morning at a local Methodist church in an oft-repeated incident. As the minister announced his text for his sermon, two white-robed Klansmen entered the sanctuary and asked to make a statement. Granted their request, they presented an envelope to the pastor containing $25 to be given to a woman church member whose home had been damaged in a fire.

Few Dallas residents or public officials had the courage or perhaps the inclination to speak out against such an organization. To criticize it was to oppose Americanism, the Bible, womanhood, motherhood, and morality. The public's reaction to the hard-hitting *New York World* series gave ample proof. Finally, however, in the spring of 1922 an event occurred in Dallas that gave rise to an aggressive but short-lived and ill-fated opposition movement. The ensuing debate between pro-Klan and anti-Klan forces became a point of contention in county and municipal politics, as it was to become in the 1924 gubernatorial election. The anti-Klan group organized after a blatant miscarriage of justice when a Jewish whipping victim positively identified one of his KKK assailants as a Dallas police officer whom he knew. Yet, a local jury quickly declared him innocent.

The courtroom drama had its vague genesis in an incident occurring in early February 1922. Two Dallas police officers attempted to arrest a Negro suspect as he left the Jewish picture framer's house and business on McKinney Avenue. An officer named J.J. Crawford, a secret Klansman, fired at Hall, but his shot accidentally struck and fatally wounded his partner, Officer Leroy Wood.

A month later the picture framer, Phillip J. Rothblum, a native of Austria who came to the United States at the age of fourteen, was abducted from his home in the presence of his wife and her eleven-year-old sister. Two men who identified themselves as police officers lured Rothblum outside by telling him that he was wanted at the courthouse. In a struggle the officers knocked out two of Rothblum's teeth. Blindfolded and gagged, Rothblum was driven outside town for a flogging by a group of about eight men. At one point during the whipping Rothblum's blindfold slipped down and he recognized one of his assailants as the same Officer Crawford who had been involved in the shooting at his house. The men warned Rothblum to say nothing of the flogging, ordered him to leave town before 6 p.m. the next day, and dumped him from their car on Ross Avenue near Lamar. Rothblum, who had lived in the city for at least nine years, was so frightened that before the next day was over he had complied with the Klan's ultimatum by selling his business and belongings at a desperation price, then with his wife fled the city before the 6 p.m. deadline. Before they left a *Times Herald* reporter interviewed Rothblum at his house. Rothblum's back was raw, his lips were swollen, he moved only with great difficulty, and he presented a "badly battered appearance." The newspaper also interviewed police officers assigned to the case, who said they believed the beating had been committed by "certain people living near him [Rothblum] who objected to his alleged moral conduct."

Two weeks later, for an uncited reason, the Klan apprehended another alleged transgressor, the manager of a lumber yard, Frank H. Etheredge, forty-seven, also a white man, from his house at 1814 Moser Avenue. Etheredge, described by one newspaper as "wealthy," fought back and knocked down one of the kidnapers before they overpowered him. Once again the two men who appeared at his door had identified themselves as police officers. The two, joined by others, took Etheredge to the Hutchins area, tied him to a tree, lectured him on morals, and flogged him. One of the attackers told him, "You're not so bad off. Sixty-three other men have been whipped in the last few months." Upon investigation, the *News* discovered the "torture tree" near Hutchins not far from the New Zion Colored

Baptist Church. Members of a black family, living nearby, said they frequently heard screams in the night.

At this point District Attorney Hughes, evidently alarmed at the Klan's continued law-breaking, broke ranks with the organization and decided to pursue the Rothblum case against all odds. He located Rothblum in St. Louis, and after promising him an armed guard persuaded him to return twice to testify, once to the grand jury and again for Crawford's criminal trial.

At the trial in Judge Charles Pippen's Criminal District Court No. 2, Rothblum was unwavering in his identification of Crawford as one of his attackers. Aside from the shooting incident at his house, he said he knew Crawford from previously having sold him a picture and from attempting in vain to be paid. The judge refused to permit jurors to hear Rothblum testify that just two days prior to his abduction and flogging he had visited the police department and had been warned there by a friendly officer that policemen were passing the word that they were going to "Ku Klux" him. It was revealed that Crawford had made repeated inquiries as to whether or not Rothblum actually had left town after the attack as ordered. Rothblum withstood on cross-examination a withering attack on his own character. He denied that he had kept prostitutes years earlier in the reservation, and he denied that he had solicited Negroes and Mexicans to sleep with his wife for pay.

Defense attorney Barry Miller led Crawford and half a dozen other witnesses to characterize Rothblum as an immoral character. A social settlement worker who said she had known Rothblum for nine years testified that his reputation was "bad, very bad." Immediately after testifying and before a verdict could be returned, Rothblum was escorted by an armed deputy sheriff to the train station, where he departed once more for St. Louis. Rothblum's quick return was precautionary: anonymous threats had been made that he once again would be abducted and beaten. The jury on its first ballot declared Crawford innocent. Crawford, twenty-four years of age and the father of two small children, shook each juror's hand in thanks.

AN ANTI-KLAN MOVEMENT

The jury's verdict outraged a large number of influential Dallas residents who had been watching with great interest. Evidently prepared for the worst, a self-appointed committee of twenty-five, headed by attorney and former judge C.M. Smithdeal, immediately gathered 400 signatures on a powerfully worded anti-Klan statement, and announced on the day after the verdict a public campaign to discredit the Klan. Citizens who signed the statement expressed alarm at the Klan's powerful presence in the city and its infiltration into the police department and sheriff's office. "Some of our citizens have been driven from the communities in which they live by threats of personal violence," the statement said. "Others have been seized in the presence of their wives and daughters and dragged away to some secluded spot and there brutally beaten and otherwise maltreated. Some of those committing these crimes admit that while disguised they have punished at least sixty-three, presumably in this county. Many of those doubtless were afraid to report the fact of their punishment for fear of greater violence, or probably death. Yet, not one of these marauders has been indicted....We must demand of our officers undivided allegiance....We can not now, therefore, afford to commit the protection of our people to officers sworn to obey the laws of this land who at the same time recognize their obligation to the superior officers of the Ku Klux Klan as paramount to the laws of the Union and the Imperial State of Texas." All those who agreed were asked to attend a mass meeting on April 4 at Dallas City Hall. Both the *News* and the *Times Herald* published all 400 names and promised to print the names of all other citizens who submitted them. Among the signatories were G.B. Dealey of the *News*, Glenn Pricer of the *Dispatch*, former commissioner Dan Sullivan, Ben Cabell, and leading Jewish merchants Alex Sanger, Charles Sanger, Arthur Kramer, Herbert Marcus, and Leon Harris.

Mayor Aldredge, who did not sign the statement, urged all City of Dallas employees who belonged to the Klan to resign from it. Texas Governor Pat Neff sent a telegram to Aldredge offering the assistance of the Texas Rangers in bringing law and order to Dallas. Neff told the mayor pointedly that the city's own law-enforcement machinery needed overhauling. "It seems to me," he wrote, "that for some reason your law-abiding people have been forced to bend their knees to the lawless element of your city." The mayor and other officials declined the offer. The governor perhaps had been influenced by a recent visitor to his office, lumberman Frank H. Etheredge, who complained to him first-hand about his beating at the hands of the Klan. A contingent of Texas Rangers, headed by Frank Hamer, already was in town, and rumors persisted that it was poised to act, although ostensibly its purpose was to investigate a burglary ring rather than Klan activities.

So many people attended the April 4 anti-Klan rally that they could not fit inside the city hall auditorium. The 2,000 who managed to get inside were outnumbered by 3,000 on the outside, for whom the speakers repeated their comments. Those attending organized themselves into a body known as the Dallas County Citizens League. They widely denounced the Klan as an un-American organization, called on all public officials who belonged to it to resign, and elected as their chairman the former lieutenant governor and former attorney general of the state, Martin M. Crane. Other speakers included former Texas governor O.B. Colquitt, Dr. J.B. Cranfill, and Sam P. Cochran. On the advisory committee were such people as Karl Hoblitzelle, Mrs. E.P. Turner, W.G. Sterett, Alex Sanger, and Manning B. Shannon.

While the large turnout suggested widespread public opposition to the Invisible Empire, a weekly Klan newspaper that had arisen in Dallas carried a banner headline saying, "Anti-Klan Meeting Proves Big Fizzle." The newspaper, entitled awkwardly the *Texas 100 Per Cent American,* gleefully ridiculed the speakers. Dr. Cranfill, it was said, told the crowd "how MUCH he loved the Catholics and especially about his filial feeling for the negro." Those on the podium were said to be so eager to point to the "menace" of 100 percent Americanism that they "forgot the 100 per cent Catholic whose political designs are hidden in the heart of a man elected Big Papa." The newspaper declared that "every man joining the Masons, Odd Fellows or any secret society takes a more binding oath than the one this nasty little nigger daily [*The Dallas Morning News*] charges to the Klan." Editor and owner J.W. Hutt proposed a counter meeting in which Dallas residents could show their support for the sheriff and police commissioner in their crime-fighting efforts. Hutt's virulent and propagandistic newspaper, supported eagerly by the growing members of the Klan, was destined to thrive in the next two and a half years before a new owner re-located it in Washington, D.C.

The League sought to expunge Klan members from the roster of city and county officials, to prevent the election of other Klansmen to office, and to educate citizens as to the menace of the Klan. The organization prepared a questionnaire asking city and county employees if they now belonged to the Ku Klux Klan, whether they intended to affiliate with it, and whether they were in sympathy with its purpose, practices, and objectives.

One official who publicly spurned the questionnaire was Louis Blaylock, finance and revenue commissioner. "I am responsible to the public through my official oath as to the conduct of my office and not to any certain committee," he said. The *Texas 100 Per Cent American* praised Blaylock for his stance, as it was to do frequently in the years ahead: "No other man in Dallas stands higher in the confidence of the voters as a 100 per cent American....Now the [Dallas] *Dispatch* excommunicates him because he will not kneel to Pope Crane, Cardinal Colquitt and Father Cranfill."

The *Times Herald* had been ordered by publisher E.J.Kiest to "go down the middle" in its coverage of the Klan because "many solid citizens are members." After the Rothblum incident the newspaper began to criticize the Klan, but never so much as the *News*, the *Journal*, and the *Dispatch*. The *Texas American* responded with caustic and false accusations that the unfriendly newspapers, especially the *News*, were controlled by Catholics. The local Klan singled out Catholics as no less than a foreign power themselves presided over by the Pope, or "Big Papa." This was the Klan's usual direct response to critics who claimed that Klan members owed their allegiance to the "Invisible Empire" above local or state laws. "Catholicism Is Sworn to Overthrow Our Government," read one big headline in the *Texas American*. Of O.B. Colquitt the newspaper wrote: "Nobody knows how DEEP his hand is in the pope's pocket."

Catholics and Catholicism clearly were the Klan's primary target, far more so than Negroes and Jews. Despite the heavy concentration of Klansmen in Masonic lodges (and despite the lodges' Protestantism), two Jewish leaders, Julius Schepps and Rabbi David Lefkowitz, attended Masonic meetings with some regularity. They argued there that accepting Klansmen within the Masons hindered the organization's growth. Schepps, in his effort to combat the Klan, even paid membership fees for some fifty of his employees so that they could infiltrate it and keep him informed as to its activities.

Without a doubt, a large number of Dallas residents and Americans identified with the Klan's announced goals and purposes. Klan activities quickly expanded. In early 1922 applications for Klan membership in Dallas were said to be averaging better than 100 a day. Four days after the Dallas County Citizens League was formed, 2,342 new Klansmen enrolled at a mass meeting. Later that summer on August 18 the Klan initiated 3,500 members at Fair Park Stadium in a spectacle complete with a huge fiery cross, a 125-piece Klan band, a massed chorus of Klansmen, and a Klan drum and bugle corps. Dallas Klan No. 66, soon to be the largest chapter in the nation, opened offices on Young Street, and by 1923 at least two full-time staff members were working there. George K. Butcher was secretary and Edward M. Nelson was office manager. By 1924 a local Klansman, Zebina E. (Zeke) Marvin, owner of Marvin's Drugstore in downtown Dallas, had become grand dragon of the entire state with headquarters in Dallas in the Marvin Building. Butcher had become the state's great titan. A Ku Klux Klan Junior chapter, under the direction of M.W. Parker, had offices at 310 Andrews Building, and the Women of the Ku Klux Klan maintained an office on North Harwood. Mrs. A.B. Cloud was imperial klaliff of the latter organization, and Mrs. D.H. Mahon was kligrapp. Small towns surrounding Dallas also were hotbeds of Klan activity. A mass initiation in Farmersville north of Dallas saw 721 new members enrolled.

The Citizens League created an ambitious program of anti-Klan publicity, publications, and speeches to warn the public about the dangers of the Invisible Empire. Spokesmen who visited neighborhoods and nearby small towns to spread their message often encountered considerable hostility, though. Leading businessmen and citizens in Lancaster held a mass meeting and signed a petition demanding that League speakers stay away from their town. In Richardson angry citizens followed a League spokesman and tore up the anti-Klan cards he was distributing. A thirty-page miniature booklet, "The Case Against the Ku Klux Klan," was prepared and distributed by the League, but it was no match against the emotionalism generated by burning crosses, the Bible, and 100 percent American declarations.

Concerned about the number of "special" part-time officers authorized by the Dallas Police Department who were believed to be Klansmen or Klan sympathizers, the League asked Mayor Aldredge for a list of the 350 or so men. The mayor referred the matter to Commissioner Turley, who declined to turn over the names. Turley said the list would be available to any private citizen who came by the police station. Sheriff Harston, also asked to make public the names of deputies who were Klansman, refused.

KLAN IN POLITICS

The futility of the League's battle against the Klan became obvious after the 1922 Democratic primary when Klan-supported candidates, touted by the *Texas American,* won every local race, gaining control of the courthouse. On the state level, Earle B. Mayfield, a secret Klansman who was supported openly by the Klan in the race for the U.S. Senate, won a place in the run-off against former Governor James E. Ferguson, then defeated Ferguson to win the Senate seat. Notable among the local candidates were three admitted Klansmen, Felix D. Robertson, who advanced from municipal court to Criminal District Court; Dan Harston, re-elected as sheriff; and Shelby S. Cox, a young resident of Oak Cliff and a political unknown who upset former Klan-supporter Hughes in the race for district attorney. Fifty thousand copies of an election "special" promoting these and other Klan-endorsed candidates were printed and distributed by the *Texas American* prior to the July 22 primary. Candidates who publicly opposed the Klan gained the endorsement of the *News*, the *Dallas Journal*, and the *Dallas Dispatch.* The *News* castigated Cox as a "river bottom advocate" and Harston a "bedsheet sheriff."

Harston, Robertson, and other Klan candidates won outright primary victories, tantamount to election since the Republicans were never a factor in the fall general election. Cox's win over Hughes for district attorney had to await a run-off. Klan winners and their supporters marched triumphantly in downtown Dallas the night of the primary, pausing at the *News* to refer to it as that "dirty, slimy, Catholic-owned sheet," and then stopping at a truck outside the friendlier *Times Herald* for speech-making. First on the platform was none other than the exalted cyclops of Klan No. 66, Alex C. Parker, who had made a fortune in the oil business in the Burkburnett field but recently had become pastor of Rosemont Christian Church. Parker, flamboyant and flush with victory, asked those in the crowd if they knew who he was. Before anyone could answer he introduced himself as the exalted cyclops of Dallas Klan No. 66. Shelby Cox also spoke and made no secret of his Klan affiliation, proudly telling the crowd that he had marched with the Klan in Dallas and other North Texas cities.

With every Klan-endorsed Democratic candidate winning the county's general election that fall, the *News* acknowledged that the vote gave "striking evidence" of the Klan's political strength. The *Texas American* crowed that "we have just won a most glorious victory....No event since the signing of the Declaration of Independence will have a more far reaching influence upon the history of this beloved country of ours than with the victory of our cause at the polls." The Klan's victory spelled an effective end to the Citizens League's efforts against it.

The News Becomes a Target

The Klan's false attacks against the *News* as a Catholic-controlled newspaper and a boycott which peaked in the spring of 1922 brought about alarming declines in circulation and advertising revenue. Klan members and sympathizers cancelled subscriptions, dropped their advertisements, flooded the newspaper with irate and accusatory letters, and boycotted businesses that continued to advertise in the newspaper. The Klan's popularity in rural areas caused special concern because the newspaper's agents in small towns were reporting sharp drops in sales. The *News'* afternoon paper, the *Journal,* also suffered. The agent in Frisco advised that all twenty-eight subscriptions to the *Journal* had been cancelled.

Reader after reader wrote Dealey to ask specifically how many of the *News'* editors and officials were Catholics. Dealey patiently responded to each letter, listing the religious affiliations of all editors as well as those who owned more than 1 percent of the stock. (Only a handful of individuals owned more than 1 percent of the stock—one of them was a surprise—the Klan-supported Louis Blaylock.) None of these individuals were Catholic. Dealey always asked for a reply to his responses, and when they were not forthcoming he sent a second letter to remind the writer that he had requested an answer. Exaggerated rumors were rampant. A man in New York wrote to ask Dealey if it were true, as he had heard, that "all towns between Fort

Worth and Amarillo had quit selling the *News*." An advertiser in Whitesboro heard that 700 subscribers in Sherman alone had quit the *News*, and that in the past forty days the newspaper had lost $20,000 in subscriber dollars.

By 1923 the *News'* circulation had declined by 3,000, and its cash surplus of $200,000 had dwindled to nothing. *News* officials pondered their plight, and considered but rejected as inappropriate a plan to publish full-page declarations that the newspaper was not controlled by Catholics. Nevertheless, the accusations prompted internal studies which revealed that 89.5 percent of the newspapers 500 employees and 150 carriers were Protestants. One editorial writer, Alonzo Wasson, was Catholic, and the circulation manager, M.W. Florer, was Catholic. "Our conscience will not permit us to change front even if 50% of our readers quit," Dealey wrote in March 1922 to an alarmed circulation agent who was among those reporting falling sales in towns such as Greenville and Rusk.

Hugh Fitzgerald, an editorial employee of Irish ancestry and Catholic background, was visited in his office by a suspicious committee of Protestant preachers who asked him what church he belonged to. He answered: "No priest, preacher or other outsider is permitted to dictate the policies of this paper, and furthermore I have never been willing to apologize for the religion in which my mother lived and died. Good day." Fitzgerald told Tom Finty Jr. that as a result of this visit he promptly reinstated himself in the Catholic church.

On May 4, 1922, the *Brownwood Bulletin* sent this telegram to the shell-shocked newspaper: "Do either Jews or Catholics own any of the stock in the Belo publications? If so, how many and how much...?" Dealey responded with the usual form letter, but closed with an added comment: "Suppose Jews or Catholics do own stock in any of our publications, what of it?"

A few agents in small towns, especially to the south and east of Dallas, began reporting bodily threats. The *News* advised them to take special care for their safety. By mid-July Dealey was so alarmed about physical threats and boycotts that he conferred with an attorney about the possibility of bringing civil or criminal action against those responsible. He alerted agents and employees to write down specific details with names of those making threatening statements.

The deteriorating economic situation prompted the daughter of the late Colonel A.H. Belo, Mrs. Jeannette Peabody, to come to Dallas from Massachusetts for a series of conferences. Mrs. Peabody and her mother, Belo's widow, were the primary owners of the newspaper. In the midst of the meetings came a fortuitous offer from W.L. Moody Jr. of Galveston to buy the *Galveston News*. The *Galveston News*, the original partner in the combination between the two newspapers, had founded the *News* as an adjunct in 1885, but by now the Galveston paper was by far the smaller of the two. The sale, consummated on March 23, 1923, improved the *News'* financial situation greatly. The Klan, interpreting the transaction in a different way, boasted that the newspaper was up against the wall and soon would be bankrupt or be forced to sell out. While such did not occur, the *News* had suffered enough. It pulled back its claws in the battle against the Klan, not to extend them for more than a year.

The *Dallas Dispatch*, livelier and more irreverent than the *News*, also suffered from the Klan boycott. Between April and October 1921, the *Dispatch* lost approximately 2,500 subscribers, almost as many as the *News*, but from a far smaller base. A noted example of the *Dispatch's* coverage occurred when managing editor Glenn Pricer and some of his reporters went to Fair Park during a Klan rally there. They circulated among the parked cars, recorded the license-plate numbers, then checked out the ownership records and published the names to a great hue and cry. While the *Dispatch*, the *News* and the *Journal* lost circulation, the sympathetic *Times Herald* gained more than 1,500 subscribers in the same six-month period that saw the others sharply declining.

KLAN INFLUENCE IN MUNICIPAL GOVERNMENT

As the May municipal elections of 1923 loomed the only organized political force to stand up to the Klan was the business-dominated Citizens Association. The Cits' executive committee early in the year endorsed for mayor the veteran office-holder and finance commissioner, Blaylock, now seventy-three years of age. Also gaining endorsement were the three other remaining incumbent commissioners, Louis Turley (despite his Klan membership) for a second term as police and fire commissioner, J.D. Rose for street commissioner, and Fred Appel for a third term as water commissioner.

John C. Harris was nominated to fill Blaylock's position as finance commissioner.

The Dallas City Democrats, sympathetic to Klan interests, determined to field their own slate of candidates. They endorsed three of the five Citizens Association candidates as their own: Blaylock, Turley, and Harris. To the consternation of the Citizens Association, these three accepted the Democratic endorsement and indicated that they would support the full City Democratic ticket rather than the Citizens Association slate. Enraged by this snub, the Citizens Association executive committee withdrew its support of all three men and began searching for replacements. After several weeks they announced Marvin E. Martin as their new candidate for mayor, Arthur J. Reinhart for police and fire commissioner, and T. Walter Scollard for finance commissioner.

The Cits' candidates energetically criticized the Ku Klux Klan and the Democrats' implied approval of that organization. Blaylock and the other Democrats refused to disown Klan support or Klan objectives; yet in their four-column advertisement in the *Dallas Express* they pledged to rule honestly and fairly for all people "without regard to color, race, religious or other affiliations." The question for the voters, said Dwight L. Lewelling, chairman of the Cits' executive committee, was "whether the people want a Ku Klux Klan administration or a government by and for all the people." Blaylock, Lewelling charged, had aligned himself with "secret and partisan" politics. Citizens Association campaign manager T.F. Monroe was more candid, saying that those on the Democratic ticket were either members of the Klan or sympathetic to it.

Martin, a businessman with interests in the electrical industry who had served as first president of the Dallas Rotary Club, and Reinhart, former state adjutant of the American Legion, were especially outspoken during the campaign on the issue of the Klan. In one speech Martin charged that the Klan had warned him that if he agreed to run for mayor they would "crucify" him. Reinhart, a distinguished-looking attorney, described Turley's previous term in office as one of "river bottom administration," a direct reference to the Klan whippings. As to a Turley claim that he had solved all major crimes occurring in Dallas during his term, Reinhard said: "There are sixteen known cases where citizens of Dallas have been taken from their homes and beaten or tarred and feathered and sixty-three cases boasted of. These are major crimes and he has not solved them, nor made any appreciable effort to do so."

As the April 3 election date drew near Citizens Association rallies began to be attended by large numbers of Klansmen and Klan sympathizers whose purpose was to heckle the speakers. Fistfights sometimes were only narrowly averted. On one occasion police reserves had to be called out to keep the peace.

Two days before the election a member of the Klan women's auxiliary, the Kamelia, exchanged sharp taunts with Reinhart at a huge rally at Elm and Stone streets. Disruptions at this rally became so intense that Citizens Association campaign manager Monroe threatened to have the numerous police officers scattered about fired if they did not perform their duty and control the crowd. Reinhart castigated the officers directly as Klan sympathizers. "There stands a member of Louis Turley's police department—and there another—and there another—and if they don't tend to their business properly, and allow the speakers to proceed without interrupting, their heads are liable to come off," he said, asserting power which he lacked. When Reinhart made critical references to Turley many in the crowd cheered Turley. Responding to rumors that he was Jewish, Reinhart felt obliged to stress that he came from "one of the best old Baptist families that ever grew up under the eaves of the Baptist church."

The April 3 election saw a landslide victory for all Klan-endorsed candidates, just as had occurred the previous year at the courthouse. It was the first complete defeat of the C.A. ticket since its inception eighteen years before. Blaylock led the City Democratic ticket, trouncing Martin, 14,386 to 5,209. Turley defeated Reinhart, the Citizens Association's most outspoken candidate, 14,282 to 5,433, and the other City Democratic candidates won by margins nearly as wide. Backers of the winning candidates organized that night the inevitable parade, marching through the downtown streets bearing American flags at each end of the column and singing a hymn widely favored by Klansman throughout the nation, "Onward Christian Soldiers." According to the *Times Herald*, the landslide "virtually wiped out" the Citizens Association. "It is difficult to say whether the so-called Citizens Association committed suicide, or whether it was assassinated by its executive committee," said attorney W.L. (Jack) Thornton of the Democratic executive committee and also a member of the Klan's Steering Committee of One Hundred. "However, it is dead."

This was true. The Citizens Association was finished as the monopolistic force in municipal politics, a victim of the Ku Klux Klan. None of the candidates offered by the Citizens Association in the next two municipal elections would be elected. The organization withered away to nothing. But its philosophy of a municipal leadership dominated if not dictated by the city's businessmen would be revived when the Citizens Charter Association emerged a few years later to promote the adoption of the council-manager form of government.

The *News*, conspicuously quiet during the heated 1923 campaign, expressed no apprehension about the results: "Sensible men will not doubt, now that the excitement of the campaign has passed, that Mr. Blaylock and his associates are ambitious to serve Dallas with the same high degree of fidelity and efficiency that has characterized the service of their predecessors ever since Dallas has had a commission government."

KLAN SEEKS RESPECTABILITY

With municipal and county politicians in office who were either Klansmen themselves or friendly to the interests of the Klan, and with the Klan by now de-emphasizing its abductions and whippings because of widespread criticisms and official investigations, the organization began to concentrate on less controversial projects. A notable project for which it raised money through special events and concerts was establishing a home for foundling children, Hope Cottage. Another was the sponsorship in 1923 of a special day for the Klan at the State Fair of Texas, under the direction of Klansman George K. Butcher. As it happened, the home for children was completed and ready for formal dedication simultaneously with Ku Klux Klan Day at the Fair. For these special events Grand Wizard Hiram Wesley Evans, surrounded by an entourage of Klan officials from Atlanta, returned to Dallas. A widely distributed handbill promoted Ku Klux Klan Day with a drawing of a hooded Klansman holding high a flaming torch from atop a hooded horse.

Ku Klux Klan Day thus began with an outside dedication at the children's home itself. The crowd of some 1,500 Klansmen and Klan women who attended saw Grand Wizard Evans, the mayor of Dallas, and a host of other Klan and local public officials sharing the platform. Dallas Klansmen included J.D. Van Winkle, a bookstore owner who presided over the ceremony; the Rev. Alex C. Parker, the grand cyclops; and Z.E. (Zeke) Marvin, owner of Marvin's Drug Store at Main and Akard (and later president of Gulf States Life Insurance Co.), now the titan of the Realm of Texas. Marvin had been responsible for starting the Hope Cottage project. With Mayor Blaylock were Dallas commissioners Turley, R.A. Wylie, and Harry H. Gowens, and Judge Felix D. Robertson. Marvin presented the institution, "free of any encumbrance," as a gift to the city to be administered by the Hope Cottage Association. Approximately $80,000 in Klan money had gone into the development of Hope Cottage, making it the single largest charitable Klan enterprise in the Southwest. A five-pointed star with the inscription, "K.K.K. 66," decorated the reception hall.

In his opening comments Van Winkle welcomed Grand Wizard Evans and others with this provocative remark: "Your majesty, members of the imperial household, ladies and gentlemen, fellow Klansmen, sympathizing friends, one and all....There will be no flogging parties in Dallas tonight, neither will there be any river bottom tar and feather parties." Van Winkle's comments were considered to be of such import that they were reprinted in full in the *Times Herald*, as were speeches by Marvin and Evans.

At the fair grounds Ku Klux Klan Day was a spectacular success, attracting a record-setting attendance for any weekday in the history of the fair. Klaverns from adjoining states came in great numbers, some via special trains. Special events of all sorts with Klan themes were presented throughout the day and evening. Even the rodeo performers wore Klan regalia. An afternoon football game was billed as a battle between Fort Worth Klan No. 101 and Dallas Klan No. 66. Actually, the two were represented on the gridiron by two high school teams, Sulphur Springs for Fort Worth and Oak Cliff for Dallas. At a 1 p.m. ceremony Evans spoke from under a striped canopy and before a huge crowd on "The Menace of Present Immigration." A reception was held honoring surviving original Klansmen of the post-Civil War era, and the Klan's drum and bugle corps, billed as the largest in the world, performed. That evening some 25,000 spectators gathered at the grandstand and watched the largest

Klan initiation ever, a total of 5,631 men swearing their fidelity to the Klan in a spectacular mounted ceremony. In an accompanying ceremony, 800 women took oaths for the Klan's female auxiliary, the Kamelia. The *News* uncritically described the spectacle, which included burning crosses at both ends of the field, as "the most colorful and unique event ever seen in the city of Dallas."

Exposition officials gave attendance figures for the day as 151,192. The *Texas American* protested that the figure was too low, claiming that from 250,000 to 300,000 persons actually had attended but that State Fair officials did not want this higher count to be known. *Literary Digest* magazine estimated that 75,000 of those in attendance actually had been Klansmen. The gathering was said to be the largest single assembly of Klansman anywhere.

THE KLAN'S DEMISE

The 1924 Democratic primary once again saw the Klan heavily involved in politics, but this time its focus was higher—on the gubernatorial race. County-wide offices were securely in friendly hands, although an unknown candidate named Schuyler B. Marshall Jr. managed to unseat veteran sheriff Dan Harston. Z.E. Marvin, as grand dragon for the state, personally sponsored his friend and Dallas District Judge Felix Robertson as the Klan-favored candidate for governor. (One of Robertson's biggest financial backers was the former boy mayor of Dallas, Frank Wozencraft, who donated the second highest amount of money given by anyone in the state, $250, to Robertson's campaign.) Robertson's candidacy caused dissension within state-wide Klan ranks because some members who preferred another Klan candidate resented Marvin's dictatorial endorsement. Robertson won enough votes in the hard-fought primary to reach a run-off against Miriam Ferguson, wife of impeached governor Jim Ferguson. Robertson carried Dallas County by a 2-1 margin, but he lost to Ferguson in the run-off race. Bigotry reigned in both camps even with the Klan as a primary issue. Robertson's failure to capture the governor's seat as the openly avowed Klan candidate signaled the beginning of a decline in the reign of the Invisible Empire in Texas. It also led to Marvin's resignation from the Klan because of controversy over his role in sponsoring Robertson.

Growing documentation of Klan abuses throughout the nation suddenly began to reverse the organization's popularity. One sensational incident bringing discredit occurred in Indiana in 1925 when the powerful Klansman David Stephenson was convicted of second-degree murder and sentenced to life imprisonment for abducting and sexually assaulting a secretary, who afterwards poisoned herself in remorse.

Texas and Dallas membership rolls collapsed overnight. Former state grand dragon Zeke Marvin said in 1926 that membership in Texas had fallen from its peak of 97,000 to 18,000. Dallas Klan No. 66, once boasting of 13,000 members, was reported that same year to be down to 1,200. So reduced were its circumstances that a Klan supervisor based in Texarkana was directing its affairs. "A Klan endorsement of any candidate now anywhere in Texas, it is said, would mean certain defeat," reported the *New York Times* early in 1926. Marvin said that attendance at Dallas Klan political meetings formerly had been as high as 3,500, but "now it would be hard to get 150 at any meeting." Still, as late as 1929, Klan No. 66 maintained a full-time office at 101 Exposition Avenue near Fair Park.

5

Daddy Lou's Dallas

Oh, yes, you can stop a mob. The Sheriff of Dallas County did it. . . . He showed himself to be a brave man who hates bloodshed but who hates cowardice and treason to official duty even more.

–The Dallas Morning News, 1925

New Sheriff Faces a Mob

Sheriff Harston's defeat by neophyte Schuyler B. Marshall Jr. came as a distinct surprise. Harston, a rough-and-tumble man who operated in the classic manner of an Old West peace officer and who was the father of nine children, had seemed certain to win his fourth term of office. He led in the Democratic primary, but failed to gain a majority, and in the run-off the youthful Marshall, supported especially by the American Legion, upset Harston by a narrow margin. Like Harston, Marshall was--or at least had been--a member of the Klan. It would be an ironic twist that the defining event of Marshall's term would be his protection of two black prisoners from a lynching mob.

As Marshall, the county's first college-educated sheriff, took the oath of office on the first day of 1925 he disdained the customary western-style garb of the office in favor of khaki trousers and an Army shirt. (Later, he sometimes donned military riding pants on duty.) He wore a wide belt around his waist, two six-shooters thrust into holsters, and a star pinned on his shirt. He was ready and eager, he announced, to battle crime and criminals. It wasn't difficult to imagine why Marshall gained a nickname: "the College Kid Sheriff."

Naive though the new sheriff seemed, he was no stranger to firearms, for he had learned to shoot by the age of five on the family farm outside Dallas. He boasted that by the time he became sheriff he could shoot a coin out of the air, heads or tails, and he could keep a croquet ball rolling with a six-shooter, turning it around and making it roll backwards.

Marshall's family was intimately involved with the old settlement of Scyene, located just east of Dallas. His father was a large landholder and farmer who also owned a brick manufacturing plant near Mesquite. Scyene was where the notorious female desperado Belle Starr grew up, and it was a frequent stopping place for outlaws such as the Younger Brothers. Marshall's father was said to have known Belle as a child. Marshall's grandfather, Charles Marshall, who moved to Dallas County from Mississippi in the late 1870s and began buying land in the Scyene area, had been a boyhood friend of Buffalo Bill Cody, and when Cody's Wild West Show came through Dallas the veteran frontiersman and showman regularly visited the Marshall household. As a high school student Schuyler rode horseback to classes in Mesquite, the newer town with a railroad which was making Scyene superfluous. After graduation he enrolled at Kansas State, played on the football team and participated in the ROTC program. His first real military experience came during college when he was summoned to active duty with the National Guard to join General John J. Pershing's expedition in Mexico against Pancho Villa. Upon completing his college studies, Marshall saw service in World War I in France, was discharged in 1919 as a captain, and returned to Scyene to take up dairy farming. By the time 1924 came along he was ready for a new challenge, and he gladly accepted the offer of support from the American Legion to oppose Harston.

Much of Marshall's work as sheriff was in enforcing prohibition. Bootlegging was widespread. A study in 1925 showed the annual earnings of a Dallas bootlegger to be about $36,000. Raids on stills occurred in residential neighborhoods, garages, barns, warehouses, and even in a South Dallas cemetery.

Marshall's single term of office was marked by the greatest civil disturbance in Dallas' history. It was an event that called upon the sheriff's every resource in courage and skill in thwarting the armed mob that sought to lynch two black prisoners. brothers Lorenz Noel, twenty-five, and Frank Noel, twenty-three, had been arrested and indicted on six counts for murder and rape. They were suspects in a series of other capital crimes. Lurid headlines labeled them as the "Black Terrors." News stories detailed their confessions.

On Wednesday morning, May 20, 1925, threatening crowds began assembling outside the "skyscraper jail" in the upper floors of the red-brick Criminal Courts Building across from the main courthouse. Through the day the crowd swelled, some of the individuals taunting county officials by saying they knew exactly where the Noels could be found. As the mob continued to grow, Marshall ran out of deputies to secure the area and jail. City policemen responded to his call for help. At nightfall the crowd had reached a size of some 5,000, by which time city firemen had joined the deputies and police officers. Firemen strung out hoses and stationed themselves at various intersections around the building to repel the inevitable attack from a mob that included large numbers of women and even children.

Containing the unruly crowd that night was difficult and uncertain. Bold individuals occasionally burst through the front lines in an effort to encourage a mass storming of the jail, only to be arrested each time. Others made impromptu, inciting speeches. Officers had to overcome shoving from the crowd as they tried to reach individuals singled out for arrest. At about 11 p.m. a well-dressed woman, shouting for the crowd to follow her, attempted to lead a charge, but a stream of water stopped her. She, too, was arrested and jailed. Firemen soon were using their hoses regularly to hold back the crowd, although some individuals took pleasure in jumping in front of the streams of water. From other parts of town people called in false fire alarms to distract the firefighters. Nine were sounded in just one hour. Random reports came during the night that groups were forming elsewhere to march on the jail building. A mob from Rockwall was said already to be en route.

At about 1:30 a.m. the long-feared assault commenced. It originated with a group of some 300 men who had gathered west of the jail at the railroad tracks. They picked up rocks, then came to the rear of the crowd and began throwing them at the lawmen and firemen. Streams of water answered the rock attack, and the men retreated to gather more rocks. This time they found an accumulation of soft-drink bottles at a nearby bottling plant. Thus armed, they returned again, showering rocks and missiles at the officers, striking and injuring many of them. The chaotic scene worsened when two men began firing pistols at officers from behind a building and telephone pole. Lawmen returned the fire, shooting mostly in the air. In a two-minute period some 150 rounds were estimated to have been fired. Sheriff Marshall, who had been manning a fire hose and wearing a large white hat, seemed to be a particular target. He narrowly escaped being hit. Five men in the crowd were wounded by gunfire; none of the lawmen were shot. One of the wounded, an eighteen-year-old "soda jerk," later died from his wounds. At least one of the leaders was arrested, but when officers saw that he was a "prominent man" they sent him home instead of to jail. News accounts failed to identify him.

When the attackers retreated to the railroad tracks, Marshall followed and implored them to return to their homes, assuring them that justice would be done to the Noel brothers. His talk, punctuated no doubt by the cries of the wounded, was effective. The men soon broke up, as did the rest of the crowd in the courthouse area.

Approximately forty deputies, policemen, and firemen suffered "battered heads and broken bones" during the melee. Unspecified amounts of property damage occurred. Officers arrested during the evening at least fifty and perhaps as many as one hundred individuals, confiscating from them twenty-three pistols and numerous liquor bottles. The sheriff's brother suffered a broken nose when struck in the face with a brick. Marshall himself did not go home; he slept the few remaining hours of the night in a jury room.

Next day it appeared that the worst was yet to come. Reports circulated that as many as 20,000 people would gather that night outside the jail and storm it. Sheriff Marshall sent an urgent request to Governor Miriam Ferguson to activate the National Guard and to send help from the Texas Rangers, too. He set up outposts at highways leading into town, made further security arrangements to protect the jail, and stored tear and ammonia gas and extra supplies of ammunition. As to his request to activate the National Guard, the adjutant general advised Marshall that state law permitted him to activate units himself in emergencies. The sheriff promptly ordered Company G, 144th Infantry, 36th Division, to report to the jail early that evening. Another unit, Troop C, 112th Cavalry, headquartered at the nearby State Fair grounds, also was summoned. A contingent of Texas Rangers appeared as well, including famed Captain Frank Hamer, who drove from Austin to Waco and then rode the interurban into Dallas. Deputy U.S. marshals arrived at the request of federal Judge William H. Atwell, who said he wanted to insure the safety of federal prisoners in the jail.

The new cyclops of Klan No. 66, Clarence S. Parker, issued a statement decrying the mob violence of the previous night and urging that an orderly trial be held for the "Black Terrors." Mayor Blaylock signed a proclamation forbidding crowds from assembling in the courthouse area or anywhere else in town with the purpose of inciting a riot, and he urged officers to be especially vigilant in their duty. His proclamation contained an odd phrasing with a reference to the mob's "attempt to *rescue* [emphasis added] certain individuals charged with capital offenses." The *Dallas Journal* criticized the mayor, noting his odd choice of words and saying that the mob clearly intended to "lynch Negroes" rather than to rescue them.

That night a huge crowd estimated at 10,000 gathered in the courthouse area. But security was strong with the addition of National Guardsmen, Texas Rangers, and federal marshals, and the crowd differed in mood from the previous evening. Those present appeared to be curiosity-seekers milling about and waiting to see someone else storm the police lines. In good-humored fashion they exchanged jokes with the lawmen. The ugliness of the previous night never developed, and the crowd's numbers by midnight dwindled to a few hundred. In the following days National Guardsmen remained on the scene, and at midnight Saturday the Texas Rangers relieved them. The crisis was over.

Marshall won praise for his work under extreme pressure. "Dallas County Has a Sheriff," was the headline for a *News* editorial. "Oh, yes, you can stop a mob. The Sheriff of Dallas County did it Thursday morning....He showed himself to be a brave man who hates bloodshed but who hates cowardice and treason to official duty even more." The *Dallas Express* opined that "every Negro citizen of Dallas now had a heightened regard for the action of the police departments of both city and county."

Judge Charles A. Pippen announced that the two brothers, who had been very much aware of their perilous circumstances from their jail cells, would stand trial the very next Thursday. They would be tried for the rape of a woman whose male companion had been bludgeoned to death with a hammer in an attack occurring near Airline Road in North Dallas. Judge Pippen first ruled that no women would be permitted to attend, for it was believed that testimony would be too graphic for them, then he broadened his order to prohibit all spectators save reporters. Texas Rangers would guard the courtroom with orders to shoot the first person who made a hostile move toward the Noels.

In what surely were the fastest two capital trials in Dallas history, the brothers were convicted and sentenced to death by the electric chair. District Attorney Shelby Cox, who had helped obtain confessions from the pair, prosecuted. Both brothers walked into the heavily guarded courtroom at 9:16 a.m. Frank Noel was tried first. A jury was selected within minutes, Noel's confession was entered into evidence, the victim identified Noel as her assailant, and the state rested its case. Noel's court-appointed attorneys, who accepted the case with great reluctance, declined to present anything in their client's behalf, refusing even to cross-examine the victim. At 10:05 a.m. the jury retired to deliberate, and at 10:12 a.m. it returned and announced its guilty verdict and a sentence of death. Frank Noel bit his fingernails. Lorenz's trial took even less time. A new jury heard virtually the same testimony from the victim. At 10:37 a.m. the jury brought in the same verdict and punishment. Lorenzo Noel burst into tears. Judge Pippen immediately sentenced both men to be executed in the electric chair at Huntsville on June 28, the earliest possible date. Total time consumed for both trials was an hour and a half.

At 3:30 a.m. on the next Saturday, Sheriff Marshall, three deputy sheriffs, and two Texas Rangers loaded the Noel brothers into two fast cars and drove them to the state prison at Huntsville. Their early departure surprised and infuriated District Attorney Cox. He claimed that he had hoped to clear several more crimes through interrogating the two men, but that Marshall refused to let him see them and now it was impossible to see them. Cox's dislike of the youthful sheriff would be manifested more visibly at the next election.

Marshall's outstanding performance in face of the lynch mob prompted Denton County's sheriff to call upon him for help three months later when members from the notorious Webb Martin gang barricaded themselves in a house near Argyle after killing a deputy sheriff. Upon his arrival Marshall immediately took command, called Martin inside the house by telephone, and arranged to go inside for a personal meeting. Marshall walked unarmed into the house, which was filled with dangerous desperadoes, and negotiated without success. Back outside, he strapped on his six-shooters and headed once more to the house to confront Martin. Both men began firing. Martin shot off Marshall's hat, but he retreated inside and brought out fifteen other men and one woman with their hands up to surrender. It was a remarkable triumph.

Less than a year later Marshall ran for re-election. District Attorney Cox campaigned vigorously against him. Despite Marshall's demonstrated courage in controlling the lynch mob and arresting the Webb Martin gang, Cox contended that he actually had not performed well. Gunfire had been unnecessary with the mob at the county jail, he argued. Also criticized for his alleged failure to be more energetic in arresting bootleggers, Marshall said he would have done better if Cox had cooperated with him. Marshall also had appointed a Catholic deputy and a Jewish deputy, earning him the enmity of the Ku Klux Klan. Marshall's chief opponent was veteran lawman Allen Seale, who upon leaving the sheriff's office after Harston's defeat had been hired by Cox as a special investigator. A four-column advertisement in the *Times Herald* portrayed Seale as a fearless lawman: "He's six feet tall, hard as nails, and homely. Doesn't know what fear is--and cares less. He's 'toted' a gun for 22 years--can use it, too."

When the votes were counted in the Democratic primary, Marshall lost to Seale by 124 votes. His brief but sensational career as Dallas County sheriff was over. Marshall returned to farming for a while, dabbled in the oil business, lived for a year in Mexico, and worked as chief of security near Cape Girardeau, Missouri, for the laying of the Big Inch and Little Inch pipe line across the Mississippi River. In April 1982 he died at the age of eighty-seven, alone in his University Park home, his single term as sheriff forgotten.

Seale would not live to finishl his term. He died in office of cancer, to be succeeded by his wife Lulu, who was succeeded herself in 1928 election by Seale's former partner in busting bootleggers, Hal

Hood. Three decades later Seale's son, Denver, would serve as a Dallas County Commissioner and would successfully nominate Shelby Cox to be a county court judge.

Municipal Election of 1925

Just one month before the lynch mob had gathered at the jail, Louis Blaylock and his four fellow incumbent commissioners all asked to be re-elected on the City Democrat ticket for April 1925. The Citizens Association offered its own slate of candidates, headed by Perry G. Claiborne, and a new political organization called the Citizens Independents emerged with a ticket led by David McCord for mayor. Having attacked Blaylock and his slate in the previous election on the basis of their affinity with the Klan, and having suffered a crushing defeat, this time the Citizens Association candidates sought to avoid personal attacks that might backfire. The result was a bland and ineffective campaign.

Far more feisty was the new Citizens Independent organization, and especially its chief spokesman, attorney Noah Roark. Roark, also avoiding specific mention of the Klan, broadly asserted "gross misconduct" and mismanagement. He spoke of things occurring under Blaylock's administration "too terrible to contemplate." He claimed that Blaylock's own building at Jackson and St. Paul streets was vastly undervalued on the tax rolls at $24,000 when it was worth hundreds of thousands of dollars. He charged that city hall had given preferential treatment, too, to the new Magnolia Building, whose owners paid taxes on $189,000 rather than on its approximate value of $3.5 million. Blaylock and his City Democrat colleagues, he said, had rewarded the friendly *Times Herald* with city printing contracts at inflated rates. Two days before the election Roark told the newspapers that an anonymous person had called his wife to warn that he would be killed if he didn't stop talking. R.M. Connell, candidate for police commissioner, said that if elected he would "make the star of a policeman a badge of honor instead of being a badge of disgrace."

Blaylock declined to campaign until less than four weeks before the election. Considering all the things he had to do, he said, that was all the time he had. "If you don't think I am the right man for the job, vote me down," he said. The *Times Herald* said that Blaylock and his fellow City Democrat commissioners had set "a record of achievement seldom, if ever, equaled." Veteran civic leader Colonel Frank P. Holland called him a credit to the city and "a beloved personality by all who know him." Wherever he went, Holland said, the mayor was "an advertisement for Dallas."

The April 8 election proved to be a lop-sided victory for Blaylock and the City Democratic Association, all its candidates winning about two-thirds of the votes cast in a small turnout. The Citizens Association candidates limped to a third-place finish behind the new Citizens Independent candidates. Blaylock became the first mayor since Holland to win two terms, and Klansman Louis Turley became the first man ever to achieve three terms as police and fire commissioner.

PORTRAIT OF DADDY LOU

He was seventy-three years old upon his re-election in 1925. His advanced years, his folksy demeanor, his white hair and mustache, and his wrinkled face earned him the nickname, "Daddy Lou." No individual served the City of Dallas in so many capacities as Daddy Lou. In pre-commission days he was the unpaid police commissioner from 1903 to 1906; from 1911 to 1915 he was the full-time police and fire commissioner; from 1920 to 1923 he was the finance and revenue commissioner; and from 1923 to 1927 he was mayor. He offered a plain-spoken, common-sense approach to the office of mayor, and whatever criticism his acceptance of the Ku Klux Klan generated, he was one of the most popular mayors the city ever had.

Daddy Lou Blaylock was basically a printer, albeit a highly successful one, whose formal education ended when he was twelve. He sometimes was called "the kissing mayor" because of his habit of welcoming visiting actresses to the city with a kiss. He chewed tobacco and he loved raw oysters. Under his two terms as mayor the city made some significant steps toward the future, including the building of a huge new water reservoir, Lake Dallas; the construction of Fair Park Auditorium; and the appointment of a citizens committee under Charles E. Ulrickson which, following up on the work of George Kessler, drew up a new long-range improvement plan for Dallas that included provisions for the construction of levees for the

Trinity River.

Blaylock was born in Sevier County, Arkansas, on October 21, 1849. When he was three years old he came to Texas with his parents in a covered wagon, following southward from the Red River the same path John Neely Bryan had taken eleven years earlier down the old Preston Trail. The family camped overnight in the small village of Dallas, but chose not to stay there, continuing on to Burnet to live in a one-room log cabin. Not far away, U.S. soldiers at Fort Hamilton, including Lt. Robert E. Lee, patrolled to protect them and other pioneers from marauding Indians. After three years in Burnet the family moved to Austin, where Blaylock's ailing father died. To keep up the family, Blaylock's mother rented and operated a hotel. Louis often played after school on the nearby capitol grounds, where he said later he met and came to admire the great Sam Houston.

At the age of twelve Louis quit school to work as a printer's devil at the *Austin Weekly Gazette*. At fourteen, in the midst of the Civil War, he took charge of a 100-mile "pony express" mail route between Austin and Brenham. He hired other boys to assist him by relay, and he continued this work until the war ended when his mother moved the family once more—this time to Galveston. Now seventeen, Blaylock returned to the printing trade. After his employer went bankrupt he persuaded his half-brother, William Shaw, to enter into a partnership with him in founding their own printing firm. The two worked diligently and with skill, and in 1877 they won a contract with the State of Texas for printing the *Texas House of Representatives Journal, Texas Senate Journal* and the *General Laws*. In 1886 the firm moved to Dallas, bringing its printing contracts with it An essential part of its work came through a contract with the Methodist church to print a state-wide newspaper, the *Texas Christian Advocate.* The firm would continue to print this newspaper until 1924. In 1894, when Blaylock and Shaw dissolved their partnership, Blaylock assumed control of the company and changed its name to Blaylock Publishing Co. In 1897 he purchased seven of the still-new automatic Linotype typesetting machines; his firm became one of the first in the state to make widespread use of them.

As his printing business prospered, Blaylock found more and more time for involving himself in community activities. He was on the building committee for the new Praetorian Building, he was a 33rd degree Mason, and he was a director of First National Bank. He and his wife, parents of five children, were active members of the First Methodist Church. Even with his widening interests, it was said that for forty years Blaylock read every proof that came off his presses.

DALLAS IN THE 1920S

The city over which Blaylock presided during the heart of the 1920s was the wealthiest in the state in terms of property valuation; it consistently ranked high in the nation in building permits issued; it had more telephones than any city in the South (the 50,000th being installed in April 1924), with one calculation showing it to have more telephones per capita than any city in the world; and its skyline--of which residents were inordinately proud--consisted of more than one hundred structures between five and twenty-nine floors. The ugly poles holding electrical wires that marred the downtown skies started being placed underground in 1924, a project completed in 1929. Some 65 million passengers rode the city's 112 miles of streetcar lines in 1925. Six interurban lines now offered more than 350 miles of track in every direction. Air-mail service to Chicago and from there on to New York began on May 12, 1926, via Curtiss "Carrier Pigeon" airplanes. After the Oriental Hotel closed in 1924, a 700-room hotel costing $5.5 million, the Baker, opened on its site the next year. Ford Motor Company that same year purchased a twenty-two acre site on East Grand Avenue from the Texas & Pacific Railway to build a huge new $1 million assembly plant that would employ 1,200 workers. A visiting real estate executive from California, impressed with the city's extraordinary growth and energy, made a far-fetched prediction that by 1940 the city would have a population of one million.

One of Blaylock's first priorities as mayor was to reduce costs at city hall. By eliminating jobs and combining various operations he was able to present a budget for 1923 that was $500,000 less than the previous one. If Blaylock had had his way he would have eliminated all municipal expenditures dedicated to welfare activities. "I'll bet the business men would stand back of me," he said, but then added that he wouldn't dare propose such cuts because of the town's club women. Despite Blaylock's pronounced tendency to pinch pennies, city parks continued to be developed, and the Dallas Zoo especially gained prominence through the acquisition of animals brought to it by famed animal hunter Frank "Bring 'Em Back Alive" Buck. At Fair Park a new above-ground, circular swimming pool opened in the summer of 1926. That same summer the mayor decided that city workers should get a break during June, July, and August, and he ordered them to work half days only.

Already the city's growth had caught up with White Rock Lake. A huge new reservoir must be built. A site was selected north of town on the Elm Fork of the Trinity just east of the little town of Garza in Denton County. Mayor Blaylock himself directed the first stroke of the steam shovel before a crowd of 1,000 spectators on October 4, 1924, thus starting the three-year task of excavating a 70-billion gallon, $5 million lake with a sixty-five mile shoreline. Since the lake was to be used for drinking water, commissioners passed an ordinance prohibiting fishing, boating, swimming, or other recreational activities. It was calculated that the lake would hold enough water for a city of from 750,000 to a million inhabitants.

The city's growth also brought a need for a large municipal auditorium. Logically, such a facility would be located downtown, and some favored this. But Blaylock and others wanted to build it at Fair Park, where parking would be more convenient. The park board and the State Fair of Texas directors agreed, and plans were drawn up for a $500,000 Spanish-style facility with a seating capacity of 5,200. The cornerstone was laid in early 1925. Most park board members favored naming it for W.H. Gaston, who originally had owned the land on which it was located. Finally, though, the name Fair Park Auditorium was selected.

Some months after Fair Park Auditorium opened Blaylock reminded Dallas residents of its rental availability for cultural presentations. When a Negro choir stepped forward to lease it, the Ku Klux Klan protested, but Blaylock said that Negroes had as much right as anyone to use the facility. "Such a protest is all a big piece of tom foolery and I will not even consider denying them the use of the Fair Park Auditorium," he said.

While leaders through the years prided themselves on their ability to accomplish whatever was needed and referred proudly to their "Dallas Spirit," the city still had many problems. A visiting city planner told members of the Kiwanis Club in 1925 that Dallas would face one of the most serious traffic problems in the nation unless something were done soon. He referred to narrow streets, insufficient connecting thoroughfares, a lack of parkways and highways, the disjointed arrangement of outlying sections of town, and the impenetrable barrier of the Trinity River. These obstacles could be surmounted, he said, except for "too much indifference on the part of too many people." In addition, many of the city's streets were crumbling, especially those paved with wooden blocks, although City Commissioner Gus Wylie said they weren't worth repairing.

The *Dallas Journal* acknowledged in an editorial in 1926 that the Dallas spirit alone was insufficient to correct a number of minor but irritating matters. Straying chickens, howling dogs, and "over-worked phonographs" were creating unrest, disturbances, and sometimes ill feelings in city neighborhoods.

Louis Turley implored his fellow city commissioners to allocate money to buy uniforms for his police officers, many of whom couldn't afford to dress themselves properly. He wanted four new uniforms a year for each officer. An officer's life was hard indeed, for the 150 or so men on the force worked eight hours a day, seven days a week. They were given one day off a month, and had an annual vacation of one week. A patrolman earned, with few exceptions, $1,680 a year.

Every fall, just before thousands of visitors came to the State Fair of Texas, the city made a determined effort to spruce up the area. This included the arrest and removal from the streets of vagrants and other undesirable individuals. Hardly any regard at all was paid to their civil rights or presumption of innocence. Plainclothes officers in late September 1925 raided five downtown rooming houses and arrested twenty-two persons as undesirables. "Charges of vagrancy may be filed against some of the prisoners," the *Dallas Journal* said, "while others, believed to be crooks, but against whom police are unable to establish cases, will be given 'hours' to leave the city."

It was not a good idea in Dallas to tangle with the law. One man who did, twenty-year-old J.L. Dailey, learned that lesson in Judge Pippen's courtroom, where a jury convicted him for robbing a couple of a pearl necklace, $21 in cash, and a watch. The judge pronounced solemnly that his penalty for this crime was the most extreme punishment permitted under the law--death. Dailey's mother fainted dead away in the courtroom without a sound save for the thud of her body hitting the floor. Dailey's sixteen-year-old bride had an opposite reaction. She shrieked hysterically. Dailey consoled his teen-age wife: "It's all right. I might just as well die now as any time." He was the youngest man in Judge Pippen's memory ever to be sentenced to death in Dallas County, and so far as anybody knew he was the first man in Dallas sentenced to death for robbery.

A coterie of wise-cracking newspaper reporters working from the police press room covered affairs of crime with flamboyancy. The scene was not unlike that portrayed in the classic play, "Front Page." Reporters raced one another to scenes of crimes, crawled through windows to steal photographs of murderers or murder victims, played practical jokes on one another, and amused themselves with cut-throat dominoes while waiting for the next story to break.

Criminals, mean-spirited though they were, had their own code of honor. Burglars who cracked a vault at a dry goods store on Elm Street found cash and checks, then realized that they could not cash the checks. They returned them to the store via the U.S. mail.

Nor were Dallas schools immune to misbehavior. High school girls raised eyebrows by dressing as "flappers." School Superintendent N.R. Crozier said, however, that those who were urging anti-rouge, anti-bare knees, and anti-peek-a-boo dress organizations need not be so concerned. No naked knees of girls could be seen on school campuses, he said, and those girls who used too much rouge were asked simply to wash their faces.

Dallas teachers in the middle of the decade wanted a raise. High school teachers earned from $1,400 to $2,400 a year in 1926-27, and elementary school teachers were paid less, $1,266 to $1,700. Teachers and their principals thought they deserved at least $300 more a year. (Black teachers were paid less than their white counterparts.)

An era of sorts ended for Dallas on September 13, 1925. Pioneer merchant Alex Sanger, the last of the five Sanger brothers who founded the department store, died at Baylor Hospital after surgery. Sanger, born in Bavaria in 1847, had joined his brothers in the United States after serving an apprenticeship in a dry goods store and traveling in steerage on a small steamer. So overcome was he on reaching New York's harbor that he foolishly and spontaneously used his last money to buy a round of refreshments for his travelling companions. He managed, however, to find his way to his brothers to join them in their dry goods business. He and his brothers had moved Sanger Bros. to Dallas in 1872 with the coming of the H&TC

Railroad at a time when just 2,500 people lived in the city. During Sanger's lifetime the city grew from that small number to 250,000. Sanger had been prominently identified with practically every civic improvement throughout those years.

KESSLER PLAN BOOSTED

One of the two major problems George Kessler had identified for the city had been solved--the Texas & Pacific Railway tracks no longer ran down Pacific Avenue. But the bigger barrier to city development, the Trinity River, remained as impenetrable as ever. The levee that Kessler had proposed still was a dream. So many things were involved in this massive project that it was too big for a single municipal government to achieve. Yet, people were at work, especially members of a new organization, the Kessler Plan Association.

No more than 10 percent of the Kessler Plan and its update had been achieved, but the association was organized in 1924 to carry out the entire plan and bring about the "scientific development of every part of Greater Dallas." Neighborhood improvement leagues banded together in the association to create a wide network dedicated to the plan's realization. One of the chief weapons was a book for schoolchildren written by former School Superintendent Justin F. Kimball. Entitled *Our City--Dallas,* the book carefully explained the benefits of city planning in general as well as Kessler's specific plan. "We now realize that if something of this kind had been begun at the time Mr. Kessler's report was adopted in 1910," wrote the secretary of the association, John E. Surratt, "and if the boys and girls at the age of 12 to 15 had been taught just what the Kessler program meant to Dallas, to-day most of the men and women in Dallas of 27 to 30 years of age and younger would be thoroughly familiar with the program, and its execution would follow just as day follows night."

The growing impetus to solve Dallas' problems prompted Blaylock in 1925 to appoint a five-man committee to carry forth the long-range planning started by Kessler, now dead, and to bring back recommendations as to how to finance specific improvements. Charles E. Ulrickson was named chairman. Other members were Alex F. Weisberg, Frank L. McNeny, Leslie A. Stemmons, and Harry A.

Olmstead. They thus began a job that would continue beyond Blaylock's term in office and culminate in a bond issue of $23.9 million that would include key components for improvements, with a particular emphasis on placing the river between levees.

Meanwhile, the city's preoccupation with means of transportation was looking in another direction--upward. First it had been the river that promised riches, then the railroads, and then the automobile. Now it was the airplane.

PART TWO

Making the Future Happen

6

Dallas' Ocean of the Air

Keep your airport--it will place you among the commercial leaders of the world.

--Charles Lindbergh, 1927

A Preoccupation with Aviation

The nation's great cities--New York, Chicago, Boston, Philadelphia, Baltimore, New Orleans, San Francisco, and many others--had one thing in common: a navigable waterway. The possibility of navigating the Trinity had inspired John Neely Bryan to found Dallas, and it had tantalized civic leaders for generations. The concern over avenues of trade had prompted the intense efforts to bring the first railroads to town. Persistent attempts to create an outlet by water had failed, though. Now Dallas joyfully realized that aviation could substitute for the missing waterway link.

This realization manifested itself early. Frank McCarroll of Oak Cliff began tinkering with aeronautical devices as early as the 1890s. In 1904 he even built an airplane behind his house which some said he managed to get into the air. McCarroll, who obtained patents on a retractable landing gear and mechanisms to alter a wing's shape while in flight, constantly pushed the city to participate in aviation. The Chamber of Commerce frequently sponsored visiting air shows, usually at Fair Park. Even before the First World War a rude landing field for aircraft had been cleared off in the Trinity River bottoms.

When in early 1917 it became known that the War Department wanted a place in the Dallas area for training pilots, the Chamber of Commerce bought and leased land south of Bachman Lake for that purpose. This bold initiative worked. The War Department leased the site, and the Army Signal Corps' Air Service constructed on it a $1.5 million training facility soon to be known as Love Field. At Fair Park another Army facility, Camp Dick, gave pre-flight training to men who then could transfer to Love Field for flight training.

When the war ended the Army declined to buy Love Field, and the Chamber found itself holding a 650-acre improved flying field with no tenant. The land could have been returned to the owners, but the Chamber decided to gamble once more and develop the property as an industrial district for civilian aviation enterprises. Again, the gamble paid off. One of the first companies to lease space and begin operations there was a passenger service and flying school called the Travel Air Agency. In 1922 Curtiss Flying School, with five pilots giving elementary and advanced flying instruction, began operations. More unusual as a tenant was the Al G. Barnes Circus, which used some of the buildings at Love Field as a winter headquarters in 1922-23 for 600 people and a menagerie of animals.

By 1925, two years before Charles Lindbergh flew across the Atlantic, aviation activity had become intense at Love Field. Curtiss Aeroplane Company was servicing and selling airplanes and offering a complete line of parts. Good and Foster also repaired and serviced airplanes. Dallas Aeroplane Co. had an aerial taxi business, and Fairchild Aerial Camera Corporation provided an aerial mapping and survey service.

The Chamber's aggressive attitude and its offer of an attractive inducement gave the airport its biggest leap forward in May 1926 when National Air Transport began flying a daily air mail route to Chicago via Curtiss "Carrier Pigeon" airplanes. To achieve this coup the Chamber guaranteed the airline at least one hundred pounds of air mail daily for six months. The new service cut two days off the time formerly required to deliver a letter from Dallas to New York or

San Francisco. The existence of regular air mail service caused the federal government to install a meteorological station at Love Field. In 1927 National Air Transport, now enjoying rent-free hangar and office space for two and a half years, again courtesy of the Chamber, carried 109,789 pounds of mail and flew 674,621 miles on the Dallas-Chicago route without a serious accident. On September 1, 1927, the state's first commercial airline passengers were carried from Love Field to Kansas City and Chicago via a National Air Transport airplane. By 1930 Dallas was second in the nation in scheduled air transport activity. The reasons for such progress were two-fold: Dallas' enterprise in promoting aviation and the city's central location.

In the fall of 1927 Dallas further focused its attention on aviation in two headline-making events. One was the tragic death of a popular Dallas pilot in pursuit of the $25,000 Easterwood Prize, and the other was the decision by the City of Dallas to involve itself directly in aviation by buying Love Field from the Chamber and developing it as a municipally-owned airport. (In this latter regard Dallas followed such cities as Kansas City, Chicago, Philadelphia, Detroit, and Boston.) A year later in 1928 the city purchased Hensley Field, west of Dallas, for the use of the Army Air Corps Reserves.

Dallas paid the Chamber $432,500 for Love Field, an amount voters approved in a bond issue despite opposition by Mayor R.E. Burt and two commissioners. Mayor Burt said Love Field was too small to be a "Class A" flying field and that the surrounding neighborhoods were so well developed it would be impossible to buy enough adjacent land to make it big enough. The mayor unwittingly had touched on what would be a sore point for years. No other Dallas mayor would acknowledge such a thought for at least four decades.

Meanwhile, however, a prominent Dallas businessman who had earned a fortune in the chewing gum business made a theatrical gesture intended to garner international headlines and further promote the city's commitment to aviation. William E. Easterwood Jr. announced a new and daring challenge open to pilots across the nation. The first pilot to fly from Dallas to Hong Kong would be awarded a gift of $25,000, the same amount Lindbergh had collected for flying solo across the Atlantic. The possibility existed for a prize twice that amount, for Easterwood tied his prize into another $25,000 award being offered by James D. Dole of Dole Pineapple for the first flight from San Francisco to Hawaii. The aviator who flew from

Dallas to San Francisco, then to Hawaii and on to Hong Kong surely would bring the city the same world-wide fame that Lindbergh's flight had brought to St. Louis. Easterwood's prize, of course, required a far greater distance, and it was surely the most dangerous of the various prizes that had been offered for flying long distances. Easterwood, a native of Wills Point, Texas, whose Orbit Listerated Gum became a national favorite (in 1925 he sold it to Wrigley), was intensely interested in aviation. Earlier, he had sought to pay Lindbergh's taxes on the $25,000 he won for flying across the Atlantic, but Lindbergh declined the offer.

The fact that the Easterwood Prize required the most hazardous flight yet known to man did not dissuade the improbable William P. Erwin, also a Dallas resident, from immediately responding. Erwin, nicknamed "Lone Star Bill," declared the day after the prize was announced that he would be an enthusiastic claimant. The fact that he had no suitable airplane was beside the fact. One could be built.

Only thirty-one years of age, Erwin was a renowned aviator, the third-ranking American fighter pilot ace of World War I. A native of Royan, Oklahoma, he had graduated from high school at Amarillo in the Texas Panhandle, then studied music in New York City and Chicago to become an accomplished pianist and composer. When the United States entered the war he enlisted for aviation training, and after earning his wings compiled a fantastic record in Europe. He gained credit for shooting down nine enemy aircraft and two "probables." He persistently flew into enemy territory to harass German ground troops with machine-gun fire from as low as fifty feet at the Chateau-Thierry and St. Mihiel salients. For his heroism he earned the Distinguished Service Cross. After the war he returned to Texas and became a barnstorming pilot, going from town to town and selling rides to the curious and courageous.

Now he wanted to bring honor and glory to Dallas as well as to himself not only by winning the Easterwood Prize, but also by grabbing the Dole Prize and then flying on around the world from Hong Kong for a triumphant return to Dallas. Plenty of prominent people believed that he could do it, and they contributed the money to build a proper airplane for Erwin in Wichita, Kansas. Contributors included George B. Dealey, Karl Hoblitzelle, Fred Florence of Republic National Bank, John W. Carpenter of Texas Power & Light Co., and eleven others. Erwin's new airplane was similar to the *Spirit of St.*

Louis. On August 6, 1927, before a crowd of some 10,000 people at Love Field, the green and silver monoplane was unveiled and christened the *Dallas Spirit*. The program was broadcast live over the state by radio station WFAA. Mayor Burt declared the moment one of the greatest in Dallas history. Dealey said that Erwin surely would make the fabled Dallas spirit known the length and breadth of the world. Easterwood drew cheers when he pledged to give Erwin an additional $5,000 if he won the $25,000 prize. Banker Fred Florence introduced Erwin and his parents, the Rev. and Mrs. W.A. Erwin of Pawhuska, Oklahoma. Texas Governor Dan Moody spoke, too, and a band played the national anthem as the white drapery covering all but the big tires on the *Dallas Spirit* was slowly pulled back.

Three days after its unveiling Erwin lifted the *Dallas Spirit* off Love Field runway en route to San Francisco. But trouble occurred with the fuel pump system and he turned back for repairs after having gone 252 miles. Next day Erwin was airborne again, and this time he completed the flight despite the same problem. Because of it he had to manipulate a "wobble pump" with his thumb for the entire flight. When he landed at the California airport he was woozy and tired and he had a huge blister on his thumb. He declared, though, that the worst part of winning the Easterwood Prize now was over. Fifteen other pilots competing for the Dole Prize were arriving at the same approximate time from various parts of the nation.

A personal problem developed. Erwin had planned for his young wife, twenty years of age and pregnant, to be his navigator. However, Dole requirements stipulated that all entrants must be twenty-one years of age. So instead of his wife a man named Alvin Eichwaldt joined Erwin for the flight across the Pacific.

Of the fifteen other entrants, for various reasons contest officials permitted only seven to depart on the long-awaited take-off day. With the heavy fuel loads required for such a journey, getting aloft was a dangerous ordeal itself. One of the seven airplanes crashed on the runway. Another failed to lift off on its first attempt, then crashed on its next try.

The *Miss Doran*, piloted by a twenty-two-year-old female flying school teacher named Mildred Doran, returned fifteen minutes after departing for quick repairs. The young aviatrix was tearful and obviously shaken over the unexpected problems. Many begged her to climb out of her cockpit and forget the attempt. But she would not, and with the repairs completed she departed once more with two crew members. The *Miss Doran* was never heard from again.

Erwin, too, encountered problems. Shortly after his take-off the wind ripped off the green and silver fabric covering the *Dallas Spirit,* leaving its skeleton bare. Erwin returned to correct the situation. But the repairs took too long. Before they could be completed word came that two airplanes already had made it safely to Honolulu, claiming both the first and second prizes. Another airplane, the *Golden Eagle,* was missing. Despite pleas from Dole officials not to depart since the prize already had been won, Erwin and Eichwaldt insisted that they wanted to search for the missing aviators en route to Honolulu and then fly on to Hong Kong for the Easterwood Prize.

George B. Dealey's son, Ted, who was there as a reporter to cover the event for his father's newspaper, helped Erwin put on his flight suit. Dealey noted that Erwin carried a small Bible. Erwin left behind separate poignant messages for his mother and for his Dallas sponsors. In the message to his sponsors he wrote, "I believe with my whole heart that we will make it....We will win because *Dallas Spirit* always wins."

A radio message was picked up from the *Dallas Spirit* some 400 nautical miles out. Eichwaldt advised that the two had encountered a storm and their airplane had fallen into a tailspin from which they had feared they could not recover. He was pleased to report that this had not been the case. But then came a frantic message: "We're in another tailspin." Only silence followed. Erwin, Eichwaldt, and the *Dallas Spirit* disappeared beneath the waters of the Pacific. The death toll among participants for the Dole prize rose to ten.

The federal government, alarmed at the casualties in such flights, soon issued a warning against similar contests, and announced stringent guidelines to regulate them. This signaled an end to an era in American history.

The loss of the *Dallas Spirit* and its two aviators cast a momentary pall over the city, but the tragedy did not halt efforts to develop aviation. The city managed to attract none less than the famed Lindbergh to come to Love Field to dedicate it as a municipal airport. Lindbergh was touring the nation in the *Spirit of St. Louis,* greeted everywhere by thousands of clamoring admirers. In agreeing to come to Dallas, he sent advance word for the speakers to please avoid "hero worship" in referring to him in their remarks.

Some 10,000 spectators were there when Lindbergh landed at Love Field on a rainy, chilly September afternoon in 1927. Dallas Mayor R.E. Burt and other dignitaries welcomed him officially, and then escorted him on a parade through downtown Dallas witnessed by as many as 100,000, the largest crowd in the city's history. Dallas was enthralled; Lindbergh, on the other hand, appeared bored. "A glassy stare and a mechanical lifting of his hand to his bare head were his only reactions to the cheers of his admirers," a newspaper account stated. Admirers packed the sidewalks, peered through windows, lined the tops of buildings, climbed on fire escapes, and elevated themselves in every way imaginable to get a glimpse of the famed aviator. Among the spectators were 40,000 children who had been turned out of school just to see the aviator.

Even the newspaper reporters, about thirty of them, stood awe-struck at Lindbergh's press conference in the Adolphus Hotel. After Lindbergh shook hands around the room, a long, nervous silence ensued. Finally, a shaky voice piped up to ask him lamely about the future of aviation. The next questions came easier but continued to be unusually simple. "How does it feel to fly, colonel?" "What makes that little paddle go round?" "How long will it be until Fords have wings?" Lindbergh answered all questions with courtesy.

That evening some 700 people attended a banquet for the visitor in the Adolphus. Lindbergh concluded his short remarks, broadcast over KRLD radio, by saying, "Keep your airport--it will place you among the commercial leaders of the world." When he returned to his fifteenth floor suite afterwards, a pretty local dancer leaped from behind a corner to try to kiss the world's most eligible bachelor. Lindbergh's manager roughly pushed her away. It was the second time in half a day that a Dallas woman had been thwarted in an effort to kiss the flyer. The earlier incident had occurred in the hotel lobby after the afternoon parade. Next morning, Lindbergh flew away to Oklahoma City, still unkissed, and his future wife, Anne Morrow, still unknown to him.

While such events as the Easterwood Prize competition and Lindbergh's visit garnered the largest headlines, Dallas continued to work quietly to advance its aviation interests. This was summed up dramatically in 1931 by the Chamber of Commerce's manager, M.J. Norrell, who gave the Dallas Rotary Club a message that would never be forgotten. "As an inland city, let the air be our ocean and let the influence of this city enlarge itself, carried upon the wings of the planes that already write across our skies the story of a new era of transportation. If the people of Dallas ever blind themselves in the delusion that aviation is just a whim or passing fancy; if they illogically think of airports and airport development as an investment upon which immediate financial returns must be realized; if they refuse to take the long look into the midst of the years ahead; hiding before their eyes the curtain of an immediate present; if Dallas is to hear and heed the insistent call of the new day in transportation, then every succeeding year will see our position less secure; and future generations which otherwise would enjoy the results of clear thinking and clear vision will realize that we of today were unequal to the tasks imposed and our vision was too narrow to hold within its perspective the more splendid achievements that lie just ahead."

A Theatrical Success

While the instant world-wide acclaim that had been imagined from the the ill-fated *Dallas Spirit* flight never came, another entirely different endeavor during these years grew from a modest beginning to one bringing national attention. It developed almost unintentionally through the work of amateur thespians whose love of the theater prompted them to begin staging plays for their own enjoyment. In 1920 the enthusiasts organized themselves as the Little Theatre of Dallas and initiated a regular program of dramatic presentations.

The Little Theatre players appointed as their "coach" a cotton broker from England, Talbot Pearson, who directed them in their first series of plays in such places as the Unitarian Church, the Scottish Rite Cathedral, and school auditoriums. In that first January-to-May season five plays were presented. Those attending the earliest productions were mostly friends and relatives. Word of their surprisingly high quality spread. Audiences grew larger and larger.

By 1923 the group had progressed to the point where it could hire for pay a director with solid professional training and experience. Oliver Hinsdell, who arrived from New Orleans, looked around, talked to a few people, and declared: "I've got the hang of things in just a few hours to know that I'm in the right place." He was right, for under Hinsdell, who remained for eight years, the Little Theatre of

Dallas entered a golden era which was to provide for Dallas a strong identification as a city of culture. In the same year that Hinsdell took over, a playhouse that seated 242 persons and cost $25,000 to build was constructed at 417 Olive Street.

The Little Theatre of Dallas was part of a national movement of theaters with similar names which sought to demonstrate that good drama could be presented by amateurs in places far from the bright lights of Broadway. In 1923 a competition was begun for these theatrical groups, and one year later Dallas' amateur thespians decided to venture to New York City and enter the competition. The Dallas group, one of sixteen entrants, presented a one-act play written by one of its own members, John William Rogers Jr., the amusements editor of the *Times Herald*. The play, "Judge Lynch," dealt with mob hysteria in the South and the lynching of a black man who afterwards was proved innocent of the crime. Local artist Olin Travis designed the set. In this national competition, judged by theatrical personality David Belasco himself, Dallas won first place over its Eastern seaboard competitors. The prize was $100 and the right to keep and display the Belasco Cup Trophy for a year. Back in Dallas the actors presented "Judge Lynch" at the Majestic Theater for ten sell-out performances, attracting more than 23,000 theater-goers. Mayor Blaylock proclaimed a Dallas Little Theatre Week.

Next year the actors returned once more to New York and performed a portrayal of Negro life in the South by Paul Green entitled "No 'Count Boy." Astonishingly, once again they won first place. In 1926 the players went back for a third try with an entirely different sort of play, a religious drama by Margaret Larkin entitled "El Christo" with a setting in New Mexico. For the third consecutive year the Little Theatre of Dallas won first place. Back in Dallas the actors gave a special performance of "El Christo," and in the accompanying celebration director Hinsdell proposed building a new and bigger playhouse. The general manager of the Chamber of Commerce, master of ceremonies that evening, endorsed the idea heartily. Merchant Arthur Kramer urged a fast start at fund-raising.

It had been understood by the Little Theatre that its third consecutive victory in New York earned for the troupe the right to have permanent possession of the Belasco Cup Trophy. Contest authorities, however, said that this was a misunderstanding, that the trophy had to be returned. The disgruntled Dallas actors decided not to return to New York City for the next year's competition.

Anyway, ambitious plans were progressing for the new playhouse to be built on Maple Street at a cost of $110,000 and with a seating capacity of 408. To help raise funds the Olive Street property was sold. Proceeds from that were $65,000 short of the total amount needed, and Dallas financier and civic leader Louis Lipsitz agreed to guarantee that amount himself. However, Lipsitz, on holiday at the Crazy Hotel in Mineral Wells, collapsed after a round of dancing and died of a heart attack without uttering a word. No provisions could be found for his pledge to the Little Theatre. Theater officials were forced to sign a mortgage to finance the amount needed for their new facility. On April 9, 1928, the ornate new theater, built in Mediterranean style with fancy interiors, opened with a presentation of Ferenc Molnar's "The Swan." The gala opening night was attended by Governor and Mrs. Dan Moody and by Mayor and Mrs. R.E. Burt.

A subtle change, however, had occurred. Now, regular payments had to be made on a financial obligation which by 1931 had swelled to $120,000. No longer was the Little Theatre of Dallas a group of happy troupers enjoying themselves immensely and carrying along others with their inspirational acting. They began to feel that their plays must cater to the tastes of the audience, and the works offered came to be dominated increasingly by comedies. Beyond that, the fancy new facility brought with it an implied sophistication and feeling of exclusivity which discouraged ordinary folks from attending. On top of these factors came the crash of 1929 and the Depression which followed, closing many theaters throughout the nation and causing attendance to plummet at others. Season subscriptions for the Little Theatre fell in the tenth season from 750 to 350. In 1931 Hinsdell resigned as director. The Little Theatre struggled through the Depression until finally in 1943 it collapsed. Meanwhile, it had created a lasting legend, having won three consecutive national championships, erected two new playhouses, and created in Dallas an enduring interest in the theater.

DEEP ELLUM

In a part of town that rarely earned headlines, even the modest ones of a theatrical group, a culture of a different sort was evident in

Dallas. This was the area east of town along Elm Street and Central Avenue, where the all-but abandoned H&TC tracks ran. "Deep Ellum" it was called. Its origin lay in the days following the Civil War when freed slaves settled there. The H&TC depot further prompted its development and character. Here was a lively street scene reminiscent of Harlem, an area of pawn shops, night clubs, domino halls, shoeshine parlors, walk-up hotels, cafes, and--for some reason--an abundance of furniture stores. Rows of two-story structures on either side of the street housed such occupants as the Day & Night Pawn Shop, the Green Parrot Dance Hall, the Indian Herb Store, Slim's Barber Shop, and the Home Cafe. At the Cotton Club, a popular cabaret, patrons entered through two wooden tunnels--one for men and a separate one for women. Here, as late as the 1940s, was an "undercurrent of jungle law; superstition, hatred and passion." Here in the alleys and shacks were transplanted farm Negroes and urban-born ones. The "reefer man" worked comfortably, dispensing marijuana cigarettes as a cheap stimulant. Deep Ellum was predominantly black in its people and culture, but there was a strong influx of Jews, many of whom owned and operated pawn shops.

In 1909 black musician Huddie "Leadbelly" Ledbetter arrived from Louisiana and sang in Deep Ellum cafes for the next eight years. One of his songs, "Deep Ellum Blues," went this way:

When you go down on Deep Ellum,
Put your money in your socks,
'Cause them women on Deep Ellum
'Sho will throw you on the rocks.

Later, of course, songs such as "The Midnight Special" and "The Rock Island Line" would bring Leadbelly and his twelve-string guitar great fame. On Deep Ellum he encountered another musician, Blind Lemon Jefferson. They began performing together, continuing until 1917 when Leadbelly was sentenced to prison for killing a man over a woman. While these two performers worked in obscurity in Dallas, their reputations over the years as seminal performers of blues music gained international reputations.

While Deep Ellum seemed representative to all too many people of what Negro life in Dallas was about, it was at best only a partial representation, a tiny but highly visible aspect. Most blacks in Dallas were more concerned about their families, their jobs, their churches, and improving their situations in a segregated society.

PROBLEMS AT CITY HALL

City politics was at an interregnum. The Citizens Association was shattered. City Democrats had been in power since 1923, but their grip on local affairs was tenuous and riddled by dissension. Even their former supporter, Frank Wozencraft, now called them "boss-ridden." Other groups, sensing a void in power, emerged in 1927 to seek control of city hall.

That spring five different groups announced slates of candidates. Twenty-seven individuals vied for the five council positions. Among them were at least two who had been active Klansmen, Dan Harston and J.D. Van Winkle. Harston, deposed sheriff, now was seeking the job of police and fire commissioner. Van Winkle wanted to be street commissioner. Both were on the All-Dallas Association ticket. Arthur Reinhart, the former candidate for police commissioner who had fought a fiery but losing battle against Klansman Louis Turley in 1923, was in the race again, as was Colonel S.E. Moss, a noted fisherman who tipped the scales at 398 pounds and who wanted to be water commissioner.

Favored in the mayor's race was the two-term commissioner of revenues and taxes, John Harris of the City Democrats. Harris recently had split with Blaylock by opposing a rate hike for the gas company, and Blaylock now supported Robert E. Burt, an oilman and candidate on the Non-Partisan slate. Harris, who once had enjoyed the enthusiastic support of the Ku Klux Klan, now was accused of being so solicitous of the black vote that he was "feeding them ice cream and cake and having his picture flashed on the screen of a negro picture show."

Dallas' municipal government had problems. They seemed not very different from the problems cited in 1907 when the old alderman plan was discarded. Now, twenty years later, it was realized that the commission format, far from bringing business-like efficiency, had created a labyrinth of political fiefdoms. The administration of four separate departments by four separate commissioners brought little cooperation in municipal work. The charter gave the mayor veto power and general supervisory control over the entire city government, yet, each commissioner not only was charged with supervising his own department but also with overseeing those of the others in a scheme of shared responsibility. Commissioners frequently smarted over supposed intrusions into their own departments by others. Jealousies and "buck-passing" were endemic. The city routinely began each fiscal year in the red, for taxes were not collected until several months later. There was no formal personnel system, and jobs often were awarded to campaign workers who displaced experienced performers. Records generally were poorly maintained. Separate departments maintained their own vehicles, generally refusing to lend their idle equipment to another one that might have a temporary overload. Only a few departments even permitted their automotive equipment to be repaired in the central garage. By 1931 things had deteriorated to such an extent that a careful study concluded the city to be in serious difficulty:

"A million-dollar deficit had been accumulated in the public works department; the water department was in the red by $460,000; annual fire losses were ranging above five dollars per capita, a figure much higher than that for most American cities; the health department was disorderly and inefficient; housewives were never certain when garbage cans would be emptied; the enforcement of laws, particularly for the building and fire codes, was sporadic."

Early in 1927 the *News* published a series of fifteen articles, "Measuring the Efficiency of a City's Government," which outlined these and other inadequacies. Under the direction of Tom Finty Jr., reporter Louis P. Head wrote articles concluding that the commission government no longer could cope with the size and complexities of Dallas. What seemed better was the council-manager form of government, already adopted by scores of cities, in which a professional city manager would oversee the administration of the various municipal departments. The goal was to remove politics from administration, to conduct city business as a business. In an editorial the *News* summarized the council-manager plan as "simply the adaptation of the same idea of private business management in public affairs." During the campaign the various candidates' positions on what form of government best suited the city were widely covered, and the Non-Partisans and City Democrats pledged, if elected, to submit the council-manager possibility to the voters.

When these two parties failed to gain a clear majority in any race, a run-off attracted more than 23,000 voters, the largest turnout in the city's history. One of the Non-Partisan's interesting contentions was that for years the Dallas Police Department had been dominated by three men--Z.E. Marvin, George K. Butcher, and Mike T. Lively. Marvin and Butcher had been prominent Klansmen. In the run-off the Non-Partisans defeated the City Democrats in every race.

Within a month after his election, Mayor Burt appointed a committee to study the adoption of the council-manager plan for Dallas. In the same month, the *News'* Louis Head began a second series of articles which described the results achieved in various cities where the council-manager plan had been adopted.

In the summer of 1928 a major step toward realizing Kessler's plan was taken. The Ulrickson Committee, whose members had been re-appointed by Burt, submitted its final report, recommending a capital improvement program of $23.9 million to be spread over a nine-year period. The largest portion, some $8.5 million, was designated for water system improvements, storm water drainage, and the sanitary sewer system. An additional $5.5 million was for street openings, widenings, and underpasses. Many of these seemingly prosaic items were tied into the construction of the levees, including new viaducts spanning the river and representing the city's contribution to the joint effort of several agencies to re-channel the Trinity between levees. The most important street project recommended was the construction of Central Boulevard (not to be known as Central Expressway until two decades later), for which $450,000 was allocated. The citycouncil and the Chamber of Commerce both enthusiastically endorsed this "Forward Dallas" program.

Mayor Burt announced a ballot for January 1928 on which voters would consider both the bond program and the council-manager plan. On further reflection it was believed best to hold two separate elections for these important matters so that each could be promoted properly. Thus, it was decided to offer first the Ulrickson bond proposal. On December 15, 1928, voters approved the bond program and twenty-four related charter amendments by a handsome margin.

Attention now focused once more on the adoption of the council-manager plan. Burt appointed Hugh Grady to head a committee to make necessary recommendations concerning it. Grady appointed a subcommittee chaired by Louis Head, the reporter who had written the two series, to complete the work needed for a new city charter. In late February 1929 Head's subcommittee recommended a nine-member city council, a mayor elected by the majority of the council rather than by the citizens, a city manager to be hired by the city council, and only nominal compensation for the council members. A vote on this charter change was called for December 1929.

Another municipal election had to be held before this could be carried out, though, and the supply of candidates for the five positions seemed endless. Thirty-five candidates, a record high, announced for office. All but ten were independents. The two organized parties for this election, both business-oriented, were the United Dallas Association, which offered for mayor the grandson of Sam Houston, Temple Houston Morrow, and the Greater Dallas Association headed by mayoral candidate W.C. Everett. From all candidates the *News* obtained pledges in which they agreed to permit the citizens to vote on the charter revision.

The leading independent candidate for mayor was J. Worthington (Waddy) Tate, whose campaign was characterized more by eccentricities than by substance. Tate, a retired railroad agent and drugstore owner, had been running for mayor since 1917. His campaigns always centered on recreational improvements for White Rock Lake. Tate bore a resemblance to the comedian W.C. Fields, and he displayed the same unpredictable temperament. He said he wanted the votes only of those who "liked to fish or owed money," and although he thought of himself as the "people's candidate" he affected a morning coat over a striped vest, wore a diamond stick pin, twirled a gold-headed walking stick, and smoked tailor-made cigarettes from a holder. To show his disdain for pretense and people of means (although he was a man of means himself), he carried in his pocket a yo-yo to play with at opportune moments. He had cheerfully accepted in 1927 the derogatory description of himself as a "hot dog" philosopher because he ridiculed a proposal to build a glitzy entertainment facility at White Rock Lake, saying he preferred to see a stand "where a hungry fisherman or tired picnicker could get a hot dog sandwich for 5 cents, than to see a place where they charged $1 for a chicken sandwich and made a $2 cover charge to sit at a table and listen to a jazz band." Capitalizing on the ensuing ridicule, he had thrown one campaign party in 1927 in which he gave away 5,000 free hot dogs. There is a lesson in the hot dog, he said, and that was to live within your means. "We can't ride in a Pierce-Arrow car on a wheelbarrow pocketbook." One of his more colorful campaign ploys was to advocate putting donkeys in Dallas parks for children to ride.

With so many candidates in the race a run-off was inevitable. But the fact that Tate led in the election was a surprise. More startling, he won the runoff, beating Morrow by a vote of 12,082 to 8,557 and becoming at last the mayor of Dallas.

From the beginning Tate set unforgettable examples in office. As he marched proudly down the aisle for the swearing-in ceremony at city hall supporters began chanting, "Hot Dog, Hot Dog, Hot Dog." For his inaugural ball Tate chose the Automobile Building at Fair Park so the "plain people" could attend. He charged a dime per person for admission and donated the proceeds to an orphans' home to buy milk. In office, one of his first acts was to order the spikes removed from the low wall around city hall so citizens and loafers could sit there. In the same spirit he removed signs at city parks which said "Keep Off the Grass." He abolished the office of Censor of Movies, ordered the city attorney to find out why ice cost more in Oak Cliff than north of the Trinity, announced that he was toying with the idea of selling Love Field, and appointed a public defender (an act which his critics dubbed a "payoff" to his supporters.) He ordered that no married women be employed at city hall, then agreed to permit them if their husbands were invalids.

Tate's preference for the "plain people" extended--at least to an extent--to Negroes. He worked to improve park and library facilities for them. He encouraged the library board to purchase a site at Thomas Avenue and Washington Street for the Dunbar Branch Library. He also created a Negro Welfare Council with whom he conferred on matters of education, parks, streets, sanitation, and civic conditions.

In Sepember 1929 Tate and the commissioners approved after two years' preparatory work and months of discussion the city's first comprehensive zoning ordinance. It was heavily weighted in favor of commercial, retail, and industrial uses by allotting too much land to those areas--a reflection of the city's concern for economic growth --and it relegated Oak Cliff from its once-proud status as a planned residential area to one dominated by small residential lots of 4,000 or 6,000 square feet. This assured its future status as a neighborhood for people of modest means. As the ordinance related to Dallas proper, it was far more generous in permitting a variety of development.

While Tate had signed the same pledge as other candidates to submit a charter vote to the electorate, he, unlike the others, had not specified a date. And now he changed his mind. Putting the city's affairs into the hands of a city manager, he said, would be tantamount to having a Russian czar. When Grady's committee submitted the final draft of the proposed charter change, Tate refused to present it to the voters. This was a crushing disappointment to the many business and civic leaders who had worked so long and hard for it and who had anticipated its approval. Tate demonstrated his disdain for the charter leaders when they visited his city hall office to persuade him to call the election. After greeting them cordially, he pulled out his yo-yo and began bobbing it up and down. Tate's attitude was the best possible argument for a new government, said the *News*, for the mayor had shown himself to be more of a czar than a city manager could ever be. In the spring of 1930 Tate once again vetoed the charter proposal, contending now that the charter commission had been illegally formed.

The stage was set for the emergence of the organization that was to dominate Dallas' municipal politics into the 1970s. The high-powered members of the charter commission determined to force Tate's hand by organizing as a group called the Citizens Charter Association and going directly to the voters to obtain the required number of signatures to force the election. The leaders of the charter commission, Hugh Grady and Louis Head, became president and vice president respectively. A total of 5,919 voters signed the petition, more than the 10 percent of the qualified voters required, and an election was set for October 10, 1930.

A massive campaign was launched in favor of charter amendments that called for nine councilmen (three elected at-large and six from council districts) with token salaries for their part-time work, a mayor to be elected from among themselves, and a full-time city manager hired by the council to carry out its policies. All the newspapers supported the change with editorials and favorable news coverage. Tate, with his oddball antics as mayor, was an easy target for ridicule. The Citizens Charter Association hired a young lawyer, John Erhard, to be campaign manager, and gave him a clerical staff of five. Lieutenants were assigned in each of the city's fifty-nine precincts to make personal calls and hold neighborhood meetings. The Chamber of Commerce directors unanimously supported the charter change. The Junior Chamber of Commerce distributed pamphlets, arranged for radio talks, and solicited support for the movement. A "flying squadron" of speakers made brief talks at industrial plants and large businesses which were asked to call their workers together to hear them. Not one of them refused. The same privilege was not extended to opponents of the plan. Service clubs invited speakers who favored the proposal, and church groups went on record as favoring the amendment because they wanted stricter moral regulations from the police than the commission government was providing. Women's organizations endorsed the plan and helped with precinct organization.

On the day before the election the *News* summed up the issue as merely another aspect in the continuing movement for a progressive Dallas, tying it tightly to the Kessler Plan, the Ulrickson plan, and the levee movement. The adoption of the charter would determine the city's destiny; it would signify whether Dallas would remain in the small city class or move up into the big city class. The council-manager government would permit the businessmen of the city to take control, as should be the case, because "the biggest business in Dallas is Dallas itself."

On election day the echoes of the most thorough campaign in the city's history were ringing in the ears of the voters. They approved the proposed amendments by a vote of 8,899 to 4,239. Dallas became the state's thirty-third city to adopt the council-manager form of government.

The original purpose of the Citizens Charter Association had been achieved. It had been assumed that the organization now would cease to exist. But as the Citizens Association in 1907 decided to become a permanent organization, so did the CCA. "We cannot permit the work we have done to be wasted by turning the government over to the politicians," said campaign manager Erhard. The organization would include a one-hundred member executive committee to elect officers and approve candidates, six vice-presidents (one from each council district), and a president. The theory was that forward-looking citizens wanted an organization to protect Dallas from politicians, that the citizens would depend upon the leadership of the Citizens Charter Association to select candidates with wisdom and integrity rather than those advocating specific issues.

7

Changing City Hall

[Dallas has the] hospitality of the South, the broad vision and daring enterprise of the West, the shrewd business sense and indefatigable energy of the North, and the culture and refinement of the East.

—Dallas Chamber of Commerce, 1931

A New Form of Government

Just as the Citizens Association in 1907 had felt it necessary to do, the Citizens Charter Association closed its doors to select in secret its candidates for the April 7, 1931, election. To the surprise of no one, the CCA executive committee nominated without exception prominent, substantial, conservative, and well-known businessmen. All but one either owned a business or held a high-level executive position. Their prestige far overshadowed that of any slate ever presented in Dallas city politics, considerably higher even than the handpicked business-oriented candidates of 1907. All had been "drafted" to fulfill a civic duty by assuming a public office that paid just $20 a week.

No politicians were these; they disdained the term. They offered no platform, made no promises, and gave no speeches. Having made no promises, boasted CCA President Hugh Grady, they could break none. Disdaining the podium, the candidates did consent at least to appear at three strategic rallies, sitting there quietly while others praised their perspicacity and especially their business acumen.

The "flying squadrons" of speakers who had been so successful in promoting the council-manager plan continued to work to elect the CCA slate. Once again, the city's large industrial and business establishments such as the Ford Motor plant, Magnolia Petroleum Co., Butler Bros. wholesalers, and Olmsted-Kirk Paper Co. assembled their workers to let them hear the benefits to be derived from voting for CCA candidates. Women's groups enthusiastically joined the campaign, as well. Local Democratic and Republican officials, in a show of unity for the good of the city, both endorsed the CCA slate. All Dallas seemed of one mind.

In such an atmosphere hardly anyone dared oppose the CCA power. Only five of the nine seats were contested, one of the challengers being the long-time Dallas Socialist activist George Clifton Edwards. None of the independents gained newspaper attention, and before the election the *News* published prominently for several days a list of CCA candidates with specific instructions on how to vote for them only. The independents struggled alone.

There could be no doubt about the outcome. CCA candidates won by overwhelming numbers, generally 9-1 margins in the contested races. Incumbent Mayor Tate, not a candidate this time, received one solitary write-in vote.

The best known new council member was Thomas L. Bradford, sixty-one-year-old chairman of the board of Southwestern Life Insurance Co. Bradford, a self-made man, had been in the retail grocery business in Dallas before joining the insurance firm that the founder of the Citizens Association, Henry Lindsley, had organized. Bradford, though, generally received credit for masterminding Southwestern Life's growth in Dallas alone from twenty to 260 employees between 1912 and 1931. He had won a special place in the city through his philanthropy, having donated the funds necessary for building Bradford Hospital for Babies at a cost of more than $100,000.

Other councilmen, hardly less prominent, included E.R. Brown, president of Magnolia Petroleum Co.; T.M. Cullum, owner of Cullum & Boren; Joe C. Thompson, secretary-treasurer of Southland Ice Co.; W.H. Painter, secretary-treasurer of United Fidelity Life Insurance Co.; Arthur B. Moore, president of Cox-Moore Drug Co.; Victor H. Hexter, vice-president of Union Title & Guaranty Co.; and Charles E. Turner, a real estate man and the only native son among the candidates.

On the day after the election the new council met privately to choose a mayor from among themselves. They passed over the leading vote-getter, Moore, and selected Bradford for the top position. The council met several other times before assuming office on May 2, but these sessions also were "executive," closed to the public.

These closed sessions were important, far more important than electing a mayor, who after all would do little more than preside over the council sessions. For the new council-manager plan to work, a strong, knowledgeable city manager must be hired, and he must be prepared to go to work on the day the government changed format on May 1. All agreed that this individual must be skilled in the science of administering the day-to-day operations of a municipality; he must be a "professional." It was also agreed that the city manager would not be a local person because such a person would have allegiances difficult to overcome.

Just days after the election, a leading candidate emerged. He was John North Edy, who had just resigned as city manager at Flint, Michigan, following a controversial election in which he found himself the chief campaign issue because of his tight-reined, by-the-book administrative approach. This, to the Dallas council-elect, seemed to be a positive trait. Edy, a native of Missouri with a civil engineering degree from the University of Missouri and a master's degree from the University of California at Berkeley, also had been the first city manager at Berkeley, serving there from 1923 to 1930 before moving to Flint. Only a week after the election he was in Dallas amidst much publicity being interviewed by the incoming council. During his private session with the council-elect he asked his would-be employers two critical questions of his own: (1) Would the council permit him to enforce the law as required by the charter, especially laws against vice? and (2) would the body support him in taking measures necessary for the city to live within its income? Such questions made his interviewers smile with pleasure. Their affirmative answers were obvious.

Newspaper reporters quizzed the candidate, too. They found the white-haired Edy, who constantly filled and re-filled his pipe, to have an easy smile despite his reputation for firmness. His aim as city manager, he said, would be to give efficient service at the lowest possible cost. News stories pointed out that his adept handling of financial and police problems as Berkeley's first city manager had gained for him international attention. His innovative system of budget control was said to have become a standard among city managers in regulating public expenditures.

Dallas acted quickly before the city of Oakland, California, could hire Edy, offering him the position at $16,500, an amount which later would bring criticism for being too high. Edy accepted the offer, and returned to Michigan to gather his wife, son, and belongings.

Edy's job, and that of the city council as well, began on May 1. Outgoing City Attorney James J. Collins, who administered the oath of office, recalled that he had done the same when the new commission form of government was introduced in 1907. Mayor Tate, who relinquished his office along with the other three commissioners after a short ceremony that morning, was genial throughout the meeting and wished the new council and city manager well.

On this special day and for months to follow the strong-minded city manager was the center of attention. The mayor and council assumed the back-seat roles that they preferred, far away from headlines and commentary. This was a posture they would continue. The difficult work ahead of Edy undoubtedly would generate criticism and ill-will, but with the certain backing of the council he stepped vigorously into the task. He began transforming city hall from one that had smacked of politics and favoritism into one based on professionalism and efficiency. Edy, prone to self-righteousness, later recalled that his first job was to "clear the chiseling politicians and loafers from the corridors of city hall." His first impressions on the job were of disorderly departments, of uncertain and suspicious employees, of overstaffed divisions, and of deficits in the treasury.

The wholesale reorganization of city hall was not easily achieved. Edy's essential job was to integrate separate departments into a unified structure under his own direction, a dramatic turnabout from the old plan in which four elected officials had created their own independent organizations with inevitable disharmony and inefficiency.

Newspaper headlines told of hirings and firings, cuts in budgets, reorganizations of departments, collections of back taxes from delinquent citizens, studies on the efficiency of the city's garbage collection, and new efficiency goals. Edy instituted biweekly meetings of department heads, explaining to them that they must live within their budgets and that to do so they must cut their payrolls. Some 10 percent of city employees, or about 300 individuals, lost their jobs. Performance records were established for individual employees. The city's health officer, identified as a political henchman of Tate's, was dismissed and replaced by a junior officer in the department, Dr. J.W. Bass, destined to serve for more than three decades. The city engineer was demoted and replaced by an administrator holding a new title, director of public works. Centralized purchasing procedures and a budget control system to oversee spending were instituted. Manuals of procedure were written and distributed to city employees. Improvements in hiring were instituted through the civil service commission. Edy insisted as a matter of course that employees attend strictly to their work without indulging in politics. Employees thus were emancipated from previous needs to be loyal to the elected city commissioner who oversaw their department.

One of Edy's early targets was the police department. Before his first week ended he handed a stiff broom with encouraging words towards a clean-up to Police Chief C.W. Trammell. Trammell's authority had been undermined during his seven-year tenure by a system of campaign contributions by gamblers and bootleggers. In his first acts, without alleging past improprieties but with the message clear, he downgraded the captain of plainclothes detectives to detective and reduced many detectives to the rank of patrolman. "There will be no crusading or staging of wholesale raids with a lot of fanfare and trumpeting," Chief Trammell said, "but I do mean that bootleggers, professional gamblers and others who profit by commercializing of vice must either change their occupations at once or be prepared for a long siege and a lot of trouble." Some respectable citizens soon suggested that the crackdown against vice went too far, that it harmed the city's best interests. Resentment against Edy reached such proportions that Chief Trammell placed a 24-hour-a-day guard outside the city manager's residence. When the city's leading gambler committed suicide it was attributed to economic hardships brought on by the crackdown.

Some compromises had been made in drawing up the ordinances creating Dallas' particular council-manager plan. Certain departments and individuals were appointed directly by council members rather than by the city manager, including the park board, library board, city planning commission, city attorney, city secretary, and supervisor of public utilities. Edwin J. Kiest, long-time chairman of the park board and publisher of the *Times Herald,* won an independent park board in exchange for his newspaper's support of the new charter. The extent to which Edy could exercise authority over the work of the park board and the other "independent" boards was open to interpretation. Frictions inevitably resulted in these gray areas. In selecting the individual to succeed the veteran city attorney Collins, CCA council members made a choice which opened them to criticism for injecting politics into administration. They chose CCA president Hugh Grady, a former assistant city attorney.

With City Manager Edy so firmly in control of most affairs at city hall, the unexpected death of Mayor Bradford in August, 1932, tragic though it was, caused hardly a ripple in the management of municipal affairs. Bradford, while chatting with friends at the City Club, suddenly had complained of a headache. He asked his friends to call Dr. W.W. Samuell, then was taken to St. Paul Hospital, where at the age of sixty-three he died before the night was over, victim of a heart attack. Council members elected real estate man Charles E. Turner, a former cowboy born north of town in Richardson, to succeed him.

It was clear by the time of the next municipal election in 1933 that city hall was being operated efficiently. Yet, problems had arisen. The most serious was the growing sense that city government had become too far removed from the citizens, that it was impersonal and without feeling. City council members, in an effort to be absolutely faithful to the dictates of the council-manager form of government, had assumed a total hands-off posture; they were unavailable or non-responsive to citizens' complaints about such matters as street paving or garbage collection because such matters were the province of the city manager. The self-righteous Edy often tended to suspect sinister purposes behind visits from outsiders. George B. Dealey made an appointment to see Edy at city hall, and as he was being escorted into Edy's office, the city manager greeted him by saying, "Oh yes, I know who you are, Mr. Dealey, but if you think that your work in the campaign will get you any favors, you are sadly mistaken." Dealey, who of course had been responsible perhaps more than any other person for the city's adoption of the council-manager form of government, never again visited the city manager. Edy probably had anticipated that Dealey's visit was prompted by his keen interest in the levee project. He may have been right, for the levee project continued to be one of Dealey's high priorities, one reflected regularly on the *News'* pages. It also was being lobbied privately with council members by *News* editorial writer Sam Acheson. Another *News* executive, J.M. Moroney, also had become a major property holder in the levee district. Edy had shown a reluctance to complete the city's portion of the project, a posture that infuriated levee district officials.

By the time the 1933 municipal elections came complaints about city hall and its administration were being heard more and more, although no one suggested abandoning the council-manager plan. An opposition party to the Citizens Charter Association arose, the Home Government Association, headed by a former member of the City Plan Commission, Jim Dan Sullivan. Its members campaigned hard on a platform of returning the control of city government to Dallas citizens. Edy himself became a principal campaign issue, just as he had become at Flint. Edward J. Railton said that Edy had caused more sorrow in Dallas in the shortest length of time than any man to sit in a public seat. Sullivan promised a "home man" for city manager as well as reductions in utility rates and reductions in salaries for top city employees. Such talk infuriated Edy, whose $16,500 salary had become a special target, and he privately vowed to resign if his pay were reduced.

Such criticisms forced at least a couple of the CCA candidates to speak out, breaking the precedent set in the 1931 election. Victor H. Hexter declared Edy to be a "godsend," sent to Dallas when it "had no more idea how to set up a government than how to take cheese out of the moon." All the city's improvements were due to him, Hexter proclaimed. "If we lose him it will be a great loss for the city." Mayor Turner, responding to the attacks on "Edyism," also spoke, saying that "'Edyism' means that all day, every day, nights and Sundays there is a trained man on the job of protecting the public interest against the multitude of grafters and moochers who would get their filthy paws in the public purse."

Sam Acheson of the *News* told Dealey in a memo that he had never seen a more "politically conscious city council than in January 1933." The newspaper now was refusing to endorse the CCA slate, a viewpoint expressed in a series of editorials. An up-and-coming power broker in the city, Fred Florence of Republic Bank, pleaded in vain for Dealey to publish "just one editorial" supporting the CCA ticket. But the newspaper would not. Typical of several editorials on the upcoming election was the one of March 25, 1933: "There are undoubtedly capable citizens in the ranks of the opposition who could do excellent work if elected to the council. Just why the introduction of a minority of new Councilmen would shake to its foundations the present smoothly functioning city organization is something of a puzzle. It might be supposed that the introduction of new blood and new ideas would be of benefit to the best interests of the city." A few days later the newspaper said that the "only sure means of preventing the entry of politics into the management of official Dallas" was for voters to refuse to adhere to any prescribed lists of candidates. The *Times Herald*, meanwhile, in two consecutive front-page editorials strongly urged the election of every CCA candidate. On the morning of the election the *News* proclaimed obstinately that "partyism has no part in the day's act of citizenship."

Edy was convinced that the *News'* coverage of city hall was designed deliberately to place him in a bad light. He was considering suing the newspaper for libel because it quoted one of his critics who called him a "dog." On the day of the election he told reporter Barry Bishop that he was considering a long vacation so he could begin looking for another job. "It would be nice to go out to the coast and wire my resignation back," he said. As to the proposed pay cut he would receive if Home Government Association candidates won, he said, "I would rather take a job with the University of Southern California as a $3,000 a year instructor than be city manager of Dallas at $10,000."

As it happened, the entire CCA slate was re-elected on April 4 without the necessity of a single run-off. While the margins were closer than in 1931, they were substantial, on the order of 2-1. All CCA incumbents except T.M. Cullum, who chose not to run again and who had been replaced by William A. Webb, had stood for re-election. Voters also returned Alex Camp, who had replaced Bradford in Place 9, to office.

The *News* commented after the election: "It is about time to think of Mr. Edy as a Dallas man....The proper business of the council is to choose the city manager and leave to him as much as possible of the government of the city. With a little more freedom of action and a little less heckling by factions, The News believes, Mr. Edy will be able to proceed with confidence and with a corresponding advantage to all Dallas."

OIL TYCOONS

The concern of Dallas' leaders was to establish a framework at city hall to accommodate and to encourage the city's rapid and welcome growth. Growth, without a doubt, was occurring. Census figures for 1930 placed the city's population at 260,475, 64 percent higher than the

1920 population, a growth that very nearly matched the optimistic predictions made by Chamber of Commerce officials a decade earlier. Just under 20 percent of the total population was black; less than 5 percent was Hispanic.

There was something about the fast tempo of downtown life that reminded some of a large Eastern city. In one of his novels Rex Beach wrote that if a New Yorker should arrive in Dallas at night, the next morning he would have to rub his eyes to make sure he was not still in sight of Broadway. Akard Street, looking south, was the city's "grand canyon," where skyscrapers towered on either side above the narrow street until it ended at the Baker Hotel on Commerce. This view was a favorite postcard picture. The Chamber of Commerce thought Dallas contained a part of all sections of the nation. It had the "hospitality of the South, the broad vision and daring enterprise of the West, the shrewd business sense and indefatigable energy of the North, and the culture and refinement of the East." Elm Street, the city's theater row, was lined with brightly lit movie houses: the Capitol, Circle, Fox, Majestic, Melba, Old Mill, Palace, Queen, and Ritz. Already, though, the movies had invaded the suburbs, often taking the name of the street upon which they were located: the Columbia, the E. Grand, the Forest, the Haskell, the Oak Lawn, and the Peak.

Within the city were certain spectacular individuals whose exploits soon would bring them reputations familiar from the Atlantic to the Pacific. One was a tall, slightly paunchy former cotton farmer and compulsive gambler who for several years had been wildcatting with some success in the oil fields of Arkansas and Louisiana. The 1931 *Worley's City Directory for Dallas* gave his name as Franklin F. Hunt; the same entry listed his wife as Frances and gave their place of residence as 4230 Versailles in Highland Park. The couple had moved to the two-story brick house in the fall of 1930 from Shreveport. They now had three small children, none of them yet of school-age, Harold, Haroldina, and a new-born daughter, Helen. Although Frances or Frania had been married since 1925 to "Major," as so many called him, and she had borne him these three children, he very frequently was away from home for long periods of time. Frania believed it necessary because of the nature of the oil business.

In El Dorado, Arkansas, another woman with five children had the same sort of marriage. In fact, this woman, Lyda Bunker Hunt, was married to the same man. She knew her husband by his real name,

Haroldson Lafayette Hunt. She had married him in 1914, eleven years earlier than his Dallas wife.

These two women, neither of whom knew about the other, and these eight children under separate roofs kept Haroldson Lafayette Hunt stepping lively as he moved from house to house and from one oil hot spot to another in the Ark-La-Tex fields.

Fate was to bring Hunt into contact with another colorful oilman who in 1925 had moved to Dallas from Oklahoma to conduct his relentless quest for black gold. Columbus Marion Joiner, virtually penniless at the moment although he had had plenty of good times in his varied past, was among the scores of oilmen and "lease-hounds" who had descended upon Dallas because of its central location and because of its abundance of venture capital. He was a man later described by one admiring biographer as one who lived in a "spiritual and intellectual world of his own." Joiner worked out of an office eight floors above Zeke Marvin's popular pharmacy in Marvin's Gulf States Building at 109 N. Akard.

By 1930 Joiner, now seventy and bent over at the waist from an attack of rheumatic fever, had become convinced for no scientific reason at all that a huge reservoir of oil, the largest in the world, lay beneath the ground in Rusk County in the Woodbine sands. His colleague, "Dr." A.D. Lloyd, a colorful old coot himself, had prepared for Joiner an extensive though palpably false report providing detailed descriptions of anticlines, faults, and saline domes under the surface in this East Texas area. With this report and based upon his own firm though instinctive convictions, Joiner had managed by hook or crook to obtain oil leases for several thousand acres in and around Rusk County.

In the fall of 1930 on farm property owned by a widow, Mrs. Daisy Bradford, Joiner began drilling for oil. By now he was financially exhausted; the first two wells had been dusters. His workers were too poor to own cars, so they slept on the site. A banker from a nearby town moonlighted on the night shift as a roughneck. The hole was 3,400 feet deep when on October 3, 1930, waves of oil shot over the top of the derrick. The Daisy Bradford No. 3 was such a sensational success that it attracted the attention of speculators and oilmen from a wide area. No one could imagine such a thing at the time, but Joiner's discovery opened up what would be the biggest, most prolific oil field in the entire world for the next two decades.

Before he could develop his property, though, Joiner found himself in court facing creditors. The judge obliged his request to delay the proceedings so he could have time to earn profits from his new field. One of the onlookers in the courtroom for that hearing was none other than H.L. Hunt, who had been present when the Daisy Bradford No. 3 was brought in. Sensing opportunity because of Joiner's financial vulnerability and the tenuousness of the judge's decision, and being able after years of high-stakes poker playing to choose the right moment for a psychological ploy, Hunt arranged a meeting with Joiner in November 1930 to negotiate the purchase of his East Texas leases. The two men, who had much in common despite their age differences, engaged in a marathon thirty-six hour session in the Baker Hotel. As the negotiations went on, Hunt had informers who kept him posted as to the progress of Daisy Bradford No. 3 and its potential. With the confidential information he received, which he did not share with Joiner, he was inspired to complete the deal. Later, when the immense value of the properties was fully realized, Joiner claimed that Hunt had deceived him, contending that Hunt's information concerning the well's capabilities was even more current than his own.

Whether the selling price was fair or not, Hunt paid Joiner $30,000 in cash as part of a transaction in which the total sales price was $1,335,000 for leases on more than 5,000 acres in Rusk County. Ironically, Hunt himself was at a low ebb in his own fortunes at the moment, and he had to raise the money to make the cash payment. But it was surely the best deal that Hunt ever made, for the oil properties he bought from Joiner served as the principal cornerstone for the huge fortune he amassed which ultimately gained for him the sobriquet of richest man in the world.

Within two years of his deal with Joiner, Hunt moved his first wife and family to Tyler, where they began to engage in social life. Not until 1934 did his Dallas wife, Frania, learn that her husband, whom she believed to be "Major Hunt," actually was the oilman whose name she had begun to see in the newspapers. She moved in distress with her children to Great Neck, New York, to live in a house Hunt bought for them, and there in October she gave birth to her fourth child by Hunt. A few years later Hunt moved his first family—Lyda and their six children—from Tyler to Dallas, where he established headquarters for his oil company. He purchased as a residence a replica of George Washington's Mt. Vernon on the west shore of White Rock Lake. This highly visible mansion would be the Hunt family home for years, continuing to be so even after Hunt's death.

As for Joiner, in 1933 he went to Juarez, Mexico, divorced his wife of fifty-two years, and married his young secretary. Returning to Dallas he purchased a home on Preston Road. Although the riches of his great find went primarily to Hunt, Joiner had enough assets to be described in 1934 as of the "millionaire class."

And as for the great East Texas oil field, it transformed Dallas' economic base from cotton to petroleum. The vast quantities of nearby oil prompted a sensational boom which contrasted sharply with the declining cotton prices. More than ever Dallas became a convenient headquarters for independent producers, corporations, wildcatters, promoters, investors, pipeline operators, oil-well scouts, lease hounds, and drilling contractors. This injection of fresh money into the economy helped the city escape the worst aspects of the Depression being felt so severely in other parts of the nation. During the first two months alone of 1931 a total of twenty-eight oil-related companies either began operations in Dallas or moved there. A year later new oil companies were said to be moving "almost daily" to the city. The Chamber of Commerce declared that Dallas had "definitely become the most important oil city in the world." By August of 1932 the Chamber directory listed 787 companies that were dedicated to the oil business, a ten-fold increase within two years. Dallas' emergence was signified by the American Petroleum Institute's decision to hold there its annual convention in 1934. For that important occasion Magnolia Petroleum Company placed atop its twenty-nine story building a double-sided flying red horse. The mythological winged horse "Pegasus" became a lasting and colorful icon for the entire city rather than merely a symbol for a single oil company.

By 1941 it was estimated that 18 to 20 percent of greater Dallas' population depended on the oil industry for income. A bank vice-president calculated that one out of every eight buildings or houses and one out of every three borrowers in local banks could be traced to oil. Dallas' banks, accustomed to lending money for prospective cotton crops that were dependent on good weather, found no problem in financing deals based on oil reserves that lay protected beneath the surface of the earth. The oil industry and the banks both prospered as they together developed an enterprise that was to become central to Dallas' existence, not to mention that of the entire nation.

BABE DIDRICKSON

In the same year that Dad Joiner sold his oil leases to H.L. Hunt, another deal was being made which brought to Dallas the woman who was to become the greatest female athlete in American history. Mildred Ella (Babe) Didrickson, a fifteen-year-old Beaumont schoolgirl phenomenon on the basketball court and one of seven children of Norwegian-born parents, was "discovered" by Colonel M.J. McCombs of Employers Casualty Company of Dallas. Early that year McCombs was scouting for players for his company's Golden Cyclones women's team. Reading in the newspapers about Babe's prowess, he scouted the high-spirited youngster at a high school basketball playoff game in Houston. Immediately impressed, McCombs decided to persuade her to come to Dallas to play on the company-sponsored team, the Golden Cyclones, which had finished second the previous year in the women's national A.A.U. tournament.

Although their daughter was still a senior in high school, Babe's skeptical parents made arrangements with school authorities for her to depart a few months before graduation to come to Dallas in February 1930. She was four months short of her sixteenth birthday. "I'd never been more than a few miles from my home," she later recalled. "I'd hardly ever been so dressed up either. I was wearing the blue silk dress with the box pleats that I'd made and won a prize at the Texas State Fair, I had on my patent leather shoes and socks and the little hat I'd got for graduation exercises at junior high school. I was carrying a black patent leather purse. It had my entire fortune in it — the $3.49 change from the money they'd given me to buy the railroad tickets."

In her first game Babe was the team's leading scorer. The Golden Cyclones lost the national championship that spring by one point, but won it the next year and made the finals in the following year. Babe, at just over 5 feet 6, was shorter than most of the girls on the team, but she was named All-American all three years.

After that first national tournament, Babe had gone back to Beaumont, finished high school, then returned to Dallas to resume work at the insurance company, as was required of the players. She found a $5-a-month room on Haines Street in Oak Cliff and began working in a clerical position at Employers Casualty's offices in the downtown Interurban Building. At night she practiced with the team. In an effort to keep the women in shape during Babe's first off-season, McCombs decided to sponsor a women's track and field team. It was only now, McCombs later recalled, that Babe learned that "track and field" referred to something other than cotton fields and railroad tracks. A few months later the new team, prominently including Babe, entered the national A.A.U. track meet in Dallas. The phenomenal youngster broke existing world records in three events: the broad jump, baseball throw, and javelin throw. In the summer of 1931 she repeated her exploits in Jersey City, New Jersey, capturing this time first place in the 80-meter hurdles, baseball throw, and broad jump, setting world records in the latter two events. Sports writers suddenly discovered her. Some proclaimed her instantly as the greatest woman athlete in America. In 1932 Babe went alone as Employer Casualty's one-person track and field "team" to the Olympic tryouts in Evanston, Illinois. She entered eight of the ten individual events, including two in which she had never before participated, the shot put and discus throw. By the end of that day Babe, all alone, had scored 30 team points, winning the team championship by herself. Her effort topped the second-place team by eight points. She won first place in five events: the javelin throw, 80-yard hurdles, shot put, broad jump, and baseball throw. She tied for first place in another, the high jump. The crowd cheered wildly for this solitary young woman from Dallas who earned on this remarkable day the right to participate in the 1932 Olympics in Los Angeles.

Unfortunately, she was prevented there from displaying her virtuosity in all these categories by International Olympic Committee rules that forbade contestants from entering more than three events. Babe chose the 80-meter hurdles, the javelin, and the high jump. Now eighteen years old, she proceeded to set new world records in all three events, although her record-setting high jump was disallowed because a judge ruled that her head had crossed the bar before her body. Moving pictures of the jump, as reviewed by the press, later showed the judge to be wrong. Judges awarded her second place. Later, of course, head-first jumps over the bar were authorized as a legal technique.

Babe returned to Dallas the triumphant hero. A welcoming crowd of more than 3,000 spectators cheered as she bounded off the airplane at Love Field on August 12, 1932. A band played and many in the crowd waved flags. Babe, wearing blue and white beach pajamas and an upturned beach cap, was carrying the javelin with which she had broken the world record. Alongside her were two prominent Dallas men:

banker Robert L. Thornton, a one-time country boy who had emerged as one of the city's leaders through his Chamber of Commerce work, and businessman George Schepps. WFAA radio station broadcast the welcoming ceremonies. Afterwards, a downtown parade was held in which Babe, surrounded with floral arrangements, rode in the fire chief's bright red car. A large truck carried all the trophies the young female athlete already had won. Among those in the parade were Babe's Golden Cyclone basketball teammates, city and county officials, Chamber of Commerce members, and the all-Dallas high school band. At the steps of the city hall, where the parade ended, City Manager John Edy and District Attorney William McGraw welcomed her. The day still was not over, though, for the main event was a luncheon held in the Adolphus Hotel and sponsored by the Chamber of Commerce and Salesmanship Club. A celebratory mood continued for days, but Babe returned to her job at Employers Casualty Company.

The next year Babe unexpectedly lost her amateur standing because her picture appeared in an advertisement for the new 1933 Dodge automobile. She now decided to become a golfer, having been introduced to the sport by writer Grantland Rice. She obtained a membership at the Dallas Country Club and took lessons after work from golf pro George Aulbach. In 1935 she achieved her first goal in golf, winning the Texas Women's Championship. She moved to California in 1938 after meeting and marrying George Zaharias, a professional wrestler. Throughout the rest of the 1930s, 1940s, and early 1950s Babe dominated women's golf, winning eighty-two golf tournaments. Six times she was named "Outstanding Woman Athlete of the Year." Her career was cut short when she died of cancer in 1956 at the age of forty-two. By then she was generally acknowledged to be the greatest woman athlete who had ever lived.

BONNIE AND CLYDE

The aggressive banker and civic leader who had appeared on the platform with Babe at Love Field, Robert L. Thornton, was a poorly educated Ellis County cotton-picker before migrating from the tiny hamlet of Bristol to Dallas in search of a better life. This he had found. Another Ellis County farm emigrant who had moved to Dallas with his wife and their eight children had not fared nearly so well. Henry Barrow and his wife Cumie had come from Telico, less than ten miles from Thornton's last home in Ellis County. After first settling in a make-shift camp underneath the Houston Street viaduct, the Barrows began operating a small filling station on Eagle Ford Road in the impoverished section known as West Dallas. Although it was just across the river, because of its poverty and lack of amenities West Dallas had never been annexed into Dallas. The couple made out the best they could selling red or white gas from their outside pumps, and soft drinks and canned goods on the inside. What made the Barrows' life more tormented than it possibly could have been back on the farm in Ellis County were their two mean-spirited boys, Buck and Clyde.

Clyde Barrow, twenty-one years of age in 1930, already was known to Dallas police as a petty thief with a penchant for stealing automobiles. The closest he had come to a criminal conviction, though, had been in Waco, where his plea for mercy on an auto theft charge persuaded a jury to let this well-dressed and seemingly earnest youth go free.

It was this winsome side of Clyde Barrow that surely was on display when he began to frequent a little cafe on Houston Street just down from the courthouse and attracted the attention of a high-spirited, tiny waitress named Bonnie Parker. Bonnie, a year younger than Clyde, also had to come to Dallas from the farm, arriving in 1914 with her recently widowed mother, two sisters, and an older brother. The family moved in with Bonnie's grandmother in a house in "Cement City," a rude collection of shanties near the site of the old utopian community of the 1850s, La Reunion. Bonnie already had been married and divorced, but that union's most lasting impression was her husband's name tattooed on her thigh. The match-up of Bonnie and Clyde seemed to be one of true love. A close bond developed between them that endured untold hardships as they embarked on their violent life of crime.

It began when the distraught Bonnie visited Clyde in county jail before he could be transferred to the state penitentiary in Huntsville to serve time for an auto-theft conviction. She slipped him a Colt .32 revolver which he used to escape. Before long he was back in prison, though, and when he was released in 1932 he and Bonnie launched their crime spree in earnest, a crime spree which before it ended in 1934 saw twelve persons, including nine lawmen, shot to death. Dallas police wiretapped the Barrow telephone at the Eagle Ford Road house in April 1934, and while they overheard Mrs. Barrow and Mrs. Parker discuss the tribulations of "the kids," they learned nothing of note other than the families' general disdain for officers of the law. One of their momentary "kidnap" victims was the ace crime reporter for the *News,* Harry McCormick. McCormick got an exclusive interview during his brief stay with the pair, and before they turned him loose in his own car he persuaded Barrow to press his fingers against the windshield to prove his story.

After Bonnie and Clyde were ambushed and slain by law officers in Louisiana, their bodies were returned to Dallas and displayed to the public in separate funeral homes. It was estimated that 30,000 people saw Clyde's bullet-ridden body at the Sparkman-Holtz-Brand Chapel on Ross Avenue (now occupied by the Dallas Bar Association), and that about 40,000 people saw Bonnie's body at the McKamy-Campbell Funeral Home. An "extra" published by the *Dallas Dispatch,* complete with graphic photographs of the slain pair, said in bold page-one headlines, "BODIES OF BONNIE AND CLYDE UNDER GUARD IN DALLAS." Thus ended a saga that far overshadowed the petty crimes of the earlier Dallas desperado who also became a national legend, Belle Starr.

COMPLICATIONS AT CITY HALL

At city hall the council-manager plan was encountering difficulties. The undertone of criticisms that had surfaced in the 1933 election was growing in intensity. Inevitably, Edy's cost-reducing efforts had alienated many, especially those who had been deprived of jobs or city contracts. Council members, having no political aspirations and determined to stay away from political aspects of their duties, made no concessions to popular sentiment.

Some of their more difficult policy decisions earned for them enemies of their own, including more than a few business leaders who once had supported them. A particularly controversial decision was their reluctance, under Edy's guidance, to finance without question sewer improvements associated with the Trinity River levee project.

Further tension emerged over the question of utility rates. Edy pushed for reduced rates from Dallas Power & Light Co., but council members, friendly and sympathetic to the company, rejected the plan. A rift grew between DP&L officials, Edy, and the Citizens Charter Association.

Some of the city's alienated businessmen, joined by a number of former city employees, began meeting quietly in such places as the downtown Elks Club to discuss their grievances. Known at first simply as "The Organization," they began to spread their network to each city precinct, appealing especially to members of various lodges, and soon adopted a name very similar to that of the Citizens Charter Association — the Citizens' Civic Association. Not many weeks had passed before the behind-the-scenes organizers were given a term of opprobium: the "Catfish Club," so-called because their critics said they lived out of sight "like catfish in the mud." This description they accepted with a measure of glee, responding that they intended to "clean the political stream of Dallas" by offering a slate of their own candidates. A principal Catfish leader was Jim Dan Sullivan, a genial, red-haired Irishman who had headed the Home Government Association in its 1933 campaign to unseat the CCA and who was on friendly terms with Dealey.

At its first public meeting in January 1935, the Citizens' Civic Association attracted some 300 supporters. Speakers announced that if their candidates won in the April election they would send Edy "back to the Pacific coast," and their new city manager would be a Dallas man who would put local people instead of outsiders on the payroll. At least one speaker complained that Edy was so inaccessible to the public that he had an unlisted telephone number.

As campaign manager the organization selected Hal Moseley, the same man who had had been elected city commissioner in 1919 while he was in France. He also was a former city engineer. Moseley had a score to settle: in 1931 he had been rejected by Edy for the position of director of public works. Some now believed that Moseley wanted to be city manager.

The Civic Association had no intention of abolishing council-manager government, and it proclaimed that fact in its platform. The party pointedly called for a new city manager who could exhibit "courtesy." The selected candidates, generally small businessmen, represented a broad spectrum of the city. Most of them were prominent in church, lodge, and service club organizations.

As for the Citizens Charter Association, only five of the nine incumbents chose to stand for re-election. Mayor Turner was not one of them. Having accepted an appointment to be financial director of the Texas Centennial celebration in 1936, he announced in January that he would not run for another term. Unlike the CCA's first prestigious slate, the new candidates and the holdovers did not represent the city's absolute top echelon of businessmen.

Although not a candidate, Turner campaigned hard for the Citizens Charter Association slate. He predicted that a defeat for the CCA would cause the greatly anticipated Texas Centennial Exposition to "fold up" and make Dallas the laughing stock of the nation. A new regime would interfere with Centennial preparations, he contended, and he pleaded with voters not to "change horses in the middle of a stream." In defending Edy, who was the focus for so much of the Civic Association's ire, Turner pointed out that Edy had not been given the raise originally promised and that in fact he had taken a voluntary 20 percent reduction in pay as an economy measure.

The charges and counter-charges, frequently made over the powerful new medium of radio, (the opening addresses by both parties were given on the radio), caused the *News* to label it "one of the most vigorously contested political campaigns in the city's annals." Shelby Cox, the former KKK district attorney, was one of the CCA's chief spokesmen (many pointed out that some of the Catfish Club members also were former KKK members). Behind the Citizens' Civic Association, Cox charged, was a group of "discharged, disgruntled and disgraced" city employees. Both parties accused the other of being favored by the city's criminal interests and holding secret agendas for unleashing organized vice. Throughout the campaign both sides accused the other of having ulterior motives. CCA president W.D. Jones stressed that the past four years at city hall had been free of graft and corruption, and he suggested that the opposition was mostly interested in a return to the old days when favor could be purchased. As for the issue of Edyism, CCA campaign manager John Erhard announced in his first statement in February that Edy definitely would be retained by the CCA council. Erhard himself, who had managed the 1933 campaign as well, became a target of the Civic Association because he was an outsider who did not reside within the city limits.

On the eve of the election the *News* published a fence-straddling editorial which pointed out that those who were not satisfied with the present city government should vote for the Citizens Charter Association slate. Those who were not satisfied could assure changes by voting for the Civic Association.

More than half the city's 40,000 eligible voters cast ballots on the April 2 election day. The result was a surprising clean sweep by the upstart Citizens' Civic Association, each candidate winning by an approximate 5-4 ratio. "Civic Ticket Runs Away With Election; Edy Quits Today," recorded the *News'* banner headline. Catfish strength was especially evident in the predominantly blue-collar South Dallas and Oak Cliff areas, while CCA support in the higher-income areas of the city declined substantially from 1933 and 1931.

The new slate of councilmen, meeting next day in their headquarters in the Santa Fe Building, promised among other things to give full, courteous, and prompt hearings to all citizens who appeared at city hall. They also appointed a new city manager, their own campaign manager, Moseley. In keeping with the complaints about Edy's salary, Moseley's annual pay was reduced to $10,000. Moseley's appointment was a disquieting note to some, including the *News*, because it clearly compromised the theory of council-manager government by rewarding one who had played a major role in the political campaign.

However, Moseley showed his mettle early when he met in a hotel room with the council-elect and several Catfish Club members. Moseley listened to their proposals as to whom he should appoint as police chief and as heads of several other departments. For police chief the Catfish Club wanted one of their own, a sheetmetal manufacturer named Jim Railton. But Moseley balked at being compromised at the start through hack political appointees. In the ensuing quarrel, five of the nine council members stood behind him and his position. Thus, the proferred candidates were not accepted, and notions of a Catfish Club patronage system were thwarted. Moseley selected his own choices to head the major departments, including a director of public works whom Edy himself had concluded to be one of three persons qualified for the job.

As mayor the council elected from among themselves the top vote-getter, George A. Sergeant. He was a lawyer, a former city judge, and former chief justice of the Texas Court of Civil Appeals . Sergeant twice had been around the world, and as a boy of sixteen he had lived with the Cheyenne and Arapaho Indians.

Thus began a new regime at city hall which was to extend until the Citizens Charter Association could re-invigorate itself and regain control of city hall in 1939. Still, the council that took office in 1935 acquitted itself very credibly, and individual councilmen participated more freely in the general affairs of the community.

8

Centennial Triumph

"What we need is the boss men organized so we can act quick."

–Robert L. Thornton, 1937

Moving the Trinity

The 1930s were for Dallas a decade of triumph. Before these years—so bleak for so many—had ended, the image of the city had undergone as if by magic a transformation. From a rather nondescript town with agrarian ways it became a smart city of sophistication and accomplishment. The transformation was recognized and even embellished by the nation's press. Actually, real changes had occurred. Two of them we have seen. One was the adoption and successful implementation of the council-manager system, a change that was to bring great fruit in the decades ahead. The second was the introduction of the oil industry as a powerful component to the city's economic base. Three other significant events during the decade added to this mix: the realization of the long-time dream to tame the Trinity, the formation of the powerful Citizens Council, and the accomplishment that was the most crucial for the city's image transformation—sponsorship of an acclaimed world's fair, the Texas Centennial Exposition of 1936. It was the decade when Dallas became "Big D."

Achieving George Kessler's recommendation for the Trinity was far more complicated than merely bulldozing a straight new river channel between two high mounds of dirt. It was an immense, expensive, complex, and politically sensitive project requiring re-routing and re-building storm sewers, moving railroad lines and switches, re-laying utility lines, creating a new confluence of the river's West and Elm forks, digging a straight and different channel for the river bed, constructing twenty-five miles of thirty-foot high earthen levees, and erecting four new high bridges to cross the levees.

All this did far more than save central parts of the city from flooding. It reclaimed and made available for use approximately 10,000 acres of previously worthless flood plain in a strategic area adjacent to downtown. These acres now could be developed as a planned industrial district along the outer levees.

A project such as this in the center of a large city required the cooperation of municipal, county, state, and federal governments, of a newly formed public levee district, and of public utility companies, railroads, and private enterprise. The Chamber of Commerce bragged that probably never before had an American city coordinated expenditures of such magnitude from so many different sources.

The first work toward achieving Kessler's recommendations had been inspired by Dealey, who with a handful of other men, including especially Henry D. Lindsley, in 1914 paid several thousand dollars of their own money toward preliminary engineering studies. The onset of World War I ended their plans.

The next specific step toward accomplishing the goal had been achieved in April 1920 through the organization of an entity called the City of Dallas and Dallas County Levee Improvement District No. 10. Anticipated costs of some $50,000 for its operations were underwritten by leading individuals and businesses of the city, including Dealey, whose $2,500 contribution was as much as anyone's.

After a period of little or no progress, this organization was replaced in 1926 by the City and County of Dallas Levee Improvement District. This would be the entity that finally saw the project to completion. An engineering firm, Myers and Moyes, was hired to prepare initial plans for the project. Funding for construction and related aspects came in 1928 from the City of Dallas through the Ulrickson bond issue of $23.9 million, augmented by another bond issue of $6.9 million approved by county voters, and by an agreement by levee district property owners to issue $6.5 million in bonds to construct the actual levees.

Even with all this financing through the ballot an accomplished fact, opponents tried to stop the levee project before a single shovel of dirt could be dug. Although 85 percent of levee district property owners approved their bond issue, a dissenting minority threatened an injunction to halt the sale of the bonds. Levee district supervisors determined to sell the bonds without fanfare before their opponents could tangle up the matter in the courts.

The three supervisors, chairman John J. Simmons, W.P. Dumas, and Leslie A. Stemmons, arranged to print the bonds in Galveston instead of Dallas, then delivered them discreetly to the attorney general in Austin for his routine approval. There, the three stuffed the bonds into eight suitcases and brought them to Dallas by automobile in a high-speed drive. So concerned were they about the possibility of a highway interception as well as for their own safety that as a precaution they armed themselves for the ride. They pulled up without incident at Stemmons' Oak Cliff home, and Stemmons' ninety-year-old mother was picked up to take to Union Terminal to board a train for Chicago, ostensibly to visit relatives. They placed the suitcases stuffed with bonds in Mrs. Stemmons' stateroom car. In Chicago the bank officials who had been engaged to sell the bonds met Mrs. Stemmons at the depot with an armored car, collected the suitcases, and conducted as quickly as they could a private sale of the entire bond issue. All this was done before opponents could devise their legal strategies and get to the courthouse.

A petition signed by a majority of the levee property owners, most of whom stood to make substantial profits with their land rendered usable, authorized similarly the "private" awarding of a contract for the levee work to Trinity Farm Construction Co. George B. Dealey, appropriately, was the speaker for groundbreaking in June 1928. He acknowledged that his own inspiration for the projection had come on that day in 1902 (he incorrectly stated 1903) when he had been smoking a cigar on the old Commerce Street bridge and suddenly realized the possibilities inherent in reclamation. As for this groundbreaking event, he said it was "one of the most important in its potential effects" that he had seen during his forty-three years in the city. "A blot on the landscape near the heart of Dallas will be removed, and a great industrial development will gradually follow. Not only this, but near the heart of our splendid city there will be developed a park containing hundreds of acres, with a clear channel in the middle of it—a park equal in width to ten city blocks and miles long," he optimistically proclaimed.

Once under way, the immense project employed an average of a thousand men at a time. Up to fifteen huge dragline machines worked twenty-four hours a day to move twenty-one million cubic yards of dirt in re-aligning the river and building up the levees. It was calculated that if this dirt were piled along a three-and-a-half-mile stretch of Commerce Street it would have been eighty feet wide and as high as the Magnolia Building.

The new viaducts crossing the river, four graceful concrete structures, were modeled after the original 1912 Houston Street viaduct. The four, Cadiz Street, Lamar-McKinney, Corinth Street, and Commerce Street, were completed in that order between 1929 and 1931. To connect these viaducts Industrial Boulevard was laid out along the east side of the levee.

In these heady days great dreams were envisioned for the 3,300 acres of floodplain between the levees. This acreage, as Dealey had said in his ground-breaking speech, was to be transformed into a huge park system, available for use except for occasional times of high water. The slanted sides of the levees would be covered with beautiful wildflowers, especially bluebonnets, and on the flat lands between these verdant banks would be sunken gardens, baseball diamonds, polo grounds, golf courses, bridle paths, archery ranges, trapshooting spaces, winding drives, and a two-mile long lake with a Coney Island atmosphere. Even a landing field for airplanes was projected for a space northwest of where Turtle Creek entered the river. Alas, as future Dallasites would see all too well, such noble dreams were only made of pipe.

As the work commenced, by 1930 the entire project became mired in an intense political struggle, a struggle which was the source of the *News'* antagonism toward Edy. In June 1930 some 1,000 Dallas citizens met to protest the city's involvement in the project and especially a proposal to increase city taxes because of it. The meeting was organized by an impromptu anti-tax committee whose members included such prominent individuals as Karl Hoblitzelle, Felix Harris, C.C. Weichsel, and Dr. E.H. Carey. Towards the end of the stormy meeting levee district supervisor John J. Simmons sought to respond, but the crowd hooted him down and then walked out on him.

Dealey and other levee proponents, who regularly communicated concerning strategy, were furious with Edy and the City of Dallas because they believed they were deliberately dragging their heels. Others, though, such as Hoblitzelle and Dr. Carey, had an opposite conviction--that the City of Dallas was unfairly biased in favor of the project. Growing sections of East and South Dallas, they argued, desperately needed municipal services, and these should not be neglected in favor of a river bottom populated only by frogs and snakes. "Certain big interests...are trying to force the City to spend bond money to complete a project in the face of all of the needs of these people on Mill Creek, and other sections of Dallas who have been suffering for years for lack of this protection," complained John E. Surratt, who spoke in February 1932 at a meeting of several improvement leagues. These comments were meant to include Dealey and the *News*, whose support for the project the *Dallas Dispatch* labeled as being strictly because of selfish interests. The *Times Herald* also sided with those who charged the levee project sought to enrich the pockets of floodplain property owners at taxpayers' expense.

Levee proponents, including the three levee district supervisors, took the view that the project helped all citizens. They charged Edy with reneging on the Ulrickson bond program, which voters had approved. Leslie A. Stemmons, one of the three levee district supervisors and also the president of Industrial Properties Association (the private firm which would develop the property), said the levee district had been subjected to "broken promises, repudiation, and bad faith." Edy's attitude, he said, was "comparable to dictatorships now operating in Europe."

By 1932, despite delays and debate, the basic levee work was completed except for a small gap on the east side. This awaited the City of Dallas' completion of drainage work at the Coombs Creek-Kidd Springs area, the source of much debate. On February 29, 1932, the three levee supervisors filed a $70,973 law suit against the City of

Dallas for failure to use bonds authorized by the Ulrickson program to complete the storm sewer drainage system, a failure which they said caused city floodwaters to be discharged onto an area that should have been reclaimed.

On the same day they filed the suit the trio, all of whom had served without pay for six years, resigned, saying that it was time to let others take over to try to bring harmony into the plan. Dallas County Commissioners Court named three new supervisors, compromises were reached, and the remaining work on the levee district was completed sometime after the *News* published an eleven-part series by Lynn Landrum in May 1933 that was highly critical of the city's reluctance to cooperate with the levee district.

A final element in the overall levee project came in 1936 with the bringing together of Main, Commerce, and Elm streets into a "Triple Underpass" at what formerly had been the bed of the river. This realignment permitted traffic entering downtown Dallas to separate according to designation, greatly alleviating traffic problems.

It was estimated that the value of the reclaimed Trinity bottom land jumped from $3.2 million to $47 million. Total cost of the project was approximately $25 million.

Here, as promised, lay an immense amount of usable land, zoned for industrial use, and adjacent to the strategic downtown area. The actual development of the great industrial district did not come about instantly, however. Stemmons, the major developer as president of Industrial Properties Corporation and a guiding force on the levee project, had a great personal incentive in seeing it to completion. He had organized his company in 1928 for the specific purpose of developing "industrial sites, business properties, manufacturing and switch properties." He died in 1939 before he could fully develop his holdings. His sons, John and Storey Stemmons, carried on their father's work, but the continuing Depression and then World War II delayed the district's development. After the war, however, the pent-up demand for commercial property exploded and brought a boom lasting many years. The first development, the Trinity River Industrial District, spread in orderly fashion along the new Industrial Boulevard over some 10,000 acres of the once-worthless floodplain. In following years the area farther expanded as the West Trinity Industrial and Brook Hollow industrial districts along the new Stemmons and Carpenter freeways and Irving Boulevard. Here arose an immense, impressive collection of commercial enterprises, manufacturing facilities, warehouses, office buildings, corporate headquarters, and hotels.

While the commercial aspects of the reclamation of these floodplains became an obvious and spectacular success, the strip of land between the levees was to remain virtually untouched. Into the 1990s it continued to be a sterile, artificial wasteland with no public effort to develop the far-reaching recreational purposes envisioned as a complement to the industrial park.

THE CENTENNIAL IDEA

The idea for Texas to observe its centennial anniversary of independence had been around at least since Governor James S. Hogg in 1903 suggested a fitting celebration for the occasion. But the direct suggestion that catalyzed the idea and led directly to the centennial occurred in Corsicana in 1923 at a joint meeting of the Texas Press Association and the tenth district of the Associated Advertising Clubs of America. One of the speakers, ironically a New Yorker, stirred the crowd with his talk, "What Texas Has to Advertise and How to Advertise It." The speaker, Theodore H. Price, publisher of a business weekly, stressed the state's romantic history as a theme that could focus the nation's attention on the neglected state. He painted a fantasy-like picture of a huge, new exposition city. So appealing and so persuasive were Price's suggestions that the 400-plus delegates voted unanimously to begin campaigning for a centennial observance for 1936. These delegates, who included so many of the state's leading newspaper publishers and editors, would continue to push the idea on their editorial pages in the next years.

Governor Pat Neff endorsed the centennial movement in a proclamation drafted by *Dallas Morning News* reporter Harry Benge Crozier, who had covered the Corsicana meeting. A committee formed to assess public sentiment on the project mailed 10,000 questionnaires to leading citizens throughout the state. All these developments gained headlines in the state's sympathetic newspapers.

Various problems and strategies concerning the centennial celebration were discussed and explored over the next years. Some believed that the best celebration would be a series of smaller events scattered about the state rather than a major celebration in one location. But with the matter settled in favor of a central exposition at a specific location, the Texas Legislature in 1934 authorized creation of a centennial commission to select the site. There was no legislative hint as to where it should be other than that the centennial should be located in "the city offering the largest financial inducement and support."

Dallas could not resist such a temptation. It suffered a distinct handicap, though. When the Republic of Texas declared its independence in 1836 the area that would become Dallas was no more than a wild, unsettled land in a remote part of the nation. Unlike Houston and San Antonio, both of which had strong historic claims as logical centennial sites, Dallas could not boast of such names and deeds as General Sam Houston and the battle of San Jacinto or William Barret Travis, James W. Fannin, and Davy Crockett at the Alamo.

Helpful though historical romanticism might be, however, it was not a prerequisite to be the host city. What would be required were these important items: (1) the availability of approximately 200 acres of land suitable for development as a centennial site, (2) provision of all utility services to the site, and (3) submission of a monetary offer with an inventory of all properties available. These things Dallas could handle. The man who realized this more than anyone else was the man who already had aggressively solicited new industry for the city through the Chamber of Commerce's half-million dollar national advertising program, Industrial Dallas, Inc. He was Robert Lee Thornton, president of Mercantile National Bank.

ROBERT L. THORNTON

Thornton, founder of his own bank and an enthusiast of state fairs and world expositions, garnered the support of other leading businessmen and launched a vigorous and successful campaign to win the plum of hosting the centennial. His background was rural Texas. He was born in Hamilton County in Central Texas on August 10, 1880, in a half-roofed sod dugout used by the family as a temporary dwelling after their farm house, recently purchased, had been destroyed by a fire. A few years later more trouble came. The title to the farm turned out to be faulty; the family was rendered homeless. The Thorntons moved to Ellis County, immediately south of Dallas County, where cotton-picking was good and plentiful for a tenant farm family. Practice made perfect, and as Thornton grew bigger he developed a prodigious capacity for this backbreaking labor, bagging as many as 500 pounds of cotton in a single day. The money that could be earned from such labor was more important to the family in these hard times than schooling. Before starting classes each year Bobby Lee Thornton waited until after Christmas when there was no more cotton to pick. There weren't many of these years; his own son later said he dropped out after the third grade, others said the eighth grade.

Thornton's affection for Dallas—and his fondness for fairs and expositions—may have stemmed from his first visit to the Texas State Fair in 1888. His father hitched up a team of mules to a wagon, drove Bobby Lee and a brother to nearby Ferris, and then boarded a train with them for the eighteen-mile ride to Dallas. After spending fifty cents each at the fair, the trio returned home at dark.

As he grew toward manhood young Thornton realized that he must escape the cotton fields if he was to amount to anything. But there was a great gap between his lowly station in life and the sorts of achievements he envisioned. His first step away from cotton-picking came when he took a laborer's job helping build roads. Then, following a pattern set by a young Abe Lincoln, he obtained a job as a clerk in a country store in the community of Bristol. After a couple of years there he borrowed money from his employer to take an eight-week course in bookkeeping at a business school in Dallas. Later, he would boast of possessing just one educational degree—a CC&M, which stood for corn, cotton, and mules. Forever Thornton's conversation would reflect his rural roots; he referred to his plain speech as "cotton-pickin' talk."

In 1904 the World's Fair in St. Louis proved to be an irresistible lure. With a few dollars somehow saved, Thornton went there to savor its wonders. He got involved in a crap game with some city slickers, lost his money, and had to sell his return train ticket for meal money. One of the young gamblers, taking pity on the luckless lad, introduced him to his father, who gave him a job as a travelling candy salesman in his company's worst district, the Indian Territory (now Oklahoma). In the year that followed Thornton improbably became the company's top seller, then continued his travelling salesmanship abilities with the National Candy Company. After several more years on the road in which he worked out of Dallas (first showing up in the city directory in 1906), Thornton became secretary-manager of the Commonwealth Land & Mortgage Co. When that company failed he bought part-interest in a book store for $500 at an unfortunate time—just prior to the state of Texas' decision to issue free textbooks to students. He and his partner had to close down the Thornton and Bracey Bookstore.

Someone suggested that he try banking. "Well, I've tried everything else," Thornton said, although he acknowledged he knew nothing about it. He had $6,000 of his own in cash, though, and he traveled to Shreveport to see an uncle who had some oil money. The uncle, A.C. Stiles, obligingly put up $12,000 in notes in his possession and agreed to join the venture. Thornton, now thirty-six years of age, arranged for a third partner who had experience in banking, Martin C. Lund, and a fourth associate, Harry Susman. The four men bought used fixtures for $350, which they repaired and revarnished themselves, and in October 1916 the bank opened at 704 Main Street as Stiles, Thornton, and Lund. Thornton was manager (soon re-titled as president); Stiles, assistant manager; and Lund, cashier.

What the new bank offered that was distinctive in a city already top-heavy with banks was long operating hours; it kept its doors open "day and night." What Thornton lacked in banking expertise he more than made up with his uncanny instinct in recognizing customers who could pay him back. This failed him, however, at an early moment. One of Thornton's first major loans was for $16,000 for thirty days to a man who used as collateral mules, equipment, and his contract to build some levees. Being comfortable about his knowledge of mules, Thornton inspected them and the equipment, and he approved the loan. On the due date neither the man nor the money were to be found. Upon inquiry Thornton learned that the man had slipped away to Kansas City, so he went there, found him, and collected the money he was owed plus interest. The new bank was on its way; its chief had displayed the tenacity that would serve him and Dallas for the next decades.

The bank, soon re-named Dallas County State Bank, prospered especially through "jitney" (early taxis) loans, then by being the first institution in the city to lend money for automobile purchases.

Located at Main and Lamar, the bank promoted its location as the place "where all the cars pass." Thornton's outgoing personality led him to join the Rotary Club, the Shriners, the Wholesale Merchants Association, and the Chamber of Commerce. By 1921 his success was such that he was able to boast as a vice president on his staff the former mayor of Dallas, William M. Holland. And if Thornton had belonged in the early 1920s to an organization noted for intolerance --the Ku Klux Klan--even at that time he had recruited three Jews, Charles L. Sanger, Harry Sigel, and Lawrence Kahn, for the board of directors of his "KKK Business Firm 100%." By the end of the 1920s Thornton had emerged as one of the Chamber of Commerce's most dedicated leaders, especially effective as president of the Chamber's program to lure new industry to town, Industrial Dallas, Inc. In 1929 his bank moved into the tallest structure in town, the Magnolia Building.

One fledgling entrepreneur who came to Dallas, Conrad N. Hilton, credited Thornton with proposing one of the greatest gambles he ever took. Hilton was short of the cash he needed to lease Dallas' Waldorf Hotel, and Thornton suggested that he play "double-or-nothing" with the $55,000 that he did have. Hilton did, and he won. He took over the hotel, the biggest he had ever operated, and launched a fabled career in inn-keeping.

WINNING THE CENTENNIAL

Because of his leadership in the Industrial Dallas program, Thornton was acutely aware of the advantages the centennial celebration could bring. To pursue his goal Thornton carefully covered all bases. He secured the backing of the Chamber's board of directors; he won the approval of Mayor Charles E. Turner; and, more importantly, he got the endorsement and cooperation of the presidents of the two largest banks in town, Nathan Adams of First National Bank and Fred F. Florence of Republic National. Adams and Florence joined Thornton as the key leaders in the movement. In early August Thornton arranged for a luncheon at the Baker Hotel's Crystal Ballroom for all citizens interested in supporting the project. More than 500 business leaders attended and pledged their help. As Thornton and his committee raised money at such meetings it was reminiscent of the scene years earlier in 1908 when the city's leaders raised money for flood victims. Only the names had changed. Thornton would plead and cajole from the podium, "Come on, Bill, make it $15,000. Bill make it $15,000." Bill would hesitate, and Thornton would snap, "Put Bill down for $20,000." Before Bill could protest Thornton already would be working the next man.

The blue-eyed, gravel-voiced Thornton commanded in his practical head ample economic facts to argue convincingly for Dallas as the best site for the exposition The facts he had learned well through his leadership of Industrial Dallas, Inc. They were the same sort of facts used in 1912 to get the regional Federal Reserve Bank. When the Dallas City Council met to hear Thornton, Florence, and Adams urge approval of a bond election to raise between $2.5 million and $3 million to enlarge and improve Fair Park if the city was selected, Thornton put it plainly: "From a cold-blooded dollars and cents view, this exposition will mean more to Dallas than anything else." Nathan Adams threw in a warning: if the centennial went elsewhere future implications for the state fair would be troublesome. The council agreed to hold a bond election, if necessary.

As the September 1 deadline for submission of bids approached Thornton learned that the city of Houston would ask for an indefinite delay. Houston's committee contended that it would be "absolutely impossible to get a credible celebration ready by the early part of 1936." Thornton objected in a strongly worded telegram. Any delay, he argued, would cause problems in getting any site ready because of all the legal, political, and financial problems to be overcome. Moreover, the state-wide enthusiasm for the project would wane. Dallas, he pointed out, enjoyed a solid base of community support and it was ready to move forward. Delay was unacceptable. Thornton's protest won the day; the September 1 deadline stood firm. But before an award could be made the committee had to make on-site inspections.

The inspections began in Dallas on September 6. State Fair officials, accompanied by local architect George F. Dahl, escorted the twenty-one commission officials. Dahl elaborated on the advantages of Fair Park, where so many state fairs had been held, carefully pointing out locations for proposed new buildings and additional acreage that would be annexed along Second Avenue and east of the grounds. After lunch at the Baker Hotel, the commission heard final arguments in a meeting room on the ninth floor.

Thornton gave what surely was the most inspirational, the most persuasive talk of his life. Of the several who spoke, he stood out as the unparalleled star. Dallas banker George Waverley Briggs, who was present, summarized it as "a masterpiece of vivid color and cogent argument...[that] enraptured everyone who heard it. He talked for an hour and his audience called for more....If we [Dallas] win it will be attributed to him." Surrounded by maps, charts, graphs, and six of Dahl's romanticized colored renderings, Thornton stressed with fervor all the basic data he knew so well in promoting Dallas: its leading role in manufacturing, finance, and insurance; its central location and the abundant surrounding population; its experience in putting on huge state fairs; its excellent transportation facilities; its financial resources; the unification of its citizenry in seeking the centennial; and its ample hotel accommodations.

A spokesman from the Dallas Hotel Association assured the commission that the city's present hotel rates would be maintained throughout the centennial year, not exceeding $5 for a single room and $6 for a double.) Thornton pointed to U.S. Highway 80, a great east-west artery running from the South through the entirety of Texas, and said that a traffic check of this "Broadway of America" showed that 730,000 cars with out-of-state guests already were passing through Dallas annually via the highway, more than through any three other cities in the entire state. As to the historical issue and Dallas' deficiencies here, Thornton pointedly said that history must be viewed through the economic progress made possible through the patriotic sacrifice of the state's founders. No place better than Dallas could show progress.

A central question was how much the state and federal governments would appropriate for the exposition. If such appropriations were less than desired, Thornton was asked, how would this impact Dallas' determination to host the event. Thornton, possibly overstepping his authority, said with conviction: "We pledge you this, that if we are designated as the central centennial city there will be a centennial held, whether the State of Texas or the government of the United States contributes one cent because Dallas never fails."

From Dallas commission members went directly to Houston by overnight train to hear that city's presentation. Thornton and Dahl decided to check out the competition; they drove overnight to

Houston by car, arriving in time for the morning reception at the Rice Hotel and the rest of the day's activities. At the historic San Jacinto battlefield commission members listened to Judge Clarence R. Wharton extoll on that historic moment of 1836 when Sam Houston's Texan forces routed Santa Anna's invading soldiers from their early-morning slumber. As the judge verbally recreated this historic experience, the wind suddenly shifted. It carried from the swamps a thick swarm of mosquitoes. Women in low-neck dresses began battling the insects with folded newspapers, swatting here and there to keep them away. Thornton and Dahl watched in growing amusement. Judge Wharton, flustered, protested: "How can I deliver a romantic speech to you as long as you are waving those damn newspapers at me? It's those fellows here that came down from Dallas; they're the ones that brought these gallinippers in." The comedy of the moment broke up the meeting.

Later, Mayor Oscar Holcombe responded to the same question about state and federal appropriations which Thornton had answered so confidently in Dallas. Holcombe's response was markedly different. If such aid were not forthcoming, Holcombe said, Houston would not be interested because the exposition would be merely a "Houston fair" and not a Texas centennial.

Commission members next went to San Antonio. There, Mayor C.K. Quinn complained to the commission about the "highest bidder" aspect of the competition, referring to the requirement that the competing cities submit monetary bids. As to the question of state and federal aid, Mayor Quinn said his city would need at least $1 million.

On September 9 the committee met in Austin's Driskill Hotel to select the winning bid. Waiting in the lobby during the day-long deliberations were representatives from the three competing cities. All of Dallas' campaign leaders, Thornton, Florence, and Adams were there. Late in the afternoon Centennial Commission Chairman Cullen F. Thomas announced the winner: Dallas. The city had led from the first ballot, which gave Dallas 13, Houston 8, and San Antonio 6. From there Dallas picked up additional votes, and on the third ballot the commissioners voted unanimously for the city. "We accept this honor in a spirit of humility and thankfulness," Thornton said in his acceptance speech. "It is a heavy obligation. It will require all we have of strength, of cash and of credit to portray faithfully and adequately the century of achievement in this great empire of Texas." Only now were the amounts of the various cities' bids revealed. Dallas had submitted the highest, $7,791,000, followed by Houston's $6,507,000, and San Antonio's $4,835,000.

San Antonio's committee members expressed bitterness. They charged that the decision had been based unfairly on regional considerations and that South Texas had not been adequately represented on the selection committee. While they said that a "commercialized exposition" might be all right, appropriations also should be given to a city in the "historical region of Texas."

Houston's delegation was more accepting, but the city's Chamber of Commerce expressed fears as to what the decision said about the city's leadership. J.E. Josey, a commission member from Houston, wrote to Thornton afterwards that he had told his fellow commission members that "Houston stood no chance in their half-hearted, unorganized effort against the united support of Dallas, led by such men as you."

Kenneth Ragsdale, who fully chronicled the history of the centennial celebration, wrote that the competition revealed "vastly different urban personalities" among Texas' leading cities. He contrasted the ineffective presentations and disunity in Houston and San Antonio, and concluded that while Houston had more than ample reasons to have been chosen, its decision-makers simply were no match for the high calibre of those in Dallas.

Perhaps the more demanding aspects of the Centennial Exposition still lay ahead for the triumvirate of Thornton, Florence, and Adams, all of whom took executive titles in the newly formed Texas Centennial Central Exposition. Thornton, as chairman of the executive committee, held the senior title.

Adams, the senior member of the trio in terms of age and a key participant in the successful drive to win the Federal Reserve Bank, was chairman of the board. Born in 1869 in Pulaski, Tennessee, Adams had moved to Dallas in 1887 to work in the auditor's office of Texas & Pacific Railway. Soon he entered banking, and in 1924 he had become president of American Exchange Bank, which had evolved into the First National Bank in Dallas, the largest in the Southwest. He was now sixty-six years of age.

Florence, who grew up in East Texas, was president of the exposition corporation. He had been a small-town banker in East

Texas before moving to Dallas in 1920 to be the chief assistant to the president of a new bank that eventually would become Republic National. He became president in 1929. Despite his small-town background and a formal education that had stopped upon graduation from high school in 1907, Florence was a polished, sophisticated banker whose urbane manners contrasted sharply with that of the folksy Thornton. In 1931 Florence had become official treasurer for the City of Dallas, a position he was to hold for two and a half decades as a complement to his bank. Over the years he was to play an important behind-the-scene role in civic affairs.

Other civic, city, and county leaders assisted this trio in facing a myriad of problems in arranging for the enormous project. A genuine hero who emerged was architect George L. Dahl, who designed the exposition setting at Fair Park and supervised the work of more than a hundred architects, artists, and craftsmen. In just ten months, a time-table that was almost literally impossible, Dahl and his crew worked an around-the-clock schedule to tear down old buildings and construct or completely remodel seventy-seven structures. Total cost was approximately $25 million. Dahl's Fair Park architecture in recent years has been hailed as perhaps the single greatest collection of "art deco" buildings extant. It was inspired by the 1925 Exposition des Arts Decoratifs in Paris. Unlike structures commonly associated with other expositions, many of these at Fair Park were built as permanent additions, including the centerpiece Hall of State, the Museum of Fine Arts, the Museum of Natural History, an aquarium, an outdoor theater, and exhibition buildings along the esplanade.

Amidst this frenzy of construction, a $500,000 advertising and publicity campaign called attention to the goings-on in Dallas. It included national radio spots, newspaper advertising both in and out of the state, and a plethora of special folders, posters, and specialty items. A corps of approximately twenty-five attractive female Texas Centennial Rangerettes, attired in red, white, and blue cowboy regalia traveled the country over to promote the Centennial. In the process they became celebrities themselves. A contingent of them issued direct invitations to President Franklin D. Roosevelt, Vice President John Nance Gardner, Congressman Sam Rayburn, and FBI Director J. Edgar Hoover. They "lassoed" Hoover in his office to try to bring him to the Centennial, and a photograph of the event appeared next day in newspapers all across the land.

Triumph at Fair Park

The Centennial, buttressed by $3 million appropriations from both the state and federal governments, opened June 6. More than 250,000 spectators witnessed the inaugural parade. The noon opening ceremony was broadcast across the nation over the two radio networks. Six days later President Roosevelt visited the grounds at Fair Park, and proclaimed that the Centennial Exposition was not just for Texans but for the people of all the other forty-seven states as well.

Visitors did come from every state in the union and from many nations of the world to see the Centennial's wide variety of attractions. These included an outdoor theater with a historical pageant entitled "The Cavalcade of Texas," theatrical shows, music, and a midway with rides and games. Bare-breasted female dancers—and at least one bottomless one, "Lady Godiva"—entertained adults in special attractions along the midway.

Still, Centennial exhibits predominantly were educational, historical, futuristic, and cultural rather than titillating. Fort Worth, in contrast, developed in competition its own Frontier Centennial Exposition produced by showman Billy Rose and stressing entertainment with such attractions as Paul Whiteman's band and Sally Rand's Nude Ranch. To woo Centennial visitors away, the city developed the slogan, "Go to Dallas for Education, Come to Fort Worth for Entertainment."

Fort Worth's apparent success bothered Dallas. A traffic study revealed that an unduly large number of automobiles coming into the area headed for Fort Worth. An unofficial city council meeting was called in a downtown office to review the situation. As Dr. J.W. Bass, the city health director later recalled, he and Police Chief Bob Jones received news of the unofficial council meeting later that day. In order to compete with Fort Worth, Dr. Bass said he was told: "We've got to open up the town. Mr. Thornton is in a hole for a lot of money and going in deeper all the time." As a result, the decision was made to loosen enforcement, to permit bookies to operate, to stop closing bars for illegal liquor sales, and to "keep the whores as safe as possible....keep them in the houses and off the streets." In less than a month Dr. Bass's office issued 2,400 health cards to prostitutes. Madams operating houses along Griffin Street and near the downtown hotels required the cards for their "girls."

Certainly the Centennial was the crowning achievement in all the city's years of self-promotion. The public relations value was incalculable. And while the Centennial itself actually lost money, its economic benefits were enormous: hotel business was up 35 percent; restaurant sales increased by 50 percent; wholesale sales ranged upwards from 22 to 40 percent; and local bank deposits soared. Just one month after the Centennial opened bank deposits in the city increased more than $30 million. A total of 6,353,827 people attended the Centennial before it closed on November 29. City Manager Moseley reported in mid-summer, 1936, that the previous twelve months—in the depths of the Depression—had seen "probably the most spirited building growth" of the city's recent history. A consensus of businessmen interviewed by a *News* reporter was that the city generally had made more progress in the six months of the exposition than in all its previous existence. Dallas could never be the same; indeed, neither could the state.

"Examined in any context," observed the closest student of the affair, "the 1936 Texas Centennial and its broad spectrum of experiences—social, cultural, and economic—had helped change the face and mood of Dallas forever....Texas had begun to turn an important corner and was now headed down untrodden paths toward 'that new era which lies ahead.'"

So pleased was the city that in the following year, 1937, the exposition was re-opened as the Greater Texas and Pan American Exposition. Its theme was the celebration of cooperation—as opposed to the revolution—of Texas with Mexico and the nations of Central and South America. On opening day physicist Albert Einstein started an electrical impulse from his home in Princeton, New Jersey, which fired a field gun to signal exposition technicians to turn on the electricity. It was expected that profits could be generated out of the Exposition since the physical plant now was in place, but the event failed to generate the excitement of the Centennial.

Dallas now comfortably viewed itself in a new way, a way reinforced by glowing descriptions appearing in the nation's press. The city became a favorite subject for feature stories. Between July

1935 and June 1937 twenty-five articles on aspects of the city or about the Texas Centennial observance appeared in national publications, and over the next two years eighteen more articles appeared. For the same number of months in the 1933 to 1935 period, the *Reader's Guide to Periodical Literature* lists only one article about the city.

Dallas' ties to its western heritage never again would be part of its promotional program. That would be left to Fort Worth, "where the west begins." Nor would the city's one-time identification as a part of the South again be promoted. Dallas was becoming "Big D," an entity unto itself that was neither Southern nor Western.

One article that had an early and important impact in portraying the city as sophisticated and cultured appeared in the November 1937 issue of *Fortune*. Entitled "Dallas in Wonderland," it described with unrestrained enthusiasm and with numerous color photographs the success and impact of the city's high-class specialty store, Neiman-Marcus, celebrating that year its thirtieth anniversary. Exclusive merchandise offered at Neiman-Marcus and eagerly purchased by knowledgeable Dallasites and Texans, it was reported, could be found only in a few stores like I. Magnin's in San Francisco and Saks Fifth Avenue in New York City. Marcus family members were portrayed as cultured and intellectual as well as astute merchandisers with impeccable taste. The fact that such a store and such people could be found in Dallas, Texas, seemed to make a profound statement about the city's character.

An article that followed in 1940 in the influential *Atlantic Monthly* was almost as enthusiastic in describing the entire city. Here was a new kind of city not restricted by old patterns; a city that faced each day a new world of its own creation; a "new town in a new world"; a place where "nearly everything is still fluid"; and a place where the visitor had the sensation of being in a "new, energetic, and somehow strangely innocent world." The city's leaders tended to be more intelligent than intellectual, more money-minded than their Southern forefathers, and also more aggressive. Here one saw a marriage between the tall beaver topper of the East and the ten-gallon hat of the West, and the union had "turned out well." Repeated was a theme introduced in the *Fortune* article—Dallas was famous for its well-dressed women, a comment reinforced by syndicated columnist Walter Winchell, who avowed that Dallas had the "best-dressed" women in the nation.

Readers were told that none of this should be surprising, for Dallas families had more purchasing power than those anywhere in the nation except Washington, D.C., and New York City. The average family income was $3,600, which meant that an average Dallas family could spend more in a single month than an average Mississippi family in a full year.

These and other articles in similar veins created a stereotype of Dallas, albeit one that was especially pleasing. The Chamber of Commerce's promotional material took on a new confidence. In 1930 the *News* had referred to Dallas as being in the small-city class. Chamber publicity now began describing it as "friendly, cosmopolitan, [and] big," and as "one of the best known cities in America." The chamber's 1938 annual report said, "To MOST of the Southwest DALLAS is simply 'BIG D.'" The future had arrived.

CITIZENS COUNCIL FOUNDED

Thornton's hard work in coordinating the Centennial effort and the success of that enterprise gave him an idea. Why not organize a handful of powerful executives who could handle other civic projects and problems that arose, just as he, Adams, and Florence had done for the Centennial. Problem-solving could be streamlined if these individuals gathered in a single room, thrashed out issues, devised solutions, and then exercised their authority to implement their goals. Only the "yes or no" men could be a part of it—men who did not have to run back to their offices for permission—men with the power to commit themselves and their company resources to whatever project they deemed worthy. With this idea Thornton went to see his friend Adams at First National. He told him that he was tired of having to run up and down Main Street, raising money for this, that and every other project. "Nate," he said, "what we need is the boss men organized so we can act quick...*dydamic* kind of organization ...*stupendjious* effort...people doin' things." Adams, a reflective man, listened patiently until Thornton ran down a bit, then laid down his cigar in a big glass ash tray. Funny, he said, he had been thinking the same thing.

On November 22, 1937, Thornton's idea was incorporated by the state as the Citizens Council, an organization established for "wholly educational and civic" purposes. The charter stated that it would be "absolutely non-political in character." Membership was by invitation only. To be eligible one had to be the chief executive officer or president or the top executive of a firm doing business in Dallas. This included especially the city's leading bankers, insurancemen, manufacturers, merchants, and the publishers of the daily newspapers. It largely excluded professional people such as lawyers, doctors, and teachers, as well as labor leaders and citizens without portfolio. The inclusion of the newspaper publishers into the inner circle—and their willingness to join it—meant that the city's media would wholeheartedly support approved projects or goals for the city. Since both the *News* and the *Times Herald* owned radio stations (and ultimately television stations), this was important in giving these projects a sense of widespread support. A twenty-two member board of directors was formed, including the same triumvirate of influential bankers who had led the Centennial effort, Thornton, Adams, and Florence. No more exclusive, influential organization ever had been formed in the city's history.

In decades to come the Citizens Council, with bankers always prominent, working quietly behind the scenes, endeavored to ensure progress for Dallas by putting its money and muscle behind the projects it deemed important for the city. While the organization had no official powers, it exercised far more influence over municipal and civic affairs than the elected city council, but without the publicity. While it abstained from endorsing political candidates or ostensibly from becoming involved in politics, much of its membership duplicated that of the Citizens Charter Association. The CCA inevitably, and with justification because of its less prestigious status, came to be identified as the political arm of the Citizens Council.

Not until 1963 with the assassination of President Kennedy would the Citizens Council become widely recognized as a dominant force. This occurred when outside journalists began to examine the manner in which the city functioned. Much of their attention was critical of the Citizens Council's insular nature and its failure to include all parts of Dallas in its decision-making. Yet, the Citizens Council had never sought to be representative of the citizens. It was the kind of organization Thornton had envisioned—a group of powerful men who had the authority to put not just their own stamp of approval on projects but that of the business organizations they headed as well. In that goal its success was undeniable.

9

Jim Crow Holds Its Grip

There is a strange quality in the attitude of Dallas towards the appointment of Negro police officers.
--Dallas Express, 1939

Discrimination--By Law and By Practice

Life for the nearly 50,000 black residents of Dallas did not differ markedly these years from life for those in most Southern cities or, for that matter, in many cities in the nation. One may safely generalize that these minority citizens, about 16 percent of Dallas' population, worked hard to better their economic situations, believed in and expressed a need for self-improvement and education, centered many of their activities around approximately 130 churches, and promoted especially the positive values of happy, strong family life. Although segregation, discrimination, and chronic depressed economic status were staples of their existence, they bore these burdens with patience. They believed that as they worked and studied to prove their worthiness, segregated barriers gradually would be removed and they would slowly enter the mainstream of society.

These days, their complaints about discrimination continued to center around the failure to provide equal facilities rather than the maintenance of strict segregationist policies.

Unfortunately, since the turn of the century discrimination in the South had increased rather than decreased. Community after community had adopted "Jim Crow" laws drawing rigid segregationist lines for residential neighborhoods, schools, transportation facilities, restaurants, stores, and public facilities. Dallas had followed the same pattern.

Negro neighborhoods were not confined to any one section. They existed in small but densely populated pockets scattered throughout town: parts of South Dallas, the east side of Love Field, adjacent to the levee in Oak Cliff, Deep Ellum, and the State Street-Thomas Avenue area off of Hall Street. Deep Ellum and Hall Street thrived especially as centers of business and entertainment. The State Street-Thomas Avenue area, while surrounded by row houses and alley courts, was a neighborhood just north of downtown where handsome Victorian houses with expansive front porches were pleasantly situated. It was the finest of the residential areas. (It later would be designated a historical district.)

Negro housing, inadequate and in short supply, had been strictly segregated by a city ordinance adopted in 1916 and re-affirmed in a series of ordinances in the 1920s that specified individual residential blocks as either white or colored. The last of these ordinances, passed in 1927, was reaffirmed by the 1931 charter election. While it was clear that these ordinances already had been found unconstitutional, the boundaries between black and white neighborhoods now were being enforced as social custom rather than law. On at least one South Dallas street a tall, solid, wooden fence defined the line between the black and white sectors. Tensions inevitably arose as Negro families, growing in numbers, could not find sufficient housing within designated areas and spilled over into "white" areas.

Segregation in other areas of life was just as severe. Dallas parks became segregated in 1915 when the park board voted to create two specific facilities for Negroes, Oak Cliff Negro Park at Sabine and Cliff streets and Hall Street Negro Park (later named Griggs Park). A glaring inequity now existed: less than thirty of the 4,000 acres in the park system were designated for Negroes. "Jim Crow" streetcars kept the races separated, with blacks relegated to the rear. Dallas schools always had been segregated. By the 1930s the one Negro high school, named Booker T. Washington after being moved to Flora Street in 1922, served all black students even though they had to travel from all parts of town to get there. So crowded was the school that double sessions began in 1931, and by 1938 the school's 700-student capacity was being sorely taxed by some 2,100 students.

Restrooms and water fountains designated as "white only" and "colored" confronted visitors to public buildings and large stores. Restaurants either refused to serve Negroes, had separate rooms for them at the back, or sold them meals "to go" only. Black customers usually were prohibited from trying on garments at clothing stores. The Democratic Party's "all-white" primaries kept Negroes out of state politics. Those who did profess a political allegiance continued to support the party of Abraham Lincoln, but in Dallas and throughout the South the miniscule Republican Party had no impact in county or state politics. Improvements such as street pavings, electric lights, and sewage lines usually came to Negro neighborhoods only after committees of black leaders called upon the city fathers with specific requests and their hats in hand.

TWO LEADERS: SMITH AND JACKSON

But the mid-1930s saw a different mood surfacing in the black community of Dallas. Negro leaders began displaying a more aggressive stance. This came, to be sure, partially as a result of changing times throughout the nation as reflected by New Deal politics, but in Dallas it came specifically because of the energy of two youthful, well-educated, ambitious men who happened to arrive in the same year, 1933, to assume positions of influence. Both were native Texans—one had grown up in the city and retained strong family and religious ties—and the other had grown up in Texarkana. Both of the men formerly had lived in the East; neither now was willing to accept the subservient position of the Negro in the South. Together these two, Antonio Maceo Smith, a businessman with a penchant for organization, and the Rev. Maynard H. Jackson of New Hope Baptist Church, created a host of new and intertwined coalitions to strive for economic, political, and social improvements.

Smith's career in the city was to be the longer one; he was

destined to become over the next four decades Dallas' most effective activist in advancing the Negro cause. He was also the spearhead for state-wide NAACP activities. Jackson, after two decades in the city, would move in the 1950s to Atlanta, Georgia.

Smith, born the fourteenth child of a Texarkana, Texas, couple on April 16, 1903, graduated in 1924 from Fisk University in Nashville, Tennessee, then went East to obtain in 1928 a master of business administration degree from New York University while working part-time as a red cap at Grand Central Station. Upon graduation he organized a small advertising agency and began publishing a weekly newspaper. He intended to make his career in New York, seeing opportunities for advancement far beyond what seemed possible in his native South. When his father died he returned to Texarkana, intending to stay no more than three weeks. Conditions in Texarkana seemed so intolerable for black citizens, however, that he determined to take off his "New York clothes" and stay awhile to see what he could do to improve the situation.

In Texarkana he became co-owner of a realty company and organized a local chapter of the National Negro Business League. A few years later he moved to Oklahoma City to serve as general agent for a life insurance company. There he also re-vitalized the National Negro Business League chapter. In 1932 a Negro Dallas undertaker, E.J. Crawford, went to Oklahoma City and hired Smith to come to Dallas and help him organize a new insurance company and manage a burial association.

Smith arrived in Dallas ready for work on January 1, 1933. He quickly joined the nearly moribund Negro Chamber of Commerce association, and with his experience in organizational work became executive secretary that same year. He immediately began to transform the Chamber, which had been founded in November 1926 as a splinter group from the National Negro Business League chapter, into a vital force in the city in promoting economic opportunities for local Negroes.

Smith initiated a program of activities designed to encourage Negro businessmen whose enterprises, frequently undercapitalized, usually lasted less than a decade before vanishing. These businesses typically consisted of "mom and pop" grocery stores, taverns, barber and beauty shops, and small restaurants. Letters of introduction to Dallas Chamber of Commerce executive secretary

Ben Critz had preceded Smith to Dallas, and he quickly developed a working relationship with Critz.

Smith became secretary of the Dallas NAACP branch and of the Progressive Voters League. In these positions he concentrated on political advancement of Negroes and civil rights. In all his endeavors he moved naturally and easily into state-wide organizational activities. Under his leadership the Dallas branch of the NAACP was recognized as the most active one in the entire state.

The man who almost immediately became Smith's partner in many of these and other ventures, the Rev. Maynard H. Jackson, returned to his native Dallas in 1933 to take over ministerial duties at New Hope Baptist Church from his father, the Rev. Alexander Jackson, who had been pastor there since 1899. Maynard Jackson, born May 3, 1894, in New Orleans, spent his formative years in Dallas, and completed studies at the Negro high school in 1911. He graduated from Morehouse College in 1914, then earned a bachelor of divinity degree from Northwestern University's school of theology. Jackson worked as a field secretary for the Baptist Church's Foreign Missionary Board, headquartered in Philadelphia, and he also went to Africa for a while to oversee missionaries there. When his father retired after so many years' service he was called to Dallas to succeed him. He affiliated right away, as had Smith, with the Negro Chamber of Commerce, and he was elected first president of the Progressive Voters League. Later, he would be the first black candidate to run for the Dallas school board.

The Hall of Negro Life

In 1934, with news of the forthcoming Texas Centennial Exposition, Smith saw a special opportunity for Negro advancement. He called a meeting of the Chamber and persuaded members to vote their full support for the city's goal of becoming the official site. Smith's mind soon raced on to another idea. Why not sponsor an exhibition at the Centennial showing the progress of Negro life in the state? Smith, again winning the support of the Chamber as well as other Negro leaders throughout the state, decided to seek funds for such an exhibit. He and a few others gathered as many historical photographs as they could depicting Negro life, and took them to

Austin to request a $100,000 appropriation from a joint legislative committee. Smith's forty-five minute talk was warmly received, and he left feeling assured that a state grant would be forthcoming.

The situation was complicated when Governor James Allred appointed in 1935 a young Texas legislator named Sarah T. Hughes of Dallas to preside over the 14th District Court. A special election was called to select her successor, and a Negro candidate, Ammon S. Wells, was one of sixty-five candidates who filed for the office. Smith and Maynard Jackson served as Wells' campaign managers. The idea that a Negro should run for public office in Dallas was a novel one. Smith and Jackson found themselves called before two or three well-known Dallas leaders. The civic leaders demanded that they withdraw their man from the race, arguing that his candidacy would stir up trouble and worsen race relations. If Wells would withdraw, Smith and Jackson were told, the $100,000 appropriation from the legislature for the Centennial would be secure. Otherwise, they could expect nothing. They refused to yield to the pressure. Wells went on to finish fifth in the large field of candidates. And as had been intimidated, the seemingly assured $100,000 appropriation was denied. (Years later, in recalling the meeting with the civic leaders, Smith refused to identify them.)

Efforts to obtain the needed financial assistance from the City of Dallas failed as well, but Vice President John Nance Garner used his influence to see that the federal government's grant to the Centennial included $100,000 earmarked for the Negro project. The money was awarded just ninety days before the Centennial was to open.

Smith and others involved were able in this short time to organize extensive exhibits showing Negro advancements in education, health, aesthetics, agriculture, mechanical arts, business, religion, and many other fields. They were displayed in a handsome, modernistic, 10,000-square-foot facility called the Hall of Negro Life. A mural in the lobby, painted by Aaron Douglas, portrayed the transition of Negroes from slavery to the present.

Jesse O. Thomas was manager of the facility, and Smith took the position of assistant manager. Thomas later wrote that "this was the first time in the history of America the Negro was given as much freedom in planning his own participation in connection with a state celebration comparable to the Texas Centennial."

The exhibit's official opening was on June 19th, or "Juneteenth," annually celebrated by Texas Negroes as their day of freedom from slavery. On this occasion the city's first interracial track meet was held on the Centennial grounds, with white and black high school and college athletes competing. Another special event that day was the appearance of Negro entertainer Cab Calloway in the bandshell.

Overall, the success of the Hall of Negro Life seemed to be a happy harbinger for improved race relations ahead. More than 400,000 persons toured the building during the Centennial, and 60 percent of them were white. Most of them, Thomas proudly pointed out, used the building's restrooms without signs of reluctance or discomfort. This, he claimed, demonstrated the growing acceptance by white persons of Negroes as equals.

The accomplishment of the Hall of Negro Life, notwithstanding the difficulties encountered in gaining the appropriation, was not without its demoralizing aspects. While the handsome structure was first-rate in appearance, Thomas and others protested when Centennial officials, evidently with premeditation, positioned large shrubberies that obscured the building from casual passers-by. Not until mid-October did the Negroes succeed in having the offending shrubbery removed. While Negroes were welcomed to the Centennial itself on all days, restrooms were not provided for them. Many concessionaires refused to serve them food and drinks. A number of them even put up signs, "For Whites Only." Some exhibits prohibited Negroes from attending. Smith recalled that on a special Centennial day for Negroes an ice show closed its doors because its operators did not want their scantily-clad female skaters to expose their bodies to black men. These practices caused Thomas and others to send numerous letters and to make frequent telephone calls to Centennial General Manager W.A. Webb asking for a policy statement on such matters. Webb never responded.

Meanwhile, however, the Hall of Negro Life proved useful in a far more significant way. Smith's energetic effort to involve Negroes from throughout the state in the project and their ensuing visits inspired the creation of several organizations to promote the Negro cause. Through discussions concerning the Hall of Negro Life, Smith was largely responsible for founding the Texas National Association for the Advancement of Colored People. Individual branches of the NAACP in towns throughout the state also were organized at the Hall of Negro Life. Two other related outgrowths of the project were the formation of the Texas Negro Chamber of Commerce and the Progressive Voters League in Dallas.

Overall, so pleased were Negro sponsors that they expected to continue their exhibit for the following year's Greater Texas and Pan American Exposition. But they were denied this opportunity in callous fashion after some local citizens protested to the Dallas Centennial Commission that the Hall of Negro Life would be out of harmony with the spirit of the new event. The commission announced plans to dismantle the building, explaining that the space was needed for other purposes. Frantic appeals to reverse this decision failed. Dallas Mayor George Sergeant sought to save the Hall of Negro Life. He wired Senator Morris Sheppard in Washington, D.C., for his help. But the effort failed. The building was torn down. It was the only exhibit denied the right to extend from the Centennial into the 1937 exposition. The space where it once stood remained vacant. (In 1993 the Museum of African-American Life & Culture opened as a permanent structure on almost the precise location of the old Hall of Negro Life.)

Exercising the Vote

In January 1936 Smith, in his capacity with the Negro Chamber of Commerce, began a broad survey of the potential voting strengths of Negroes in Dallas. The *Express* called it "one of the most significant drives in the history of Dallas and the State of Texas." The survey was followed that year by a registration drive sponsored by the Ministers Alliance, an organization of Negro pastors headed by Maynard Jackson, which encouraged black citizens to pay their $1.75 poll taxes. All this activity, shared with the Negro Chamber of Commerce's efforts, culminated in the fall in the formation of the Progressive Voters League, an organization representing fifty-two Negro civic and social organizations. Maynard Jackson was elected president of the organization; A. Maceo Smith was secretary; an undertaker, A.A. Braswell, was treasurer. As the end of the year the Progressive Voters League announced yet another voter registration drive for 1937 with the target of qualifying 10,000 Negro voters. Its announced goals were to secure a second Negro high school, win approval for the hiring of Negro policemen and letter carriers, obtain more paved streets for Negro neighborhoods, achieve relief in the crowded elementary schools, have more and better parks, install adequate street lighting, and obtain more opportunity for employment in all branches of city government.

The League also initiated a petition calling for greater police protection in Negro neighborhoods, decrying a recent series of black-on-black murders. This, the petition stated, demonstrated the need for hiring Negro police officers. The district attorney's office, generally nonchalant about crime in black neighborhoods, was implored to prosecute Negro criminals aggressively. Juries typically were reluctant as well to treat crime in black communities as seriously as in the white community. For instance, when a twenty-five-year-old Negro man murdered his sweetheart while the two stood waiting for a streetcar, the district attorney asked the jury to assess the death penalty. The jury returned a verdict of two years.

Having no chance of electing candidates of their own race to public office, yet eager to encourage political participation, the Negro Chamber of Commerce sponsored its own election in early 1937 for the "Mayor of Negro Dallas." Braswell, treasurer of the Progressive Voters League and operator of Crawford Undertaking Co., won the election on a platform stressing small-business development. Braswell had come to Dallas in 1935 from Knoxville, Tennessee. He would be succeeded next year by a physician, Dr. E.E. Ward, but in 1939 Braswell was to be re-elected to the office whose occupant by then was known as the "Bronze Mayor of Dallas."

The successful push to involve Negro residents in the political process soon was rewarded. The opportunity came in the acrimonious and wide-open April 1937 municipal election, characterized by a multitude of slates and candidates. The Citizens Civic Association, which had ousted the CCA from power in 1935, already had dissolved, its members aligning with CCA or the new Forward Dallas party. By the March 6 filing deadline three other slates had announced candidates, the Utility Rate Reduction League, All-Dallas Association, and the Dallas Democratic Association.

During this intense competition for support, the *Dallas Journal* reported the surprising presence of a large, uncommitted bloc of registered voters. The Progressive Voters League and Negro Chamber of Commerce drive had persuaded some 5,000 Negro voters to pay their poll taxes. "This created quite a stir," Maceo Smith later recalled, for these numbers represented about one-sixth of the city's entire voting strength. Here was a new power to be reckoned with—the largest single bloc of voters in the city.

Council candidates began immediately to call on the League offices in the Crawford Building, seeking endorsements. The PVL, suddenly in a position of power, set up a series of interviews for candidates to state their cases. For these interviews the League prepared a questionnaire. Would the candidates, if elected, support the League's program? Its five points were: (1) Negro police officers, (2) a low-cost public housing program, (3) a new recreation center to be administered by blacks, (4) a second high school for Negroes, and (5) increased employment opportunities in municipal government. All candidates of the two leading slates, the Citizens Charter Association and the new Forward Dallas Association, endorsed the entire PVL platform. (During the campaign the Forward Dallas Association accused the CCA of being a "silk stocking" group; the CCA charged Forward Dallas candidates as being friendly to the vice interests.)

The major daily newspapers endorsed the CCA candidates, but the Progressive Voters League chose to support the Forward Dallas Association, which was less closely tied to the downtown business leadership. Negro voters accordingly cast their ballots overwhelmingly for Forward Dallas candidates. When the election and ensuing run-off campaign ended, the Forward Dallas candidates had won five of the nine council seats. One of their candidates, George Sprague, the father of two popular Southern Methodist University football players, led in popular votes and was chosen mayor. Former mayor Sergeant was re-elected to a council seat.

"For the first time in the history of the South, the Negroes voted as a block to turn the tide," reported the *Dallas Express*. The payoff was not long in coming. Within weeks City Manager Hal Moseley announced that Negro policemen would be hired at the same salary as white officers as soon as the Civil Service Board could hold examinations. (More than seventy-five Negroes applied for the examinations.) Within three months an announcement was made that a new Negro high school would be constructed in South Dallas, more convenient to a growing number of black residents who lived far from Booker T. Washington High School. (This was to be Lincoln High School, constructed at a cost of $416,000 and opened in January

1939.) The Park Board said that it would purchase land for two or more new parks for black citizens to use. Before the year was out came the announcement that a new community house and recreation center would be built at Wahoo Park in Southeast Dallas. The *Express*, reflecting on these developments, observed that while streets in their neighborhoods still needed improvements, Negro residents soon could say truthfully, "It's a privilege to live in Dallas."

In June 1937, primarily because of Smith's energy and vision, NAACP delegates from five branches in the state came to Dallas for a state conference. Delegates stressed the need to overturn white primaries and to create better educational opportunities. Smith was elected secretary.

THE EXPRESS PUSHES FOR HOUSING

These and other matters relevant to the Negro community were being fully reported in the weekly newspaper which billed itself as "The South's Oldest and Largest Negro Newspaper," the *Dallas Express*. Its quality indeed was excellent. W.E. King founded the *Express* in 1892, and he operated it until his death in 1919. In the 1930s the newspaper's page-one nameplate showed a fast-moving locomotive, meant to symbolize the progress of Negroes. A promotional slogan proclaimed the newspaper "A Champion of Race Development." A large portion of the activities reported by the *Express* emanated from the Negro Chamber of Commerce, the Progressive Voters League, the Moorland Branch of the YMCA (where the PVL had been formed), Booker T. Washington High School (which was graduating more than 200 seniors each year), and local churches—especially New Hope Baptist.

The *Express* provided more than just local news; it carried personal columns filled with names of people from correspondents in small towns throughout the state. It also prominently featured national news relevant to its readers, never neglecting reports of racial injustices, mob violence, and lynchings. Its advertising columns mostly contained small notices from local Negro businesses, although the largest advertiser by far during these years was the white-owned-and-operated Hart Furniture Store. The Southwestern Negro Press was listed as the newspaper's publisher, but the company was controlled by whites who had owned the newspaper since 1930 when it encountered financial difficulties.

In February 1938 Smith, Jackson, and three other prominent black leaders purchased the newspaper from the white ownership. Joining Smith and Jackson as new owners were Dr. E.E. Ward, now the "Bronze Mayor of Dallas"; Henry Strickland, president of Excelsior Life Insurance Co.; and C.F. Starkes, president of Peoples Undertaking. While the *Express*, despite its former white ownership, had unabashedly and consistently championed Negro causes, the fact that blacks now owned the newspaper was cause for jubilation. The *Express* never had been timid in its coverage of controversial subjects, but the ownership change signaled a far more aggressive period for the newspaper, especially on its editorial pages where more pertinent, more vigorous, and more timely commentary began to appear regularly.

An opportunity to exercise more biting commentary presented itself soon in the controversial campaign to bring to Dallas low-cost federal housing for Negroes. The city already had one federal housing project, Cedar Springs Place, completed in 1937 for 181 families at a cost of $1,020,000 with the aid of a grant and long-term loan from the Public Works Administration. But Cedar Springs Place was strictly for low-income white families, and even it had been accomplished over the heated protests of Dallas real estate brokers.

Further public housing units were made possible in 1937 by passage of the U.S. Housing Act, which authorized the U.S. Housing Authority to buy 90 percent of the bonds issued by a municipal authority for housing projects for low-income families. As the *Express* pointed out clearly, federal housing for Negroes would represent a symbol with far greater meaning than mere shelter. "It would set up a new direction in the thinking of such people who now too often felt they were foredoomed to live in the city's alleys in close proximity to the open toilets with which Dallas is generously studded." The Negro, the editorial went on, was continually confronted by the "ugliness and filth" underlying the city's supposed beauty. "We could point to a dozen sections...which would shame any fifth-rate city."

The Dallas Housing Authority, appointed by Mayor Sprague in March 1938, was seeking a $3 million appropriation for a low-cost housing project for Negroes. Approval had to be obtained from city council, where the debate centered. While the elected councilmen had pledged to the Progressive Voters League that they favored a housing project, there remained formidable opposition. The chairman of the City Plan Commission, George Burgess, declared the idea "a lot of hooey" and drafted a resolution for the Commission to oppose the plan because it would compete with private interests. Lovell Turner, president of the Dallas Real Estate Board, warned the council that federal subsidies might "change the living habits of the American people." He also had opposed Cedar Springs Place. Councilman Willis Gunn decried trends toward socialism and complained that the federal government already was ruining many farmers and businessmen. Questions also were raised as to whether the federal housing project was actually needed. In the midst of such questions and debate, Negro sentiment became increasingly frustrated and irate.

The *Express* began a series of angry page-one editorials in scathing terms. "Are Negroes To Be Condemned to Filth?" was the title of the first. It went on to say that when the Chamber of Commerce advertises the wonders of Dallas, "nothing is said of the OPEN PRIVIES within the city limits or the HOVELS without sewerage, light or heat. The FHA survey made here in 1935 showed Dallas to be one of the sore spots of the South when it comes to housing for colored people." The *Express* vowed to highlight the abundance of slum housing until remedies were effected. Just a hundred feet off State Street, one of the black community's model streets, one could find "one of the ROTTENEST GHETTOS in America," the editorial continued. The *Express* was incredulous that some city leaders could be so naive as to request a survey to determine if federal housing actually was needed. "By all that is decent and Christian, perhaps, Kind Sirs, maybe, as it were, we might need it."

A graphic picture in the *Express* reminiscent of Jacob Riis' photos of slum housing in New York City showed two rows of crowded, tiny tenement houses separated by a dark and narrow passageway no more than five feet wide. Within this dark passageway just off Bryan Street more than 200 persons were said to live. Fifteen families shared one toilet. "This condition actually exists," the *Express* said, "while the seeming indifference of city fathers threatens to cause Dallas to lose a $3,000,000 housing and slum clearance program to eliminate these moral and health menaces from our great city."

As the moment arrived for the council's decision on housing, the *Express* said there was little else now for the Negro community to do but pray. Mayor Sprague was on record in favor of it, pre-election promises had been made to the Progressive Voters League, and the newly formed group of prominent businessmen, the Citizens Council, also had supported it. In October all council members save Sergeant and Gunn voted to approve the request for federal funds for low-cost housing. "The Council Is Humane," said the *Express* in its appreciative editorial.

Construction on the project, which would be named Roseland Homes, began in January 1941. It was followed by other low-rent housing developments such as Little Mexico Village, Washington Place, Frazier Courts, and Cedar Springs Place Addition. Roseland was completed in the summer of 1942, and the others were finished before the end of the year.

The *Express'* editorials soon broadened to include the poor quality of Negro education in public schools, the failure to pay Negro teachers on the same basis as white ones, the need for higher standards in the classroom, and the lack of proper equipment and supplies. "We want the superintendent of schools to give a typewriter to a school office without a petition from all the Negroes in town," the *Express* observed sarcastically. Readers were encouraged to send copies of the editorial to the school superintendent. The *Express* sent him two.

A Move to Hire Black Officers

Negroes found reason for optimism that summer through one of the more sensational crimes in the city's annals. Headlines described how Highland Park police rescued a beaten, hungry, blindfolded and bound Negro man from the attic of a prominent couple's home in exclusive Highland Park. The man, twenty-four-year-old Mickey Ricketts, was the former yardman for the couple, Dr. F.H. and Cosette Faust Newton. The Newtons had beaten and bound him to coerce a confession for allegedly stealing several valuable rings from their house at 4005 Miramar. Highland Park police took Ricketts, who had been held for five days, to a hospital where he was treated for injuries from the beating and for malnutrition. The Newtons were arrested on charges of false imprisonment, beating, starving, kicking, and threatening. Dr. Newton's brother, a private investigator, and two other Negro servants were also implicated and arrested. The Newton couple were released on $10,000 bond; the others on lesser amounts. "One of the surprising aspects of the case," wrote the *Express*, "has been the apparent disposition of the law to bring to justice white citizens of influence and wealth whose alleged infractions of the law involved a Negro."

A week later Cosette Faust Newton, the private investigator, and two of the Newton Negro servants were indicted for false imprisonment, a misdemeanor. In a sympathetic feature story appearing in the *News*, Cosette Faust Newton was identified as an educator, traveler, and lecturer. She said one of the rings was a priceless jade given to her by a Chinese princess. Loss of the ring, she said, was "greater than death."

Before the criminal case could be tried, Ricketts sued the couple in a civil suit for $57,300. The matter was settled out of court when Mrs. Newton paid him $400. Afterwards, the criminal misdemeanor charges were dropped. (Cosette Faust Newton, who claimed to have earned a Ph.D. from Harvard at age nineteen and also a law degree from the University of Chicago, later would emerge as one of Dallas' most eccentric characters. In 1941 she and her husband constructed in their back yard a huge replica of a boat containing three decks and a ballroom. The boat, dubbed the "S.S. Miramar," proved to be an irritant to neighbors, who complained that it violated city zoning ordinances. By the 1950s the boat had become dilapidated and subject to vandalism. Still, Mrs. Newton stubbornly insisted on her right to maintain the now unsightly structure. When a suit was filed to make her comply with the zoning ordinances she defiantly put a "For Sale" sign on her house with the stipulation that it could be sold only to Negroes. As a result, on two separate occasions flaming crosses were placed in her front yard at night by anonymous persons. The legal dispute between Mrs. Newton and the City of Highland Park was not resolved until 1956 when the Texas Supreme Court ordered the structure razed.)

While City Manager Moseley and the city council had announced a plan to hire Negro police officers, its accomplishment had been stalled. Some seventy-five Negroes applied for the civil service examinations, but a Dallas lumber dealer obtained a temporary injunction in state court to prevent civil service examinations being given for special groups. He claimed that hiring Negro officers would incite riots.

By 1939 there still were no black officers in Dallas, a fact that continued to irritate Negro leaders such as Smith and Jackson. The *Express* editorialized two weeks before examinations were scheduled for mid-March 1939 to qualify Negro officers that practically every Southern city with the exception of Dallas by then had two or more black officers serving in Negro neighborhoods. "Negroes are interested in this project purely as a crime reduction measure," the editorial stated. Six months later there still were no black policemen on the Dallas force. "Dallas Stands Alone on Negro Police," the *Express* headlined an editorial, stating that Beaumont, Galveston, Houston, Austin, San Antonio, and other Texas cities already had black officers. "There is a strange quality in the attitude of Dallas towards the appointment of Negro police officers," the newspaper said.

Despite such discouragements, Smith, Jackson, and others continued to work together in the years ahead through the Progressive Voters League, the Negro Chamber of Commerce, and other black organizations to create opportunities and equality for blacks in the city.

Smith served as the chamber's executive secretary until 1939, then held other offices, including the presidency. His well-composed, thoughtful letters to influential individuals and organizations contained specific requests and recommendations on such matters as employment opportunities and park and street improvements. In 1939 he was named regional racial adviser for the U.S. Housing Authority for a six-state area, a position which gave him a travel budget and prompted him to use the authority of his office to further the goals of the NAACP and to work extensively on its organization. The following year he became regional vice president of the National Negro Business League. In 1942 he became president of the Texas Negro Chamber of Commerce, a position he held for a number of years, and in 1943 he assumed the presidency of the Dallas Negro Chamber of Commerce.

Jackson succeeded Smith as executive secretary of the Negro Chamber of Commerce, and continued as pastor at New Hope Baptist. He was just as diligent as his predecessor in corresponding with influential individuals and agencies in behalf of Negro opportunity and advancement. Through his family he set an example by stressing the need for education and seeing all six of his children earn advanced college degrees. In 1954 Maynard assumed the pastorship of a prominent Baptist church in Atlanta, Georgia. His son, Maynard, born in Dallas in 1938, was to become Atlanta's first black mayor and its youngest ever.

CCA RETURNS TO POWER

Affairs at city hall continued to be hectic. There had been some question after the 1937 election as to whether City Manager Moseley would retain his job. A group called the Legion of Honor, led by former Catfish clubber Jim Railton, determined to see Moseley fired, evidently because he had refused to name Railton as police chief in 1935. The Legion of Honor had waivered between supporting the CCA and Forward Dallas, then had thrown its support to the latter group. With the 5-4 margin gained in the election by Forward Dallas, it was felt that Moseley would be replaced. Mayor Sprague, though, elected as part of the Forward Dallas slate, determined to be a compromiser during his term. He sided with the four CCA councilmen, and Moseley was retained. In a spirit of compromise he and the majority of the council agreed to appoint Railton to the park board.

Railton, still not appeased because of his snub over the police chief's job, in early 1938 sought to organize a movement to abolish the council-manager form of government. He prepared petitions for four charter amendments to create a scheme of city government more comparable to the commission form. These amendments provided for a full-time mayor with an annual salary of $7,500; six councilmen who would be paid $2,400 annually; an elected park board; and a clarification of city purchasing procedures. The movement died when Railton and others could not secure enough signatures to force the election.

Railton's headline-making days were not finished. From this point, however, they were to be even more negative. In December 1938 rumors circulated about improprieties on the park board concerning Railton and Harry E. Gordon, a defeated Forward Dallas council candidate who like Railton had been named to the board. The allegations, spurred by an investigation by park board member George A. Ripley, involved payoffs from contractors, diversion of park-owned materials for personal use, and sale of public properties for private gain. City council members asked Ripley to present a full report of his inquiry to a combined council-park board meeting in January 1939.

These events earned bold page-one headlines in the city's newspapers. They so stirred emotions that Ripley feared for his own safety, and he requested and received protection from the Texas Rangers for the meeting. Just before it got under way in the crowded council chambers, where some 300 spectators had gathered, the Rangers searched Railton and Gordon for weapons. Ripley charged that Gordon's home had been extensively repaired and remodeled by Park Department employees using Park Department materials. Affidavits and testimony from Park Department employees corroborated his charges. Ripley promised more revelations as he continued his investigation.

At the January 21, 1939, meeting, held again in crowded chambers and with Texas Rangers there once more to protect him, Ripley detailed astounding charges concerning payoffs from contractors, fixed specifications, nepotism, and illegal sales of city property. He also said that Railton had ordered a load of Park Department sod to be delivered to the home of the chairman of the Legion of Honor, and that an employee had collected rent from city-owned houses and kept the money for himself. Railton and Gordon denied these and other charges and called the city council a "kangaroo court." Railton demanded that the charges be presented to the grand jury. He became so enraged during the meeting at one point that he shouted "liar" at witness Al Simpson, who admitted participating in the illegal schemes.The Rangers had to restrain Railton from attacking the witness.

Finally, after some machinations, both Railton and Gordon were removed from the park board while protesting their innocence. A number of Park Department employees were fired, and in March 1939 the Dallas County grand jury indicted Railton, Gordon, and three employees. Railton was sentenced to two years in prison and assessed a $500 fine. Gordon was not convicted, but his career as a certified public accountant was ruined. The other three were given minor sentences. Mayor Sprague declined to fill their vacancies, saying, "We have already made too many mistakes." On the following day he suggested that the Park Department's separate public works staff be merged with the city's public works department.

Because of these scandals many of the city's leading businessmen as well as others became convinced that a thorough shake-up was needed in municipal government. The chance to achieve this lay immediately ahead in the April 1939 election.

The Citizens Charter Association, encouraged by what seemed to be a fortuitous opportunity to re-gain control of the city council, nominated a slate of businessmen whose collective prestige was the highest since 1931. They campaigned with no apology for the fact that they were "nine businessmen." As CCA president R.L. Thomas said, "Dallas voters are tired of politics instead of business methods at city hall." Both major newspapers fully supported the slate.

With the demise of the Forward Dallas Association, a new party combined of its remnants and parts of the old Civic Association emerged—the Citizens' Nonpartisan Association. Its avowed purpose was to "clean up city hall," and its leaders argued that if the CCA candidates were elected the "bankers will get a stronghold on city hall." A third party, the Progressive Civic Association, advocated a return of city government to the people; its leader was Tony Brignardello. As the Legion of Honor member upon whose yard the Park Department sod had been so controversially deposited, Brignardello's candidates faced an uphill struggle for voters support.

"This is an emergency," insisted the *News* in an editorial. "The good name of Dallas has been dragged in the mud," it said in reference to the park board scandal. The newspaper, as well as the *Times Herald*, enthusiastically endorsed the entire CCA slate. The theme was reminiscent of 1931—"Not a single [CCA] man sought the office. Most were unwilling to make the race. All were carefully selected."

The campaign, a lengthy one that started early in the year, was described as one of "slander and villification." Thirty-three candidates vied for the nine council seats, making the prospects of a run-off high. However, the CCA slate easily won all nine seats, generally winning twice as many votes in each race as the other candidates combined. Incumbent Mayor George A. Sprague sought re-election as an independent, but he finished third in his race. Nonpartisan

Association candidates were a distant second in all races.

Businessman Ben E. Cabell Jr., who several years earlier had started a dairy with his brother Earle, led all candidates. This, according to recent tradition, gave him an indirect right to be mayor, and it was speculated in the newspapers that he was the favorite. Another precedent also could be cited—both Cabell's father and grandfather had been mayors of Dallas. Instead of electing Ben Cabell mayor, though, council members chose J. Woodall Rodgers, a lawyer. He was to hold the office for four terms throughout the coming world war. Cabell swallowed but did not forget his hurt.

10

Brilliant In Achievement

There is no north Dallas because of the Park Cities on the north drawing the blood from the heart of Dallas. This is an anemic situation.

—J. Woodall Rodgers, 1944

On the Eve of the War

Between the 1936 Centennial triumph and Pearl Harbor, Dallas adopted a favorite symbol that overflowed with raw energy. It was a dazzling night-time photograph of downtown Dallas, a horizontal view showing the heavy concentration of towering buildings—their windows brightly lit—up and down Main, Elm, and Commerce streets. Not a wisp of smoke or fumes obscured the view; the city's use of natural gas assured at almost all times a crisp, unfettered skyline. The photograph's title, "Dallas: Brilliant in Achievement," aptly summed up the city's confident mood. The confidence seemed well-placed, and the photograph was reprinted widely in promotional materials.

The thousands who came for the Centennial created a new and

permanent level of visitor activity that was immediately about 50 percent higher than before. In the year preceding the Centennial, 85,400 convention-goers had come to Dallas; in 1939 the figure was approximately 122,000. Dallas would never relinquish its new status as one of the nation's favorite sites for conventions.

In the summer of 1940 came an announcement that the Dallas area had been chosen for "the greatest industrial development in the history of Texas." North American Aviation of Inglewood, California, would build a $7 million plant for the emerging national defense program employing more than 12,000 workers. Twin-engined bombers and other aircraft would be built at a facility in Grand Prairie at the edge of Mountain Creek Lake. North American would be "far and away the biggest single industry in the state." Dallas' location in the center of the continent would rule out surprise enemy air attack, but the availability of an adjacent military airfield, owned by the City of Dallas but leased to the Navy, also had been an important factor--a reward from the city's emphasis on aviation.

The number of manufacturing jobs in the city was growing rapidly. It would reach 75,600 by 1944, a figure that would increase over the next years at an average of 7,000 jobs annually until 1970.

One of the key employers, Ford Motor Company, which had started assembling Fords in Dallas before the First World War, now revealed plans for a $450,000 expansion of the assembly plant it had built on East Grand Avenue in 1925. The East Grand plant had replaced the facility built on the edge of downtown in 1914.

Robert L. Thornton realized a long-term dream in March 1941 when he announced that Mercantile National Bank would construct its own skyscraper at the site of the old post office at Main and Ervay. It would be the city's tallest building, thirty stories, higher than the Magnolia Building, where the bank had been located for a number of years. The structure would be of masonry, the last such major skyscraper to go up in Dallas.

Thornton's building would be air-conditioned, of course. This had come to be expected for all new buildings constructed in Dallas since the mid-1930s. Even residential dwellings these days were being cooled by refrigerated air. The air-conditioning industry in Dallas was so significant that the Chamber of Commerce magazine devoted an entire issue to it in April 1938.

Another harbinger of the future came in 1941 when Sanger Bros.

became the first Dallas department store to open a suburban branch. The site was the Highland Park Village, which when it had opened in 1931 was the nation's first planned, single-owner off-street shopping center. Sanger's move signaled the beginning of a trend that would become especially pronounced after the war. (By the late 1980s not a single department store would remain downtown.)

The year 1941 also marked the hundredth anniversary of the time when John Neely Bryan had settled on the bank of the Trinity. Talk of a full-fledged city centennial celebration died down because of the somber international situation, as did the idea of constructing a downtown civic auditorium to commemorate the occasion, but the chairman of the centennial committee declared 1941 "an unforgettable milestone." He elaborated: "The city's retail stores are famous. Dallas is known far and wide as an oil center, a key industrial district, an aviation capital, fourth ranking insurance town in the United States. Can you think of any other place where so much has been achieved in such a relatively short period?"

NEW COUNCIL, NEW CITY MANAGER

At city hall the new CCA council asserted itself right away. Woodall Rodgers announced on WFAA radio three special goals: elimination of algae from the water supply, realization of Central Boulevard as a complete cross-city thoroughfare, and preparation of a master plan.

Another goal was to avoid the public controversies that had beset the council and city government during the 1930s. George B. Dealey, despite his interests in reporting the news, recommended to Rodgers on the day after his election that the council should avoid public family quarrels by meeting privately, away from the press, for an hour or so before the public meeting. Rodgers thus initiated a luncheon before each council meeting at a downtown club so that the city manager's recommendations could be heard privately and issues could be discussed away from the public's scrutiny. The council thus began a practice that would be of long duration. Rodgers, at the end of his four terms, would say that the luncheon meetings removed the temptation to use the council as a forum for cheap publicity, politics or debate. It also deprived the public of its right to see public business conducted openly and discussed freely, although no official votes were taken at these briefings.

The new regime's first major step was to replace Hal Moseley with a new and youthful city manager, James W. Aston. Although only twenty-seven years of age, Aston was a veteran of city affairs from the lowest level. As a student at A&M he had decided upon a career in municipal government after being inspired by Lincoln Steffens' muckraking exposes of corruption in cities. During one summer break from Texas A&M, Aston had worked as a laborer on the Commerce Street bridge. Upon graduation he wrote to City Manager Charles Edy to request a job in his new administration. Edy, initially negative, changed his mind after the persistent Aston offered to work without pay. Edy, who was to create a corps of promising youthful administrators, hired Aston at a token salary as the first apprentice city manager in the nation. When Edy lost his own job four years later, his successor, Moseley, asked Aston—despite his known closeness to Edy—to remain as assistant city manager. Aston later explained, "There wasn't anybody in the city hall at that time that knew as much about all facets of city government as I did. There were 1,800 employees. I had ridden garbage trucks. I had lived in fire stations." Working with Moseley turned out to be as positive an experience for Aston as it had been with Edy. But early in 1939, eager to gain experience as a city administrator in his own right, Aston accepted an offer from the City of Bryan to be its city manager. After only a few weeks there, Rodgers asked him to return to Dallas to replace Moseley. Aston accepted, becoming the youngest known city manager in the nation for a city of similar size.

Over the next five months Aston substantially overhauled city hall. He replaced top administrators, including the city judge, public utilities supervisor, public works director, police chief, and welfare director. When the director of the park department retired, another of Edy's young trainees, L.B. Houston, was promoted to that position and given unlimited authority to reorganize. Houston thus began a career in that position that continued until he retired in the 1970s.

Aston's first crisis came after some six months when Mayor Pro Tem Ben Cabell called a special council meeting to investigate erroneous billings in the sale of municipal water to Highland Park and University Park. These suburban cities regularly purchased their water from Dallas, and recently the instruments for measuring the amount of water flowing there evidently had malfunctioned and the billings had been too low. Cabell proposed to appoint a committee to investigate the water department, then to do whatever was needed to correct the situation, even to the extent of firing the water department superintendent. His motion to form such a committee gained a quick second. Before a vote could be taken Mayor Rodgers asked for comments from the city manager.

Aston, fearful of a precedent that would undermine his authority as city manager and damage the integrity of the council-manager plan, quickly spoke up. "The waterworks superintendent is my appointee," he said. "I'm responsible for him, and I'm responsible for the result. And there is not going to be a committee of this council to go into my administrative departments and make a study or a survey and determine whether or not the people are efficient or not efficient. If you vote to form this committee and investigate this department, I want the next vote to be to accept my resignation because I can't work under these circumstances." Cabell, unmoved, refused to yield. Aston remained obstinate, too, insisting that he would investigate the situation himself and report his own findings to the council. "If you don't like it, you can fire me. But you're not going to investigate my departments." Cabell reluctantly withdrew his motion, and Aston maintained his authority. The theory and practice of council-manager government in Dallas remained unsullied.

One of Rodgers' special projects, in keeping with his overall commitment to planning, was Central Boulevard. George Kessler had proposed removing the Houston & Texas Central railroad tracks at the same time he advocated removal of the T&P downtown tracks, although without the same urgency. Along the H&TC's north-south route he had urged the creation of a great thoroughfare to link both ends of the city. No progress had been made toward that goal, but the need grew more acute as the city grew. By the late 1930s Central Boulevard was recognized as one of the city's critical priorities. The Chamber of Commerce in 1937 declared that it would relieve traffic-clogged streets, wipe out blighted areas, provide a fine route through the city for U.S. Highway 75, and be a catalyst for growth.

One of the first moves of the new council and City Manager Aston in 1939 was to hire a consulting engineer, W.J. Powell, to plan the project. Next came the purchase of the downtown tracks, by then owned by Southern Pacific, which was negotiated by a Dallas delegation to the railroad's offices in Houston. Committee member R.L. Thornton won special praise by using his horse-trading skills to reduce Southern Pacific's price by $25,000. The new boulevard was planned to be seven miles long, originating in South Dallas at Holmes Street Road and U.S. 75 and extending northward to Northwest Highway. As to how it would look, Rodgers could only say in 1941 that "we don't know ourselves." An elevated road was considered for a while, but this idea was discarded. It was known that a 180-foot right of way would be required and that all cross streets would be via underpass. The city was implementing plans slowly in cooperation with the State Highway Department, for the thoroughfare must be "serviceable for years." Many enterprising businessmen already were planning new buildings and recreational establishments along the route. Predictions were made that new homes would be constructed in areas made accessible by the boulevard. "The boulevard will definitely be a boon to the real estate in its vicinity, and, of course, we are glad of this," Rodgers wrote in 1941.

Racial Tension Emerges

Amid such concern for the city's proper physical development, however, racial problems continued to brew, especially in South Dallas. The black community's success in gaining Lincoln High School was marred by new tensions arising in the transitional neighborhood where it had been placed. In this area just east of Hatcher Street neighborhood blocks continued to be sharply demarcated as white or black. Many whites felt threatened by the school's location in a neighborhood they considered to be their own, and they were especially disturbed that boundaries between white and black residents seemed to be blurring. Threats of bombings and other violence arose, and Lincoln High's opening in January 1939 was delayed several days as a precaution. On the morning of the planned opening day a temporary injunction was granted to keep its doors closed. Sheriff's deputies dutifully arrived and locked the doors. "We were in there looking out and the children were all around the building looked in," said a teacher, Thomas Tolbert. By noon the injunction was dissolved, doors were opened, and classes began.

But racial tension continued. The Negro population in Dallas and other Southern cities multiplied during the Depression of the 1930s as blacks were forced to leave rural areas in search of urban employment at an even faster rate than that of white farm workers. The 61,605 Negroes in Dallas in 1940 found themselves in an impossible situation. Their numbers were growing rapidly, yet there were few places for them to go without causing trouble. A 1940 study showed that 83.5 percent of Negro housing was tenant-occupied, and 80 percent of the units were judged to be "sub-standard." Virtually no new housing developments were designated for them—even for those who could afford them—and the white population still was unwilling to permit incursions into neighborhoods they considered their own. (A Dallas Housing Authority survey in 1940 found 19,620 tenant families living in substandard housing in Dallas. About half of these, or 10,096, were occupied by Anglo-Americans; 8,350 were occupied by Negroes; and the remaining few were occupied by Latin Americans.) In the fall of 1939 irate white residents in South Dallas began meeting to plan ways to stop encroachments into their neighborhoods. Of particular concern to them were black schoolchildren who were walking through white neighborhoods. City Councilman Bennett H. Stampes suggested restricting Negroes to designated streets. Aston agreed to seek a plan in cooperation with white and Negro leaders to solve this particular problem of passage, but the idea of street designations was not implemented.

Many white residents were becoming increasingly agitated by the expansion of Negroes into the South Dallas area around Oakland Avenue, Pine Street, and Eugene Street near the Oakland Cemetery. A self-appointed committee of white residents met at the Ascher Silberstein Elementary School on Pine Street to try to hold the lines. M.V. Vines, chairman of the group, said the residents wanted two Negro families moved from that area. Dennie Mitchell, one of the Negroes involved, pointed out to a reporter that he was living on property held by his family for more than fifty years. Some whites, including the Rev. John G. Moore of Colonial Baptist Church, proposed building an eight-foot concrete or brick wall to mark clearly the border betwen Negro and white neighborhoods.

What these debates signified, said the *Express*, was no less than a "little World War." The idea of forcing black families to move from their homes to satisfy white desires was declared outrageous. "Here in the world's greatest and perhaps its last democracy we cannot reasonably apply force to the removal of the men and women across the street any more than we would be willing to drop bombs on them in a totalitarian war." Necessity alone forced Negro families to secure homes wherever they were available, the *Express* wrote.

The tension lingered past 1939. A series of bombings, mysterious fires, hangings in effigy, and throwing of stones and bricks rocked the area in late 1940 and early 1941. In an effort to force removal of a Negro funeral home on Oakland Avenue, a mob of whites threw stones and broke its electrical sign. Several months later the city council eased the situation by purchasing the property for $2,100. Aston said that officials had sought for some time to preserve Oakland Avenue for whites, and that efforts still were being made to purchase at least two more Negro-occupied residences.

Two days before Christmas, 1940, dynamite shattered the front porch and front windows of a vacant house in the 2600 block of Hatcher that stood between two houses occupied by Negro families. Three months later the house next-door, occupied by a post office janitor and his family, was similarly dynamited. No one was injured. Dallas Postmaster J. Howard Payne reflected the general atititude of the period when he sought to compliment his nine-year employee by calling him a "hard-working darkey." Police assigned extra detectives to patrol the troubled neighborhood. Mayor Rodgers cited a resolution of inter-racial residential problems as his third highest priority for the new year of 1941.

The city council, trying to respond to the deteriorating situation, passed and then rescinded another segregation ordinance. In another feeble effort to calm the situation the City of Dallas followed through on Aston's plan to buy out several black families in ostensibly white neighborhoods. Others were induced to leave when the sellers agreed to refund their money. In at least one instance, the remaining white families on an integrated block agreed to sell their property and leave the area.

Some linked the over-flow of Negro families into previously white areas to the removal of more than two hundred black families from the site of the new $3 million low-cost housing project at the Hall and Thomas street area. A number of these Negro families themselves—unhappy over their dislocation despite predominant favorable black attitudes toward public housing—had filed a futile suit to prevent the condemnation of their property. The matter dragged on for months before its conclusion.

Completion in 1942 of the housing project which had been so controversial, Roseland Homes, provided low-cost housing for some 650 Negro families who took pride in their pleasant new surroundings. Inspired by the project's name, many of them planted roses. Roseland Home's first manager, Sam Hudson, saw the facility as one of the most prominent in public housing in the country. To be eligible to live there the head of the household had to have a job and be of good character. But the problem of black neighborhoods bulging with no place to go continued to be a source of tension. Half a dozen houses occupied by Negroes were dynamited or fire-bombed in a six-month period through March 1941, presumably by segregationists. Those responsible were never apprehended.

'Little Mexico'

Another group of minority citizens in Dallas, the Mexican-Americans, were less numerous and much less apparent as a factor to be considered in this period. Mexican-American residents generally kept to themselves, largely because of the language barrier, a factor which also limited their economic opportunities. The majority of the 6,000 Hispanic residents lived in a congested, slum-like area known as "Little Mexico" stretching on both sides of McKinney from Akard to Lamar streets. Part of this area was in the old red-light "reservation" district, where Little Mexico began developing after authorities chased out the prostitutes in 1913. Only a few Hispanics lived in the city then, the 1910 census listing just 583, a figure which jumped by 2,902 by 1920 after an influx of Mexican nationals following the revolution of 1910.

By the 1920s Little Mexico was a clearly defined area with Spanish-language signs above frame stores with long overhangs and with a small market reminiscent of those in Mexico where one could buy fruits, flowers, clothing, and jewelry in small stalls. Fixed prices were unknown; bargaining was very much the norm. By the 1930s, so stated the Works Progress Administration's history of Dallas, two and three families typically shared accommodations in a single house, with others sheltered in sheds and outhouses arranged around dirt courtyards at the rear. Even the most primitive sanitary conveniences sometimes were absent. A study in the mid-1930s reported that not a single dwelling unit in Little Mexico had hot water. Forty percent of the residential structures were declared to be "unfit for occupancy," 74 percent were overcrowded, and 75 percent had no indoor toilets. Squalor and poverty were the dominant notes, and the rate of disease was high.

Still, bright flowers and potted plants lent cheerful notes of color to the neighborhood. Among the notable establishments were a Spanish-language movie house, restaurants which included the popular El Fenix, a tamale factory, and offices for two Spanish-language magazines (*La Variedad* and *Cinemax*). Activities centered around the Pike Park Community Center which had been used almost exclusively by Mexican-Americans since the early 1930s, the Cumberland Hill school on N. Akard (where in 1935 enrollment was 92 percent Hispanic), and the Church of Our Lady of Guadalupe.

More prosperous Mexican-American families resided in the area just north of Akard Street. Here in "northern Little Mexico" lived the Cuellars, owners of the El Chico Restaurant, and the Zambranos, who operated a photography studio. Two areas showing much growth in Mexican-American population were Cement City and Juarez Heights, both in West Dallas.

At the end of 1941 Pearl Harbor changed the nation's temper; the problems of race relations in Dallas assumed secondary status, but they did not go away.

CCA Withstands a Challenge

For the spring 1941 municipal elections a new organization, the Dallas Citizens Association, put together a slate of candidates who campaigned on a familiar theme by charging CCA rule at city hall with being "elitist." They alleged it to be an organization of "special interests" dominated by a behind-the-scenes coterie of men who conducted their businesses in Dallas but who lived in Highland Park and University Park. They were the "executives of big businesses, utility companies and bankers." Their residences in Highland Park and University Park, it was charged, had caused the city to provide water for residents there at an inordinately low cost when rates were climbing for Dallas residents. A campaign charge of a totally different nature was that these same conservative businessmen were condoning widespread gambling in the city. One D.C.A. candidate, W.H. Tobin, estimated that some 85,000 gambling devices were operating in the city. "They (the big businessmen) have busted the little gambler and turned the town over to racketeers and big-shot gamblers," he charged. D.C.A. candidate Larry Walker unveiled a slot machine at one campaign rally to demonstrate the sort of devices permitted to exist. He challenged incumbent council members to name a committee of ministers to tour the city and make a report on gambling machines.

All CCA councilmen save one, R.D. Suddarth, who was being replaced by O.W. Cox, were up for re-election. They and CCA president R.L. Thomas declined to respond to their opponents' many charges, boasting instead of "honest, efficient and courteous government" at city hall and claiming a need to complete important projects already under way. Rodgers especially noted Central Boulevard in this regard as a project that could not be jeopardized. It would commence as soon as contracts could be signed. Rodgers also cited efforts to make Dallas the aviation center of the Southwest. Success in this venture was critical to the city's future progress, he said. The outcome of the election was in little doubt. The CCA council, according to the *News*, "has made Dallas a cleaner, safer and more habitable city." The newspaper pointed especially to major improvements at Love Field and the agreement with Southern Pacific to purchase right-of-way for Central Boulevard as key accomplishments. Even the Dallas Central Labor Council endorsed the CCA slate.

Voters, not surprisingly, returned the incumbents to office by an overwhelming majority, 3-1 in some races and no less than 2-1 in any race. Rodgers interpreted the results as a green light to move forward with a vast program of public improvements. But on the day after the election City Manager Aston requested a year's leave of absence to enter the Army. It was the first of many such leaves to be awarded as the war approached, but Aston's departure was especially significant, for in his absence the council and Mayor Rodgers felt obliged to assume a stronger role in the affairs of the city. Adherence to the council-manager system would not be nearly so close as before.

WORLD WAR II IN DALLAS

Pearl Harbor sent the same sort of chill through Dallas as it did throughout the nation. On that fateful Sunday, December 7, Dallas police arrested six persons of Japanese descent, only four of them Japanese nationals, and held them for immigration authorities. Three of them were cotton buyers working out of the Cotton Exchange Building with other buyers from throughout the world. The city immediately stationed armed guards at properties feared vulnerable to sabotage, including Love Field, radio station WRR, and Bachman Lake. At the latter site Texas Defense Guardsmen bearing rifles with fixed bayonets patrolled to prevent contamination of the water supply by foreign agents. On the Monday after Pearl Harbor applicants swarmed to local military recruiting offices; the Naval office handled 120 applications, eight times the normal number. Citizens were advised that in case of an air raid a siren atop the Adolphus Hotel would signal a city-wide blackout in which all lights would be extinguished. At the end of the first week a school was announced to train 5,000 air raid wardens for the city to patrol designated blocks and ensure compliance with blackout regulations. "We don't believe an air raid on Dallas or its defense industries is imminent, but nobody can be sure," Mayor Rodgers said. Acting City Manager V.R. Smitham said that as of January 1 all frills and unnecessary expenditures would be removed from the budget. In stores throughout Dallas clerks began removing Japanese-made goods from display shelves.

Before the war ended some 52,000 men and women from Dallas would serve in the armed forces; another 55,000 would work in industry to produce war goods; some 10,000 would help coordinate defense-related activities in the city. North American Aviation alone employed as many as 30,000 workers who built 24,000 B-24 bombers, P-51 Mustangs, and AT-6 Texan trainers.

Local affairs in the midst of such a monumental world-wide conflagration lost almost all sense of urgency, although a mass riot with racial overtones occurred January 3, 1943, that gave evidence to underlying tension between the races. The situation involved Negro soldiers, Negro civilians, and Dallas police officers, all of whom clashed sporadically for some three hours in the Hall-Thomas area before order could be restored. The riot began on a Sunday afternoon when three Military Police officers were called to the Midway Cafe to investigate a Negro soldier's alleged theft of a pistol kept at the restaurant. Officers found the suspect next door in the Weems Cafe drinking a beer. Upon being questioned, the suspect struck one of the M.P.s. A fight broke out which spread to patrons as well, and a Dallas police car arriving on the scene had to radio for reinforcements because a hostile crowd wouldn't permit the officers to get out of their car. Half a dozen civilian policemen and a dozen detectives responded, and they were joined by a large force of M.P.s. Many of the Negro soldiers and civilians retreated inside the State Theater as they were confronted by officers who, according to the *Express*, backed their orders with rifle butts and abusive language. Others were forced into nearby houses. Occasionally, groups would burst out of these places to confront the officers, only to be driven back inside. Finally, the provost marshall for the Dallas area arrived on the scene and managed to call a formation of the Negro soldiers. About seventy-five of them were placed in M.P. squad cars, and approximately 500 Negro soldiers were cleared from the area and sent back to their bases at Hensley Field in Grand Prairie and Camp Wolters at Mineral Wells. No one was seriously injured and no shots were fired, but a number of minor injuries had occurred. The Army immediately declared Dallas off-limits for Negro personnel, an order which was rescinded the next day.

Negro leaders were so alarmed at the outbreak of hostilities that they formed the Dallas Council of Negro Organizations, representing twenty-three city-wide black organizations, and appointed a special investigative committee which lamented the "abusive language and conduct employed by the police on innocent bystanders and passers-by." The committee called for the establishment of recreation centers for Negro soldiers in the area, and it urged the hiring of Negro civilian policemen to be assigned to the Hall and Thomas streets area.

Love Field Faces a Challenge

In the 1943 city council elections no one bothered to oppose the incumbent CCA council. It was the first time ever that no competition had surfaced for a council election. "Interest In Election Near Zero," a headline stated. The few voters who bothered to enter the polling booths—less than 3,000 among some 50,000 qualified voters—returned the entire council to office.

The election occurred on the heels of a stirring battle with the City of Fort Worth over the construction of a new airport mid-way between the two cities. Dallas' energetic development of Love Field had won for the city dominance in aviation over Fort Worth that far superseded its advantage in population. Passengers arriving and departing at Love Field numbered about five times those in Fort Worth. Dallas was trying its best to achieve its stated goal of being the gateway and port of entry for air commerce between the U.S., Mexico, and Central and S. America.

Still, talk of a single, super airport equi-distant between the two cities emerged as early as 1940. In an early plan, sponsored by Braniff and American, the two airlines agreed to buy 640 acres in Arlington, deed the property to that small city, and then lease and operate it. Dallas backed out of the plan because it believed Dallas and Fort Worth should control the airport rather than Arlington. By the spring of 1943 a new plan had been worked out by Dallas, Fort Worth, American Airlines, Braniff Airways, and the Civil Aeronautics Board to construct a Midway Airport on the new U.S. Highway 183 midway between the two cities just east of Euless in Tarrant County. This airport would have far greater space for expansion than Love Field, which was already facing the problem of surrounding congestion. The administration building would face a "neutral location," looking north on Highway 183 rather than west to Fort Worth or east to Dallas.

Unknown to Dallas, however, Fort Worth's powerful Amon G. Carter began working quietly behind the scenes to enhance his city's standing. Carter persuaded the Civil Aeronautics Board's regional director, L.C. Elliott, to recommend that the administration building's location be shifted so that instead of facing north, it would face west toward Fort Worth! Moreover, the hangars, repair and maintenance shops, and other such facilities were to be closer to Fort Worth. Pressed for an explanation for the changes, Elliott admitted they had been made to appease Carter. Dallas' leaders were stunned. This meant that the major commercial developments to be associated with the airport would line up and down the thoroughfare leading directly toward Fort Worth. Rodgers protested loudly, as did others. "It doesn't add up for a community of 420,000 supplying 80 percent of the current air traffic," he said. On March 5, 1943, thirty top civic leaders in Dallas vowed by unanimous standing ovation to join fully in a "gloves-off fight" to change the recommendation. A blue-ribbon committee chaired by Nathan Adams and including Robert L. Thornton, Karl Hoblitzelle, Ted Dealey, Tom C. Gooch, John W. Carpenter, and B.F. McClain was formed to join him. The leaders especially noted that a great aviation development inevitably was coming after the war, that Dallas must be prepared to capitalize on it at once or be left behind, and that it would be an injustice to permit Fort Worth to undercut Dallas when Dallas generated by far the preponderance of air traffic. A delegation headed by Rodgers traveled to Washington, D.C., to express to Secretary of Commerce Jesse Jones and the Civil Aeronautics Administration their strong objections about what they called a double-cross.

The *News* editorialized thoughtfully on the matter: "The controversy over the gateway has served to clarify Dallas thinking on the subject, and the clarification reveals this: A city with the natural geographic, industrial and commercial advantages of Dallas would be throwing away its opportunity of an age if it proceeded into the future without a definite aviation program. A twin-city program is only half a program under any circumstances. With fair play on both sides it might have served the purpose. But it would be less than half a program if Dallas should be forced to spend most of its energies in guarding its interests."

In early April Rodgers won a standing ovation from the Dallas Salesmanship Club when he announced that Dallas was withdrawing from the joint venture. Midway Airport "is no more," he said. It had been a symbol of a "mistake in generosity." The city had been very liberal and fair in offering to trade 77 percent of its patronage in aviation for only 50 percent consideration in developing Midway Airport. "But then, to attempt to take advantage of us by devious methods—and I'm not talking about the people of Fort Worth—was too much. We're accepting no dictates from a dictator, foreign or domestic," he said. The reference clearly was to Amon G. Carter.

Rodgers elaborated with prescience about the stakes at hand. "Inland cities will be the great transportation centers of the future. No longer will seaport towns have the great advantages they held in the past. Tomorrow it will be Chicago, Detroit, St. Louis and Dallas—the gateway to Mexico and South America—that will hold this leadership in transportation because of the airplane....But it is not necessary for us to go beyond our own area to develop our aviation facilities."

Disillusioned, Dallas withdrew its offer of cooperation in developing Midway Airport and announced plans for extensive new improvements at Love Field. But the issue of a new airport midway between the two cities would simmer for three more decades, causing great enmity, an enmity sometimes disguised as jovial play but which had a genuine basis because of the economic consequences. Both cities clearly believed that their future growth and progress were dependent on establishing a successful aviation program. Both cities, to a large degree,were correct.

Such matters aside, the first half of the decade saw commitment of local resources and energy to the war's successful conclusion. Capital projects were postponed. The city began to anticipate the expected post-war economic boom. The war years became for Dallas—as for virtually all American cities—an era of great planning. In fact, planning that anticipated the return of military men was seen as a patriotic duty. Besides, other cities were doing it, and some of them were ahead of Dallas. "Dallas Chiefs Shocked By Alertness of Other Cities on Master Plan," read a 1943 headline in the *News*. This realization came when some city leaders toured Kansas City, St. Louis, Lousville, and Memphis, all of which had the advantage of river traffic and heavier industrial development than Dallas, and all of which were farther along in their post-war planning.

"We need another Kessler Plan and have waited long enough to start," Mayor Rodgers said. "We want to be ready to put Dallas ahead when the war is over and we will have great opportunities to put a master plan in effect." Thus came the hiring in 1943 of a nationally recognized planner, Harland Bartholomew of St. Louis, to develop a new master plan in conjunction with work in progress by City Plan Engineer E.A. Wood and S. Herbert Hare of Kansas City.

At the same time the *News* launched another campaign to encourage community support for city planning. It published a series of ten articles in the summer of 1943, then issued them in pamphlet form entitled "Dallas Meets A Challenge." Beginning in late 1943 Bartholomew began issuing a series of fifteen master plan reports on subjects such as the character of the city, population, housing, streets, transportation, public buildings, parks and schools, and land use. They were based on a projected population of 670,000 in the year 1970. Bartholomew's plan, Wood summarized, would "increase the working efficiency of the city, improve living conditions, develop a more attractive city, stabilize the central business district, eliminate slums and make provisions for future expansion and other contingencies."

In his report on transportation, a critical one for a city so ambitious in such matters, Bartholomew struck a final blow against the Midway Airport scheme. The site was too far away and too inaccessible. It was too small. "It just doesn't fit into any comprehensive plan of airports to serve the future needs of Dallas," Bartholomew summarized. Instead, he recommended a site for a big new airport east of Dallas and opposite Fort Worth. This "super-airport," to be constructed on a 5,300-acre site in the unannexed Pleasant Grove area north of U.S. Highway 175, would replace Love Field as the city's major airport, expansion of which was deemed too expensive because of surrounding development. Love Field's new use, after the development of the super-airport, would be confined to private flying, industrial and service activities, and non-scheduled commercial flights. One thing seemed certain: even these two airports would not be sufficient. Dallas would need a system of twenty-one airports to accommodate what was seen as a literal explosion in aviation after the war, not including eight helicopter landing fields scattered throughout the city. Bartholomew's visionary plan anticipated the helicopter as a logical successor to the automobile.

But the automobile was not forgotten. Kessler's suggestion that a Central Boulevard should replace the H&TC railroad tracks again was emphasized.

Resurfacing in Bartholomew's plan was an old dream: canalization of the Trinity River from Galveston Bay to Fort Worth. A fifteen-year program to accomplish this would cost $59.9 million, it was estimated, but it would bring average annual benefits of $17,217,000 to the Trinity watershed.

In his report on zoning, Bartholomew stressed the importance of strong neighborhood associations to secure residential areas from commercial encroachments. Newly annexed territories should have lot sizes of no less than 10,000 square feet, he recommended, and he wanted the city to evolve toward an ideal in which the city's residential lots would average 7,500 square feet. However, his master plan retained the smaller 6,000-square-feet lots proposed by Kessler and adopted in a 1929 ordinance. This guaranteed that Oak Cliff would remain lower-middle-class in comparison to North Dallas, where the lots would be larger and more desirable.

Bartholomew especially criticized the city's 1929 zoning ordinance because of the disproportionate amount of land reserved for commercial use. He observed that the city had enough commercial space for a city of 1.75 million people instead of its 333,000. This imbalance jeopardized residential areas. In submitting his own zoning proposal in 1945 (passed in 1947), Bartholomew sought to correct this situation.

Implicit in comments concerning housing was the continued segregation of the races. Bartholomew believed that strong neighborhood associations would ensure this segregation. To help accommodate the growing Negro population, Bartholomew proposed to develop two new black neighborhoods in out-of-way locations. One would be in the northern portion of the levee district, a location convenient to the anticipated industrial area and also to domestic work in Highland Park and University Park. The other would be in far South Dallas near the Thompson School in the flood plain of White Rock Creek, a site that would be feasible only after construction of a new levee. The addition of these would give Dallas nine distinct Negro neighborhoods and eighty white neighborhoods.

While white organizations around town reviewed and discussed these plans, black residents had no such opportunities. The president of the Negro Chamber of Commerce protested. He suggested to Mayor Rodgers that Dallas Negroes might have suggestions of their own. Rodgers responded by asking the president, T.W. Pratt, to form a committee of Negroes to make their recommendations. Pratt formed seven committees, and their findings were given to the city's Bi-Racial Committee, which endorsed their report. On July 18, 1944, Rodgers and other city officials met with more than 500 Negroes to respond to questions about the master plan.

In Batholomew's view, downtown Dallas, despite its notable skyscrapers, was "quite unsatisfactory" in character and appearance. There was an unfortunate mingling of high and low buildings, of expensive and inexpensive structures, and of commercial enterprises with fine and poor character to a "far greater extent than is found in the usual American city." Public buildings were scattered and on inadequate sites; they needed to be replaced by "a fine group of public buildings with considerable open space and planting." Twenty acres would be needed for a site to accommodate new public buildings. Bartholomew suggested three sites, but the one he preferred was a N. Akard Street location between Pacific and Camp streets. Here would be constructed a twelve-story, modernistic city hall as the focal point. It would be on an axis with Akard Street, and it would be flanked by a new library, auditorium and music hall, and federal building. All of these would be placed in an imposing setting made possible by the acquisition of two city blocks in front of the buildings to be developed as parks. The entire development would be "spacious and imposing." Pools and fountains would be an integral part.

A Move to Annex the Park Cities

City officials assumed that by definition the master plan, still being formulated in a series of reports and due completion that year, required a comprehensive approach that superseded the city limits of Dallas itself. Highland Park and University Park, the exclusive incorporated suburbs north of the city, had been urged to become a part of Dallas as far back as 1917. This seemed especially important in thoroughfare planning, but also in such matters as public transportation, utilities, and the development of Love Field. Residents of Highland Park and University Park prided themselves in their high-quality residential areas firmly protected through restrictive zoning, their independent school district (combined in the two cities), their separate municipal governments, and their separate police and fire departments. Integration into the far larger Dallas community, many believed, would render them powerless to set their own standards in these matters. Such concerns could be resolved, Mayor Rodgers believed, and merger of these cities with Dallas became one of his primary goals. Rodgers saw it as essential to the full realization of the master plan to which he was so committed, and he campaigned hard for annexation. In another sense, the Park Cities stood in the way of Dallas' "manifest destiny." Rodgers told the Dallas Chamber of Commerce: "There is no north Dallas because of the Park Cities on the north drawing the blood from the heart of Dallas. This is an anemic situation, and pretty soon it will become pernicious unless corrected."

One aspect of the problem he acknowledged as early as 1943 in a speech to the Dallas Salesmanship Club. He declared—with some exaggeration—that 90 percent of the city's top business executives lived in the Park Cities. These executives, despite their obvious and direct interests in creating a prosperous and well-governed city, could not even vote in City of Dallas elections. To Rodgers this was a "distressing situation." So tantalizing was the talent pool in the Park Cities that certain of its residents quietly had been appointed to various Dallas boards and commissions. Two examples were Hugo W. Schoellkopf, chairman of the Dallas Public Library's board of trustees, and Homer R. Mitchell, chairman of the municipal radio commission. Because well-heeled residents of the Park Cities relied extensively on Love Field, they needed to assume their rightful burden in its upkeep and administration, Rodgers pointed out. The *News* had observed in 1941 that the Park Cities were "suburban hitchhikers" using Dallas' facilities free of charge.

Highland Park had been developed north of Dallas in 1907 as an exclusive, planned community. A noted landscape architect, Wilbur David Cook, who had designed Beverly Hills in California, was engaged by developers John S. Armstrong and his son-in-law, Hugh Prather, Sr., to devise a plan. Early advertisements boasted of a community "beyond the city's dusk and smoke." Another slogan was, "It's 10 degrees cooler in Highland Park." In 1924 a major new section, "Highland Park West," was opened. By 1945 Highland Park had a population of approximately 13,000 in its 2.2 square miles.

University Park, which had developed shortly thereafter around the new Southern Methodist University and immediately north of Highland Park, opened in 1915. By 1945 its 3.7-square-mile area was populated by 20,048 residents.

Yet another new community north of University Park had been started, and it, too, became part of the debate on annexation. This was Preston Hollow, where some 1,700 citizens lived in a two-square-mile area in an area intersected by Walnut Hill Lane and Royal Lane.

The matter of annexation was to be decided by voters of Dallas and the three suburban towns as a part of a simultaneous April 3, 1945, election, coinciding with the Dallas City Council election in which Mayor Rodgers and all eight of his CCA colleagues once again, as in 1943, had no opposition. Five of the incumbent council members were seeking their fourth terms. With their re-elections assured, the election's primary issue was annexation. Merger would not occur in any instance unless a majority of the voters on both sides favored it.

In February the Greater Dallas Citizens Committee, chaired by Judge C.F. O'Donnell, was formed to campaign for unification. Organized opposition to the mergers soon developed in both Highland Park and University Park. In the latter city former mayor Elbert Williams headed the University Park Antiannexation Association. The Highland Park Antiannexation Association was led by A.M. Grayson. Before the campaign ended these two organizations united themselves in an umbrella group, the Park Cities Antiannexation Association. No organized opposition developed in Preston Hollow.

Opinion in the two Park Cities was sharply divided, although University Park's entire city council went on record as favoring the merger. A majority of the Highland Park school board also favored joining Dallas. While many of Park Cities' influential citizens who were active in Dallas' affairs favored annexation, the average homeowner did not. Preston Hollow's mayor, Mart Reeves, proclaimed neutrality on the subject.

The *News* campaigned vigorously for the unification in a series of editorials as well as in "news" stories which clearly were slanted. If voters rejected unification, according to the *News*, the result would be a "serious setback" to the Dallas area's development at the very time when metropolitan problems required unity of action. "Everything possible has been done by the leaders of Dallas to reassure the suburbs, even including the passage of legislation to guarantee Dallas' promises as to the future of the Park City schools, zoning rights and police protection."

One of these guarantees was being formulated in the state legislature to still the Park Cities' concerns that their fine residential neighborhoods might suffer if unification occurred. A bill was nearing final passage to permit greater local autonomy in zoning through neighborhood councils, as Bartholomew had proposed in his master plan. This was touted as a special incentive to permit Highland Park and University park residents to protect their own communities according to their own preferences. In response to other stated concerns, Dallas had guaranteed that the Highland Park Independent School District, which also included University Park students, would remain inviolate, that there would be no change in police and fire policies, and that the difference in taxes would be neglible. Other soothing statements had been made concerning such matters as upkeep of streets and parks, prohibition policies, pension plans for municipal employees and sewage disposal. These commitments, according to the *News*, guaranteed the "maintenance of any standards they [the Park Cities] desire."

A full-page newspaper advertisement sponsored by the pro-annexation Greater Dallas Citizens Committee framed the argument as one of selfishness: "Are you going to join the thousands of Dallas and Park Cities people who are placing citizenship above selfishness, tolerance above distrust, faith above prejudice, vision above short-sightedness, and the future of their homes and Dallas above complacency? Or are you going to join the few who through misunderstanding or selfishness are unwittingly or deliberately obstructing progressive plans for a Better Dallas, who by their status-quo thinking would condemn their homes and Dallas to stagnation and decline, who by anonymous attacks betray a lack of leadership?" In another full-page advertisement the committee warned that if unification failed the suburban cities would be burdened with the "tremendous cost of a separate water supply and sewage disposal system which will increase our taxes enormously." Some 450 residents of Highland Park and University Park signed the advertisement, includingFred Florence, Karl Hoblitzelle, Edgar Flippen, Judge W.M. Holland, Umphrey Lee, Eugene McElvaney, Hugo Schoellkopf, J. Howard Payne, T.W. Cullum, and Dr. E.H. Cary.

Judge O'Donnell said that approval of the merger would "re-kindle the Dallas spirit which has waned during the past few years." The city, he said, could not continue to exist as "a divided city."

Arguments that Park Cities residential neighborhoods would be protected through the newly proposed neighborhood zoning groups were countered by Fred Penn, director of the Economic Research Bureau of the Park Cities Anti-Annexation Association. Penn, whose title suggested the level of Park Cities opposition to annexation, pointed out that the neighborhood zoning boards would be subject to the City Plan Commission's final review. He used as one example the deterioration of the once-proud Swiss Avenue area of large estates. Its decline, he said, had been brought about by the city's lax enforcement of zoning regulations and a resulting encroachment by commercial interests.

Fresh in the memory of many residents, and a recollection freshened by Penn's reminders, was the council's re-zoning the previous year of a large tract of land on Mockingbird Lane at Greenville Avenue from a planned shopping center to permit the construction of a Dr Pepper bottling plant and national headquarters. This had been done despite violent neighborhood opposition, including those living in the nearby Park Cities, who argued that the industrial facility would destroy their property values. Penn described the matter as an example of "ruthless politics" in which the "pleas of 200 angry property owners" were rejected in favor of the Dr Pepper president and his lawyer.

(One indirect reason for this zoning had been the failure to this point of the Trinity Industrial District to develop in the reclaimed flood plain. That area, despite the levees, remained a quagmire of mud. Its development had been complicated by conflicting tax and refinancing schemes and questions of clear titles. The abundant vacant land near Central Boulevard, or "Expressway," as it had come to be called, now nearing completion, and other well-serviced streets offered attractive alternative sites.)

On the eve of the election O'Donnell said his figures showed that University Park voters would favor unification by a "substantial majority." In Highland Park he foresaw a closer race, but one that would still be decisively for unification. In Preston Hollow and in Dallas he expected almost unanimous approval.

By April the contest, fanned for months through newspaper advertisements, radio speeches, and public meetings, reached a fever pitch. On election day about 50 percent of the voters in the Park Cities cast ballots. They rejected the merger, although not by an overwhelming margin. University Park turned down merger by a vote of 2,017 to 1,726; Highland Park by a count of 1,619 to 1,122. Preston Hollow favored unification by 300 to 76, and its merger with Dallas became effective immediately. Dallas' vote never was in question, and the final tally there in a light turnout saw aproval of unification by as much as 145 to 1. Not a single precinct opposed it.

The result was clearly a disappointment for Rodgers and Dallas. Inevitable post-election tensions arose. Rodgers, who had campaigned so hard for merger, had little to say other than that the re-elected council would concentrate in the next two years on the "rapid execution" of the master plan. He also denied rumors of retaliation.

"That kind of talk has no place in Dallas," he said. O'Donnell predicted that within a few weeks the Park Cities would be surrounded by Dallas. Indeed, one amendment Dallas voters approved permitted the annexation of adjacent unincorporated areas without approval of property owners in the area. And one day after the election O'Donnell's prediction came true. The Dallas City Council voted to annex all the areas surrounding the Park Cities, thus freezing their boundaries. The new areas also included the Kessler Park and Kidd Springs neighborhoods adjacent to Oak Cliff, an area in North Dallas west to Harry Hines Boulevard, and Forest Hills and Casa Linda Estates in the White Rock area. On the same day city council members climbed aboard a fire truck to tour the newly annexed Preston Hollow area. Rodgers promised that every pledge made prior to the election to Preston Hollow would be honored. A week later the city annexed more areas containing about seven square miles, including territories surrounding the suburb of Cockrell Hill in Oak Cliff. The city council, still in a punitive mood, instructed the city manager to inventory all services being rendered Highland Park and Univerity Park for which they were not paying their share.

The City of Dallas, realizing that it must look to the future without help from the affluent Park Cities, quickly adjusted. Rodgers advised the council three days after the election that none but Dallas residents now would be permitted to serve on city boards and commissions. Park Cities residents then serving—such as Schoellkopf and Mitchell—had to give up their positions. Acting City Attorney A.J. Thuss said that addresses of all appointees in the future would be checked to ensure this residency requirement. One day later Acting City Manager V.R. Smitham said that all City of Dallas employees must move into the city as soon as wartime housing conditions permitted. All employees were expected to make a diligent effort to comply with this new policy.

The annexation of lands surrounding the Park Cities was just the beginning. Before 1945 was over, Dallas' size had grown through annexation from fifty square miles to ninety. But that, too, was just the tip of an iceberg. Between 1945 and 1960 the city's square miles would grow almost six-fold, from 50.664 square miles to 283.356 square miles. This gave the city domain over a large portion of the county for planning purposes, but it also placed continuing burdens in building infrastructures and providing municipal services.

PART THREE

Post-War Explosion

11

The Mob Makes Its Move

Regardless of its registered attitude in favor of strict enforcement of dry laws, I know of no town more bold in its violation of them.

--Owen P. White, 1929

Postwar Boom

The war's end, so Dallas and the nation believed, signaled the start of a period of unparalleled prosperity and possibilities. In this new era all cities would have an equal opportunity for advancement. Since past successes would mean little, there could be no guarantees as to how Dallas would fare in the great competition among cities. Civic leaders who had assumed such confident airs after the Centennial now toned down their optimism. What Dallas believed necessary to succeed in this new competition was the same as always: growth in population, attraction of new businesses and industry, development of aviation, and a vigorous program to bring in visitors and conventions. Implementing the master plan was seen as central to these goals, especially building Central Boulevard.

The city lost no time in preparing for the anticipated boom. Ex-G.I.'s were still unpacking their duffle bags when a $40 million bond election was announced for December 8, 1945, to help support the city's growing pains toward a projected 1970 population of 750,000 (now expanded from Bartholomew's earlier 670,000 estimate). These bonds would implement vital but unglamorous portions of the master plan for the next ten years. More than half of the funds—about $25 million—would be spent on street improvements, sewers, street lights, parks, water lines, schools, and final right-of-way purchases for Central Boulevard. Earmarked for $7 million was a new downtown municipal auditorium desperately needed to accommodate the larger conventions being snared increasingly by rivals Houston and Kansas City. (A separate need in this regard, not addressed by the bond issue, was to alleviate a severe shortage of hotel rooms.) A new livestock coliseum at Fair Park, carrying a $2.5 million price tag, was believed necessary to maintain the city's position as a livestock and agricultural center. A new city hall also was needed, and $2.5 million was allotted for one. Finally, the bond program called for the construction of a fire station, a public market, and a new library to replace the old and outdated 1903 Carnegie facility at Main and Harwood streets.

City leaders described the bonds as the most important ever for Dallas. R.L. Thomas, head of the CCA since 1938, put it bluntly: "If they should not be voted, then this city is in for the biggest slump in its history and we will be classed as a city without ambition, a second-rate town which did not have the stamina to stay in the postwar race."

However, the approximately 125,000 qualified voters had their minds on other matters. No more than 5,000 of the voters bothered to cast ballots; yet they approved all seventeen propositions by margins ranging from 2-1 to 3-1.

It soon became clear that $40 million was woefully inadequate. Dallas was growing too rapidly in population and geographical boundaries. The $40 million had been projected for a ten-year period, but a 1947 survey of city departments showed their need of $54 million for the next five years. Water and sanitary sewers alone would cost $20 million.

A perplexing dilemma that would become a perennial one arose in assigning priorities for limited resources as the city struggled throughout the post-war period to keep up with its growing needs.

Although municipal budgets grew larger than ever, the additional sums had to be spent on unglamorous basics such as streets, storm sewers, sanitary sewers, and water mains. The ambitious new civic center Bartholomew recommended had no chance to be realized. Rampant inflation rendered the amount authorized for it totally insufficient.

The postwar boom and the city's aggressive annexation policy were spreading the city's outer limits far into the county. Scores of housing additions with neatly aligned bright white frame houses were popping up on flat, treeless plains just recently covered with rows and rows of cotton. Little county towns where farmers in straw hats formerly congregated on Saturday mornings to discuss their crops and the weather—Irving, Garland, Carrollton, Duncanville, Mesquite, Richardson, and Lancaster—were taking on the trappings of suburban communities. One study estimated that more than 80 percent of job-holders residing in Duncanville, Pleasant Mound, Pleasant Grove, Farmers Branch, Letot, and Rylie commuted to Dallas for their work.

Housing costs, artificially restrained during the war by government controls, escalated rapidly with the increased demand. Dallas, dubious about the wisdom of federal regulations, became one of the first cities in the nation to abolish war-time rent controls. By 1946 the price of a modest house in Dallas had climbed by 91.4 percent over the 1940 cost. The National Housing Agency reported the city to have the second highest inflationary housing rate in the country.

ARTS AND SPORT

As for cultural life, the arts prospered as never before in a city which had convinced itself that a strong artistic presence was necessary as a sign of progress and sophistication. A leading figure was the acclaimed new conductor of the Dallas Symphony Orchestra, Antal Dorati, a former ballet concertmaster of Hungarian descent who arrived in Dallas in 1945. Dorati began spending several hundred thousand dollars a year on symphony operations instead of the previous $30,000 or $40,000. With significantly higher budgets, Dorati created a first-rate orchestra recognized nationally for its qualities. John Rosenfield, the ubiquitous *News* critic, wrote that

Dallas and Dorati were "indivisible, each giving the other a glory that detonated through four continents."

Each spring the city enjoyed a series of performances by New York's Metropolitan Opera Company. These had begun in 1939 after an eight-year push by retailer and lawyer Arthur L. Kramer Sr. to bring the Met to Dallas during its annual spring tour. To underwrite the costs and guarantee the profitability of the visits, Kramer founded the Dallas Grand Opera Association.

In 1945, two years after the collapse of Dallas' once-acclaimed Little Theatre, a determined and brassy young Texan named Margaret Virginia (Margo) Jones arrived fresh from Broadway, where she had co-directed Tennessee Williams' "The Glass Menagerie." Coming in the same year as Dorati, she dedicated herself to founding a new repertory theater. The homely old Gulf Oil Building at Fair Park was the best site she could find. Its interior limitations prompted Miss Jones to establish what became a much-acclaimed "theater-in-the-round" format. Her first season in 1947 was launched by a new and noteworthy production, William Inge's "Farther Off From Heaven." Patrons from as far away as New York City and Mexico City arrived to see the initial performance. In that same first season she presented another new play by Tennessee Williams entitled "Summer and Smoke." Among other new plays she later introduced was "Inherit the Wind" by Jerome Lawrence and Robert E. Lee. The play went directly from Dallas to a successful and acclaimed run on Broadway.

Miss Jones, who had grown up in Denton and who held two degrees from the College of Industrial Arts (later Texas Woman's University), credited her childhood visits to Dallas' Little Theatre with inspiring her interest in drama. She changed the name of her theater each year—Theater '47, Theater '48, etc.—and she greatly outdistanced the old Little Theatre in achieving national attention before her tragic and unusual death in 1955, attributed to the accidental inhalation of carbon tetrachloride fumes after her carpets had been cleaned.

Only a stone's throw away from Margo Jones theater one could attend summer performances of the Starlight Operetta in Fair Park's outdoor bandshell. Here were produced such musicals as "No, No, Nanette," "Rio Rita," "The Merry Widow," and "Roberta." When the summer series first started in 1941 it was known as "Opera Under the

Stars." The summer productions boasted of such famous performers as Patrice Munsell, Allan Jones, Patricia Morison, and Jackie Gleason in leading roles. The outdoor stagelights attracted a massive number of bugs during these hot summer nights. In 1949 Nanette Fabray, who had come to Dallas to star in "Bloomer Girl," let it be known that she was deathly afraid of insects. Extraordinary precautions to protect her from them were instituted. Yet, *all* bugs could not be eliminated, and when a cricket jumped down the singer's bodice as she reached a high note at center stage, she transformed her note instantly into a hysterical scream. Miss Fabray had to be led from the stage. The performance was cancelled; rainchecks were issued. In 1951, partially as a result of this incident, all performances were moved inside Fair Park Auditorium, which turned out to be a superior setting for the musicals, and renamed the State Fair Summer Musicals.

In these post-war years "liquor-by-the-drink" was forbidden in Dallas. Each evening on Commerce Street, where so many night spots were located, revelers carried brown paper bags containing bottles of liquor to be added to the non-alcoholic "set-ups" available in bars and clubs. Pappy's Showland, Abe's Colony Club, and the Theater Lounge were popular night spots with adult entertainment, and a variety of other possibilities were available elsewhere. Dorothy Franey's Ice Revue at the Adolphus Hotel's Century Room featured attractive skaters on indoor ice within the intimate atmosphere of a hotel nightclub. The Pleasant Mound Rodeo at Buckner Boulevard and Scyene Road, a once-rural area down the road from where Belle Starr grew up but now spotted with urban developments, attracted fans of the cowboy arts each Saturday night. Every morning except Sunday on Radio Station WFAA a group of local radio performers known as the "Early Birds" offered live entertainment on the nation's "original breakfast hour program."

Elm Street had been the site for Dallas' movie row since the infancy of the film industry before World War I. The unusual number of theaters on that well-lit street had now consolidated to a handful of large ones, but they continued to be the only places in town where one could see new releases. Such Elm Street movie houses as the Majestic, Palace, Tower, Melba, Rialto, Strand, Joy, and Capitol offeredfirst-rate fare with stars such as Clark Gable and Rita Hayworth as well as double features with cowboy stars Gene Autry, Tom Mix,

Hoot Gibson, and Roy Rogers. By now, too, in this age when movie attendance was at an all-time high, some two dozen neighborhood theaters also had sprung up in all parts of town . Elm Street, though, continued to be the destination of all serious movie-goers.

Dallas' professional baseball club, nicknamed the Rebels, played home games on the Oak Cliff side of the Trinity adjacent to the levee where a stadium built in 1920 replaced the old site adjacent to Fair Park. When East Texas oilman Richard W. (Dick) Burnett purchased the club in 1948 from George Schepps he gave it a new nickname, the Eagles, and named the ballpark for himself, Burnett Field. Burnett attracted scores of spectators with special attractions as well as by putting contending baseball teams on the field. One year his team featured a one-armed outfielder named Pete Gray, who amazed incredulous fans with his dexterity in hitting, catching, and throwing.

For the season opener in 1950 Burnett determined to set a national record for attendance at a minor league game. He scheduled the opener at the Cotton Bowl, seating capacity about 72,000. The rectangular playing area, designed for football, was awfully cramped along both first- and third-base foul lines, and center field was unusually deep. To attract a huge number of spectators Burnett held a pre-game exhibition featuring some of baseball's all-time greats, including Ty Cobb, Tris Speaker, Dizzy Dean, Frank (Home Run) Baker, and Mickey Cochrane. Texas Governor Allan Shivers threw out the first ball. The event attracted a total of 53,578 fans, easily giving Burnett his minor league record.

Burnett's next plan for bolstering attendance required a special kind of courage. He decided to break the rigid color line in Texas League baseball and bring to his Dallas club a Negro player. While major league baseball had been integrated in 1947 when Jackie Robinson joined the Brooklyn Dodgers, Dallas and the Texas League remained strictly segregated. As a wealthy oilman from a small East Texas town, Burnett seemed an unlikely candidate to break the color barriers, but as he told the *Dallas Express*, he was "indebted to the colored race" for having helped him make his fortune in the oil fields, and he saw an obligation to repay his debt by helping them in their struggle for equality. After a series of pre-season open tryouts failed to produce the outstanding calibre of black player desired, Burnett borrowed from the Cleveland Indians' farm system a twenty-seven-year-old Michigan native named Dave Hoskins. That year Hoskins became the star pitcher as well as a fine hitter. He led the team to the pennant in 1952 and compiled a record of 22 wins and 10 losses. Hoskins became a popular figure among all fans—black and white. Attendance boomed—especially among the Negro fans, all of whom sat in a segregated bleacher along the left-field line.

For his work, black members of the Moorland Branch of the YMCA honored Burnett as the man who had done the most to improve race relations in 1952. Hoskins won promotion to the major leagues in 1953, where he had a brief career before returning to Dallas for his final season of professional baseball in 1957.

POLITICS AT THE COURTHOUSE

In this post-war period a large number of returning veterans decided to seek political office in the democracy they had risked their lives to save. Many were elected, for those who bore the label of ex-G.I. enjoyed formidable advantages.

The veterans' first opportunity in politics came in the 1946 county and state elections. Two of the most interesting races were for district attorney and sheriff. With the incumbent district attorney retiring, that office attracted six candidates, including two veterans who would achieve outstanding political careers in Texas. Will Wilson, a former Army major who had taken a leave from the state attorney general's office, was one leading candidate. Wilson, thirty-three, had grown up in Highland Park and graduated from Southern Methodist University.

Another war veteran candidate was Henry M. Wade, a native of nearby Rockwall, graduate of the University of Texas law school with highest honors, former F.B.I. agent, and most recently of the U.S. Navy. Wade, who had been elected district attorney at Rockwall County immediately after graduating from law school and served until joining the F.B.I., entered the race on an impulse after a fellow attorney suggested it. Having been away from the area since 1939, Wade had not established a residency in Dallas, although he occasionally spent nights in town with a brother who lived in University Park. Worried that he might fail to meet residency requirements, Wade was advised by his attorney friend that a returning veteran could declare his residency anywhere he pleased. Wade thus listed his brother's address as his residence and began campaigning for the office, using radio addresses to advantage. One of the other five candidates, Andy Priest, summarized his situation aptly in a campaign speech in Mesquite in which he critiqued all his opponents and which Wade recalled with laughter years later. "As for this man Wade," Priest said, "he came into Dallas with a suitcase in one hand and an announcement in the other."

In the race Wade finished a close third. Will Wilson led all campaigners, but a run-off was required. Wilson invited Wade to assist him in his run-off effort, explaining that he would hire Wade as a prosecutor afterwards and that he only intended to keep the job for a single four-year term before running for a state-wide office. Wade agreed to do so; Wilson won; and Wade became his chief felony prosecutor.

Four years later in 1950 Wilson entered state-wide politics, becoming an important figure for many years, and Wade was elected district attorney. Before he would retire Wade's career in that office would extend for more than thirty-five years, and he would gain national fame as a zealous and efficient district attorney.

As for the 1946 Dallas County's sheriff's election, the veteran Smoot Schmid appeared certain to win it for the eighth consecutive time since 1932. Schmid, six-feet-five and the wearer of size 14 shoes, was the son of a Swiss woodcarver who emigrated to Dallas in 1884. No man had served longer as sheriff in Dallas County than Schmid; in fact, no previous man had held the office for more than three terms. In 1938, to avoid any possibility of voter confusion at the polls, he legally changed his name from Richard Allen Schmid to R.A. "Smoot" Schmid—as he had been popularly known since his football days at Dallas High School. At age forty-nine, the popular Schmid's career seemed to have many more years to go.

Among the three novices challenging Schmid was Steve Guthrie, a former Army Air Corps sergeant and a 1931 graduate of Forest Avenue High School. Before entering the service at the onset of war, Guthrie had served as a Dallas police officer. While in the Army Air Corps he survived the crash-landing in Oak Cliff of the Flying Fortress "Suzie Q." After the war Guthrie briefly rejoined the police force before deciding to run for sheriff. In his campaign Guthrie promised to modernize the sheriff's office, and he stressed especially his military record. Schmid, who had not served in the war, could say only that a third of his office personnel were ex-G.I.'s.

As expected, Schmid led the primary election by a wide margin with 25,741 votes; Guthrie being a distant second with 14,346 votes. A run-off was necessary because of votes split among other candidates. As the underdog Guthrie appealed vaguely for voters to join him in fighting "the biggest political machine ever known in Dallas County." When the last votes were counted, to the surprise of all, Guthrie had defeated the over-confident Schmid by 805 votes.

Gambling and Benny Binion

If they hoped to live up to their campaign promises to eliminate the vice which had become quietly pervasive in the city and county, the challenge before Guthrie and Will Wilson was formidable. While there had been highly publicized raids against bootleggers and stills in the 1920s, it was true that illegal activity in booze as well as gambling had gone basically unchallenged. A *Collier's* magazine writer who investigated bootlegging in the city in 1929 reported that within a two-block stretch in the heart of downtown he found six places that would sell him liquor. "Regardless of its registered attitude in favor of strict enforcement of dry laws, I know of no town more bold in its violation of them," the author wrote, estimating that a hundred or more illegal bootleg sites existed in the city. The writer, Owen P. White, described a Chicago mob's "protection" racket in Dallas in which bootleggers paid a monthly fee in return for immunity from harassment by the law.

Dallas readers and law enforcement officials expressed outrage over White's shocking article. To prove his own commitment to law enforcement, Sheriff Hal Hood had immediately conducted a series of raids, and then participated in a public rally with the Women's Christian Temperance Union to denounce White, his article, and the magazine. At the downtown rally sheriff's deputies dramatically poured more than 5,000 gallons of contraband liquor into the gutter. Unfortunately, someone carelessly dropped a match onto the volatile stream; it ignited suddenly into a roaring river of flames. Before firemen could contain the spreading fire more than twenty automobiles had been burned and several buildings threatened. What had started as a move to combat negative publicity about lacklustre law enforcement ended up as a public relations nightmare.

The question of city and county policies concerning vice later emerged with special emphasis in 1936 in connection with the Texas Centennial when city officials decided to permit gamblers, bootleggers, and prostitutes to operate with even fewer challenges than before. Petty vice continued without much attention through the remainder of the decade, the war years, and into the post-war era. The *News'* own afternoon paper, the *Dallas Journal,* acknowledged the interest in betting on the horse races. It published each day a "sporting" edition detailing on the front page race-track results even though pari-mutuel betting had been illegal in Texas since 1937.

One of the most popular forms of gambling was something called the "policy wheel," which especially appealed to residents in poorer neighborhoods. Playing the wheel became a daily habit for many. Those operating the illegal policy wheels paid "runners" to sell numbered tickets for a nickel, dime or quarter. Winning numbers were pulled each day from a roulette wheel or box behind closed doors. Payoffs varied according to the price paid for the tickets. It was estimated in the post-war period that the dozen or more policy wheels being operated brought in more than $2 million a year, and that the annual gross from all gambling operations in the city was about $14 million a year. The battle among underworld interests for shares of this money, fought out of the public's view except for occasional violence covered by the newspapers, was spirited.

Dallas Morning News crime reporter Harry McCormick described in early 1947 his efforts to see how many forms of gambling he could find in a single day. He placed a $2 bet with a bookie on a horse race, put a nickel in a slot machine in a downtown cafe, bought two 25-cent chances on a punch board at a cashier's counter, inserted a nickel in a marble machine that paid off in cash, and bought a 25-cent ticket on a policy wheel. He declined a dice game in the downtown Southland Hotel (notorious as a gambling hangout) because he was too tired. While such gambling activities sounded decidedly penny-ante in nature, the volume of activity in Dallas was such that it represented enormous potential for profit.

The open situation attracted the attention of an organized mob in Chicago, which saw possibilities for expansion into this lucrative market. In the summer of 1946 a mobster named Marcus Lipsky came from Chicago to survey the scene. Lipsky, whose Dallas contact was an ex-convict named Paul Roland Jones, hatched a bizarre plot to murder the four top gamblers in Dallas—Benny Binion, Ivy Miller, Earl Dalton, and Buddy Miller—and to leave their bodies outside the Dallas police station in a stolen car to show the mob's resolve and toughness. Jones protested vigorously, and he successfully appealed to higher mob authorities to veto the far-fetched scheme. In July that year four other members of the same mob, Daniel Lardino, James Wineburg, Paul (Needle Nose) Labriola, and Marty (The Ox) Ochs, came to town. Dallas sheriff's deputies somehow learned of their presence, arrested them, fined them $1 plus court costs for vagrancy, drove them to the county line on U.S. Highway 67 near Rowlett, put them in their own car, and ordered them to drive away and never return. The mobsters were not identified publicly, but a newspaper photographer managed to take their picture. Because of this public humiliation, three of the four men afterwards were executed by order of their mob superiors. James Wineburg and Labriola were killed with piano wire, and Ochs was murdered in San Francisco. The fourth man, Lardino, supposedly escaped execution because his older brother had a high position in the mob syndicate.

The man who controlled the largest share of the illicit Dallas loot was round-faced Lester (Benny) Binion, who later would gain national visibility and—incredibly—a degree of respectability after moving to the new desert oasis of Las Vegas and building a prominent casino there. Born in Grayson County in 1904 into a family that sold race horses on the county fair circuit, Binion moved to Dallas in the 1920s to engage in bootlegging and various gambling activities, including craps games operated out of hotel rooms. He began finally to specialize in the policy wheel racket.

Run-ins with the law were common for Binion, although he managed to escape serious charges. Early in his career he gained an odd and short-lived nickname as "the bumper beater" because of a bizarre incident at Lamar and Cadiz streets. He became so enraged at a woman that he jerked a bumper off an automobile and attacked her with it. He accumulated other charges for vagrancy—then a catch-all offense commonly used for gamblers—and for carrying a concealed weapon. Binion killed a a Negro liquor runner in 1931 in his backyard on Pocahontas Street. He got off with a two-year suspended sentence after claiming that the man had attacked him with a knife.

Bigger headlines came in 1936 when he and his top lieutenant shot to death a rival policy wheel operator, Ben Frieden, in a brazen daylight attack on Allen Street. Binion believed that Frieden, a newcomer to Dallas, was infringing on his policy wheel territory. A few months earlier Frieden had escaped an attempt on his life by gunfire, an effort probably instigated by Binion. The fatal shooting this time occurred when Binion and his henchman, H.E. (Buddy) Malone, pulled up alongside Frieden in his parked car as he talked to one of his Negro runners. The few eyewitnesses willing to describe what they saw said Binion approached Frieden on the driver's side, exchanged harsh words with him, and then fired pistol shots pointblank at him, being joined in the shooting by Malone from the opposite side. Frieden died instantly. A pistol was found next to his body. Within an hour Binion surrendered to Chief Deputy Sheriff Bill Decker at the courthouse, displaying a flesh wound on his arm which he said he suffered when Frieden fired at him. The grand jury accepted Binion's claim of self-defense and no-billed him.

As king of the policy wheel racket in Dallas, Binion employed a large number of black men as runners. Some years later, a physician would recall his own father's work as one of them: "I remember the pride that my father showed whenever he collected his small earnings, the result of miles of walking in the community....I remember the trucks, laden with apples and oranges that Mr. Binion had parked next to the 'policy' shack behind the old State Theater during the Christmas season. Sometimes that fruit was the only gift the neighborhoods would receive from Santa."

NOVICE SHERIFF FOILS THE MOB

In his 1946 post-election remarks Sheriff-elect Steve Guthrie promised to "wear out the Dallas County jail" by arresting those responsible for organized vice and gambling. Some of these local gangsters had grown so bold, he said, that they openly dared peace officers to do anything about them.

The Chicago mobsters had a different perspective. They saw in Guthrie youth, ambition, inexperience, and naiveté—an individual who might welcome their "assistance" in making good on his claims to control crime when he took office. To discuss this possibility the Dallas representative of this Chicago gang, Paul Roland Jones, arranged a meeting with Guthrie through Dallas police detective George Butler, who had been assigned by Dallas Police Chief Carl Hansson to maintain contact with gambling operatives.

Feigning interest, Guthrie agreed through Butler to meet with the thirty-seven-year-old Jones. First, however, he and Butler secretly notified Chief Hansson, District Attorney-elect Wilson, Homer Garrison of the Texas Department of Public Safety, and the Texas Rangers. Guthrie and officials of these agencies set a trap for the mobsters. Texas Ranger W. E. (Dub) Naylor installed a hidden tape-recording system in Guthrie's modest red-brick home at the corner of Malcolm Street and Abrams Road to record the first and four subsequent meetings in November and December.

Jones, a prematurely gray-haired, smooth-talking ex-convict from Kansas, had moved to Dallas in 1940 after being paroled from a life sentence for murder. His years in prison had not purged him of his criminal ways. In Dallas he had quickly involved himself once more in criminal activities, being convicted in federal court in 1945 for selling sugar on the black market. He informed Guthrie that he represented Al Capone's resurrected Chicago gang, now under the control of Jack (Greasy Thumb) Guzik and Murray Humphries. Jones said he was authorized to offer Guthrie an estimated $40,000 monthly from gambling profits if he would allow the crime syndicate to operate exclusively and without interference. For its part, the gang would guarantee that no other unauthorized gambling activity would occur within the county. It was understood that the $40,000 would include payments that might be necessary for the district attorney. The mob would operate one large, modern gambling casino at a site already selected—the Chicken Bar at Commerce and Industrial Boulevard.

While occasional "raids" would be tolerated to keep Guthrie above public suspicion, he would tip off the mob in advance so the best equipment could be replaced with older gambling devices for public destruction. Jones would be the city's "gambling czar," and Guthrie's sole mob contact. There would be absolutely no involvement with dope or prostitution, Jones promised Guthrie. None of its activities would be new, said Jones, for the mob already controlled some of the city's slot machines, marble tables, juke boxes, and liquor interests. (Whether or not this was the same Chicago gang described in the 1929 *Collier's* article which detailed bootlegging in Dallas is interesting to speculate.) The syndicate would not want a one-term sheriff, Guthrie was told, and he was assured that he would have no significant opposition in future races. His campaign assistance would come from the highest offices in the nation, including letters of commendation and endorsement for re-election from President Harry Truman and the Democratic Party national chairman, Bob Hannegan. As to what to do about Bennie Binion, Guthrie was advised—accurately or not—that the mob already controlled him.

Jones told Guthrie that similar arrangements with law enforcement agencies were common in cities throughout the nation as well as in Mexico. The mob wanted to secure Dallas in the same way because it was a "fast-growing, prosperous city where there was money to be made." Names of Dallas politicians, county officials, lawyers, and prominent businessmen slipped easily from Jones's tongue as he discoursed in the several meetings on the possibilities. At one evening meeting Jones attempted to press upon Guthrie a huge roll of high-denomination bills as an advance "part payment" to take care of his "needs" until regular payments could begin. The sheriff-elect, fearful of the implications, managed to reject the offer without suspicion.

On December 18, with damaging tape-recordings of the conversations in hand, officers ended the ruse. They arrested Jones at his apartment on Junius Street, as well as three other men involved, including a Chicagoan named Romeo Jack Natti, 26. Justice of the Peace W.L. (Lew) Sterrett set bond for Jones and Natti at $30,000 each. Jones argued that police had unfairly entrapped him. After a twelve-day trial in April 1947 for bribery, prosecuted by new District Attorney Will Wilson, the jury found Jones guilty and sentenced him to a three-year prison term. Jones did not begin his term until May 1957 because he first had to serve a five-year federal sentence for smuggling opium into the United States.

GANGLAND WARFARE

The sensational attempt to bribe Guthrie signaled the beginning by law enforcement officials of a lengthy and ultimately successful effort to end organized gambling in the city. Guthrie, wearing a white cowboy hat, initiated a series of raids on gamblers, his first occurring on January 7 just after taking office. Mayor Rodgers concurrently announced a new City of Dallas policy: instead of filing minor charges against gamblers in corporation court, police henceforth would file felony and misdemeanor charges at the courthouse. This meant an annual loss in fine revenues of approximately $150,000 to the City of Dallas. District Attorney Wilson prosecuted vigorously the cases brought to his office, aided prominently by Assistant District Attorney Henry M. Wade. Within one five-day period in May 1947, vice officers shut down a dozen horserace bookie joints. Police also raided policy wheel operations bearing such names as "White and Green," "High Noon," "Grand Prize," and "Gold Mine." The crusade was by no means an easy one, for not until the early 1950s would the Dallas gamblers be brought under effective control.

As the *News* commented in an editorial at the onset of the raids, in earlier years Dallas had followed the policy of allowing the gambling industry to exist with only token arrests every so often. "The gamblers arrested came up, paid their fines, went back to gambling, and charged the fines off to expenses." Those to blame for the hands-off policy had been the city's churchmen, its Chamber of Commerce officers, its bankers, and its "leading people," all of whom agreed that it was good for the city's economic health.

Seeing this new resolve to curb vice, Benny Binion moved to Nevada, where gambling had been legalized, to start a new episode in his life. He located in the small desert town of Las Vegas to participate in its development as a huge entertainment center with gambling as the major component. Although physically removed from the city, Binion, however, was not willing to give up all of his illegitimate Dallas gambling earnings—estimated in 1947 to be a million dollars a year—and he left major portions of his illicit empire intact.

One of those competing with Binion for these profits was white-haired, fortyish Herbert Noble, an Oak Cliff resident who lived in a modest home with his wife and daughter. The warfare that erupted between Noble and his allies against Binion's forces made it appear for a while that the city was another Chicago in the 1920s. Before the war finally ended with his murder, Noble survived an incredible number of gangland attempts to kill him. So elusive was he that he gained the nickname, "the Cat." Noble was convinced that Binion—from his Las Vegas setting—was the man who had placed a "contract" on his life. Although he refused publicly to identify him, even to police, his statements about the attempts on his life clearly referred to Binion. The man responsible, Noble told reporters, lived 1,500 miles from Dallas. "That man...wants to get me just because his pride is hurt."

The efforts to kill Noble began on January 15, 1946, when assailants shot him several times from an automobile on a country road near his Grapevine ranch northwest of Dallas. Although badly wounded, Noble escaped death by managing to drive to a farm house and crawling under it. Two years later a would-be assassin ambushed and wounded him again as he drove near his ranch at Grapevine. Borrowing a note from the macabre Valentine's Day massacre in Chicago in the 1920s, another effort was made to kill Noble on Valentine's Day, 1949. In this instance dynamite was attached under his car so that it would explode when he started it. The plot failed when one of Noble's friends saw a strange man underneath the car, became suspicious, and summoned police, who found the dynamite.

Later that year Noble and a friend noticed a black Ford passing and re-passing the Grapevine place. Finally, the two pursued the car at a high rate of speed until the Ford failed to make a turn and overturned. The four men inside climbed out shooting. Noble suffered a shotgun wound. Sometime later police arrested a forty-four-year-old ex-convict named G.R. (Jack) Nesbit on an assault-to-murder charge.

More spectacular headlines came two months later in November at Noble's Oak Cliff house when his wife happened to take his car one morning rather than her own, not knowing that overnight someone had attached to it a powerful charge of nitroglycerin. When the thirty-six-year-old Mrs. Noble started the late-model Mercury it exploded with such force that it demolished the car down to its chassis and wheels. Mrs. Noble was dismembered, her torso falling into their front yard. Police questioned a large number of suspects, but no charges were filed. Noble and his eighteen-year-old daughter continued to live in the house, but Noble installed floodlights to sweep the yard, brought in half a dozen big dogs, and stationed weapons within easy reach.

Underworld rumors circulated that Binion had hired a tough, blond-haired mobster named Hollis Delois (Lois) Green to arrange for Noble's death. At least one member of Green's gang already had been questioned about the explosion that killed Mrs. Noble. Green, just thirty-one, for the past half dozen years had headed a mob involved in crimes less seemly than gambling—drugs, prostitution, robbery, and safecracking. Green, who also lived in Oak Cliff, had a police record three pages long for such things as robbery and burglary. He was overbearing, arrogant, and brutal.

In the past months law enforcement officials had been systematically reducing his gang's size: two had been slain, twenty had been sentenced to prison, and about ten more were in police custody. Green himself was said to be "jail proof" because of his ties to defense attorneys and bondsmen. No sooner would police stop him than Green would summon a bondsman over his mobile car telephone to meet him at the police station to arrange for his immediate release. Green and his brother had grown up in an area widely associated with criminal activities, on St. Louis Street one block over from Pocahontas Street where Binion had lived. But Green's brother was now in the penitentiary in North Carolina, and Green himself was under three indictments for robbery, burglary, and being a fugitive from justice from Idaho.

On the evening of December 22, 1949, Green and some of his cronies, including one who had been questioned about Mrs. Noble's killing, were partying at a West Commerce Street nightspot, the Sky-Vu Club. The revelry continued past midnight into the early hours of Christmas Eve. At about 1 a.m., the party over, Green stepped from the club into an alley to climb into his green convertible. A hail of shots sounded from behind a nearby parked car. Green died instantly of bullet wounds in his upper chest and throat. Police found only a few 12-gauge shotgun shells scattered about, although the mortal wounds were thought to have come from a pistol. Police believed Noble was responsible for killing Green in revenge; they questioned him extensively, but were unable to develop a case against him.

One week later on New Year's Eve, Noble stepped out of his Oak Cliff house to drive to a drugstore for a newspaper. An unknown assailant fired two shots from a 30.06 rifle at him; one passed through his left arm and lodged in his back, nestled delicately next to his spine. Noble fell backwards to safety into his living room, and his daughter summoned an ambulance. When ambulance attendants got there, Noble, fearing a ruse, refused to let them into the house until police arrived. He was taken to Methodist Hospital. Police said they hoped to question Binion in Las Vegas or at his ranch in Montana about the incident. As Noble lay recovering in Methodist Hospital five weeks later he again barely escaped death when a rifleman fired a shot into his room from outside but missed him. Six months later, having recovered, Noble was driving in an armored car near his Grapevine ranch when gunmen once again ambushed him from behind a duck blind. This time, too, he escaped harm.

From Las Vegas Binion, more and more identified as Noble's adversary, felt obliged to send a message by emissary to Noble insisting that he had nothing to do with the death of Mrs. Noble. The emissary, Harold Shimley, met with Noble in a tourist cabin near Love Field. Their conversation was recorded secretly by the Dallas Police Department's George Butler. Binion "swears and hopes his children will die" if he had anything to do with Mrs. Noble's death, Noble was told.

Noble didn't believe him, but he accepted Shimley's report that Binion already had identified the man responsible for planting the dynamite. That man since had been convicted of another crime, and he was serving time in the state penitentiary. Shimley told Noble that Binion was prepared to have the man murdered in the penitentiary if it would square matters. "Well, that's good enough for me," Noble replied. Whether or not the unidentified convict met such a fate is unknown.

Meanwhile, Dallas police and the district attorney were making their own war on the policy wheel racket. On December 28, 1949, between Green's death and the shooting of Noble on his front porch, officers conducted a series of raids on gambling operations. Less than two weeks later District Attorney Wilson filed felony charges against seven alleged kingpins of the policy wheel racket, including Binion and his Dallas lieutenant, Harry Urban Jr., the "big shots" of the scheme. Noble, who consistently described himself as a "retired gambler," was not among those charged. Binion began a long battle to avoid being extradited to Dallas for trial; Urban was tried and sentenced to four years in prison.

No sooner had the guilty verdict been returned than a Dallas man, reputedly involved in gambling, called Wade, who had tried the case, and asked him how soon Urban would be re-tried after his case was reversed. But the case has just now been tried, Wade said, and there has been no reversal. There will be, the man said, because he understood that an appeals judge had been paid $10,000 for a reversal. Wade went to the district judge who tried the case, Robert Hall, and asked him if such a thing could be possible. Judge Hall said he believed that it could be true. "They offered me $5,000 to give him a new trial," he said. Sure enough, Urban's conviction was overturned by two members of the Texas Court of Criminal Appeals because of evidence introduced into the trial concerning past gambling activities that was ruled inadmissible and irrelevant to the charges.

The efforts to kill Noble brought not just page-one headlines in bold type in Dallas, but also undesired national attention. The *Denver Post* sent its crime reporter to investigate, and in a six-part series on "the Southwest's crime and culture center" he concluded that in Dallas "mob violence and derision for the law" could "boil over any time." Dallas leaders, aghast, loudly disputed the conclusions. In retaliation the *News* sent its ace police reporter, McCormick, to Denver to write his own expose of crime in Denver.

One night in January 1951 Noble, armed with a rifle and pistol, charged into a West Dallas grocery store owned by an alleged mobster, Charles (Sonny) LeFors, and confronted at gunpoint a man named Jack Todd. Todd, one of the late Green's henchmen, had been with Green at the Sky-Vu Club the night he had been shot to death, and just one week before this confrontation he had been arrested as he boarded an airplane with nitroglycerine of the type used to blow up Noble's wife. A witness heard Noble say to Todd, "If you don't tell me what you know I'll shoot your damn brains out." Noble removed a pistol from Todd's belt and forced him into his car, then drove west on Singleton Boulevard with the lights out. A few blocks away Todd evidently struggled with Noble and forced the car into a ditch. A fierce fight ensued, and sheriff's deputies arrived in time to see them in a death struggle over a rifle and pistol. Noble's ear lobe was practically torn off his head, and Todd was bruised with tooth marks in his back.

Two weeks later a bomb was tossed under Sonny's Grocery in the middle of the night. Damage was minimal, and no one was present when it occurred.

A fortnight later a nightclub owned by Noble, the Airmen's Club on Live Oak, was shattered by a bomb. Police called it a "pre-Valentine's Day gangland greeting." No one was injured. In March 1951 Noble climbed into his private airplane to fly to New Mexico. A nitroglycerine bomb exploded as he started the engine, but a steel wall in front of the pilot's cabin was sufficient to keep the force away and prevent injury. In May 1951 yet another bombing occurred, this one at a restaurant on Lovers Lane owned by former Sheriff Guthrie. A year later three men were arrested for this explosion. They said Noble had paid them $250 to do the job, having told them that he wanted only to "irritate" Guthrie a little. Guthrie had no idea why Noble would want to do such a thing, for he said he never had dealt with him at any time.

In April 1951 Noble went to Austin to testify before a state house committee investigating crime in Texas. He asserted that Dallas was free of organized gambling as a result of Will Wilson's election, but that Binion's old gang was continuing to operate from twelve to fourteen policy wheels on a "sneak" basis. Noble said he had heard that a $50,000 price had been put on his head, and that Binion was after him simply because he wouldn't "bow down to him." A month later, Senator Estes Kefauver's crime-investigating committee estimated that gambling and policy wheel rackets in Dallas did some $14 million annually in business.

Noble's Grapevine ranch house was as well-protected as his house in Oak Cliff. A pack of Dalmatian dogs roamed the grounds to keep trespassers away. Floodlights kept the area well-lit. Wherever Noble walked on the grounds he carried a carbine rifle. But on August 7, 1951, four months after his Austin testimony, Noble's luck ended. As he stepped from his car to check his roadside mailbox a powerful dynamite explosion blew him and his car to bits. The impact left a hole three-feet deep and five feet in diameter. The forty-two-year-old gambler's body was torn asunder. His head, shoulder, and arms were left intact, but the rest of his body was shredded into pieces over a sixty-foot area. Some $550 in cash and a deck of playing cards were scattered about.

Police theorized that Noble's assailant had used a battery to activate the explosion via wire from a short distance away. A dozen or so mobsters were questioned, but no one ever was prosecuted for the crime. Benny Binion again denied any connection with the slaying. With Noble dead, gangland warfare in Dallas ended.

In Las Vegas Binion continued to live a "respectable" life. However, Dallas' new district attorney, Henry Wade, elected to succeed Wilson in 1950, was determined to bring Binion back to Dallas to face gambling charges. He developed a new case against him for evading income taxes from his share in two policy partnerships from which he allegedly received $30,252 in 1949.

But Binion's friends in high places included the foreman of the federal grand jury in Dallas, businessman Jimmy Purse, who openly opposed indicting him and who openly criticized Wade for his zeal in seeking to prosecute Binion. Just thirteen of twenty-three grand jury votes were needed for an indictment, though, and Binion was indicted over Purse's objections with a strong push from a young member of the grand jury, oilman Leo Corrigan Jr. When the indictment was returned in Federal Judge T. Whitfield Davidson's courtroom, Purse—emotionally distraught—dropped dead of a heart attack.

Desperate to avoid a return to Dallas where he knew he would be arrested to stand trial on gambling charges, Binion sought to plead no contest in Nevada to the federal charges. The U.S. district attorney for the Northern District of Texas, Frank B. Potter, was willing to permit Binion to plead no contest in Nevada and thus avoid a return to Texas. Wade went over Potter's head and appealed to U.S. Attorney General James McGranery to overrule his recommendation and to urge that Binion be made to return to Texas to enter his plea. Davidson, fortified by a lengthy memo which Wade's office had prepared for the attorney general's office concerning Binion's unsavory background, ordered him to Texas. Meanwhile, the F.B.I. received a tip that Binion had paid an underworld character to assassinate the district attorney, and the agency offered to provide personal protection for the crusading district attorney. Wade refused it, and nothing more developed concerning the threat.

Three years after the gambling charges had been filed, Binion returned to Texas. The result was that he was sentenced twice: he received a five-year sentence for income tax evasion in federal court and a four-year sentence in a state district court for his policy wheel racket. The two sentences were ordered to run concurrently, and Binion went to the federal prison at Fort Leavenworth, where he served four years before being released. He thereupon returned to Las Vegas.

Many years later in 1986, when he was eighty-one years old and in poor health, Binion told a newspaper reporter that he and his wife had greatly missed Dallas during their many years in exile, his wife more than he. "Sometimes all you do is mention the name and she almost starts crying," he said.

Upon his death on Christmas Day, 1989, he was eulogized in Las Vegas as a "man for all seasons." His funeral procession was several blocks long, and services described as "emotional" were attended by political leaders, Nevada gaming executives, and many other prominent individuals. Even in death Binion did not return to Texas or Dallas; his cemetery lots at Hillcrest Memorial Park went unused.

Organized professional gambling in Dallas had been forced out of the county. Some of Binion's old gang reportedly made their way to Fort Worth to commence operations there.

CCA AND TISTE ADOUE

At city hall, Mayor Rodgers and the incumbent city council, after holding office for eight long years, now were ready to yield their authority to a new team of CCA candidates. The council could brag of several major accomplishments: implementing major portions of Bartholomew's master plan, purchasing the needed right-of-way for the new Central Boulevard, and adopting a zoning ordinance at its next-to-last meeting which set up fourteen zoning classifications instead of eight. Rodgers had served as mayor longer than any other Dallas leader in the twentieth century, a mark which seemed destined to last indefinitely. It had been a time when war had curtailed many activities and initiatives, but one in which Rodgers and his colleagues grabbed the opportunity to turn their attention to planning. The harmony with which this had been done and the tenor of the years caused Rodgers to comment that "I do not see how men could serve together for eight years with fewer conflicts of opinions and misunderstandings."

As had occurred in the courthouse elections in 1946, the spring municipal campaign for city council, in which every seat was open, attracted a large number of returning war veterans. A record number of candidates, forty-six, filed for office. They represented parties with names such as All-Dallas, G.I. and Veterans, Greater Dallas Association, People's Party, and People's Protective Party. All were distinct underdogs to the CCA. None but the CCA candidates publicly committed themselves to returning the council-manager form of government. The People's Party pledged to put the matter to a popular vote.

The CCA's harmony was disrupted by a disagreement as to whether Mayor Pro Tem J.B. (Tiste) Adoue Jr. or attorney Robert G. Storey, recently returned from duty as a prosecutor in the Nuremberg war crimes, should head the ticket. Adoue, a stubborn and self-confident banker accustomed to leading, had feuded openly with the mayor because he disdained Rodgers' pet project, Central Boulevard, and scoffed at the value of a master plan. The issue between Adoue and Storey was resolved quietly when Storey declined to run and Adoue became ill and withdrew as a candidate.

When the votes were counted in 1947 only two candidates won clear victories. Both were CCA men: Jimmie R. Temple of Oak Cliff, who was elected at-large, and Wallace H. Savage, a Navy veteran and Harvard law school graduate chosen to represent Place 5. The remaining seven seats were thrown into a run-off. Every seat but one was won by a CCA candidate. The sole CCA loser was a young former master sergeant, Joe Golman of South Dallas, who was criticized roundly for being too young at the age of twenty-three to hold office. (Years later in 1962 he was appointed to the council, then twice won election to the council.) The winner in the South Dallas race was C.G. Stubbs Jr. of the All-Dallas Party. Prior to assuming office, the council-elect met privately in the Baker Hotel and chose Temple as their mayor and Savage as mayor pro tem.

Temple, small, energetic, and friendly, was a former auto mechanic and parts man at Ford Motor Co. He left to work for Oak Farms Dairy and worked his way to president. His wife was the granddaughter of a former mayor of Dallas, Bryan T. Barry, who had served a single term in that office from 1896 to 1898. Temple himself was destined to be a one-term mayor. In 1949 he decided not to run for re-election.

Adoue, now sixty-five and bearing a distinguished-looking full head of white hair slicked straight back, was not through with city politics. He had been appointed to the council in March 1942 upon the death of E.J. Ward Cannon, and re-elected in 1943 and 1945. During his terms on the council Adoue charted a vigorous and independent path, crossing swords with the powerful Rodgers with apparent relish over such key issues as Central Boulevard. After a two-year absence from office from 1947 to 1949 he decided to return in 1949 with his sights set squarely on the mayor's seat.

Jean Baptist Adoue Jr. was the son of a French emigrant who came to Dallas in 1879 and founded the private banking house which had become the National Bank of Commerce. Adoue, born in 1884 at the family home at the corner of Cadiz and Evergreen just south of downtown in the fashionable Cedars area, had joined his father's bank after he earned a law degree at the University of Texas in 1906. In 1924, upon his father's death, Adoue became the bank president. He served twice as president of the Chamber of Commerce.

As a younger man Adoue had won the tennis championship of the state of Texas five times, and he continued to be an avid player who had gained national attention, having been ranked nationally in both singles and doubles and being captain of the U.S. Davis Cup team in 1938. Adoue's passion for the active life encompassed automobile racing, too, and he was considered an expert on all automotive affairs. For many years he drove annually to Indianapolis to see the Indy 500.

Selecting the CCA slate was not difficult since seven of the nine incumbents announced for re-election. Their success at the polls was virtually assured. Before the election the candidates met in Robert L. Thornton's penthouse office in his new Mercantile Bank Building to plan their post-election strategy. They informally agreed that Adoue should be their mayor. As expected, the nine-member CCA slate won every council seat. It was no surprise that Adoue led the ticket with 15,527 votes, followed by G.C. Stubbs. His selection as mayor was widely assumed.

However, when the council-elect met, four of those present concluded that the younger Savage, who had been mayor pro tem the previous term, was a more comfortable choice as presiding officer than Adoue. Having worked with Savage during the previous term and having seen him preside when Temple was absent, council members appreciated his general outlook and demeanor. They also knew of Adoue's reputation as a maverick. Savage, out of town, did not attend the meeting. As the ninth councilman he held the tie-breaking vote on electing the mayor.

Consequently, the moment Savage and his wife returned to Dallas several councilmen met them at the Union Terminal train station. They quickly apprised him of the situation and persuaded him to vote for himself so that he would become mayor instead of Adoue.

Adoue, furious at his unexpected loss, loudly protested after the official vote that he had been double-crossed. As the top vote-getter, as a considerably older and more experienced man than Savage, and as the previously anointed choice, he felt betrayed. He vowed to take the matter to the voters to change the charter so that they elected the mayor themselves.

In this crusade, surprisingly, Adoue won the backing of the CCA officers, who through their president, Laurence R. Melton, petitioned the council to submit the charter amendment to the voters. Savage, as presiding officer, kept his thoughts to himself during the presentation, but four other council members voiced their strong opposition despite CCA approval. Councilman Roland Pelt feared that such a change would lead to the adoption of a "strong-mayor" plan for the city. "I'm surprised," he said, "to see such a request come from the officers of the Citizens Charter Association."

Although made up entirely of CCA members, the majority of the council rejected this request from their organization's president. The only remaining recourse to effect the change was by petition. The city charter provided for a mandatory election if 10 percent of the registered voters requested it. Adoue sent a letter and petition to every poll tax holder in the city and placed large advertisements in the newspapers urging that the petitions be signed and returned. More than twice enough signatures were obtained to force the election, and the council dutifully agreed to hold an election on the issue on November 1.

The city's two daily newspapers split on the issue, with the *News* opposing it as being ruinous to the council-manager plan and the *Times Herald* favoring it. In the campaign Adoue denounced the "powerful and influential downtown and Highland Park tycoons" for their practice of choosing mayors in secret meetings. Dallas voters agreed with Adoue. In a close election they approved the charter change, 7,260 to 6,216.

The entire episode was revealing. CCA officers had recommended one course of action, yet their own anointed council members had refused to endorse it. The CCA shook off this interal split on an important issue without lasting effect even though the council-manager plan had been significantly altered to give voters a larger share of responsibililty than had been intended originally.

Curtis P. Smith, left, was Dallas' last mayor under the old aldermanic system of city government.

Stephen J. Hay, right, became the city's first mayor under the commission form of government in 1907.

Scenes such as this on McKinney Avenue were familiar in the flood of 1908.

Just visible in the center background is the lifeless body of Allen Brooks, taken by force from a courtroom in 1912 by a lynch mob and hanged at Akard and Commerce.

Dallas businessmen are prepared for a ride. Seated at the wheel of the Chalmers automobile, left, is Hugh Chalmers, the manufacturer who was visiting Dallas in 1908.

Two Immoral Resorts at No. 2116—2114 Griffin Street, Dallas, Texas. Owned by Mr. R. M. Chastain and Dr. W. W. Samuel.

In his efforts to end prostitution, reformer J.T. Upchurch sought to embarrass the owners of properties by using names and pictures in his publication, *The Purity Journal.*

This picture of three young prostitutes also appeared in *The Purity Journal.*

Henry Lindsley, left, was the founder in 1907 of the Citizens Association, the organization which would be the forerunner of the city's "establishment."

The "boy mayor," Frank Wozencraft, right, won wide praise as the city's mayor for the single term he served, 1919-1921.

This is the 1919 graduating class of the Dallas Colored High School.

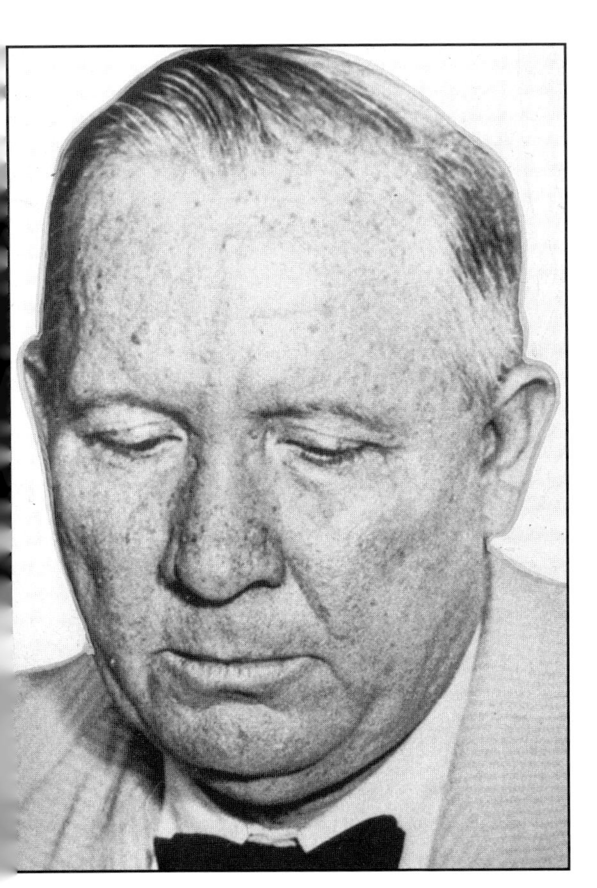

The leader of the Ku Klux Klan in Dallas was Hiram Wesley Evans, a dentist whose success led him to the Klan's national headquarters in Atlanta, Georgia, where he took over the national organization.

The extent of Klan penetration in Dallas in the early 1920s is suggested by the size of the Women KKK Drum Corps. The Klan also boasted of a junior auxiliary.

An all-male crowd gathered in 1925 for the two murder trials of the Noel brothers.

After their death sentences, the handcuffed Noel brothers were driven to Huntsville for execution.

Louis Blaylock served the City of Dallas in more capacities than any individual under the commission form of government, including two terms as mayor from 1923 to 1927.

Sheriff Dan Harston, wearing the big mustache, shows off results of raids on bootleggers.

Bill Erwin and his young wife pose jauntily not long before their fatal flight over the Pacific.

National Air Transport began carrying air mail from Dallas to Chicago in 1926.

Edwin J. Kiest of the *Times Herald*

J. Waddy Tate was a flamboyant mayor.

Clyde Barrow's parents operated this filling station on Singleton Boulevard in the 1930s.

Progressive Voters League members, seen in about 1937, activated the black community.

The Gypsy Tea Room was just one of any number of exotic places common to Deep Ellum for many decades.

The Harlem movie theater on Deep Ellum sometimes showed films with all-black casts.

Sarah T. Hughes was a well-known Dallas lawyer, legislator and state judge long before being appointed to the federal bench by President Kennedy.

Elmer Scott had a successful business career before heading the Civic Federation and championing the cause of minorities and the poor.

The Hall of Negro Life, built for the Texas Centennial only after a protracted struggle, was the only major Centennial building to be torn down prior to the 1937 Pan-American Exposition.

African-Americans for many years were given only limited access to the State Fair of Texas. This photograph, taken probably in the 1930s, shows Negro Day at the Fair.

Patrons at the Fair and during summers threw balls to drop black youths from collapsible perches into a tank of water. By the late '40s the concession was called the African Dip.

This row of shanty houses in Little Mexico points directly to downtown Dallas' towering banks.

Mexican-Americans celebrate on Cinco de Mayo in Little Mexico.

Harry S. Truman's campaign visit to Dallas in 1948 at the baseball stadium attracted a number of black supporters who were able to sit with whites on the playing field.

As this sign suggests, white and black neighborhoods were sharply delineated for years.

Dist. Atty. Henry Wade, center, early in his long career at the courthouse, is flanked by city homicide detective Will Fritz, left, and investigator Jimmy McNichol.

Gambling devices confiscated by Dist. Atty. Will Wilson await a judge's order for destruction.

Gambler Herbert Noble and his teenage daughter after the funeral of Mrs. Noble, who was killed mistakenly in an attempt on Noble's life by rivals. Noble believed that rival Benny Binion was responsible.

After more than a dozen failed attempts, mobsters finally succeeded in killing Noble in 1951 by detonating an explosive under his car as he checked his rural mailbox.

From left, oilman Eugene McElvaney, SMU President Willis M. Tate, and grocer Robert B. Cullum, helped chart Southern Methodist University's path.

The ruling elite, from left: Stanley Marcus, Fred Florence, Ben Wooten, and Robert L. Thornton.

Post-war Dallas, with the Magnolia Building, center, and Mercantile Bank the tallest buildings.

Gambler Benny Binion, finally brought back to Texas, testifies in Judge Henry King's court.

Officers examine evidence at this Eugene Street house in South Dallas, damaged by an explosion.

John Runyon of the *Times Herald,* left, and Fort Worth's Amon Carter stay on safe grounds.

This photograph, taken in about 1950, clearly shows the congestion surrounding Love Field.

Fords assembled at the plant on Grand Avenue bore the label, "Made in Texas by Texans."

These former mayors of Dallas, all involved in the project, presided over a ceremony in 1956 marking completion of Central Expressway. They are, from left, George Sergeant, George Sprague, J.B. Adoue, R.L. Thornton, Woodall Rodgers, and Wallace Savage.

Bertoia's controversial and abstract screen hangs above the circulation desk at the public library.

Robert L. Thornton, top center, is flanked by the CCA slate of councilmen after their election in 1953. They are, clockwise: Thornton, W.J. Harris, Vernon S. Smith, Arthur Kramer Jr., Roderick B. Thomas, W.C. Miller, J.R. Tevy, Milton Richardson, and O.H. Vickery.

Juanita Craft, third from right, organized pickets in 1955 to protest "Black Achievement Day" at the State Fair of Texas, an event referred to on one of the picket signs as "Negro Appeasement Day."

Black citizens had their own "Negro Achievement Day" (about 1950).

Somber-faced officials and city leaders, including Mayor Wes Wise (first from left on the third row), receive a briefing on court-ordered school desegregation.

Opening day of schools in the early 1950s at Sunset High in Oak Cliff shows a sea of white faces.

Initial desegregation of the city's schools in fall, 1961, was minimal, but it attracted widespread praise because of the peaceful manner in which it was accomplished. The arrival of the first black children was fully recorded by the press.

Thurgood Marshall, left, frequently visited Dallas as he assisted and advised the local NAACP a other organizations in their efforts to dissolve racial barriers.

By the 1960s oilman H.L. Hunt had turned his interests to right-wing political causes.

A. Maceo Smith was an effective activist and organizer for the black community.

The annual Texas-Oklahoma football game during the State Fair of Texas attracted thousands of revelers along Commerce Street. Police usually made scores of arrests.

Lee Harvey Oswald, a former U.S. Marine who had defected at one time to the Soviet Union, allegedly fired the shots that killed President John F. Kennedy at Dealey Plaza.

The presidential party departs Love Field for the motorcade drive through downtown Dallas.

nnette Strauss was a long-time
orker for civic and art causes before
ecoming Dallas' first woman mayor.

Juanita Craft, the first black woman to
serve on city council, was a veteran in
civil rights activities.

George Allen, Dallas' first elected African-American councilman, became mayor pro tem.

W.L. (Lew) Sterrett, county judge.

Raymond Nasher, NorthPark develop

Barefoot Sanders as U.S. district attorney

Robert Folsom, pro-growth may

Adlene Harrison, a CCA-endorsed councilwoman who later was elected as an independent.

Anita Martinez, Dallas' first Mexican-American councilwoman, was elected as a CCA candidate in 1969.

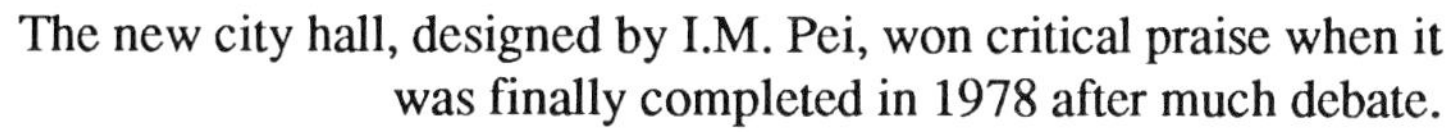

The new city hall, designed by I.M. Pei, won critical praise when it was finally completed in 1978 after much debate.

Protestors showed their anger on downtown streets when the Justice Department refused to review the incident in which a 12-year-old boy, Santos Rodriguez, was shot to death by a police officer.

As publisher of the *Dallas News*, Robert W. Decherd brought a more moderate tone to the paper.

hese four individuals were among the minority leaders who helped direct the Dallas Independent School District in the 1980s and 1990s. Top, Rene Castilla and Kathlyn Gilliam; bottom, Dr. Marvin Edwards and Yvonne Ewell. Dr. Edwards was the district's first black superintendent.

Sculptor Henry Moore's "Dallas Piece," designed for the city hall's park plaza, had become by the1990s a billboard for graffiti artists who wielded knives to carve their messages.

John Wiley Price, a county commissioner, became a familiar sight as he regularly led demonstrators to protest hiring practices by the Dallas Police Department and other agencies, including television stations.

12

The Uneasy Fifties

The plot reached into unbelievable places....There was evidence that lay and religious and community groups, through misguided leadership, entered an action, perhaps unwittingly, that resulted in violence and destruction.

—Dallas County grand jury, 1951

THE CURMUDGEON MAYOR

Dutifully and with trepidation, Citizens Charter Association leaders in 1951 endorsed the crusty, silver-haired Adoue in his great desire to become mayor. Since CCA nomination was tantamount to election, Adoue easily became the first mayor directly elected by the voters in twenty-two years. Taking office with him was a full slate of supporting CCA councilmen. Nevertheless, harmony was not destined to reign. From the first session to the last one, the council's term became the most tumultuous in memory.

Even beyond his accomplishments as a civic leader, businessman, and athlete, there was much to admire in the sixty-six-year-old Adoue. Notwithstanding his prominent social standing, his streak of independence included rebellion against stuffed shirts. A hint of this was seen in an anecdote related about him when he took office. Some time earlier a Negro porter at his bank fell prey to a con artist who smooth-talked him into lending him money to buy gasoline for his car, promising to repay him with a huge load of potatoes. The potatoes failed to arrive, of course, and two bank employees began taunting the porter unmercifully about his gullibility. Adoue learned of the situation, was furious, and without telling anyone went to a grocery store, bought its entire stock of potatoes, and had them delivered anonymously to the porter's desk. The two men never teased him again.

As a mayor ordained by popular vote, Adoue immediately sought to take advantage of what he evidently presumed to be his prerogative. On the Saturday prior to the first council session Adoue telephoned City Manager Charles Ford at his city hall office and asked him to resign. Ford refused. At the council meeting a few days later Adoue sought council support to fire Ford, reciting a list of his supposed inefficiencies, ineptness, and bungling. Not a single council member supported Adoue. Ford retained his position, and the working relationship normally required between the mayor and city manager was irreparably damaged from the beginning. (Towards the end of Adoue's term, though, Ford had had enough; he voluntarily resigned and was replaced by Elgin Crull, a former newspaper reporter who earlier had joined the city manager's staff.)

In addition to his bold move to fire the city manager, Adoue on the same day also balked against the routine re-appointment of the city's two corporation court judges. Adoue claimed that they had been automatically and improperly reducing the fines of well-heeled defendants who came to court with lawyers. Not a single council member supported him in this effort, either. Former mayor Savage and three other former council members watched this first council session from the audience in what was a preview of a two-year term that would be marked frequently by sharp clashes and 8-1 votes—Adoue on the losing side.

Soon in his term Adoue began criticizing the police department and Police Chief Carl Hansson for various alleged improprieties and inefficiencies. Under the council-manager plan, of course, Hansson was the city manager's appointee, accountable only to him and immune to council action. But Adoue's persistence caused the council to appoint a blue-ribbon committee—one Adoue promptly denounced as unqualified by training and experience—to investigate the police department. (It had been just such a committee that James Aston rejected in 1939 as an intolerable intrusion into his authority as city manager. In the decade since, however, strict allegiance to council-manager theory had eroded during Aston's absence as Mayor Rodgers and his long-term council exerted increasing authority over municipal affairs.) In its report the committee exonerated Police Chief Hansson and the department.

Adoue's crusade against alleged abuses by the police department included his personal intervention in a case in which he witnessed a Negro driver being handcuffed, arrested, and charged with failure to obey an officer and drunken driving. Unknown to police, Adoue was just behind in his own car when the incident occurred, and he fully supported the arrested man's contention that his "failure" to obey an officer's directive was nothing but a simple, unintended misunderstanding. The enraged Adoue personally went to the city jail to intervene in the man's behalf and arrange for his immediate release. The charges stood, however, and at a corporation court trial Adoue testified for the man. The man was found not guilty of the charge of failing to obey an officer, but he was fined $10 for drunken driving.

Despite the turbulence in Adoue's term, a number of accomplishments were achieved. Voters passed a $49,985,000 capital improvements bond program, the city's largest ever, and a $12.5 million bond program to expand Love Field. New sites were selected for a municipal auditorium, city hall, library, and health administration building, and the City of Dallas continued on an ambitious expansion program by aggressively annexing large surrounding areas.

A New Era Begins at the Courthouse

At the courthouse, down at the opposite end of town from city hall, incumbents were in for a hard time as the post-war mood to begin afresh set in. The victories of Will Wilson and Steve Guthrie in 1946 were an early indication of this pattern. Democrats such as W.L. (Lew) Sterrett, Henry Wade, Bill Decker, Bill Shaw, Ed Steger, Ben Gentle, and Warren G. Harding won offices to be elected time and time again over the next two decades and more.

Elected at the same time as Guthrie and Wilson in 1946 was Bill Shaw, a returned Army veteran who before the war had held the position of deputy district clerk. In 1946 he defeated his former boss, the incumbent Pearl Smith, who had served four terms. Shaw assumed office on January 1, 1947, and began a reign that lasted until his retirement thirty-four years later.

In the 1948 election Walter Lewis (Lew) Sterrett and James Eric (Bill) Decker, both of whom had worked their way up from the bottom at the courthouse, won their races for county judge and sheriff. Sterrett, born May 13, 1902, on a farm at Como, Texas, grew up there, worked in the farm fields, sold watermelons and newspapers, labored in the nearby lignite mines, and then went to Dallas to take business courses at the Metropolitan Business College, following the pattern Robert L. Thornton had set some years earlier. To help pay his way Sterrett took a temporary job at the courthouse as an assistant to the county clerk. He did so well that he was asked to stay longer. He did, and in 1938 he was appointed justice of the peace for Precinct One, a position he held until 1948 when he decided to challenge the incumbent county judge, Al Templeton, who was campaigning for his fourth term. Sterrett, endorsed by a poll of the Dallas Bar Association as best qualified, also won editorial support from the *News*. The result was an upset victory over the veteran Templeton. Sterrett thus began what would be a twenty-seven year reign as the top administrator of Dallas County government.

That same year Decker, a close friend to Sterrett and a long-term deputy sheriff who had resigned with Steve Guthrie's victory in 1946, defeated Guthrie and began a career as sheriff that would continue until he resigned shortly before his death in 1970. Decker was born in 1895 in a frame cottage at Akard and Belleview streets. His father operated a liquor store, and in that rough neighborhood just south of downtown many of young Decker's friends turned to crime. Decker himself dropped out of Bryan High School before graduation and began his career at the courthouse in 1920 as an elevator operator. Two years later he became a court clerk, then a deputy constable the following year. In 1933 Smoot Schmid appointed him chief deputy sheriff, a position he held until Schmid's defeat by Guthrie. As deputy sheriff for fourteen years, Decker earned a formidable reputation as a fearless lawman and a straight-shooter, and also as a man known and respected by the criminal element, many of whom he had known as a boy on the streets. This reputation he maintained throughout his twenty-four years as sheriff.

Also in that same 1948 election Ben Gentle, who had been appointed tax assessor-collector upon Ed Cobb's death the previous year, won the election to that office without a run-off. This also marked the beginning of a long career which did not end until twenty-five years from his initial appointment with his retirement at the end of 1972.

Henry Wade, who had lost to Will Wilson in 1946 in the race for district attorney only to become Wilson's chief felony prosecutor, ran once more in 1950 when Wilson elected to run for state office. Wade took office on January 1, 1951, and continued to be district attorney until he retired thirty-six years later on January 1, 1987. During these years he became one of the nation's most famous and successful district attorneys, noted for a sensational record of courtroom triumphs and for developing a large number of aggressive prosecutors. He also gained particular attention for his courtroom victory over famed and flamboyant defense attorney Melvin Belli in prosecuting and winning the death penalty for Jack Ruby. Later, Wade would be the famous "Wade" in the abortion case, Roe v. Wade, even though he was not an active participant in the legal battle.

Also taking office in 1950 as county treasurer was Warren G. Harding, who would continue in that position until 1977 when he was appointed state treasurer.

One incumbent who managed to prevail over his post-war challengers was Ed H. Steger, county clerk. Steger became county clerk in 1933, a position he held until 1962 when he died at the age of seventy-eight.

All these officials together brought a remarkably long and stable period of efficient management to the Dallas County courthouse.

'BOMBINGS' IN SOUTH DALLAS

As yet, race relations never appeared on priority lists of problems to solve. The 1947-48 *Negro City Directory* summarized the overall situation optimistically: "Although Dallas interracially has had its rough spots, it has been remarkably consistent for the degree to which the races have worked together for development of the city as a whole." Negroes enjoyed in Dallas, the directory said, the opportunity "to help in the planning for most of the movements in the city which affect them."

Such statements were entirely too optimistic. Problems did exist, of course, and they were becoming more apparent throughout the nation as well as in Dallas. Black leaders were beginning to demand more persistently and in louder terms better opportunities in housing, jobs, and law enforcement. Their arguments were taking on a new tone, though. Whereas they previously had concentrated on improving their separate and segregated facilities, now they began to insist on integration as their goal.

A talk by A. Maceo Smith in 1946 in Hobbs, New Mexico, demonstrated the new attitude. Smith, speaking as an official of the Federal Housing Authority, called segregation "one of the worst evils tolerated by any people." Not only did it "sectionize" the people, it created barriers of inter-racial understanding and good will. It bred "envy and hate" and ultimately caused strife, misery, and destruction.

This more aggressive language reflected one of the most important civil-rights victories to that date for black Americans—the U.S. Supreme Court's 1944 Smith v. Allwright decision declaring all-white Democratic Party primaries prevalent in Texas and the South to be unconstitutional. The exclusion of Negroes from Democratic primaries, of course, had been one of the most effective barriers to blacks in a one-party system which saw the Democrats controlling Southern politics at all levels. Fourteen months after having masterminded this legal victory, the NAACP's chief counsel, Thurgood Marshall, came to Dallas to plan an attack against segregated higher education in Texas. He enrolled the assistance of Dallas' most prominent black attorneys, W.J. Durham and C.B. Bunkley Jr. The ultimate result was another important decision, Sweatt v. Painter, in which the Supreme Court in 1950 declared the University of Texas' all-white law school to be unconstitutional.

Meanwhile, immediately following the Smith v. Allwright decision, A.G. Weems, Juanita Craft, and two other men began working diligently in the black community as deputy poll tax collectors. By 1946 an estimated 13,000 Dallas Negroes held poll taxes, and they participated for the first time in the Dallas Democratic County convention. Black delegates from eight precincts, including three Negro precinct chairmen, attended.

The Negro Chamber of Commerce's 1946 campaign for new members, under the leadership of president A. Maceo Smith, was the most intensive and profitable in the organization's history. A total of 1,574 members were recruited. The chamber enunciated specific goals that year for blacks: a first-class hotel, a technical high school, an amusements center, additional housing, police officers, an R.O.T.C. unit for high school students, and better accommodations on common carriers.

The Council of Negro Organizations, formed in October 1942 after the riot in the Hall and Thomas streets area, joined hands with the Negro Chamber of Commerce in pushing for these and other improvements. The council's first project, equal pay for black teachers, had been achieved during the war by way of a federal court order.

Another organization, buoyed by its successes in the federal courts, was picking up momentum as a force in the Dallas Negro community. This was the local NAACP, which for 1947 set an ambitious membership goal of 10,000.

Segregation in the post-war era seemed especially painful. Negro soldiers had risked their lives in uniform to help the nation preserve a democratic way of life, a way of life that so often excluded them. Discrimination was especially inconvenient to black soldiers and civilians alike who passed through Love Field but found no accommodations for food or refreshments. Towards the end of the war Weems wrote to the Love Field Airport Restaurant in behalf of the Negro Chamber of Commerce to complain about the situation. He pointed out that the Negroes were prohibited from patronizing these places, and yet had no other place to go. Through no fault of their own they suffered hunger and discomfort.

The hotel situation in town was critical, too. Weems surveyed accommodations in 1946 and found that the eight Negro hotels contained only 137 rooms. Individuals seeking accommodations had to be turned away daily because these hotels were stretched to capacity. White hotels did not accept black patrons, so the inconveniences suffered were extreme.

Federal regulations now outlawed segregated seating on interstate transportation facilities, but word of that seemed not to have reached Texas. At least that was the experience of Juanita Craft, who in 1950 was returning to Dallas from St. Louis via Texas & Pacific Railway. When the train crew changed at Texarkana the new conductor ordered Mrs. Craft to move to a segregated car two coaches ahead "with the other colored folks." She demurred, and the conductor rebuked her harshly: "You're in Texas now. If you won't get up and go where you belong, I'll stop this train and have some of these laws take you off, and they'll have a *rope* waiting for you." In Dallas Mrs. Craft informed Maceo Smith of the incident. He wrote a letter of protest to the president of T&P with specific details.

Of greater concern than all such matters, serious though they were, was an injustice that if solved would have made all the others more palatable. This was the matter of employment, an issue of critical concern to the Negro Chamber. Its staff and members devoted great attention to this problem because it caused so much suffering, hardship, and grief. A 1948 year-end report by the Chamber's Employment Division suggested the depths of the problem. Negro job-seekers were placed in fifty-four positions as follows: 15 laborers, 12 porters, 8 dishwashers, 5 cooks, 5 bus boys, 5 yardmen, 2 shipping clerks and 2 chauffeurs. One hundred and seventy-three women took these jobs: 79 as "day" workers, 52 as domestic maids, 10 as waitresses, and 8 as hotel maids.

This was not to say that all Dallas Negroes were restricted to such menial positions. In the city were a number of black attorneys, nearly two dozen physicians, half a dozen dentists, six postal clerks, six mail carriers, and a larger number of teachers. In addition, many independent entrepreneurs owned grocery stores, restaurants, barbecue stands, funeral parlors, and beauty shops. The city was home in 1947 to headquarters or branch offices of eleven black-owned life insurance companies.

A surprising development occurring in the 1940s placed Dallas in the fore as a center of production for all-Negro films. This came about through the combined efforts of a Dallas man, Alfred Sack, and a Negro actor-director named Spencer Williams. Sack, a Jew and owner of Sack Amusement Enterprises, financed the films and served as producer, while Spencer directed them and also took parts in them. The series of films included such titles as "The Blood of Jesus," 1941; "Marching On," 1943; "Dirty Gertie from Harlem,

U.S.A.," 1946; and "Juke Joint," 1947. All-white camera crews, hired from the city's oldest film studio, Jamieson Film Co., shot the movies. "We had no problem of white guys working for a black director, none," recalled one of the cameramen, Gordon Yoder. The director, Williams, was "a guy who knew what he was doing, and that's all we needed to know."

For "Dirty Gertie" an indoor sound stage in South Dallas, dubbed playfully as "Harlemwood," was used as a basic production facility. True T. Thompson of Dallas wrote the script, which was inspired by Somerset Maugham's *Rain*. Thompson also wrote "Juke Joint." Local actors were used for most parts, but Francine Everett was imported from New York City to play the part of Gertie Larue in "Dirty Gertie." Williams was in the midst of a prolific career as a director of black films and as an actor. He later became best known to general audiences for his portrayal of "Andy" in the short-lived television version of "Amos n' Andy."

The *Dallas Express* reported in 1946 that Dallas was recognized as one of four cities in the nation in which all-Negro films were being produced.

In 1939 the city council had agreed under pressure to hire Negro police officers for black neighborhoods. However, this continued to be an unrealized goal even after the war. As far as Negroes were concerned, the matter was more than one of seeking equal job opportunities. It was seen as a more effective way to combat crime in their neighborhoods. A *Dallas Express* banner headline in September 1946 stated that Negroes accounted for three-fourths of the city's violent deaths in June, July, and August. Compounding the problem was the fact that when black persons were convicted of violent crimes they typically received far lighter sentences for the same offense than did whites. The Council of Negro Organizations lamented in 1944 that of fifty-four murders occurring in the black community, only four prosecutions brought penalties to the killers. Most of those in favor of black officers, including the Negro Chamber of Commerce, specified that the officers hired would be assigned to black neighborhoods. *News* columnist Lynn Landrum, a staunch conservative, was a strong proponent for hiring black police officers.

At a qualifying exam for officers on October 3, 1946, three Negroes—accompanied by L.D. Bennett, the new executive director of the Negro Chamber of Commerce—showed up at the City Civil

Commission only to be turned away at the door because of their color. Before the month ended, at the request of City Manager V.R. Smitham and with the support of Police Chief Carl Hansson, the council voted to authorize the hiring of fourteen "apprentice" Negro officers for service in black neighborhoods. Forty-seven black applicants applied to take the next written examination on November 15; four passed. By early 1948 four Negro men had managed to qualify and were serving as Dallas officers in the Hall-Thomas streets area with instructions to deal only with their own race except in emergencies.

Nothing illustrated more dramatically the obstacles encountered by blacks to better themselves than the fact that at the close of the war there was just one licensed black plumber in the entire city. About twenty Negroes were doing work as plumbers, but they were only laborers. The one licensed plumber had obtained his license in 1920. Since then all Negroes who had taken the licensing examination failed. No cries of racism emerged to protest this situation. Instead, to remedy the situation, the Negro Chamber in 1945 organized the Dallas Negro Plumbers Association to begin formal classes in plumbing and to secure textbooks for study so that Negro applicants could pass the tests. A second step by the Negro Chamber was writing letters to established black plumbers in other towns to urge them to relocate in Dallas.

Even more explosive than any of these issues—discrimination, jobs, law enforcement, public accommodations—was the critical shortage of housing. The difficulty could be seen easily in a 1950 report. With 21,568 Negro households in Dallas, only 14,850 housing units were available to them. This meant that 6,718 families—or one out of three—were living "doubled up." A large percentage of the available housing was sub-standard. The agonizing battle over public housing that had been fought in the late 1930s continued to be debated, although proponents had made several breakthroughs. Three separate public housing facilities containing together just over 1,000 units had been constructed, the largest of which was the first, Roseland Homes.

Still, the debate over public housing waxed fierce with much emotion. Four days before Christmas in 1949 a group of businessmen appeared before the city council to argue that a Dallas Housing Authority request for a slum clearance program and $25 million in federal loans for public housing was "socialistic" and "communistic." The project, argued D.A. Frank, chairman of an organization called the Dallas Council for Free Enterprise, would be rife with "temptations for graft, corruption and favoritism." Frank insisted that he had not yet found "any place in Dallas" that he would call a slum. As to the dilapidated shacks that undeniably existed, they were—according to Frank—properly being retained by their absentee owners until such time as the free market afforded them a favorable opportunity to sell at higher prices for "commercial, industrial or other valuable purposes." Whatever the objections, at the same meeting J.W. Rice of the Negro Chamber declared public housing a greatly needed "boon" to his race.

Even private projects designed to meet the need for Negro housing came under attack. Two weeks after the public housing debate an overflow crowd appeared at city hall to denounce a proposed $14 million privately funded housing development for 2000 Negro families between Jefferson Boulevard extension and Mountain Lake Road in Oak Cliff. The houses were to sell at prices between $5,000 and $10,000. Rice, again speaking in behalf of the Negro Chamber, told the council that there was a "tragic necessity" to find 9,000 new homes for Negroes. Council members, unwilling to approve the project because of heated opposition from neighborhood residents, voted only to make further studies of the matter.

As pressures intensified among black residents to find additional housing, white residents stiffened in their determination to protect their segregated neighborhoods. The situation was becoming especially tense in South Dallas, an area with large numbers of affordable houses where several enclaves of black residents already existed. The presence in South Dallas of Lincoln High School was another incentive that prompted Negroes to look for housing in the vicinity.

Real estate agents who dared to work with prospective Negro buyers in South Dallas were either courageous or foolhardy. In March 1950 two white women agents showing property to blacks on Copeland Street—where one black family already had moved—were surrounded by several car-loads of protesting whites who began threatening and cursing them. The women, Ethel Bradshaw and Nola Kennemur, were able to leave safely only when police arrived and sent the protestors home.

Police never had solved the outbreak of "bombings," as they were commonly called, that had occurred in South Dallas ten years earlier. Now, a new series of bombings and fires broke out. Typically, the "bombs" consisted of sticks of dynamite tossed onto the roofs or front porches of houses occupied by Negroes on previously all-white streets. Sometimes firebombs were thrown. Between February 1950 and mid-1951 eleven bombings occurred, largely in an area around Oakland Avenue.

With the occurrence of the first bombing in February 1950, Mayor Savage quickly identified them as symptoms of a serious housing shortage that must be remedied. Since the end of the war, the mayor said, there had been "practically no Negro housing built in Dallas." With two, three, and four Negro families cramped together in small dwellings, it was impossible to keep them from overflowing into white areas unless other places were provided for them, Savage said.

On the Sunday evening of June 24, 1951, the quiet was interrupted by four separate explosions heard over wide distances. Three of the four were in South Dallas. One was a commercial rental property at 4301 S. Oakland Avenue purchased a month earlier by a black businessman named C.A. Galloway (later to become a well-known realtor and Dallas' first black city councilman). Galloway, his wife, and seven others had just left the property, which was being renovated, when dynamite was tossed onto the roof, causing about $200 damage. A second explosion occurred not far away at 2214 Eugene Street (just four blocks down the street from where entertainer Ray Charles would move two years later) at a vacant dwelling purchased a month earlier by a Negro, Mrs. Doris Jean Andrews. This bombing followed a typical pattern. Until a month earlier the two-block stretch of Eugene Street between Central and Waldron had been occupied by all-white residents. Two Negro families moved in one weekend, and by Monday about a dozen homeowners put out "For Sale" signs. A newspaper reporter who interviewed residents along the street wrote that all but two white families intended to move away.

The third explosion came just after midnight at Leo's Grocery, 4208 S. Oakland. The black owner, Leo Smith, was standing at the rear of his store and his wife and four-year-old son were in the living quarters behind when the explosion ripped an eighteen-inch hole in the roof.

The fourth explosion that evening, widely accepted to be the work of gangster elements and unrelated to race, occurred when someone tossed a dynamite stick onto the roof of Danceland at Corinth and Industrial.

At the city council meeting three days after that Sunday night's bombings, a group of Negroes appeared to demand police action. A representative from a Negro business school read a petition signed by every student imploring the city to use any and all means possible to halt the bombings. Council members voted unanimously to instruct Police Chief Carl Hansson to do so.

Next day the interracial committee of the Dallas Chamber of Commerce, composed of twenty-five whites and five blacks, met secretly with Chief Hansson. Afterwards, the committee publicly urged the city and civic groups to find suitable locations for more Negro housing to stop the strife in South Dallas. M.J. Norrell, the chairman, said his committee was trying to interest those with capital to invest in housing projects for Negroes. He declared the bombings "an outrage of law and public order."

Adoue, who by now had succeeded Savage as mayor, was not convinced that the bombings were racially motivated. Noting that the bombings of Danceland and two other restaurants did not occur in South Dallas, he believed that criminal gangs could be responsible. "It is one of the means of operations of gangs when they cannot buy their way or force their way into a city," Adoue said. Chief Hansson, at odds with the mayor on so many matters, would not comment on his own theories.

Pressures continued to mount from all directions to end the crisis before the city exploded into racial warfare. Adoue pleaded for anyone with "even a bare scrap of information" to bring it to the attention of the authorities.

Members of the Citizens Council and the Dallas Chamber of Commerce's biracial committee called on District Attorney Henry Wade to request that a high-powered special grand jury be appointed to investigate the crimes and to indict those responsible. Wade, agreeing to the need, persuaded a district judge to appoint the body despite the judge's belief that the investigation could not succeed. The judge, Henry King, named a special grand jury whose membership read like a who's who of the Citizens Council. Its foreman was Ray Hubbard, president of the park board and a wealthy and prominent oilman. It included as well James Ralph Wood, president of Southwestern Life Insurance Co.; B.F. McClain, president of Hart Furniture Co.; William H. Cothrum Sr., builder; Julius Schepps, wholesale liquor distributor, C.A. Tatum Jr., vice president of Dallas Power & Light; Felix McKnight of the *News;* and James F. Chambers Jr. of the *Times Herald.* Three Negro grand jurors were appointed who were anything but window dressing. One was the president of the local chapter of the NAACP, the Rev. Bezeleel R. Riley. Another was the state's outstanding black activist attorney, W.J. Durham, who through his affiliation with the NAACP had been a lead strategist in the Heman Sweatt case to desegregate the University of Texas and who also had participated in the suit which caused the U.S. Supreme Court to agree to abolish the oppressive white Democratic primary system. The third was the Rev. Robert L. Parish.

Several other aggressive steps were taken. The Texas Rangers entered the investigation to assist local authorities. The Dallas Chamber of Commerce announced a $1,000 reward for information, and the Dallas chapter of the NAACP offered an identical reward. The local NAACP chapter pondered a plan to hire its own private investigators. Thurgood Marshall of the NAACP arrived in Dallas from New York City to study the matter.

Juanita Craft sent her own summary with newspaper clippings to Walter White, executive director of the NAACP in New York. "There is existing a political fight between the Mayor, the city manager and the Chief of Police, which I think is good," she wrote. "The law enforcement officers are on the spot because of the pressure that is being placed on them....One can never know what will happen when the BRAINS of this situation are apprehended." Mrs. Craft urged White to give as much publicity to Dallas as he could because the city had had thirty-three bombings in eleven years. However, she added with glee, not a single bombing attempt had occurred since "the widow Sharpe" had raced from her house and fired shots at a fleeing car whose occupant had just tossed a bomb at her house on Crozier Street. Mrs. Craft appended the single word "smiles" to the sentence in appreciation for the woman's aggressive posture. (The bomb, fortunately, had failed to explode.)

On hearing from Mrs. Craft, White expressed pleasant surprise that the Dallas newspapers were publicizing the bombings rather than ignoring them. "Unlike Chicago," he wrote to Mrs. Craft, "the

Dallas papers certainly are letting the people know what is going on." Thurgood Marshall should be "filled up with loads of material" when he returned from Dallas, White said.

On September 9 came the first break. Police arrested for questioning two men, George Leatherwood and Floyd Foster. Both implicated others, although Texas Ranger Captain Bob Crowder announced that they were merely "messenger boys" and not the "kingpins."

Other arrests soon followed, including those of a forty-two-year-old pants presser named Claude Thomas Wright and his half-brother, Arthur Eugene Young, both of whom admitted participation in five bombings. Wright, it developed, had been the man whom the widow Sharpe tried to gun down. The two men were indicted for bombings occurring on the night of June 24—at Leo's Grocery on Oakland and at the frame house at 2214 Eugene Street. Others indicted in ensuing days were: Pete Garcia, a husky twenty-five-year-old machinist who lived in South Dallas; T.D. Peacock, twenty-four, of Fort Worth; Dowell C. (Cotton) Bailey, thirty-seven, who lived on Samuell Boulevard; Burl Foster, thirty, of Mesquite; Elmer Henry (Red) White, forty-two, of Oak Cliff; and Richard Russell Reeden, a South Dallas garage mechanic. None of these men, it was explained, were "kingpins."

The arrests of Wright and Young, who confessed that they had been paid for their deeds, brought the investigation one level higher. Police determined that a South Dallas labor and neighborhood leader named Charles O. Goff, sixty-eight, was the man who had paid Wright. Goff was a familiar speaker before city council on issues concerning preservation of all-white neighborhoods. He was chairman of the Exline Park Improvement League, a group of homeowners living in the area of the bombings, and he was the business agent for the lathers' union. In 1947 Goff had organized a slate of city council candidates to oppose the CCA. One of the South Dallas candidates, C.G. Stubbs, had upset CCA candidate Joe Golman in that race. After his arrest Goff was bailed out by none other than former district attorney Maury Hughes, who once had had ties with the Klan.

With ten individuals now indicted for the bombings, the special grand jury concluded its work, acknowledging that it had failed to indict all those responsible, especially the leaders. District Attorney Wade recalled later that the grand jury very much had wanted to indict the Baptist preacher, John G. Moore, but he had advised the members that without direct evidence linking him to the bombings he could not be prosecuted successfully. The frustrated grand jury's comments were highly suggestive. "The plot reached into unbelievable places," the body's final report stated. Some of the conspirators not yet charged or indicted, it continued, were well known and highly regarded. "There was evidence that lay and religious and community groups, through misguided leadership, entered an action, perhaps unwittingly, that resulted in violence and destruction." These comments pointed directly at the Rev. Moore's South Dallas Adjustment League and also at such South Dallas neighborhood groups as Goff's Exline Park Improvement League. The latter group had the announced purpose of raising money to buy out Negro homeowners who had moved into white neighborhoods. The unnamed conspirators in such groups had not been indicted because of "insufficient corroborating evidence."

The only one of the individuals indicted who stood trial was Pete Garcia, a member of Moore's South Dallas Adjustment League and the father of three small children. Garcia, arrested at his job as a machinist in a Grand Prairie plant, was accused of bombing a vacant house next door to his own on Marburg Street on June 3, 1951, because it had been sold to a Negro. Garcia denied responsibility for the bombing, and numerous South Dallas residents testified in his behalf as character witnesses, including the Rev. Moore. A number of others painted an entirely different portrait of him. They said that they had been crudely admonished by Garcia, sometimes while he flashed a knife, not to sell their houses to Negroes. As a member of the South Dallas Adjustment League, Garcia testified that one of his duties was to paint "For Whites Only" signs and place them on the lawns of persons who agreed not to sell their homes to blacks. He admitted strong feelings against the integration of South Dallas neighborhoods. After undergoing a vigorous cross-examination from the prosecutor, he glared menacingly at him as he took his seat. A star witness who earlier had told the grand jury that she had seen Garcia enter the vacant house about one minute before the explosion now recanted her testimony. The jury, after deliberating for twelve hours, acquitted Garcia.

By now the bombings had ceased. The urgency of the matter seemed over. Law enforcement agencies figured that their jobs were over. No other persons were indicted.

The admittedly critical need for housing for blacks in Dallas remained, but now with greater emphasis. A number of Dallas' leading citizens, including Karl Hoblitzelle, Fred Florence, John E. Mitchell Jr., J. L. Latimer, and Jerome Crossman, financed the development of a new residential project for middle-class black residents between Dallas and Richardson. It was named Hamilton Park, after the black physician, Dr. R.T. Hamilton, who had served on the biracial commission formed after the earlier 1940 series of bombings. One of the streets was named for Hoblitzelle. With brick-veneer houses, ample lawns, pleasantly winding streets, and a park and school, Hamilton Park upon its opening in 1954 became recognized as a highly desirable oasis for Negroes. While it in no way solved the housing crisis, it did offer a model community—though a segregated one—for black citizens who could afford to buy homes.

A DEVASTATING DROUGHT

Another critical issue confronting Dallas between 1951 and 1957 seriously threatened its continued prosperity, if not its very survival. The problem was an old one: shortage of water. This time, though, its magnitude was far greater than ever, for residents and industry were consuming more than 70 millions gallons of water a day.

In 1951 the water in Lake Dallas was splashing as usual over the top of Garza Dam. There was no concern about any lack of water. Yet, this was the last water to go over the dam until mid-May 1957. The effort to solve the acute water shortage that developed between these years confounded the municipal staff, divided council members, terrified residents, raised the spectre of loss of industry, and prompted lawsuits.

The enormity of the situation was not realized until September 1952 when two men cruising on Lake Dallas turned on their depth sounder and were shocked to discover that the deep water they knew should have been there was not. Instead, frighteningly close to the surface, they found mud. Much faster than anyone had supposed, the lake, less than three decades old, had silted up. Calculations showed that a scant four months' supply of water was available for a city of half a million residents.

The quickest relief—if it was to come—would be a good rainfall to fill the reservoir. In a frantic decision that would bring years of ridicule the city council in November 1952 signed a contract with a rainmaker. He was Dr. Irving P. Krick, a Denver meteorologist whose expertise was such that he had helped forecast the weather for the D-Day invasion. Now he had turned his efforts to a sophisticated form of rainmaking. Dr. Krick's procedure was to place generators in the watershed area to fog likely-looking clouds with silver iodide crystals. There was evidence that his procedure had worked elsewhere. Dr. Krick didn't claim that he could manufacture rain from nothing; he contended only that he could increase the amount of rain that fell during a rainfall. It sounded plausible enough for the council to sign Dr. Krick to a six-month contract paying him $36,505 to work his magic. Dr. Krick claimed some successes, but it was impossible to assess the degree to which he may have been responsible for the few showers that did fall. At any rate, they were not enough. The drought continued.

To conserve water the council enacted a series of emergency actions, including severe restrictions on lawn watering, washing of cars with hoses, and prohibition of defective plumbing. The measures reduced daily use from 72 million gallons to 42 million gallons by November 1952. New deep wells were drilled; downtown buildings which had shut off their own water wells were encouraged to put them back into use; and private wells were purchased and in some cases added to the municipal water supply.

If a terrible calamity were to be avoided, though, major new sources of water soon had to be developed. Water engineers identified two possibilities: the convenient but contaminated West Fork of the Trinity, which merged with the Elm Fork just west of downtown to form the Trinity proper, and the Red River, nearly a hundred miles to the north. The nasty West Fork had been tainted for many decades by Fort Worth's sewage, by other excrement from that city's stockyards and meat-packing companies, and by industrial pollutants. While clean-up efforts had progressed since the 1920s, the water's murky appearance and stench did not at all commend it. The Red River lacked these contaminants, but it had an unpalatable and undesirable high mineral content. It also was far away. Still, with few other alternatives available beyond prayer and Dr. Krick, Water

Superintendent Karl Hoefl and City Manager Elgin Crull began plans for tapping both of these sources. The water department determined that the polluted West Fork water could be treated sufficiently to meet health standards. Henry Graeser, the water department's assistant superintendent, dramatically demonstrated this to council members by holding up a glass of the treated water and drinking it. Dallas residents, unconvinced, complained loudly. Mayor Adoue promised that West Fork water would not be used unless the State Health Department approved. Graeser repeated his act at the State Health Department in Austin, and won there a half-hearted endorsement.

Less than two months later the mayor abruptly reversed his position. Adoue claimed that Crull and Hoefle had lied to him and to the council about the acceptability of West Fork water. Actually, he said, instead of endorsing it, both city and state health authorities were advising the city to look elsewhere. After a torrid exchange in which Crull said the mayor attacked his integrity, Crull demanded and received a vote of confidence from city council.

The information Adoue contended had been distorted soon began to surface. A letter from the State Health Department's Bureau of Sanitary Engineering assessing both the West Fork and the Red River had been interpreted favorably at city hall, but it was filled with conditions. The bureau's senior engineer wrote that "under normal conditions" neither the West Fork nor the Red River could be considered desirable as a water supply because of excessive bacteria and chemicals. "However, when water supply conditions appear critical and time is limited, it is always possible to meet recommended standards." The use of the West Fork water should be considered only as a "final alternative," and it would be feasible from a public health standpoint *if* [emphasis added] sufficient storage were provided and sufficient water released to reduce bacterial densities to acceptable values." Did this letter constitute a go-ahead for Dallas? Crull and Hoefle believed it did. On their recommendation the city council had approved plans to build a storage basin for holding and purifying West Fork water before treating and processing.

A private citizen, attorney Tom Howard, complicated the matter by filing a suit to prevent use of West Fork water. He alleged that the city could not by filtering or any other process make the water fit for human consumption. To attempt to do so, he argued, would endanger the health of all Dallasites. He contended that water officials were hiding and suppressing critical facts.

Two councilmen, Dr. George Schenewerk, a physician, and clothier W.B.(Bart) Ring, now joined Adoue in adamantly opposing the use of West Fork water. Schenewerk insisted that he would be derelict in his calling as a physician not to do so. He pointed out that the State Health Department's ostensible letter of improvement was sprinkled with "if" clauses that could not be met. It would be better, Dr. Schenewerk maintained, to shut down all Dallas industries and get along with limited supplies of pure water than to use impure water.

The suppression of facts to which Howard and also Adoue referred alluded to a report by Dallas' own city health director, Dr. J.W. Bass, which the city manager chose to withhold from the public. Bass had written that the city would encounter extreme difficulties in fulfilling all the contingencies outlined by the State Health Department for using West Fork water. Pressured by reporters, Crull released the report and acknowledged that he earlier had placed Dr. Bass under a "suggested ban" not to make public comments about the controversial situation.

Dr. Schenewerk, meanwhile, also was muzzled from making further criticisms. City Attorney Henry Kucera warned him that he should not make further public comments on the matter because of Howard's pending lawsuit. Schenewerk complied with the request.

At this critical point, spring city council elections loomed. Adoue appeared ready to run for a second term as mayor as he began mailing post cards to voters soliciting their support. Some talk surfaced that he might campaign as an independent rather than accept a CCA endorsement. CCA officials were not at all pleased with Adoue's independent ways and his penchant for controversy. A growing number of businessmen complained privately that they could not continue to support the CCA if it endorsed him. The *News* editorialized that Adoue was fundamentally opposed to the council-manager form of government and had dealt a "severe blow" to it. With powerful anti-Adoue sentiment growing, a past president of the organization, S.J. Hay (son of the former mayor), was delegated to bargain with him. Adoue later gave his version of the visit: "He [Hay] called on me at my office and asked me to get out of the race. He said the businessmen would not support the CCA ticket if I were on it. He said they didn't want me because I was responsible for stirring up too much dissension at the City Hall. He added that the Charter Association would let me name the ticket, if I agreed to stay out of the race." Next day Hay did not deny the visit, but he declared absolutely that no offer had been made for Adoue to name the CCA slate. "That just couldn't be done. No one in the Charter Association would have such authority."

Except for the years 1947 to 1949, Adoue had served on the council since 1941. His turbulent two-year term as mayor was not without accomplishments. But at the end of January, three days after voters approved a $12.5 million expansion of Love Field—a project which Adoue had enthusiastically supported—Adoue announced that on doctor's orders he would not be a candidate for re-election in 1953. Nor, for that matter, as it turned out, would any of the other incumbents.

A strong mayor who knew how to pull city leaders together in a time of crisis now was needed. The CCA turned to the trusted warrior, Robert L. Thornton, seventy-two, who in his lengthy career of civic involvement had yet to hold elected office. Thornton accepted the nomination. In the campaign that followed, the water crisis and how to confront it was a major issue. Thornton effectively removed from consideration the controversial proposal to use West Fork water, vowing that it would not be used under any circumstances.

Despite spirited opposition from an independent candidate who claimed that he could solve the water crisis with a plan to bring Red River water to Dallas in ninety days, Thornton won the 1953 election easily by a better than 2-1 margin, capturing eighty-four of the city's ninety-seven precincts. As the *Times Herald* observed, Thornton showed "amazing strength" in his first bid for office.

The drought, though, despite Uncle Bob Thornton's formidable presence, continued. White Rock Lake dried up totally. A person could walk from one shore to the opposite one without muddying his shoes. Pumps were installed to send water from the Red River to Lake Dallas, where its undesirable mineral content was diluted but not eliminated. Loud complaints about the water's taste and the damage it caused to evaporative home coolers arose. Many residents dug their own backyard wells; many of them placed signs in their yards saying that they were watering their lawns from private wells. In 1954 the new Lewisville Dam was finished, the reservoir behind it ready to be added to the city's supply. But it could not be helpful without rain. Meanwhile, Mayor Thornton named a high-powered committee to develop plans for dams, reservoirs, treatment plants, and accessories that would be needed through the year 2000. While the long-range plans they submitted in 1955 did not help for the moment, their recommendations among other things included the construction of Lakes Tawakoni, Ray Hubbard, and Aubrey. These, when completed, would solve the city's water problems for the rest of the century.

In August 1956 an alarmed city manager announced that only 22.49 billion gallons of water remained in Lake Dallas. Unless good rains arrived, the supply would be reduced to seven to eight billion gallons by the next summer. Then, in late summer 1956, as if by signal, the skies opened and heavy rains fell. More downpours came in the spring of 1957. Water began flowing over the new dam at Lewisville for the first time. Lake Dallas filled up, too. The great and memorable drought of the 1950s had ended.

THORNTON BEGINS LONG REIGN

"I said in the beginning that I am no politician, don't want to be one, and won't be one." Thus spoke Robert L. Thornton after being elected mayor of the city that he loved so much.

Yet, Thornton was beginning a long reign as mayor during years of great growth and development. These would be the crowning years for the benevolent reign by businessmen who joined together in the CCA or who used their influence from the even loftier plateau of the Citizens Council. Thornton would be re-elected three more times, thus sitting as mayor from 1953 to 1961, equalling Woodall Rodgers in years spent in office.

At his swearing-in ceremony Thornton vowed to provide "as efficient and business-like government" as humanly possible. He tightened the reins on the council-manager theory by urging citizens with problems to contact the pertinent municipal departments rather than their council representatives. Council members were to be approached "only when relief is not obtained from the regular sources." His goal was to reduce the heavy work load that increasingly was being placed on the shoulders of council members, all of whom continued to serve with token pay, with no personal staff support, without private offices at city hall, and without giving up their gainful and full-time occupations. The emphasis in Thornton's stated desire for "businesslike yet democratic administration" was definitely on the former. Thornton announced that prior to each Monday's session council members would gather behind closed doors for briefings on issues they were to confront in the public meetings. This was a return to the earlier practice of excluding the press, originally recommended by Dealey, that Adoue had abandoned fourteen months earlier. The press duly noted the decision to exclude journalists, but did not protest.

Two years later in the spring 1955 election no one deigned oppose the CCA office-holders; Thornton and the CCA slate were returned to office routinely. In 1957 a ticket arose under the name of the Peoples Candidates to challenge the incumbents, but Thornton and all but one of his CCA mates again easily won re-election. The exception was Mrs. Carr P. Collins Jr., the first woman ever nominated by the CCA for city council, whose ultimate victory was delayed by a run-off. With her win, Mrs. Collins became Dallas' first female council member.

The 1957 election day was marked by a devastating tornado which danced across Dallas skies for forty-six minutes, killing ten people, injuring at least 170 others, destroying more than 800 homes and businesses, and causing some $4 million in damages. The black funnel could be clearly seen for miles around. Television cameramen caught it for the evening news. It was one of the most fully documented tornadoes ever to occur anywhere.

AIRPORT DISPUTE ARISES

The age-old schemes to make the Trinity River navigable continued to linger in these years—as they would for many years to come—but no longer was navigation deemed the critical factor for the city's prosperity. Aviation had replaced it. "The air is our ocean," the ringing statement made in 1931 by Chamber president M.J. Norrell, had been taken to heart. No longer was it valid to believe that there was a ceiling on the growth of any city lacking navigable waters. The airplane had changed all that, and Dallas had been one of the first cities to recognize that fact. The city's role in the growth of the aviation industry was a large one, for it included the emergence of such airlines as National Air Transport and Texas Air Transport, which after some mergers would become two of the nation's biggest carriers, United and American.

Almost all residents supported the city's commitment to Love Field. They had approved by substantial majorities every bond election ever held to improve the facility since the city took it over in 1927. By 1953 Love Field was generating more air passenger traffic than any two Texas airports combined, and more mail and cargo tonnage than any three airports in the state combined. It was fourth in the nation in enplaned passengers on local service airlines, and tenth in the nation in total number of enplaned passengers. The effort ten years earlier to build a unified airport with Fort Worth, in retrospect, would have been a "serious mistake," the Chamber of Commerce concluded. The nearby convenience of Love Field was a blessing.

Fort Worth had continued to push for a mid-city airport since 1943, and failing to obtain Dallas' cooperation, it had done so unilaterally. On April 26, 1953, Fort Worth opened its own mid-city airport, the Greater Fort Worth Airport. Amon Carter was the key figure in this venture. He was the organizer and majority owner of the firm which leased the property to the airport. Federal regulations prohibited the naming of the airport after a living man, otherwise the airfield would have been named for Carter. As a compromise, the terminal building alone was named for him, but the popular name for the entire facility became Amon Carter Airport. As a director of American Airlines, now headquartered in Fort Worth, Carter owned more stock in that firm than all other directors combined. Dallas became alarmed that American Airlines, through Carter's influence, was pushing federal authorities to transfer more and more flights from Love Field to Greater Fort Worth.

The construction of Fort Worth's new airport signaled another intense chapter in the rivalry of the two cities over aviation. The diversion of a number of American Airlines flights to Greater Fort Worth from Dallas drew strong protests from the Dallas Chamber of Commerce with a warning that a complaint would be filed with the

Civil Aeronautics Board.

Fort Worth remained hopeful that Dallas would cooperate with its mid-city venture. It offered to sell one-half interest in the airport to Dallas for only $2.7 million, and to change its name to Dallas-Fort Worth International Airport, giving first billing to Dallas. Dallas City Council voted unanimously to reject the offer.

The preponderance of flights remained at Love Field, and Fort Worth residents often had to drive there to catch a flight. Fort Worth appealed to the CAB for more routes. In defending Love Field against further encroachments, Dallas submitted to the CAB documented studies showing that when airline services moved to more distant airports a substantial part of the traffic was lost. Elaborate tables were prepared to document savings derived by travelers when they did not have to travel to distant airports. The on-going feud over these matters was accompanied by intense publicity.

Fort Worth's position was detailed in a careful letter to the editor of the *News* in 1955. "The time will come, within less than the next ten years, when there will be two million people in Dallas and Tarrant Counties, and we wonder just how they are going to be handled by the present facilities [at Love Field], some of which cannot be adequately enlarged. However, we do know that the Greater Fort Worth International Airport can be doubled in capacity without the acquisition of any additional land and at a very reasonable figure. So, time, patience, and facts will tell the story, and Fort Worth is adequately supplied with all these requisites. Many substantial citizens consider that quite a lot of the derogatory, inaccurate propaganda spread against Fort Worth's new airport has been more beneficial than detrimental.... Self-sufficient people and dictators have usually paid the penalty in the long run."

There was no denying the disproportionate number of passengers being generated by the two cities. Dallas supplied far more per capita. These figures, coupled with what appeared to be the grasping nature of Fort Worth's desire to siphon off some of Dallas' flights and Amon Carter's dictatorial role, convinced Dallas residents almost without exception that their pro-Love Field position was correct.

However, disquieting arguments could be heard—if one cared to listen—from neutral sources. One who sought to put the matter into perspective was the Washington, D.C.,-based editor of *American Aviation*, Wayne W. Parrish, who told *News* columnist Lynn Landrum that it was his impression that Dallas was putting an "awfully high price on city pride to the detriment of both the air transport industry and the air traveling public." But at least nobody could say the controversy was dull, he said resignedly. He elaborated further in a prophetic letter. No one was disputing the numbers on passengers which overwhelmingly favored Dallas, he said, but "I just have the strong feeling that Love Field is not destined to be the big airline airport for the area ten years from now in the next stage of equipment ....[Dallas] is likely to miss a bet to join hands for a midway airport and eventually will have to spend a lot more dough building another field farther out....It is just the simplest, most sensible thing in the world to conclude that the midway airport, connected to both cities with expressways, is the answer for the future."

Another aviation expert closer to home, George Haddaway, publisher and editor of *Flight* magazine in Dallas, reprimanded the *News'* managing editor, Felix McKnight, for that newspaper's "epidemic of errors" in its aggressive pro-Dallas assertion of Love Field's quality, including a claim that Love Field's runway was the longest in the southwest and that Love Field was the only profitable municipally-operated airport in the nation. "Felix," he wrote, "these kind of statements are making the *Dallas News* ridiculous among a host of aviation people because they are simply not true."

Fort Worth's continuing push to pull more and more traffic to its airport at Dallas' expense was monitored very carefully by the Dallas Chamber's aviation committee. More "evidence" of Fort Worth's success was revealed in mid-1956 when the Chamber's air mail service committee discovered that just over half of Dallas' air mail was being trucked past Love Field to Greater Fort Worth Airport for delivery. Not only did it cost taxpayers extra money, but the mail was counted as originating from Fort Worth instead of Dallas. "Outrageous" was the aviation committee chairman's description of this news in a strong protest to Dallas Congressman Bruce Alger. The Post Office's explanations were convoluted and unsatisfactory.

The dispute between the two cities was nowhere near being resolved. The issue would continue to flare over the next years. While the rivalry between the two cities generally was portrayed as friendly—accompanied by such antics as Amon Carter bringing a sack lunch to Dallas for meetings—in the matter of aviation the cities could not have been more serious in their disagreements.

13

Uncle Bob's Reign

I am bucking the machine that has been in power in Dallas for 27 years and bucking the present incumbent who is positive of the fact that he has a God-given right to that office.

—Earle Cabell, 1959

A Transformation

A different kind of place was Dallas now. It was more than just being bigger, although certainly its expanding size was significant. The 1950 census showed a huge population jump of about 50 percent over 1940, and the city limits were in the process of being extended by an amazing six-fold between 1945 and 1960.

What was really so different was Dallas' changed economy and character. Practically invisible now were the city's long-time ties to the surrounding rich agricultural area, so essential and visible in the establishing years. The thousands of farmers who had tossed aside their plows and moved to Dallas during the hard times of the Depression long since had been assimilated into the work force. Cotton had been surpassed in importance by oil, and now electronics and manufacturing were rapidly emerging. More and more transplanted Easterners, many of them brought by relocating companies, lived in the city. Chance Vought's decision to come to Dallas from Connecticut in 1948, billed as the largest industrial move in the nation's history, had been a harbinger of the next decades. (As had been the case with North American Aviation in 1940, the decision had not been entirely spontaneous; it was a government strategy to decentralize defense contractors from the East Coast.) From Cleveland in 1950 came Dresser Industries, a firm historically entrenched in the oil and gas industries with world-wide operations. In 1953 General Motors began building a $35 million assembly plant west of town in Arlington. Several attractive factors brought these and other companies to Dallas and the surrounding area. An important reason was the convenience of Dallas' central location between the East and West coasts, an attractive feature to major corporations with far-flung interests. This was a geographical advantage not overlooked in the city's careful development of Love Field. Another was the city's mild climate. Yet another was its proximity to so many major oil and natural gas fields. There was also a favorable public attitude toward the free-enterprise system, an attitude which had fostered low taxes and a labor force that was largely non-union. Besides all that, the city looked clean; its constantly growing downtown skyline was unsullied by the smoke of coal-burning furnaces common to Eastern cities.

Something else was new: some home-grown businesses were becoming major national firms. This included especially Southland Corporation and its chain of Seven-Eleven stores. From its modest beginning in Oak Cliff the company had tied its destiny to the automobile by providing convenient outlets for customers to buy ice on their way home, then had begun supplying milk and bread. The formula was perfect. Seven-Elevens now could be found throughout the nation. Another local giant was Texas Instruments, founded in the 1930s to provide seismic services for the oil industry. Encouraged by a huge line of credit from Republic National Bank, the company broadened in the 1950s to include the electronics industry, and especially the transistor. TI's development of the integrated circuit in 1958 became an essential part of the computer revolution.

Dallas had achieved what it wanted: national recognition as a growing and progressive city. A song popularizing its now-common nickname, "Big D," could be heard every night on Broadway by theater-goers who saw Frank Loesser's musical, "The Most Happy Fella." Occasionally, for the first time now, a character in a movie might casually mention the city by name. "I'm flying to Dallas for a business meeting next week," or some such. Local audiences, happily surprised at this novelty, invariably broke into applause and whistles.

Recognition now encompassed the arts in new areas. The brightest new achievement came with the founding in 1957 of the Dallas Opera by two men from Chicago, Lawrence Kelly and Nicola Rescigno. The company assumed from its very first days a vivid presence in the world of opera, featuring frequently the acclaimed Maria Callas and attracting audiences and critics from throughout the world.

A second accomplishment came in 1959 when the Dallas Theater Center began operations at a facility designed by Frank Lloyd Wright at a heavily wooded site along Turtle Creek. Paul Baker of Baylor University assumed directorship of the Theater Center's permanent crew of professionals. The Center began mounting boldly conceived productions, and it was cited widely as proof that good professional theater could be found in places far from Broadway.

Some Key Leaders

Dallas' civic leaders had reason to be proud. Never had their carefully controlled plans for civic advancement seemed more successful. Much of the credit belonged to the Citizens Council. The organization was exerting a far more central and powerful role in decision-making than the elected city council. Yet, few residents even knew of its existence. And that was how the Citizens Council wanted it to be.

Its overriding influence dominated municipal politics, public schools, bond issues, industrial development, housing projects, and civic endeavors such as the symphony orchestra, the zoo, and charitable fund drives. The body's central authority lay in an executive committee of some twenty-five members who met monthly. Of these few, the very top echelon was composed of bankers. The backing of any project by the Citizens Council guaranteed substantial financial support not only from the influential bankers but also from other members, all of whom were required by charter to be the chief executives of their organizations. These men could guarantee the support of their organizations and their employees for any project. These projects also automatically gained backing from the city council, and they were accompanied by positive news coverage and editorials from newspapers and television and radio stations, for their chief executives also were members of the Citizens Council.

A long-time Citizens Council member, C.A. Tatum of Dallas Power & Light Co., took an emerging civic leader to lunch and explained step-by-step to him how one accomplished community projects in Dallas. First, he said, you visit the chief executives of the top three banks and win their support. Next, you pay calls on the publishers of both daily newspapers for their approval. Then you persuade the chiefs of the three utility companies about the project's merits. Next in line were the heads of the big downtown department stores, then a couple of businessmen who fell into none of the categories such as Robert B. Cullum and Julius Schepps. "After you've got these ten or twelve people on board everything just falls into place," Tatum told his avid listener.

The Citizens Council's operating principle always was to do what was best for Dallas. What was best, of course, was a determination made by its members, not by labor, minority groups, members of professions such as medicine, law, and teaching, or the average working citizen. For that matter, elected politicians did not qualify for membership either.

According to its charter, the Citizens Council refrained from political activity, not just traditional partisan politics, but municipal politics as well. However, the CCA, even though it was an older organization than the Citizens Council, was the council's political arm, albeit indirectly. A sudden crisis involving Chance-Vought Aircraft's move from Connecticut to a facility adjacent to Dallas' Hensley Field illustrated this arrangement. Chance-Vought's decision was jeopardized when the head of the company suddenly realized that the Hensley runway was too short for some of its aircraft operations. He telephoned the president of the Citizens Council, D.A. Hulcy, with his concern. Hulcy went to work on the CCA council, and less than four hours later he called back Chance-Vought and said that the Dallas City Council had just voted $256,000 in an emergency meeting to extend the runway to the required length.

The CCA's dominance at city hall continued to be rarely

challenged. In 1947 voters had elected one lonely non-CCA councilman, the first time in ten years. They would not do so again until 1959 when another lone independent, Joe Geary, won office. Not another independent held office during the 1940s or 1950s.

During municipal political campaigns the CCA always boasted of the fact that it had brought corruption-free governance to city hall throughout its years in power. This was true, remarkably so. And unlike the case in so many other cities, this was achieved without the necessity of a patronage system in which jobs were delivered in return for political support. With the city's steady record of economic growth and progress for so many decades, CCA and Citizens Council leaders had no temptation to add to their well-being through corruption. They were making plenty of money honestly through free enterprise.

In recognition of the CCA's success at city hall and the benefits it believed this control had brought to the city, the Citizens Council started a similar organization to bring the same kind of leadership to the Dallas Independent School District. This was the Committee for Good Schools, founded by a handful of leaders in Fred F. Florence's office at Republic National Bank. The organization began selecting business-minded slates of school board candidates and providing the finances necessary for their elections. The CGS' success at the school board was immediate and long-term.

The organizer and founder of the Citizens Council, Robert L. Thornton, was widely recognized as "Mr. Dallas" by the 1950s. His folksy, avuncular ways earned him alternately the affectionate title of "Uncle Bob," and he was the subject of a flattering profile in the *Saturday Evening Post*, the first Dallas leader to be so honored. Yet, for all his presence and power over four decades, his multiple terms as mayor, and his presidency of the State Fair of Texas, those in the inner circles of the Citizens Council did not consider him to be their most influential member. The single individual whose support was deemed most important and most necessary for the success of any civic project, was that banker in whose office the Committee for Good Schools had been founded, Fred F. Florence. This was the opinion of Citizens Council members themselves, who were interviewed anonymously by the author of a scholarly study of the organization. Considering the Citizens Council's wish to stay out of headlines, it was fitting that a man who never held public office was recognized as the most powerful of all. The fact that Florence also headed the city's—and the state's—largest bank, Republic National, was no coincidence.

Florence was the son of Jewish Lithuanian emigrants who moved from New York City to East Texas less than a year after their child was born. Florence grew up in the small town of Rusk, where he studied hard in the public schools, freely participated in Methodist church activities since there was no synagogue, and earned extra money selling copies of the *Dallas Morning News*. Upon completing all ten grades offered at school, Florence began working at First National Bank of Rusk, doing everything from sweeping floors to keeping books.

After four years and promotion to assistant cashier, Florence went to Dallas in 1911 to attend a business school, as had Thornton. After completing its brief course he took a job as bookkeeper with the American Exchange Bank in Dallas, a position he held briefly before re-entering small-town banking. At the Alto State Bank in Cherokee County, he began developing a reputation as a shrewd banker . Soon he became president. There, he attracted the admiration of W.O. Connor of Dallas. When Connor assumed the presidency of the new Guaranty Bank and Trust Co. in 1920 he persuaded Florence to join him as his first vice president. Nine years later the hard-working Florence had become president of the bank, by then known as Republic National Bank. This position he was to hold for three decades until his death on December 25, 1960. Under his capable leadership Republic became the state's dominant financial institution, and Florence's acumen was called upon regularly by fellow civic leaders in Dallas.

Although they had much in common in background, Florence and R.L. Thornton were dissimilar in personality. Florence was sophisticated in manner and appearance, polished in speech, and a lover of the symphony and orchestra. Like Thornton, he developed an early reputation for astuteness through his special knowledge of the cotton industry, gained from his boyhood in cotton-rich East Texas. As the 1930s developed he became even better known for his knowledge of the growing oil industry and his willingness to commit resources to its operations.

In 1954, under Florence's leadership, Republic opened a new 598-foot building, the tallest in the state. It replaced Thornton's Mercantile as the city's tallest skyscraper. When Florence died in 1960 he was succeeded by James W. Aston as Republic Bank's president, who also assumed Florence's powerful role in the Citizens Council.

Another highly influential member of the Citizens Council was a colleague of Florence's at Republic, Karl Hoblitzelle, who after making a fortune in the movie industry became chairman of the board of directors at Republic in 1945. Thus, Republic Bank had two key members on the Citizens Council. Hoblitzelle's involvement with Republic had become so thorough that he now was becoming known mostly as a banker.

Thornton, Florence, Hoblitzelle, and other Citizens Council members such as C.A. Tatum of Dallas Power & Light Co. were thoroughly committed to the betterment of Dallas as they conceived it, determined as always to foster economic progress and growth, and opposed to any disruptions or disorders which might endanger the city's good name. Yet, the city already was too diverse for the organization to force its will on the city in all matters. A growing segment of Dallas—minorities whose ambitions were expanding and newcomers from other parts of the country—simply fell outside the reach of the organization. If the Citizens Council could have had its way, no controversy ever would have reared its head to mar the city's reputation for collegiality. This never had been the case, and certainly it would not be true as the 1950s moved into the 1960s.

Bruce Alger Breaks Tradition

Perhaps the first indication of a break from Dallas' old system came from Casa Linda, one of the town's many new sections, where there emerged a realtor who typified the ultra-conservative, Republican political tone that would characterize the city through much of the 1950s and into the 1960s. New to town, not a part of the familiar coterie of downtown businessmen, he was beholden to none of their traditions. This was Bruce Reynolds Alger. Born in Dallas, Alger had left the city as an infant with his parents when they moved to Webster Groves, Missouri, where he grew up. As a child he witnessed the tragic death of his sister in a dancing recital fire, an event which Alger later said triggered in him a "constant search for meaning." After high school, Alger went to Princeton University on scholarship, played varsity football for three years, and graduated in 1940 with a degree in an unusual field, the philosophy of art, which further exposed Alger to intellectual thought. As an undergraduate Alger came to know Albert Einstein, in residence at Princeton, and the two frequently discussed ideas. With the war Alger became an Air Corps pilot, flying low-altitude bombing raids over Tokyo. During this period he met and married a woman from Dallas, and with the end of the war they moved to Dallas with their first-born child. Alger began selling residential real estate and involved himself in a full range of neighborhood civic activities. Handsome, polished, tall, ambitious, and blessed with a mellifluous voice, Alger, the father now of three children, became the first president of the White Rock Kiwanis Club, president of the White Rock Chamber of Commerce, health club chairman of the downtown YMCA, handball doubles champion at the Dallas Athletic Club, and a participant in other neighborhood civic and school activities.

One day four fellow members of the White Rock Chamber of Commerce urged Alger to run for Congress. "It was a surprise to me, and I didn't even believe them," Alger later said. Before accepting his refusal, the four persuaded him to come to a noon meeting which turned out to be a political gathering of Republicans. Alger accepted the draft, and announced in 1954 as a candidate.

The election of a Republican to Congress in Texas was exceedingly rare, and certainly none had been elected from Dallas. Neither was it anticipated that a Republican could be elected this time, although in 1952 a Republican, Grover Hartt Jr., had been elected judge of County Court at Law No. 2, and Dwight Eisenhower had carried the state in the presidential election. Alger himself seemed at first to disparage his own chances. Despite his leadership in neighborhood and civic organizations, Alger was almost entirely unknown to most of Dallas.

Just the opposite was the case for his formidable Democratic opponent, Wallace Savage, who upon leaving the mayor's office in 1951 became state chairman of the Democratic Party's executive committee. Savage was himself a conservative, as was true for most Southern Democrats. Having already defeated a liberal Democrat, Leslie Hacker, in the spring primary, his election in the 5th Congressional District seemed certain.

The general election, then, was a battle between two conservative candidates: Savage, the downtown establishment lawyer and resident of prestigious, mansion-lined Swiss Avenue, versus Alger, the newcomer with a shopping center office in Casa Linda Plaza and a small home on North Lake Drive just above White Rock Lake. Confident that his primary triumph was tantamount to election, Savage sat back to await his inevitable victory in November.

Realizing the difficulty of overcoming Savage's familiar name, Alger began an early campaign based on his full support of Eisenhower. "You Elected Ike—Now Support Him," read one of Alger's cards. He distributed a bumper sticker that read: "Back Ike—Vote for Alger for Congress." A photograph of Alger shaking hands with Eisenhower was widely reprinted in his campaign literature. As Alger pointed out at every opportunity, he was the only candidate who could give unequivocable support to Eisenhower. Because of party ties Savage would be forced to support Democrat Sam Rayburn for speaker of the house rather than Eisenhower's preference, Republican Jim Martin.

To spread his message Alger used billboards, newspaper advertising, bumper stickers, direct mail, yard signs, and especially radio and television commercials. He tirelessly knocked on doors in residential areas, and spent hours walking through downtown office buildings to introduce himself. Savage spurned Alger's offer to debate issues, and at his solo appearances Alger frequently placed an empty chair next to him as a reminder to voters.

One day on these office rounds, Alger happened into his opponent's law office, shook his hand, and offered him a fistful of campaign literature. The amused Savage amiably observed, "I guess I'd better get busy if you're campaigning like this." Alger replied, "If what people tell me is true, you have it in the bag. You have nothing to worry about."

After graduating from Princeton, Alger's first brief job before the war had been as a management trainee for RCA. His first assignment was a novel one—talking on television for RCA at the New York World's Fair. He now took advantage of that experience by appearing in his own television commercials. During the last week of the campaign he appeared at 9:30 a.m. each morning in a series of relaxed commercials entitled "Coffee With Bruce Alger."

The *News*, traditionally Democratic, had supported Eisenhower over Adlai Stevenson, but it followed its usual pattern and endorsed the Democrat Savage for Congress. Even though Savage must vote with the Democrats in organizing the House, the newspaper observed, afterwards he would be "an aid, not a handicap, to the President."

Savage was slow in recognizing the threat that Alger posed to his re-election. Not until a few days before the election did he realize that he might lose. The realization came too late, for the "political infant" Alger scored a shocking upset victory, 28,010 to 24,950. On election night the transformation was complete, reported Associated Press. A politician who had "appeared supremely confident of winning" suddenly became a "beaten, bewildered candidate."

Alger's astonishing win gained national headlines. As the only Republican Congressman elected in all of Texas, he was hailed widely as the new leader of the state's Republican Party. His election also signified, it was believed, the long-awaited beginning of a two-party system in the South.

His victory seemed untarnished by the debt he owed to liberal Democrats, who, upset over Savage's bitter primary campaign against the Hacker, had crossed party lines to vote for Alger. Voters in Negro precincts, who remembered Savage's attacks against integration and the NAACP, also gave Alger a majority. Yet another factor in Alger's victory was the influx of new residents in Dallas who, unlike Texans and Southerners, felt no special allegiance to the Democratic Party.

Suspected at first of having won a fluke single-term victory, Alger would disprove that in the years ahead. In five terms in office he gained a reputation as one of the most conservative Congressmen in the nation. He spoke ardently against creeping socialism, communistic tendencies, and communism. He sponsored bills to withdraw from the United Nations and to break diplomatic relations with the Soviet Union. He strongly favored the supremacy of local authority rather than federal, and his opposition to federal expenditures even included the popular school lunch programs. Consistent with his belief in limited government, he initiated practically no legislation in Congress, and he even voted against federal funds for Garza-Little Elm Dam when Dallas was suffering from the drought. He became noted for his widely proclaimed yardstick in deciding whether to vote for or against Congressional bills: (1) Is it a function of the federal government, and (2) Can we afford it? If the answer to either question was negative, Alger voted no. This he carried to such an extreme as to be charged with failure to support a federal building in Dallas, a stance which the dismayed city leaders were powerless to change since he was outside their sphere of influence. Alger took pride in a voting record that consistently earned him the lowest possible marks on the AFL-CIO scoreboard. His political stances attracted to him a faithful corps of rabid followers; yet, he showed little interest in using that advantage to promote the creation of a two-party system in the state. That would await the election of John Tower to the U.S. Senate in 1961.

Until his ultimate loss in 1964, the nearest Alger came to defeat was in 1956 when District Attorney Henry Wade conducted a strong campaign, attacking Alger for his refusal to vote for federal programs to help Dallas County and for not making the city's voice heard in Congress. Wade also criticized Alger for failing to protect segregationist traditions, and for "running on the coattails of a member of the NAACP." This was a reference to Alger's support of Vice President Richard Nixon, an honorary member of the NAACP. He noted that Alger had refused to sign a pledge made by Southern Democrats to muster every legal option available to oppose the 1954 Brown v. Topeka decision. He attacked Alger for favoring the "gradual integration" of Negro children into the public schools. Despite Wade's own popularity and a hard-hitting campaign in which Wade lost fifteen pounds, Alger won re-election to a second term. He became seemingly invincible in winning again in 1958, 1960, and 1962.

ART AND COMMUNISM

The old Carnegie Library, built in 1901 at Harwood and Commerce, was woefully inadequate for a city of Dallas' size. There was some money for a new building—$342,000 from the 1927 bond issue and another $1 million approved in the 1945 bond election—but this was insufficient. "Friends of the Dallas Public Library" began pushing hard in 1951 for supplemental funds, and in 1952 voters approved a bond program for an additional $1.25 million. After some controversy over where to place the new building , the council in 1953 voted to tear down the old library and to erect the new one at the same site. In 1955 the modern structure, designed by

George L. Dahl in striking contrast to its aged predecessor, opened.

The new library soon became the focus of lengthy debates over modern art and politics, arguments of whether or not tax money should be used to exhibit the works of communists or communist sympathizers. The argument gave early evidence to the existence in Dallas of fanatical right-wing elements.

The first debate arose over a controversial piece of abstract art chosen for the library's interior. Dahl had managed to divert earlier suggestions for works that he believed too trite—a huge bluebonnet landscape, a mural of the city's leading businessmen, or a photo-mural of Dallas' skyline. The library board instead accepted Dahl's recommendation to commission an abstract work, and for a fee of $12,000 Dahl hired sculptor Harry Bertoia of Philadelphia to create a modernistic metallic screen to hang from the ceiling. The screen, measuring 10 by 24 feet, consisted of a series of vertical bars with varied projecting shapes that formed interesting patterns of shadow and light. Dahl arranged to unveil the work before Mayor Thornton and a handful of other city officials, surely a risky proposition since Thornton was notorious for his unsophisticated artistic instincts. The mayor's reaction was immediate and painfully honest: "My God, it looks like a bad welding job," he exclaimed. Mayor Pro Tem Vernon Smith thought that people would forget why they came to the library when they saw "this pile of junk."

Such comments, reported in the press with great fanfare, spawned a sometimes bitter public debate which focused not just on the abstract nature of the sculpture, but on the $12,000 fee which many believed exorbitant. Dahl, disgusted, finally bowed to pressure and ordered the contractor to "take the damn screen down." Dahl stored the work in his garage and paid Bertoia with his personal check.

Then came a counter-reaction from those offended by the mayor's brutal rejection of the sculpture. Who was Uncle Bob Thornton to set himself up as an art expert? Art patrons appeared before the city council and offered to raise the money to pay for the screen if it were returned to its original position. Their argument was persuasive. The sculpture was retrieved from Dahl's garage and placed once more and permanently in the library.

Shortly afterwards, yet another question of artistic appropriateness arose. Sculptor Marshall Fredericks submitted to the library board his model of a sculpture to be placed on the front of the new building. It was a huge pair of hands on which stood an unclad male youth reaching to the sky with a book. This represented, according to the artist, "the hands of God supporting youth reaching for learning through the medium of literature." The nakedness offended some members of the library board, objections were stated, and when the completed full-size sculpture arrived Fredericks had clothed the youth in a pair of jeans.

These debates over art, marked by a degree of naiveté, bordered on the humorous, but in the same year another controversy arose that more seriously injected ultra-conservative political notions into artistic standards. In an era in which the American democratic system was perceived to be struggling for survival with communism, right-wingers challenged the patriotism of the Dallas Museum of Fine Arts and the Dallas Public Library boards for exhibiting such artists as Pablo Picasso, Diego Rivera, Joseph Hirsch, George Grosz, Ben Shahn, and others who were accused of being communists or communist sympathizers. Since these artists' works were predominantly "modern" or "abstract," in the debate modern art was portrayed as subversive and traditional art as pro-American. Among the organizations leading the charges against the library were the Dallas Patriotic Council, the American Legion, the Veterans of Foreign Wars, and the Public Affairs Luncheon Club.

The issue exploded in March 1955 when Colonel John W. Mayo, who as head of the city's Civil Defense program began promoting an ultra-conservative political agenda, objected loudly because the art museum was patronizing and supporting artists whose political beliefs were "dedicated to destroying our way of life." Mayo's accusations gained instant headlines. Many in Dallas supported Mayo and joined him in the battle against art by communists. The Public Affairs Luncheon Club helpfully issued lists of artists who were communists or who presented communist concepts. Beleaguered art museum trustees, hearing their patriotism questioned and unable to mount an effective defense, surrendered. They unanimously declared that henceforth the museum would not exhibit or acquire the work of any person known to be a communist or member of a communist-front organization.

To many, this was an unfortunate and improper retreat from objective artistic standards which should be free of political considerations. A counter-attack arose from individuals across the nation and from such authorities as *Art News*. The trustees now engaged in more deliberate discussions over the relationship between art and politics. They concluded that their acquiescence to those who had questioned their patriotism had been wrong. In December 1955, eight months after Colonel Mayo's initial salvo, the trustees rescinded their previous action and voted 17-9 to exhibit and acquire works of art "only on the basis of their merit." This policy was in keeping with those of other major museums throughout the nation.

The Dallas Patriotic Council demanded that the city council withdraw financial support of the museum. This the council declined to do. When a touring exhibit, "Sports in Art," was scheduled for the museum, the Patriotic Council again urged the trustees to purge from the exhibit the works of several artists, including Ben Shahn, Leon Kroll, and William Zorach. The trustees refused, reaffirming their adherence to their December policy statement opposing censorship on political grounds.

Many of the prominent trustees, especially oilman Eugene McElvaney, civic leader Jerome Crossman, Gerald C. Mann, and Waldo Stewart, effectively argued against those who would censor the arts. They won support from the city council, which joined the park board in endorsing the museum's stand against censorship.

In November 1956 the persistent issue surfaced once more, this time at the Dallas Public Library, where an exhibition of paintings and rugs included works by Pablo Picasso. Public pressure mounted to take down the Picasso works because he previously had expressed his sympathy for communism. Library director James D. Meeks, hoping to avoid a prolonged controversy, agreed to remove a Picasso painting and rug from the exhibit. The library board supported his action in a resolution acknowledging that a "mistake" had been made in displaying them. Then came an outpouring of protests against the library for yielding so easily, but the board stood firm in supporting Meeks.

Cabell Shakes Up the CCA

In the spring of 1959 Mayor Thornton, now seventy-five years of age, decided that three terms were enough. He was ready for a rest, but he wanted a hand in selecting his successor. Thornton privately approached Earle Cabell, whose father, Ben E. Cabell, and grandfather, William L. "Old Tige" Cabell, both had served Dallas as mayor. Would Cabell accept the CCA nomination for the 1959 election? The answer was a quick yes. Earle remembered 1939, the year his brother had been thwarted when council members chose Woodall Rodgers to be mayor, denying the Cabell family the honor of having three successive generations represented in that office.

Earle's grandfather, "Old Tige," had moved to Dallas in 1872 to practice law. A former Confederate general, he lost no time in making friends. Two years after he arrived he was elected mayor of the city. Voters returned him to the office two more times. His son, Ben E. Cabell, also a lawyer, was elected mayor in 1900. He, too, won a second term.

Although Ben E. Cabell, Earle's father, was an attorney, the family lived on a farm in Oak Cliff. All three Cabell sons, Ben E. Jr., Charles Pearre, and Earle, born in 1906 and the youngest, spent their formative years there. Earle graduated from North Dallas High School in 1925, then studied one semester each at Texas A&M and Southern Methodist University. In 1926 he quit college to go to work, taking a job with Morning Glory Creameries in Houston washing out milk cans. Within a few years he had found a much better job: superintendent of a milk plant in Amarillo. From there he moved in 1930 to Pine Bluff, Arkansas, and bought a small milk plant. When the Depression came the local bank folded and Cabell was wiped out. He and his wife, Elizabeth Holder Cabell, returned to Dallas, where Earle and his older brother Ben went into business together. Earle contributed $150 in cash and an old car that could be converted into a truck; Ben had $1,000 worth of ice-cream equipment. The third and eldest brother, Pearre, invested $1,000 of his savings. Thus was established Cabell's, an ice-cream company specializing in five-cent double-dip ice cream cones, a welcome treat in the dark Depression days. Ben was the first president, and Earle was vice president. The company was an immediate success, and the brothers built the operation into a full-line dairy business. By the 1950s Cabell's Dairies was serving a thirty-county area in North and East Texas. It also had a chain of some six-dozen "Minit Market" drive-in food outlets similar to Southland Corporation's Seven-Eleven stores. Ben retired from the business in 1952 and Earle succeeded him as president.

Earle's participation in civic activities, in addition to his business success, had given him the traditional qualifications to be mayor. Most importantly, perhaps, he was a member of the Citizens Council. He belonged as well to the Dallas Sales Executives Club, the Dallas Crime Commission, and the Dallas Crusade for Freedom. He had served as president of the Texas Manufacturers' Association.

Before the anointing of Cabell became publicly known, however, a movement emerged to draft Thornton for a fourth term as mayor. Thornton, flattered and involved in a number of city projects that now he felt he could not leave, acceded. Cabell would have to wait until the next election . As a consolation prize the CCA offered him a council nomination that had occurred after a sudden opening on the ticket. Cabell declined. Hurt, irritated, and believing that he had been treated unfairly, he kept his feelings to himself.

But he didn't forget his disappointment. As the 1959 elections approached he and his brothers sold Cabell, Inc., to Southland Corporation, and Earle announced as an independent candidate for mayor. Thornton's decision to seek a fourth term did not deter Cabell from his own decision to run, but the prospect of a race between these two "establishment" men concerned the CCA. One hour before Cabell was scheduled to open his campaign headquarters on March 6, one of the city's "Big Banker Bosses" (so Cabell later described him) approached him with an unusual offer. If Cabell would postpone his race until the next city election, the CCA would agree to nominate him for mayor, place a large sum of money in escrow for his campaign, and obtain fifty sworn pledges of support from prominent businessmen. Cabell was furious at this behind-the-scenes effort to manipulate affairs. He flatly refused. He was ready to take on the man known as "Mr. Dallas" as well as the powerful establishment.

In a letter to his brother Pearre, Cabell summarized his feelings. "I am bucking the machine that has been in power in Dallas for 27 years and bucking the present incumbent who is positive of the fact that he has a God-given right to that office....Whatever the outcome I will not be subjected to the kind of double-cross that was handed to Ben in 1939." It would be difficult to raise funds for the fight ahead, he said, because the heavy downtown contributors are "part of the machine and don't think that I am worthy of any investment."

Thus began one of the most torrid campaigns in Dallas history. Cabell's plan, as strategized by campaign adviser Ed C. Schwille, followed this line: "The C.C.A. candidates are the candidates only of the C.C.A. machine. CABELL is EVERYBODY'S candidate. This is YOUR city and CABELL is YOUR candidate." Cabell quickly embellished on this basic theme, boldly denouncing the arrogance of city hall, challenging the CCA's "machine politics," decrying the long duration of their rule, and swearing to end their habit of holding secret sessions. He vowed, if elected, to improve city services in Casa View, Casa Linda, South Dallas, and other neglected areas. The fact that Cabell was anything but a liberal challenging conservative leadership was suggested by one item on his platform generally associated with a goal of far-right fringe groups: his adamant opposition to putting fluoride in the municipal water supply.

Even the city's recent capital improvements programs had been far from satisfactory, he contended. The 1957 Love Field improvements had been thoroughly botched; the layout was a "nightmare" because travelers had to walk half a mile from entrance to airplane gate. Noise pollution was another problem there. Elsewhere in the city, too much concrete had been poured. The six new lanes for Walnut Hill Lane had converted that once-pleasant thoroughfare into a menacing speedway, and now he complained that the same was in store for Royal and Forest lanes.

As the campaign progressed Cabell blasted the "machine politics" that had dominated the city and suggested that its insiders were accruing huge personal profits. He urged voters to pick up their brooms and "sweep out these vicious slanderers and character assassins" who were "nothing more than a syndicate of downtown landlords, bankers and millionaires who pick the candidates, tell them what to say and after elected tell them what to do."

He was especially critical of what he termed a "land grab" on Griffin Street by the "fat cats." His reference was to the decision to extend tiny Griffin Street across Commerce, Main, Elm, and Pacific streets and to broaden it into a major thoroughfare, running adjacent to the *Times Herald* building on Pacific. Why not change Griffin Street's name to "Times Herald Boulevard"? It was strange, Cabell observed, that just two days after the newspaper had editorialized in behalf of the CCA ticket that the CCA-controlled city council had put into action the plan for improving Griffin Street through two acres of property owned by that newspaper.

When the fiery campaign ended Cabell had done what seemed impossible: force Thornton into a runoff. Cabell trailed "Mr. Dallas" by only 2,000 votes out of 60,000 cast. Another independent candidate for mayor, George F. Fox Jr., had earned enough votes to deprive Thornton of a majority. Similarly, strong races by independents Elizabeth Blessing, Joe Pool, and Joe Geary had forced their CCA opponents into run-offs. An analysis of returns showed that, as usual, Oak Cliff voters had voted against the CCA candidates, as did Southeast Dallas. But Cabell's fiery campaign had cut into the CCA's usual dominant strength in North Dallas.

Cabell, in a radio address, spoke directly to his listeners: "I need your help. Your help in breaking up a political machine in Dallas that is dominated by millionaires, bankers, and downtown landlords. They have run this city for 29 years. Don't you think it's time for a change?"

He charged that the "biggest political and economic squeeze in Dallas history" was being applied in behalf of Thornton. He intimated that Thornton might resign if elected, and he wondered who had been handpicked to succeed him, mentioning as possibilities Jerome K. Crossman and Dub Miller.

Thornton, stung by such comments, sharply denied Cabell's charges. "Too frequently," he said, "those who cry boss where there is no boss or machine, have a hidden motive. Just what is his motive? Would he create a machine; does he want to become boss?" As to Cabell's suggestion that he would resign as mayor once elected, Thornton absolutely denied it. CCA council candidate Walter Cousins Jr. spoke on local television and called Cabell a man with "an overpowering and ill-conceived obsession to become mayor of Dallas."

Of the city's two newspapers, the *Times Herald* now was more closely attuned to local events than the *News*, and it strongly supported the CCA. Cabell believed that the newspaper was guilty of "slanting and distortion" in its stories concerning his candidacy. He vented his ire in a letter to the editor: "I shall win this election despite your venomous attacks, and I shall give the people of Dallas a square and impartial administration despite the carping and needling that I know will be forthcoming from your newspaper." The newspaper printed the letter in its letters-to-the-editor column, but on the same page it carried an ardent pro-CCA editorial praising the city's "amazing progress" under its rule. The *News*, concerned these days mostly with national and international affairs and espousing an increasingly strident right-wing philosophy, remained quiet on its editorial page, observing only on the eve of the general election that "an unusual number of good candidates" were competing.

On the Sunday prior to the Tuesday run-off election the *Times Herald* published a page-one editorial supporting Thornton and the other three CCA candidates and lamenting the worst "low level, name-calling political campaign...in many years," one marked by falsehoods, half truths and damaging innuendoes. Most unforgiveable, most insulting of all, according to the newspaper, was Cabell's unsubstantiated charge that Thornton might resign once elected. Another front-page editorial on Monday strongly supported Thornton and his three CCA colleagues, and it was accompanied by yet another on the editorial page.

When the votes were counted, Thornton won by a margin of 37,013 to 34,037. Cabell's aggressive and nearly successful campaign, however, showed that the CCA and even so revered a figure as Robert L. Thornton were vulnerable. While CCA candidates Walter Cousins Jr. and George Mixon Sr. also won their run-off races, independent Geary upset CCA incumbent Tom L. Beauchamp to become the first non-CCA winner since 1947. Geary, a thirty-five-year-old attorney, was a resident of Lakewood who had broken with the CCA after having headed its speakers' bureau in the 1953 city race. He had split with the organization, he said, because "there is such a thing as any group being in office too long." Cabell, having lost, expressed thanks for the support he had earned, and he hinted at a second race in 1961.

Cabell's near-win and his stinging accusations against "machine politics" shocked the CCA leaders into a reassessment of their methods of selecting candidates. Long-time CCA president Laurence Melton, much maligned during the campaign for his role as a behind-the-scenes "boss," resigned. He was replaced by W.H. Pierce, who was from a section of town which never had provided energetic support for the CCA, Oak Cliff.

Attorney Robert L. Clark prepared for CCA members a thoughtful eight-page critique of the organization's past methods, arguing that the CCA must open its operations to the public to deflect future charges of bossism. In his memo, "Times Have Changed," Clark argued that the new type of Dallas voter was not satisfied with being taken for granted. "To live down the image of 'bossism,' 'machinism,' and 'downtown dictatorism,' the old-style domination must be well submerged to win elections for a charter slate in the future. Looking at the 1959 city election as a whole, it seems crystal clear that the Citizens Charter candidates ran weakest where the boss image was strongest....The boss image and battle cry of put an end to 'orders from downtown bosses' would have done decisive damage to the candidacy of our Mayor in the election had he not proved himself in the runoff election the master of the charges that bosses and downtown big-business dictated to him." The time had come, Clark argued, for those who wanted "top-notch, gilt-edged city administration and good, clean, progressive city government" to "wake up and take positive measures to revitalize and rearm the bulwark before the city's political body, as we have known it, is a thing of the past." Clark's memo bore the endorsement of four former mayors: Rodgers, Sergeant, Temple, and Savage.

CCA members agreed that a re-organization was in order. They created a new procedure in which nomination to the CCA slate was ostensibly opened to the public. W.H. Cothrum, appointed to lead the campaign to re-vitalize the CCA, sent a copy of the plan to Cabell for his thoughts and comments. Cabell's response, if he made one, is unrecorded. A brochure, "Your Choice, Your Voice," was prepared and distributed widely to explain how any qualified voter now could propose a candidate to his CCA district committee.

Pierce, the new president, publicly called for a "grass roots" movement. He expressed his belief that every qualified Dallas voter should be a CCA member, an interesting if unlikely proposition which would have effectively eliminated municipal political campaigns. In the fall of 1960 "grass roots forums" were held in all parts of the city "to dispel the notion," as the *Times Herald* phrased it, "that the CCA was an exclusive organization with a selfish ax to grind."

This reform effort failed to bring Cabell into the CCA camp. In 1961 he once again announced for mayor, again as an independent ready to battle whomever the CCA nominated. This time it would not be Thornton. Having served four terms, at last he had had enough. To succeed him the CCA nominated none other than Joe Geary, the energetic independent councilman who had defeated a CCA incumbent but who now agreed to return to the CCA fold to head its ticket.

Thornton could look back with pride on the eight years he had spent in office. He had "kept the dirt flying" just as he had promised. More public improvements were initiated during his years in office than in any similar period in the city's history. New city hall facilities were built adjoining the old Municipal Building; a new public library was constructed on the site of the old and outmoded Carnegie Library; Dallas Memorial Auditorium was built; Love Field continued to be defended, expanded and improved (including the addition of a new terminal building); the long-range water committee initiated reservoir projects that would remove the danger of drought from the 1960s to the year 2000; and the geographical boundaries of the city exploded. If the years had been controlled by a handful of leaders, they had been productive. Few residents had complaints.

The 1961 campaign between Cabell and Geary repeated the fireworks of 1959. Cabell's campaign was buoyed this time by the editorial backing of the *News*. Despite the CCA's public effort to democratize its selection process, Cabell continued to pound away on the theme of machine politics, of "windfall profits" being made by members of the CCA or their friends through municipal projects, of special favors such as zoning exemptions, of problems concerning the transit system, of the need for privately funded slum clearance and urban renewal, and of inadequacies at the new Love Field terminal.

One night prior to a televised debate before the Junior Chamber of Commerce at the Adolphus Hotel, reporters were tipped that a new development would be revealed. The surprise came when Geary produced a police report showing that Cabell had been arrested for disorderly conduct at the Red Barn Restaurant on Hillcrest Avenue because of a fight in the parking lot. Cabell responded to the new information by dramatically asking the crowd, "Is there any man here who would not fight to protect the honor of his wife?" The crowd burst into applause; Cabell's reputation as a battler for just causes was enhanced.

On election day Cabell beat Geary by nearly 3,000 votes, 41,468 to 38,725. He was the first non-CCA mayor to gain that office since 1937. Moreover, Mrs. Elizabeth Blessing, who had mustered such a strong campaign as an independent in 1959, did so again, but this time successfully. She was joined on the council by yet a third independent, feisty Joe Moody of Pleasant Grove.

The CCA had never been stronger than in the 1950s. Yet, clearly, as the turbulent decade of the 1960s loomed, maintaining its hold on municipal politics likely would be difficult.

Earle Cabell went on to be elected as well to a second term as mayor. If he did not become as beloved a figure as his predecessor, his pragmatism and direct assault on municipal problems earned him a great measure of respect from all quarters. His experiences as mayor also pulled him from the tent of the conservatives into the camp of the moderates. During Cabell's first term he established a city-wide emergency ambulance system, ending the practice of private funeral homes responding to emergency calls. He encountered fierce opposition when he proposed the construction of 3,000 public housing units for the disabled and elderly. (His plan was put to the voters, who rejected it in a 1962 referendum.) With the city's privately owned transit company struggling with losses, Cabell engineered in his second term the acquisition of the company by the municipal government. One of the special problems faced during Cabell's terms was the matter of integrating the city's public schools. Here was a problem not easily solved, despite a promising beginning.

Desegregation of the Public Schools

By 1960 Dallas was one of the largest cities in the South with a completely segregated school system. Maintaining separate white and black schools in the face of a historic and rising tide of legal challenges and federal court rulings was becoming increasingly difficult. Negro residents had begun their efforts to integrate Dallas' schools immediately after the monumental 1954 Brown v. Topeka decision. Shortly after that ruling the local chapter of the NAACP petitioned the Dallas school board to take "immediate steps" to comply with the Supreme Court mandate. In declining to do so, School Superintendent W.T. White said that since Dallas schools operated under state rather than federal law, any such changes would have to await the authority of the Texas legislature.

A year later in 1955 attorney W.J. Durham, representing the Dallas chapter of the NAACP, filed suit in federal court to force the public schools to desegregate in compliance with the Supreme Court's 1954 ruling. Federal Judge William Hawley Atwell, who in

1923 had argued in behalf of a Negro client that Dallas' segregationist residential ordinances were unconstitutional, ruled against the NAACP, observing that equal opportunities for schooling already were offered to both white and black children.

In the following year Atwell once again was confronted with a school desegregation suit. In rejecting the plaintiffs' arguments, the eighty-five-year-old jurist made clear his own belief that integrating the schools was wrong. His decision was reversed in 1957 by the 5th Court of Appeals, which sent the case back to him for further action. The appeals court explained the case in simple terms: "The basic facts were simple and undisputed. Rosa Sims, ten years of age, and Maude Sims, nine, applied for admission to the John Henry Brown School, four blocks from their home. The school principal showed their father a directive from the School Board saying that no Negro children could go to school with the whites, and denied them the right to enter because they were Negroes." Instead of being able to attend the school in their neighborhood, the children were required to go to a Negro school eighteen blocks away across heavy traffic.

Following his directive from the appeals court, Atwell ordered the school board to desegregate in January 1958. The school board appealed, beginning a federal court battle that would be repeated for more than thirty-five years as the highly complex issue of integrating the schools unfolded and presented for Dallas one of the most difficult dilemmas of modern times.

While the majority of Dallasites clearly agreed with the school board's intention to maintain its traditional policy of separate school boundaries for blacks and whites, there were those—including some whites—who did not. In the spring of 1958 some 300 white Protestant Dallas ministers signed a statement calling enforced segregation "morally and spiritually wrong." In a press conference a number of them asked that churches, service clubs, newspapers, and broadcasting stations promote a spirit of harmony and peace as the inevitability of desegregation took place in Dallas. The decades to come would be marked by anguished debates, great racial tension, some student disturbances in the schools, and large-scale white flight out of the district. Ultimately, though, Dallas residents would accept the integration of public schools without resorting to violence or defiant refusal to follow the mandates of the courts.

By 1960 the ensuing legal battle had lasted for five and a half years, moving back and forth between the federal district court in Dallas and the 5th U.S. Court of Appeals in New Orleans. Finally the appeals court ordered the school district to file a desegregation plan no later than May 1960. Its chief justice complained that after five years in litigation the first step toward integration in Dallas still had not been taken.

Aside from its admitted reluctance to integrate the schools, the school board faced an unusual dilemma. The Texas legislature, in an obvious effort to thwart the Brown v. Topeka decision, passed a law stipulating that no school district could desegregate unless its voters approved the action in a referendum. Dallas accordingly held a referendum on August 6, 1960. The result was a better than 4-1 vote against desegregation. In light of this vote, if Dallas integrated its schools it would lose more than $3 million a year in state funds. This quandary was resolved when State Attorney General Will Wilson, Dallas County's former district attorney, ruled that a school district under federal court order could integrate without losing state funds and accreditation.

Finally, with its May 1960 deadline approaching, the board conceived of a "stair-step" plan by which selected schools would be integrated one grade at a time, starting with the first grade in 1961 and proceeding one grade each year. The plan was submitted to Federal Judge T. Whitfield Davidson, who had taken over the case upon Atwell's retirement. Davidson made it clear that he, too, opposed integration. "No country in history has ever amalgamated the two races without both races being the loser," he said in a speech. Davidson rejected the school board's stair-step plan and substituted his own "salt-and-pepper" plan in which just one white school and one black school would be integrated on a test basis. The 5th Court of Appeals rejected his plan, and instead approved the stair-step concept, ordering its implementation beginning that fall.

How Dallas residents would react even to this token amount of first-grade desegregation was impossible to determine. The turmoil accompanying desegregation in Little Rock had caused the very mention of that city to be identified instantly around the world with an ugly image of bigotry and violence. There was no particular reason to believe that Dallas' residents would react in a calmer way than those in Little Rock. And if turbulent scenes did accompany desegregation, the city's image would be damaged for years to come.

Mayor Thornton, nearing the end of his time in office, believed the situation to be so critical that the Citizens Council should exercise its power to assure success. He reminded members of the losses suffered in reputation and business in Little Rock and New Orleans. Unless the problem could be solved quickly and peaceably in Dallas, the same could happen. The question was not one of morality or equity, for most citizens obviously did not favor integration of the schools. It was a matter of dollars and of preserving the good reputation that had been so carefully nurtured through the years.

Acceding to the mayor's request, the Citizens Council agreed in 1960 to assume as a special project the successful integration of Dallas schools. While precise details of implementation, of course, would be the school district's responsibility, the Citizens Council would prepare the overall community for its acceptance. The essential work was delegated to a powerful seven-member committee headed by the Council's president, C.A. Tatum Jr. of Dallas Power & Light. As a major element of its strategy the Citizens Council initiated a massive public relations campaign to educate Dallas residents as to the importance of peaceful desegregation. This came under the direction of committee member Sam Bloom, owner of a large advertising agency bearing his name. The two newspapers and the radio and television stations, whose chief executives were Citizens Council members, agreed to stress news concerning the benefits of peaceful desegregation and to avoid stories that might disturb readers or viewers. Under this agreement some important news was suppressed.

Convinced that all racial controversy must be avoided to keep the white public from being antagonized during this delicate period, the committee believed cooperation from Dallas Negroes to be essential. It decided to augment its seven white members with seven prominent Negro members. Thus was formed a bi-racial committee whose members included white leaders such as Karl Hoblitzelle, James W. Aston, and Carr P. Collins Sr. and black leaders such as W.J. Durham, A. Maceo Smith, and George Allen.

Black members of the committee were expected to persuade Negro organizations not to protest or embarrass desegregation plans or incite others to action. This was not an easy task; the committee members could not realistically speak for all Negroes in Dallas. In the months ahead black committee members would face accusations of "selling out" to the white leadership. The NAACP generally maintained the desired low profile, but it was a force in behind-the-scenes negotiations during the delicate months prior to integration.

The day already had passed when Dallas' Negro population would accept proferred tokens without consultation. By now the push to integrate the nation's public schools and all public facilities had become so intense that it was truly impossible to stifle all manifestations of the movement, including those in Dallas. One special target had been the State Fair of Texas, whose president was Mayor Thornton himself, and which had been integrated only through pressure. A significant battle had been won in May 1953 when the State Fair's board of directors voted to integrate the midway rides for all sixteen days of the Fair rather than only on "Negro Achievement Day." This applied only to rides where no contact was involved among the riders.

It turned out that at least two rides did not qualify for integration under these terms, and in 1955 the Youth Council of the NAACP, under the leadership of Juanita Craft, announced intentions to picket the entrances to the Fair on Negro Achievement Day. The intent was not only to protest the segregation of the two rides but also to discourage black support of Negro Achievement Day. The NAACP saw the day as a subterfuge to encourage Negroes to attend the fair only on that day and on no others. On the weekend prior to the picketing, C.B. Bunkley, president of the Negro Chamber of Commerce, personally tested the Fair's acceptance of Negroes. When he found himself excluded from the two rides and subjected to other discriminatory practices, he prevailed upon the Negro Chamber in a Saturday night meeting to cancel its endorsement of the Fair. On the next night, alarmed Fair officials attended yet another Chamber meeting to ask members to rescind their vote. In a session that lasted until 1 a.m. the Chamber directors agreed at last to reverse their stand. Bunkley immediately resigned in protest. When the Fair opened at 7 a.m. that morning the twenty-two members of the NAACP Youth Council, mostly Lincoln High students, took their positions at the entrance gates with pickets. The customary Negro Achievement Day parade of black organizations and schools moved down Second Avenue to the Grand Avenue entrance, but instead of proceeding into the grounds as expected a number of the marching bands refused to cross the picket lines, including those of Booker T.

Washington High and Wiley College. Thornton, having explained earlier that the two rides had been closed because they might create situations leading to physical violence, now yielded and declared that for the balance of the Fair the two restricted rides would be open to all.

Thus, there was no certainty in the black community that patience was better than pressure. One of the new firebrand Negro leaders refusing to go along with the bi-racial committee's plea for patience was the Rev. H. Rhett James, who had taken over at New Hope Baptist Church after Maynard Jackson moved to Atlanta. Beginning in October James organized regular picket lines outside the downtown H.L. Green Department Store to force it to integrate its lunch counters. A number of white liberals joined the pickets. Occasionally, the scene became ugly when hecklers appeared. James spoke not only from his church pulpit and from the picket lines, but also in a regular column he was writing for the *Express*. He was the most vocal critic of the Negro members of the bi-racial committee, accusing NAACP attorney Durham in particular, of selling out to the whites. These events largely were ignored by the Dallas press.

In early January 1961 the effort to integrate Dallas lunch counters broadened when a Negro SMU theology student named Earl Allen and a white friend decided to challenge the University Drug Store's segregated lunch counter across the street from the campus. Upon being denied service they departed and returned with a group of approximately thirty other white theology students to begin a "sit-in" at the counter. The drugstore owner retaliated by fumigating his store. As he thoroughly sprayed the students, they remained seated with only handkerchiefs over their faces for protection. They stayed until he closed the store about an hour later. Later that afternoon they returned with pickets. This event was reported by wire services in Fort Worth, but not in Dallas. This was the kind of news, it was feared, that might spark angry whites to retaliate.

On the following day, Sunday, some 500 Negroes heard Durham announce that talks between the seven Negroes and the seven Citizen Council members on the bi-racial committee had "broken down." He said he and other committee members were deeply disappointed because Mayor Thornton had rejected their plan to totally integrate Fair Park on a year-round basis. Durham urged the crowd to boycott Dallas businesses that practiced discrimination and to prepare themselves for sit-ins and demonstrations.

On Monday Rhett James led five Negroes in a demonstration at the downtown Titche-Goettinger Department Store, a larger and more prominent department store than Green's. On the same day some 200 students returned to the University Drug Store at SMU to demonstrate for five hours against its white-only seating policies.

In February the Dallas NAACP's youth council, in observance of Lincoln's birthday, staged demonstrations at two downtown theaters to protest segregation, and a few days later the same group congregated at Ferris Plaza opposite Union Terminal in commemoration of the NAACP's fifty-second anniversary. The protests soon included an effort to boycott downtown department stores by a mass turning-in of credit cards and a refusal to buy new Easter clothes at any of them.

Under such growing pressure, the Citizens Council bi-racial committee recognized that part of their strategy for integrating the schools without incident would have to be to gradually desegregate other areas, including the midway at Fair Park and lunch counters of downtown restaurants. On August 2 A. Maceo Smith announced at a mass meeting at the Good Street Baptist Church that as a result of the bi-racial committee's work some forty business enterprises throughout the city had removed all discriminating signs, symbols, and practices, and they had extended their food service to include all customers, regardless of race.

Without question, though, the activist tactics of Rhett James and Earl Allen, coupled with the aggressive actions of the NAACP, working outside the umbrella of the bi-racial committee, had been an important factor in the breakthrough. It was an indication of the times to come when the mantle of leadership in the black community shifted to a new generation. James would be elected president of the NAACP in 1962. Allen, after graduating from SMU's theology school, became minister of Highland Hills Methodist Church and a leader of the local chapter of the Congress on Racial Equality (CORE). He continued to pursue integration through confrontational tactics, including the picketing of the Piccadilly Cafeteria in downtown Dallas in 1964 which ended the ban there on black customers.

Meanwhile, Sam Bloom's public relations committee completed work on a skillfully produced thirty-minute film, "Dallas at the Crossroads," narrated by the familiar and nationally respected figure

Walter Cronkite, which elaborated on the harm that would come to the city and its children if violence or disruptions accompanied school desegregation. The message was clear: those who failed to cooperate would be damaging the best interests of their town. The film was shown widely and under careful guidelines to community groups and on television. A printed manual under the same title and bearing the same information also was distributed widely.

The city council passed an "anti-mob ordinance" to prohibit persons from "standing, remaining or congregating on any public street or sidewalk...so as to obstruct, prevent, or interfere...with its use." The city's police officers received "mob control training" in anticipation of trouble. On the Sunday before the first day of school almost all of the city's ministers, inspired by Dr. Luther Holcomb of the Greater Dallas Council of Churches, made references from their pulpits to the critical need for peaceful cooperation.

Finally, on Wednesday, September 6, 1961, eighteen Negro first-graders enrolled in eight previously all-white elementary schools. Their numbers had been kept small by a complicated transfer system in which the burden on integration lay on Negro parents to initiate the enrollment of their children in all-white schools. The most black children in a single school was four at City Park Elementary. Two police officers were assigned to each integrated school, and a riot squad of 100 officers was ready to move rapidly if trouble erupted at any place. Only a few minor, isolated incidents were recorded on the first day of school, none requiring the officers' presence. "No one congregated except newspaper people," School Superintendent W.T. White said. School children expressed puzzlement at the presence of reporters and photographers, although the newsmen were kept at a distance.

President John F. Kennedy and Attorney General Robert Kennedy singled out Dallas for public praise in its peaceful handling of school integration. *Life* magazine also saluted the city's success. In a lengthy report on the day's events the *New York Times* said the city's peaceful integration "contrasted sharply" with the violence at Little Rock and the distasteful scenes at New Orleans.

Dallas' Negro community reacted cautiously over the token amount of school integration that actually had occurred. Of the system's 128,563 enrollment, about 20 percent, or 24,317, were blacks. Of those black students, only eighteen had been integrated. James pointed out in his column in the *Express* that it had come only through Negro initiative. "We have yet to see just how much integration will take place in Dallas," he wrote.

C.A. Tatum seemed touched by the public role the Citizens Council had played in the tense situation. He hoped, he told the *News*, that the organization now could return to its more characteristic pattern of conducting quiet, unobtrusive action for the betterment of Dallas.

Under the stair-step plan, integration of the Dallas schools would not be completed for eleven more years. Negro residents became more restive as the obvious turtle-like pace grew clear. By 1964 only 131 out of 9,400 Negro students in the affected first three grades had been integrated. Pickets organized by the Congress of Racial Equality (CORE) began appearing outside the DISD administration building. In 1965 the 5th U.S. Court of Appeals ruled that this pace—which they had approved themselves—was too slow. It ordered all elementary schools to be desegregated by the beginning of school in 1965, and that two years later all junior high and senior high schools in the city be fully integrated. Meanwhile, a cautious beginning had been made to integrate the school faculties as well. By 1967 fourteen of the 172 schools had integrated faculties.

PART FOUR

Boom and Bust

14

November 22, 1963

I sure wish to hell you'd persuade Kennedy not to come. It is a grave mistake to come to Dallas.
--Stanley Marcus to Lyndon B. Johnson, 1963

LBJ and Lady Bird Face a Mob

Four days before the 1960 election in which John F. Kennedy and Lyndon B. Johnson became president and vice president, Johnson and his wife Lady Bird came to Dallas for a noon Democratic Party luncheon at the Adolphus Hotel. They were confronted by an angry, screaming crowd of demonstrators who shook insulting signs and began taunting the couple from the moment they emerged from their automobile. Mrs. Johnson no sooner had got out of the car than one of the women demonstrators snatched away her gloves and threw them into the gutter. The taunting persisted as the crowds surrounded the Johnsons while they crossed the street, and then congregated so tightly about them in the hotel lobby that the couple had to push and shove for thirty minutes before they could reach the Grand Ballroom. Lady Bird Johnson was genuinely frightened for her life in what she later recalled to be her worst hour in politics ever. Spittle and insults were flying. A reporter who was there described the scene as the "nearest thing to an uncontrollable mob" in Dallas since the wilder days of the Texas-Oklahoma pre-game activities.

Police officers tried to clear a path through the demonstrators for the prominent couple, but Johnson ordered them away. "If the time has come when I can't walk through the lobby of a hotel in Dallas with my lady without a police escort, I want to know it," he said. Johnson already had rejected an offer to be slipped into the hotel through a side door. "Down With Lady Bird," read one sign which was poked into her face. "Smiling Judas Johnson," read another placard bearing the senator's photograph. Vainly seeking an impromptu, face-to-face debate with Johnson in the lobby was Republican candidate John Tower, who was campaigning for Johnson's senate seat.

The man primarily responsible for the demonstration, Bruce Alger, stood on the street bearing a sign, "LBJ Sold Out to Yankee Socialists." At the front of the mob were his well-dressed Republican "Alger Girls," who had come downtown at the Congressman's call for "Nixon Tag Day." Their original purpose was to pin Nixon buttons that morning on downtown pedestrians. Afterwards, though, they gathered at the Commerce and Akard intersection to give the Johnsons a keen sampling of their Republican fervor. Dressed colorfully in red, white, and blue outfits, they were, Alger recalled, "the prettiest bunch of women I ever saw in my life."

This raucous affair, recorded by television cameras, caught the Johnsons, Dallas, and the nation by surprise because of its intensity. The nation's press played up the tumultuous scene with all the details it could muster. The surprising manner in which a Texas crowd treated its own vice presidential candidate and a Senate powerhouse was big news. Johnson's critics claimed that he had immediately sensed a political advantage from the scene, and prolonged it for television cameras by refusing police assistance.

The fervor of the anti-Johnson demonstration—whatever it meant for the GOP—was an embarrassing setback to Dallas' reputation for cordiality. In a front-page editorial the *Times Herald* wrote that the scene was "completely foreign to usual Dallas manners and hospitality—even in the heat of dying campaign days."

Bruce Alger refuted the press' graphic descriptions of the incident by taking a full-page advertisement in the newspaper on

November 7. In Alger's point of view, there was no violence and very little jostling other than what one normally experience in a tight crowd; the "goon squad" was 300 young ladies who had volunteered for the Nixon Tag Day; there was no spitting, no profanity, and no interruption of Johnson's speech; Johnson's arrival was coincidental to the Tag Day event; and the demonstration was "good-natured and courteous."

Both the *News* and the *Times Herald* endorsed the Nixon-Lodge ticket, and on election day Dallas voters proved themselves of like mind. Texas as a whole supported the Democratic ticket, but Dallas' conservative voters gave the majority of their votes to Nixon and Lodge, as they had done for Eisenhower and Nixon in 1952 and 1956—and for Herbert Hoover in 1928.

THE FAR RIGHT IN DALLAS

In an era when fanatical right-wing extremism was gaining strength throughout the nation, few if any cities seemed to encourage it more than Dallas. When Army General Edwin A. Walker resigned his commission in 1961 after heavy criticism for indoctrinating his troops with a "pro-blue" John Birch Society political program, he chose to settle in Dallas, where he instantly became the darling of the far right. Walker, a bachelor, moved into a large two-story house on Turtle Creek Boulevard where he regularly flew his American flag upside down as a distress signal that the nation was in danger from being taken over by the Communists. From his house Walker, a member of the Birch Society, began making solemn pronouncements about government officials selling out to Communists. When he contemplated campaigning in 1962 for governor, Alger privately advised him that he could be far more helpful to the "cause" if he would stay out of politics and not become the "tool of any special interest group." Walker ran anyway, but he proved to be an ineffective campaigner and speaker, and he finished last in a field of six. This poor showing tarnished his reputation somewhat, but to many zealots it did not diminish his stature as a patriotic military man whose warnings against the perils of communism had been muzzled by his superiors.

Assorted right-wing individuals other than Edwin A. Walker

also found Dallas a congenial setting. H.L. Hunt, still a maverick rather than a man who worked within organizations, was writing and publishing conservative tracts with titles such as *We Must Abolish the United Nations* and *Hitler Was a Liberal*, sponsoring a radio commentary show known as LIFELINE (spelled always with capital letters), bombarding newspapers and magazines with letters to the editor decrying liberalism, and funding since 1952 a tax-exempt organization called Facts Forum. Now aged considerably from his energetic days as an aggressive oilman, Hunt's extremist views as well as his peculiar personal habits were bringing him a reputation as an ineffective eccentric, but his steady stream of far-right diatribes bombarded Americans for more than two decades.

Another far-right spokesman in the city was Dr. Robert B. Morris, the president of a new Catholic university, the University of Dallas. Morris's fulminations brought doubts as to just what was the purpose of this new institution.

More far right activity came through the founding and meteoric rise of the National Indignation Convention (later Conference). A thirty-two-year-old Dallas man named Frank McGehee began the group in outrageous indignation when he learned that Communist Yugoslavian pilots were being trained at Perrin Air Force Base in Texas. Chapters of the Dallas-based organization sprang up all across the nation as a move to force Congress to cease granting military aid to any Communist regime anywhere and to seek the dismissal of all government officials responsible for such actions.

Especially strong in Dallas was the John Birch Society. Its membership included some of the city's oil-rich, notably H.L. Hunt's son, Nelson Bunker Hunt, who also supported many other conservative political and religious causes. The Society put its regional headquarters in Dallas under the leadership of Rex Westerfield. Independent oilman Joseph P. Grinnan was the local coordinator. The Society operated in the city its own American Opinion Book Store, where a large collection of right-wing material was sold to the public. Robert Welch of Massachusetts, the organization's founder, made periodic visits to the city to make speeches and to give seminars to receptive audiences.

None of these ultra-right organizations or points of view were promoted or endorsed by the city's civic leaders, at least not openly. Extremist political views did not bring the favorable sort of attention that these leaders and their predecessors had sought to cultivate for so many years. Nor, on the other hand, did they seek to disown or to discourage these groups.

Any mention of the arch-conservatives in Dallas would have to include the pastor of the powerful First Baptist Church of Dallas, the Rev. W.A. Criswell, who from his pulpit in July 1960 declared that "the election of a Catholic as president would mean the end of religious liberty in America." Criswell, who believed in the inerrancy of the Bible in every respect and who preached against the evils of school integration as contrary to biblical command, endorsed Nixon over Kennedy in a sermon.

Overall, Dallas was undeniably out-of-step with the rest of the state in the depths of its conservatism. The *News* had grown especially adamant in its crusades against what it perceived to be Kennedy's socialistic tendencies and also the civil rights movement. It had nodded approvingly as extremist elements gained strength in the city and nation, and its editorial stances were being cited widely as examples of ultra-conservative thinking. Publisher E.M. (Ted) Dealey, son of the late George B. Dealey, raised eyebrows across the nation when at a White House luncheon he shocked fellow publishers in attendance with a display of bad manners. He pointedly told his host, President Kennedy, that the people in Texas and the Southwest needed and wanted a strong president who would get off Caroline's tricycle and lead the nation from horseback. Kennedy was quietly furious, especially at the use of his daughter's name. The incident prompted a *Times Herald* vice president to apologize for his colleague's bad behavior. Kennedy replied that he was certain the people of Dallas were glad when afternoon (and the *Times Herald*) came.

A Mob Confronts Adlai Stevenson

There were organizations in the city that were at least mildly liberal in their outlook. One such organization was Dallas' Council on World Affairs, which began planning a public event to honor United Nations Day in Dallas. The special day, set for October 26, 1963, would feature an address from the U.S. ambassador to the United Nations, Adlai E. Stevenson. The United Nations, of course, was anathema to the far right. To display their scorn for the organization, Edwin A. Walker and the National Indignation Convention announced a counter-event they called "U.S. Day" to be held one night before the U.N. event and in the same downtown Memorial Auditorium. At first glance, "U.S. Day" seemed innocuous enough, so much so that Texas Governor John Connally, who had been Kennedy's secretary of the Navy, officially sanctioned it as a matter of routine. What it actually became was an occasion for the gathering of some 1,400 die-hard extremists to make fierce attacks against the United Nations and President Kennedy, including reckless accusations of treason. (One of those who attended that evening's speech-making was definitely not a right-winger. He was a young Marxist named Lee Harvey Oswald, who six months earlier had attempted to assassinate the former general with a rifle from an alley behind Walker's house. The shot had barely missed Walker, who was working at his desk late at night when it occurred.) Walker told the U.S. Day crowd that the Communists and Alger Hiss "and that crowd" had been behind the founding of the United Nations. The real battle being fought in this Cold War was taking place inside the United States, and it was the U.S. versus the United Nations, he said. Walker asserted that every street corner in Dallas was a virtual battleground to fight the Communists and the red-controlled U.N. Historian and rancher J. Evetts Haley won loud applause when he announced that he didn't want to impeach Chief Justice Earl Warren, as the Birch Society was urging, he wanted to hang him. Messages of support were read at the meeting from Bruce Alger, Dr. Morris of the University of Dallas, political commentator Dan Smoot, and Senator Strom Thurmond.

Next day, on the morning of Stevenson's address, handbills were circulated on the city's streets bearing pictures of Kennedy with the words: "Wanted for Treason. This Man is wanted for treasonous activities against the United States." There followed a listing of such charges as permitting "known Communists" to abound in federal offices.

On the evening of U.N. Day in Dallas, a capacity crowd of 1,770 filled Memorial Auditorium. Stanley Marcus give a glowing introduction to Ambassador Stevenson, but as Stevenson came to the podium to speak a man with a bullhorn stood up in front of the auditorium and demanded answers to specific questions. He was

Frank McGehee, founder of the National Indignation Convention. Many in the crowd attempted to shout down the incessant McGee, but he persisted until finally police officers had to remove him from the auditorium.

The traumatic events of the evening had only begun, though. Right-wing extremists in the auditorium equalled in number those supporters of the United Nations, and they consistently sought to humiliate and disrupt Stevenson by waving placards, booing, shouting interjections, laughing derisively, coughing incessantly, displaying miniature American flags upside down, and walking up and down the aisles clicking their "crickets." "How about Cuber?" was a frequent shout, imitative of Kennedy's accent. "How about Hungary?" "How about Katanga?" The evening became a struggle of wills between the two groups, one determined to cheer on Stevenson and the other intent on disrupting him. While Stevenson was speaking, someone climbed high on a catwalk behind the stage and flipped over a huge banner so that the friendly "Welcome Adlai" message now revealed on the opposite side an entirely different one: "U.N. Red Front." The banner had been planted there the night before at the U.S. Day rally.

After the speech, about a hundred demonstrators waited outside to confront Stevenson. They carried anti-U.N. signs which had been stored overnight at Edwin A. Walker's house. When finally Stevenson emerged at a side door the crowd spotted him and rushed towards him, shouting. Cries of "Communist" and "traitor" were heard. Stevenson paused at his car to reason with one screaming woman, but this only gave another woman the opportunity to hit him on the head with her sign, a deed recorded clearly by television and by a newspaper photographer. A college student spat on the ambassador. As police broke through the crowd to rescue him, Stevenson wiped his face with a handkerchief and was heard to say, "Are these human beings or are these animals?" Stanley Marcus, escorting Stevenson, managed to push him into the car, but crowd members began rocking it. At Marcus' urging, the driver managed to speed away despite the congestion. Police arrested the woman who had hit Stevenson, but soon released her at the ambassador's request. They apprehended and jailed the spitting college student.

The fierceness of the mob, both inside and outside, brought national headlines to the city, even more so than the 1960 incident concerning Lyndon B. Johnson. ABC radio commentator Edward P. Morgan said that "Big D now stands for disgrace." He suggested to his national audience that the *News'* editorial preoccupation with the extreme right "may in a very real sense have encouraged the crackpots." *Time* magazine's relation was entitled "A City Disgraced." *Christian Century* published an article recapping the success of right-wing extremists under the title, "The Dallas Image Unveiled," and blamed the situation on the refusal of civic leaders to respond to right-wing extremists. It singled out the *News* for "following the party line of the radical right" and publishing naive editorials on enormously complex matters of international affairs.

The city's leaders were aghast at the incident and its immediate injury to the city's reputation. Mayor Cabell, Citizens Council president J. Erik Jonsson, Chamber of Commerce president Robert B. Cullum, and a hundred other leading citizens sent a telegram of apology to the ambassador. "The City of Dallas is outraged and abjectly ashamed of the disgraceful and discourtesies you suffered at the hands of a small [sic] group of extremists."

Mayor Cabell recalled the days in which the Ku Klux Klan had reigned in the city and made it the "hate capital" of the Southwest. He urged Dallas residents to reject the radical right just as it ultimately had rejected the Klan.

"Dallas has been disgraced," read a front-page *Times Herald* editorial. "There is no other way to view the stormtrooper actions of last night's frightening attack on Adlai Stevenson" which amounted to a "senseless inability of some of the residents of Dallas to tolerate those with whom they disagree." The display was a "misguided brand of 'patriotism'" dragging Dallas' good name through the "slime of national dishonor."

Editorial comment and letters to the editor reprinted in the newspapers for days afterward probed the significance of the affair. For four consecutive days the event received front-page newspaper coverage. The *Times Herald* asked: "What has happened to Dallas?" The display of malevolence "has brought sensible Dallas to the sickening realization that 'harmless extremists' can not only cause physical harm but create destructive havoc....We must quit preaching hate. We must stop spreading and believing the ridiculous stories of suspicion and distrust of our fellow citizens from the seeds of uncontrolled frenzy." In contrast to the *Times Herald*'s fulsome editorial laments, the *News* apologized conditionally: "If the time has come when a distinguished gentleman in his position cannot express his beliefs without abuse, then this city should examine itself."

APPREHENSION ABOUT JFK'S SAFETY IN DALLAS

The most immediate and critical aspect of the Stevenson affair was obvious. President Kennedy himself, the primary target of the extreme right, was due in Dallas within weeks. When Kennedy had his aide, Arthur Schlesinger, convey to Stevenson his congratulations for maintaining his presence of mind and coolness under such extreme circumstances, Stevenson joked about it, then added seriously, "But, you know, there was something ugly and frightening about the atmosphere." He had talked with some of the leading people in Dallas afterwards, he said, and they "wondered whether the President should go to Dallas, and so do I."

One of the leaders, identified only as a "prominent" businessman, wrote to Stevenson and said that the incident had had "serious effects" on the entire community. "Your visit has had permanent and important results on the City of Dallas."

In the days that followed Stevenson sought to downplay the mob's hostility and its size, probably as a courtesy to the embarrassed city. In letters to friends he reduced the numbers of the demonstrators to "a minute handful" and "a few zealots." Forgetting that the auditorium's capacity was just 1,770 and that within these numbers a desperate struggle had ensued for control, he contrasted 5,000 cheering supporters inside with just fifty outside who were jeering.

People in Dallas knew better. The news director of WFAA-TV, Bob Walker, wrote to Stevenson with a pessimistic observation that the idiot fringe elements were "winning their fight in Dallas." Stevenson forwarded this letter to Kenneth O'Donnell, Kennedy's appointments secretary, and said he doubted Walker's conclusion. "On the contrary, my guess is that the President will have an enthusiastic and sincere reception," he now wrote. But Stanley Marcus, who had been there, too, shared the news director's pessimism. He urged that President Kennedy omit Dallas from his upcoming Texas political tour. "I sure wish to hell you'd persuade Kennedy not to come," Marcus told Vice President Johnson. "It is a grave mistake to come to Dallas." But he recalled the vice president's strong response: "I don't care what you think, nor does it make any difference what I think about the President coming down to Dallas. He is coming to Dallas, so go out and raise the money."

The White House spokesman announced on the day after the Stevenson melee that the president's plans to visit Dallas would not be cancelled. The trip seemed important, not just for raising political funds but also to mend the Texas Democratic Party feud between the conservative John Connally forces and the liberal Senator Ralph Yarborough element.

The *Times Herald* addressed itself directly to the possibility of a recurrence of misbehavior in a news story under the headline, "Repeat of Demonstration for JFK Visit Not Likely." The story warned that the White House Secret Service detail had studied the Stevenson incident in order to prevent a similar incident, and that its agents would be "very knowledgeable about his [Kennedy's] zealous critics." Mayor Cabell strongly urged the city to redeem itself by being on its very best behavior on the president's visit.

To ensure success at this critical juncture, the Citizens Council once again stepped forward. The organization announced that it would assume sponsorship of the luncheon at which the president would speak. Certain members of the Citizens Council, despite the fact that many of them were Republicans, already had been involved in a preliminary strategy session. Governor John Connally had met in Dallas with them to discuss the visit before he flew to Washington, D.C., for a briefing with the White House staff. The Dallas session, held in the Adolphus Hotel, included J. Erik Jonsson, president of the Citizens Council and a staunch Republican; Robert Cullum, president of the Chamber of Commerce and an influential Citizens Council member; the venerable R.L. Thornton; Joe Dealey, son of Ted Dealey; and Albert Jackson of the *Times Herald*. Connally told the Dallas group that his purpose in consulting with them was to remove the presidential visit from politics. He wanted a nonpolitical body—such as these men represented—to sponsor the visit. The impact of this decision was to place authority for the presidential visit to Dallas in the hands of men who were predominantly Republicans and conservatives. Loyalist Democrats protested loudly, to no avail, about their exclusion from a luncheon for a president whom they had helped elect. Stanley Marcus, a Citizens Council member and a prominent Kennedy supporter, complained that Dallas' business leadership "froze" even him out of the preparation plans.

The Citizens Council, determined as always to be successful, initiated a broad campaign to promote a successful presidential visit, free from ugly incidents, knowing full well that the nation's attention would be sharply focused on Dallas for evidence of its hostility to Kennedy. To "broaden" its base, as it had done in preparing for integration of the schools, two new organizations were added as sponsors. Both, however, were intimately tied to the Citizens Council. One was the Dallas Assembly, a "junior" Citizens Council for younger business executives destined one day to assume regular membership, and the other was the Science Research Center, a collection of scientists who had been organized by Jonsson and other top executives at Texas Instruments. (Later, the Science Research Center would form the nucleus of the University of Texas at Dallas.) Through its powerful membership, the Citizens Council caused the city to be saturated with a series of newspaper articles and television reports emphasizing the need for a cordial reception. The message, also carried forth from the city's pulpits and civic clubs, reached a peak during the six days preceding Kennedy's visit.

Three days before the president's arrival Alabama Governor George Wallace came to town to speak to the conservative Public Affairs Luncheon Club at the Baker Hotel. In the audience were H.L. Hunt and Edwin A. Walker. During Wallace's speech a television newsman, George Phenix of KRLD-TV, inched closer and closer as he photographed the general at his table in the middle of the dining area. Walker, irritated, suddenly stood up and shoved the newsman into the laps of diners at the next table, sending chairs, dishes, glasses, and silverware flying. The audience broke into spontaneous applause.

A day later the *Times Herald* carried a front-page headline, "Police Chief Puts Dallas on Notice." Chief Jesse Curry asked citizens to report to police any suspicious activities during the presidential visit or to take preventive actions themselves "if it becomes obvious someone is planning to commit an act harmful or degrading to the President." On November 18 the City Council adopted an ordinance which prohibited individuals from interfering with lawful assemblies. Even former vice president Richard M. Nixon, visiting the city briefly, joined police in "urging Dallas to give

President and Mrs. Kennedy a courteous reception."

THE PRESIDENTIAL VISIT

On the morning prior to the president's November 22 arrival crude handbills accusing him of treason were spread about the downtown area. A close associate of Walker's had printed 5,000 of the leaflets for distribution about town prior to Kennedy's arrival. The handbills had "mug shots" of Kennedy under the headline, "WANTED FOR TREASON." Beneath were a series of irrational, treasonous charges. Typical was a claim that the president had turned over the nation's sovereignty to the United Nations. A more personal charge alleged that Kennedy had lied to the American people about a previous marriage and divorce he had experienced before marrying Jacqueline Kennedy.

Other direct accusations of treason appeared on the morning of the president's arrival in a shocking full-page advertisement in the *News*. The advertisement, surrounded by funereal black borders, addressed twelve rhetorical, accusatory questions to the president. Typical were these two: "Why has Gus Hall, head of the Communist Party praised almost every one of your policies and announced that the party will endorse and support your re-election in 1964?" "Why have you ordered or permitted your brother Bobby, the Attorney General, to go soft on Communists, fellow-travelers, and ultra-leftists in America, while permitting him to persecute loyal Americans who criticize you, your administration, and your leadership?" When Kennedy saw the advertisement in Fort Worth that morning, he shook his head and told his wife, "We're really in 'nut country' now."

The advertisement had been devised and placed in the newspaper by three men, dedicated ultra-conservatives, who arbitrarily called themselves "The American Fact-Finding Committee." To help pay for the advertisement they had approached oilman Joseph P. Grinnan, local coordinator for the Birch Society. Grinnan raised money for placing it in the *News* and helped polish the final draft in his office. Two of those who contributed money and helped solicit other donations were H.L. Hunt's son, Nelson Bunker Hunt, and H.R. "Bum" Bright, chairman of the board of a trucking company who later would become owner of the Dallas Cowboys and a director of RepublicBank. The advertisement was approved for publication by *News'* publisher Ted Dealey. (Afterwards, he defended his decision to his irritated son Joe, now the newspaper's president, who told his father that the action was akin to inviting a guest into your home and then hitting him in the face with a cream meringue pie. The younger Dealey had been out of town when his father made the decision. Dealey told his son that the advertisement merely represented what the *News* had been saying editorially.)

After a short hop that morning from Fort Worth on Air Force One, President John F. Kennedy and his wife arrived at Love Field at 11:40 a.m. on a crisp, sunshiny day. Travelling with them were the eyes and ears of the world—sixty-eight journalists. (*Dallas Times Herald* executive editor Felix McKnight had stepped out of his role as a newsman to handle press arrangements for the visit.) A welcoming crowd of several thousand spectators roared their approval at the sight of the presidential couple. Mayor Cabell's wife Dearie handed the first lady a huge bouquet of red roses as she stepped from Air Force One. The president and his wife walked up to a chain-link fence to greet exuberant spectators behind it. Ten minutes later the presidential motorcade departed along a route planned for maximum exposure on the way to the luncheon at the Trade Mart. Some 250,000 spectators were estimated to have gathered along the route, cheering and holding up signs of greeting. Their enthusiasm and displays of affection for the president, all agreed, were exceptional.

The open-topped presidential limousine, surrounded by police motorcycles and followed by cars and buses bearing the other political dignitaries, journalists, and communications equipment, passed slowly down Main Street through the center of town amidst the biggest crowds of all. Just beyond the shadows of the downtown buildings at Dealey Plaza, at the very site where John Neely Bryan had founded the town, the motorcade turned from Main to Houston Street for one short block and then turned sharply again in front of the Texas School Book Depository Building so that it could head directly to Stemmons Freeway and the Trade Mart.

Now occurred the most horrendous event in the city's history. Shots rang out. Few were certain as to how many. Some mistook them for firecrackers. A handful of people close to the presidential limousine could see the dreadful impact of a rifle shot hitting the president's head. Abraham Zapruder, a dress manufacturer whose business was across the street from the School Book Depository, saw the president's head explode "like a firecracker" as he recorded the event with his 8 mm. camera. The driver of the presidential limousine, escorted by Police Chief Curry and others, sped away to Parkland Hospital, carrying the stricken president, wounded Texas Governor John B. Connally, and their horrified wives at speeds estimated to be between 70 and 80 m.p.h.

At the Trade Mart the silk-stocking crowd of businessmen waited impatiently for the president's arrival. Instead, they saw pulling up two bus-loads of bewildered reporters who had been separated from the fast-moving presidential limousine and its motorcycle escort. The journalists themselves were uncertain of what had happened, although some had heard shots. They began scurrying about, questioning one another and commandeering telephones. Luncheon guests, themselves uncertain and confused, listened fearfully to Erik Jonsson as he made a cautious announcement about reports of shots fired. "We believe it is not serious at this time," he said. The Rev. Luther Holcomb prayed. Jonsson, shaken, soon returned to the podium. The president had been seriously wounded by the gunfire. "Those damn fanatics," a man shouted, "why do we have to have them in Dallas?" The shock of the moment was more than many could bear. An immediate assumption was shared that those responsible for the act had been over-zealous right-wingers who had carried their protests to the ultimate extreme.

Minutes after the shots had been fired at Dealey Plaza, an order-filler in the Texas School Book Depository, twenty-four-year-old Lee Harvey Oswald, walked out of the building, got on a bus, abruptly abandoned it, and caught a taxi to take him across the Houston Street viaduct to his room on North Beckley Street in Oak Cliff. There, he picked up a jacket, grabbed a pistol which he hid on his person, and began walking toward Jefferson Boulevard. Confronted after a few blocks for some unknown reason by police officer J.D. Tippit, Oswald shot and killed him, then hurried down Jefferson Boulevard, slipped into the Texas Theater without paying, and sat quietly in the audience as the movie played. Officers, summoned there by spectators who had seen Oswald hurrying down the street and trying to hide at the sound of police sirens, entered the theater at 1:45 p.m. and arrested him. In the brief ensuing scuffle Oswald once more pulled his pistol and tried to shoot the nearest officer.

At Parkland Hospital, twelve minutes before Oswald's arrest, presidential aide Malcolm Kilduff announced to reporters that President John F. Kennedy was dead, victim of an assassin's gunfire. Federal Judge Sarah T. Hughes, a Kennedy appointee, was summoned to Air Force One on the Love Field runway, where she swore in her old friend Lyndon Johnson as president. Air Force One then departed for the nation's capital, bearing among others the new president, his wife, the body of the slain president, and the martyred president's widow.

By Friday afternoon the astonishing revelation had come that Oswald once had defected from the United States as an avowed Marxist to live in the Soviet Union. During the rest of the afternoon and evening and throughout Saturday, law enforcement officers at the Dallas police station interrogated him for a total of some twelve hours over several sessions. The suspect resisted with surprising force and dexterity, denying any involvement with the deaths of the president or Officer Tippit. Police, however, gathered evidence linking him to both murders. Reporters, their numbers now multiplied to as many as three hundred, packed the third floor of the police station on Friday evening and Saturday. Feeling an obligation to let the nation and world know that they had arrested the man they were convinced was the actual assassin, Chief Curry, District Attorney Henry Wade, Homicide Captain Will Fritz, and others held impromptu press conferences in the hallway to pass along developments in the case. Late Saturday, pressured by the weary newsmen for assurance that Oswald would not be transferred from the temporary city jail to the more permanent county jail without their knowledge, Curry promised not to do so before 10 a.m. the next day.

The chief kept his word. Not until 11:20 a.m. on Sunday did officers escort Oswald from his cell into the policement basement toward a waiting car for the trip to the county jail at the other end of downtown. A crowd of reporters, photographers, and police officers watched. As Oswald came through a basement doorway, handcuffed to a detective for security, a local nightclub owner named Jack Ruby stepped from the front of the crowd with his .38 caliber Colt revolver and fired once into the abdomen of the suspect. Oswald lapsed into unconsciousness. The unbelievable event was seen live on nation-wide television.

Once again, a shooting victim was rushed to Parkland Hospital, and once again, the wound proved to be fatal. Oswald was pronounced dead at 1:07 p.m. He died without regaining consciousness, carrying secrets of the assassination with him.

The city, the nation, and the world again were plunged into despair. The murder of the suspected assassin while in police custody in the police station was an event almost as shocking as the president's death. No three days in Dallas' history, probably no three days in the nation's history, had been so startling, so surprising, so devastating, so jolting to the public psyche. Certainly no other event had possessed such immediacy or had been assimilated so quickly.

A Nation Angry With Dallas

Oswald's death compounded the fury that many citizens already were feeling against Dallas. In the eyes of many, the city was not only a haven for right-wing zealots, its police department was hopelessly incompent. An avalanche of hate mail began pouring into the mayor's office. Harsh long-distance telephone calls began to flood the police station. The city was under siege; its leaders quickly assumed a defensive posture in their reactions. There are maniacs all over the world and in every city of the world, Cabell stressed. "This could have happened in Podunk as well as in Dallas." It was a theme that would be emphasized repeatedly.

Although no one dared utter such a thought, a great feeling of relief arose that Lee Harvey Oswald had been a Marxist instead of a right-winger. A Marxist could not have been inspired by the ultraconservativism that the city had tolerated but already was beginning to feel guilty about. More solace was found in an exaggerated rationalization that Oswald had been an "outsider" with no ties to Dallas. Conveniently forgotten was the fact that he had lived in Dallas and Fort Worth periodically since childhood, that he had attended—however briefly—a Dallas elementary school and a Dallas high school, that when he returned to the United States in June 1962 with his Soviet wife and infant child he flew immediately to Love Field to settle in the area, and that he had been living and working in Dallas for more than a year when the assassination occurred.

The city could not easily accept the world-wide opprobium that came. Although little could be done when an Eastern author or a European newspaper blamed the city for the assassination, local critics who spoke too harshly faced retribution. The Rev. William A. Holmes' self-critical sermon at Northaven United Methodist Church was one such message. In that sermon, parts of which were televised nationally, he refuted what city leaders already were saying—that Dallas need take no responsibility for the death of the president. Minutes after his sermon the Rev. Holmes was besieged with death threats. Police sent guards to his house, and he and his family followed police advice to stay away from their home for a week.

A fourth-grade teacher also paid a price for her negative assessment of the city's political climate. In a letter published in *Time* the teacher, Eleanor Cowan, wrote that for several years she had seen the seed of hate being planted by the newspapers and many of the leaders of Dallas. "Don't let anyone fool you. Dallas is as responsible as anyone." Dallas School Superintendent W.T. White immediately suspended her. She was reinstated days later only after the national press reported her suspension and the Dallas chapter of the American Civil Liberties Union exerted pressure in her behalf.

A senior vice president for American Petrofina of Texas, John Martin Shea, made similar observations in a first-person article for *Look* magazine. For his observations, Shea found himself under attack by Chamber of Commerce President Robert B. Cullum as one of the "gratuitous defectors and journalistic buzzards that are still circling our town." Others joined in persecuting the executive for his critical essay. One day, his wife and three children found a load of cement in their backyard swimming pool. After pressure from many, evidently including the management of his own company, Shea resigned his position.

More acceptable were the views of Stanley Marcus, who in a half-page newspaper advertisement coupled his criticisms with a positive outlook. In his advertisement, entitled "What's Right in Dallas?" he acknowledged that the city indeed had suffered from the spirit of "absolutism" in recent years. Now, he emphasized, there must be a new mood in which fair play would be accorded for all legitimate differences of opinion. (When Marcus had announced his support in 1960 for Kennedy, he was shocked by a deluge of letters from customers who closed their Neiman-Marcus accounts in protest.)

In fact, the impact of the assassination on Dallas was as Marcus suggested. The new mood which was to dominate the city for the coming years was one of moderation, rejection of extremism, and encouragement of introspection. "We are a tormented town," said Joe Dealey. "All I could do was pray," said Robert L. Thornton, now eighty-four. The *Times Herald* described the city as "undergoing the dark night of the soul," its citizens gripped by "an inexpressible feeling that all of us have contributed something to the atmosphere which has caused or allowed these acts to take place here." More pointedly, the Rev. Holmes had asked from his pulpit on the Sunday after the assassination, "In the name of God, what kind of city have we become?" The extremist groups that once had been so vocal in their convictions against Kennedy, now in disrepute, quickly stopped making headlines in Dallas.

DALLAS REACTS

It was a foregone conclusion in this new era that Bruce Alger, who epitomized and gave cheer to the far-right even though he himself did not belong to the Birch Society, must be replaced with a more moderate candidate.

The individual with the best chance to beat him was the mayor himself, a man whose equanimity and composure in the midst of tragedy had enhanced his already-positive standing. Cabell declared himself ready for the challenge. According to the city charter, he would have to resign as mayor to campaign for office. The charter also required that a majority of the council appoint his replacement. With the city's continued prosperity and reputation now in apparent jeopardy because of the assassination, a strong, visionary replacement seemed essential. The selection of the new mayor clearly lay in the hands of the majority of six CCA council members. Those six, joined by Citizens Council president John Stemmons, privately visited the recent Citizens Council president, Erik Jonsson, and drafted him for the office.

On Monday, February 3, 1964, at the conclusion of the City Council meeting, Cabell resigned as mayor. Council members immediately voted for Jonsson to succeed him, and within minutes the wealthy, self-made industrialist who had played a key role in transforming Texas Instruments into a world-wide firm, took the oath to be the city's new mayor. Independent council members Elizabeth Blessing and Joe Moody objected because they had been excluded from the private deliberations to draft Jonsson. "This may be a benevolent oligarchy—but it isn't representative government," complained Mrs. Blessing. Jonsson's appointment, rather than a spontaneous gesture, she said, had been "a power structure decision."

The suddenness of Jonsson's accession and the behind-the-scenes, secretive maneuver which preceded it indeed were surprising. It was an example of the power structure working at its most efficient—and also most exclusive—level.

Cabell, undeniably a conservative himself when he first defied the CCA, had become more and more moderate as his experience in office led him to recognize the need for such things as public housing, a stance which brought him much criticism. Now he campaigned for Congress with the editorial backing of both the *News,* which had deserted Alger, and the *Times Herald,* which after having opposed Cabell earlier now beat the drums loudest in his support. Cabell's steering committee suggested the depth of his support in the business community. It included John Stemmons, Robert B. Cullum, Robert Strauss, R.L. Thornton Jr., Raymond Nasher, and the former CCA president, Laurence Melton. The *Times Herald* published a lengthy, highly critical series on Alger concerning which *Times Herald* editor Felix McKnight had conferred closely with Cabell's political consultant, Sid Pietzsch.

It was a campaign against extremism and against Alger's alleged failure to adequately represent the city's needs in Congress. No piece of Alger's legislation, it was pointed out, ever had been passed by Congress. Perhaps worst of all, Alger had not supported projects seen as vital to Dallas' interests such as federal funds for the long-sought Trinity River canalization plans and the defense of Love Field in the continuing struggle with Fort Worth over a regional airport. The fact that Congress refused to appropriate money for a new federal building in Dallas was widely cited as retribution against the city because of Alger's refusal to support other federal appropriations projects for other Congressmen.

Actually, Alger had not been derelict as a Congressman in representing his district. He simply had the pronounced conviction of a conservative who sought to keep the federal government's involvement in the lives of private citizens at an absolute minimum.

He managed successfully to follow this conviction even when it impacted his own district. Dallas voters had supported him consistently in that practice even if the city's key leaders often fretted. One leader who had not frowned, however, had been Erik Jonsson, who had supported Alger in the past and had intended to do so publicly in 1964 until becoming a non-partisan mayor and deciding that an endorsement would be improper.

Cabell's victory over Alger in November was surprisingly easy; his margin was some 44,000 votes out of nearly 200,000 votes cast. Cabell billed his election as "a return to sanity on the part of the people of Dallas County." Alger commented: "I see us moving into a socialist dictatorship."

Dallas indeed was entering yet another era. Not only was the long-time Republican leader Alger defeated by a Democrat, but Democrats also defeated the city's eight Republican incumbents in the Texas Legislature. Now all nine delegates to the Legislature were Democrats. In the presidential race, Johnson easily defeated Barry Goldwater in the county, reversing Nixon's 1960 county win.

Cabell, fifty-six years of age, would go on to serve a total of four terms as Congressman. Not until 1972 after the 5th Congressional District lines were redrawn would he be defeated. His successor, Alan Steelman, a one-term Republican Congressman, successfully introduced legislation to have the city's new federal building named after Cabell, honoring him for the diligent work he had done to bring the center to Dallas.

15

The Erik Jonsson Years

We were determined to build the best airport that anybody had built up to that point.

–Erik Jonsson, recalling 1965.

A Boom Period

The year 1963 marked the beginning of a time that distinctly altered America's people, politics, and culture. The shots fired at the Triple Underpass ended in a large sense the long and domestically stable post-World War II era. They introduced a period marked by political violence, disillusionment, rebellious youth, new cultural standards, experimentation with drugs, and accelerating demands for civil rights. Sobered by its historical role as the first lightning rod in signalling these changes—accidental though it may have been—Dallas managed to avoid the negative headlines given other cities as these dramatic manifestations took place. Even so, while the city experienced a prolonged period of prosperity and growth with many genuine accomplishments, underneath lay rumblings of discontent.

Despite widespread publicity characterizing Dallas in demeaning terms, the city's worst fears about the harmful impact of the assassination failed to materialize. It prospered more than ever, missing nary a step. Statistics showed that in the first nine months of 1964 Dallas experienced a 14 percent increase in business activity compared to the same period in 1963. This was more than Houston or San Antonio. In the decade following the assassination 143 major office buildings were constructed as the downtown skyline constantly spiked higher into the sky.

These boom times would continue through the 1970s and into the 1980s. Dallas became the nation's eighth largest city, up from fourteenth a decade earlier. Now it was bigger even than St. Louis or Boston, cities which always had overshadowed Dallas. Growth was concentrating especially on the north side, creating an imbalance that brought problems of its own.

The changes also included a dramatic shift in the shopping habits of residents, signalling enormous consequences for the health of the downtown area. Enclosed, air-conditioned retail malls such as NorthPark now provided attractive alternatives to downtown shopping. Soon after its 1965 opening NorthPark began hosting more shoppers than the entire downtown area. Yet another development in the 1960s that de-emphasized the importance of downtown was the emergence of "garden office buildings" which placed employment opportunities outside the central business area in landscaped, garden-like settings.

The move away from town soon extended beyond city limits into the suburbs of Richardson, Carrollton, Farmers Branch, Garland, Irving, and even Plano in Collin County. As more and more residents departed Dallas for these suburban cities, they left behind growing percentages of racial minorities, deteriorating housing, a declining school system and an eroding tax base. Of great moment was a rate of growth in the city that saw the proportion of minorities dramatically rising and that of whites falling.

However, these complications were only emerging. So well did things seem to be going that in 1970 towards the end of Jonsson's term as mayor *Look* magazine declared Dallas an "All-America City," an honor not taken lightly. In 1974, with new Mayor Wes Wise at city hall, *Newsweek* labeled it "the city that works." While the instant identification of Dallas's name with the assassination lingered, it began fading quickly as similar isolated tragedies occurred in places like Memphis and Los Angeles.

JONSSON AND THE AIRPORT

Erik Jonsson presided as mayor from 1964 to 1971. The fifteen months he originally intended to serve stretched to three additional terms as he began to see progress. His major accomplishments in office helped ameliorate the trauma of 1963. This included the lead role in creating the enormous, forward-looking Greater Dallas-Fort Worth International Airport, in planning a spectacular new city hall designed by I.M. Pei, and in establishing a Goals for Dallas program which itself spawned many positive changes. So busy did Jonsson and his fellow council members become that for the first time full-time clerical workers were assigned to assist them, an unthinkable thought in earlier, purist days of the council-manager form of government. In the years to follow the staff would grow even bigger, with councilmen being assigned their own personal aides and private offices at city hall. Jonsson's terms in office would represent the brilliant final act of a long era in Dallas history, for despite his many acknowledged accomplishments he was destined to be its last CCA mayor.

Born in Brooklyn as the only child of Swedish immigrants, Jonsson as a small boy moved with his parents to Montclair, New Jersey, where his mother and father operated a tobacco shop and newsstand at the train depot. An energetic boy, young Erik saved enough money doing odd jobs to buy his own motorcycle at the age of fourteen. Keeping it in repair gave him good mechanical abilities. Rejected as an applicant at Columbia University, Jonsson instead attended and graduated from Rensselaer Polytechnic Institute in Troy, New York. His first job was with the Aluminum Corporation of America, but at nights he began repairing radios and learning hands-on about electronics.

In 1930, during its first year of existence, a company which used seismic waves to map structures below the earth's surface for the oil industry hired Jonsson to supervise its laboratory above an automobile showroom in Newark. While its shop and laboratory were in Newark, Geophysical Services established its main office in Dallas. In 1934, with the oil industry booming in East Texas and Dallas emerging as a major center for operations, Jonsson and the lab moved to Dallas. Seven years later in a reorganization on December 6, 1941, the company split into two parts. Jonsson, Eugene McDermott, Cecil Green, and H.B. Peacock assumed control of what remained of Geophysical Services. In the post-war era the company entered a new phase by supplying airborne radar and sonar systems for the U.S. Navy. In 1951 it changed its name to Texas Instruments, Jonsson was named president, and electronics became the biggest part of the company. In 1952 Texas Instruments began manufacturing transistors, and in 1958 one of its engineers developed the integrated circuit which revolutionized the electronics and computer industry. TI had established itself on the ground floor of a new era of technology impacting the entire globe. The company entered a period of dramatic, world-wide growth. By 1964, when Erik Jonsson became Dallas' mayor, TI had become a giant corporation with annual revenues of $850 million and much greater days ahead.

Jonsson entered the mayor's office as a visionary industrialist, comfortable with global concepts, long-term planning, and goal-setting, and accustomed to dealing with huge projects involving immense sums of money. He also had developed a sincere affection for his adopted city, for when he had moved there in the midst of the Depression he saw a remarkable contrast between the disheartened populace of the East and the more optimistic outlooks of Dallasites, who, Jonsson said, "hadn't begun to give up." Jonsson found that they instead had "just dug in and worked a few hours longer each day." They were, he thought, "completely devoid of gloom or fear of consequences."

For Jonsson, presiding over a city government with an annual budget of $162 million was small potatoes. However, all his skills and attributes were required to handle a problem that confronted him two months after he replaced Cabell. This was the sudden escalation of the long-simmering feud with Fort Worth over a regional airport located somewhere between the two cities.

Civil Aeronautics Board Examiner Ross Newman, in rejecting the latest Fort Worth bid for its mid-cities facility to be designated as the regional airport, observed on the other hand that Dallas' plans for an improved runway at Love Field presented "an extremely serious problem" for all the usual reasons—population density and safety. He suggested earnestly that the two cities once more attempt to cooperate in creating an area airport authority.

A few months later in August FAA Administrator Najeeb Halaby made a far tougher statement. Testifying before a Senate subcommittee, he accused Dallas of "unadulterated childish civic pride" in persisting with further development of Love Field. The FAA, he said, would not give it "another nickel" of federal money. Two days later an FAA assistant administrator announced that Halaby's remarks meant that the FAA would not install navigational safety devices on Love Field's planned new runway.

Fort Worth, taking quick advantage of this opening, announced a rebuilding of its suffering airport, now renamed Greater Southwest International, so that it would be adequate for both cities. The CAB further complicated the situation by ordering an investigation to determine whether airlines should be required to serve both cities through a single airport. Following a familiar pattern, the Dallas City Council responded with a unanimous resolution declaring its intent to hold on to Love Field as its airport, to proceed with its master plan for its further development, and to fight this battle, as before, to victory. The city council and the Chamber of Commerce asked the CAB to reconsider and to vacate its order for an investigation.

Instead, the CAB sent a telegram announcing that the two cities had six months to determine a site for a joint airport. If they could not come together, the CAB itself would designate a site.

To those not blinded by civic pride, it long since had become evident that Love Field would face a severe handicap in the future. As early as 1933 Leslie A. Stemmons had lobbied G.B. Dealey to support a new "downtown airport" in the reclaimed Trinity River flood plain because Love Field was "already overcrowded." Because of its "insufficient size" Dallas, he believed, soon would find itself "without adequate facilities to become an aviation center." However, Love Field's status as one of the busiest airports in the nation, its convenient, near-downtown location for Dallas passengers, its undeniable success, and its source as an object of pride understandably clouded the vision of many.

The limited amount of space for runways in a densely populated area was a fact which could be avoided only at the peril of the city's future as an aviation center. Love Field was not a prize to be yielded easily, though, especially not to a smaller city which forever seemed too grasping and covetous.

Jonsson thought hard about the CAB telegram and Love Field's limitations, and he decided finally that the city must proceed with

Fort Worth as a partner to build a new regional airport. He secretly initiated discussions with Fort Worth's mayor and a few chamber of commerce officials from both cities to get their reactions. Amazingly, harmony prevailed. The talks progressed, and in 1965 both city councils agreed to create a regional airport authority to build and operate a facility at a site straddling the Dallas and Tarrant county lines.

Jonsson was the obvious choice as chairman of the authority, a position he would hold beyond the airport's opening eight years later. The many complicated aspects to such a lengthy, major undertaking required delicate negotiations between the two cities. As Dallas' mayor and as chairman of the airport board, Jonsson was afforded virtually unquestioned approval from the Dallas City Council for the many phases of the project.

"We were determined," he later wrote, "to build the best airport that anybody had built up to that point; to think it through as far ahead as we could see or what airplanes we could envision were coming into use and what might be coming down the line; to have enough land to expand and add runways, widen and lengthen them, for safe accommodation of larger and heavier planes without difficulty."

Work on it continued through Jonsson's years as mayor, but its opening would not come until 1974 during Wes Wise's administration. Built at a cost of $750 million, it covered 17,500 acres, about twenty-seven square miles. Instead of having a huge single terminal with fingers extending for multiple gates, it was built as a series of half circle terminals spread out to give passengers easy access by automobile. It was larger than Manhattan Island, six times the size of Los Angeles International Airport, and three times as big as Kennedy Airport.

SETTING GOALS FOR DALLAS

Jonsson's penchant for goal-setting was best exemplified through his introduction of a bold program entitled Goals for Dallas, patterned after the Goals for America program under President Eisenhower. Goals for Dallas, which Jonsson announced in November 1964, involved brain-storming by thousands of Dallasites from all sectors to establish common goals in such areas as local government, design of the city, transportation, health and welfare, education, cultural activities, recreation, and public safety. Jonsson avowed that he was "totally unimpressed with the phenomenon of great size"; what interested him was becoming "the best city in the United States." He asked participants to paint "an idyllic picture of what we would like our city to be if money, manpower, and other resources were of little consequences." A permanent, full-time office coordinated the effort, which involved not merely setting goals but implementing them and charting their progress. Some influential insiders privately expressed skepticism about the idealism of Goals for Dallas. It was seen as "window-dressing." But the force of Jonsson's personality carried the program forward, and grandiose ideas were converted to realities.

The process was slow and deliberate. As consensuses formed, a series of books were published to describe them, determine their overall priority, and establish deadlines for their achievement. The most significant step toward achieving the program's capital goals was a $175 million "Crossroads" bond issue passed in 1967, including $42.4 million for a new city hall with adjoining park-plaza and underground parking garage. In 1969 a $41.2 million bond issue satisfied another simple but important goal: air-conditioning the city's public schools. Implementation of a kindergarten system in the elementary schools achieved yet another goal.

Five years after the program began more than 100,000 citizens had participated in Goals for Dallas, and still it continued. The program involved regular revisions of the goals in recognition that priorities constantly changed in a growing city. Through the sixties, into the seventies and eighties and into 1992 the Goals program operated before finally closing its doors. Goals for Dallas was the primary basis on which *Look* magazine declared Dallas an "All-America City" in 1970, the only city in its size category to be so honored.

The new city hall, park-plaza, and underground parking garage was another Jonsson pet project. A committee of prominent citizens selected one of the world's most renowned architects, I.M. Pei, who had designed the Kennedy Library in Boston and the Earth Sciences Building at MIT, the latter paid for by Jonsson's colleague at Texas Instruments, Cecil Green. Jonsson, who had attended the dedication of the MIT building, was impressed by both the building and its personable architect. He and Pei developed a close working relationship over the next years. In planning the new city hall Pei talked to many citizens and atttended city council meetings. He also participated in a three-and-a-half-day "Goals for Dallas" retreat in Central Texas. There he concluded that all the Dallas people he met—rich and poor—were very proud of their city. "They felt that Dallas was the greatest city there was, and I could not disappoint them. They were entitled to have something that represented their pride," Pei said.

To satisfy this goal Pei drew up plans for a unique, massive, bold, concrete structure with a slanting front that grew bigger towards the top until it appeared so top-heavy that it might tumble to the ground. It contrasted sharply with the city's towering skyscrapers which it faced, for Pei had concluded that the city's public sector needed a symbolic, massive strengthening to balance the city's high-rise commercial concentration. For a buffer between the building and the rather dismal surroundings immediately before it, Jonsson conceived of a series of public buildings surrounding Pei's park-plaza to be built later, the main one being a new library.

Pei's novel design for the city hall instantly created two separate camps—enthusiastic supporters and detractors who thought it too unconventional. The $42.4 million allotted for it in 1967 seemed sufficient, but an early indication of greater expense came when Pei sent a $3.1 million bill to the city for architectural designs alone. When the first bids were received in the spring of 1970, detractors instantly gained the upper hand, for the low bid was $50.2 million, far more than available.

Thus began a protracted struggle in revising the plans and obtaining lower bids. Some said that if the new city hall ever were to be built, a redesign would be required to eliminate its slanted front in favor of a conventional design. In September 1970 Jonsson diplomatically withdrew his support for the project "for a time," even though new bids for a pared-down building had come in at a figure just over the available funds. City council members, obviously relieved because the project had become controversial, readily agreed to postpone the expensive project.

However, this abrupt curtailment seemed not in keeping with the city's tradition. Did Dallas no longer dare great dreams? Many asked this question, and Jonsson's decision to retreat spurred renewed support to go ahead with the building. Within a month the council seemed ready to call for a supplemental bond election to get additional funds.

Desperate to get the project approved before his last term as mayor ended, Jonsson went to the Citizens Council executive committee to win its backing for the supplemental bonds. Those opposed to Pei's building included powerful members of this body. In a stormy session, committee members deadlocked in a 7-7 vote on whether or not to back the bond program. Jonsson, mortified, was in tears. If the Citizens Council could not support the new city hall, then he would not attempt it alone. He decided once more to pull back on the project.

But the groundwork for this spectacular new city hall had been laid. Getting started on it became a matter of obtaining satisfactory bids. This would await until after Jonsson left office.

DALLAS COWBOYS MOVE TO IRVING

One especially helpful factor in creating a new post-assassination image for Dallas was the emergence in the 1960s of the highly publicized Dallas Cowboys professional football team. Before the Cowboys became a national success, however, the city experienced painful struggles as three separate teams tried to win a following. In 1952 the New York Yankees National Football League team franchise was awarded to a group of Dallas investors. The team, nicknamed the Dallas Texans, played most of its home games that year in the Cotton Bowl. Crowds were sparse, though, and the team's performance dismal. Before the season ended the team's ownership was forced to give the franchise back to the NFL, and the Texans played their last games that season on the road. The next season they were transferred to Baltimore, where they were given a new nickname—the Colts. Within a few years they were the champions of the National Football League. One interesting aspect of the team's experience in Dallas occurred when the Texans held a banquet at the segregated Adolphus Hotel. Two Negro players were served without incident and without even realizing that they had integrated the hotel's dining facility.

H.L. Hunt's son, Lamar, was responsible for bringing another professional football team to the city. Thwarted in his efforts to secure an existing National Football League franchise, he decided to start his own league and to field in it a Dallas team of his own. His American Football League was founded in 1959, with league play beginning in 1960. Meanwhile, the NFL awarded an "expansion" franchise to Clint Murchison Jr. in Dallas, and the two teams competed weekend after weekend for fan loyalty. Both teams shared the Cotton Bowl as their home stadium. It was obvious that the city could not support two professional teams. In the third season of competition, Hunt's team, nicknamed the Dallas Texans (as had been the first team), won the American Football League championship in a thrilling double overtime against Houston. Yet, attendance at home games that season averaged just over 22,000, which was slightly more than the Cowboys' average. Hunt, discouraged, announced in May 1963 that his Texans would move to Kansas City, where they took on the nickname of the Chiefs.

Murchison and the Cowboys stayed, and after struggling for the first years against superior opponents, soon began to enjoy unusual success. The team, under the presidency of Tex Schramm, the coaching of Tom Landry, and the quarterbacking of former SMU star Don Meredith and Roger Staubach, became a glamorous powerhouse team appearing regularly on network television and drawing the highest TV ratings of any NFL team. The Cowboys brought fame to the city, but success also created a situation which did not enhance one of its brightest attractions, Fair Park.

During its first years the Cowboys played their games in Fair Park's Cotton Bowl, as did the Southern Methodist University football team. Although the Cotton Bowl seated some 75,000 spectators, it was aging. Seating was uncomfortable, locker rooms were outmoded, parking was inadequate, press accommodations were inferior, and surrounding neighborhoods for over-flow parking were high-crime areas. Cowboys owner Clint Murchison Jr. began exploring the possibilities of building a new downtown stadium, perhaps adjacent to a new art museum and music hall. To do so required Jonsson's support.

Jonsson conferred with city hall architect I.M. Pei and with Vincent Ponte and Warren Travers, urban planners with futuristic ideas about in Dallas' downtown. "I got a unanimous answer from them," Jonsson later said. "If you put the stadium downtown, you'll hate it so much, you'll tear it down in ten years for what it does to your traffic and because it's dead space only used once a week." Instead, Jonsson wanted the Cowboys to refurbish the Cotton Bowl, an idea Murchison rejected as "pouring money into a hopeless situation." Murchison argued that a new stadium would revitalize the downtown area at precisely the times when it needed activity—Saturday nights and Sunday afternoons. Stadium parking lots could be used weekdays by downtown workers to help subsidize the costs.

In his Dallas Cowboy newsletter Murchison wrote: "I exposed the plan to civic leaders. Great, they said. Merchants liked it; hotel operators liked it; restaurateurs liked it; convention promoters liked it; the president of the Dallas Citizens Council liked it so much he even proposed expanding the concept; both newspapers loved it. Erik Jonsson hated it." Jonsson's verdict came, Murchison said, "as sure and swift as a Turk's scimitar." The mayor, he believed, had a more pressing priority: the new city hall.

Murchison gave up on the idea. He announced in early 1967 that he would build a new stadium outside of Dallas in Irving, a facility so good that it would be the envy of the National Football League. One last time, though, he met with Jonsson and State Fair President Robert B. Cullum. "If you take the Cowboys out of Fair Park, what are you suggesting we put there instead?" Murchison was asked pointedly. "How about an electronics plant?" he responded wryly.

Murchison built his new stadium in Irving as planned. In 1971 the Cowboys began playing in a modernistic new facility, Texas Stadium. Its unique semi-dome covered and protected spectators as they watched the athletes play under the sun—or in the rain. Southern Methodist University decided to play its home football games at Texas Stadium. The Cotton Bowl was virtually abandoned. Now its only big-time football games were the annual New Year's Day contest and the Texas-Oklahoma rivalry during the State Fair.

Meanwhile, the Cowboys went on to even greater heights on the gridiron, reaching the Super Bowl in 1972, winning it the next year, setting an enviable record for consecutive playoff appearances, and gaining widespread acknowledgment as one of the nation's premier sports franchises. The team gained a sobriquet, "America's Team," that was not as unrealistic as one might think.

Jonsson's dreams for downtown Dallas were less successful,

although the plans that Ponte and Travers presented as consultants in late 1969 sounded grand. They included a pedestrian network above and below street level. The idea of removing pedestrians from streets ultimately would worsen the problem of a downtown that suffered from a lack of people and was deemed by many as a hostile environment for them.

BREAKING COLOR BARRIERS

In 1966 black attorney Joseph Lockridge, thirty-three years of age, won election from Dallas County to the state legislature. His election and that of a black man from Houston the same year broke the color barrier that had existed in the state for legislative office since Reconstruction. A Democratic supporter of Governor John Connally, Lockridge won the endorsement of Dallas' business leadership, of labor, and of both daily newspapers in his campaign for the State House of Representatives. His outstanding service during his first term in Austin caused his fellow legislators to name him their "Rookie of the Year." Lockridge's promising career was cut short by a tragedy. In 1968 he died in an airplane crash. His successor was another black man, the Rev. Zan W. Holmes Jr., a graduate of SMU's Perkins School of Theology.

In all of Dallas' history, though, there still had never been a black city council member. Despite the progress that had been made toward integrating Negroes into mainstream society following the Civil Rights Act of 1964, the election of a city councilman seemed unlikely under Dallas' at-large system. City-wide voting effectively precluded almost any independent challenge, whether the candidate be black or white or Hispanic. Few independents could raise enough money to campaign on such a wide scale.

Recognizing the need for change, however, in 1967 the CCA decided to make a gesture toward black representation on the council. The opportunity arose before the April 1967 election after the feisty independent councilman from Pleasant Grove, Joe G. Moody, resigned. Moody's seat remained unoccupied for five weeks until the CCA-dominated council appointed black realtor C.A. Galloway to succeed him. Only two weeks remained for the term, so his tenure was brief and in years to come often forgotten. The choice of Galloway had an interesting historical footnote: he had been one of the property owners in South Dallas whose place of business was bombed in 1950 by segregationists. Galloway's brief period on the council was virtually meaningless, though, for a white man, Jesse Price, already held the CCA endorsement for the election two weeks hence.

Price's successful campaign for election and its aftermath opened a new chapter in the question of how city councilmen were elected. Price, a Pleasant Grove businessman, faced another Pleasant Grove man, Max Goldblatt, an independent who had been operating a hardware store in the area since just after World War II. Price won the election and the council seat because of his city-wide majority. Goldblatt, though, had won the majority of votes in Pleasant Grove, where both men lived and worked. Voters in other parts of the city—particularly North Dallas—had in effect deprived Pleasant Grove voters from selecting their own council representation. Goldblatt thought this an injustice. He filed a suit in federal court to change the system so that residents from individual districts could elect their own council members.

By the time three federal judges heard Goldblatt's case in 1968 Dallas voters already had approved a charter change which amounted to the first tentative step away from the old at-large system. The amended charter increased the council size from nine to eleven members, but most important, it established residency requirements for the first time. Now, eight of the eleven council members had to live in designated districts. Even so, they still would be elected by city-wide vote. Those elected to the other three seats, which included the mayor, could live anywhere they chose.

One of the eight new districts, Place 8, was predominantly in South Dallas. In this district resided George L. Allen, a native of New Orleans who had earned a business degree from Xavier University and moved to Dallas in the late 1930s to organize a life insurance company for Crawford Funeral Home. Allen had aligned himself with Dallas' NAACP leaders while an insurance district manager in Austin, and under their sponsorship he tested the rigid color barrier at the University of Texas by seeking to enroll. To his surprise, Allen was permitted to enroll with no questions for a seminar in business psychology and salesmanship. After ten days, though, the university realized what it had done and cancelled his enrollment. The NAACP then was able to follow through on its intended goal by filing a suit against the state, causing the legislature to pass a law giving scholarships to black graduate students so that, being denied admission to Texas institutions, they could attend out-of-state schools.

With that civil rights work completed, Allen busied himself with establishing a career in insurance. So well did he do over the next years that in 1955 he was named the first Negro director of the Dallas Community Chest Trust Fund. When he showed up for the first meeting in a downtown hotel the doorman refused to admit him through the front door. Allen refused to use the suggested back entrance, and finally Community Chest officials summoned the hotel manager who ordered that Allen be admitted through the front. In 1965 and 1966 Allen ran for city council as an independent, failing both times, but he subsequently gained appointment to the city plan commission and then to the board of adjustment. In both instances he was the city's first black man so chosen.

When the charter change enlarging the council from nine to eleven members took effect in late 1968, the CCA council appointed Allen to one of the two new posts. He thus became the city's first meaningful black city councilman. The appointment gave him a head-start for the upcoming April 1969 election, for which he gained CCA endorsement. Voters proceeded to elect him for what would be the first of four terms at city hall.

The person endorsed by the CCA in 1969 for the second new post, Henry Stuart, a North Dallas businessman, was challenged by an independent, a well-known former radio and television newsman, Wes Wise. The popular Wise, bolstered by his long familiarity to television viewers throughout the city, defeated the CCA candidate.

Noteworthy as well in that 1969 race was the election of the city's first Mexican-American to the council, Anita Martinez. The CCA endorsed Mrs. Martinez, as it did Allen, in seeking to broaden its appeal and to counter the growing criticism about its exclusivity.

THE GUARD CHANGES AT DISD

Racial barriers also fell in 1967 on the Dallas Independent School District board when a black surgeon, Dr. Emmett J. Conrad, was elected. Conrad, who also had broken racial barriers in medicine by becoming the city's first black hospital staff surgeon and the first black hospital chief of staff, would serve ten years before leaving the board. Significant though Conrad's election was, it represented just one part of a momentous change occurring at DISD. A group of liberal-minded persons, disenchanted with school policies which they felt were regressive and a handicap to the city, organized the League for Educational Advancement (LEAD) in 1965 to campaign for school board seats and establish more progressive educational policies. The organization had endorsed Dr. Conrad for office.

Founded primarily by Dr. Norman Kaplan and Milton Tobian, LEAD began endorsing a diverse slate of candidates to challenge the conservative, business-oriented nominees of the Citizens for Good Schools which, as the educational arm of the Citizens Council, had won since its formation in 1950 every seat on the board. Part of the LEAD program was its contention that the CGS was not receptive to Goals for Dallas programs, including the need for public kindergarten classes and air-conditioned schools. Even though the CGS was sponsored by the Citizens Council, its conservatism in such important matters alienated many city leaders, including Erik Jonsson (who privately was deemed by some to be a "closet liberal" when it came to public school matters). Thus, the first LEAD trustee elected was none other than the personnel director of Texas Instruments, Dr. Marvin Berkeley, who defeated Field Scovell in 1967. He was followed by Dr. Conrad, who had to wait for a run-off victory that year before taking office. In 1968 three more LEAD-endorsed candidates were elected, and for the first time it held a 5-4 majority on the board. Berkeley was elected president.

The meaning of their election was clear: change. The first significant change was the inevitable retirement of W.T. White, Dallas' school superintendent for twenty-three years, who had been adverse to innovation and an ardent foe of school integration. To replace him the LEAD-controlled board hired Dr. Nolan Estes, an associate commissioner in the U.S. Office of Education, and gave him a mandate for change. Under LEAD and Estes, the board initiated a number of expensive innovations and paid special attention to the growing number of minority students. Innovations included the introduction for the first time of public kindergarten classes, a free-lunch program for the poor, and additional minority teachers.

In the 1969 and 1970 annual school elections LEAD further

strengthened its grip on the school board despite CGS newspaper advertisements bearing such captions as "DANGER. BEWARE. LIBERAL-LABOR NEGRO EXTREMISTS TAKING OVER OUR SCHOOLS." By 1971 only one CGS board member, attorney John Plath Green, who had helped found the organization in Fred Florence's bank office in 1950, remained. (For eight years Green had managed the Committee for Good School campaigns; in 1961 he had been elected himself to the board.) Meanwhile, another black man, Joe Kirven, president of the Negro Chamber of Commerce, had been appointed to the board.

In the 1971 election, with four of the nine school board seats open, the opportunity arose for the CGS to regain its lost majority. Its chances were bolstered three days before the election when a *News* reporter somehow acquired a report revealing a sharp decline in the reading comprehension of Dallas students. Average scores, the report indicated, had fallen drastically in the three years under the innovative programs of LEAD and Estes. Arguments reverberated about the validity of the test results, but newspaper summaries reported that Dallas students had fallen from the top 30 percent of the nation to the bottom 35 percent. This was shocking news to a city that prided itself on the excellence of its school system. It also was a political bonus for the CGS candidates, for it seemed to verify their charges that LEAD's innovations had harmed rather than helped the students.

LEAD board members denounced the report as "misleading, politically inspired and questionable." Kirven, up for election, called publication of the report a "conspiracy involving the CGS, a newspaper reporter and somebody at the school administration." CGS candidates took an opposite approach, charging that the report previously had been concealed from the public "for political reasons." The possibility that demographic changes in school enrollment had lowered the average scores was not mentioned.

Whatever the case, the report heaped fuel onto a growing concern in Dallas about problems in the classrooms of "disruption, drugs and discipline." Committee for Good Schools candidates hit hard on these issues, which they said were caused by LEAD's permissive policies.

Another issue in the election was that of rising taxes. School taxes under LEAD had climbed to the highest level allowed under the law.

Per pupil costs rose from $422 in 1966-67 to $598 in 1969-70, a fact CGS candidates constantly emphasized. The times called, they argued, once more for a "business approach" to running the school district.

Election day brought a dramatic upset win for three of the four CGS candidates, dividing the board evenly between CGS and LEAD. A run-off would determine which group would control the board with a 5-4 margin. The run-off was between CGS candidate James Jennings and Kirven, whose vote in the black community had been split with challenger Kathlyn Gilliam. In the largest run-off vote in school board history, Jennings, a public relations man for Coca-Cola and a former police officer, won. The Committee for Good Schools regained its majority control of the board. John Plath Green was elected the new president.

CGS would maintain a majority on the board which it would not relinquish until it disbanded in 1977 following a change which paralleled what had happened at city hall. Beginning in 1974 trustees were elected from single-member districts instead of at-large over the entire city.

SCHOOL DESEGREGATION

Integration of Dallas schools still was not fully accomplished, but the token amount that had occurred already had precipitated the beginning of "white flight" to the suburbs. Meanwhile, the city's black population continued to grow dramatically. By 1970 almost 30 percent of the population was black. During the 1970-71 school year 42 percent of DISD students were minorities, and the rate of change was such that it was calculated that black students would be in a majority by 1975. The situation was entirely different in the county's suburban school districts, where 93 percent of the students were white.

Although the federal courts had ordered full desegregation of the city's junior high schools by 1965 and of high schools by 1967, it had not been achieved. There remained a large number of predominantly black schools. Twenty-one of these schools had black enrollments of between 98 and 99 percent; seven more were all-black in enrollment. Eight out of ten African-American students in DISD attended schools that had black enrollments greater than 90 percent.

Conversely, there were sixty-one schools in DISD with not a single black student. Because of the city's segregated housing patterns, the remedy for this situation, as mandated by federal courts in other cities, seemed clear: busing.

In October 1970 the Dallas Legal Services Project, an agency spawned by President Lyndon Johnson's War on Poverty, filed a suit (Tasby v. Estes) contending that Dallas still was operating a segregated school system. The plaintiffs, eight parents and twenty-one students, charged that DISD was perpetuating segregation through assignment of students and teachers in sites chosen for school construction and by discrepancies in the quality of predominantly white and black facilities. On August 2, 1971, Judge William Mack Taylor ordered DISD to begin busing some 15,000 junior and senior high school students, an order soon modified to include just 7,000 students. Busing thus began in the nation's eighth largest school system. White flight now accelerated. Private schools began springing up, and the move to the suburbs intensified. In the fall of 1971 the school population was 54 percent white, 36 percent black, and 9 percent Mexican-American. Two years later white students were a minority in the public schools.

Transporting students across town for classes with others of a different race, background, and economic status was not without its difficulties. In the 1972-73 school year a number of racial confrontations occurred, with some 200 students involved in a single incident on the first day of school at Bryan Adams High. A survey taken in September revealed that most Dallasites—whites and blacks alike—opposed busing. This represented a change among blacks, for a similar survey the previous year showed that a majority of them favored busing.

As part of his order Judge Taylor created a tri-ethnic committee composed of white, black, and Hispanic members to oversee the desegregation progress. The "tri-ethnic" title acknowledged the emergence of the Mexican-American students as a rapidly growing and distinct group with special needs in addition to whites and blacks.

The committee, chaired by the Rev. Zan Holmes, a black minister, began to play a major and often controversial role in DISD decisions. René Martinez, assistant director of the Human Relations Commission, and David Kendall, a white businessman, were the other members. The aggressive outlook on the part of at least a portion of the staff could be seen in its office in the Federal Building. A poster on the wall showed the black militant, H. Rap Brown, with a quote: "At a certain point, caution becomes cowardice. No slave should die a natural death." When a white committee member protested that the poster was offensive, a spirited debate arose. The result, finally, was to remove from the walls the posters of both Brown and President Richard Nixon.

ACTIVISTS ASSERT THEMSELVES

There were no Rap Browns in Dallas, but the sudden militancy of new groups such as the Blank Panthers, the Southern Christian Leadership Conference (SCLC), the Bois d'Arc Patriots, the Student Nonviolent Coordinating Committee (SNCC), Black Citizens for Justice, the Angela Davis Liberation Party, and federal VISTA volunteers assigned to Dallas surprised and disturbed many. With racial disturbances occurring in many cities throughout the nation, it was feared that Dallas might suffer from them as well. Police quietly made plans for such an eventuality. (In the summer of 1968 the *Times Herald* handed out contingency assignments to reporters outlining their responsibiities and duty stations if rioting broke out.) Older organizations which had worked within the system, the Negro Chamber of Commerce, the NAACP, and the Progressive Voters League, faded into the background as new activists took center stage and began making headlines through provocative confrontation.

One such example was SNCC's aggressive boycott in 1968 of the white-owned OK Supermarkets in South Dallas. The campaign included not just picketing, but such tactics as loading up shopping carts with groceries, then abandoning them in the aisles for reshelving. Police began making arrests, and the movement's leaders, Ernest McMillan and Matthew Johnson, gained high visibility. In order to end the boycott the harassed OK Supermarket officials agreed to sell all ten of their South Dallas stores to black businessmen.

The growing militancy of such groups set a pattern soon followed by the city's Mexican-Americans, who by 1970 constituted 8 percent of the population, or about 40,000 residents. Grievances they began to express included discrimination, a disproportionate amount of poverty, and an abnormally high drop-out rate in the schools. Mexican-American adults suffered not so much from unemployment as under-employment. While the Dallas Police Department had more than 1,600 officers, only twelve of them were Mexican-Americans; the fire department had not a single uniformed Mexican-American on a staff of more than 1,300. Anita Martinez had broken the barrier on the city council and continued to serve there, but some anxious Hispanics complained that she was reluctant to address issues specifically related to their community. René Martinez, a member of the tri-ethnic committee, emerged as an aggressive and articulate spokesman for Mexican-American rights and needs.

Little Mexico as a distinctive community by now was little more than a memory. The tiny, crowded alleys once existing there had been cleared out through an urban renewal program in the mid-1950s, after which code enforcement maintained new standards. Then, in the 1960s, the Dallas North Tollway cut through the heart of the neighborhood. In the mid-1970s Woodall Rodgers Freeway even further decimated the community.

The activist Hispanic organizations which emerged in the early 1970s, such as the Brown Berets, Los Barrios Unidos, and Mexican-Americans for Progressive Action, were based in West Dallas, where there existed a growing Mexican-American population.

The primary public forum for the new activism, especially among the black spokespersons, became the once-a-week meetings of the city council. Determined, sometimes irate minority leaders began grabbing the podium for extended harangues about needs and injustices in the black community, making demands and questioning at length affairs that once had been considered routine business. Sometimes Jonsson summoned police officers to remove speakers who refused to relinquish the microphone. It was a new phenomenon, one that had developed during Jonsson's tenure as mayor. He coped with the often volatile situation with considerable patience, sometimes suffering in the process unexpected dignities.

An SCLC speaker, angered by the council's refusal to create a human resources department to combat hunger, handed the mayor two loaves of bread and some fish and challenged him to "go out and feed the multitudes." To further dramatize the issue, the Rev. Peter Johnson, who recently had moved to Dallas to be regional director of the Southern Christian Leadership Conference, took a seat on the outside steps of the municipal building and began a one-man hunger strike. For two weeks he fasted there, sometimes surrounded by supporters but often a solitary, forlorn-looking figure. He ended his fast after the council agreed to support a community anti-hunger movement called Operation Assist.

The most persistent individual with regular city hall appearances and ultimately the most effective of all was Albert Lipscomb, a Dallas native and 1942 graduate of Lincoln High School who had a flair for the flamboyant. Lipscomb, or "Lip," styled his hair in the huge "Afro" popular at the time, wore a goatee, and decorated himself with beads and buttons touting activist causes. Despite his formidable appearance and aggressive demeanor in public, he was in private a gracious, approachable individual. Lipscomb often clashed with Jonsson at council meetings. Sometimes, when he persisted in talking despite the mayor's admonitions, he found himself escorted by police from the council chambers.

Lipscomb had served with the Army during World War II in California. He remained there afterwards and got in trouble for using and selling drugs, serving ten months on a work farm for drug dealing. In 1950 he returned to Dallas, married, and settled down as an excellent waiter at the city's finest restaurants. In 1966 he began to involve himself in community activities by working as a neighborhood organizer for the War on Poverty, and then for the Block Partnership program sponsored by the Greater Dallas Council of Churches.

The single issue most responsible for galvanizing new black activists such as Lipscomb, Peter Johnson, J.B. Jackson, and Elsie Faye Heggins was the proposed expansion in the late 1960s of Fair Park. The plan required the condemnation of modest homes owned by blacks in a fifty-acre area between Pennsylvania and Fitzhugh. Many of the residents had moved into the area in the 1950s as South Dallas made a transition from a predominantly white to a predominantly black area. With the prospect now of forced removal from their homes, the residents found their cause championed not only by black activists who grew increasingly vocal, but also by a core of white supporters from University Park Methodist Church, who had affiliated with the South Dallas neighborhood through Block Partnership. Protests concerned not just the expansion itself but especially the amounts of payments awarded homeowners through the condemnation process. The awards, they claimed, were so low that they would be unable to find comparable housing anywhere in the city. It was alleged that the expansion, planned primarily to increase parking accommodations, was racist with its intent to remove Negroes from Fair Park's immediate boundaries. An official 1966 report, "Redevelopment Program for the State Fair of Texas," stated that the acquisitions were necessary because the substandard and low-income housing around Fair Park did not project the image of prosperous, progressive, and pleasant Dallas. It also was argued that the city had encouraged the neighborhood's deterioration through spot zoning decisions which adversely affected its residential character.

The controversy nearly erupted into major headlines just before the 1970 nationally televised New Year's Day Cotton Bowl Parade. Residents and their leaders, having sought in vain a personal meeting with Jonsson to discuss their complaints, now sent him an ultimatum: either meet with them or they would sit down in the street and embarrass the city by blocking the parade on national television. On the night before the parade nearly 500 determined individuals gathered at a nearby church for last-minute preparations to make good their threat. Late that night, hours before the parade was to begin, Jonsson agreed to meet with their representatives. In the midnight session Jonsson agreed to investigate personally the homeowners' point of view. As a sign of his good faith he also agreed to share his mayor's car in the parade that morning with Fair Park homeowner J.B. Jackson. This he did.

The Fair Park homeowners' issue dragged on, though, capturing even the attention of the CBS television show, "Sixty Minutes," whose Mike Wallace interviewed J.B. Jackson. In November 1970 some of the residents filed a federal lawsuit against the city to halt condemnation proceedings. It failed, however, and ultimately expansion plans were enlarged to wipe out a large section of Second Avenue, a major thoroughfare lined with small businesses, so that State Highway 352 could be extended from Scyene Road to serve as the park's southern boundary. This caused the loss of still more dwellings. The activists who opposed the expansions had not achieved their particular goals, but they gained confidence in their ability to mount sustained battles for future battles at city hall.

'NEWSROOM' BREAKS TABOOS

While the Fair Park controversy gained regular newspaper headlines, for the most part the doings of people such as Al Lipscomb and the organizations they represented were ignored by the news media. The managing of news that sometimes occurred in Dallas was rarely overt. Generally, it was so subtle as to be undetectable to the average reader. Still, news deemed harmful to the best interests of the city was subject on occasion to manipulation or—at worst—suppression. Publishers of both daily newspapers were key members of the Citizens Council. Their newspapers owned the major television stations (KRLD-TV and WFAA-TV) and two of the most prominent radio stations. A word from the publisher relayed through top executives of the newsrooms sufficed to play up, play down, or—more rarely—to suppress a story. In 1961 newspapers refrained from covering the lunch-counter demonstrations across from SMU because it was believed that the stories might prompt further demonstrations. More subtle news management occurred through the placement or special emphasis of stories. This occurred after the Adlai Stevenson incident when newspapers and broadcasting stations joined the Citizens Council crusade to ensure a welcome reception for President Kennedy by providing a publicity blitz of appropriate news stories.

Another instance occurred when the Rev. Martin Luther King Jr. came to Dallas to speak at Southern Methodist University. Pressure from conservatives arose to cancel his speech for fear it would incite demonstrations in Dallas and possibly harm a fund-raising drive at the university. SMU's president, Willis M. Tate, refused to cancel his appearance. And while the newspapers did not avoid all mention of King and his speech, by apparent agreement stories concerning it were relegated to a few paragraphs on inside pages.

In February 1970 a television news program began which refused to play by the agreed-upon rules. This was *Newsroom*, a Monday-through-Friday program on public television station KERA-TV. The goal of the show, which soon expanded from thirty minutes each day to a full hour, was not so much to report the basics of news—newspapers and broadcasting stations already did that—but to tell the story *behind* the news or even the story that might otherwise be avoided. On *Newsroom*, for the first time, sensitive news stories were no longer subject to manipulation from above; grievances of the minority community found a forum; race relations and the criminal justice system were assigned to reporters on a regular basis; regular media criticism began for the first time in the city. *Newsroom*, a program of "local news, analysis, and opinion," departed from its local news format only when a guest with suitable credentials appeared for conversation on a topic of national or international interest.

The program was begun by a former reporter who had experienced first-hand examples of news management during his years at the *News* and then the *Times Herald*. In fact, he had abruptly resigned at the *News* when a series he prepared on the county's civil defense program was held back because of its sensitive nature. The reporter was James C. (Jim) Lehrer, who recently had left the *Times Herald* as city editor to concentrate on a writing career. As a side-line venture he had affiliated on a part-time basis with the public television station, KERA-TV. Then his role expanded to full-time as the station's news and public affairs director. At the behest of the station manager, Robert A. Wilson, Lehrer wrote a proposal to the Ford Foundation requesting funding for a new local news television program that would go beyond superficial reporting. Lehrer was determined to put on a news show free of artificial restraints.

Lehrer, Wilson, and the station's chairman of the board, Ralph Rogers, a prominent Dallas businessman and civic leader, were called to New York City for a grilling by Fred Friendly, the Ford Foundation's television news consultant and former president of CBS News. Taking aim at Rogers in his capacity as chairman of the board, Friendly impressed upon him thoroughly and pointedly the importance of journalistic enterprise in American society and management's obligation to permit newsmen to operate on a professional basis without undue, non-professional direction from non-journalists. Rogers agreed that Lehrer would be able to exercise a free hand in news decisions, and Ford Foundation gave KERA-TV a $500,000 grant to get the show under way.

Lehrer assembled a dozen or so talented journalists and several filmmakers and photographers. None of the reporters had on-air television experience. Most of the staff had newspaper backgrounds; a few had no journalistic experience. Blacks, Hispanics, women, and men with long hair were prominent in a format which positioned Lehrer inside a circle of desks occupied by reporters who were encouraged to participate in around-the-circle discussions.

Newsroom's non-traditional approach to news coverage attracted many followers, and also many detractors. It was perceived by many, with considerable justification, to be a liberal voice in the city. *Newsroom*'s presence meant that controversial stories or those deemed harmful to Dallas' "best" interests could no longer be ignored by the other media, for they could not be certain that *Newsroom* would not cover them. As Lehrer later recalled, "We broke a lot of reporting and personnel taboos that very much needed to be broken in that conservative city, and for this I am unashamedly proud. Our main value was in our influence on the two daily newspapers."

The program's immunity from traditional journalistic restraints became especially evident during its first year after the Dallas County Commissioners Court refused to permit *Newsroom* reporter Mike Ritchey to attend a meeting. This action was in apparent violation of the then little-known Texas Open Meetings Act. In behalf of *Newsroom*, Ritchey filed a criminal complaint against the commissioners for holding a closed meeting. Such a complaint had never been made in Dallas, and rarely in the state. For stepping out of what had then been considered the traditional role of a news organization, Lehrer and his reporters came under fierce attack as wild-eyed hippies and leftist radicals.

County Judge W.L. (Lew) Sterrett, who had presided over the Commissioners Court since his election in 1948 and was a defendant in the complaint, led the attack. A Dallas banker joined him by organizing a drive to force *Newsroom* off the air. Ralph Rogers had been out of the country when the complaint was filed against the commissioners, and he returned to a full-blown crisis. The financial integrity of the station, which as a non-profit institution largely relied upon community contributions for its existence, seemed jeopardized. He declared *Newsroom*'s official complaint an awful mistake. After several agonizing days in which the matter was debated back and forth internally, Lehrer decided to withdraw the complaint. The crisis ended. *Newsroom*'s dedication to playing "hard ball" remained, though, and its growing core of fans swelled in number.

Lehrer moved from Dallas to Washington, D.C., to continue his career in public television, ultimately becoming the co-anchor for the widely acclaimed McNeil/Lehrer NEWSHOUR as well as a writer and novelist. As the Ford Foundation's financial support for *Newsroom* decreased annually in accordance with the original plan, local support was not sufficient for its continuation. The program began to cut its staff and finally disappeared altogether after several years.

16

Last Days of the CCA

The establishment, as it once was, is dead and we can't put it together again.

–John Schoellkopf, 1973

WES WISE UPSETS THE 'ESTABLISHMENT'

As Erik Jonsson approached in the fall of 1970 the end of his third full term in office, CCA leaders began looking for a strong, conservative businessman to succeed him. An unusual problem arose: for years Republic National Bank's executives, board members, and principal customers had dominated the highest local decision-making bodies. One of them, James W. Aston, was becoming president of the Citizens Council in 1971. Fred Florence, Karl Hoblitzelle, and Jonsson all had been Republic officers or board members. Another key civic leader who worked closely with Jonsson, Robert B. Cullum, was a Republic board member. First National Bank executives and board members now believed the time had come to have a mayor who identified more closely with them. After all, First National was about as big as Republic and it had a long tradition of leadership.

Some of the antagonism evidently arose because Jonsson, a long-time Republic customer and board member, had been confiding in too many people his belief that Republic's officers and directors of late had been far more faithful in devoting themselves to civic causes than First National, which he suggested was dominated by "oil types." Such talk, when it got around to First National, irritated them and made them all the more determined for the next mayor to have an affiliation with their bank.

Yet, the first candidate mentioned prominently as Jonsson's successor was recent two-term City Councilman Charles Cullum, a Republic customer who with his brother Robert was on the bank's board. Cullum was receptive to overtures, but his candidacy was unacceptable to First National. As the Cullum boomlet thus quietly was allowed to fade away, a candidate acceptable to First National Bank was presented—Tom Unis, a former two-term councilman and a former president of the CCA. Unis, however, soon announced that the press of his law practice prohibited him from considering the position. Yet another candidate favored by First National, Warren Woodward, was rejected by Republic. Next emerged a compromise candidate from Oak Cliff, Avery Mays, president of his own construction firm. Mays, fifty-nine years of age, had a good record of traditional civic involvement, including a term as CCA president. Drawbacks included his lack of experience on the city council and his quiet, non-assertive demeanor, a trait that would not have been a handicap in earlier years when council meetings were conducted among friends. But he was acceptable to both First National and Republic.

With indecision in the CCA camp and with the emergence of the new anti-establishment mood in the city, the door to the mayor's office seemed far more open than ever before. Independent Councilman Wes Wise, who had defeated CCA nominee Henry Stuart in 1969, announced early that he intended to run for mayor. Jonsson sought to discourage him, citing his lack of a strong business background. Wise complained to the *Times Herald:* "Does this mean no lawyer, no accountant, no journalist can ever be mayor of the City of Dallas?" No, he would not defer to Jonsson.

What was certain for 1971 was the hottest mayor's race in years. For the first time in more than thirty years the election of a CCA mayor was not a foregone conclusion.

The CCA needed a candidate who could generate enthusiasm from both major banks, one with the traditional business background of CCA candidates, and one who could overcome Wise's popularity and strong name identification. To add to the dilemma, at the biennial meeting before the election CCA president Dow Hamm, a retired oil company executive, decided to yield his office after a single term in hopes that the organization would "select someone from the younger group" to succeed him.

That person turned out to be John Schoellkopf, thirty-two, descendant of a pioneer Dallas family, and former reporter and Washington correspondent for the *Times Herald*. Schoellkopf had resigned as an executive at the newspaper after it had been purchased in 1970 by the Times-Mirror Corporation. He saw that for the CCA to fit into the new voter mood in Dallas and retain its leadership role without entirely jettisoning its traditional values it would have to continue its process of liberalization. Yet, when the slate was announced in February, it was Avery Mays, admittedly a traditional type of CCA candidate, who headed the ticket. Schoellkopf could boast, though, that the overall slate was a balanced one with three young men in their thirties, a black man (George Allen), and a Mexican-American (Anita Martinez) to go with the half a dozen men who headed large companies.

Never had the CCA appeared so vulnerable and the times so propitious for political change. An unusual number of independents, all of them unique, entered the mayor's race. For the first time, perhaps inspired by *Newsroom*'s generous coverage of all the candidates, each and every one of them received a share of newspaper space. The two primary candidates, though, Wise and Mays, gained by far the most attention. Wise, a former sportscaster who had started on radio with Gordon McLendon's KLIF re-creation of baseball games and who had covered sports on television for KRLD-TV and WFAA-TV, was everywhere—exuding an air of confidence in his public appearances. Mays, unaccustomed to the limelight, took on the air of a reluctant campaigner. Lipscomb, the activist, announced as the city's first black mayoral candidate. He paid an immediate price: suspension for ten weeks from his Block Partnership job. Other candidates were Dave Moeller, a bearded, twenty-five-year-old "flower child" and odd-job specialist (including a long stint as a window washer on high-rise buildings); Joe Bock, an accountant who expressed concern over how the backward-slanting windows on the proposed city hall would be washed; Herbert Green Jr., who was to become a perennial candidate; and David Wade, a well-known television chef who suggested the creation of a rapid transit system which he proposed could be called DART (Dallas Area Rapid Transit). (This was surely the first usage of the term which later would be adopted and become widely known.)

In the key battle between Mays and Wise, both candidates agreed on the need to proceed with the new city hall as well as promising full support of the work toward D-FW Airport. Wise emphasized his ability to relate to all peoples of Dallas and his experience on the council. Mays, in espousing the CCA's economic-based "Agenda for Action" platform, stressed his business and civic experience. "I'm not a news analyst or a sportscaster," he said in comparing his own personality with that of the dynamic Wise. "I'm just old Avery Mays." Wise capitalized on Mays' reluctance to debate him by carrying an empty chair to his speaking engagements.

In the April election the numerous independent candidates split the vote several ways and prevented a clear winner from emerging. Mays was the top vote-getter, but he failed to get enough votes to escape a run-off. He was followed by Wise. Third was Lipscomb, whose ten-week suspension from his job now became an outright termination. Lipscomb blamed CCA domination of the Block Partnership program for his dismissal. The program director, Don Johnson, also black, acknowledged that Lipscomb was fired by the board for being "disruptive." In the run-off Wise collected the votes of the other independents, winning a resounding victory over Mays, 57,776 to 39,947, and becoming the first non-CCA mayor in more than three decades.

In the other council races, CCA candidates won nine of the other ten council seats. Such a majority suggested that the organization had lost little of its vaunted power. Yet, only three of the eleven positions had been seriously contested, and the CCA lost two of those three despite outspending the independents by large amounts. Besides Wise, the other independent to win was Jesse Price, who first had been elected as a CCA nominee but had failed to get a second endorsement after losing Jonsson's favor.

In assessing the overall election and the CCA's lacklustre performance, second-term winner Garry Weber, himself a CCA man but one with a more liberal tint, said that the organization should recognize that the "old-style traditional politics and political campaigning it has practiced are now a thing of the past....It isn't enough to put up a lot of signs, print a lot of folders and slate cards and rely primarily on pushing the name of the candidates and the name of the organization." He believed that many voters were "sick" of having CCA candidates "crammed" down their throats.

Concerned itself, the CCA immediately commissioned a poll to assess its image in the community. The results indicated that the CCA must broaden its base of support if it hoped to continue as the major force in municipal politics. The report, prepared by the firm of Louis, Bowles & Grace, pointed out that Dallas had changed substantially since the CCA had been founded and that the old presumptions no longer were valid. In 1931 enthusiastic business participation in politics had been a formidable force. As Dallas had grown, though, an increasingly greater proportion of the population fell outside the business community's domain. "Today there is no longer the possibility of the business community alone guiding and directing the growth of the city," the study concluded.

THE OLD SYSTEM STRUGGLES

The new council's first job was to select a mayor pro tem. This was a position George Allen openly sought. When council members instead voted 8-3 for Ted Holland, the outraged Allen jerked his All-America City badge from his lapel, threw it on the table, and exclaimed that All-American city or not, his failure to win the post was a sign of blatant racism. Accompanied by his wife, he stormed out of the room. Mayor Wise promptly said he wanted to make it clear that his vote had nothing whatever to do with race. "No excuses," shouted someone from the audience. After lunch Allen returned to the council table, and—borrowing a note from J.B. Adoue—proposed that in the future the majority of the citizens rather than the council elect the mayor pro tem. The council took the matter under advisement, thus stalling the issue indefinitely.

A more direct threat to the CCA was a lawsuit filed by Lipscomb, Peter Johnson, J.B. Jackson, Elsie Faye Heggins, Pancho Medrano, and others. It contended that the city-wide method for electing councilmen was unconstitutional. (The suit had been filed before the recent council election in an attempt to postpone it, but a federal court rejected it. A recent Supreme Court decision prompted the 5th U.S. Court of Appeals to revive the case for a hearing.) At issue was the very basis by which the CCA had controlled municipal politics since 1931: the at-large system. With all residents being able to vote for all council candidates, an advantage was awarded to those areas with the highest turnout despite the still-new residency requirements for candidates. Since turnout in middle-class and affluent white neighborhoods far exceeded that of minority neighborhoods, black residents never had had the power to elect their own candidates. This system, the plaintiffs contended, had the "invidious effect of diluting the vote of the ghetto residents living in the ghetto voting area" in violation of the Equal Protection Clause and the 15th Amendment.

There is a possibility, the Court of Appeals noted, that Lipscomb and the other plaintiffs "might succeed in proving that the Dallas City Council election plan is a purposeful attempt by the white majority or the Dallas city fathers to fence ghetto area residents out of the City Council." Thus began a lengthy, years-long battle in the federal courts, one of critical importance to the minority community in its effort to gain more council representation.

In August 1972 Schoellkopf, still seeking to modernize the CCA, announced his intention to establish a broad-based leadership committee that for the first time would include liberal, labor, and minority figures. This was followed by the CCA's new "open door" policy in which candidates from all walks of life were encouraged to offer themselves for endorsement. This practice contrasted sharply with the old philosophy of shunning those who sought office in favor of drafting businessmen to fulfill their civic duty. Schoellkopf said the CCA now would be seeking a "diversified City Council with members of different ages, races, groups, vocations, and professions."

As mayor, Wise was managing to maintain a delicate balance in working side-by-side with the CCA-dominated council while still being receptive to the increasing demands of minorities. He had vowed in the campaign to be a "full-time" mayor, and this he was. Once a week he opened his office door to receive any citizen who wanted to see him. This policy attracted a large number of visitors who heretofore had never had an opportunity to meet personally with their mayor.

Work continued under Wise on the city's ambitious construction projects. In the fall of 1973 he shared center stage with Jonsson and Fort Worth's mayor when Greater Dallas-Fort Worth International Airport was dedicated with great fanfare as the world's largest airport. As for the new city hall, a third request for bids successfully attracted one that made construction possible. Groundbreaking for the building, underground parking garage, and park plaza took place in August 1972 with Wise, Jonsson, and I.M. Pei as key participants. In the adjoining block an ambitious $37 million expansion of the Convention Center was under way.

Wise's tenure was not harmed either by the phenomenon of so many corporations transferring their headquarters to Dallas. By 1974 the city had become headquarters for 626 firms with $1 million or more in net worth, a ranking that was third in the nation. New office buildings were going up that constantly altered the skyline, rendering inconspicuous Thornton's Mercantile Bank and the Magnolia Building's Flying Red Horse. Wise was proving to be a very effective ambassador for a city that continued, based on all evident signs, to prosper.

Dislodging the popular mayor in 1973, CCA leaders recognized, would be difficult if not impossible. Their "solution" was not to endorse anyone. As for the remainder of the CCA slate, it was broadened to include for the first time two black candidates, Allen and Lucy Patterson; a second woman, Adlene Harrison; and another Mexican-American, Pedro Aguirre, to replace Anita Martinez after two terms.

This was the third time Allen had gained CCA endorsement, a precedent for a councilman. The CCA had a firm policy of limiting councilmen to two terms in its determination to avoid "professional" politicians. When Allen, despite the policy, demanded a third term, the screening committee balked. A Negro columnist for the *Dallas Morning News*, Julia Scott Reed, clashed with John Stemmons. "You white folks are all the same. Just as soon as we get a leader in our community that we can follow and that can get a job done for us, you want to kick him out and give us another leader. Well, we're not going for that." Stemmons and the committee yielded; Allen received the endorsement.

Another CCA candidate, Garry Weber, also wanted a third term.

But Weber had shown evidence of political ambitions beyond council service. The CCA refused to endorse him again. Weber announced anyway for a third term as an independent.

In the election Wise won a second term as mayor, and voters returned Weber for a third term. The CCA held a 9-2 majority. Yet, candidates bore little resemblance to those CCA councils of old. The nine members included a liberal Jewish woman, Harrison; two blacks, Allen and Patterson; and a Mexican-American, Aguirre. Once again, Allen lobbied to be mayor pro tem. This time he was successful.

"The establishment, as it once was, is dead and we can't put it together again," Schoellkopf said. This pronouncement by the president of the CCA seemed to be confirmed as his organization began a desperate search for a candidate to campaign against Wise in 1975. Schoellkopf offered in September to make the race himself, and he resigned as CCA president to prepare for a campaign. Jonsson did not prefer Schoellkopf as mayor, who as a member of a wealthy family did not fit the preferred self-made mold, and he continued to search personally for a candidate more to his liking. James W. Aston declined the honor. So did Robert Folsom, a successful developer and former captain of the SMU football team, who said the CCA had "lost touch with the people."

Next, Jonsson beseeched Louis Weber Jr., president of the Dallas Bar Association, to accept a draft. Weber also refused. Speculation appeared in the *News* that if Jonsson persisted in insisting on his own candidate the organization would be seriously split, for another influential CCA leader, John Stemmons, favored Schoellkopf as a candidate

Stemmons and a group of like-minded members had their own agenda on another matter, too, reinforcing the picture of internal CCA discord. This contingent threatened to withdraw from the organization if it endorsed for a second term Adlene Harrison, a very atypical CCA council member who had charted a fiery, often abrasive path in her first term. Mrs. Harrison soon solved the dilemma herself by rejecting the CCA label for her second race.

It was clear that the political group was struggling as it had not since the days of the Catfish Club in the mid-1930s. What amounted to its eventual death knell came on January 17, 1975, when federal Judge Eldon Mahon, acting on Lipscomb's suit, declared Dallas' at-large system of voting unconstitutional. The system, he said, "diluted" minority voting strength, gave undue power to white-dominated groups "such as the Citizens Charter Association," and made the cost of running a city-wide race prohibitive.

Mahon ordered the city council to draw up a new plan for the upcoming April election. The council quickly devised an 8-3 scheme, approved by the judge, in which eight council members would be elected from specific "single-member" districts rather than by city-wide vote. The remaining three, including the mayor, would be elected "at-large." While those elected from districts might feel allegiance to their particular constituents, it was reasoned that the two at-large council members and the mayor would look to the needs of the entire city.

The scene was set for what would be the CCA's last attempt to control the Dallas City Council. The slate of candidates offered by the organization in the April 1 election had little resemblance to the business-dominated tickets of old. Schoellkopf, the CCA mayoral candidate, was a former reporter with little business experience. Two candidates, Russell Smith and John Leedom, had been political operatives in the Republican Party, a background always avoided by earlier CCA policy. Two candidates were African-Americans. Another was a Mexican-American. This was not the kind of group to march lock-step to an agenda pushed from behind the scenes by the Citizens Council or even by its own CCA officers and members.

Yet, even with this liberalized group, election results confirmed the CCA's worsening predicament. Wise thoroughly defeated Schoellkopf to win his third term. The CCA held on to just six of the eleven seats. Two incumbent CCA council members were defeated, and a third soon lost in a run-off with a young Oak Cliff housewife who campaigned on an anti-busing platform. Another CCA councilman, L.A. Murr, managed barely to defeat the independent Max Goldblatt by distancing himself as far as he could from his CCA endorsement.

Clearly, the CCA's last days were near. The organization's tenuous council advantage disappeared when later in the year George Allen resigned to accept a commissioners court appointment as justice of the peace. (Named at the same time as justice of the peace was another black man, Cleo Steele. The two became the first two black men in the county's history to hold that office.) Allen's successor was the veteran NAACP organizer Juanita Craft, now seventy-three years of age and undeniably an independent, who won over six opponents. The CCA found itself in a minority on the council, outnumbered 6-5, the first time since 1935-39.

When Wise resigned in early 1976 to run for Congress as a Democrat, a special election was called to replace him. (Wise, new to partisan politics, would be defeated in an upset by attorney Jim Mattox, a state representative and long-time Democratic Party worker.) Robert Folsom, who had rejected Jonsson's bid to run for mayor in 1975, now felt ready—but he had decided that he would fare better without CCA endorsement. When he heard that the CCA was prepared to nominate R.L. Thornton Jr., he called Robert Cullum to tell him that if the organization would not nominate Thornton he himself would announce for the office as an independent. The CCA, although having been spurned once by Folsom, preferred him in office even as an independent, accepted his terms, and rescinded the offer to Thornton, who felt that he had been betrayed.

Meanwhile, activists at city hall sometimes were creating pandemonium at council sessions as illustrated by one incident which occurred in March 1976 after Wise's resignation. It took place during a presentation by one of the most disruptive and controversial of all the activist groups, the Bois d'Arc Patriots, whose white leaders dedicated themselves to championing the cause of the poor in East Dallas. The group's co-founder, Charlie Young, a former filmmaker for *Newsroom*, appeared before the city council to protest policies affecting low-income groups and sub-standard housing. To dramatize his point Young concluded his presentation by upending a model house, purposely pouring onto the floor hundreds of swarming cockroaches. He was promptly arrested. Later, the Patriots would protest a proposed ordinance that would make tenants responsible for eradicating rodents from their premises by threatening to invade the neighborhoods of individual council members and releasing scores of rats.

Folsom ran against another independent, Garry Weber, in a high-profile campaign dubbed cynically as the "million-dollar" race because both sides spent huge amounts of money. Folsom's business ties, his conservatism, his personal friendships, and his support base strictly conformed to CCA candidates of old. A developer of the exploding far North Dallas area, Folsom was favored by most "establishment" businessmen. Weber, an incumbent council member and a stockbroker who had made a fortune through his own firm, sought the support of minorities and more liberal voters. One of the issues in the campaign was the Comprehensive Land Use Plan of 1975, which City Planning Director James Schroeder had devised as an orderly guide to growth. Weber enthusiastically endorsed the plan as a necessity and a comfort to homeowners. Folsom opposed it as too restrictive and likely to force new development to the suburbs.

Folsom won in a run-off by 1,225 votes, with the results showing a dramatic contrast: Folsom predominantly carried precincts north of downtown and Weber carried precincts south of downtown. Never before had the city been so sharply divided. During more than four years in office Folsom became widely acknowledged as the "establishment" mayor despite his "independent" status. The Comprehensive Land Use Plan was never adopted, leading Schroeder later to comment that the city council "doesn't want to do anything to interfere with doing what it wants to do on any given day." Schroeder was quietly demoted, and for two years the city had no planning director. Weber afterwards won election as county judge for the Democratic Party, where he served as the county's chief administrative officer.

At the end of 1976 the new president of the CCA, Dave Braden, announced that the organization probably would not again make political endorsements. It would be given a new name and structure. But in February 1977 it was clear that the CCA would never be revived in any form. Braden blamed the media, the "naive" business community, single-member districts, and CCA candidates themselves for its demise. Council campaigns, he said, pointing to the "million-dollar race" between Folsom and Weber, had become expensive personality contests in which serious issues were secondary to public relations image-making. The next step, he predicted, would be a deterioration in the quality of council members to the extent that highly skilled administrators and staff members would leave city service.

His assessment as to how the CCA had lost its immediate grip was accurate and colorful: "In a four-year period, via the media we have allowed the independent candidates and their PR counsel to create a public image of the CCA as a power-hungry anachronistic group floundering in contemporary times, and allowed them to place the city in a class war of the little man versus the big man."

There were, of course, more long-term and far-reaching reasons for the CCA's demise. Most important, the culture had changed in Dallas as well as in the nation. A rising tide of public opinion was identifying with and supporting the goals of those who for too long had been denied a fair share in all aspects of society. New organizations representing such groups, particularly minorities, were striving hard to participate in the city's governance. Many middle-class persons supported them. If new ideas emerging were not entirely anti-business, they did contain a perception that for too long business in Dallas had had its way. The CCA's efforts to accommodate these forces by broadening its candidate-selection process not only was insufficient to change the image which Braden so graphically described, but it also alienated some important CCA members. Beyond all this, however, no longer could traditional downtown Dallas businessmen control the city's destiny through decisions made at a luncheon or at a series of luncheons. Dallas' thriving economy over the years had been accompanied by the emergence of many successful entrepreneurs outside the downtown area who, unlike the traditional leaders, had not grown up together, joined clubs together, nor conducted business together. They had natural desires to be their own persons, to do things their own way or in a different way.

As a former president acknowledged, for all its power the CCA was never very well-organized. It never developed—nor had it desired—a patronage system common to many cities in which jobs could be offered as rewards for supporters. The closest it came to such a thing, critics might observe, was a form of patronage through favorable zoning decisions for developers.

Erik Jonsson was reluctant to accept the loss of power which the organization's dissolution meant for the business community. The CCA's demise, he said, would open the door for something the organization had always sought to avoid: partisanship in municipal affairs. "There is going to be a real tendency for the politicians to move in," he said. "I'm talking about people who are self-serving rather than wanting to serve the public's interest." To maintain their voice in city affairs Jonsson urged the city's businessmen to form political action groups.

Still in operation as a powerful group of business leaders was the

Citizens Council. But with its direct CCA tie to city hall severed, no longer could its luncheon decisions be greeted at council meetings with immediate acceptance and implementation. Yet, few people in Dallas seemed to realize that the "establishment" no longer ruled by fiat. This, though, was the new reality. The city was entering a period to be distinguished by something uncommon to its history—an absence of control by any organized group.

THE SANTOS RODRIGUEZ INCIDENT

A tragic incident in July 1973 marked the nadir of the increasing hostility minority groups were feeling towards the Dallas Police Department. It prompted an outbreak of mass violence that was as close as the city would come in experiencing the widespread rioting which already had occurred in so many American cities. The cause of the turmoil was the shooting of a twelve-year-old Mexican-American boy by a Dallas police officer.

Two police officers had picked up the boy, Santos Rodriguez, and his thirteen-year-old brother after midnight from their eighty-year-old grandfather's home in Little Mexico. They wanted to question the boys about an attempted break-in earlier that night of a Fina Service Station on Cedar Springs and the looting of its outdoor soft-drink machine. Returning the boys to the scene, Officer Darrell L. Cain attempted to frighten Santos into confessing by placing his pistol against his head and pretending to play Russian roulette with him as he sat handcuffed in the car. When Cain pulled the trigger after the second spin of the cylinder, his .357 Magnum pistol discharged, fatally wounding young Rodriguez. Cain claimed that he did not realize a bullet was in the chamber.

Dallas Police Chief Frank Dyson arrested the officer, stripped him of his badge, and filed murder charges against him. A municipal court judge sat bond for him at the surprisingly low amount of $5,000.

The irate Mexican-American community, joined by blacks, immediately decried the shooting and the circumstances around it as an example of the low value police officers placed on the lives of members of the minority community. The $5,000 bond was denounced especially as ludicrous. (Within days a judge raised it to

$50,000.) The Brown Berets and the Southern Christian Leadership Conference together demanded that the second officer in the car with Cain also be charged with murder.

Making the incident all the more aggravating was the fact that Cain earlier had been involved in another highly controversial shooting which had inflamed the black community and left a lingering discontent. In that instance in 1970, Cain and a partner responded to a silent burglary alarm at a bar and grill, saw a suspect fleeing the scene, and shot and killed him. He was an eighteen-year-old black youth, Michael Moorhead. Both officers were cleared by the grand jury, but the shooting of a suspect who seemed to be posing no threat to the officers touched off loud protests and demonstrations from the black community.

The Santos Rodriguez shooting similarly prompted groups in the Mexican-American community to commence a series of vigils and meetings, culminating on Saturday, July 28, with a mass march sponsored by the Brown Berets from the Kennedy Plaza to city hall in memory of the slain youth. More than a thousand demonstrators marched down the city streets to city hall, where they heard several talks, then headed back toward Kennedy Plaza. At this point others arrived to join them, small groups began to form and to linger, and then they marched once more toward city hall, this time their mood far angrier. Some leaders tried to calm the crowd, but they could not be heard. To amplify their comments a plainclothes police car with a public address system pulled onto Harwood Street, and City Councilman Pedro Aguirre climbed atop the car to talk. The crowd booed him, and when State Representative Sam Hudson tried to speak a black woman grabbed the microphone from him and began exhorting the crowd: "We want justice.... We want Cain." She claimed that police earlier had shot her own "baby boy," and she further incited the crowd by shouting obscenities at officers. A Mexican-American youth replaced her at the hand-held microphone and urged the crowd to "never let them [the police] forget Santos Rodriguez." When a police official tried to clear demonstrators from the car a black man jumped on his back and began pummelling him. Others climbed on top of the car and began stomping their feet, crumpling the roof. Crowd members turned on other officers, kicking, hitting, and throwing objects at them. Two police motorcycles were turned over and set on fire. Mob members smashed the windows of a television news car and hurled bottles through city hall windows. As rioters began running through downtown streets they broke windows of more than forty stores and looted their displays. Neiman-Marcus, Titche-Goettinger's, Zales Jewelry, Everts Jewelry, Jas. K. Wilson, Woolf Bros., and H.L. Green all suffered damages and losses. Police were reluctant at first to move against the demonstrators, fearful of inciting further violence, but finally they arrested thirty-eight demonstrators, including twenty-three Mexican-Americans and thirteen blacks. Five officers suffered injuries.

In the agonizing aftermath of these events Councilman Aguirre introduced a resolution which the city council adopted. It recognized officially that "unequal law enforcement, dual justice, and unequal treatment for the different segments of the community and different races" did exist. Dyson, a youthful chief considered to be one of the most progressive to hold that office in Dallas, became embroiled in the bitter disputes that followed the incident and eventually resigned his position.

A jury found officer Darrell Cain guilty for the murder of Santos Rodriguez, but when the former officer was sentenced to just five years in prison (he served less than three) complaints once again surfaced about a double-standard in law enforcement. Pressures mounted for federal authorities to prosecute Cain for violating the boy's civil rights, but in 1978 as the statute of limitations expired the U.S. Justice Department announced that it would not do so. Further demonstrations promptly broke out in Dallas in protest of the decision. The Santos Rodriguez incident would not be forgotten in the years ahead.

SCHOOL BUSING BEGINS

Those many in Dallas who believed that their public schools already had been "integrated" learned otherwise in July 1975 when the 5th Court of Appeals ruled to the contrary—school desegregation, in fact, had *not* been achieved. There were simply too many black students continuing to be enrolled in one-race schools. The court ordered that the school system must eliminate all vestiges of the existing unsatisfactory plan. School trustees returned to the drawing board. The new plan they submitted to Judge Taylor still permitted the continuation of forty-six all-black schools. Taylor declared the proposal "patently unconstitutional" and unacceptable. The judge now assumed responsibility for drawing up a satisfactory plan himself.

In his comments Taylor sharply rebuked the city's business leadership for neglecting its responsibility toward the city's school system in these difficult times. There would be little hope, he observed, for attracting new industry to Dallas if its schools were inferior and if the city were torn apart by racial strife. "It's time for the business leaders to stand up and be counted," he said.

While for years the business community had dominated public school affairs, that had ended a decade earlier with LEAD's triumph. And although the Committee for Good Schools had regained a majority on the board in 1971, that instrument of the Citizens Council had ceased to function in 1974 when single-member districts replaced the at-large method of electing school board trustees. Stung by the judge's critical remarks, though, the Dallas Alliance, a new group of business leaders representing a broad array of community organizations, began to participate in the effort to further desegregate the schools. Under the leadership of businessman Jack Lowe, who earlier had helped establish the Block Partnership program, a task force composed of seven whites, six blacks, seven Mexican-Americans, and one native American began meeting frequently and at length to find a satisfactory plan for mixing the school children.

In his 1976 hearings Judge Taylor had several proposals to consider. Among them were those of the school board, the Dallas Alliance task force, and the NAACP. He chose the basic plan submitted by the task force, ordering its implementation that fall. Under the plan, some 17,000 students between the fourth and eighth grades were to be bused, and four new senior high magnet schools were to be created to entice voluntary busing at that level. Some 10,000 high school students did choose to ride buses to the new schools which specialized in business and management, creative arts, health professions, and transportation. In addition to busing students, the plan called for ethnic ratios to be established among school administrators so that within three years they would be 44 percent white, 44 percent black, and 12 percent Mexican-American.

Among whites and Mexican-Americans, response to the plan was positive, but the black community was divided in its assessment.

What was worrisome to many of them was the fact that the plan left in place a large number of all-black schools containing some 27,000 students. Al Lipscomb, an outspoken critic of the plan, picketed the federal courthouse to protest. The NAACP opposed the decision, appealed it, and eventually succeeded in having the 5th Court of Appeals agree that the continuation of so many one-race schools was improper.

The legal battle did not end here, for it was appealed to the U.S. Supreme Court, where in 1979 school board and NAACP attorneys presented arguments. DISD lawyers argued that the dwindling number of white students (32 percent in 1979) made further efforts at desegregation through busing impractical. NAACP attorneys argued that the exclusion of high school and grades K-3 in the busing order rendered it too narrow to achieve desegregation. In January 1980 the Supreme Court decided that it should not make a ruling in the case. It remanded the case to the 5th Court of Appeals.

By now, even many black parents were beginning to frown on the use of busing as a device for school desegregation. This became especially apparent in November 1980 with the emergence of a new group of black leaders, the "Black Caucus to Maximize Education," led by Robert Price as chairman. Another member was Kathlyn Gilliam, now the school board president and the first black person to hold that position. This group, unhappy with the NAACP's aggressive, pro-busing stance, believed that children should be returned to their neighborhood schools. Judge Taylor accepted the group as an intervenor equal to the NAACP in standing before the court.

Not long afterwards, having been challenged by the NAACP as being too closely tied to the city's business leadership to be an impartial judge in the desegregation hearings, Taylor agreed to yield his authority to another judge. Taylor had been involved in the matter for more than a decade.

Judge Barefoot Sanders assumed jurisdiction over the matter, his name having been drawn from a hat. He was the fourth federal judge to be directly involved in the case that was now twenty-six years old. Other changes in the major participants already had occurred. Nolan Estes had resigned as school superintendent to be replaced in 1978 by Linus Wright, former Houston school superintendent.

On August 3, 1981, Sanders concluded that additional busing would serve no useful purpose, even though he believed Dallas' schools still showed evidence of segregation. The district now was 70 percent minority; the number of white students was continuing to decline every year.

The long, debilitating struggle to desegregate the schools to meet the requirements of federal judges and law continued. The amount of busing decreased as new one-race remedial centers were opened in minority neighborhoods with court approval in an effort to raise test scores. Even with a school enrollment that was 77 percent minority in 1985, with successive school board presidents who were black and Hispanic, and with a black school superintendent who replaced Linus Wright, the district continued to be monitored by the federal courts for its desegregation efforts. Unsuccessful efforts in 1988 and 1989 by five white trustees and one Hispanic to have Judge Sanders declare the DISD "desegregated" and end the court's long supervision generated great outbursts and new accusations of racism. The board itself appeared to be hopelessly mired in politics and racial tension.

The black superintendent, Dr. Marvin Edwards, had been hired after Wright resigned in 1987 to become undersecretary of education in Washington, D.C. Wright was discouraged after having struggled for nine years and still being confronted with charges of racism. Dr. Edwards came to Dallas from a similar position in Topeka, Kansas. The selection by the school board of DISD's first black school superintendent was unanimous.

17

One Era Ends, Another Begins

Not even the most unrepentant free-enterprisers could ignore the chaos in far North Dallas. The area was strangling in a noose of its own devising, abetted by a city council that over the years has caved in to developer requests for major zoning variants.

—David Dillon, 1985.

Keeping the Dust Flying

Many now reluctantly recognized a disturbing reality—Dallas was not immune to the difficult problems which had been plaguing older Eastern cities for many years. The evidence was all-too clear. More and more middle-class residents were moving to newer and safer suburban surroundings—Plano, Irving, Richardson, Garland, Mesquite—and leaving behind those who were less affluent, less educated, and in greater need of social services. Established businesses were moving there, as well, and the same was especially true of new business and industry. It was clear that African-American and Hispanic citizens soon would overtake the number of white residents and constitute a majority of Dallas proper's population.

Minority leaders were increasingly restive about their lack of proportionate representation in public affairs and loudly proclaimed that a pattern of racism permeated the entire city. Dallas's major crime rate, one of the highest in the nation, seemed immune to efforts at reducing it. Public schools were buffeted with problems accompanying desegregation and the exodus of white students. "Re-segregation" was just one of these problems; among others were low scores on state-wide, standardized tests. North Dallas continued to be developed far out of proportion to the languishing southern sector. Dallas's tax base surely would decline at the same time municipal obligations rose. The city was becoming the hole in a donut. Unfortunately, none of these disturbing trends would be reversed as the decade of the 1980s became the 1990s. Instead, they accelerated.

But these problems, which were to become all too apparent in the late 1980s, were camouflaged in the late 1970s and early 1980s by a remarkable economic boom. So prosperous was the Dallas area that large numbers of out-of-work people were renting trailers and hauling their belongings to the city to find work. R.L. Thornton, who had always wanted to "keep the dirt flyin'," surely would have been pleased at the proliferation of construction dust in the air. In 1983 and 1984 alone 29.3 million square feet of new office space was created in Dallas. That rather remote number becomes more meaningful by a comparison: it was the equivalent of all the office space in Miami. The Metroplex, a new term coined to encompass the Dallas-Fort Worth area, now ranked third behind New York and Chicago as headquarters for companies with more than $1 million in assets.

When the new city hall opened in 1978 after twelve long years in the making, it won rave compliments for its design and for the philosophy behind the design. The project covered seven acres instead of an original five; its cost had climbed from $42 million to nearly $70 million. But *New York Times* architecture critic Ada Louise Huxtable declared it one of the most important public buildings in the country. In front of the structure, balancing its eight floors just as the building itself was intended to balance the skyscrapers in its foreground, was a massive sculpture by Henry Moore entitled simply, "The Dallas Piece." For Jonsson, the new city hall truly represented the people of Dallas. "It's strong, and the people of Dallas are strong people. Concrete is simple, and they are simple people—in the best sense of the word, plain people," he observed.

Across the street from city hall was a new library, built at a cost of approximately $42.7 million, opened in 1982, and conceived by Jonsson to complement the city hall building as an attractive buffer. Jonsson co-directed the drive to raise private money for the facility, and the library later was named in his honor.

Many grand notions arose during these years that were designed to keep Dallas moving ahead culturally as well as economically. Indicative of the mood was an idea that the city's major cultural institutions should be located in an arts district. The suggestion had arisen first in 1971 when Mayor Wise appointed Councilman Garry Weber to chair a committee to examine the possibility. An ill-conceived 1978 bond election that included this notion failed—an ominous sign since it was the first such failure in memory. But in November 1979 voters approved a new package which included $24.8 million for a new art museum and $2.25 million for a concert hall site, both to be located north of the immediate downtown area.

In 1983, following an energetic push from Mayor Jack Evans for private land donations, the city council approved creation of the Arts District itself on a sixty-acre tract of land along Ross Avenue. By that time its first occupant, the Dallas Museum of Art, was nearly ready to move into a new building. Designed by architect Edward Larrabee Barnes and built at a cost of more than $50 million in public and private money, the museum opened in 1984 to wide praise. In the following year ground was broken nearby for a new concert hall designed by I.M. Pei. It, too, was financed jointly by public and private funds. By the time it opened in 1989 its cost had grown to $81.5 million, with the largest private donor being H. Ross Perot, who was permitted to name the facility for his friend and long-time business associate, Morton H. Meyerson. The spectacular hall won instant praise as one of the world's finest concert facilities. It was an ornament for the city, but its creation at such great expense was condemned by some as indicative of misplaced priorities which favored the privileged few rather than the economically disadvantaged many.

Other public structures springing up during these heady times also made spectacular additions to the landscape. A new all-purpose arena was built, and with its opening in 1980 came a National Basketball Association franchise, the Dallas Mavericks. Reunion Arena, located just behind the revitalized Union Terminal and spectacular Reunion Tower with revolving restaurant, had a seating capacity for basketball of 17,134.

Regional planning for transportation began in 1983 when Dallas voters and those in most adjoining suburban cities authorized the creation of Dallas Area Rapid Transit (DART). The road ahead for creating a regional mass transit system turned out to be filled with many twists and turns, for many of DART's expensive projects generated much public controversy, including the inevitable charges of racism.

Dallas-Fort Worth International Airport was a resounding success, ranking sixth in total passengers in the entire world for the year 1982, and serving as a major reason for the relocation to the area of such major corporations as American Airlines, Caltex, Diamond Shamrock, and J.C. Penney. Love Field was still in operation too, and although restricted in the range of its commercial flights, it flourished as the sixty-eighth ranking airport in the world in terms of passenger traffic.

All these tax-supported ventures, however momentous, were dwarfed by the magnitude of private developments. Striking, modernistic new buildings dramatically changed the downtown skyline. That popular old landmark, the building with the flying red horse, was lost in a forest of skyscrapers that dwarfed it. The northward momentum that had begun with Central Expressway continued as modernistic office parks, super-regional shopping malls, and fancy condominiums sprang up in Far North Dallas and in places such as Las Colinas in Irving, Richardson, Addison, and Plano. In many ways, Far North Dallas held the development spotlight. In 1974 the area had some 1.5 million square feet of office space; by the end of 1982 it had grown by almost ten-fold to 14 million square feet with an additional 7.1 million square feet announced or under construction.

All this prosperity needed showing off, and to do so Dallas vied for and won the honor of being host city for the 1984 Republican Party's national convention. Attention was focused intensely on the city that summer as GOP delegates from throughout the nation met in the new Convention Center and nominated Ronald Reagan for a second term as president.

The city's economic boom found confirmation in fiction. A television series that attracted a phenomenal world-wide audience added yet another dimension to the city's reputation for up-scale prosperity. The series began on April 2, 1978, when millions of evening television viewers saw the first hour-long show of a CBS program revolving around the antics of a powerful, oil-rich, and much-agonized Dallas family, the Ewings. Before the series ended thirteen years later in 1991 the Friday evening prime-time show, entitled simply "Dallas," had been broadcast for 356 episodes, making it second only to "Gunsmoke" as the longest-running prime time television drama in American history. The Ewing family—J.R., Sue Ellen, Bobby, Pamela—and their enemies became powerful symbols of the fast-paced life in Dallas.

The show was fiction, but as a depiction of Dallas life it had—despite frequent absurdities—more than just a touch of reality in portraying the excesses of the new-rich. It reinforced the growing notion that Dallas was a place where wheeler-dealers reigned, where women were beautiful, sophisticated, and tantalizing, and where the architecture was dazzlingly modern.

Business-Minded Mayors

In these exciting days, the CCA, its long rule, and its demise were largely forgotten. With free-enterprise flourishing in Dallas, the CCA's loss of power at city hall was mitigated by the presence of three consecutive business-minded mayors who struggled to maintain order over city council sessions that were increasingly hectic. Even though they did not wear the CCA tag, these men, Robert Folsom, Jack Evans, and A. Starke Taylor Jr., fit comfortably into traditional profiles of civic leadership.

It was Folsom's expensive 1976 victory over Garry Weber in the special election to succeed Wes Wise that returned the city to this series of "establishment" mayors. During his four years in office, Folsom led the drive to build Reunion Arena and concentrated on the city's economic growth to the detriment of urban planning. As a developer prominently associated with the Far North Dallas boom, Folsom faced frequent criticism from homeowner groups who believed that in zoning decisions he favored developers over residential neighborhoods, a belief reinforced by his refusal to endorse the Comprehensive Land Use Policy Plan of 1975. He came under special attack for an alleged conflict of interest when he led the council to annex the town of Renner despite personal property holdings there. The annexation included exclusive North Dallas developments such as Bent Tree, which Folsom's development company had begun in the early 1970s, and it extended far into Collin County. At a time when demands upon a mayor's ability to interact with varying constituencies were growing, Folsom—who described himself as basically a shy person—maintained a no-nonsense, business-like approach to city affairs. Minority advocates complained that he was insensitive to their needs and difficult to communicate with.

As the end of his last term drew near in 1980 Folsom approached grocer Jack Evans and told him that people were saying he was the most qualified person in town to succeed him. Evans was interested. After a long and successful career in the grocery business dating back to his childhood, public service now was on his mind. He had developed and sold a chain of grocery stores to the Kroger Company before becoming president of the Cullum Company, whose principal owners, Robert and Charles Cullum, were integral participants in the city's traditional establishment.

Evans accepted the challenge, and he won the mayor's position easily. As mayor he played a leading role in bringing the 1984 GOP Convention to Dallas, helped organize and win approval for the new Arts District, and worked toward the successful bond election which authorized the creation of and implementation of a 1 percent sales tax for DART. Evans was more inclined than Folsom to reach out to diverse groups in the city, but after one term he declined to seek a second one.

Evans' successor was Bob Folsom's former campaign manager, A. Starke Taylor Jr., challenged in the 1983 race by former mayor Wes Wise, who wanted to make a comeback. Absent from public office and television cameras for half a dozen years, Wise had lost his name-identification advantage of the early 1970s and he could not match Taylor's campaign chest. To win the election Taylor spent just under a million dollars compared to Wise's $65,000. Taylor had made his fortune in the cotton brokerage business, but recently he had involved himself deeply in developing Far North Dallas, as had his friend Folsom. Taylor went on to serve a second term as well, beating Councilman Max Goldblatt in a colorful, close campaign. Under Taylor the city appointed its first black city manager, Richard Knight, who replaced Charles Anderson when he resigned to become executive director of DART.

While the mayor's office remained in the hands of these three strong businessmen between 1976 and 1987, individual council members reflected the independent voices that had foreshadowed the CCA's collapse. Businessmen on temporary, two-term loan from fancy downtown offices no longer were the norm. Council members debated sharply over zoning for homeowner groups and developers, pension fund investments in South Africa, matters related to DART, police-minority relations, powers of the police review board, and especially over redistricting plans that would enhance opportunities for minority representation on the council.

More and more, as a natural concomitant to the politicization of their offices, council members identified with the needs of their constituents rather than those of the overall city. They were less and less inclined to work through the city manager's office as the charter specified, eroding the council-manager theory in a way that would have been unthinkable in previous decades. Some spent nearly all their working hours at city hall, where they now had private offices and aides. Proposals appeared periodically to increase their pay to a regular salary rather than the $50 per meeting they earned as "citizen volunteers." (Between 1973 and 1993 voters rejected this plan five times, but the idea still did not die.) Being uttered by some councilmen was their growing belief that the council-manager plan had outlived its usefulness. Dallas was the largest city in the nation giving administrative authority to its appointed city manager rather than to the elected mayor.

ACTIVIST COUNCIL MEMBERS

It had become routine since 1973 for the council to have two black members and one Hispanic, no more and no less. Federal requirements of 1975 that eight councilmen be elected from geographical districts had not altered that fact. This was a matter of concern for many minority activists, for by 1980 minority population in Dallas was 41 percent of the total. Neither did it matter that minorities—African-Americans especially—held highly visible positions that would have been impossible just a few years earlier. By 1987 minorities held one-third of the jobs at city hall, and there was a sizeable percentage of minority workers at the courthouse. About one in five police officers were minority, and 12 percent more were female. Dallas had a black school superintendent and black city manager. There were minority judges, minority journalists, and minority television anchors. A major courthouse building had been named for George Allen; a high school for A. Maceo Smith. Despite such gains, the stridency of minority spokesmen accelerated. Their struggle for equality had evolved to another level—that of seeking proportionate representation in all aspects of public affairs, especially elective offices and government contracts.

Dallas' first minority city council members—George Allen and Juanita Craft—were transitional figures who, having achieved office after years of struggle against bitter odds, proved to be moderates when in power. They measured the needs and desires of their ethnic constituents against what they perceived to be the overall needs of the city, and gained great respect. Allen, who had boldly attempted to desegregate the University of Texas in the 1930s, worked comfortably with fellow white councilmen in his pioneering role. So did Juanita Craft, who had been active in the NAACP since 1935, leading protests, registering voters, organizing pickets to desegregate the State Fair in 1955, pushing for the desegregation of Dallas restaurants and lunch counters, and helping establish more than 180 branches of the NAACP in Texas between 1946 and 1957. But the conciliatory approaches of Allen, Craft, and other early minority council members—Anita Martinez, Lucy Patterson, Pedro Aguirre, and Fred Blair—often brought them harsh criticisms from impatient activists.

The election of Elsie Faye Heggins in January 1980 signaled the arrival of a far more aggressive type of minority council member, a type that continued throughout the decade to win voter approval. A close associate of Al Lipscomb's, Heggins was a part of the South Dallas group that had been deliberatively confrontational in seeking its goals. Her predecessor in District 6, Juanita Craft, endorsed a more moderate candidate, Mabel White, but Heggins won in a run-off by eighteen votes. Unlike Allen and Craft, she had no significant ties to any group outside the black community, nor did she seek them. As a councilwoman she appeared to examine every major issue in terms of its impact on the black community. Her insistence on this was widely understood to have driven Folsom to distraction. When Starke Taylor, seeking to bolster the economic development of South

Dallas, appointed a blue-ribbon committee made up of blacks and whites for that purpose, Heggins skeptically countered by naming her own all-black economic development committee. In several tense instances after Dallas police officers were involved in shooting incidents with minorities, she was quick and loud in citing police racism as the cause. In such times, her regular community forums in South Dallas became in the words of Police Chief Billy Prince a platform for "irresponsible people who were telling untruths and causing rumors and unrest." The chief said, "She's gonna end up creating a Watts in South Dallas."

Dallas Morning News columnist and former city hall reporter Henry Tatum wrote concerning Heggins: "Never in the history of municipal government have so many racial connotations been attached to so many city issues. If a consultant needed to be hired to review a serious city problem, she wanted to know how many minorities were on its staff. If Dallas officers shot and killed a black suspect she publicly aired rumors that the shooting was unjustified, that officers were 'trigger-happy' and more willing to shoot blacks." Still, the councilwoman's aggressive, uncompromising stances won for her faithful support from voters in the black community. Her single-minded approach to the office set a pattern for a series of black council members who followed her.

In the same year that Heggins was elected, voters also sent to city hall a moderate black city councilman, Fred Blair, a real estate broker. Blair took a more traditional approach to his job, akin to that of George Allen and Juanita Craft, and he was chosen mayor pro tem in 1983.

In 1984 both Heggins and Blair resigned their council offices to campaign for the same Dallas County commissioners court seat representing the county's southeast quadrant. The head-on race between the moderate and the activist was complicated by the presence of another black activist candidate, John Wiley Price, a former Heggins supporter. Price's background as an administrative assistant for a justice of the peace and his work in Democratic politics gave him an advantage in the partisan election. Voters in the predominantly black area rejected Blair and sent the more activist Heggins and Price into the runoff. In the run-off Price defeated Heggins, who—consistent with her past uncompromising record—refused to concede, would not congratulate her one-time supporter, and blamed her defeat on voting irregularities. Price thus began a highly controversial career at the courthouse marked by a series of arrests for his aggressive behavior, including assault, that no Dallas black leader yet had exhibited. Blair in 1986 won a seat in the Texas Legislature. Heggins moved from the city.

The special election to replace Heggins and Blair at city hall brought to the council two more black representatives, Al Lipscomb and Diane Ragsdale, who more than matched Heggins for being outspoken on racial matters. Since his loss in the mayoral race of 1971 Lipscomb had unsuccessfully launched low-budget campaigns for the commissioners court in 1972, the Dallas Independent School District board in 1974, and for city council in 1973, 1975, and 1983. Several months before his election he had been thrown out of a council meeting by Mayor Taylor for his disruptive behavior. Lipscomb, the long-time activist and perennial candidate, earned Blair's vacated spot by defeating a more moderate candidate in a run-off.

Having won a council seat, Lipscomb vowed to change his confrontational antics. And, to a degree, he did, but he retreated not a step in his advocacy of African-American rights, and he continued to denounce racism—often in a loud voice—as a source for many of Dallas' problems. Yet, despite his frequent intemperate outbursts, he displayed an innate conservatism in many of his votes for the city's economic development. His council career, which extended to 1993, included election as mayor pro tem for his last term. When he retired from office it was revealed that he had been supported financially by a number of wealthy local patrons, including the woman who would become mayor, Annette Strauss. Not a word of criticism could be heard.

Diane Ragsdale, who succeeded Heggins, was a nurse who had been involved in civil rights work since childhood. Ragsdale, at thirty-one years of age, was younger and more abrasive than either Heggins or Lipscomb in her public utterings and behavior. Yet, she was elected deputy mayor pro tem for all three of her terms. Ms. Ragsdale's demeanor on the council, which included a highly publicized shouting match and near fisticuffs with a white woman in a debate over the police review board, made Mrs. Heggins appear to be a model of decorum by contrast.

THE NEWSPAPER WAR

During these years a significant change had occurred in how controversial matters at city hall and elsewhere were covered by the local media. Both newspapers had become far more aggressive and virtually immune from pressures to downplay news that some perceived as harmful to community interests. What lay behind this new stance was the collapse of the former comfortable and long-existing relationship between the *Dallas Morning News* and the *Times Herald* in which each newspaper had left the other alone to its respective morning and afternoon monopolies. Since the demise of the merged *Dispatch* and the *Journal* in 1940, the *News* and *Times Herald* had maintained a friendly, cooperative sharing of the market.

The *News* , holding the more distinguished position as well as greater overall circulation, had concentrated on its role as a statewide newspaper. The *Times Herald* had been content to emphasize local coverage and local circulation, and to leave the morning market to its competitor. Its readership had a blue-collar tint compared to that of the *News.* Both newspapers prospered in this arrangement; both enjoyed a partnership relationship with the city's traditional leadership. Each could be counted on to put its muscle behind any civic goal.

But the *Times Herald* ownership changed in 1970 when the Times Mirror Corp., publisher of the *Los Angeles Times,* purchased it and its two broadcasting outlets for $100 million. (As a condition of the transaction the FCC required the Times Mirror Corp. to sell one of those stations, which turned out to be KRLD Radio.) The new owner pledged not to interfere with local management other than in providing greater financial resources, but in time that was bound to change.

That moment came in 1973 with the appointment of a new executive editor and vice president, W. Thomas Johnson Jr., a former aide to President Lyndon B. Johnson. Two years later when he became publisher he recruited two key news executives from outside: Kenneth P. Johnson from the *Washington Post* as executive editor and Will Jarrett of the *Philadelphia Inquirer* as managing editor. Next came an influx into the newsroom of aggressive reporters from other states, especially the East Coast, none of whom had any special ties or allegiance to the decision-makers of Dallas. Veteran editors and reporters departed. Previous tendencies to minimize coverage of news that might be inimical to the "best interests" of Dallas were replaced by a passion for the First Amendment.

This new spirit included a new attitude toward the *News*. No longer was the *Times Herald* willing to take second seat in prestige, in circulation, and in advertising revenue. It aimed to be first in Dallas.

By the late 1970s a full-scale newspaper war had developed which would reach into the 1990s. The *News* responded to the *Times Herald* challenge by revving up its own operations with new personnel and bigger news budgets. Changes at the top had occurred there, too. A reorganization of ownership brought in a new and youthful publisher, Robert W. Decherd, whose family had held a substantial interest in the newspaper and its parent company, A.H. Belo Corp., for many years.

In 1980 Decherd hired a new executive editor, Burl Osborne, former managing editor of the Associated Press, who became president and editor in 1985. The editorial page became a voice of moderate reason rather than rigid ultra-conservatism. All departments were upgraded, and a sophisticated printing plant was built in Plano to ease the burdens of serving the northern suburban area. Unlike what had happened at the *Times Herald*, there was no widespread departure of veteran journalists; they instead were given added encouragement to write more penetrating news stories. In both newspapers probing, hard-hitting series began to examine sensitive local issues. By 1992 the *News* had won four Pulitzer Prizes, something it never had done until the reorganization under Decherd. (Fifth and sixth ones came in 1993 and 1994.) Both newspapers opened new bureaus in far-away places. Many new columnists appeared; their images began showing up on billboards throughout the city. Conflicting claims of circulation superiority by both newspapers confused readers, most of whom did not understand that while the *News* had more readers overall, the *Times Herald* for many years enjoyed a larger circulation within the county.

The battle escalated to a still higher level when the *Times Herald* confronted the *News* directly by offering its own morning edition. It sought to convert as many afternoon subscribers as possible to its morning edition, which was identical to the afternoon paper except for the addition of some late-breaking news. This effort to switch afternoon readers to the morning edition was prompted, at least partially, by the fact that afternoon papers throughout the nation were declining.

During the peak years of this newspaper battle Dallas readers enjoyed a far higher level of journalism than they had ever seen. If the era of "honest" journalism had been introduced by *Newsroom*, its audience had been small, and, moreover, *Newsroom* now was gone. The newspaper war brought hard-hitting journalism to far larger audiences and with much greater scope and depth.

And yet, the outcome was not a favorable one for the city's newspaper readers. In opening the battle the *Times Herald* had made a splashy and energetic start, capturing much attention and holding the favor of many who were slow to recognize the editorial changes and more moderate voice at the *News*. But in the long stretch the *Times Herald* could not sustain its energy, especially after the Times-Mirror sold it in 1986 to a group with less resources. Two years later the *Times Herald* once again changed owners.

As the city experienced economic problems it was the *Times Herald's* advertising revenues that suffered the most. The newspaper instituted cost-cutting measures which began to impact its quality. It decided to abandon altogether its traditional afternoon edition, offering only the morning edition. This irritated many of the afternoon subscribers, who felt betrayed after years of loyalty. Towards the end of the decade rumors began spreading about the *Times Herald's* declining condition and sagging staff spirits, but it still came as a surprise when on December 9, 1991, the newspaper announced cessation of publication in a huge headline, "Goodbye Dallas." The newspaper's assets had been purchased by the *News'* parent company, the A.H. Belo Corp. Like so many American cities, Dallas now was a one-newspaper town.

BOOM TURNS TO BUST

The awesome development and construction boom in the Dallas area in the late 70s and early 80s was fueled at first by profits from skyrocketing oil prices, always handy for Texans, and then carried further after deregulatory policies of the Reagan administration permitted savings and loans institutions to build up their deposits overnight by offering extra-high dividends. Recognizing the endless possibilities emerging in this heated market, aggressive entrepreneurs and developers gained control of many of the "thrifts" and converted their once-conservative operations into roaring engines of speculation. Instead of lending money for the purchase of family homes, government-insured deposits were used to finance speculators' acquisition of raw land and construction. Development loans went for new office buildings, apartments, condominiums, and shopping centers. Banks, too, became involved in these high-risk developments, turning to them especially after a sharp drop in oil prices in 1982 following the historic highs of the late 1970s.

The seemingly endless possibilities in real-estate development attracted all sorts of participants; caution was cast aside as raw land changed hands from one speculator to the next with enormous profits. Appraisers, often friendly to the speculators, confirmed the seemingly upward spiral of values. Huge loans were approved to "insiders" on grossly inflated appraisals. When the heated economy cooled down it became clear that massive over-building had occurred. Loans worth millions of dollars were defaulted, but the value of the foreclosed properties rarely if ever came close to the indebtedness. Midway through the 1980s it was clear that a savings and loan collapse of unprecedented dimensions was occurring, one that was nation-wide in scope but that was centered in Texas, and especially in the Dallas area. Failure after failure of financial institutions—both thrifts and banks—took place at a cost to taxpayers estimated as much as $300 billion for the thrifts alone. Scores of the participants in the ill-conceived schemes found themselves bankrupt; many wound up in prison. Litigation continued into the 1990s.

The first significant failure of a savings and loan institution in Dallas was that of Empire Savings and Loan of Mesquite in 1984. Its collapse raised dark clouds of suspicion that all was not well in the industry and that the development bubble might burst. Empire, under new ownership, had multiplied its assets in a single year from $40 million to $320 million. In this process, as in many others, out-and-out fraud was involved, with four principal participants making an estimated $136 million profit in the twelve months following September 1982 and ultimately being convicted of fraud with prison sentences ranging from 10 to 20 years and forfeitures of millions of dollars.

The key figure was the somewhat unusual personage of David Lamar (Danny) Faulkner, a former housepainter and son of sharecroppers who seemed perversely proud of saying—as he wheeled and dealed his way up the ladder of speculation—that he was illiterate. (Whether or not this was literally true was doubtful.) Faulkner got his start after being befriended by a prominent insurance executive whose house he had painted and whom he had impressed with his courteous manners. He expanded his work as a painting contractor into the development of condominiums along Interstate 30 northeast of Dallas toward Lake Ray Hubbard. One success led to another, and Faulkner began multiplying that success time and time again along that same I-30 corridor, financing his projects through Empire Savings and several affiliated savings and loan firms.

A central part of Faulkner's scheme, and an essential ingredient to the frenzied activities of the period, was the "land flip" which involved the cooperation of a number of insiders. A piece of vacant land worth maybe $125,000 would be purchased for $200,000, then sold immediately to a second set of buyers who might pay $400,000. The second buyers would immediately resell it for $600,000. By the end of the day the parcel may have gone through six sales and ended up with an alleged market value, supported by courthouse records, of $2 million. With this documented value, someone like Faulkner could approach Empire Savings or another institution, use the land as collateral, and borrow $2 million on it. Before Faulkner's scheme collapsed, the I-30 corridor had a twelve-and-a-half year oversupply of housing that was poorly built and largely vacant. Faulkner and his associates used only a portion of the loans for the developments, pocketing millions of dollars themselves.

Faulkner gloried in his overnight riches, especially at his regular Saturday morning breakfast sessions at the Circle Grill at I-30 and Buckner Boulevard. There, among old and new friends, he gave away as many as thirty $5,000 Rolex watches and cut favorite pals in on lucrative business deals. Texas Governor Mark White and Attorney General Jim Mattox showed up; both of them received campaign contributions. When his son married, Faulkner hired the entire Oklahoma City Symphony Orchestra to play for the wedding. A fleet of eighteen Rolls-Royces carried guests to the reception.

When Empire Savings was shut down in 1984, the FSLIC had to

pay out some $300 million to insured depositors. Faulkner ultimately was sentenced to twenty years in prison and ordered to forfeit approximately $40 million. Empire's chairman, Spencer Blain Jr., and the former mayor of Garland, James L. Toler, also received twenty-year sentences.

Empire was by no means the largest thrift to collapse, though, merely the first; Vernon Savings and Loan had deposits of almost $1 billion when it failed. Nor was Faulkner the most flamboyant or extravagant of the new-rich, for Dallas' savings and loan executives bought Rolls-Royces, helicopters, 727 jets, expensive paintings, mansions, beach houses, airplanes, European tours, and bevies of high-priced prostitutes for parties in Las Vegas. By 1992 some two-thirds of the state's approximately 300 savings and loans institutions operating in the mid-1980s had disappeared through mergers and failures. In Dallas this included such familiar names as First Texas, Bright Banc, Sunbelt, Murray, Western, and Skyline. More than a hundred officials were convicted for their illegal activities in a series of highly publicized cases that stretched over many years.

It became apparent that banks were not to escape difficulties associated with development loans. Oil prices had plummeted to less than $10 a barrel in 1986, down from $35 in 1981, and the major Dallas banks, as always, had loan portfolios heavy in the energy industry. With opportunities in energy lending severely limited, the banks naturally turned their attention to the thriving real estate developments. Their loan commitments to speculative developments had become top-heavy when the economic troubles of the mid-1980s showed up. First National Bank, now renamed InterFirst, began reporting massive losses. In December 1986 came sensational news, widely interpreted as the rescuing of a struggling bank by a prosperous one: the merger of InterFirst and RepublicBank, the city's two largest and most prominent bank holding companies. A suggestive press release declared that the union between InterFirst Corporation and RepublicBank created an organization, to be named FirstRepublic, that was "strong enough to withstand the current economic conditions in the Southwest." Mergers had been common in earlier years to both these banks, but none had approached the magnitude of this one. It created the nation's twelfth largest banking organization with assets of more than $35 billion.

Even more shocking news from this supposedly powerful new

entity came at the end of the first year when the 1987 financial report showed losses of $656.8 million, the largest ever recorded by a Texas bank holding company. The *Wall Street Journal* reported that the situation and related news reports caused a "siege mentality" to set in at bank headquarters. The bank chairman invited the *Dallas Times Herald*'s publisher and key editors to his office with a request that they hold back on their news coverage. Interrogations were conducted inside the bank to find sources of information being leaked to the press. One executive proposed lie detector tests for employees.

This bleak situation worsened as huge loans were defaulted and the foreclosed properties, largely vacant and worth nowhere near what had been thought, yielded little possibility of repayment. FirstRepublic losses in the first quarter of 1988 amounted to $1.5 billion, then $758 million in the second quarter. As the struggle to survive progressed, the Federal Deposit Insurance Corporation injected $1 billion into the bank to try to save it. Drastic cost-cutting measures were introduced with scores of employees terminated, including a reduction of the board of directors from thirty-three to sixteen. The dreaded denouement occurred on July 30, 1988. Federal regulators seized FirstRepublic and sold it on the same day to a North Carolina banking firm, NCNB (later Nations). At a cost to taxpayers of $3.6 billion, this was the most expensive bank failure in United States history.

To add to the humiliation, thirty-nine former officers and directors of FirstRepublic's Dallas operations, including some of Dallas' most elite citizens, were named in a $500 million suit filed by the Federal Deposit Insurance Corp. They and their counterparts in First Republic's Houston bank were cited for having "utterly abandoned" their responsibilities to oversee the banks and permitting inaccurate appraisals of collateral. Those named included former mayor Jack Evans, Ray L. Hunt (one of H.L.'s sons), former Dallas Cowboys' owner H.R. "Bum" Bright, Texas Instruments chief executive officer Jerry R. Junkins, and Robert H. Dedman. Damages from them of $200 million were sought, but in January 1993 the defendants and twenty-seven other defendants from the bank's Houston operation settled out of court for $23 million.

If the state's largest bank could fail, lesser banks had to be in trouble, and they were. While FirstRepublic's failure was the biggest, it was by no means isolated. Throughout the city others failed: Texas

National Bank, Security Bank, Northwest National Bank, Highland Park National Bank, Bank of Dallas, Merchants State Bank, Parkway Bank and Trust, Commerce Bank of Plano, Texas Bank of Plano, Oak Lawn Bank, Union Bank and Trust, and still others.

So did Robert L. Thornton's old Mercantile National, now MBank (with its holding company known as MCorp). The "momentum" bank and nineteen other MBanks were declared insolvent in March 1989 and sold to an outside group. (The omission of the space between corporate names had become trendy: Mercantile National Bank was changed to MBank, Republic National Bank became RepublicBank, First National had become InterFirst, and Raymond Nasher's shopping mall was NorthPark.) FDIC regulators claimedthat the directors and officers of MBank had been negligent in their policies, and in 1993 twenty-six bank directors and officers agreed to pay $39.2 million to settle the matter. Once again, some of the city's most prominent individuals were a party to the settlement, including former Dallas Cowboy quarterback Roger Staubach, Southland Corporation's Joe C. Thompson, Leo F. Corrigan Jr., and MBank's Gene Bishop.

Banks throughout the state collapsed, too—fifty in 1987 and 113 in 1988. The number of banks operating in Texas in the mid-1980s had shrunk by 1992 from about 2,000 to 1,200. Of the ten largest banking companies existing in the mid-1980s, all but one had been forced to merge with stronger out-of-state banks or had been rescued by the federal government. Independent banking in Texas and in Dallas virtually had ended.

Aside from the obvious economic losses and the humiliating aspects of the debacle after such a long period in which Dallas had taken pride in being the acknowledged banking center of the Southwest, the long-term impact of the failures was profound. Throughout the city's history bank executives had provided the most important leadership for virtually every civic endeavor. Now these banks were owned by companies located outside the state. Their interest in Dallas, aside from their existence as profit centers, was understandably far less intense than that of people such as Nathan Adams, R.L. Thornton, Fred Florence, Karl Hoblitzelle, James W. Aston, and Robert H. Stewart Jr.

DESPAIR IN DALLAS

Dallas' boom days were over. Jubilation turned to gloom; prosperity to depression. Joblessness skyrocketed. Bankruptcies reached record highs. Entire shopping centers were shut down. Condominiums along I-30 were bull-dozed. Construction virtually ceased. Property values—residential as well as commercial—declined. By the end of 1987 almost 40 million square feet of office space was vacant. This was more than all the office space in Boston's central business district. The city's tax base, so critical for providing revenues sufficient to fund municipal services, began what appeared to be a long-term decline. To prevent reductions in services, tax increases had to be enacted.

Downtown's future, an object of concern for many years, seemed even more uncertain. About one-third of all available downtown office space was vacant by 1991, compared to less than 10 percent in 1980. R.L. Thornton's once-proud Mercantile Bank—both the office building and the skyscraper—were empty. RepublicBank's 36-story building and the adjoining 50-story tower were almost totally vacant. The drop in value of the once-proud and still shiny Republic buildings was dramatic and frightening. In 1989 the asking price for the two buildings was somewhere between $50 million and $75 million; when the buildings were sold to a Houston man in late 1992 the sales price was about $8 million. Small retail stores were closed and boarded up. Many of the empty, deteriorating buildings were simply demolished by the owners to save money, leaving ugly, littered open spaces. (In 1992 a record 913 buildings were demolished in the city, more than twice the number of 1991.)

Spectacular though the huge new skyscrapers were, they were too dominating, occupying entire blocks with no space for shops and cafes to entice a passer-by to linger. In fact, many pedestrians had been removed by design from the downtown streets through a series of futuristic skybridges above the streets and pedestrian tunnels beneath the streets. Second thoughts emerged about the advisability of that. The park plaza in front of city hall—built with such high hopes as a setting for throngs of happy people—was usually devoid of signs of life. It was merely a gigantic empty space.

William Whyte, in his 1988 book, *City: Rediscovering the Center*, wrote that the American city that had done the most to kill off its streets was Dallas: "One gathers that the proponents [of the tunnel and skybridge system] would be delighted if pedestrians could be eliminated from the streets altogether." This was an unhappy legacy of the high-minded dreams of planners Vincent Ponte and Warren Travers, who had sought to streamline downtown Dallas and had influenced Jonsson in rejecting Clint Murchison's plan for a downtown football stadium. All the department stores had forsaken downtown for suburban malls, leaving only Neiman-Marcus as a major retail outlet. Not a single movie theater could be found in the downtown area that in the 1950s boasted of more than a dozen on Elm Street's great white way. The only downtown apartments were the high-rise Manor House's 252 units. Homeless people wandered downtown side streets, asking pedestrians they managed to find for handouts, sleeping in random unoccupied spaces or homeless shelters, and using the public library as a "headquarters." What if anything should be done about these homeless people was a practical and moral dilemma in Dallas and in cities across the nation.

The dramatic, uncontrolled growth of Far North Dallas and adjacent suburbs not only had resulted in over-building with widescale vacancies, it had generated monumental traffic jams miles away from the center of town. Commercial development there had outpaced the city's ability to accommodate it as the council had granted zoning request after zoning request. Tens of millions of dollars then had to be spent to widen streets and provide city services. David Dillon, architecture critic of the *News*, summarized the situation: "Not even the most unrepentant free-enterprisers could ignore the chaos in far North Dallas. The area was strangling in a noose of its own devising, abetted by a city council that over the years has caved in to developer requests for major zoning variants." It was, Dillon believed, "the most dramatic example of the consequences of irrational development."

Another legacy of the building boom was more surprising. Many of the handsome, modernistic structures were poorly constructed. By the early 1990s problems were reported to be common: leaks, improperly fitted outside panels, and glitches in the heating, ventilating, and cooling systems. Sloppy workmanship by improperly supervised crews and penny-pinching developers were cited as the root of the problems.

Two bright spots on opposite sides of downtown did give

encouragement. The West End area behind the old School Book Depository had developed as a tourist attraction where trendy restaurants, bars, and nightclubs operated out of old warehouse buildings. On the east end of town a similar thing had happened along Deep Ellum. Where Blind Lemon Jefferson and Huddy Ledbetter once played and sang, now could be found avant-garde night spots and art galleries. First, the area's uniqueness had attracted "skinheads" decked in all-black clothing and Doc Marten boots, but by the late 1980s the territory had been claimed by less bizarre youths and by ritzy and inquisitive folks from North Dallas.

THE FIRST WOMAN MAYOR, ANNETTE STRAUSS

When first elected to the city council in 1983, Annette Greenfield Strauss was the eleventh woman to hold that office since Mrs. Carr P. Collins first broke the gender gap twenty-six years earlier. After serving two terms in her at-large seat, Strauss declared ready for the mayor's office after Starke Taylor said in 1987 that he would not seek a third term.

She was one of nine candidates in a wide-open race reminiscent of 1971 when seven men sought to succeed Erik Jonsson. Four of the nine were credible candidates with significant chances at winning. They had plenty of money to run good campaigns. All four were millionaires; all four lived in North Dallas. Combined, they were to spend $3 million in the general election. Besides Strauss, the main candidates included Fred Meyer, former chairman of the Dallas County Republican Party and a long-time executive with Tyler Corp.; Jim Collins, who had served as a Republican Congressman from North Dallas for sixteen years after a career in the family insurance business; and Jim Buerger, publisher of a travel magazine who promised to spend what was necessary to begin his public career at the top in the mayor's office.

Among the traditional business leadership, Meyer was the favored candidate, holding the endorsements of four former mayors: Erik Jonsson, Robert Folsom, Starke Taylor, and Wes Wise. Strauss, though, was hardly an outsider in establishment circles. She had years of experience as a civic worker, especially as a fund-raiser for arts organizations, and she had served faithfully on many of the city's boards and commissions. Her husband Theodore was a wealthy investment banker; her brother-in-law was Robert Strauss, former chairman of the Democratic National Party and prominent Dallas attorney. Jim Collins, though a staunch conservative, was not tied as closely to the business community as was Meyer, and at the age of seventy he was a newcomer to municipal politics. Buerger, virtually unknown until announcing for office, was the only one of the four major candidates who favored changing the charter to require direct election of all council members. His lack of experience in public affairs was a handicap, but he was an engaging, aggressive campaigner.

Strauss finished first in the general election, but did not win a majority. Placing second and joining her in the runoff election was Meyer. There were no dramatic differences for voters other than a choice between a traditional, business-minded leader and a woman whose experience was largely in council service and volunteer work. From another perspective, though none would say it, the election basically was between a Republican and a Democrat.

Voters chose Strauss by a 56 to 44 percent margin, the city's minority precincts giving her overwhelming majorities. Meyer carried only precincts that were heavily Republican.

Dallas' first woman mayor was sixty-three years of age, a resident of Preston Hollow, a grandmother, and the holder of a bachelor's degree from the University of Texas and a master's degree from Columbia University. Not until recent years had she held a paying job, having parlayed her extensive civic involvement into a vice presidency at the city's largest advertising and public relations firm. On the night of her election triumph her husband described her as "the loveliest, strongest, brightest and toughest steel butterfly I have ever met in my life."

Of those characteristics, the one Strauss most needed during her two terms as mayor was "steel." Her task was not easy. With the city's economic boom ended, painful cuts in the budget at city hall were essential. Yet, public sentiment concerning crime demanded greater expenditures for police operations and salaries. Race relations were more tense than ever, centering around the continuing complaints that police officers were "trigger-happy" when dealing with minority suspects. A second key issue increasing racial tension was the growing determination of minorities to create a redistricting plan that would guarantee the election of more African-Americans and Hispanics to city council.

Debate over these two issues dominated Strauss' tenure as mayor. Further deteriorations in police-minority relationships nearly brought the city to a boiling point. Because of so many questions raised, Michigan Congressman John Conyers brought a House subcommittee to Dallas for a hearing. Testimony given by a large number of officials and citizens demonstrated wide disparities in their assessments of the situation. The hearings were resented by many as an undue interference in local affairs by a Congressman from Michigan. In fact, the hearings contributed little if anything toward easing the situation, and perhaps worsened it.

With tensions continuing to grow, Strauss appointed a widely diversified, eighty-eight member blue-ribbon committee to recommend ways to promote racial harmony. When the "Dallas Together" committee reported its findings in January 1989 it identified five broad areas for easing racial tension, notably the need for enhanced opportunities for political participation by minorities. In this regard, the committee concluded that the 8-3 system did not provide sufficient opportunity for all citizens to be fairly represented at city hall.

To address this specific concern Strauss appointed another body, the Charter Review Commission, a fourteen-member group chaired by attorney Ray Hutchison and including two minority vice chairmen, Joe May, a Hispanic, and Pettis Norman, an African-American, as well as six other minority members. There followed months of anguished, lengthy deliberations to devise a system for electing council candidates in a way to assure greater minority representation. Finally, a unique 10-4-1 plan was endorsed which would have ten council members elected from single-member districts, four from larger quadrants of the city, and the mayor city-wide. The committee was not unanimous in its recommendation. Some minority participants, such as René Martinez and Pettis Norman, favored the plan; however, four minority members, including Al Lipscomb and Diane Ragsdale, opposed it as insufficient. Lipscomb denounced it as something that must have come "from the North Dallas Chamber of Commerce," and Ragsdale called it "elitist." They preferred a plan under which all candidates would be elected from specific districts.

Angry, name-calling debates ensued in the newspapers and over the airwaves. Positions hardened, alternate plans were proposed and discussed, and hostilities had grown rather than diminished when the city council met in June 1989 to vote on whether or not to submit the 10-4-1 plan to the electorate as a charter change. Two dozen adamant opponents of the plan, both minorities and whites, took a standing position in the front of the seated council, refused to leave, locked arms, and sang "We Shall Overcome" as extra police officers stood by. In this dramatic setting the council defied the protesters and voted 7-4 to submit the 10-4-1 plan to voters. After a bitter campaign, two-thirds of Dallas voters approved the plan on August 12, 1989. Sharp divisions along racial lines were apparent: some 85 percent of white voters favored the plan, but 95 percent of African-Americans and more than 70 percent of the city's Hispanic voters were against it.

Meanwhile, a federal lawsuit that had been filed in January 1988 was destined to render moot all the divisive furor. Two African-American men, Marvin Crenshaw and Roy Williams, contended in their suit that the city's 8-3 scheme was unconstitutional. Unsuccessful themselves as past council candidates, they argued that the system diluted the voting strength of Dallas' minorities, who now constituted about one-half of the city's population but who had never held more than three of the eleven council positions.

Crenshaw and Williams had similar backgrounds. Both were U.S. Army veterans who had served three-year stints in W. Germany, both had been active in the civil rights and anti-Vietnam war demonstrations of the 1960s, and both were regular city council speakers who loudly decried racism. Crenshaw, a former member of the Dallas chapter of the Black Panthers, had campaigned without success four different times since 1983 for election to the council.

Williams, too, had failed in his bid to win election to the council in 1987. He had been spurred to activist appearances at city hall after a Dallas police officer shot a black man accused of being a drug dealer and a controversy arose. The incident led Williams to attend one of Elsie Faye Heggins' lively South Dallas forums, where he encountered Crenshaw and other leading black activists: Lipscomb, Ragsdale, John Wiley Price, Peter Johnson, J.B. Jackson, Dallas Jackson, and Heggins. Williams and Crenshaw were named to an impromptu citizens' committee created to investigate police brutality. In the months and years to follow, Williams joined Crenshaw in speaking to the city council, in participating in public demonstrations, and in pushing especially for a stronger police review board, a proposal vehemently opposed by police officers.

In March 1990 U.S. District Judge Jerry Buchmeyer, responding to the Williams-Crenshaw suit, ruled that the 8-3 system was unconstitutional. While he did not rule specifically on the pending 10-4-1 plan, his critical comments about it seemed to jeopardize its ultimate chances of being upheld. City council, seeking to settle the Williams-Crenshaw suit, now placed a 14-1 plan with single-member districts on the ballot in a December election. In one of the highest turnouts ever for a city charter referendum, voters rejected the 14-1 plan by just 372 votes. This popular vote had no impact on Judge Buchmeyer, who three months later ordered a council election to be held May 4 under the 14-1 plan. The City of Dallas appealed this decision, and submitted the 10-4-1 plan to the U.S. Justice Department for approval. The suddenly revived local chapter of the SCLC urged a nation-wide boycott of Dallas by conventions, businesses, and tourists until the city halted its appeal. In May the Justice Department agreed with Buchmeyer that the 10-4-1 plan was inadequate. At this point, the City of Dallas yielded, having spent more than $1 million in legal fees to support the 10-4-1 plan, and agreed in a settlement with Williams and Crenshaw to adopt the 14-1 plan.

Even after all this, though, the hardest days lay ahead. What would be the boundaries of the new districts? How could they be drawn to accommodate an appropriate mix of African-Americans, Hispanics, and whites? How would Oak Cliff be divided? Pleasant Grove? Would there be five predominantly African-American districts or six? Two or three Hispanic districts? Which council districts would suffer the most dismemberment as the entire map was dissected into fourteen rather than ten sections? As plans shifted and pressures mounted, council members' tempers grew shorter. Charges of racism, of double-crossing, and back-stabbing were common.

When finally agreed upon, the borders of the fourteen new districts zig-zagged up and down city streets, sometimes in narrow corridors, making odd, surprising turns as they located appropriate racial mixes instead of traditional communities of interest. District 5, for example, was a crooked east-west pipeline extending from Red Bird Airport in deep Oak Cliff to the eastern city limits at Mesquite. Each new district, however contorted in boundaries, held carefully calculated majorities of either whites, African-Americans, or Mexican-

Americans so that in theory the voters in them should send to city council seven whites, five African-Americans, and two Mexican-Americans.

18

Coming Apart in the '90s

[Dallas has] a bad case of such urban ills as crime and poor race relations.

–Fortune Magazine, 1992

A Babel of Voices

On New Year's Day, 1993, outside a main entrance to Fair Park where thousands of visitors were converging to see the Cotton Bowl football classic between Texas A&M and Notre Dame, County Commissioner John Wiley Price led more than eighty supporters in a protest demonstration lasting three hours. Their announced purpose was to highlight racism in the city. "Welcome to Dallas. This is just like Johannesburg," Price shouted over and over. "Dallas is the most racist city in the country." On his "liberation radio" show that evening he called one white police official a "racist cracker" and an elected black leader a "pointy-headed Negro."

Surprising though such actions may have seemed for one of the county's highest elected officials, residents were well accustomed to the demagogic commissioner's statements and actions. Indeed, the provocative subject of race relations dominated public discussion in

Dallas in the early 1990s, even more so than in previous years.

Some elected officials—of whom Price was the most flamboyant and outspoken—seemed committed to the difficult task of eradicating every last trace of racial prejudice from the city. This determination carried with it a cost, for the demonstrations and persistent charges of racism created a backlash among many white residents who believed many of the claims to be exaggerated and self-serving. Police Chief William Rathburn, whose resignation in 1993 came in the midst of aggressive, African-American demonstrations against his administration, said that he had never worked in a city where people so quickly ascribed racial motives to every action. Certainly the preooccupation with such a volatile subject meant that other matters of pressing concern were either neglected or unduly complicated, and it caused *Fortune* magazine in 1992 to eliminate Dallas from its "top-ten" list of the best cities in the nation for doing business. The magazine cited "poor race relations" as the reason.

That racism would continue as the foremost topic of public debate in the 1990s was unexpected, for considerable progress had been made in Dallas and in the nation as well in expanding opportunities for minorities. The preoccupation with the issue--both in Dallas and the nation--seemed to be a reflection of a common historical phenomenon so frequently accompanying the liberation of oppressed people: a revolution of rising expectancies. Progress escalated hope for more progress, and more progress brought anticipation of greater progress, and greater progress brought expectations of ultimate progress. The inevitable result, no matter how much had been accomplished in the process, was one of disappointment and frustration. This, it seemed, was the situation in Dallas.

The adoption of the 14-1 plan especially was a resounding victory for minorities who had believed an enlarged city council with all districts single-member to be critical to their aspirations. The first council elected under this plan, the most ethnically diverse in the city's history, devoted much of its energies toward redressing past injustices. Despite all the clamor to the contrary, Dallas' record in expanding opportunities for minorities was one that well could have been extolled rather than condemned. A new city manager chosen in 1993 was an African-American, the second member of his race to hold that position in recent years. Over the past several years the

Police Department had achieved the second-best record in the nation in its size category for increasing the percentage of minority officers on the force. In 1988, 71.8 percent of new police officers hired were African-American and 6.7 percent were Hispanic. By September 1993 about 30 percent of the 2,800-plus member force were minorities. Beginning in 1990 minorities made up more than half of every new police recruiting class. By 1993 the interim police chief was a youthful African-American who a few years earlier had skipped two promotion grades as part of an affirmative action plan. DART's interim executive director was a black man. Five of the nine DISD trustees responsible for overseeing the education of the city's youth were minorities, including the school board president. The school superintendent (he resigned in 1993) was an African-American, and a majority of school administrators were members of minority groups. The city attorney and the director of public housing were African-Americans. The executive director of the Dallas-Fort Worth International Airport, Vernell Sturns, was an African-American. Six of Dallas County's thirty-seven state district judges, or 16 percent, were minorities. Forty-five percent of the sheriff's employees; 43 percent of the district clerk's employees; and 65 percent of the county juvenile office's employees were minorities. Average citizens of the city's various ethnic groups worked together, dined in restaurants together, attended cultural and athletic events together, and in some cases—despite largely segregated housing patterns—lived together. In these patterns of daily living there appeared to be few significant problems; yet, none of this was acknowledged in public discourse. The prideful boosterism that had characterized Dallas for so many decades had been drowned out by the deafening protests about what was wrong with the city.

THE 14-1 PLAN

Judge Jerry Buchmeyer's ruling that the council be enlarged and that all candidates be elected from single-member districts was the final triumph for those who for so many years stood on the outside while an elite, close-knit group of businessmen dominated city affairs. His judicial order was, in effect, an extension of Federal Judge Eldon Mahon's 1975 decision requiring eight of the eleven council members to be elected by voters in single-member districts. From 1931 until Mahon's ruling the charter had required all council candidates to be elected at-large by voters from all over town. Once in office they were presumed to vote in accordance with what was best for the overall city rather than as champions of a particular neighborhood, group, or special interest.

While the Dallas establishment's admittedly exclusive way of doing things had brought civic accomplishments that an assortment of independents likely could not have, critics always had argued that for a truly representative council, members must be elected from specific neighborhoods. Buchmeyer's 14-1 plan accepted that proposition and then went beyond it. His plan implicitly if not expressly required that council representation be based on ethnicity. It held that a white person was most likely to vote for a white person, that an African-American would vote for an African-American, and a Hispanic would favor a Hispanic. Moreover, it held—and Buchmeyer cited abundant local political history in his ruling to support his position—that constituents could be represented adequately *only* by persons of their own color. Therefore, new districts somehow must be drawn (actually "gerrymandered," although no one used that negative term) to guarantee racial or ethnic majorities. The 14-1 plan was pragmatic, even cynical, a plan far removed from idealistic dreams of representation conceived of by the nation's founding fathers. It was based instead on the pressures of multi-cultural, multi-ethnic urban life. Its ultimate effect, it seemed likely, would be to reinforce segregated residential patterns because of ethnic classification of neighborhoods.

The first 14-1 council was a remarkably diverse assortment of individuals. With the day of organized city political parties long since passed, all of them were independents. Members ranged from the conservative Republican mayor to an outspoken Mexican-American activist (who once had been slugged by the incumbent Mexican-American councilman when he accused him of being an establishment lackey) to a white-haired North Dallas banker to a matronly black woman from West Dallas to a bearded white liberal who had presided over a city-wide homeowners' group.

In all but one district, the plan for ethnic representation had followed theory. The exception was in the 4th District, where white liberal Larry Duncan, who had been one of those who two years earlier stood with arms locked at city hall and sang "We Shall Overcome" to protest the 10-4-1 plan, defeated African-American Marvin Crenshaw. (Roy Williams, who with Crenshaw was largely responsible for the 14-1 plan, also was defeated in his bids for office.)

Thus, the council which took office in December 1991 consisted of nine whites, four blacks and two Hispanics. Six of the members (five of them white) had been re-elected as incumbents. While ideological definitions could not be precise, liberals held a numerical advantage. Without a doubt the council was the most liberal group ever to sit as a policy-making body over City of Dallas affairs.

The council assumed office at a time when the city's overall situation continued to be unusually challenging. The discouraging economic and social conditions of the late 1980s had continued to deteriorate. By the spring of 1993 downtown Dallas had the highest rate of office vacancy in the nation--35.4 percent. Much-maligned Detroit, by contrast, had a downtown office vacancy rate of 22.6 percent. Between 1980 and 1990 the percentage of Dallas residents living in poverty increased from 14 to 18 percent. Construction was virtually nil; municipal services had been curtailed; the amount of violent, random crime was frightening and seemingly uncontrollable; many of the wayward youth had aligned into gangs in which violence was accepted or encouraged behavior; metal detectors had been introduced to keep firearms out of the public schools; corporate relocations were going to the suburbs instead of the central city; and Dallas had lost to suburban cities in both its efforts to win a class-one pari-mutuel horse-racing facility and to be the site of a new baseball stadium for the Texas Rangers.

Perhaps the most vexing long-term result of this distressing picture was one that neither elicited emotions nor drew huge crowds to council sessions: a dwindling tax base in the face of growing demand for expensive social services. By 1993 the city's tax base had declined for five consecutive years, requiring higher property taxes to generate enough money for municipal operations. In the fiscal year 1986-87 the tax rate was 50 cents per $100 assessed property value; the tax base, $51.1 billion. By 1992-93 the rate had climbed to more than 67 cents; the tax base had fallen to $43.2 billion. Even the higher taxes were not enough to maintain previous standards, though, and budgets for all city departments other than police were being reduced. This trend was disturbing. No longer was the tax base primed through the relocation of new businesses. More than a decade had passed since a major company had moved to Dallas.

A particular problem was the dearth of residential housing downtown and in the immediate area. In the 1960s about 70,000 people had lived within a two-mile radius of city hall. By the early 1990s that number had declined to about 30,000.

The mayor, Steve Bartlett, was—as had been the case for so many past mayors—a conservative. He had sat on the council between 1977 and 1981 before being elected to Congress as a Republican, representing a district which included the northern part of the city. After ten years in Washington he yielded his Congressional seat to campaign for and win the mayor's office, a position that paid him just $50 per meeting. The politicization of city hall could be seen in the fact that Bartlett felt it necessary to hire three political advisers, each of whom he paid more than he earned himself as mayor. These three served Bartlett in addition to a regular office staff provided at taxpayers' expense. Two of his advisers were Republican Party operatives; the third was a black man whom Bartlett also appointed to the Park and Recreation Board.

Chosen mayor pro tem was the venerable Al Lipscomb, in his fourth and last term as a councilman and still aggressively pursuing any manifestations of racism he perceived. (This was his last term because the 14-1 court settlement had limited incumbent council members to four terms.) The deputy mayor pro tem, attorney Chris Luna, was a newcomer, elected from a district designated as Hispanic.

As dictated by the council-manager plan, the administrative head of the City of Dallas was not the mayor but the $143,000-a-year city manager, Jan Hart, who oversaw some 12,000 city employees and a $1.2 billion annual budget. While the mayor was the titular head of the city, Bartlett held no administrative authority other than what he could finesse away from the city manager. Given the political aspects of the mayor's job, that temptation was ever-present unless he foreswore further ambitions in elective office, which he did not do. Tensions between the mayor and city manager thus arose, as they did between the mayor and the council, and in the summer of 1993 reached headline status. The mayor's chances in such endeavors had been improved by a new provision that gave him a four-year term instead of a two-year one. Yet, even before the new council's first term was over, members who were upset with Bartlett were seeking to reduce the mayor's term of office once again to two years. Just how long the council-manager plan could survive under such tensions was uncertain. At least three and probably more council members were ready to abandon it in early 1993, expressing grave concerns because under the council-manager plan they were restrained from interacting directly with city departments in behalf of their constituents. Even the conservative mayor was openly critical of the system. Less than half of the city's residents favored the council-manager system, according to a *Dallas Morning News* poll.

The council's own restiveness with the council-manager plan could be seen as well in its never-ending push to be paid a regular salary. Even though voters in the spring of 1993 rejected the idea for a fifth time since 1973, the notion still would not die. The sentiments favoring salaries were diametrically opposed to the theory of the council-manager plan, which was to eliminate political considerations from decisions at city hall.

Yet, for two consecutive years the magazine *Financial World* declared Dallas to be the best-managed city in the nation for handling its resources, a direct compliment to the city manager and her staff. In both 1992 and 1993 the publication placed Dallas at the top of its list, declaring it to be a "model of effective city management in the areas of accounting, budgeting, care for infrastructure, and evaluation of programs."

As the council-manager plan lost support from both the council and citizens, as the notion of civic duty began to be replaced by a sense of obligation to a specific group of constituents, and as election to the council came to be accepted as a step in a political career, so did commitment to another former ideal rapidly fade away. This was the concept of making decisions based on "what was good for Dallas," admittedly a hazy concept but one that was not without value. It had lost credibility because critics had demeaned it thoroughly for more than two decades as a self-serving tool by those wielding exclusive power. Instead, the *modus operandi* now had become—and none disputed it—"What's good for my constituents?"

DEMONSTRATIONS HEIGHTEN TENSION

John Wiley Price had graduated from high school in nearby

Forney, then began working in Dallas as a salesman at Sanger-Harris. He soon enrolled in computer programming classes at downtown El Centro Community College, got his first taste of politicking by winning election to the student council, and then took a series of jobs at the courthouse, winding up as a clerk to Justice of the Peace Cleo Steele, himself an African-American. From the courthouse Price involved himself thoroughly in behind-the-scenes politics, working into a leadership position of the Progressive Voters League. Upon election as the commissioner for the Third District, Price established a reputation as a conscientious official who worked well with his fellow commissioners in governing Dallas County, although he admittedly was far flashier in his expensive wardrobe and in the exotic Ferrari and Lotus sports cars he drove. His work earned him re-election to a second four-year term as commissioner.

Beginning in March 1990 he took a far more activist turn, consistently courting controversy through a series of headline-making episodes. In the first incident he and a group of supporters—under the gaze of television cameras and reporters—whitewashed a number of privately owned billboards advertising liquor and cigarettes in the Fair Park area, products which they believed were harmful to the community's well-being. Charged and soon convicted for damaging private property, Price was placed on probation for six months. Next he began a regular series of provocative demonstrations at two television stations, WFAA and the Dallas office of KXAS, accusing both of racist policies in hiring and promoting employees. In December 1990 at the KXAS building parking lot he attempted to prevent a woman from driving her van across his picket line by breaking her windshield wipers. For this he was sentenced to 75 days in jail and fined $1,000, a judgment upheld by the Texas Court of Criminal Appeals. In the fall of 1993 he served his sentence in the county jail, being released after twenty-four days for "good time." Within the span of an hour on August 1, 1991, he was involved in two altercations in separate incidents. In the first one, he tackled and struck a jogger who attempted to pass through his picket line outside WFAA. Immediately afterwards and just a few blocks away, Price got into a fight with a carpenter working outside a courthouse building and broke the man's ankle. In the first incident he pled no contest, was found guilty of assault, and was fined $500. As to the confrontation with the carpenter, he was acquitted in a trial. In March 1992 he was charged with attacking a KXAS cameraman and damaging his equipment. In October 1992 he was charged with assault on a police officer during a demonstration outside a police substation.

His quick temper also involved him in several confrontations with individuals, including accusations that he struck a justice of the peace, threatened a black county judge, shot a man in an altercation over a woman, pulled an automatic weapon on an off-duty police officer, and raped one of his female office workers. Despite mounting criticisms, Price remained undaunted in his behavior and pronouncements concerning the continued "oppression" of African-Americans in Dallas and the institutional "violence" being perpetrated against them. As his forum he used not only the influence of his elected office, but also hosted a "talk" radio show each evening on a black-oriented station. (The producer of his show was head of the Dallas' New Black Panther Party, a militant organization whose members spoke of the need for "urban guerrilla warfare.") Price became without question the most controversial figure ever to hold elected office in Dallas, far surpassing Heggins, Lipscomb, and Ragsdale. (Ragsdale no longer held office. She had been defeated by a moderate black woman, Charlotte Mayes, who then withstood a recall election inspired by Ragsdale and beat her a second time.)

In all the complaints against him, Price inevitably proclaimed that he was guiltless, that charges and accusations against him were inspired by racism, and that he and all African-Americans were themselves the victims. His trial for the alleged assault of the carpenter followed shortly after riots in Los Angeles when police officers were acquitted of charges that they had beaten motorist Rodney King. It was widely feared that if the jury found Price guilty, rioting might erupt in Dallas.

While Price was a figure who generated unusual antagonism in the white community because of his strident, exaggerated behavior, he undoubtedly had developed a core of largely African-American followers who believed his actions were fully warranted. Moreover, by winning his second four-year term as the county commissioner well after he had become so controversial, he seemed to prove that a majority of voters in his district favored his actions.

Demonstrations against television stations were superseded and escalated by Price's next target—the Dallas Police Department. In these demonstrations, beginning in September 1992 and continuing into 1994, Price and his group of activists, whom he dubbed the "Warriors," were joined by members of the predominantly black Texas Peace Officers Association (TOPA).

In light of so much evidence documenting special efforts to achieve racial balances in police department personnel, the hostile demonstrations puzzled many. A study at the University of Nebraska showed that between 1983 and 1992, among the nation's forty-one largest cities with more than 10 percent black population, Dallas ranked second in increasing its percentage of minority officers. The percentage more than doubled from just under 13 percent to 28 percent. (One out of five officers now was African-American; one in twelve Hispanic.) To achieve this percentage improvement in such a larg department, new hires were being weighted heavily in favor of minorities. In 1992 a total of 60 percent of all officers hired were minorities--34 percent black and 26 percent Hispanic. (As of September 1993 African-Americans held 20 percent of police administration jobs, and Hispanics 12 percent, or one-third of all executive positions. This was up from 8 percent in 1988. The percentage of sergeants, lieutenants, and captains who were minorities had climbed in the same period from 7.5 to 18.5 percent. Minorities holding the rank of senior corporal rose from 21.9 percent in 1988 to 32.1 percent in 1993.)

Yet, protestors' complaints centered around alleged discrimination in hiring, promoting, and administering discipline. The president of the officers' group, Senior Corporal James Allen, presenting Police Chief Rathburn with thirteen demands, including a moratorium on promoting white officers, threatened to lead a national boycott against Dallas unless his group's demands were met. Rathburn accused the organization of being "dishonest" and misleading. "We cannot allow a few employees to drive this department," he said.

Racial tensions were acknowledged to be rising within the department itself as demonstrators began to rotate their Saturday picketing from one police substation to the next. The assistant chief at the Southeast sub-station was transferred in an effort to achieve harmony there. Those marching with picket signs, including many off-duty TOPA members, were predominantly African-Americans, a contrast to the presence of many whites in the demonstrations of the 1960s and 1970s. The nastiness of the mood was suggested at one substation demonstration when John Wiley Price wore a placard asserting that Monica Smith, the female Hispanic president of the Dallas Police Association, and other officers also identified by name were "life members" of the Ku Klux Klan.

Tensions rose as officers on duty attempted Saturday after Saturday to maintain crowd control and to keep the streets cleared for traffic. When demonstrators adopted a policy of deliberately marching slowly to disrupt traffic, police began blocking off streets adjacent to the substations—even such major throughfares as Northwest Highway—to avoid confrontations. This infuriated many inconvenienced motorists. It caused some council members to complain. As a further accommodation the city painted a crosswalk across Northwest Highway at the spot used by the demonstrators. When on October 3, 1992, police arrested a demonstrator for allegedly striking an officer, Rathburn feared that it might cause a riot. To avoid that possibility, he ordered the arrested demonstrator released. This infuriated many officers who complained of a double standard for the demonstrators.

The following weekend an even greater riot-threatening situation occurred when Dallas City Councilman Don Hicks, a black attorney in his first term of office, defied officers' orders not to cross their line at the Southeast Dallas station, and then resisted vigorously when they arrested him for doing it. Television cameras recorded the unexpected confrontation as several officers brought the city councilman to the ground and handcuffed him. Afterwards, he was briefly jailed. Incensed because he argued that he had been at the scene as an official observer not subject to police orders, Hicks announced his intention to ask the U.S. Justice Department to investigate, contending that racist police had targeted him because he was an elected black official.

Many African-Americans quickly rose to support Hicks. So volatile was their mood that an emergency five-hour city council session was held. Hundreds of African-Americans protested bitterly at the meeting, not just about Hicks' arrest but about alleged routine racial discrimination by police. Threats of violence punctuated the raucous meeting and forced Mayor Bartlett at one point to call a fifteen-minute recess.

With charges still pending against Hicks, it appeared that any new untoward incident might spark rioting. At this point the Dallas Citizens' Council—reduced to a new role as peacemaker instead of power-broker—negotiated behind-the-scenes and defused the situation. Rathburn withdrew charges against Hicks and apologized for arresting him; Hicks agreed to cancel his request for an investigation by the Department of Justice.

Price expressed embarrassment that Hicks could be bought off so easily with the chief's apology, and he continued every Saturday to lead demonstrations at police substations. The possibility that they could erupt into violence seemed ever-present, a possibility that escalated in late February when white counter-demonstrators began marching.

In April 1993 the city council approved settlements in two lawsuits alleging police department discrimination against African-American officers. In one of them nineteen black officers maintained that they had been illegally passed over for promotion in favor of whites. In the other, forty-eight white officers maintained that they had been illegally passed over for promotion by minorities. A month later Federal Judge Barefoot Sanders dismissed a lawsuit filed by six African-American officers who claimed that the city had discriminated against them because of their race. Sanders cited a lack of evidence to back up such claims.

A shocking event in early February 1993 seemed to confirm the worst fears that racial violence lay just beneath the city's surface. It was unexpectedly associated with what had been planned as a triumphant day for the city—a downtown ticker-tape parade to honor the Dallas Cowboys football team after its resounding victory in the 1993 Super Bowl game. A mid-day crowd estimated at 300,000 to 400,000, many of them truant schoolchildren, swarmed the streets to cheer their heroes. So great were the numbers that all order was lost. The parade's end was marked by a series of random and brutal attacks by groups of young, predominantly black male youths against innocent, individual whites and Hispanics in full view of crowds of people. Television cameras recorded shocking scenes of these youths singling out victims, more than half of them female, chasing, hitting, and knocking them down, then kicking them. Thousands of viewers saw young females bleeding from their faces, saw a television cameramen beaten to a semi-conscious state, and even saw homeless persons being pummeled unmercifully. Local hospitals treated twenty-one people for injuries; an identical number of persons reported minor injuries. Of the forty-two victims, all but seven were either white or Hispanic. Suspects in thirty-two of thirty-three of the crimes were listed as African-Americans.

As it had happened, Police Chief Rathburn was in Atlanta, Georgia, on the day of the parade, discussing the new job he planned to assume there. Reeling from constant pressures after just two years as chief and failing in his effort to get a contract from the city manager guaranteeing his job security, Rathburn had submitted his resignation several days before the parade riots occurred. He had been the city's third chief since 1988; each had departed amidst controversy related to race-related problems. In June 1993 City Manager Hart named an officer from Phoenix, Arizona, Bennie R. Click, to be the the new chief. While under the city charter the choice was hers alone to make, Councilman Hicks made unprecedented attacks against Hart during a regular council session, calling her a "queen" member of an elitist conspiracy like the one in Nazi Germany. Hicks said the choice of Click amounted to racism. Others on the council expressed concern in far milder terms that she had not consulted them adequately. Disgruntled council members hurriedly held a job-performance review for the city manager, but she emerged from it with her job intact if less secure. The council appeared ready to abandon the city charter so that they could have a direct hand in hiring officials who reported not to them but to the city manager, a move that inevitably would inject politics into the process.

By October 1993 Hart had had enough. She resigned to become an investment banker. The council quickly hired John Ware, the African-American first assistant city manager, to succeed her.

During Rathburn's tenure, major crime in the city had declined. More significantly, he had continued the work of his recent predecessors, Billy Prince and Mack Vines, in bringing to the department large numbers of minority officers. Yet, this was not enough for the protestors. Indeed, the progress still fell short of the city's ambitious five-year plan to have personnel in both the police and fire departments match the city's ethnic makeup. Each Saturday protestors marched at police sub-stations, and then began to focus on the Northeast Dallas facility on Northwest Highway. Their marches generated much debate over the right of the protestors to demonstrate versus the rights of drivers to pass unrestricted.

RACIAL ISSUES DOMINATE COUNCIL

Hicks' aggressive, flamboyant championing of minority rights followed an early lesson he learned in his first days as a councilman. Eager to bring jobs to the depressed southern part of the city, he had joined with Mayor Bartlett in seeking for the area a new Texas Department of Corrections facility--a prison. As far as near-by residents were concerned, though, bringing in convicts in striped clothing would not enhance their neighborhood despite any jobs it might create. Comments that a southern Dallas facility would be convenient for family visits for the many prisoners from that area only exacerbated the situation because of perceived implications of racism. Hicks and Bartlett did not realize the full extent of the residents' anger, however, until they held a community meeting. Some 700 protestors loudly accused Hicks of selling out to the white power structure by trying to place an undesirable facility in their black neighborhood. Hicks quickly dropped the project, as did the mayor. No more was heard of it.

The strong feelings generated by the proposed prison facility were duplicated soon afterwards by another emotional session at city hall concerning the Police Department rule against hiring gays and lesbians. Hundreds of people packed the council chambers to urge that the policy be dropped. The meeting lasted until past midnight as council members heard scores of speakers. Finally, though, the council decided to uphold the hiring ban.

It soon became apparent that Hicks and the new council would concentrate their efforts not on economic development but on perceived inequities towards minorities. Almost every issue before the council was considered in that regard. When a special presentation was made on ways to encourage inner-city residential housing, a critical need, the first question asked by a council member was why minorities had not been included on the list of cited housing experts.

A major effort to increase the participation of minority businesses in municipal work, one championed especially by Hicks, came through the council's adoption of a policy to give minority-owned firms a greater percentage of city contracts. The goal for awarding contracts to minority-owned businesses became 32 percent—23 percent for firms owned by blacks and 9 percent for firms owned by Hispanics. These figures equaled the percentage of available minority contractors in Dallas. While there had been specific goals for minority contracting since the late 1970s, these new goals were much higher.

They were also more difficult to achieve, as controversy surrounding a project to renovate the Cotton Bowl for the 1994 World Cup soccer games demonstrated. In March 1992 Dallas had won the distinction of being named one of nine host cities for the games, the world's largest sporting event. It was anticipated that the soccer matches would generate $200 million in spending by visitors to Dallas. But extensive renovations were needed to make the Cotton Bowl suitable for the six scheduled games, and a multi-million contract was awarded Dal-Mac Construction Co. of Richardson. Just as work was to begin in December 1992, the weekly *Dallas Observer* charged that the firm used deception in reporting the percentage of sub-contracting work awarded to minority-owned firms. A firestorm broke out. With Mayor Bartlett away on vacation, an irate Mayor Pro Tem Lipscomb called an emergency city council meeting to halt work until investigations could be made into the charges, even if it meant the Cotton Bowl could not be ready for the games. Several of the white council members did not attend the meeting, and the lack of a quorum prevented decisions from being made. The absences drew the ire of some minority council members who charged that they had deliberately conspired to prevent a quorum from being present. Days later, in a regular council session described by the *News* as a "wrenching meeting filled with allegations of racism," Dal-Mac satisfied the majority of the council with figures showing that 43 percent of its sub-contractors were owned by minorities or women. Lipscomb's request for work stoppage failed, and he complained that the city's opportunities for minority-owned companies amounted only to "another form of sophisticated sharecropping."

Meanwhile, the city's goals for hiring minority firms, criticized by some as a quota system, prompted large numbers of complaints from some big contractors who claimed that the requirements were unwieldly, expensive, and unrealistic. City Auditor Daniel Paul created a backlash of protests when he labeled the goals as unachievable because they were based on flawed data. Abuses were occurring because of the unrealistic goals, he claimed. One of his several recommendations was that white contractors who employ a high percentage of minorities should be certified to do business as minority employers. Paul's public comments prompted council members to immediately schedule an evaluation of his job performance. His observations clearly placed his job in jeopardy.

As was true for hiring minority police officers, the city had made significant advancements in broadening minority participation in city contracts. In 1987 minority participation, excluding women, had been 8.5 percent of the total. In 1992 that figure had climbed to 26.4 percent, and 1993 seemed certain to be even higher.

Another effort to spread resources among minorities was seen in funds awarded to arts organizations. Councilman Domingo Garcia sought in 1992 to re-distribute the city's allocations according to the approximate percentages of minority population. His plan would have awarded 52 percent of the funds to minority art groups. This would have drastically reduced amounts given to such organizations as the symphony orchestra and the art museum. Garcia's arguments assumed that these major cultural institutions failed to serve minorities, a point of view vehemently denied by spokespersons for these groups. While he was unsuccessful in his efforts, Garcia promised not to abandon his goal.

The concern about minority participation in public contracting was a major part of the council's continuing hassles with DART, whose representatives often asked for approval of zoning changes related to construction of a light-rail line into Oak Cliff. Council members Chris Luna and Garcia, chafing at what they believed was DART's failure to use a sufficient number of minority contractors, at one point sought to halt all work on the Oak Cliff line. Suburban cities which were integral parts of the DART system complained that the council was treating DART as if it were a City of Dallas agency instead of a cooperative regional effort serving the entire metropolitan area. Tensions during city council sessions became so high in 1992 that the council announced a ninety-day moratorium in dealing with DART as an effort to de-fuse the volatile situation.

Yet, DART's record with minority contractors was not that far from the city's. During 1992 the agency awarded 17.6 percent of all its contracts to minority, women, and disadvantaged businesses. Its overall goal was 25 percent minority participation (excluding women), a figure which an internal study in May 1993 calculated was too high because there were not enough minority-owned companies to achieve it. The result, according to the study, was either to discourage white contractors from submitting bids or causing them to inflate them because of the difficulties in meeting the quotas.

Concerns about alleged racism caused internal problems at DART as well. One instance revolved around the board's choice to hire former city councilman Dean Vanderbilt to replace retiring executive director Jack Evans. Vanderbilt, as president of the Dallas Tennis Association, had alienated some African-Americans through his handling of a racial discrimination complaint in the tennis center at Samuell-Grand Park. As a result, some board members insisted that they would accept Vanderbilt only if he agreed to appoint an African-American as his general manager. Vanderbilt refused to accept the position with this condition attached, and he withdrew his name. A disappointed Evans said afterwards that politics on the DART board was threatening its entire operations. "Some members of the board believe this should be a social service agency and not a transit agency," he said, lamenting that a "racial factor" had prevented DART from hiring a strong and effective executive director. An African-American interim executive director replaced Evans, and when a San Diego transit executive who was white was hired in 1993 as DART's new director, his selection was decried as an example of racism by former mayor pro tem Lipscomb and by the president of the city's NAACP chapter.

Yet another complication in race relations, one that appeared to have been brewing for some time, emerged clearly in 1993. This involved a rivalry of sorts between the city's African-Americans and the rapidly growing numbers of Hispanics. The problems especially were manifested on DISD campuses. In February 1993 about one hundred youths from the two groups fought openly for some twenty minutes at Boude Storey Middle School. Fights with racial overtones also were becoming common at Pinkston and Sunset high schools. Parents, fearful for their children's safety, flooded a special meeting to urge an end to the hostilities. A Hispanic neighborhood association president who spoke blamed John Wiley Price and African-American school board members Yvonne Ewell and Kathlyn Gilliam for encouraging the violence through their aggressive rhetoric.

Soon after this meeting School Superintendent Marvin Edwards spoke on the school system's cable television channel to all students. He urged them to "help end the violence." Domingo Garcia, Al Lipscomb, and John Wiley Price visited schools to make personal pleas to stop the fighting.

The same sort of racial discord sometimes was evident at city council. In one public dispute Deputy Mayor Pro Tem Chris Luna heard Mayor Pro Tem Lipscomb belittle him as a "Tio Taco." Luna received harsh criticisms from other African-Americans when he sought to eliminate a trust fund he cited as an example of "pork-barrel" politics. The South Dallas / Fair Park fund had been established to inject economic development money into the predominantly black neighborhood. Luna quickly retreated from his comments, although later city council members agreed to place more controls on the fund.

When the 1993 council members took office in June, there was hope that greater harmony might prevail. Domingo Garcia, who became the first Hispanic to be mayor pro tem, spoke of a "reborn" Dallas. Deputy mayor pro tem was Charlotte Mayes, an African-American. While there was some turnover in council membership, the ethnic breakdown continued to be the same. One councilman had campaigned openly as a member of the gay community. Yet, council sessions sometimes erupted. Early in December 1993 black Councilman Hicks openly threatened to put Councilman Paul Fielding "in the hospital" because of his alleged racism. In May 1994 the council banned activist Marvin Crenshaw from its meetings for two months after guards twice had to subdue him after he reacted violently when the council rejected his proposal to change the name of Illinois Avenue to Malcolm X Boulevard.

SCHOOLS CONTINUE TO STRUGGLE

It was an astonishing fact that in 1993—after more than two decades of close supervision by a federal court to achieve that purpose—the Dallas Independent School District still was not officially desegregated. Just how much additional integration could be achieved with a white student population that now was less than 15 percent and still declining seemed highly questionable. Five white and one Hispanic trustee sought in 1988 and 1989 to have Judge Sanders declare the DISD desegregated and terminate his supervision of it. Black trustees disagreed. They accused their colleagues of being motivated by racism, and the effort to end federal supervision failed. The same possibility arose in early 1993 when white and Hispanic trustees voted once more to ask Judge Sanders to declare that the

Dallas schools had achieved a "unitary" or desegregated status. Their motion carried by a 6-3 vote; all three black trustees opposing it. Once again, the final decision was left to the judge.

Even more so than the city council, the school board viewed issue after issue in terms of racial implications. A state-appointed consultant who monitored the board's actions for a year and a half concluded that "racial and gender tensions" on a daily basis reduced the board's effectiveness, marred its public image, and confirmed the widely held perspective that they were unable to govern.

Problems in the school district--desegregation and test scores--were increasingly complex. The number of white students was declining annually. Their continuing exodus from DISD had reduced their enrollment by 1992 to just 14.8 percent. As the school system changed from one that had been predominantly white and middle-class to one dominated by less affluent minority students, standardized test scores declined. Dallas' scores were significantly below those in surrounding suburbs, and they also failed to match state and national averages. (Scholastic Aptitude Test scores for the Dallas schools in 1992 were a median 793, compared to a national median of 899.) Only 29 percent of Dallas high school graduates were enrolling in colleges or universities.

In the spring of 1993 the Texas Assessment of Academic Skills (TAAS) revealed that just 26 percent of DISD's eighth-grade students passed the standardized mathematics examination. Only 38 percent of fourth-graders and 41 percent of eighth graders passed the reading section, scores that were far below state-wide averages.

Sanders cited low scores registered by minority students compared to white students as a primary reason for his reluctance to declare the system "unitary" or desegregated. For example, 72 percent of the district's eighth-grade white students were reading at grade-level compared to 35 percent for black students and 38 percent for Hispanics.

To boost test scores among minorities Sanders approved the opening of a number of one-race remedial centers. This had the effect of reducing the numbers of students being bused. In a further move to raise minority scores, Sanders imposed a quota on talented and gifted classes and magnet programs—decreeing that enrollment must be 40 percent African-American, 40 percent white, and 20 percent Hispanic.

In addition to student enrollment, desegregation of the administrative staff and faculty also was under federal court jurisdiction. Significant progress had been made here. By 1992 more than half of school-level administrators, 51.3 percent, were African-Americans; 17.9 percent were Hispanic. Of central staff administrators, 36 percent were African-American and 17.5 Hispanic. Nearly half the district's teachers were minorities—37.2 percent African-American and 8.1 percent Hispanic.

In 1987 School Superintendent Linus Wright, after nine years in office, resigned to become undersecretary of education in Washington, D.C. He was replaced by the city's first black superintendent, Dr. Marvin Edwards, who came from a similar position in Topeka, Kansas. Edwards' selection by the school board was unanimous. In 1993 Edwards resigned his position to take a superintendent's job with a much smaller town in Kansas. His successor was Chad Woolery, a veteran administrator with twenty-five years' experience in DISD. Woolery, a white man, won support from all segments of the board, an encouraging sign that more harmonious times might be ahead.

Despite on-going conflict among school trustees and the other difficulties widely reported in the district, Dallas residents gave DISD a resounding vote of confidence in December 1992 by passing a $275 million bond package for capital improvements. The largest single item in the program was a new super magnet Townview high school in Oak Cliff which had been ordered by Judge Sanders more than a decade earlier. Its original projected cost of $45 million had been reduced—despite much opposition from minority trustees—to a more manageable $29.9 million, the difference used to construct two additional schools. With 68 percent of the voters approving the bond program, a remarkable record remained intact: Dallas residents had never failed to pass a school bond program.

By the 1990s the challenge of yet another major ethnic change was approaching for DISD. African-American students, who only a few years earlier had replaced Anglos as the largest ethnic group, were destined to be replaced themselves in that role by Hispanics. Figures for 1992-93 showed Hispanics, already with 38.2 percent of the total enrollment, moving up rapidly. They compared to 44.9 percent African-American and 14.8 percent white students. Demands were being made that the district accommodate these changing ratios by hiring more Hispanic administrators and teachers and making related curriculum changes.

A GROWING SCHISM

Related to problems of race relations was an awkward situation which for decades had posed complex problems for Dallas. This was the continuing economic and sociological gulf between north and south; the existence, in effect, of two separate cultures and lifestyles, one rich, one poor. This situation showed no signs of improvement in the 1990s. Despite official efforts to enhance the economy of the southern sector, the differences between the two parts of town seemed even more pronounced in 1990 than a decade earlier. To a certain extent, it was a contrast between life as a white person and life as a minority in Dallas. White residents overall enjoyed per capita incomes two-and-a-half times that of African-Americans and three times that of Hispanics.

In the northern half the predominantly white residents held college degrees and earned comfortable incomes. Census tracts of 1990 showed almost all North Dallas neighborhoods with median family incomes of at least $40,000, many between $60,000 and $80,000, and nearly a dozen of more than $80,000. By the end of 1992 homeowner groups in eighteen of these North Dallas neighborhoods, alarmed by the high number of residential burglaries, had established regular programs for hiring off-duty Dallas police officers to cruise their streets in marked squad cars as a supplement to regular police patrols.

In the poorer southern sector lived 83 percent of the city's African-Americans. More than half of these lacked high school diplomas. In huge sections of the area more than 30 percent of them lived in what was defined officially as poverty. Crime was rampant, but neighborhoods here could not afford their own off-duty police officers. Many of the residents doubted the wisdom of city policies which permitted North Dallas neighborhoods to have—even at their own expense—greater police protection.

Another complicating factor, the rapid growth of suburbs, was placing greater demands on Dallas in providing basic urban essentials which transcended municipal borders—thoroughfares, libraries, sanitation, police protection, and other services. Moreover, residents who moved from Dallas to the suburbs tended to be replaced by less affluent newcomers in greater need of social services. They included large numbers of immigrant laborers from Mexico. So rapid was the growth of the Hispanic population that—just as their children were close to becoming the largest group in the school system—the day was approaching when they would constitute the city's biggest ethnic group.

Among those departing the central city for suburban areas were African-American families moving up the socio-economic ladder. These families particularly were choosing suburban cities in the southern half of the county: Cedar Hill, Duncanville, Lancaster, and DeSoto. Between 1980 and 1990 the percentage of African-American residents in those cities increased from single figure digits to between 12 and 32 percent. Black suburban population in the area increased by 120 percent in the decade of the 80s, the second-fastest rate in the nation.

A Mood Change for Dallas

Upon bursting so firmly and so positively into the national consciousness during the Texas Centennial, Dallas had become accustomed to hearing accolades about its desirability as a place to live and work. These praises the city had enjoyed for more than half a century. As late as 1990 *Fortune* magazine listed Dallas as the nation's best location for conducting business. Two years later, though, the magazine struck Dallas from its top-ten list, citing the reason as "a bad case of such urban ills as crime and poor race relations." Two weeks later came news that Moody's Investors Service had lowered its bond ratings for the city and the school district from triple A to double A. At the end of 1992 an alarming real-estate report confirmed that the struggling downtown area had deteriorated further. For the second consecutive year the amount of unoccupied downtown office space had increased, confounding those who had hoped for a turnaround. One day later it was reported that the annual Artfest, a weekend event at Fair Park which attracted some 80,000 patrons, henceforth would be held at Texas Stadium in Irving. Late in 1993 the situation downtown once again had deteriorated. Almost 37 percent of the central business district office space was vacant, up from 32 percent at the same time in 1992.

Dallas once had prided itself on shaping its own destiny. No longer could that be said. Negative news no longer surprised, no longer alarmed. The city which once had been reluctant to accept federal money for fear it meant loss of independence now had seen federal courts and agencies take control of its central institutions. Federal authorities had changed the way Dallas elected its council members; they had supervised its public schools for more than two decades; they had shut down its biggest financial institutions and sold them to out-of-state owners. Property values were eroding; taxes were climbing; crime was rampant. Obscenities and threatening language had found their way into the public discourse of elected officials. Even physical altercations occurred, including one in which the city's public housing director, an African-American, attacked a white councilman after a fiery and profane confrontation at city hall. Flames of racial unrest were being fanned at alarming levels. A change in the format of municipal government seemed likely in the not-too-distant future, but with uncertain results.

Even more frightening was the fact that so many urban residents in Dallas as well as elsewhere in the nation feared for their personal safety as armed gangs of youths began making "drive-by" or random shootings a regular occurrence. What once had been a rarity became common. In 1984 just two youths under the age of seventeen had been charged with homicide. In 1992 that number had grown to sixty-four.

These problems, many of them common to other large cities in a time of national economic recession and unrest, were too complex for a city divided in leadership and seemingly lacking in affection for it to surmount. Few of the new public leaders spoke admiringly of Dallas as their primary concern; few of them valued it as something whose whole was greater than its separate parts. Anyone daring to express such a sentiment stood the possibility of ridicule, for this kind of rhetoric had been used in past years to rationalize unfair treatment for those outside the protective umbrella of the ruling power group. Still, by the 1990s, with so many of the historic inequities gone, one could safely wish for a revival of something as hackneyed as the old "Dallas spirit." The city was in need of a sharp, inspirational jolt.

THE METROPLEX THRIVES

"Keep your airport—it will place you among the commercial leaders of the world." So Charles Lindbergh told Dallas' leaders in 1927. His words were prophetic. Dallas built upon aviation as the essential key to its future. Eventually, it ended its feud with Fort Worth and created a partnership in the enterprise. Thinking big and innovatively had paid dividends far greater than expected. By 1992 D-FW International Airport, with more than 49 million travelers a year, had become in terms of passenger travel the second busiest airport in the world. Nearly 150,000 persons passed through the airport each day, a figure expected to top 285,000 daily in the year 2010.

This activity helped spur tremendous growth in the surrounding areas. The Dallas-Fort Worth area was transformed from a regional center to one that held the third largest number of Fortune 500 company headquarters in the nation, thirty-two. Since 1980 more than 150 companies had relocated to the area, and a survey of their chief executives showed D-FW Airport to be the main reason. These companies included the gigantic Exxon Corp., the world's second largest energy company with revenues of more than $116 billion a year, which located in Irving; J.C. Penney Co., which moved its headquarters from New York City to Plano, where it built a spectacular $200 million facility; and AMR Corp., parent company of American Airlines, the nation's largest carrier, which left New York City for a campus-like facility adjacent to Dallas-Fort Worth International Airport.

The airport also played a key role in helping the Dallas Market Center grow into the largest wholesale merchandise mart in the world, with some forty markets being conducted annually. Some 7.5 billion wholesale dollars a year were being spent there, an amount second only to New York City.

The availability of so many direct flights to cities across the nation, coupled with a constant expansion in convention accommodations, was a boon for Dallas' convention business, too. More than three million persons attended conventions in the city in 1992, making Dallas the second most-favored site in the nation.

While the central convention facility was in downtown Dallas, many tourist attractions were outside the city—Six Flags Over Texas, Wet 'N Wild, the Texas Rangers' old Turnpike Stadium and its handsome new stadium, "The Ballpark at Arlington," Texas Stadium, and others. Such a dispersion of assets prompted Dallas, Fort Worth, Arlington, Grand Prairie, Arlington, and Addison to unite in a marketing campaign entitled "The Texas Metroplex: Dallas-Fort Worth, One Exciting Place."

It no longer was realistic to think of Dallas as a separate city standing alone. That Dallas was gone, irretrievable. The energy that once had concentrated at its center had been redistributed to the edges. Now Dallas, the nation's seventh largest city, was the center piece of a large patchwork of growing municipalities. This situation was not unique. Large cities everywhere were losing their separate identities and their dominance as forces in American life. During the decade of the 1980s it had been the medium-sized cities, those with populations between one-fourth and one-half a million, which had shown the greatest growth, an average of 20 percent. Cities with populations between 150,000 and 250,000 had increased in population by 15 percent. Cities such as Dallas with more than half a million in population grew by just 6 percent.

The urban sprawl encouraged by the automobile had erased practically all traces of what once had been well-defined city limits. This fact had been recognized as early as 1950 by the U.S. Census Bureau when it introduced the concept of the Standard Metropolitan Statistical Area, "an integrated economic and social unit with a large population nucleus."

In the greater Dallas area, with major business and commercial centers now widely dispersed, the significance of a downtown was largely lost. And despite strong sentiment to revive it through various economic incentives and schemes, there was little reason to believe that the forces which had brought its decline--stronger even than what was presumed would be a temporary economic downturn --could be reversed. Suburban cities had gained so much sophistication and power that they had more to offer than Dallas in capturing economic prizes such as a new baseball stadium, a pari-mutuel horse-racing track, and new corporate headquarters.

So if the city itself was struggling to recapture lost vitality under these new terms, the suburbs which it clearly had spawned were thriving. While Dallas bettered the national average for cities in its size category by growing during the 1980s at a rate of 11 percent, the entire Dallas-Fort Worth area increased in size by 32.6 percent. This made it the second-fastest growing major urbanized area in the nation. Five of the fastest growing cities in the nation surrounded Dallas: Plano, Arlington, Mesquite, Irving, and Garland. The suburban town of Arlington was in 1990 a bigger city than Dallas had been in 1930 and nearly as big as it had been in 1940. In housing starts, the Dallas-Fort Worth area ranked third nationally during 1991 and 1992, and it was projected to be fourth in 1993. The area gained 55,800 new jobs in 1993, the second best growth rate in the nation. Although *Fortune* magazine had dropped Dallas from its top ten list, the overall Dallas-Fort Worth area for two consecutive years in 1992 and 1993 was deemed by one leading forecaster to be the nation's very best location for real estate investment and corporate relocations. All the things that once had attracted new industry to Dallas still held true for the metropolitan area at large—good schools, low taxes, a good work force, a fine climate, a location in the center of the nation, and especially an outstanding airport with direct flights to major cities all over the world.

THE NEW CHALLENGE FOR DALLAS

By the standards of those who early had dreamed of such great things, the twentieth century had been good to Dallas. The boosters—Henry Lindsley, George B. Dealey, Nathan Adams, Fred Florence, Robert L. Thornton, Erik Jonsson, and others—had wanted growth and economic prosperity. Through their good works Dallas had grown—far more than they ever could have imagined. They also had wanted recognition for the city, and that had come. Some others—Alexander S. and Maynard Jackson, A. Maceo Smith, W.J. Durham, Juanita Craft, and Albert Lipscomb—had dedicated their lives toward improving the lot of Dallas' neglected minorities and creating equal opportunities for all races. Stymied for so many years, they, too, eventually had seen far more of their goals realized than they likely had imagined possible.

Now, awaiting the next generation of leaders as the twentieth-first century approached, were difficult, more intangible challenges.

But first there was unfinished business from the twentieth century: to merge the separate goals of earlier generations into a unified one, thereby creating an atmosphere that encourages and permits all citizens to work together to achieve prosperity and happiness. With this achieved, all other problems would be diminished. With this achieved, citizens of Dallas and surrounding areas could concentrate on the new challenges of the twenty-first century, recalling both the good memories and hard lessons of the past.

Acknowledgements

My debts for this work must begin with my late parents, Burnice Wylie Payne and Sallie Myrtle Jones Payne, who brought me to Dallas when they, along with scores of others, gave up farm life in East Texas in the 1930s to move here. I was six months old when they came in 1937. My sisters, June and Sally, and I grew up very happily among close relatives and friends in South Dallas, many of whom also had come from East Texas. In 1950, when I was in the eighth grade, we moved a few miles away to the new neighborhood of Pleasant Grove, where I graduated from high school in 1955. I feel a great sense of debt to this city for having provided for me and my family such a happy and stimulating environment, not only as a child but for these many years afterwards as an adult. Certainly, I have much affection for Dallas.

The most important and the most accessible resource for any study of Dallas' history is the Texas/Dallas History and Archives Division of the downtown J. Erik Jonsson Central Library. The times spent there over the years have been entirely enjoyable. Marvin Stone, Joan Dobson, Jimm Foster, and the entire staff there are knowledgeable, helpful, courteous, and friendly. Other researchers, I know, share my great appreciation for this fine group of people and the resources that they oversee. Most of my photographs came from the library's fine collection. (A full listing of photo credits is on Page 426.)

Another invaluable source was the Dallas Historical Society, whose collections, located in the basement of the Hall of State building at Fair Park, also are essential to any serious student of local history. I am indebted to Mary Ellen Holt and others there for their knowledge and assistance.

Closer to me on the Southern Methodist University campus was the DeGolyer Library, which holds a number of important archival sources for the study of Dallas history. For me, this included especially the Earle Cabell and Lynn Landrum collections. David Farmer, director of the DeGolyer, is always a congenial host for researchers.

Much of my basic work has been done, too, in SMU's Fondren Library. Throughout my teaching career at SMU it has been a hospitable and invaluable source for research as well as for leisurely reading. To all the librarians there I owe a great debt.

A new resource in town is the Museum of African-American Life and Culture at Fair Park. I obtained a number of photographs there through the assistance of W. Marvin Dulaney.

Vivian Castleberry, my former colleague at the *Dallas Times Herald*, graciously lent me photographs from her private collection.

A still-young publication which has been immensely useful to me and to others who are interested in this area's history is *Legacies: A History Journal for Dallas and North Central Texas*. This journal, edited ably by Michael V. Hazel, is a publication of the Dallas County Heritage Society and the Dallas Historical Society.

A number of individuals have taken a serious interest in this city's history and have published articles and books concerning it which have been helpful. All of them cannot be mentioned, but they include Kent Biffle, Dorothy D. DeMoss, W. Marvin Dulaney, Elizabeth York Enstam, Robert Fairbanks, A.C. Greene, Michael V. Hazel, Jackie McElhaney, Gerald D. Saxon, Philip Seib, Thomas H. Smith, Suzanne Starling, and William H. Wilson.

My colleagues at Southern Methodist University's Center for Communication Arts, where I teach journalism, all have been cheerful and supportive companions as they have seen me working on this manuscript. Curtis Matthews was particularly helpful as I encountered miscellaneous problems on the computer, and he is responsible for translating my own rough ideas for the dust jacket into a polished and professional product. Fellow faculty members Kathy R. Fitzpatrick and Laura Hlavack were boon companions and helpful readers. Others who assisted by reading chapters included Greg Brown, Susan Krasnow, David McHam, Peggy Montgomery, Barbara Scribner, Susan Springfield, Don Umphrey, and Rick Worland. Ted Carlin, John Carstarphen, John Gartley, Lynn Gartley, Alice Kendrick, Kathy LaTour, Janie Loveless, Jim Morris, Don Pasquella, Philip Seib, David Slayden, Sharon Thomas, Barry Vacker, and Rita Whillock also saw this book in the making and were gracious in sharing time on the printer.

Another SMU colleague, Glenn Linden of the History Department, graciously permitted me to read and cite from his work-in-progress on the desegregation of the Dallas Independent School District.

Over the years I have been teaching a seminar in Dallas history through the Master of Liberal Arts program at Southern Methodist University. My students have been especially inspirational to me as they have eagerly undertaken to research and to write term papers on aspects of the city's history. My thanks, too, to those who oversee the Master of Liberal Arts program, Robert Patterson, Shirley Smith, and Judith Montague, and for their encouragement in offering my course in Dallas history.

A number of individuals read parts of this manuscript and made important suggestions, some of which I followed. These individuals included David C. Frailey, John Schoellkopf, Philip Seib, Gary Shultz, Bill Sloan, Henry Tatum, and Stanley Marcus. John Schoellkopf and Henry Wade consented to interviews.

Marvin Steakley of the SMU Book store also has been a helpful friend who has been gracious in sharing his knowledge about publishing and bookselling.

There are, of course, dozens of others who have contributed in other ways to this book. They include my wife, Phyllis, and my children, Sarah and Hannah, who are still at home, and Mark and Scott, who now are grown up. All of them have provided different windows through which I have seen this city.

Finally, I want to thank all those individuals, primarily public officials and public figures, who have participated in oral history interviews or who have donated their letters, files, and other documents to the several research outlets which are working so hard to preserve basic sources for this city's history. Without them, the best part of our local history would dissolve without a trace.

Darwin Payne
Dallas, Texas

Notes
Bibliography
Index

Source Notes

PART ONE

1. What Mattered Was Growth

3 - "A city of skyscrapers": G.H. Wheeler in *The Western Trail,* a publication of the Chicago, Rock Island and Pacific Railroad, quoted by *Daily Times Herald,* March 17, 1907. On Sept. 13, 1954, the *Daily Times Herald* changed its name to *Dallas Times Herald.* (The newspaper will be cited under both titles hereafter as DTH.)
3 - "Where the wheels of enterprise": Preface to *Worley's 1907 Directory of Greater Dallas.*
4 - "[Gould] predicted its population": Darwin Payne, *Dallas: An Illustrated History* (Woodland Hills, Windsor Publications, 1982) 122.
6 - "the purchase of a parcel of land": DTH, March 12, 1907.
6 - "This ordinance forbade": Ibid., March 2, 1907.
7 - "Hurry back": Folder 2, Box 6, Florrie Wade Collection, Texas/Dallas History and Archives Division, Dallas Public Library. (The Texas/Dallas Division will be cited hereafter as DPL.)
7 - "In the spring of 1890": Folder 1, ibid.
7 - "situated at the head of navigation": Preface to *Worley's 1907 Directory of Greater Dallas.*
8 - "There is scarcely a more slovenly": Typewritten article dated Dec. 17, 1902, "Early City Planning Data" folder, George Bannerman Dealey Papers, Dallas Historical Society. The Dealey Papers will be cited hereafter as GBD.
8 - "A careful student, Delos F. Wilcox": Wilcox, *Great Cities in America: Their Problems and Their Government,* (New York: The Macmillan Co., 1913), 311.
9 - "In less than twelve months": DTH, May 12, 1907.
10 - "The mayor had arrived": *Memorial and Biographical History of Dallas County, Texas,* (Chicago: The Lewis Publishing Co., 1892), 907-909.
11 - "To create that format": DTH, March 5, 1907.
12 - "'the good of the city'": Ibid., March 6, 1907.
12 - "On the stage this night": Ibid., March 9, 1907.
12 - "In opening comments": Ibid.
12 - "No clique or faction": Ibid.
13 - "I do not propose": Ibid.
13 - "especially from the 'laboring classes'": Ibid., March 11, 1907.
13 - "a declaration of 'principles'": Ibid., March 24, 1907.
13 - "This Fort Worth had done": Richard G. Miller, "Fort Worth and the Progressive Era: The Movement for Charter Revision, 1899-1907," in Robert F. Oaks, et al, *Essays on Urban America* (Austin: University of Texas Press, 1975), 89-121.

13 - "For mayor the nomination went": DTH, April 28, 1907.
14 - "There is not a dishonest": Ibid., May 5, 1907.
14 - "Citizens Association promotional": Ibid., April 14, 21, 1907.
15 - "'one of the bitterest' campaigns": Ibid., April 19, 1907.
15 - "'lawbreakers and grafters'": Ibid., March 29, 1907.
15 - "'Conservatism will be'": Ibid., April 25, 26, 1907.
15 - "The most vigorous spokesman": Ibid., April 28, May 15, 1907.
16 - "'secret political organizations'": Ibid., May 19, 1907.
16 - "'If a frog at the bottom'": Ibid., May 16, 1907.
16 - "The city hall overdraft": Ibid., May 8, 1907.
16 - "'It has been easy'": Ibid., May 12, 1907.
17 - "Overcrowding was an acknowledged": Walter J.E. Schiebel, *Education in Dallas* (Dallas: Dallas Independent School District, 1966), 39-40.
17 - "A rumor circulated": DTH, May 15,1907.
17 - "Five days before the election": Ibid., May 16, 1907.
17 - "Voter turnout was": Ibid., May 14, 22, 1907; *Dallas Morning News* (cited hereafter as DMN), May 22, 1907; John H. Cullom, " Biographies of the Mayors of Dallas Since 1917," typescript, Dallas Historical Society.
18 - "Smith, watching election returns": DTH, May 22,1907.
18 - "'you cannot throw a mob'": Ibid., May 26, 1907.
18 - "Installation of the new": Ibid., June 1, 1907.
18 - "'My mind goes back'": Ibid.
19 - "'He made a first-class mayor'": Ibid.
19 - "Three days after": Ibid., May 24, 1907.
19 - "a massive two-volume book": Philip Lindsley, *A History of Greater Dallas and Vicinity,* (Chicago: The Lewis Publishing Co., 1909) I, 312.
19 - "In the early hours of": DMN "extra," May 25,1908.
20 - "As he crossed once again": Ibid.
20 - "The special edition": Ibid.; Jack Brown, "Electrifying Dallas: Early Impressions and Societal Impacts," SMU Seminar Paper, 1992.
21 - "The greatest single horror": DMN, May 26, 1908, May 9, 1933; Maxine Holmes and Gerald D. Saxon, eds., *The WPA Dallas Guide and History* ([Dallas] Dallas Public Library, Texas Center for the Book [Denton] University of North Texas Press), 62.
21 - "Volunteers on that same Monday": DMN, May 26, 1908.
22 - "All of Dallas suffered": Ibid.
22 - "Everywhere carcasses": Ibid., May 26, 1908, June 2, 1908.
23 - "Homeless men, women and children": Ibid., May 27, 1908, June 2, 1908.
23 - "If all these troubles": Ibid.
23 - "As the water gradually": DTH, June 16,1908.
23 - "With the Trinity still swollen": Ibid., June 1, 1908.
24 - "'I telephoned Colonel'": DMN, June 1, 1908.
24 - "'When you need money'": Ibid.

25 - "by June 5 the relief fund": DTH, June 5, 1908.

2. Eliminating the 'Social Evil'

27 - "Dallas had been a 'border' town": "The March of the Cities," *World's Work*, January 1914.
27 - "It was an 'emerging' metropolis": Blake McKelvey, *The Emergence of Metropolitan America* (New Brunswick: Rutgers University Press, 1968), 4 .
28 - "'There are windy corners'": *Dallas Dispatch*, Sept. 27, 1913.
29 - "An inspiration suddenly came": "Recollections—Trinity Valley," October, 1929, Folder 398, Box 42, GBD.
29 - "'When I went home'": Ibid.
30 - "'In exaggerated form'": George E. Kessler, "A City Plan for Dallas: Report of Park Board," May 1911, 7.
30 - "'As I understand your ideas'": Dealey to Kessler, Feb. 28, 1919, Folder 398, Box 42, GBD.
30 - "As for the railroad tracks": Dealey typescript, "Recommended by Mr. Kessler," [Feb. 15, 1919] Folder 393, ibid.
31 - "The construction of an all-weather": Payne, *Dallas:*, 148; William H. Wilson, *The City Beautiful Movement* (Baltimore: The Johns Hopkins Press, 1989) 267-68.
31 - "The people of Dallas": *Worley's Directory of Dallas*, 1913.
31 - "Crime existed, certainly": City of Dallas Annual Report, May 1, 1912, to May 1, 1913, 174-75; T.P. Finnegan, ed., *Souvenir: Dallas Police Department* ([Dallas] A. Zeeze Engraving Co., 1910), 43.
32 - "1913 was the greatest year": DMN, Jan. 1, 1914.
32 - "two 99-year leases had been signed": Ibid.
32 - "A fine nine-room, two-story": Ibid., Dec. 3, 1913.
32 - "On a wooded tract of land": Ibid., Feb. 1, 1987.
32 - "Other real estate news": Ibid., Jan. 1, 1914; Dec. 6, 1915; March 23, 1913.
33 - "A new, red-brick eight-story jail": Ibid., Jan. 1, 1914.
33 - "$475,000 Is Sum Voted": *Dallas Dispatch*, Sept. 15, 29, 1913.
34 - "At one point": Notes, Folder 1, Box 6, Florrie Wade Collection, DPL.
34 - "wrote W.E. Hancock": DTH, April 3, 1911.
34 - "'Never before in all'": DMN, Jan. 1, 1914.
34 - "Traversing this maze": Gwen Simpson, "Early Automobiles in Dallas: Heralds of a New Age," *Heritage News*, Winter 1984-85.
35 - "This would be an inconvenience": DMN, Dec. 5, 1913.
35 - "was working 'like a charm'": Ibid., Dec. 18, 1913.
35 - "They were building": Ibid., Dec. 7, 1913.
35- "a mammoth volunteer project": *Dallas Dispatch*, Oct. 30, 1913.
35 - "A twelve-foot wide bitulithic road": DTH, April 5, 1913.

36 - "Fourteen liveries": *Worley's 1913 Dallas City Directory.*
36 - "These dances, said Blaylock": DTH, April 5, 1913.
36 - "'chicken ordinance'": DMN, March 29, 1913.
37 - "the city's first native-born mayor": The senior Holland is described in *Memorial and Biographical History of Dallas County,* 244. W.M. Holland is profiled in Sam Acheson, *Dallas Yesterday,* (Dallas: SMU Press, 1977), 167-69.
37 - "had been achieved with no tax increase": DMN, April 1, 1913; Cullom, "Biographies of Mayors of Dallas Since 1917," 30-32.
38 - "Though small in number": Patricia E. Hill, "Origins of Modern Dallas," Ph.D. diss., University of Texas at Dallas, 1990, 148-49.
38 - "The 'token' Socialist candidate": George Edwards, *Pioneer-at-Law* (New York: W.W. Norton & Co., 1974), 20-27; DMN, Sept. 7, 1947.
38 - "'There is no home for'": Edwards, *Pioneer-at-Law,* 22-23.
39 - "a black man...named Allen Brooks": Ibid., 28-30.
39 - "The *Dallas Dispatch* noted": April 2, 1913.
40 - "He was Alexander S. Jackson": Peter W. Agnew, "Making Dallas Moral: Two Baptist Pastors," *Heritage News,* Summer 1987; *Dallas Express,* Jan. 25, 1936.
41 - *"The Rebirth of Negro Ideals":* The book was published by National Baptist Publishing Board, Nashville, Tenn.
42 - "The area included": *Worley's 1913 Dallas City Directory.*
42 - "'practically unclothed'": Henry Bruere, *The New City Government,* (New York: D. Appleton and Co., 1919), 283.
42 - "Judge W.W. Nelms, in making": DTH, March 28, April 1, 1907.
42 - "In 1910 Dallas' city commissioners": Minute Book, City of Dallas, Book 5, 1910-1911, 312-13.
43 - "'despoiling of virtue'": [J.T. Upchurch], "The Tribute Dallas, Texas, Pays to Vice," *Purity Journal,* October 1912.
43 - "Crib 'girls' would sit": J.T. Upchurch, *The Unchained Demon, and the Tribute Dallas, Texas Pays to Vice* (Arlington: Barachah Printing Co., 1912) 7.
43 - "One Saturday night": J.T. Upchurch, *Traps for Girls and Those Who Set Them,* (Dallas: Berachah Printing Co., 1904), 9
44 - "'Why not erect a monument'": [Upchurch], "The Tribute Dallas, Texas, Pays to Vice," *Purity Journal,* 21.
44 - "he reproduced in his publication": Ibid., 2-19.
45 - "meningitis epidemic": "Notes and Draft of History," Dallas Health Department, Folder 6, Box 2, DPL.
45 - "Dr. Samuell had taken": Harry Jebson Jr., et al, *Centennial History of the Dallas, Texas Park System, 1876-1976* (Lubbock: Department of History, Texas Tech University, 1976) 524; DMN, Aug. 26, 1957.
45 - "The profits to be earned": Bruere, *The New City Government,* 283.
45 - "Bruere called the reservation": Ibid.

45 - "in a speech to this influential organization": DMN, Sept. 22, 1913.
45 - "the city's Council of Churches decided": Ibid.
46 - "'one of the most severe excoriations'": *Dallas Dispatch,* Sept. 29, 1913.
46 - "urging the dissolution of the reservation": DMN, Oct. 6, 1913.
47 - "'home for fallen women'": *Dallas Dispatch,* Nov. 4, 1913.
47 - "'A veritable parade of'": DMN, Nov. 4, 1913.
47 - "where had the women gone?": DMN, Nov. 5, 1913; DTH, Nov. 3, 1913.
47 - "The Council of Churches": Ibid.
48 - "Scattered reports": *Dallas Dispatch,* Nov. 10, 21, 22, 1913.
48 - "the grand jury reported confidently": DMN, Jan. 1, 4, 1914.

3. The Boy Mayor Takes Over

50 - "quickly moved to win this plumb": DMN, Jan. 1, 2, 1914, Oct. 1, 1935.
50 - "Houston commented that the twelve": Nathan Adams, *The First National in Dallas* (privately printed, 1942), 42.
50 - "prepared an elaborate booklet": DMN, April 3, 1914.
50 - "Dallas spokesmen argued": Payne, "Dallas: The Story of Determined Citizens and How They Made the Improbable Dream of 1841 Come True," *Dallas,* July 1976.
51 - "Then came an important break": Sharpe, *G.B. Dealey of the Dallas News,* (New York: Henry Holt and Co. 1955), 172.
51 - "a solid citizen with impeccable credentials": DMN, Feb. 24, 1939.
51 - "Finty, a native of Illinois": Ibid., April 26, 1929.
52 - "Dealey devised a secret code": Sharpe, *G.B. Dealey of the Dallas News,* 172-73.
52 - "'destined to become'": Quoted by Payne, "Dallas: The Story of Determined Citizens and How They Made the Improbable Dream of 1841 Come True."
52 - "'for his goodness in giving'": Ibid., 16.
53 - "'It is repugnant to me'": DTH, April 5, 1915.
54 - "'the bat boy of the corporations'": Cited by Acheson, *Dallas Yesterday,* 173.
54 - "'intimidate, cajole, and browbeat'": DTH, April 5, 1915.
54 - "PIPs' campaign manager protested": Ibid., April 6, 1915.
54 - "Voter turnout was": Acheson, *Dallas Yesterday,* 174.
55 - "These new franchise arrangements": *Street Railway and Light and Power Franchises,* a pamphlet prepared by the City of Dallas, 1916, 2, 88.
55 - "His speech, however, contained": DTH, March 1, 1917.
55 - "Dallas' business leaders...were shocked": DTH, March 2, 1917.
56 - "whose duty was to elect": Ibid., March 15, 1917.
56 - "A clean-shaven man": Ibid., March 8, 1917.
57 - "'Lindsley talks about the'": Ibid., March 19, 1917.

57 - "he would rather cut off his right arm": Ibid., April 1, 1917.
57 - "described by Lindsley as a 'meddler'": Ibid.
57 - "'No man ever tried'": Ibid.
57 - "'How to Vote for Lawther'": Ibid.
58 - "a 'bolter' and a 'traitor'": Ibid., March 23, 1917.
58 - "Lindsley halted campaigning": Ibid., March 25, 1917.
58 - "Balloting that day": Ibid., April 4, 1917; DMN, April 4, 1917.
58 - "'kicked brass band methods'": DTH, Feb. 8, 1919.
59 - "The long-sought goal": Extract of letter, Mayor Lawther to J.L. Lancaster, July 17, 1917, Folder 393, Box 42, GBD.
59 - "rough-and-ready Dan Harston": O'Byrne Cox Jr., *Sheriffs of Dallas County, Texas, 1846-1985* (privately printed), 65-66.
59 - "Some 220 saloons and beer parlors": Kuberski, "Prohibition in Dallas," in *Sketches of a Growing Town: Episodes and People of Dallas From Early Days to Recent Times*, ed. Darwin Payne (Dallas: Southern Methodist University Master of Liberal Arts Program, 1991), 137.
60 - "raided a mammoth still": Owen P. White, "Dripping Dry Dallas," *Colliers*, July 20, 1929.
60 - "'This is not a gamble'": DTH, Feb. 2, 1919.
60 - "An expectant crowd of 5,500": Charles C. Alexander, *Ty Cobb* (New York: Oxford University Press, 1984), 131-32; DTH, April 1, 1917.
61 - "Lawther announced early": DTH, Feb. 7, 1919.
61 - "'The only thing wanting '": Ibid., Feb. 8, 1919.
62 - "sent word to Lindsley": DTH, Feb. 9, 10, 1919.
62 - "'Brass collars are for dogs'": Ibid., Feb. 15, 1919.
62 - "Gross Scruggs was the next choice": Ibid., Feb. 19, 1919.
62 - "the two parties chose not just Wozencraft": DMN, Feb. 24, 1919.
62 - "Although only twenty-six years of age": Mrs. Frank Wozencraft and Frank M. Wozencraft Sr. Oral History, DPL.
63 - "Captain Wozencraft's nomination": Acheson, *Dallas Yesterday*, 177-78; DMN, April 2, 1919.
63 - "'I am not so fortunate as'": DTH, March 3, 1919.
63 - "needed to elect a mayor with 'business ability'": Ibid., March 9, 1919.
64 - "by placing an empty chair beside him": Wozencraft oral history, DPL.
64 - "'If Frank will say to me'": DTH, March 26, 1919.
64 - "the *News* praised Lawther's courageous": DMN, April 1, 1919.
64 - "Captain Frank W. Wozencraft, lawyer": Ibid., April 2, 1919.
65 - "he did far more than merely watch this progress": Holmes and Saxon, *The WPA Dallas Guide and History*, 68.
65 - "he was with police officers": Acheson, *Dallas Yesterday*, 178-81; Wozencraft Oral History, DPL.
65 - "Wozencraft's performance": Acheson, *Dallas Yesterday*, 180; Wozencraft Oral History, DPL.

66 - "Wozencraft soon had an office": *Dallas Journal,* Aug. 28, 1934.

4. Embracing the Ku Klux Klan

67 - "Proud Chamber of Commerce officials": DTH, May 8, 1921.
67 - "Workers maneuvered about the steel beams": Ibid.
68 - "*Dallas* magazine declared that thousands": "What Oil Industry Means to Dallas," *Dallas,* February, 1922.
68 - "Hoblitzelle declared it the greatest": DTH, April 12, 1921.
68 - "Hoblitzelle, forty-one years of age": Ibid., Feb. 5, 1956; DMN, March 9, 1967.
69 - "the famous 'Dallas Spirit'": Ted Jones, *Dallas, Its History, Its Development, Its Beauty,* (Dallas: Lamar & Barton, 1925), 7.
69 - "Charles Saville...presented his list": DMN, Jan. 2, 1921.
70 - "an aggressive wolf": DTH, May 1, 1921.
70 - "'I don't know whether I'll buy a horse'": Ibid., May 8, 1921.
70 - "Mayor Aldredge announced that": Ibid., May 15, 1921; *Dallas Express,* April 2, 1921.
71 - "Municipal charges were filed against Williams": DTH, May 10, 19, 1921.
71 - "A series of seven ordinances": William Neil Black, "Empire of Consensus: City Planning, Zoning, and Annexation in Dallas, 1900-1960," Ph.D. diss., Columbia University, 1982, 146-150.
72 - "A survey of available Negro housing": Justin F. Kimball, *Our City—Dallas,* (Dallas: Kessler Plan Association, 1927), 198-99; Harold A. Stone, Don K. Price, and Kathryn H. Stone, *City Manager Government in Dallas* (Chicago: Public Administration Service, 1939), 2; T.J. Woofter Jr., *Negro Problems in Cities,* (College Park, Md.: McGrath Publishing Co., 1969),126; *Dallas Express,* May 18, 1925.
72 - "'It is proof that there are'": *Dallas Express,* May 25, 1925.
72 - "This was exemplified through the experiences": Hill, "Origins of Modern Dallas," 38-39; Richard K. Dozier, "Black Architects and Craftsmen,"*Black World,* May 1974; Richard K. Dozier, "Architects,"*Black Enterprise,* September 1976.
73 - "In 1918 two black men": W. Marvin Dulaney, "Whatever Happened to the Civil Rights Movement in Dallas, Texas?" In John Dittmer, George C. Wright and W. Marvin Dulaney, *Essays on The American Civil Rights Movement* (College Station: Published for the University of Texas at Arlington by Texas A&M Press, 1993), 69.
73 - "On April 1, 1921, a sensational event": DTH, April 2, 1921.
74 - "won the tacit approval of local law enforcement agencies": Ibid., April 2, 4, 1921.

74 - "the 'Black K.K.K.'": DTH, April 4, 1921.
75 - "Typically, a prospective recruit": Kenneth T. Jackson, *The Ku Klux Klan in the City, 1915-1930,* (New York: Oxford University Press, 1967), 67.
75 - "Many charter members": Norman D. Brown, *Hood, Bonnet, and Little Brown Jug* (College Station: Texas A&M Press, 1974), 51.
75 - "Certainly this was true in Dallas": The names and businesses of leading Dallas Klansmen were printed on an oversized paper evidently intended for members only since membership was secret. "Dallas KKK," [spring 1922] A42166, Dallas Historical Society.
76 - "A young Rockwall boy": Author's telephone interview with Henry Wade, Feb. 18, 1993.
76 - "A large proportion of Dallas police": The list is included with a letter from Klan official Elmer Bieser of Atlanta, Georgia, to Ben E. Cabell of Dallas as a solicitation for his membership. "Police Department Klansmen," Folder 40, Box 1, Earle Cabell Collection, DeGolyer Library, Southern Methodist University.
76 - "The Klan was quite a threatening": Lois Torrence, "The Ku Klux Klan in Dallas," M.A. thesis, Southern Methodist University, 1948, 52.
77 - "it probably was Evans": Jackson, *The Ku Klux Klan in the City,* 71.
77 - "'high grade dentistry at moderate prices'": DTH, May 10, 1907.
77 - "'Gold crown, $4.'": *Dallas Dispatch,* Oct. 30, 1913.
77 - "*Outlook*...called him a 'natural orator'": Stanley Frost, "When the Klan Rules," *Outlook,* Dec. 26, 1923.
77 - "One of Evans' personal friends": Supplement to DTH, "100 Years of Gathering News in Dallas," May 6, 1979, 17,19.
77 - "The Klan made its public debut": DMN, May 22, 1921; DTH, May 22, 1921; *Dallas Express,* May 28, 1921.
78 - "The newspapers gave broad coverage": Ibid., May 22, 23, 1921; DMN, May 24, 1921; *Dallas Express,* May 28, 1921.
78 - "'This organization is composed'": DTH, May 22, 1921.
78 - "'Dallas Slandered'": DMN, May 24, 1921.
79 - "the Klan struck again in a flagrantly lawless manner": DTH, May 24, 1921.
79 - "Neither did this incident disturb": Ibid.
80 - "From Dallas pulpits choruses of approval": *Texas American,* March 9, 1922; DMN, April 3, 1922.
80 - "one Sunday morning at a local Methodist church": *Texas American,* March 31, 1922.
80 - "The courtroom drama had its vague genesis": DTH, Feb. 6, 1922. (One of the two officers who apprehended Hall two hours later was identified as "Fritz," later famous as homicide chief Will Fritz, who conducted interrogations of Lee Harvey Oswald, November 22-24, 1963.)
81 - "was abducted from his home": DTH, March 7, 1922.

81 - "a *Times Herald* reporter interviewed": Ibid., March 8, 1922.
81 - "the Klan apprehended another alleged transgressor": DMN, March 28, 29, 1922.
82 - "At this point District Attorney Hughes": Ibid., March 30, 1922.
82 - "At the trial in Judge Charles Pippen's": DMN, April 1, 1922; *Texas American,* April 7, 1922.
82 - "The jury on its first ballot": Ibid.
82 - "The jury's verdict outraged a large number": DMN, April 2, 3, 1922.
83 - "urged all City of Dallas employees": *Texas American,* April 7,1922.
83 - "'It seems to me,' Governor Neff wrote": DMN, April 4, 1922.
84 - "So many people attended": Ibid., April 5, 1922.
84 - "carried a banner headline saying": *Texas American,* April 7, 1922.
84 - "The League sought to expunge": Ibid., April 21, 1922.
85 - "I am responsible to the public": Ibid., April 28, 1922.
85 - "'No other man in Dallas'": Ibid., June 16, 1922.
85 - "'Catholicism Is Sworn to Overthrow Our Government'": Ibid., May 19, 1922.
85 - "'Nobody knows how DEEP his hand'": Ibid., April 7, 1922.
85 - "Two Jewish leaders, Julius Schepps and Rabbi David Lefkowitz": Marilyn Wood Hill, "A History of the Jewish Involvement in the Dallas Community," M.A. thesis, Southern Methodist University, 1967, 52-53.
86 - "were averaging better than 100 a day": *Texas American,* April 7, 1922.
86 - "2,342 new Klansmen enrolled": Ibid., April 21, 1922.
86 - "on August 18 the Klan initiated": Ibid., Aug. 25, 1922.
86 - "opened offices on Young Street": *Worley's City of Dallas Directory,* 1923 and 1924.
86 - "The Citizens League created": *Texas American,* May 26, June 30, 1922.
87 - "Turley said the list would be available": Ibid., June 16, 1922.
87 - "Sheriff Harston, also asked": Brown, *Hood, Bonnet, and Little Brown Jug,* 73.
87 - "Fifty thousand copies of an election special": *Texas American,* June 30, 1922.
87 - "The *News* castigated Cox as": Quoted by Jackson, *The Ku Klux Klan in the City,* 72.
87 - "that 'dirty, slimy, Catholic-owned sheet'": Ibid., 73.
87 - "First on the platform": *Texas American*, Aug. 25, 1922; Jackson, *Ku Klux Klan in the City,* 73.
88 - "'striking evidence' of the Klan's political strength": Quoted by Jackson, *Ku Klux Klan in the City,* 74.
88 - "'we have just won a most glorious victory'": *Texas American,* Oct. 6, 1922.
88 - "The agent in Frisco advised": Ben Winfrey to G.B. Dealey, May 31, 1922, Folder 314, Box 36, GBD.

88 - "'all towns between Fort Worth and Amarillo'": R. Clyde White to Dealey, Aug. 5, 1922, Folder 317, ibid.
89 - "An advertiser in Whitesboro": A.J. Harris to M.W. Florer, May 3, 1922, Folder 314, ibid.
89 - "the accusations prompted internal studies": E.D. Gavin to G.B. Dealey, July 11, 1922, and Dealey to Fred W. Bott, July 14, 1922, Folder 315, ibid.
89 - "'Our conscience will not permit us'": Dealey to P.L. Sherrill, March 3, 1922, Folder 314, ibid.
89 - "'No priest, preacher or other outsider'": The anecdote was related by Finty to Dealey, July 3, [1922], ibid.
89 - "the *Brownwood Bulletin* sent this telegram": Unsigned letter from *News* to *Bulletin*, May 6, 1922, Folder 316, ibid.
89 - "A few agents in small towns": E.D. Cavin to Dealey, July 11, 1922, and Dealey to Fred W. Bott, July 14, 1922, Folder 315, ibid.
89 - "The deteriorating economic situation": Sharpe, *G.B. Dealey of the Dallas News*, 198-201.
90 - "The *Dallas Dispatch*, livelier and more irreverent": Torrence, "The Ku Klux Klan in Dallas," 55, 57; *Texas American*, May 19, 1922.
91 - "After several weeks they announced": DMN, Feb. 21, 1923.
91 - "they pledged to rule honestly and fairly": *Dallas Express*, March 31, 1923.
91 - "'whether the people want a Ku Klux Klan'": DMN, March 13, 1923.
91 - "were either members of the Klan": *Texas American*, March 6, 1923.
91 - "Martin charged that the Klan": DMN, March 19, 1923.
91 - "'There are sixteen known cases'": Ibid., March 13, 1923.
92 - "police reserves had to be called out": Ibid., March 29, 1923.
92 - "'There stands a member of Louis Turley's'": DTH, April 1, 1923.
92 - "'one of the best old Baptist families'": DMN, March 21, 1923.
92 - "marching through the downtown streets": Ibid.
92 - "'It is difficult to say": DTH, April 4, 1923.
93 - "'Sensible men will not doubt'": DMN, April 5, 1923.
93 - "A widely distributed handbill": Reproduced in Payne, *Dallas*, 168.
93 - "Ku Klux Klan Day": Alexander, *The Ku Klux Klan in the City*, 76-77.
94 - "In his opening comments": DTH, Oct. 24, 1923.
94 - "Ku Klux Klan Day was a spectacular success": Jackson, *The Ku Klux Klan in the City*, 76-77; DTH, Oct. 25,1923.
94 - "some 25,000 spectators gathered": Holmes and Saxon, *The WPA Dallas Guide and History*, 70.
95 - "who donated the second highest amount": DMN, July 2, 1924.
96 - "'A Klan endorsement of any candidate now'": *New York Times*, Feb. 21, 1926.
97 - "as late as 1929": *Worley's City of Dallas Directory, 1929.*

5. Daddy Lou's Dallas

97 - "the county's first college-educated sheriff": DTH obituary, April 11, 1982.
98 - "he was no stranger to firearms": Bettye McLaughlin, "A Profile of Schuyler Bailey Marshall Jr., Sheriff of Dallas County, 1925-1926," SMU seminar paper, 1990.
98 - "Marshall's family was intimately involved": Ibid.
98 - "Bootlegging was widespread": Brian Kuberski, "Prohibition in Dallas," SMU seminar paper, 1990.
99 - "threatening crowds began assembling": DMN, May 21, 1925; DTH, May 21, 1925; *Dallas Journal*, May 21, 1925.
99 - "the long-feared assault commenced.": *Dallas Journal*, May 21, 1925.
100 - "it appeared that the worst was yet to come": DMN, May 22, 1925; DTH, May 22, 1925.
101 - "The new cyclops of Klan No. 66": DTH, May 22, 1925.
101 - "The *Dallas Journal* criticized the mayor": *Dallas Journal*, May 22, 1925.
101 - "'Dallas County Has a Sheriff'": DMN, May 22, 1925.
101 - "'every Negro citizen of Dallas'": *Dallas Express*, May 30, 1925.
102 - "the fastest two capital trials in Dallas history": DTH, May 28, 1925; *Dallas Express*, June 6, 1925.
102 - "loaded the two Noel brothers into two fast cars": *Dallas Journal*, May 30, 1925.
103 - "Webb Martin gang members": McLaughlin, "A Profile of Schuyler B. Marshall Jr."
103 - "had not performed well": *Dallas Journal*, June 25, 1926.
103 - "'He's six feet tall, hard as nails'": DTH, July 21, 1926.
103 - "Marshall returned to farming": DMN, Dec. 28, 1956; DTH, April 11, 1982.
104 - "broadly asserted 'gross misconduct'": DTH, April 3, 4, 5, 1925.
104 - "'If you don't think I am the right man'": *Dallas Journal*, March 21, 1925, cited by Byrdette M. Peterson, "Louis Blaylock, Mayor of Dallas," SMU seminar paper, 1990.
105 - "'a record of achievement'": DTH, April 3, 1925.
105 - "'a beloved personality'": Ibid., Dec. 16, 1924.
105 - "He was seventy-three years old": Details of Blaylock's life are from "Personalities," *The Dallasite*, Oct. 26, 1929; and Peterson, "Louis Blaylock, Mayor of Dallas." The latter source took advantage of a huge scrapbook of clippings gathered during Blaylock's career as mayor and now in possession of his great-grandson, Charles C. Blaylock.
107 - "The city over which Blaylock presided": Data about Dallas come from various issues of *Dallas*, April 1924 through May 1926.
107 - "a budget for 1923": DTH, July 13, 1923, cited by Peterson, "Louis

Blaylock, Mayor of Dallas."
107 - "'I'll bet the business men would stand back of me'": *Dallas Journal*, May 28, 1925.
108 - "city workers should get a break": Ibid., June 4, 10, 1926.
108 - "A huge new reservoir": Peterson, "Louis Blaylock, Mayor of Dallas"; "What New Reservoir Means for Dallas," *Dallas*, September 1924.
108 - "a need for a large municipal auditorium": DTH, April 1, 1925; *Dallas Dispatch*, April 3, 1925, cited by Peterson, "Louis Blaylock, Mayor of Dallas."
108 - "'Such a protest is all a big piece'": DMN, Feb. 27, 1926, cited by Peterson, "Louis Blaylock, Mayor of Dallas."
108 - "A visiting city planner": *Dallas Journal*, May 26, 1925.
109 - "Gus Wylie said they weren't worth": Ibid., Sept. 12, 1925.
109 - "The *Dallas Journal* acknowledged": Ibid., June 9, 1926.
109 - "Louis Turley implored his fellow": James Robert Curtis, "The Dallas Police System," M.A. thesis, Southern Methodist University, 1929, 59, 67.
109 - "'Charges of vagrancy may be filed'": *Dallas Journal*, Sept. 25, 1925.
109 - "a jury convicted him for robbing": Ibid., Sept. 23, 1925.
110 - "wise-cracking newspaper reporters": DMN, April 19, 1925.
110 - "Burglars who cracked a vault": *Dallas Journal*, Sept. 8, 1925.
110 - "Nor were Dallas schools immune": Ibid., Sept. 28, 1925.
110 - "Dallas teachers in the middle of": Ibid., June 8, 1926.
110 - "Pioneer merchant Alex Sanger": Ibid., Sept. 14, 1925.
111 - "the 'scientific development of every part'": "Selling City Planning to Dallas," *The American City*, July 1925. Kimball, *Our City—Dallas: A Community Civics* was published in 1927 by the Kessler Plan Association of Dallas.
111 - "to appoint a five-man committee": DMN, Oct. 1, 1935.

PART TWO

6. Dallas' Ocean of the Air

115 - "This realization manifested itself early": Payne, *Dallas*, 139-143.
116 - "a $1.5 million training facility named Love Field": Love Field was named for First Lt. Moss Lee Love of Virginia, an Army pilot who had been killed in 1913 in a training flight in California.
116 - "the Chamber found itself holding": James E. White, "Aviation in Dallas, 1919-1939," SMU seminar paper, 1983.
116 - "the chamber decided to gamble once more": Ibid., 3-4.
116 - "aviation activity had become intense": Ibid., 4-5; "Getting Closer to New York," *Dallas*, February 1930.
116 - "the chamber guaranteed the airline": "Dallas Love Field: Dallas' Community Aviation Program," a Chamber of Commerce document in the

Lynn Landrum-Love Field Papers, A 80.230, DeGolyer Collections.
117 - "109,789 pounds of mail": White, "Aviation in Dallas, 1919-1939"; *Aircraft Year Book,* 1928, U.S. Aeronautical Chamber of Commerce.
117 - "Mayor Burt said Love Field was too small": DMN, March 15, 1928.
118 - "had sought to pay Lindbergh's taxes": Laura Fishman, "William E. Easterwood Jr.," SMU seminar paper, 1987.
119 - "the green and silver monoplane": DMN, Aug. 7, 1927.
119 - "he was woozy and tired": DMN, Aug. 12, 1927.
120 - "Erwin, too, encountered problems": An excellent description of Erwin, the *Dallas Spirit,* and its difficulties is in Ted Dealey, "'The Dallas Spirit': The Last Fool Flight," *Southwestern Historical Quarterly,* July 1959. Contemporary newspaper accounts also have good details.
121 - "Some 10,000 spectators": DTH, Sept. 27, 28, 1927.
121 - "'a glassy stare'" Ibid., Sept. 28, 1927.
121 - "'How does it feel to fly, colonel?'": Ibid., Sept. 28, 1927.
121 - "'Keep your airport'": Ibid., Sept. 28, 1927.
121 - "'As an inland city, let the air be our ocean'": His talk was reprinted in "Prophecy," *Dallas,* February, 1956.
122 - "The Little Theatre players": Helen Jo Potts, "A Study of the Little Theatre of Dallas: 1920-1943," M.A. thesis, Southern Methodist University, 1968, 27-31.
122 - "'I've got the hang of things'": DMN, Sept. 14, 1923, cited by Potts, "A Study of the Little Theatre of Dallas, 1920-1943," 33.
123 - "a playhouse that seated": Payne, *Dallas,* 183.
123 - "the play, 'Judge Lynch'": Potts, "A Study of the Little Theatre of Dallas," 38-40.
124 - "civic leader Louis Lipsitz agreed": Ibid., 50-51.
124 - "Now regular payments": Ibid., 51-66.
125 - "'Deep Ellum' it was called": Holmes and Saxon, *The WPA Dallas Guide and History,* 270-73.
125 - "rows of two-story structures": *Worley's City of Dallas Directory,* 1925 and 1927.
125 - "'When you go down on Deep Ellum'": Holmes and Saxon, *The WPA Dallas Guide and History,* 272-73.
125 - "They began performing together": Ibid., 87-88; Lee Ballard, "The Rise and Decline of Deep Ellum," *Westward,* DTH, Sept. 25, 1983, 28; Alan Govenar, *Meeting the Blues* (Dallas: Taylor Publishing Co., 1988), 19.
126 - "'feeding them ice cream and cake'": The quote is by mayoral candidate H.L. Goerner as reported in the DMN, April 1, 1927.
127 - "a careful study concluded": Stone, et al, *City Manager Government in Dallas,* 14-17.
127 - "In an editorial the *News*": DMN, April 23, 1927.
127 - "the Non-Partisans and City Democrats pledged": Louis P. Head,

"Measuring the Efficiency of a City's Government by the Munroe Criteria," *The American City*, June 1927.
128 - "One of the Non-Partisan's interesting contentions": DMN, April 13, 1927.
128 - "Within a month after his election": H. Clifford Long, "Citizens Charter Association," SMU seminar paper, 1983.
128 - "The Ulrickson Committee...submitted its final report"; Holmes and Saxon, *The WPA Dallas Guide and History*, 73; DMN, Aug. 24, 1947.
128 - "Attention now focused": Long, "Citizens Charter Association."
129 - "the *News* obtained pledges": Acheson, *Dallas Yesterday*, 186; Stone, et al, *City Manager Government in Dallas*, 22.
129 - "J. Worthington (Waddy) Tate": DMN, March 13, 1968; Tom Peeler, "Hot Dog Mayor," *D*, October 1989; Cullom, "Biographies of the Mayors of Dallas Since 1917"; DTH, April 3, 1927, April 9, 19, 24, 1929.
130 - "Tate set unforgettable examples in office": Peeler, "Hot Dog Mayor"; DTH, April 24, 1929; Holmes and Saxon, *The WPA Dallas Guide and History*, 73; DMN, Oct. 13, 1929.
130 - "Tate's preference for the 'plain people'": *Dallas Express*, Feb. 12, 1938.
130 - "In September 1929 Tate": Black, "Empire of Consensus," 156, 161, 171-72, 180.
131 - "And now he changed his mind": Peeler, "Hot Dog Mayor," 72.
131 - "he pulled out his yo-yo": Ann P. Hollingsworth, "Reform Government in Dallas, 1927-1940," M.A. thesis, North Texas State University, 1971, 13.
131 - "the mayor had shown himself to be more of a czar": DMN, Dec. 20, 1929.
131 - "Tate once again vetoed": Long, "Citizens Charter Association"; Stone, et al, *City Manager Government in Dallas*, 22-23.
131 - "A total of 5,919 voters signed": Stone, et al, *City Manager Government in Dallas*, 22-23.
131 - "A massive campaign was launched": Ibid., 24-25.
132 - "the *News* summed up the issue": DMN, Oct. 9,1930.
132 - "'We cannot permit the work'": Long, "Citizens Charter Association"; Stone, et al, *City Manager Government in Dallas*, 48.

7. Changing City Hall

134 - "There could be no doubt": Details about the election are from Stone, et al, *City Manager Government in Dallas*, 26; and DMN, April 1, 3, 5, 7, 1931.
134 - "The best known new council member": Acheson, *Dallas Yesterday*, 190-92; DMN, Aug. 23, 1932.
135 - "the new council met privately": DMN, April 9, 1931.
135 - "A leading candidate emerged": Stone, *City Manager Government in*

Dallas, 26-27; DMN, April 16, 1931; DTH, April 17, 1931.
135 - "Newspaper reporters quizzed the candidate": DMN, April 17, 1931.
136 - "Dallas acted quickly": Ibid., April 29, 1931.
136 - "was genial throughout the meeting": Ibid., May 2, 1931.
136 - "the strong-minded city manager": Stone, et al, *City Manager Government in Dallas*, 28.
136 - "hirings and firings, cuts in budgets": Ibid., 28-48.
137 - " One of Edy's early targets was the police department": DMN, May 9, 1931; Stone, et al, *City Manager Government in Dallas*, 51-52.
137 - "Edwin J. Kiest...demanded": Hollingsworth, "Reform Government in Dallas, 1927-1940," 8-9.
138 - "he died before the night was over": DMN, Aug. 23, 1932.
138 - "elected real estate man Charles E. Turner": Cullom, "Biographies of Mayors of Dallas Since 1917."
138 - "George B. Dealey made an appointment": Hollingsworth, "Reform Government in Dallas, 1927-1940," 18-19.
138 - "It also was being lobbied privately": Sam Acheson to George B. Dealey, Jan. 11, 1933, Folder 401, Box 43, ibid.
138 - "J.M. Moroney, also had become a major property holder": L.A. Stemmons to R.E. Simond, March 19, 1937, Folder 398, Box 42, GBD.
139 -"Edy himself became a principal campaign issue": Hollingsworth, "Reform Government in Dallas, 1927-1940," M.A. thesis, 18-19; DMN, April 1, 1933.
139 - "vowed privately to resign": Memo, Barry Bishop to Mr. Barrett [Nov. 21, 1932], Folder 404, Box 43, GBD.
139 - "Hexter declared Edy to be a 'godsend'": DMN, April 1, 1933.
139 - "a more 'politically conscious city council'": Acheson to George B. Dealey, Jan. 11, 1933, Folder 401, Box 43, GBD.
139 - "pleaded in vain for Dealey": Memo from E.B. Doran to Dealey, March 17, 1933, Folder 403, ibid.
140 - "'only sure means of preventing the entry of politics'" DMN, March 31, 1933.
141 - "'partyism has no part'": DMN, April 4, 1931.
140 - "Edy was convinced that": Memo from Bishop to Mr. Barrett, April 4, 1933, Folder 403, Box 43, GDB .
140 - "'I would rather take a job'": Memo from Joe Murray to Mr. Withers, April 3, 1933, ibid.
140 - "'It is about time to think of Mr. Edy'": DMN, April 6, 1933.
141 - "Rex Beach wrote that if a New Yorker": Quoted in introduction to *Worley's City of Dallas Directory, 1931.*
141 - "'hospitality of the South'": Ibid.
141 - "a tall, slightly paunchy former cotton farmer": Harry Hurt III, *Texas Rich: The Texas Dynasty* (New York: W.W. Norton & Co., 1981), 18, 73.

142 - "lived in a 'spiritual and intellectual world'": Everett Lloyd, "Colonel C.M. Joiner, Ideal American," *Dallas,* November 1934.
143 - "Hunt paid Joiner $30,000 in cash": James A. Clark and Michel T. Halbouty, *The Last Boom* (New York: Random House, 1972), 90-95.
143 - "Within two years of his deal": Hurt, *Texas Rich,* 114.
143 - "Hunt moved his first family": Ibid., 122-23.
144 - "Joiner had enough assets": Ibid, 102; Lloyd, "Colonel C.M. Joiner, Ideal American."
144 - "it transformed Dallas' economic base": The classified directory in *Dallas,* April 1930, lists the growing number of businesses related to the oil business. See also "Yellow Gold From Black," *Dallas,* March 1932; and "Oil Industry Grows," *Dallas,* August 1932; Payne, *Dallas,* 192.
144 - "By 1941 it was estimated that": Payne, *Dallas,* 192.
145 - "'I'd never been more than a few miles'": Babe Didrickson Zaharias, *This Life I've Led* (New York: A.S. Barnes & Co., 1955), 7.
146 - "The phenomenal youngster": Zaharias, "This Life I've Led," (excerpt of autobiography of same title appearing in *Saturday Evening Post,* June 25, 1955.)
146 - "Babe returned to Dallas the triumphant hero": M.J. McCombs, "World's Greatest Athlete, Man or Woman," *Dallas,* September 1932.
147-48 - "Henry Barrow and his wife Cumie": John Treherne, *The Strange History of Bonnie and Clyde* (New York: Stein and Day, 1985), 33-43.
148 - "was known to Dallas police as a petty thief": Ted Hinton, *Ambush: The Real Story of Bonnie and Clyde* (Austin: Shoal Creek Publishers, 1979), 9-10.
148 - "Dallas police wiretapped the Barrow telephone": A paraphrased transcript of the intercepted phone calls is in the "Day Book," Dallas Police Department Archives, DPL.
148 - "One of their momentary 'kidnap' victims": "Turnabout," *Time,* March 20, 1950.
149 - "An 'extra' published by *Dallas Dispatch*": May 24, 1934.
149 - "Further tension emerged": Stone, et al, *City Manager Government in Dallas,* 54-56.
150 - "'like catfish in the mud'": Ibid., 65; DMN, March 20, 1935.
150 - "A principal Catfish leader": Hollingsworth, "Reform Government in Dallas, 1927-1940," 33-34.
150 - "At its first public meeting": DTH, Jan. 25, 1935, cited by Hollingsworth, "Reform Government in Dallas, 1927-1940," 29-32.
150 - "the organization selected Hal Moseley": Hollingsworth, "Reform Government in Dallas, 1927-1940," 32-33; Stone, et al, *City Manager Government in Dallas,* 66.
151 - "He predicted that a defeat": DMN, March 23, 1935.
151 - "In defending Edy": Ibid., March 29, 1935.
151 - "'one of the most vigorously contested'": Ibid., April 2, 1935.

151 - "'discharged, disgruntled and disgraced'": Hollingsworth, "Reform Government in Dallas, 1927-1940," 38-39.
151 - "Edy definitely would be retained": Hollingsworth, "Reform Government in Dallas,1927-1940," 29.
151 - "because he was an outsider": DMN, March 24, 1935.
151 - "a fence-straddling editorial": Ibid., April 2, 1935.
152 - "'Civic Ticket Runs Away With Election'": Ibid., April 3, 1935.
152 - "Catfish strength was especially evident": Stone, et al, *City Manager Government in Dallas,* 67-70.
152 - "Moseley's annual pay was reduced": DMN, April 3, 4, 1935.
152 - "was a disquieting note to some": Ibid., April 5, 1935.
152 - "Moseley showed his mettle": Stone, et al, *City Manager Government in Dallas,* 71; Hollingsworth, "Reform Government in Dallas, 1927-1940," 49.
152 - "the top vote-getter, George A. Sergeant": DMN, April 5, 1935.

8. Centennial Triumph

154 - "Anticipated costs...were underwritten": L.V. Sheridan to G.B. Dealey, May 31, 1920, Folder 395, Box 42, GBD.
155 - "arranged to print the bonds in Galveston": DMN, May 16, 1933. A good summary of these events is found in the DMN, Oct. 1, 1935.
155 - "George B. Dealey...was the speaker": "Dealey's Speech at the groundbreaking for the Trinity Levee Project on July 24, 1928," Folder 401, Box 43, GBD.
156 - "the immense project": *Dallas,* November 1929.
156 - great dreams were envisioned": "Dallas' Great Improvement Project," *Dallas,* August 1929; "Possibilities Made Practical by Reclamation," *Dallas,* November 1929.
156 - "became mired in an intense political struggle": DMN, June 8,1930.
157 - "Dealey and other levee proponents": E.D. Hurt statement, March 2, 1932, Folder 406, Box 44, GBD.
157 - "comments were meant to include": John Stemmons Oral History, DPL.
157 - "'broken promises, repudiation, and bad faith'": L.A. Stemmons to Storey Stemmons, March 18, 1938, Folder 398, Box 42, GBD.
157-58 - "a $70,973 law suit": DMN, March 1, 1932.
158 - "an eleven-part series by Lynn Landrum": This series was initiated on May 8, 1933.
158 - "This realignment permitted traffic": C.B. Beckenbach, "The New Triple Underpass in Dallas," *American City,* November 1936,.
158 - "It was estimated that": "Growing Dallas Moves River Away," *Business Week,* March 12, 1930.
158 - "He had organized his company": The slogan is on the company's

letterhead, Folder 398, Box 42, GBD.

159 - "The idea for Texas to observe": Kenneth B. Ragsdale, *The Year America Discovered Texas* (College Station: Texas A&M University Press, 1987), 3-6; Don Dorsey, "Winning the Texas Centennial Exposition for Dallas," SMU seminar paper, 1983.

160 - "'the city offering the largest financial inducement'": Ragsdale, *The Year America Discovered Texas*, 32.

160 - "What would be required": Ibid., 46-47.

160 - "Thornton, founder of his own bank": Details of Thornton's early life come from George Session Perry, "The Duke of Dallas," *Saturday Evening Post*, June 11, 1955; Thornton's obituary in the DMN, Feb. 16, 1964; and especially from the Robert Lee Thornton Jr. Oral History, DPL.

162 - "Someone suggested that he try banking": Undated DMN clipping, circa 1941, Florrie Wade Collection, Folder 4, Box 7, DPL.

163 - "credited Thornton with proposing": Payne, *Dallas*, 213.

163 - "Thornton arranged for a luncheon": Dorsey, "Winning the Texas Centennial for Dallas."

164 - "'From a cold-blooded dollars and cents view'": DTH, Aug. 10, 1934.

164 - "objected in a strongly worded telegram": Ragsdale, *The Year America Discovered Texas*, 52-54; Dorsey, "Winning the Texas Centennial for Dallas."

165 - "'a masterpiece of vivid color'": Briggs made the comment in a telegram to Thornton's wife. Cited by Ragsdale, *The Year America Discovered Texas*, 56.

165 - "Thornton stressed with fervor": "Address Before the Texas Centennial Commission, Made on September 6, 1934, in Room 950, Baker Hotel, Dallas, Texas," R.L. Thornton Scrapbook, Vol. I, DHS, cited by Dorsey, "Winning the Texas Centennial"; Ragsdale, *The Year America Discovered Texas*, 54-55; DMN, Sept. 7, 1934.

166 - "'How can I deliver a romantic speech'": George Dahl Oral History, DPL.

166 - "Holcombe's response was markedly different": Ragsdale, *The Year America Discovered Texas*, 57.

166 - "Mayor Quinn said his city would need": Ibid., 58.

166 - "'We accept this honor'": Ibid., 58-59.

167 - "San Antonio's committee members": Ibid., 59.

167 - "'Houston stood no chance in their half-hearted'": Ibid., 60.

167 - "'vastly different urban personalities'": Ibid.

167 - "Adams, the senior member": Adams, *The First National in Dallas*, 23.

167 - "Florence, who grew up in Rusk": Carol Estes Thometz, *The Decision-Makers: The Power Structure of Dallas* (Dallas: Southern Methodist University Press, 1963), 79, but see especially H. Harold Wineburgh, *The Texas Banker: The Life and Times of Fred Farrel Florence* (Dallas, n.p., 1981), for a full treatment of Florence's life.

168 - "a $500,000 advertising and publicity campaign": Ragsdale, *The Year America Discovered Texas*, 116.
168 - "They 'lassoed' Hoover": Ibid., 145-46.
169 - "'Go to Dallas for Education'": Ibid., 260-293.
169 - "'We've got to open up the town'": Ibid., 287-88.
170 - "Albert Einstein started an electrical impulse": Karen Matney Brown, "The Forgotten Fair," SMU seminar paper, 1993.
170 - 'its economic benefits were enormous": Ragsdale, *The Year America Discovered Texas*, 300-301; Introduction, City of Dallas General Budget for Fiscal Year, 1936-1937, p. II.
170 - "'Examined in any context'": Ragsdale, *The Year America Discovered Texas*, 306.
171 - "Between July 1935 and June 1937": Articles counted were those appearing in the indexes to the *Reader's Guide to Periodical Literature.*
171 - "in the influential *Atlantic Monthly*": David L. Cohn, "Dallas," *Atlantic Monthly*, October 1940.
172-74 - "Citizens Council":- Details largely from McCombs and Whyte, "The Dydamic Men of Dallas"; and Thometz, *Decision-Makers of Dallas.*

9. Jim Crow Holds Its Grip

176 - "Negro neighborhoods": Dallas Housing Survey, 1940, Housing Authority of the City of Dallas, 4.
176 - "strictly segregated by a city ordinance": Black, "Empire of Consensus," 126, 150.
176 - "a tall, solid, wooden fence": This is based on the author's recollection as a very small boy. The fence stood between houses on Rutledge Street just off Second Avenue. Houses on the south side of the fence were for black residents; those on the north side for whites. The author lived with his parents on the first house north of the fence.
176 - "less than thirty of the 4,000 acres": Jebsen, *Centennial History of the Dallas, Texas, Park System, 1876-1976*, 321.
177 - "So crowded was the school": DTH, Feb. 12, 1991; Schiebel, *Education in Dallas*, 31.
177 - "Improvements such as street pavings": Mamie L. McKnight, *African American Families and Settlements of Dallas: On the Inside Looking Out* (Dallas: Black Dallas Remembered, Inc., 1990), II, 150.
178 - "Smith, born the fourteenth child": Details about Smith's life come from A. Maceo Smith Oral History and A. Maceo Smith clippings file, DPL.
179 - "he concentrated on political advancement": Gillette, "The NAACP in Texas, 1937-1957," Ph.D. diss., 5-6, 12.
180 - "Smith's forty-five minute talk": A. Maceo Smith Oral History.
180 - "Smith refused to identify them": Ibid.

180 - "'this was the first time in the history'": Jesse O. Thomas, *Negro Participation in the Texas Centennial Exposition* (Boston: Christopher Publishing House, 1938), 37.
181 - "This, he claimed, demonstrated": Ibid., 36-37; Ragsdale, *The Year America Discovered Texas*, 248, 305.
181 - "its operators did not want their scantily-clad female": A. Maceo Smith Oral History Interview on Tape, DPL.
181 - "caused Thomas and others to send numerous letters": Thomas, *Negro Participation in the Texas Centennial Exposition*, 121-23.
181 - "proved useful in a far more significant way": A. Maceo Smith Oral History Interview on Tape, DPL; Juanita Craft Oral History, DPL.
182 - "The building was torn down": Thomas, *Negro Participation in the Texas Centennial Exposition*, 37.
182 - "began a broad survey": The survey and voter registration drives are described in the *Dallas Express*, Jan. 1, 1936; Oct. 10, 1936; and Nov. 21, 1936.
183 - "the need for hiring Negro police officers": Gunnar Myrdal pointed out that the hiring of Negro policemen in the South was rare. The states of Mississippi, South Carolina, Louisiana, Georgia, and Alabama had not a single Negro officer when he wrote his classic study, *An American Dilemma: The Negro Problem and Modern Democracy* (New York: Harper & Bros., 1944). Maryland, Delaware, Tennessee, and Texas together had a total of thirty-nine Negro officers, or one to every 41,000 Negroes.
183 - "was implored to prosecute": *Dallas Express*, Dec. 19, 1936.
183 - "returned a verdict of two years": DMN, Oct. 12, 1939.
183 - "'Mayor of Negro Dallas'": *Dallas Express*, Feb. 6, 1937, Dec. 25, 1937, and Nov. 12, 1938.
183 - "'This created quite a stir'": A. Maceo Smith Oral History.
184 - "the League prepared a questionnaire": Ibid.
184 - "the Progressive Voters League chose to support": Hollingsworth, "Reform Government in Dallas, 1927-1940," 74-78; A. Maceo Smith Oral History .
184 - "'For the first time in the history of the South'": Quoted by Stone, et al, *City Manager Government in Dallas*, 79.
184 - "The payoff was not long in coming": *Dallas Express*, July 10, 17, 1937.
185 - "'It's a privilege to live in Dallas'": Ibid., Jan. 1, 15, 1938.
185 - "NAACP delegates from five branches": Gillette, "The NAACP in Texas," 8.
185 - "'The South's Oldest and Largest Negro Newspaper'": *Dallas Express*, Feb. 19, 1938.
186 - "purchased the newspaper from the white ownership": Ibid.
186 - "The city already had one federal housing project": Charles Blaylock, "Dallas: The Struggle to Get Public Housing," SMU seminar paper, 1992.
186 - "'a symbol with far greater meaning'": *Dallas Express*, March 5, 1938.

187 - "'a lot of hooey'": DMN, Aug. 5, 1938.
187 - "'change the living habits'": Ibid, Oct. 22, 1938.
187 - "decried trends toward socialism": Ibid.
187 - "The *Express* began a series": *Dallas Express,* Aug. 20, 1938.
187 - "'This condition actually exists'": Ibid., Oct. 1, 1938.
188 - Mayor Sprague was on record in favor of it": Blaylock, "Dallas: The Struggle to Get Public Housing."
188 - "all council members save": *Dallas Express,* Oct. 15, 29, 1938.
188 - "Construction on the project": Blaylock, "Dallas: The Struggle to Get Public Housing."
188 - "the poor quality of Negro education": *Dallas Express,* Aug. 28, 1938.
188 - "one of the more sensational crimes": Ibid., Aug. 6, 13, 1938.
189 - "Cosette Faust Newton was identified": DMN, Aug. 2, 1938. Also see DTH, Feb. 2, 1926, in Cosette Faust Newton clippings file, DPL, for Ms. Newton's background and education.
189 - "Ricketts sued the couple": DMN, Aug. 2, 1938; *Dallas Express,* Aug. 13, 1938.
189 - "The boat, dubbed the 'S.S. Miramar'": See clippings file on Cosette Faust Newton, DPL, for details on the dispute.
189-90 - "obtained a temporary injunction": *Dallas Express,* March 4, 1939.
190 - "'Negroes are interested in this project'": Ibid.
190 - "'Dallas Stands Alone'": Ibid., Sept. 23, 1939.
190 - "Smith served as the chamber's executive secretary": Gillette, "The NAACP in Texas," 14.
190 - "The following year he became": A. Maceo Smith Correspondence Files, Dallas Negro Chamber of Commerce Collection, Box 2, DPL; also A. Maceo Smith clippings file, DPL.
191 - "Affairs at city hall": Hollingsworth, "Reform Government in Dallas, 1927-1940," 78-79.
191 - "Railton, still not appeased": Ibid., 82.
192 - "These events earned bold": Ibid., 83-84.
192 - "Ripley detailed astounding charges": Ibid., 84-85.
192 - "both Railton and Gordon were removed": Details about the removal and aftermath are from ibid., 86; Jebsen, *Centennial History of the Dallas, Texas, Park System, 1876-1976,* 501; DMN, Feb. 3, 7, 8, and 18, 1941.
193 - "'Dallas voters are tired of politics'": DMN, April 4, 1939; Hollingsworth, "Reform Government in Dallas, 1927-1940," 88.
193 - "'the bankers will get a stronghold'": Ibid.
193 - "A third party, the Progressive Civic Association": Hollingsworth, "Reform Government in Dallas, 1927-1940," 87.
193 - "'This is an emergency'" DMN, April 2, 1939.

10. Brilliant in Achievement

196 - "the figure was approximately 122,000": "122,000 Visitors in 1939," *Southwest Business,* November 1939.
196 - "'the greatest industrial development'": "Dallas Wins Plane Factory," *Southwest Business,* September 1940.
196 - "The number of manufacturing jobs": David R. Braden, "Architecture for Industry: Dallas," Alan R. Sumner, ed., *Dallasights: An Anthology of Architecture and Open Spaces* (Dallas: American Institute of Architects, Dallas Chapter), 1978, 164.
196 - "plans for a $450,000 expansion": "Ford Spends $450,000 on Dallas Plant," *Southwest Business,* February 1941.
196 - "Mercantile National Bank": "Like a Diamond in the Sky," *Southwest Business,* June 1941.
197 - "the nation's first planned": E.G. Hamilton, "Dallas Shops: Dry-Goods Stores to Regional Malls," *Dallasights,* 36; W.J. Brown as quoted in Payne, *Dallas,* 217.
197 - "announced on WFAA radio three special goals": DMN, April 15, 1939.
197 - "the council should avoid public family quarrels": Woodall Rodgers, "Luncheon Meetings Promote Harmony in Dallas," *American City,* February 1947; Henry Kucera Oral History.
198 - "'There wasn't anybody in the city hall'": James W. Aston Oral History; DMN, Dec. 6, 1939, in the Florrie Wade Collection, Folder 6, Box 7, DPL.
198 - "Aston substantially overhauled": DMN, Oct. 7, 8, 1939.
198 - "Aston's first crisis": James W. Aston Oral History.
199 - "Central Boulevard was recognized": "Editorial," *Southwest Business,* December 1937.
200 - "'we don't know ourselves'": Rodgers, "Central Boulevard," *Dallas,* June 1941.
200 - "'We were in there looking out'": McKnight, *African American Families and Settlements of Dallas,* II, 149, 159.
201 - "A 1940 study showed": Cited in "1950 Negro Housing Market Data," Dallas Negro Chamber of Commerce Papers, Folder 4, Box 1, DPL.
201 - "A Dallas Housing Authority survey": "Dallas Housing Survey, 1940," a pamphlet published by the Housing Authority of the City of Dallas, 6.
201 - "restricting Negroes to designated streets": DMN, Oct. 5, 1939.
201 - "becoming increasingly agitated": *Dallas Express,* Oct. 7, 21, 1939.
201 - "'little World War'": Ibid., Oct. 7, 1939.
202 - "a series of bombings, mysterious fires": DMN, Dec. 23, 1940, March 6, 1941.
202 - "'a hard-working darkey'": Ibid., March 8, 1941,
202 - "passed and then rescinded": "Racial Dynamism in Dallas," *New*

Republic, March 24, 1941.
203 - "to be eligible to live there": Julie Lyons, "Brown Jesus (and other tales from the projects," *Dallas Observer,* Aug. 6, 1992.
203 - "Another group of minority citizens": Gwendolyn Rice, "Little Mexico and the Barrios of Dallas," *Legacies,* Fall 1992, 21-22.
203 - "Little Mexico was a clearly defined area": DMN, April 19, 1925, Oct. 1, 1935; Holmes and Saxon, *The WPA Dallas Guide and History,* 184-86; Walter T. Watson, "Mexicans in Dallas," *Southwest Review,* July 1937; Simpson, *Pike Park,* 6.
204 - "More prosperous Mexican-American families": Rice, "Little Mexico and the Barrios of Dallas," 23.
204 - "an organization of 'special interests'": DMN, March 25, 27, 1941.
205 - "All CCA councilmen save one": Ibid., March 22, 25, 28, 1941.
205 - "Rodgers interpreted the results": Ibid., April 2, 3, 1941.
206 - "On that fateful Sunday": Ibid., Dec. 7-13, 1941.
206 - "52,000 men and women from Dallas": Payne, *Dallas,* 217.
206 - "a mass riot with racial overtones": DMN, Jan. 4, 1943; DTH, Jan. 4, 1943; *Dallas Express,* Jan. 9, 1943.
207 - "they formed the Dallas Council of Negro Organizations": "Dallas Council of Negro Organizations," typescript, Jan. 9, 1943, Folder 2, Box 7, Dallas Negro Chamber of Commerce Papers, DPL.
207 - "'Interest In Election Near Zero'": DMN, April 1, 1943.
208 - "A stirring battle with the City of Fort Worth": Ibid., July 21, 1943.
208 - "a single, super airport": Ibid., March 1, 1943.
208 - "Amon G. Carter began working quietly": Ibid., March 1, 4, 1943.
209 - "The *News* editorialized thoughtfully": Ibid., April 2, 1943.
209 - "Midway Airport 'is no more'": Ibid.
210 - "plans for extensive new improvements": Ibid.
210 - "The city began to anticipate": E. A. Wood,"A City Looks to the Future," *Southwest Review,* Spring 1944.
210 - "'Dallas Chiefs Shocked.'": July 1943 DMN clipping from Florrie Wade Collection, Folder 4, Box 7, DPL.
210 - "'We need another Kessler Plan'": DMN, April 2, 1943.
211 - "'increase the working efficiency'": Wood, "A City Looks to the Future."
211 - "In his report on transportation": Harland Bartholomew & Associates, *A Master Plan for Dallas,* Report No. 6, "Transportation Facilities," 35, 41, 45.
211 - "an old dream: canalization": Ibid., 51-52.
211 - "In his report on zoning": Bartholomew & Associates, *A Master Plan for Dallas,* Report No. 9, "Zoning," 14-15.
212 - "Bartholomew especially criticized": Black, "Empire of Consensus," 180-81.
212 - "comments concerning housing": Bartholomew & Associates, *A*

Master Plan for Dallas, Report No. 9, "Zoning," 8, and Report No. 7, "A System of Parks and Schools," 6.
212 - "The president of the Negro Chamber of Commerce": T.W. Pratt to National Negro Business League, Sept. 11, 1944, Folder 9, Box 3, Dallas Negro Chamber of Commerce Collection, DPL.
212 - "downtown Dallas...was 'quite unsatisfactory'": Bartholomew & Associates, *A Master Plan for Dallas,* Report No. 11, "Public Buildings," 26-27, 29-30, and 36-39; Black, "Empire of Consensus," 185.
213 - "'There is no north Dallas because'": Chamber of Commerce minutes, April 21, 1944, quoted in Black, "Empire of Consensus," 278.
214 - "One aspect of the problem": DMN, Dec. 24, 1941, and April 2, 7, 1945.
214 - "Highland Park had been developed": Acheson, *Dallas Yesterday,* 52-56; DMN, April 2, 1945.
214 - "populated by 20,048 residents": DMN, April 2, 1945.
214 - "Preston Hollow": Ibid.
215 - "'Everything possible has been done'": Ibid., April 1, 1945.
216 - "'maintenance of any standards they'": Ibid.; Black, "Empire of Consensus," 186.
216 - "A full-page newspaper advertisement": DMN, April 2, 3, 1945.
216 - "'rekindle the Dallas spirit'": Ibid., April 3, 1945.
216 - "Arguments...were countered by": Black, "Empire of Consensus," 276.
217 - "an example of 'ruthless politics'": Ibid., 182.
217 - "would favor unification": DMN, April 2, 1945.
217 - "On election day": Ibid., April 4, 1945.
218 - "'That kind of talk'": Ibid.
218 - "voted to annex": Ibid., April 5, 12, 1945; Black, "Empire of Consensus," 282.
218 - "Dallas...quickly adjusted": DMN, April 6, 7, 8, 1945.
218 - "The annexation of lands.": Black, "Empire of Consensus," 286.

PART III

11. The Mob Makes Its Move

222 - "'If they should not be voted'": DMN, Dec. 4, 1945.
222 - "they approved all seventeen propositions": Ibid., Dec. 9, 1945.
222 - "Water and sanitary sewers": Ibid., April 24, 1947.
222 - "A perplexing dilemma": Wallace Savage Oral History.
223 - "One study estimated": DMN, April 20, 1947.
223 - "the price of a modest house": Ibid., May 12, 1946; Wallace Savage Oral History.

223 - "Antal Dorati.": Payne, *Dallas*, 233-35.
224 - "Kramer founded the Dallas Grand Opera": Acheson, *Dallas Yesterday*, 213-14.
224 - "a determined and brassy young Texan": *Handbook of Texas*, III, (Austin: The Texas State Historical Association, 1976) 454-55.
224 - "Starlight Operetta": DMN, May 20, 1990.
226 - "He decided to break the rigid color line": Larry Bowman, "Breaking Barriers," *Legacies*, Spring 1991.
226 - "'he was indebted to the colored race'": *Dallas Express*, June 28, 1952.
228 - "'as for this man Wade'": Interview with Henry Wade by author, Feb. 23, 1993.
228 - "he only intended to keep the job": Ibid.
228 - "the veteran Smoot Schmid": Cox, *Sheriffs, Dallas County, Texas*, 81-82.
229 - "'the biggest political machine'": DMN, Aug. 25, 1946; Cox, *Sheriffs, Dallas County*, 93.
229 - "'Regardless of its registered attitude'": White, "Dripping Dry Dallas"; DMN, July 16, 1944.
230 - "city officials decided to permit gamblers": Stone, et al, *City Manager Government in Dallas*, 52, 77. Details on gambling in the pages that follow are gleaned largely from "Organized Crime" clippings files, DPL.
230 - "One of the most popular forms of gambling": *Dallas Journal*, Sept. 14, 1936; DMN, Dec. 10, 1945.
230- "to see how many forms of gambling": DMN, April 7, 1947.
231 - "hatched a bizarre plot": DTH, July 17, 1958; various clippings from "Organized Crime" clippings file, DPL.
231 - "Lester (Benny) Binion": DTH, Dec. 27, 1989.
231 - "Run-ins with the law": *Dallas Journal*, Sept. 14, 1936; DMN, Sept. 13, 1936.
232 - "'I remember the pride that my father'": Emerson Emory, M.D., described his feelings in an an article in the DTH on Jan. 29, 1990, shortly after Binion's death.
232 - "The Chicago mobsters": DMN, Dec. 19, 1946; April 11, 1947.
233 - "was authorized to offer Guthrie": The nature of the offer was brought out in tape recordings introduced in court during Jones' trial in April 1947, with portions of it being reprinted in newspaper stories during the twelve-day trial which ended on April 18, 1947.
234 - "Jones told Guthrie that similar": Ibid.
234 - "They arrested Jones at his apartment": DMN, Dec. 21, 1946.
234 - "Jones did not begin his term until": Ibid., May 30, 1957.
235 - "effort to end organized gambling": "Gambling I, Crime and Criminals" clippings file, DPL; DTH, Dec. 28, 1949; DMN, May 21, 1947.
235 - "'gamblers arrested came up, paid their fines'": DMN, Jan. 27, 1947.
235 - "white-haired, fortyish Herbert Noble": DTH, Dec. 18, 1949. Many of

the details that follow concerning Noble come from the Herbert Noble clippings file, DPL.
236 - "The efforts to kill Noble": DMN, Sept. 9, 1946.
236 - "noticed a black Ford passing": Ibid.,
236 - "More spectacular headlines": Ibid., Nov. 30, 1949; DTH, Dec. 18,1949.
237 - "Hollis Delois (Lois) Green": DMN, Dec. 24, 1949; Jan. 1, 1950.
237 - "Noble stepped out of his Oak Cliff": DMN, Jan. 1, 3, 1950.
238 - "gunmen once again ambushed him": DTH, June 14, 1950.
238 - "'swears and hopes his children will die'": DMN, May 2, 1951; Aug. 8, 1951.
238 - "making their own war": Ibid., Jan. 17, 1952.
239 - "asked him how soon Urban would be retried": Interview with Henry Wade by author, Feb. 23, 1993.
239 - "undesired national attention": "Turnabout," *Time,* March 20, 1952, 41-42.
239 - "charged into a West Dallas grocery store": DTH, Jan. 24, 1951.
240 - "was shattered by a bomb": Ibid., Feb. 13, 1951, May 3, 1952; DMN, Aug. 8,1951.
240 - "Noble went to Austin to testify": DMN, April 4, 1951; May 2, 1951.
240 - "a powerful dynamite explosion": Ibid., Aug. 8, 1951.
241 - "dropped dead of a heart attack": Interview with Henry Wade by author, Feb. 23, 1993.
241 - "Desperate to avoid a return": Various clippings, "Crime and Criminals—Organized Crime" file, DPL.
241 - "Binion returned to Texas": DTH, Dec. 15, 1953.
242- "'Sometimes all you have to do is mention'": Ibid., June 19, 1986.
242 - "His funeral procession": DMN, Dec. 29, 1989.
242 - "made their way to Fort Worth": Albert S. Johnson statement to Dallas Crime Commission, Feb. 14, 1955, Folder 3, Box 2, EC Papers.
242 - "'I do not see how men'": DMN, May 1, 1947.
242-33 - "A record number of candidates": Ibid., April 1, 1947.
243 - "The CCA's harmony was disrupted": Ibid., April 2, 16, 1947.
243 - "Temple, small, energetic, and friendly": Ibid., April 20, 1947.
244 - "Jean Baptist Adoue Jr.": Adoue clippings file, DPL; Payne, *Dallas*, 224.
244 - "They informally agreed": Adoue clippings files, DPL; Wallace Savage Oral History.
245 - "Savage and his wife returned": Wallace Savage Oral History; DMN, July 23, 1949.
245 - "Adoue won the backing": DMN, July 23, 1949.
245 - "Adoue sent a letter and petition": Ibid.,Aug. 21, 31, 1949.
245 - "'powerful and influential downtown'": Acheson, *Dallas Yesterday,* 198.

12. The Uneasy Fifties

248 - "fell prey to a con artist": DTH, May 1, 1951.
248 - "At the council meeting": DMN, May 2, 1951.
248 - "Adoue claimed that": Ibid.
248 - "Adoue began criticizing the police": Acheson, *Dallas Yesterday,* 200; DMN, Sept. 5, 1951.
249 - "he witnessed a Negro driver": *Dallas Express,* Aug. 11, 18, 1951, Sept. 1, 1951.
250 - "Bill Shaw": Shaw clippings file, DPL.
250 - "Walter Lewis (Lew) Sterrett": Sterrett clippings file, DPL.
250 - "James Eric (Bill) Decker": Cox, *Sheriffs of Dallas County,* 98.
251 - "*Negro City Directory* summarized": *Negro City Directory,* 1947-48, 36.
252 - "'one of the worst evils'": *Dallas Express,* June 15, 1946.
253 - "an estimated 13,000 Dallas Negroes held poll taxes": Dallas Negro Chamber of Commerce Papers, Folder 7, Box 1, DPL.
253 - "The chamber enunciated specific goals": Annual Report, 1946, Dallas Negro Chamber of Commerce Papers, DPL.
253 - "equal pay for black teachers": "Letter to All Teachers," March 16, 1943, Folder 3, Box 7, DNCC Papers, DPL.
253 - "the local NAACP": *Negro City Directory, 1947-48,* 36.
253 - "to complain about the situation": Weems letter to Love Field, Jan. 17, 1945, Folder 7, Box 7, DNCC Papers, DPL.
253 - "The hotel situation": Weems to J. Oak Smith, Jan. 3, 1946, Folder 8, Box 1, Ibid.
254 - "ordered Mrs. Craft to move": A. Maceo Smith to W.J. Vollmer, July 25, 1950, Folder 16, Box 19, Juanita Craft Papers, DPL.
254 - "A 1948 year-end report": The report, dated Dec. 16, 1948, is in Folder 19, Box 3, ibid..
254 - "a number of black attorneys": *Negro City Directory, 1947-48,* 38.
255 - "'We had no problem of white guys'": G. William Jones, *Black Cinema Treasures: Lost and Found* (Denton: University of North Texas Press, 1991), 175. Other details that follow about the films also come from *Black Cinema Treasures.*
255 - "Dallas was recognized as": *Dallas Express,* Oct. 19, 1946.
255 - "A *Dallas Express* banner headline": Ibid., Sept. 7,1946.
255 - "only four prosecutions brought penalties": "Council of Negro Organizations, Meeting Held Nov. 27, 1944," Folder 3, Box 7, DNCC Papers, DPL.
255 - "Lynn Landrum...was a strong proponent": DMN, June 24, 1946.
255 - "At a qualifying exam for officers": *Dallas Express,* Oct. 12, 26,1946;

Nov. 9, 30, 1946.
256 - "one licensed black plumber": A.G. Weems to Mr. Nichollas, Oct. 15, 1945, Folder 8, Box 7, DNCC Papers, DPL.
256 - "critical shortage of housing": "Report on Negro Housing Market Data, 1950," Folder 4, Box 1, ibid.
257 - "public housing was 'socialistic'": DMN, Dec. 21, 1949.
257- "an overflow crowd appeared": Ibid., Jan. 11, 1950.
257 - "two white women agents": Ibid., March 16, 1950.
258 - "'practically no Negro housing built in Dallas'": Savage is quoted in Jim Schutze, *The Accommodation: The Politics of Race in an American City (Secaucus, N.J.: Citadel Press, 1986),* 14.
258 - "On the Sunday evening of June 24, 1951": The explosions are described in newspaper accounts of the following day. Ray Charles' stay in South Dallas is described in his autobiography, *Brother Ray: Ray Charles' Own Story* (New York: The Dial Press, 1978), 160.
259 - "a group of Negroes appeared": DMN, June 27,1951.
259 - "'an outrage of law and public order'": Ibid., June 29,1951.
259 - "'It is one of the means of operations'": Ibid., June 27, 1951.
259 - "'even a bare scrap of information'": Quoted by Schutze, *The Accommodation,* 20.
259 - "a high-powered special grand jury": Interview with Wade, Feb. 23, 1993.
259 - "membership read like a who's who": DTH, Sept. 23, 1951.
260 - "Thurgood Marshall of the NAACP": Juanita Craft to Walter White, Aug. 4, 1951, and White to Craft, Aug. 7,1951, Folder 1, Box 9, Juanita Craft Papers, DPL.
260 - "'Unlike Chicago'": White to Craft, Aug. 7,1951, ibid.
261 - "merely 'messenger boys'": DMN, Sept. 9, 1951.
261 - "Other arrests soon followed": DTH, Sept. 21, 23, 1951.
261 - "they had been paid for their deeds": DMN, Sept. 23, 1951; Schutze, *The Accommodation,* 26.
261-62 - "had wanted to indict the Baptist preacher": Wade interview with author, Feb. 18, 1993.
262 - "'The plot reached into unbelievable places'": DTH, Sept. 23, 1951; Schutze, *The Accommodation,* 26, 71.
262 - "Garcia denied responsibility": DTH, Dec. 3-9, 1951; Schutze, *The Accommodation,* 71-72.
263 - "It was named Hamilton Park": Schutze, *The Accommodation,* 77-82.
263 - "There was no concern about": Bolding and Bolding, *Origin and Growth of the Dallas Water Utilities,* 149.
263 - "were shocked to discover": Ibid., 152; DTH, Nov. 12, 1952.
264 - "Dr. Irving P. Krick": Bolding and Bolding, *Origin and Growth of the Dallas Water Utilities,* 157.

264 - "To conserve water": DTH, Nov. 11, 1952.
265 - "holding up a glass of the treated water": Ibid., Nov. 12, 1952; Bolding and Golding, *Origin and Growth of the Dallas Water Utilities*, 156.
265 - "the mayor abruptly reversed his position": DTH, Jan. 30, 1953.
265 - "'under normal conditions'": C.H. Billings to Elgin Crull, quoted in ibid., Feb. 26, 1953.
265 - "A private citizen, attorney Tom Howard": Ibid., Feb. 25, 1953.
266 - "adamantly opposing the use of West Fork water": Ibid., Feb. 26, 1953.
266 - "Crull released the report": Ibid., Feb. 27,1953.
266 - "also was muzzled": Ibid., Feb. 27,1953.
266 - "Adoue later gave his version": Acheson, *Dallas Yesterday*, 200.
267 - "he would not be a candidate": DTH, Jan. 30, 1953.
267 - "vowing that it would not be used": Ibid., April 1, 1953.
267 - "Thornton showed 'amazing strength'": Ibid., April 8, 1953.
268 - "Mayor Thornton named a high-powered": Bolding and Bolding, *Origin and Growth of the Dallas Water Utilities*, 160-65.
268 - "an alarmed city manager announced": Ibid., 174-77.
268 - "'I said in the beginning'": DTH, May 2, 1953.
268 - "'as efficient and business-like government'": Ibid., May 1, 1953; May 4, 1953.
269 - "The 1957 election day": Ibid., April 3, 1957.
270 - "more air passenger traffic": "Dallas Love Field: Dallas' Community Aviation Program," a publication of the Dallas Chamber of Commerce aviation committee, [1954,] Lynn Landrum-Love Field Papers, DeGolyer Special Collections, SMU.
270 - "Dallas became alarmed": Ibid.
271 - "it offered to sell one-half interest": *Fort Worth Star-Telegram*, Dec. 1, 1954, clipping in Lynn Landrum Scrapbook, 1955, Ibid.
271 - "Elaborate tables were prepared": "Dallas Love Field: Dallas' Community Aviation Program," 1954, ibid.
271 - "'The time will come'": R.L. Bowen to The Editor, DMN, March 8, 1955, in Lynn Landrum-Love Field, Scrapbook, 1955, ibid.
271 - "'an awfully high price'": Parrish to Landrum, Jan. 11, 1955, ibid.
272 - "'I just have the strong feeling'": Ibid., Jan. 17, 1955.
272 - "'epidemic of errors'": Haddaway to McKnight, Jan. 11, 1955, ibid.
272 - "'Outrageous'": H.L. Nichols to Alger, June 13, 1956, Lynn Landrum-Love Field, Scrapbook, 1956, ibid.

13. Uncle Bob's Reign

274 - "the largest industrial move in the nation's history": DTH, June 2, 1991.
275 - "powerful role in decision-making": Thometz, *The Decision-Makers*, 62.
276 - "'After you've got these ten or twelve'": Interview by author with John

Schoellkopf, Dec. 1, 1992.
276 - "a sudden crisis": Warren Leslie, *Dallas, Public and Private: Aspects of an American City* (New York: Grossman Publishers, 1964), 70.
277 - "Committee for Good Schools": Thometz, *The Decision-Makers*, 64-65; DMN, March 7, 21, 1973.
277 - "the single individual": Thometz, *The Decision-Makers*, 79.
278 - "Florence was the son": Wineburgh, *The Texas Banker*, 10, 18-20.
279 - "'a constant search for meaning'": Bruce Alger Oral History.
280 - "came to know Albert Einstein": Ibid.
280 - "involved himself in a full range": Biographical sheet, Folder 1, Box 1, Bruce Alger Collection, DPL; DMN, Nov. 4, 1954.
280 - "'It was a surprise to me'": Bruce Alger Oral History.
281 - "full support of Eisenhower": Various campaign literature, Folder 7, Box 1, Bruce Alger Collection.
281 - "placed an empty chair": Bruce Alger Oral History.
281 - "'I guess I'd better get busy'": DMN, Nov. 4, 1954.
281 - "'Coffee With Bruce Alger'": Ibid.; Bruce Alger Oral History.
281 - "endorsed the Democrat Savage": DMN, Nov. 2, 1954.
282 - "scored a shocking upset victory": Ibid., Nov. 3, 4, 1954.
282 - "'beaten, bewildered candidate'": The AP story appeared in the *Lubbock Evening Journal*, Nov. 3, 1954, a clipping of which is in the Bruce Alger Collection, Folder 6, Box 1, DPL.
282 - "His victory seemed untarnished": DMN, Nov. 4, 1954.
283 - "'running on the coattails'": Campaign literature in Folder 21, Box 2, Bruce Alger Collection, DPL.
283 - "The old Carnegie Library": Larry Grove, *Dallas Public Library: The First 75 Years* (Dallas: Dallas Public Library, 1977), 67-73.
284 - "'My God, it looks like a bad welding job'": George Dahl Oral History.
284 - "'this pile of junk'": Grove, *Dallas Public Library*, 81.
284 - "'take the damn screen down'": George Dahl Oral History.
284 - "Then came a counter-reaction": Dahl recalled some years later that the group was able to raise only $700 of the $12,000, and that he insisted that the money be used to buy books for the library instead of going to him. Thus, the screen became Dahl's gift to the city. George Dahl Oral History.
284 - "another question of artistic appropriateness": Grove, *Dallas Public Library*, 81.
285 - "had clothed the youth": George Dahl Oral History.
285 - "another controversy arose": Jerry Bywaters, *Seventy-Five Years of Art in Dallas*, (Dallas: Dallas Museum of Fine Arts, 1978), [35-36]. The debate over politics and art is treated at length in Leslie, *Dallas Public and Private*, 165-178.
285 - "'dedicated to destroying'": Bywaters, *Seventy-Five Years of Art in Dallas*, [36].

286 - "'only on the basis of their merit'": Ibid. [37].
286 - "'Sports in Art'": Ibid., [37].
286 - "the persistent issue surfaced once more": Grove, *Dallas Public Library*, 81.
287 - "Would Cabell accept the CCA nomination": Notarized affidavit by Cabell, March 22, 1959, reproduced in campaign leaflet, "So That the Truth May Be Known!" Folder 4, Box 6, Earle Cabell Collection, DeGolyer Special Collections, Southern Methodist University.
287 - "Earle graduated from North Dallas High": A summary of Cabell's life is in the Guide to Earle Cabell Collection.
288 - "As a consolation prize": The CCA offer went next to attorney Tom Unis, who accepted and was elected.
288 - "believing that he had been treated unfairly": March 22,1959, affidavit, Folder 4, Box 6, Earle Cabell Collection.
288 - "If Cabell would postpone his race": Ibid.
288 - "'I am bucking the machine'": Cabell to Pearre Cabell, March 4, 1959, Folder 3, Box 6, ibid.
289 - "CABELL is EVERYBODY'S candidate": Ed C. Schwille to Cabell, Feb. 18, 1959, Folder 13, Box 6, ibid.
289 - "challenging the CCA's 'machine politics'": "This is the Earle Cabell Platform," Folder 4, ibid.
289 - "the layout was a 'nightmare'": Various campaign literature and clippings, Folder 2, ibid.
289 - "Cabell blasted the 'machine politics'": DMN, April 3,1959.
289 - "a 'land grab' on Griffin Street": News release from Cabell, March 18, 1959, Folder 4, Box 6, Earle Cabell Collection; DTH, April 4, 1959.
289 - "When the fiery campaign ended": DTH, April 8, 1959.
290 - "'I need your help'": Undated radio script, Folder 10, Box 6, Earle Cabell Collection.
290 - "'biggest political and economic squeeze'": DTH, April 12, 13, 1959.
290 - "sharply denied Cabell's charges": Ibid., April 12, 1959.
290 - "Thornton absolutely denied it": Ibid., April 13, 1959.
290 - "'an overpowering and ill-conceived obsession'": Ibid., April 14, 1959.
290 - "guilty of "slanting and distortion'": Ibid., April 14, 1959.
291 - "'an unusual number of good candidates'": DMN, April 7, 1959.
291 - "'low level, name-calling political campaign'": Ibid., April 19, 1959.
291 - "'there is such a thing as any group'": DTH, April 22, 1959.
291 - "Cabell...expressed thanks": Ibid.
291 - "shocked the CCA leaders": Various documents, Folder 29, Box 16, Earle Cabell Collection.
291 - "a thoughtful eight-page critique": Clark, "Times Have Changed," Folder 29, Box 6, Earle Cabell Collection.
292 - "sent a copy of the plan to Cabell": "Organizational Plan and Operat-

ing Procedure for the Citizens' Charter Association," ibid.
292 - "'Your Choice, Your Voice'": A copy of the brochure, dated Oct. 27, 1959, is in ibid.
292 - "'that the CCA was an exclusive organization'": DTH, Sept. 12, 1960, clipping in ibid.
293 - "of 'windfall profits'": The theme is repeated in various speeches and documents in Folders 36 and 37, Box 6, Earle Cabell Collection.
293 - "Geary produced a police report": Allison Cheney, *Dallas Spirit: A Political History of the City of Dallas* (Dallas: McMullan Publishing Co., 1991), 49-50.
294 - "the NAACP petitioned the Dallas school board": DTH, Sept. 2, 1954.
294 - "ruled against the NAACP": Glenn Linden, "Desegregating the Dallas Schools: A Generation of Court Battles," an unpublished manuscript, 27.
295 - "'The basic facts were simple and undisputed'": Ibid., 32.
295 - "some 300 white Protestant ministers": William R. Carmack and Theodore Freedman, *Dallas,Texas: Factors Affecting School Desegregation* (New York: Anti-Defamation League of B'nai B'rith, 1962), 28.
296 - "the appeals court ordered the school district": Ibid.
296 - "This quandary was resolved": Ibid., 6-7.
296 - "'No country in history'": Linden, "Desegregating the Dallas Schools," 46.
296 - "The 5th Court of Appeals rejected his plan": Ibid., 7.
297 - "the situation to be so critical": Warren Leslie, *Dallas Public and Private: Aspects of an American City* (New York: Grossman Publishers, 1964), 72-73.
297 - "some important news was suppressed": Carmack and Freedman, *Dallas, Texas: Factors Affecting School Desegregation*, 22-23.
297 - "embarrass desegregation plans": Ibid., 11.
298 - "voted to integrate the midway rides": Nancy Wiley, *The Great State Fair of Texas* (Dallas: Taylor Publishing Co., 1985), 158.
298 - "at least two rides did not qualify": *Dallas Express*, Oct. 15, 22, 1915.
299 - "now yielded and declared": Wiley, *The Great State Fair of Texas*, 164.
299 - "James organized regular picket lines": DMN, Jan. 10, 1961.
299 - "a 'sit-in' at the counter": Carmack and Freedman, *Dallas, Texas: Factors Affecting School Desegregation*, 22-23; "SMU Students Stage Sit-Ins," *Texas Observer*, Jan. 14, 1961; "Dallas Picketing," ibid., Oct. 7, 1960; "Dallasites Picket Store," ibid., Oct. 14, 1960.
299 - "heard Durham announce that": DMN, Jan. 9, 1961; *Dallas Express*, Feb. 4, 1961.
300 - "On Monday Rhett James led": *Dallas Express*, Jan. 14 and Feb. 4, 1961.
300 - "demonstrations at two downtown theaters": Ibid., Feb. 25, 1961.
300 - "boycott downtown department stores": Ibid., March 4, 1961.
300 - "removed all discriminating signs": Ibid., Aug. 5, 1961.
300 - "the activist tactics": Dulaney, "Whatever Happened to the Civil

Rights Movement in Dallas, Texas?" *Essays on the American Civil Rights Movement*, 79-85.
301 - "passed an 'anti-mob ordinance'": Thometz, *The Decision-Makers*, 67-68.
301- "'No one congregated except newspaper people'": DTH, Sept. 6, 1961; *New York Times*, Sept. 7, 1961.
301 - "singled out Dallas for public praise": DTH, Sept. 7, 1961; *New York Times*, Sept. 7, 1961.
302 - "C.A. Tatum seemed touched": Carmack and Freedman, *Dallas, Texas: Factors Affecting School Desegregation*, 25.
302 - "By 1964 only 131": Linden, "Desegregating the Dallas Schools," 62.
302 - "all elementary schools must be desegregated": Schiebel, *Education in Dallas*, 160.
302 - "By 1967 fourteen of the 172 schools": Linden, "Desegregating the Dallas Schools," 72.

BOOM AND BUST

14. November 22, 1963

305 - "snatched away her gloves": Carl L. Phinney describes this incident in Merle Miller, *Lyndon: An Oral Biography* (New York: Ballantine Books, 1980), 270.
305 - "worst hour in politics ever": Ibid.
305-06 - "spittle and insults were flying": Stanley Marcus to author, Feb. 11, 1993.
306 - "'nearest thing to an uncontrollable mob'": DMN, Nov. 5, 1960.
306 - "'If the time has come'": Miller, *Lyndon*, 271.
306 - "Republican candidate John Tower": DMN, Nov. 5, 1960.
306 - "Bruce Alger, stood on the street": Ibid.
306 - "'the prettiest bunch of women I ever saw'": Bruce Alger Oral History.
306 - "'completely foreign to usual Dallas manners'": DTH, Nov. 6, 1960.
306 - "a full-page advertisement": A copy of the Nov. 7, 1960, advertisement is in Folder 24, Box 10, Alger Papers, DPL.
307 - "Army General Edwin A. Walker": "Thunder on the Right," *Newsweek*, Dec. 4, 1961.
307 - "the 'tool of any special interest group'": Alger to Oscar Korn, Feb. 27,1962, Folder 23, Box 10, Alger Papers.
308 - "Frank McGehee began the group": "Who's Who in the Tumult of the Far Right," *Life*, Feb. 9, 1962.
309 - "'the election of a Catholic as president'": Chandler Davidson, *Race and Class in Texas Politics* (Princeton: Princeton University Press, 1990), 213-14.

309 - "raised eyebrows across the nation": A.C. Greene, *Dallas USA* (Austin: Texas Monthly Press, 1984), 103; Arthur Schlesinger, *A Thousand Days: John F. Kennedy in the White House* (Boston: Houghton Mifflin, 1965), 752.
310 - "the shot had barely missed Walker": *Hearings Before the President's Commission on the Assassination of President Kennedy,* 26 vols. (Washington: U.S. Government Printing Office, 1964), XI, 424 (cited hereafter as Warren Commission).
310 - "Walker told the U.S. Day crowd": DMN, Oct. 24,1963.
310 - "every street corner in Dallas": DTH, Oct. 24, 1963.
310 - "he wanted to hang him": Schlesinger, *A Thousand Days,* 753.
310 - "'Wanted for Treason'": Walter Johnson, ed., *The Papers of Adlai E. Stevenson: Ambassador to the United Nations, 1961-65* (Boston: Little , Brown and Co., 1979), VIII, 460.
310 - "as Stevenson came to the podium to speak": The author was present on this occasion. The events left a vivid impression. They are described in Darwin Payne, *The Impact of the Press on Events in Dallas Related to the Assassination of President John F. Kennedy,* Journalism Monograph No. 15, Association for Education in Journalism, February 1970, 21-22. Details also come from newspaper accounts on Oct. 25, 1963, in the DMN and DTH.
311 - "signs which had been stored overnight": DTH, Oct. 27,1963.
311 - "Are these human beings": Schlesinger, *A Thousand Days,* 1020.
311 - "crowd members began rocking it": Marcus to Payne, Feb. 11, 1993.
311 - "Police arrested the woman": Johnson, ed., *The Papers of Adlai E. Stevenson,* VIII, 460; DTH, Oct. 25 , 1963.
312 - "'Big D now stands for disgrace'": Quoted in DMN, Oct. 26, 1963.
312 - "'A City Disgraced'": *Time,* Nov. 1, 1963.
312 - "'The Dallas Image Unveiled'": *Christian Century,* Nov. 20, 1963.
312 - "'The City of Dallas is outraged'": Quoted in DMN, Oct. 26, 1963.
312 - "Mayor Cabell recalled the days": DTH, Oct. 27,1963.
312 - "'Dallas has been disgraced'": Ibid., Oct. 25, 1963.
312 - "'What has happened to Dallas?'": Ibid., Oct. 26,1963.
313 - "'If the time has come'": DMN, Oct. 26, 1963.
313 - "'But you know, there was'": Johnson, Ed., *The Papers of Adlai E. Stevenson,* VIII, 461.
313 - "'Your visit has had permanent.'": Quoted by Schlesinger, *A Thousand Days,* 1020-21.
313 - "Stevenson sought to downplay": Stevenson to John Connally, Nov. 1, 1963, to Earle Cabell, Oct. 30, 1963, and speech to American Jewish Committee, Nov. 7, 1963, as quoted in Johnson, ed., *The Papers of Adlai E. Stevenson,* VIII, 462, 465.
313 - "'the President will have an enthusiastic'": Stevenson to O'Donnell, Nov. 4, 1963, ibid., 466.
314 - "'I don't care what you think'": Marcus to Payne, Feb. 11, 1993.

314 - "'Repeat of Demonstration for JFK Visit Not Likely.'": Quoted by Payne, *The Impact of the Press on Events in Dallas*, 24.
314 - "He wanted a nonpolitical body": William Manchester, *The Death of President: November 20-November 25, 1963* (New York: Harper & Row, 1967), 22; Stanley Marcus, *Minding the Store: A Memoir* (Boston: Little, Brown and Company, 1974), 254.
315 - "Walker, irritated, suddenly stood up": The author was present at the luncheon in his capacity as a reporter for the DTH. News articles concerning the incident appear in the Nov. 19 and 20 editions of the paper.
315 - "'Police Chief Puts Dallas on Notice'": DTH, Nov. 20,1963.
315 - "urging Dallas to give'": DMN, Nov. 22,1963.
316 - "WANTED FOR TREASON'": Manchester, *Death of a President*, 64; Greene, *Dallas USA*, 108-109; Robert A. Surrey testimony before the Warren Commission in Volume V, 420-449, and testimony of Robert G. Clause, V, 535-546.
316 - "'We're really in "nut" country now'": Sorenson, *Kennedy*, 750.
316 - "Grinnan raised money": Testimony of Bernard Weissman, Warren Commission, V, 504-506; DTH, Sept. 28, 1964.
316 - "Two of those who": "All Eyes Turn to Dallas," from a special section in DMN, "Nov. 22: Twenty Years Later" Nov. 20, 1983; Manchester, *The Death of a President*, 109.
317 - "hitting him in the face": Manchester, *The Death of a President*, 109; Joe M. Dealey Oral History .
318 - "'like a firecracker'": Zapruder's comment was made just after the assassination to the author when he was a reporter for the *Dallas Times Herald* .
318 - "'Those damn fanatics'": DMN, Nov. 23, 1963; "Twenty Years Later," DMN, Nov. 20, 1983.
320 - "'This could have happened in Podunk'": DMN, Nov. 23, 1963.
321 - "Police sent guards to his house": "All Eyes Turn to Dallas," DMN, Nov. 20,1983.
321 - "W.T. White immediately suspended her': The incident is described in ibid.
321 - "'gratuitous defectors and journalistic buzzards'": Ibid.
321 - "'What's Right in Dallas?'" DMN, Jan. 2, 1964.
321 - "closed their Neiman-Marcus accounts": Marcus, *Minding the Store*, 252-53.
322 - "'We are a tormented'": Cited by Payne, *Dallas*, 248.
322 - "'All I could do was pray'": Ibid.
322 - "'undergoing the dark night of the soul'": Quoted in "All Eyes Turn to Dallas," DMN special section, Nov. 20,1983.
322 - "'In the name of God, what kind'": Ibid.
322 - "drafted him for the office.": Cheney, *Dallas Spirit*, 52-53.

323 - "'This may be a benevolent oligarchy'": DMN, Feb. 1, 4, 1964.
323 - "the depth of his support": Document in Folder 45, Box 114, Earle Cabell Collection.
323 - "Felix McKnight had conferred closely": See the five-page memo of suggestions from Pietzsch to McKnight, Fall 1964, Folder 46, ibid.
324 - "an endorsement would be improper": Alger Oral History.
324 - "'a return to sanity'": DTH, Nov. 4, 1964.

15. The Erik Jonsson Years

326 - "It prospered more than ever": DTH, Nov. 22,1964; *New York Times,* Nov. 24, 1973.
327 - "Jonsson as a small boy": Molly Ivins, "Dallas' 'Big Daddy' Figure," *New York Times Magazine,* Sept. 16, 1973.
328 - "TI had become a giant corporation": *50 Years of Innovation: The History of Texas Instruments,* a pamphlet published in 1980 by Texas Instruments; *Christian Science Monitor,* Nov. 24, 1970.
328 - "'hadn't begun to give up'": Carter Wiseman, *I.M. Pei: A Profile in American Architecture,* (New York: Harry N. Abrams, Inc., 1990), 121-22.
328 - "'an extremely serious problem'": "Traffic Pattern," *Flying,* June 1964.
329 - "'unadulterated childish civic pride'": "Airport," typescript summary of the situation written for the DMN, undated, Folder 40, Box 6, Earle Cabell Collection.
329 - "the CAB sent a telegram": Erik Jonsson Oral History, 48.
329 - "As early as 1933": Stemmons to Dealey, Dec. 1, 1933, Folder 403, Box 43, GBD Papers.
329 - "he decided finally": Erik Jonsson Oral History.
330 - "'We were determined'": Ibid., 50.
331 - "'totally unimpressed with the phenomenon'": Jonsson essay, "Days of Decision," *Goals for Dallas,* (Dallas: Goals for Dallas, 1966), 308-309.
331 - "'an idyllic picture'": Erik Jonsson Oral History.
331 - "The process was slow and deliberate": Bryghte Goldbold Oral History.
332 - "'They felt that Dallas was the greatest city'": Quoted by Wiseman, *I.M. Pei,* 125.
332 - "Jonsson conceived of a series": Ibid., 125, 127.
332 - "the low bid was $50.2 million": DMN, Sept. 18, 1970.
332 - "Jonsson diplomatically withdrew his support": Printed statement by Erik Jonsson, Sept. 21, 1970, in possession of author.
332 - "City council members, obviously relieved": DMN, Sept. 22, 1970.
333 - "committee members deadlocked": Interview with John Schoellkopf, Nov. 30, 1992. Schoellkopf, who was to head the drive to approve the supplemental bond election, was present at the Citizens Council meeting.

333 - "Two Negro players were served without incident": Tim Cowlishaw, "Right Place, Wrong Time," undated DMN clipping, in author's possession.
334 - "'I got a unanimous answer from them'": The dispute over the stadium is described in Jane Wolfe, *The Murchisons: The Rise and Fall of a Texas Dynasty* (New York: St. Martin's Press, 1989), 296-304.
335 - "'I exposed the plan to civic leaders'": DMN, Oct. 10, 1970.
335 - "'If you take the Cowboys out of Fair Park'": Wolfe, *The Murchisons,* 303.
336 - "the plans that Ponte and Travers presented": Walter G. Dahlberg, "Growth, Planning, and the CBD," *Dallasights,* 26.
337 -"George L. Allen": George Allen Oral History.
337 - "Allen was permitted to enroll": Michael L. Gillette, "Blacks Challenge the White University," *Southwestern Historical Quarterly,* October 1982; Kevin J. Shay and Roy Williams, *Time Change: An Alternative View of the History of Dallas* (Dallas: To Be Publishing Co., 1991), 75-76.
338 - "Anita Martinez:" For Ms. Martinez' background see the register prepared for the Anita Martinez Collection, DPL.
340 - "'DANGER. BEWARE'": Quoted by Lee Clark, "Dallas' Oligarchy and Fateful '68," *Texas Observer,* March 1, 1968.
340 - "Its chances were bolstered": DMN, March 31, 1971; DTH, March 31, 1971.
340 - "a report revealing a sharp decline": DMN, April 26, 1971.
340 - "the highest level allowed under the law": Ibid., March 21, 1971.
341 - "'business approach'": DTH, March 2, 1971.
341 - "Election day brought a dramatic upset": Ibid., April 4, 1971.
341 - "the largest run-off vote": Ibid., April 25, 1971.
341 - "the city's black population": DMN, Feb. 12, 1971.
341 - "black students would be in a majority": Ibid., Nov. 8, 1970.
341 - "There remained a large number": League of Women Voters of Dallas, *Implementing School Desegregation* (Dallas: League of Women Voters, 1971), 6.
342 - "White flight now accelerated": Linden, "Desegregating the Dallas Schools," Table 5 [n.p.].
342 - "This represented a change": Ibid., 116-17.
343 - "'At a certain point'": DMN, Jan. 25, 1972.
343 - "handed out contingency assignments": Interview with Bill Sloan, Dec. 9, 1992.
343 - "agreed to sell all ten": Estes, "Black Power in Dallas," *Texas Observer,* Aug. 6,1968.
344 - "Anita Martinez had broken the barrier": DTH, July 20, 1970.
344 - "Little Mexico as a distinctive": Rice, "Little Mexico and the Barriers of Dallas," 25, 27.
344 - "'go out and feed the multitudes'": DTH, March 16, 23, 1971.

345 - "Albert Lipscomb": DMN, April 22,1984, July 29, 1990, and June 6, 1993, July 29, 1990, April 23, 1984.
345 - "a core of white supporters": Elizabeth Durham Davies, "Fair Park Expansion: A Case Study of Political Bias and Protest in Urban Dallas," M.A. thesis, North Texas State University, 1974," 19-20.
346 - "An official 1966 report": Ibid., 17-18.
346 - "nearly erupted into major headlines": Ibid., 34-35; Williams and Shay, *Time Change,* 99-100; Schutze, *The Accommodation,* 167-173.
346 - "filed a federal lawsuit": Fred and Dorothy Joiner, et al, v. City of Dallas, et al, Nov. 24, 1970, U.S. District Court for the Northern District of Texas.
347 - "Martin Luther King Jr.": Jim Lehrer, *A Bus of My Own* (New York: G.P. Putnam's Sons, 1992), 87-88.
347 - "This was *Newsroom*": Ibid., 102-104.
349 - "'We broke a lot of reporting'": Ibid., 107.
349 - "as wild-eyed hippies and leftist radicals": Despite the characterizations of Sterrett and others, most of *Newsroom*'s reporters were competent professionals with deep ties to the community. Lehrer became co-host of public television's McNeil-Lehrer NEWSHOUR program and author of numberous books and plays. Other reporters included A.C. Greene, historian and writer; Lee Clark Cullum, daughter of Charles Cullum and eventual editor of *D* magazine, editor of the *Times Herald*'s editorial page, and *Dallas Morning News* columnist; Martin Frost, who became Democratic Congressman from Dallas; Rene Castilla, who became president of the Dallas Independent School District board; Bob Ray Sanders, who became perhaps the city's foremost black journalist in his continuing work at KERA-TV and later at KLIF radio; Patsy Swank, former *Life* correspondent and prominent figure in Dallas arts; Ron DeVillier, former Methodist minister; John Tackett, who continued a career in newspaper journalism; Ken Harrison, who became a noted filmmaker; and Darwin Payne, author and chairman of the journalism department at Southern Methodist University.

16. Last Days of the CCA

352 - "had been confiding in too many people": Private interview.
352 - "'Does this mean no lawyer, no accountant'" DTH, July 26, 1970.
353 - "'select someone from the younger group'": Ibid., Dec. 30, 1970.
353 - "Schoellkopf could boast": Ibid., Feb. 18,1971.
354 - "'I'm not a news analyst'": DMN, March 10, 1971.
354 - "was fired by the board for being 'disruptive'": DTH, April 17, 1971.
354 - "failed to get a second endorsement": Ibid., May 6, 1971.
355 - "'It isn't enough to put up a lot of signs'": Ibid., April 29, 1971.
355 - "'Today there is no longer the possibility'": Quoted in Ibid., Jan. 10,

1972.
355 - "the outraged Allen jerked": Ibid., May 4, 1971.
355 - "a lawsuit filed by Lipscomb": DMN, April 28, 1972.
356 - "'might succeed in proving'": Ibid.
356 - "a broad-based leadership committee": DTH, Aug. 3, 1972.
356 - "'a diversified City Council'": DMN, Sept. 1, 1972.
357 - "corporations transferring their headquarters": *New York Times*, Nov. 24, 1973; Payne, *Dallas*, 277.
357 - "'You white folks are all the same'": George Allen Oral History.
358 - "'The establishment, as it once was'": *New York Times*, Nov. 24, 1973.
358 - "'lost touch with the people'": DTH, June 21, 1974, and July 20, 1974; Robert S. Folsom Oral History.
358 - "Speculation appeared in the *News*": DMN, Oct. 20, 1974.
358 - "threatened to withdraw": Ibid., Feb. 18, 1975.
359 - "'diluted' minority voting strength": Ibid., Nov. 25, 1990.
359 - "distancing himself as far as he could": DTH, April 2, 4, 1975.
360 - "if the organization would not nominate": Robert S. Folsom Oral History.
360 - "hundreds of swarming cockroaches": DMN, Aug. 20, 1978, Dec. 17, 1978.
360 - "releasing scores of rats": Ibid.,
361 - "Weber enthusiastically endorsed": David Dillon and Doug Tomlinson, *Dallas Architecture, 1936-1986* (Austin: Texas Monthly Press, 1985), 128-29.
361 - "'doesn't want to do anything'": Ibid., 129-130.
361 - "Braden blamed the media": DTH, Feb. 10, 1977.
361 - "'In a four-year period'": Ibid.
362 - "'There is going to be a real tendency'": DMN, Feb. 27, 1977.
363 - "A tragic incident": Details of the Santos Rodriguez shooting and its immediate aftermath come from ibid., July 24, 25, 29, 1973.
365 - "Aguirre introduced a resolution": Williams and Shay, *Time Change*, 108.
366 - "'patently unconstitutional'": Linden, "Desegregating the Dallas Schools," 140.
366 - "'It's time for the business leaders'": DMN, Sept. 17, 1975, as quoted by Linden, "Desegregating the Dallas Schools," 141.
366 - "the Dallas Alliance": Linden, "Desegregating the Dallas Schools," 141-47.
366 - "He chose the basic plan": Ibid., 153.
367 - "What was worrisome": Ibid., 168.
367 - "It remanded the case": Ibid., 175.
367 - "'Black Caucus to Maximize Education'": Ibid., 182-83.
367 - "additional busing would serve no useful purpose": Ibid., 197.

17. One Era Begins, Another Ends

369 - "a disturbing reality": Darwin Payne, "The Future Is Here," *Dallas,* July 1975.

370 - "29.3 million square feet of new office space": Paul Zane Pilzer, *Other People's Money: The Inside Story of the S&L Scandal* (New York: Simon and Schuster, 1989), 82.

370 - "it won rave compliments": Terrell R. Harper, "Dallas City and County Buildings," *Dallasights,* 84, 90-91.

370 - "'It's strong, and the people of Dallas'": Quoted by Wiseman, *I.M. Pei,* 137.

371 - "The suggestion had arisen first": Wes Wise Papers, File 228, Box 21, DPL.

372 - "Dallas-Fort Worth International Airport": *Dallas, A Profile and Fact Book for the Media,* a pamphlet prepared for the 1984 Republican Party Convention by the Dallas Welcoming Committee, 24.

372 - "Far North Dallas held the development spotlight": Ibid., 9.

373 - "Folsom faced frequent criticism": Dillon and Tomlinson, *Dallas Architecture,* 147.

374 - "Folsom—who described himself": Robert S. Folsom Oral History.

374 - "grocer Jack Evans": Robert S. Folsom Oral History; Jack Evans Oral History.

374 - "Taylor spent just under a million dollars": Chaney, *Dallas Spirit,* 66.

376 - "Juanita Craft": Biographical sheet in "Prominent Blacks of Dallas: Professional Profiles," I, typescript, DPL. A biographical summary of Juanita Craft is in the register prepared for the Juanita Craft Collection, DPL.

377 - "'irresponsible people'": DMN, Nov. 17, 1983.

377 - "'She's gonna end up creating'": Ibid., Nov. 18, 1983.

377 - "'Never in the history'": Ibid., Feb. 10, 1984.

379 - "the *Dallas Morning News* and the *Times Herald*": An early summary of the newspaper battle is in Darwin Payne, "Goliath vs. Goliath at the Newsstand," *Dallas,* January 1980.

382 - "The first significant failure": James Ring Adams, *The Big Fix: Inside the S&L Scandal* (New York: John Wiley & Sons, Inc., 1990), 206.

383 - "A central part of Faulkner's scheme": Ibid., 206, 211.

383 - "When his son married": Ibid., 206.

384 - "Nor was Faulkner the most flamboyant": General details come from ibid and Pilzer, *Other People's Money.*

384 - "'strong enough to withstand'": News release from Republic Bank Corporation, Dec. 16, 1986, in "Banking" clippings file, DPL.

385 - "losses of $656.8 million": *Wall Street Journal,* Feb. 22, 1988.

385 - "proposed lie detector tests": Ibid.

385 - "Drastic cost-cutting measures": DMN, April 30, 1988.

385 - "the most expensive bank failure": *Wall Street Journal,* July 29, 1991; DMN, Jan. 30, 1993.
385 - "'utterly abandoned' their responsibilities": Ibid.; DMN, Dec. 3, 1992.
386 - "all but one had been forced to merge": Ibid., Nov. 1, 1992.
387 - "almost 40 million square feet": Pilzer, *Other People's Money,* 82.
387 - "About one-third": DMN, Dec. 9, 1991; Oct. 14, 1992; chart in "The Peirce Report, DMN, Oct. 27, 1991.
387 - "the sales price was about $8 million": Ibid., Dec. 1, 1992.
388 - "'One gathers that the proponents'": Cited by Ibid., Dec. 8, 1991.
388 - "'Not even the most unrepentant'": Dillon and Tomlinson, *Dallas Architecture,* 139.
388 - "were poorly constructed": DMN, Oct. 23, 1992.
389 - "they were to spend $3 million": Ibid., April 5, 1987.
390 - "only precincts that were heavily Republican": Ibid., April 19, 1987.
390 - "'the loveliest, strongest, brightest'": Ibid.
391 - "'Dallas Together'": Williams and Shay, *Time Change,* 138-39.
391 - "the Charter Review Commission": Ibid.,147.
391 - "Angry, name-calling debates": Ibid., 153.
392 - "Marvin Crenshaw and Roy Williams": Ibid., 11, 14-17.
393 - "the City of Dallas yielded": DMN, May 12, 1991.

18. Coming Apart in the '90s

395 - "'Welcome to Dallas'": DMN, Jan. 2, 1993.
396 - "he had never worked in a city": Quoted by Rena Pederson in "Our dysfunctional city family, DMN, Feb. 7, 1993.
397 - "In 1988, 71.8 percent of": Ibid., Oct. 28, 1993, Nov. 18, 1993.
399 - "the percentage of Dallas residents living": *Washington Post National Weekly,* March 15-21, 1993.
399 - "highest rate of office vacancy ": According to a survey conducted by Oncor International Inc., as cited by Steve Brown, "Dallas' office vacancy rate leads U.S., survey says," DMN, Feb. 12, 1993, June 4, 1993.
399 - "the tax base had fallen to $43.2 billion": Ibid., Feb. 23, 1993, May 12, 1993, March 1, 1994.
400 - "had declined to about 30,000": Reid, " Public-private partnership can spur inner-city housing," ibid., March 14, 1993.
400 - "three political advisers": Ibid., Dec. 6, 1992.
401 - "Just how long the council-manager": Ibid., Jan. 28, 1993, Feb. 23, 1993, April 26, 1993.
401 - "*Financial World* declared Dallas": Ibid., Nov. 17, 1992.
402 - "John Wiley Price": Laura Miller, "The Hustler," *D,* March 1991, summarizes the controversial aspects of Price's career.
402 - "upheld by the Texas Court of Criminal Appeals": DMN, May 13, 1993.

403 - "of the need for 'urban guerrilla warfare'": Ibid., May 30, 1993.
404 - "Dallas ranked second": The study was conducted by Professor Sam Walker of the University of Nebraska at Omaha, as cited by DMN, Oct. 13, 1992.
404 - "as of September 1993": DMN, Oct. 28, 1993, Nov. 18, 1993.
404 - "weighted heavily in favor of minorities": DMN, Jan. 30, 1993.
404 - "'We cannot allow a few employees'": Ibid., Nov. 20, 1992.
405 - "'life members' of the Ku Klux Klan": Photograph in DMN, Nov. 14, 1992.
405 - "infuriated many inconvenienced motorists": Ibid., Jan. 28, 31, 1993.
405 - "Threats of violence punctuated": Ibid., Oct. 14, 1992.
406 - "Hicks agreed to cancel": Ibid., Oct. 25, 1992.
406 - "passed over for promotion": Ibid., April 16, 1993.
405 - "lack of evidence to back up such claims": Ibid., May 4, 1993.
406 - "A shocking event": Ibid., Feb. 10, 11, 12, 16, 1993.
408 - "a new Texas Department of Corrections facility": Ibid., Jan. 7, 1992.
408 - "rule against hiring gays and lesbians": Ibid., Jan. 23, 1992.
408 - "why minorities had not been included": Ibid., Feb. 7, 1993.
408 - "minority-owned firms": Ibid., Oct. 15, 1992.
409 - "'another form of sophisticated sharecropping'": Ibid., Jan. 7, 1993.
409 - "labeled the goals as unachievable": Ibid., May 18, 20, 1993.
409 - "the city had made significant advancements": Ibid., June 6, 1993.
409 - "promised not to abandon his goal": Ibid., May 28, 1992.
410 - "DART's failure to use": Ibid., May 29, 1993; *Profile & Update,* February 1993, a DART publication.
411 - "'Some members of the board believe'": DMN, Dec. 16, 1992.
411 - "when a San Diego transit executive": Ibid., Nov. 27, 1993.
411 - "Fights with racial overtones": Ibid., Feb. 20, 22, 23, 1993.
411 - "Domingo Garcia, Al Lipscomb, and John Wiley Price": Ibid., Feb. 27, 1993.
412 - "belittle him as a 'Tio Taco'": Ibid., Aug. 22, 1992.
412 - "put...Paul Fielding in the hospital": Ibid., Dec. 9, 1993.
413 - "'racial and gender tensions'": Ibid., Feb. 14, 1993.
413 - "The number of white students": Ibid., Nov. 11, 1992.
413 - "Dallas' scores were significantly below": Ibid., Dec. 12, 1992.
413 - "only 29 percent of Dallas high school": Ann Melvin, "Educators Always Have an Excuse," DMN, Oct. 31, 1992.
413 - "only 38 percent": Ibid., May 29, 1993.
413 - "Sanders cited the low scores": Linden, "Desegregating the Dallas Schools," 257.
413 - "72 percent of the district's": DMN, Jan. 28, 1993.
413 - "decreeing that enrollment": Ibid., Nov. 11, 1992.
414 - "significant progress had been made": Ibid., Nov. 11, 1992.

414 - "a resounding vote of confidence": Ibid., Dec. 6, 1992.
414 - "the difference used to construct": Ibid., July 6, 1992.
415 - "three times that of Hispanics": Bernard Weinstein, "Cities and Suburbs Changing," DMN, Nov. 10, 1992.
415 - "Census tracts of 1990": Ibid., July 6, 1992.
415 - "hiring off-duty Dallas police officers": Ibid., Jan. 17, 1993.
415 - "In the poorer southern sector": "The Peirce Report," ibid., Oct. 27, 1991.
416 - "the second- fastest rate in the nation": Ibid., Nov. 1, 1992.
416 - "'a bad case of such urban ills'": Ibid.
416 - "lowered its bond ratings": Ibid., Oct. 27, 1992.
416 - "for the second consecutive year": Ibid., Jan. 15, 1993.
416 - "the annual Artfest": Ibid., Jan. 16, 1993.
417 - "the situation downtown": Ibid., Nov. 11, 1993.
417 - "In 1984 just two youths": Christine Wicker, "The Death Beat," *Dallas Life Magazine*, DMN, Feb. 6, 1991.
418 - "helped spur tremendous growth": Dean Vanderbilt, "D/FW airport must adopt to new challenge," DMN, Jan. 10, 1993.
419 - "'The Texas Metroplex'": Ibid., Jan. 16, 1993.
419 - "'an integrated economic and social unit'": Quoted by Daniel Boorstin, *The Americas: The Democratic Experience* (New York: Vantage Books, 1974), 267.
420 - "Five of the fastest growing cities": Weinstein, "Cities and Suburbs Changing," ibid., Nov. 10, 1992.
420 - "In housing starts": DMN, Dec. 18, 1992.
420 - "55,800 new jobs in 1993": DMN, March 11, 1994.
420 - "the nation's very best location": Baring Advisors of New York, as quoted in DMN, Feb. 15, 1993.

Sources Consulted

Books

Acheson, Sam. *Dallas Yesterday*. Dallas: SMU Press, 1977.

Adams, James Ring. *The Big Fix: Inside the S&L Scandal*. New York: John Wiley & Sons, Inc., 1990.

Adams, Nathan. *The First National in Dallas*. Privately published, 1942.

Aircraft Year Book, 1928, U.S. Aeronautical Chamber of Commerce.

Alexander, Charles C. *The Ku Klux Klan in the Southwest*. Lexington: University of Kentucky Press, 1965.

______. *Ty Cobb*. New York: Oxford University Press, 1984.

Boorstin, Daniel. *The Americas: The Democratic Experience*. New York: Vantage Books, 1974.

Braden, David R. "Architecture for Industry: Dallas." In *Dallasights: An Anthology of Architecture and Open Spaces*, ed. Alan R. Sumner. Dallas: American Institute of Architects, Dallas Chapter, 1978.

Brown, Norman D. *Hood, Bonnet, and Little Brown Jug: Texas Politics, 1921-1928*. College Station: Texas A&M Press, 1984.

Bruere, Henry. *The New City Government*. New York: D. Appleton and Co., 1919.

Bywaters, Jerry. *Seventy-Five Years of Art in Dallas*. Dallas: Dallas Mu seum of Fine Arts, 1978.

Calvert, Robert, Randolph Campbell and Donald Chipman. *The Dallas Cowboys and the NFL*. Norman: University of Oklahoma Press, 1970.

Carmack, William R., and Theodore Freedman. *Dallas, Texas: Factors Affecting School Desegregation*. New York: Anti-Defamation League of B'nai B'rith, 1962.

Charles, Ray, and David Ritz. *Brother Ray: Ray Charles' Own Story* (New York: The Dial Press, 1978.

Cheney, Allison A. *Dallas Spirit: A Political History of the City of Dallas*. Dallas: McMullan Publishing Co., 1991.

Clark, James A. and Michel T. Halbouty, *The Last Boom*. New York: Random House, 1972.

Cox Jr., O'Byrne. *Sheriffs of Dallas County, Texas, 1846-1985*. Privately published, n.d

Dahlberg, Walter G., "Growth, Planning, and the CBD." In *Dallasights: An Anthology of Architecture and Open Spaces*, ed. Alan R. Sumner. Dallas: American Institute of Architects, Dallas Chapter, 1978.

Davidson, Chandler. *Race and Class in Texas Politics*. Princeton: Princeton

University Press, 1990.

Dillon, David, and Doug Tomlinson. *Dallas Architecture, 1936-1986.* Austin: Texas Monthly Press, 1985.

Dulaney, W. Marvin. "Whatever Happened to the Civil Rights Movement in Dallas, Texas?" In *Essays on The American Civil Rights Movement,* John Dittmer, George C. Wright, and W. Marvin Dulaney. College Station: Published for the University of Texas at Arlington by Texas A&M University Press, 1993.

Edwards, George. *Pioneer-at-Law.* New York: W.W. Norton & Co., 1974.

Fairbanks, Robert B. "Dallas in the 1940s: The Challenges and Opportunities of Defense Mobilization." In *Urban Texas: Politics and Development,* ed. Char Miller and Heywood T. Sanders. College Station: Texas A&M University Press, 1990.

Fielding, Don. *Assassination and Education: A Guide to Dallas.* New York: Carlton Press, 1968.

Fifty Years of Innovation: The History of Texas Instruments. Dallas: Texas Instruments, 1980 (pamphlet).

Finnegan, T.P., ed. *Souvenir: Dallas Police Department.* Dallas: A. Zeeze Engraving Co. 1910.

Goals for Dallas. Dallas: Goals for Dallas, 1966.

Govenar, Alan. *Meeting the Blues.* Dallas: Taylor Publishing Co., 1988.

Greene, A.C. *Dallas, USA.* Austin: Texas Monthly Press, 1984.

Grove, Larry. *Dallas Public Library: The First 75 Years.* Dallas: Dallas Public Library, 1977.

Hamilton, E.G., "Dallas Shops: Dry Goods Stores to Regional Malls." In *Dallasights: An Anthology of Architecture and Open Spaces,* ed. Alan R. Sumner. Dallas: American Institute of Architects, Dallas Chapter, 1978.

Harper, Terrell R., "City and County Buildings." In *Dallasights: An Anthology of Architecture and Open Spaces,* ed. Alan R. Sumner. Dallas: American Institute of Architects, Dallas Chapter, 1978.

Hinton, Ted. *Ambush: The Real Story of Bonnie and Clyde.* Austin: Shoal Creek Publishers, 1979.

History, Dallas Negro High School. Dallas [n.p.], 1938.

Holmes, Maxine, and Gerald D. Saxon, eds., *The WPA Dallas Guide and History.* [Dallas]: Dallas Public Library, Texas Center for the Book, [Denton] University of North Texas Press, 1992.

Hurt , Harry III. *Texas Rich: The Hunt Dynasty From the Early Oil Days Through the Silver Crash.* New York: W.W. Norton & Co., 1981.

Jackson, Alexander. *The Rebirth of Negro Ideals.* Nashville: National Baptist Publishing Board, 1920.

Jackson, Kenneth T. *The Ku Klux Klan in the City, 1915-1930.* New York: Oxford University Press, 1967.

Jebsen, Harry Jr., Robert M. Newton, Patricia R. Hogan, *Centennial History of the Dallas, Texas Park System, 1876-1976*. Lubbock: Department of History, Texas Tech University, 1976.

Johnson, Walter, ed. *The Papers of Adlai E. Stevenson: Ambassador to the United Nations, 1961-1965*, VIII. (Boston: Little, Brown and Co., 1979.

Jones, G. William. *Black Cinema Treasures: Lost and Found*. Denton: University of North Texas Press, 1991.

Jones, Ted. *Dallas, Its History, Its Development, Its Beauty* . Dallas: Lamar & Barton, 1925.

Kimball, Justin F. *Our City—Dallas* . Dallas: Kessler Plan Association, 1927.

Knight, Oliver. *Fort Worth: Outpost on the Trinity*. Norman: University of Oklahoma, 1953.

League of Women Voters of Dallas. *Implementing School Desegregation.* Dallas: League of Women Voters of Dallas, 1971 (pamphlet).

Lehrer, Jim. *A Bus of My Own*. New York: G.P. Putnam's Sons, 1992.

Leslie, Warren. *Dallas Public and Private: Aspects of an American City*. New York: Grossman Publishers, 1964.

Lindsley, Philip. *A History of Greater Dallas and Vicinity*, 2 vols. Chicago: The Lewis Publishing Co., 1909.

Manchester, William. *The Death of a President, November 20-November 25, 1963*. (New York: Harper & Row, Publishers, 1967.

Marcus, Stanley. *Minding the Store: A Memoir* . Boston: Little, Brown and Company, 1974.

McDonald, William L. *Dallas Rediscovered: A Photographic Chronicle of Urban Expansion*. Dallas: Dallas Historical Society, 1978.

McKelvey, Blake. *The Emergence of Metropolitan America, 1915-1966*. New Brunswick: Rutgers University Press, 1968.

McKnight, Dr. Mamie L., project director. *African American Families and Settlements of Dallas: On the Inside Looking Out*, II, Dallas: Black Dallas Remembered, Inc., 1990.

Memorial and Biographical History of Dallas County, Texas . Chicago: The Lewis Publishing Co., 1892.

Miller, Merle. *Lyndon: An Oral Biography*. New York: Ballantine Books 1980.

Miller, Richard G., "Fort Worth and the Progressive Era: The Movement for Charter Revision, 1899-1907." In *Essays on Urban America*, ed.Robert F. Oaks, et al. Austin: University of Texas Press, 1975.

Myrdal, Gunnar. *An America Dilemma: The Negro Problem and Modern Democracy*. New York: Harper & Bros., 1944.

Payne, Darwin *Dallas: An Illustrated History* . Woodland Hills, Calif.: Windsor Publications, Inc., 1982.

_________, ed. *Sketches of a Growing Town: Episodes and People of Dallas From Early Days to Recent Times.* Dallas: Southern Methodist University Master of Liberal Arts Program, 1991.

_________. *The Press Corps and the Kennedy Assassination.* Journalism Monographs, No. 15, February 1970. Lexington, Ky.: Association for Journalism Education.

Pilzer, Paul Zane. *Other People's Money: The Inside Story of the S&L Scandal.* New York: Simon and Schuster, 1989.

Ragsdale, Kenneth B., *The Year America Discovered Texas: Centennial '36.* College Station: Texas A&M University Press, 1987.

Rumbley, Rose-Mary. *The Unauthorized History of Dallas, Texas.* Austin: Eakin Press, 1991.

Schlesinger, Arthur. *A Thousand Days: John F. Kennedy in the White House.* Boston: Houghton Mifflin, 1965.

Schiebel, Walter J.E. *Education in Dallas: Ninety-two Years of History.* Dallas: Dallas Independent School District, 1966.

Schutze, Jim. *The Accommodation: The Politics of Race in an American City.* Secaucus, N.J.: Citadel Press, 1986.

Seib, Philip. *Dallas: Chasing the Urban Dream.* Dallas: Pressworks, 1986.

Sharpe, Ernest. *G.B.Dealey of the Dallas News.* New York: Henry Holt and Co., 1955.

Shay, Kevin J., and Roy Williams. *Time Change: An Alternative View of the History of Dallas.* Dallas: To Be Publishing Co., 1991.

Simpson, Amy. *Pike Park: The Heart and History of Mexican Culture in Dallas.* Dallas: Los Barrios Unidos Community Clinic, [1982].

Sorenson, Theodore. *Kennedy.* New York: Harper & Row, Publishers, 1965.

Stone, Harold A., Don K. Price, and Kathryn H. Stone. *City Manager Government in Dallas.* Chicago: Public Administration Service, 1939.

Sumner, Alan R., ed. *Dallasights: An Anthology of Architecture and Open Spaces.* Dallas: American Institute of Architects, Dallas Chapter, 1978.

Thomas, Jesse O. *Negro Participation in the Texas Centennial Exposition* . Boston: Christopher Publishing House, 1938.

Thometz, Carol Estes. *The Decision-Makers: The Power Structure of Dallas.* Dallas: Southern Methodist University Press, 1963.

Treherne, John. *The Strange History of Bonnie and Clyde.* New York: Stein and Day, 1985.

Tuccille, Jerome. *Kingdom: The Story of the Hunt Family of Texas* . Ottawa, Ill: Jameson Books, 1984.

Upchurch, J.T. *Traps for Girls and Those Who Set Them.* Dallas: Barachah Printing Co., 1904.

_______.*The Unchained Demon, and the Tribute Dallas, Texas, Pays to Vice*.. Arlington: Barachah Rescue Society, 1912.
Walker, Stanley. *The Dallas Story*. Dallas: Dallas Times Herald, 1956.
Wilcox, Delos F. *Great Cities in America: Their Problems and Their Government*. New York: The Macmillan Co., 1913.
Wiseman, Carter. *I.M. Pei: A Profile in American Architecture*. New York: Harry N. Abrams, Inc., 1990.
Wiley, Nancy. *The Great State Fair of Texas*. Dallas: Taylor Publishing Co., 1985.
Wineburgh, H. Harold. *The Texas Banker: The Life and Times of Fred Farrel Florence*. Dallas: [n.p.], 1981.
Wilson, William H. *The City Beautiful Movement*. Baltimore: The Johns Hopkins Press, 1989.
Wolf, Jane. *The Murchisons: The Rise and Fall of a Texas Dynasty*. New York: St. Martin's Press, 1989.
Woofter , T.J. Jr. *Negro Problems in Cities*. College Park, Md.: McGrath Publishing Co., 1969.
Zaharias, Babe Didrickson . *This Life I've Led*. New York: A.S. Barnes & Co., 1955.

Magazine, Journal Articles

Agnew, Peter W. "Making Dallas Moral: Two Baptist Pastors," *Heritage News*, Summer 1987.
Ballard, Lee. "The Rise and Decline of Deep Ellum," *Westward* (magazine section of the *Dallas Times Herald*), Sept. 25, 1983.
Beckenbach, C.B. "The New Triple Underpass in Dallas," *American City*, November 1936.
Bowman, Larry. "Breaking Barriers," *Legacies*, Spring 1991.
Cohn, David L. "Dallas," *Atlantic*, October 1940.
Clark, Lee. "Dallas' Oligarchy and Fateful '68," *Texas Observer*, March 1, 1968.
Dealey, Ted. "'The Dallas Spirit': The Last Fool Flight," *Southwestern Historical Quarterly* , July 1959.
Dozier, Richard K. "Black Architects and Craftsmen," *Black World*, May 1974.
_______. "Architects." *Black Enterprise*, September 1976.
Estes, Sue Horn. "Black Power in Dallas," *Texas Observer*, Aug. 6, 1968.
Evans, J. Claude. "The Dallas Image Unveiled," *Christian Century*, Nov. 20, 1963.
Frost, Stanley. "When the Klan Rules," *Outlook*, Dec. 26, 1923.
"The Klan's Challenge and the Reply," *Literary Digest*, Nov. 17, 1923.

Gillette, Michael L. "Blacks Challenge the White University," *Southwestern Historical Quarterly*, October 1982.
Hazel, Michael V. "The Critic Club," *Legacies*, Fall 1990.
Head, Louis P. "Measuring the Efficiency of a City's Government by the Munroe Criteria," *The American City*, June 1927.
Ivins, Molly. "A Texas-Scale Airport," *New York Times Magazine*, Sept. 16, 1973.
_______. "Dallas' 'Big Daddy' Figure," *New York Times Magazine*, Sept. 16, 1973.
Lloyd, Everett. "Colonel C.M. Joiner, Ideal American," *Dallas*, November, 1934.
Lyons, Julie. "Brown Jesus and Other Tales from the Projects," *Dallas Observer*, Aug. 6, 1992.
McCombs, Holland, and Holly Whyte. "The Dydamic Men of Dallas," *Fortune*, February 1949.
McCombs, M.J. "World's Greatest Athlete, Man or Woman," *Dallas*, September 1932.
Miller, Laura. "The Hustler," *D* magazine, *March 1991.*
Neff, Pauline. "A Bargain in the Cost of Living," *Dallas*, April 1975.
Nettleton, Douglas A. "First Expressway for Dallas," *American City*, February 1947.
Payne, Darwin. "The Future Is Here," *Dallas*, July 1975.
________. "Dallas: The Story of Determined Citizens and How They Made the Improbable Dream of 1841 Come True," *Dallas*, July 1976.
_______. "Goliath vs. Goliath at the Newsstand," *Dallas*, January 1980.
Peeler, Tom . "Hot Dog Mayor," *D* magazine, October 1989.
Perry, George Session. "The Duke of Dallas," *Saturday Evening Post*, June 11, 1955.
Rice, Gwendolyn. "Little Mexico and the Barrios of Dallas," *Legacies*, Fall 1992.
Rodgers, Woodall. "Central Boulevard," *Dallas*, June 1941.
_______. "Luncheon Meetings Promote Harmony in Dallas," *American City*, February 1947.
Short, Violet. "Personalities: Louis 'Daddy' Blaylock, *The Dallasite*, Oct. 26, 1929.
Simpson, Gwen. "Early Automobiles in Dallas: Heralds of a New Age,"*Heritage News*, Winter 1984-85.
Smith, Richard. "How Business Failed Dallas," *Fortune*, July 1964.
[Upchurch, J.T.], "The Tribute Dallas, Texas, Pays to Vice," *The Purity Journal*, October 1912.
[_______.] "Save the Girls, Close the Brothels, Protect the Home, *The Purity Journal*, October 1912.

Watson, Walter T. "Mexicans in Dallas," *Southwest Review*, July 1937.
White, Owen P. "Dripping Dry Dallas," *Collier's*, July 20, 1929.
Wicker, Christine. "The Death Beat," *Dallas Life Magazine*, supplement to *Dallas Morning News*, Feb. 6, 1994.
Wood, E.A. "A City Looks to the Future," *Southwest Review*, Spring 1944.

Magazine Articles (author not listed)

American City. "Selling City Planning to Dallas," July 1925.
Business Week. "Growing Dallas Moves River Away," March 12, 1930.
Dallas. "What Oil Industry Means to Dallas,' February 1922.
_______. "What New Reservoir Means for Dallas," September 1924.
_______."The Story of the Little Theatre," October 1928.
_______. "Dallas' Great Improvement Project," August 1929.
_______. "Trinity River Flood Control," October 1929.
_______. "Possibilities Made Practical by Reclamation," November 1929.
_______. "Getting Closer to New York," February 1930.
_______. "Classified Directory," April 1930.
_______. "Yellow Gold From Black," March 1932.
_______. "Signs of the Times," August 1932.
_______. "Prophecy," February 1956.
Flying. "Traffic Pattern," June 1964.
Life. "Who's Who in the Tumult of the Far Right," Feb. 9, 1962.
Literary Digest. "The Klan's Challenge and the Reply," Nov. 17, 1923.
New Republic. "Racial Dynamism in Dallas," March 24, 1941.
Newsweek. "Thunder on the Right," Dec. 4, 1961.
Southwest Business, "Editorial," December 1937.
_______. "122,000 Visitors in 1939," November 1939.
_______. "Dallas Wins Plane Factory," September 1940.
_______. "Ford Spends $450,000 on Dallas Plant," February 1941.
_______. "Like a Diamond in the Sky," June 1941.
Texas Observer. "Dallasites Picket Store," Oct. 14, 1960.
_______. "SMU Students Stage Sit-Ins," Jan. 14, 1961.
Time. "Turnabout," March 20, 1952.
_______. "New Men for Detroit and Atlanta," Jan. 14, 1974.
World's Work. "The March of the Cities," January 1914.

Newspapers

Christian Science Monitor
Dallas Dispatch

Dallas Express
Dallas Journal
Dallas Morning News
Dallas Observer
Dallas Times Herald
Denver Post
The Laborer (Dallas)
The New York Times
Texas 100 Per Cent American (Dallas)
Wall Street Journal
Washington Post National Weekly

Archival and Manuscript Sources

Texas/Dallas History and Archives Division, Dallas Public Library:
Bruce Alger Collection
Juanita Craft Collection
Dallas Police Department Archives
Dallas Negro Chamber of Commerce Collection
Robert S. Folsom Mayoral Papers
Anita Martinez Collection
Max Goldblatt: Dallas City Council Papers
Florrie Wade Collection
Wes Wise Mayoral Administrative Papers, 1971-1976.

Dallas Historical Society
George Bannerman Dealey Papers

DeGolyer Special Collections, Southern Methodist University
Earle Cabell Collection
Lynn Landrum-Love Field Papers

Dissertations, theses

Black, William Neil. "Empire of Consensus: City Planning, Zoning, and Annexation in Dallas, 1900-1960." Ph.D. diss., Columbia University, 1982.

Curtis, James Robert. "The Dallas Police System." M.A. thesis, Southern Methodist University, 1929.

Davies, Elizabeth Durham. "Fair Park Expansion: A Case Study of Political Bias and Protest in Urban Dallas."(?) M.A. thesis, North

Texas State University, 1974.
DeMoss, Dorothy Dell. "Dallas During the Early Depression," M.A.(?) thesis, University of Texas at Austin, 1966.
Gillette, Michael Lowery. "The NAACP in Texas, 1937-1957." Ph.D. diss., University of Texas at Austin, 1984.
Hill, Marilyn Wood. "A History of the Jewish Involvement in the Dallas Community." M.A. thesis, Southern Methodist University, 1967.
Hill, Patricia E., "Origins of Modern Dallas." Ph.D. diss., University of Texas at Dallas, 1990.
Hollingsworth, Ann P. "Reform Government in Dallas, 1927-1940." M.A. thesis, North Texas State University, 1971.
McFerrin Jr., Stowe William. "Vaudeville at the Majestic Theater of Dallas, 1905-1910," M.A. thesis, Southern Methodist University, 1972.
Payne, B. Darwin. "The Impact of the Press on Events in Dallas Related to the Assassination of President John F. Kennedy, November 22, 24, 1963," M.A. thesis, Southern Methodist University, 1968.
Potts, Helen Jo. "A Study of the Little Theatre of Dallas: 1920-1943," M.A. thesis, Southern Methodist University, 1968.
Torrence, Lois. "The Ku Klux Klan in Dallas, 1915-1928," M.A. thesis, Southern Methodist University, 1948.

Oral History Interviews

From the Texas/Dallas History and Archives Division, Dallas Public Library
Bruce Alger, George Allen, James W. Aston, Juanita Craft, George Leighton Dahl, Joe M. Dealey, Jack Evans, Robert S. Folsom, Bryghte Goldbold, Erik Jonsson, Henry Kucera, Wallace Savage, George Sergeant Jr., A. Maceo Smith, Robert Lee Thornton Jr., John Stemmons Sr., Mrs. Frank Wozencraft and Frank M. Wozencraft Sr.

Seminar papers

Master of Liberal Arts program, Southern Methodist University
Blaylock, Charles. "Dallas: The Struggle to Get Public Housing," December 1992.
Brown, Jack, "Electrifying Dallas: Early Impressions and Societal Impact," December 1992.
Brown, Karen Matney,"The Forgotten Fair," December 1992.
Cline, Judith. "Babe Didrickson Zaharias, Female Athlete Legend and Her Life in Dallas," May, 1990.

Dorsey, Don. "Winning the Texas Centennial Exposition for Dallas," May, 1983.
Fishman, Laura."William E. Easterwood Jr., " December, 1987
Hoffman, Rita. "The Adolphus Hotel: Beautiful Lady With a Past," November, 1987.
Kuberski, Brian. "Prohibition in Dallas," May 1990.
Long, H. Clifford. "Citizens Charter Association: Its Birth and Early Struggle to Survive," December, 1983.
McLaughlin, Bettye. "A Profile of Schuyler Bailey Marshall Jr., Sheriff of Dallas County, 1925-1926," May 1990.
Peterson, Byrdette M. "Louis Blaylock, Mayor of Dallas, 1923-1927," May, 1990.
White, James E. "Aviation in Dallas, 1919-1939," December, 1983.
Wilson, Angela. "Dallas Pastors Chase the Floozies Away," December, 1992.

Unpublished Manuscripts

Glenn Linden, "Desegregating the Dallas Schools: A Generation of Court Battles."
"Prominent Blacks of Dallas: Professional Profiles," I, typescript, Texas/ Dallas History Division, Dallas Public Library.
John H. Cullom, "Biographies of the Mayors of Dallas Since 1917," typescript, Dallas Historical Society.

City of Dallas Reports and Documents

Harland Bartholomew & Associates, "A Master Plan for Dallas" [Reports Submitted to the City Plan Commission], St. Louis: H.Bartholomew & Associates, 1943-45.
George E. Kessler, "A City Plan for Dallas: Report of Park Board," May 1911.
City of Dallas Annual Report, May 1, 1912, to May 1, 1913.
City of Dallas Health Department records, Texas/Dallas History and Archives, Dallas Central Public Library.
City of Dallas Minute Book, Book 5, 1910-1911.
City of Dallas Ordinance Book 16, 1911-1912.
Street Railway and Light and Power Franchises, an informational pamphlet prepared by the City of Dallas in 1916
City of Dallas General Budget for Fiscal Year 1936-1937.
Dallas Housing Survey, 1940. (The Housing Authority of the City of

Dallas).
Bolding, M.E., and Ernie H. Bolding. "Origin and Growth of the Dallas Water Utilities. Dallas," 1981.

Interviews

Henry Wade, Feb. 18, 1993 (telephone), and Feb. 23, 1993.
John Schoellkopf, Nov. 30, 1992, and Dec. 1, 1992.
Bill Sloan. Dec. 9, 1992.

Letters to Author

Henry Tatum, Dec. 30, 1992.
Stanley Marcus, Feb. 11, 1993.

Reference Works

Handbook of Texas, 2 vols., Austin: The Texas State Historical Association, 1952.
________, A Supplement. Austin: The Texas State Historical Association, 1976.
Hearings Before the President's Commission on the Assassination of President Kennedy, 26 vols. Washington: U.S. Government Printing Office, 1964.
Worley's Dallas City Directory. (annual directories with minor variations in titles) Dallas: John F. Worley Directory Co.

Miscellaneous

Dallas, A Profile and Fact Book for the Media, pamphlet prepared for the 1984 Republican Party Convention by the Dallas Welcoming Committee.
Negro City Directory (various years)
Poster promoting Dallas with the title, "Dallas in 1873: An Invitation to Immigrants." Reproduced in 1980 by Stone-Inge Books, Dallas
R.L. Thornton Scrapbook, Vol. I, Dallas Historical Society
Pamphlet entitled *History, Dallas Negro High School* (Dallas, n.p., 1938)

Index